After the Cold War

Written under the auspices of
the Center for International Affairs
Harvard University

After the Cold War

INTERNATIONAL INSTITUTIONS AND STATE

STRATEGIES IN EUROPE, 1989–1991

Edited by

Robert O. Keohane

Joseph S. Nye

Stanley Hoffmann

Harvard University Press

Cambridge, Massachusetts, and London, England

1993

Design by Marianne Perlak

Library of Congress Cataloging-in-Publication Data

After the Cold War / international institutions and state strategies
   in Europe, 1989–1991 / edited by Robert O. Keohane, Joseph S. Nye,
   Stanley Hoffmann.
            p.   cm.
   Written under the auspices of the Center for International
Affairs, Harvard University.
   Includes bibliographical references and index.
   ISBN 0-674-00863-4. — ISBN 0-674-00864-2 (pbk.)
   1. Europe—Politics and government—1989- 2. International
agencies—Europe. I. Keohane, Robert O. (Robert Owen), 1941–
II. Nye, Joseph S. III. Hoffmann, Stanley. IV. Harvard University.
Center for International Affairs.
D860.A38 1993
320.94—dc20

92-35682
   CIP

Preface

The dismantling of the Berlin Wall in the autumn of 1989 stimulated debates in Europe and the United States about the future shape of a post–Cold War world. At the Harvard Center for International Affairs (CFIA) many of these debates focused on the different analyses and forecasts of realist and institutional students of world politics. This focus was quite natural, since Harvard was a center of institutionalist thinking yet also included a number of realist analysts among its faculty and students, and among fellows and visitors to the CFIA. Even before the end of the Cold War, the Center's programs had included one on international institutions, funded by the Ford Foundation, along with a variety of other programs that involved policy-relevant basic research from more realist perspectives.

In the spring of 1990 Europe seemed to be a perfect real-time laboratory in which to test realist and institutionalist approaches. The key events ending the Cold War—the withdrawal of Soviet forces from central Europe and the reunification of Germany—occurred in Europe. Furthermore, Europe had dense institutional networks, implying that institutionalist arguments about the impact of institutions on state strategies should apply there, if anywhere. With these notions in mind, a group of scholars of varying ages began to meet regularly over lunch. Eventually we decided that realist and institutionalist theories were too imprecisely specified to be rigorously tested in a scientific way; but the framework that we devised during the spring of 1990 and the fall of 1991 nevertheless owes a great deal to this initial theoretical impetus. The principal purpose of this volume is description and interpretation—to help us understand state strategies in Europe between the dismantling of the Berlin Wall in November 1989 and the collapse of the Soviet Union after the coup attempt of August 1991. Yet formulating cogent questions depends on a background of theory, and this volume reflects that relationship between theory and empirical inquiry.

From the outset this has been a joint project. Its major ideas have come from a large number of people, and key decisions about which analytical themes to pursue, what the organization of the volume should be, and which press to submit our work to have been made collectively and democratically. Although the lineage of ideas is difficult to trace, it is safe to say that there was no clear relationship between the age or reputation of a participant and the significance of the ideas that he or she contributed to our joint enterprise. All of the authors represented in this volume made important conceptual contributions. Futhermore, in the early discussions that set the framework for the project, major intellectual contributions were made by a number of people who were unable to write papers for this volume, among them Abram Chayes, Peter Feaver, Yuen Foong Khong, Ron Mitchell, Craig Murphy, Robert Paarlberg, Beth Simmons, David Spiro, and Fareed Zakaria. We are especially grateful to Will Wade-Gery for staff support during 1990–91 and to Daniel Philpott for similar support during 1991–92. Christina Willemsen, Assistant to the Chair of the Government Department, has played an important role in coordinating the various activities that have led to this book. Robert O. Keohane was responsible for the final editing of the entire volume.

Real research costs money. Without the help of the Avoiding Nuclear War project of the Carnegie Corporation, it would have been impossible to go beyond theorizing to empirical work. Carnegie support allowed a number of the members of the study group to travel to Europe to conduct interviews and helped others to hire assistance for documentary searches. We are most thankful to David Hamburg and Frederick Mosher of the Carnegie Corporation for their support of this work. Aida Donald of Harvard University Press had faith in this project from the moment she read the manuscript that we originally submitted. We are most grateful for her moral support as well as her assistance in shepherding this project through the press's review process.

Most of the empirical work reported in this volume was carried out in 1991. A conference was held at the Center for International Affairs in November 1991 to discuss preliminary drafts of the chapters. At this meeting we agreed that we would focus our chapters on the critical period between the fall of the Berlin Wall in November 1989 and the collapse of the August 1991 coup which began the final disintegration of the Soviet Union, although each author was free to include references to events up to the end of 1991. We are particularly indebted to people who served as discussants at this conference, including Suzanne Berger, Abram Chayes, Peter Katzenstein, Tony Levitas, Lisa Martin, Kenneth Oye, Stephen Rosen, Helen Wallace, and Philip Zelikow.

The ultimate consequences for state strategies and international institutions of the end of the Cold War are still unclear, and may remain so for some time. We hope, however, that this volume will be of some lasting significance in helping to establish a benchmark for the understanding of what is sure to be a continuing process of change.

Robert O. Keohane, Joseph S. Nye, and Stanley Hoffmann

Contents

After the Cold War

Introduction: The End of the Cold War in Europe

Robert O. Keohane

Joseph S. Nye

Dramatic changes took place in Europe during the twenty-one months between the crumbling of the Berlin Wall in November 1989 and the coup attempt that foreshadowed the demise of the Soviet Union as a state in August 1991. During that period the bipolar structure of military power that had characterized world politics for forty years collapsed. Germany was reunified within the North Atlantic Treaty Organization (NATO), and all communist governments in eastern Europe either fell or were reconfigured and relabeled. Established governments in the west and newly autonomous governments in eastern Europe sought to develop appropriate strategies to cope with the sharp decline in Soviet power, and then the collapse of the Soviet Union itself. The events of 1989–1991, which profoundly altered international politics, also deeply affected international institutions: international organizations such as the International Monetary Fund (IMF) or NATO, and the rules (international regimes) governing state action in particular domains. This volume explores the nexus between institutions and state strategies: how international institutions affected state strategies, as well as vice versa.

The changes discussed in the chapters that follow were set off by the "end of the Cold War." What does this phrase mean? For the contributors to this volume it has two dimensions: first, the withdrawal of Soviet military power

1

from central Europe, especially Germany, Poland, Czechoslovakia, and Hungary; and second, the reunification of Germany. When the structure of politics—that is, the resources available to actors and therefore their capacity to exercise influence—is thus transformed, state strategies and the characteristics of institutions can be expected to change as well. This volume examines those changes in state strategies and international institutions by using two complementary frameworks for analysis. Part I asks how the major western powers and the Soviet Union used international institutions to achieve their objectives. Part II investigates the institutional arrangements that have begun to emerge in functional issue areas linking eastern and western Europe: trade, public financial assistance, direct foreign investment, environmental policy, and the provision of security.

Institutional Analysis and the End of the Cold War

The west European international system at the end of the Cold War was highly institutionalized: state behavior was to a considerable extent governed by rules. This system therefore only distantly resembled the textbook portrayal of sovereign states pursuing self-help policies under conditions of anarchy. One essential set of rules was a legacy of World War II: full German sovereignty was not restored until October 3, 1990. Major international organizations, such as NATO and the European Community (EC), had been created in the shadow of superpower rivalry and therefore reflected the alliance patterns of the Cold War. Yet both organizations were quite strong: NATO had become the most successful and most highly institutionalized multilateral alliance in history, and the EC had evolved into an international institution that was unparalleled for the legal status of its directives and the ambition of its bureaucracy. West European and North American governments were also influential participants in a number of global economic institutions, including the General Agreement on Tariffs and Trade (GATT), the Organization for Economic Cooperation and Development (OECD), the International Monetary Fund (IMF), and the World Bank. Furthermore, scores of other international organizations and regimes, and many more transnational organizations and networks, connected the Atlantic countries and their people to one another and to the rest of the world.[1]

These institutions were not imposed on states, but were created and accepted by them in order to increase their ability to seek their own interests through the coordination of their policies. Typically, such international institutions do not enforce rules on powerful states, although they may serve as the agents of powerful states to enforce rules on the weak. Among the powerful they encourage agreement, and compliance with agreements, by establishing overall rules and practices that make negotiations easier, and by facilitating the exchange of information about the actual behavior of states with reference to the standards to which they have consented. Thus they constrain opportunistic behavior, and they provide focal points for coordination. They make a difference not by imposing order "above the nation-state" but by creating valued networks of ties between states. Among potential adversaries they may alleviate the security dilemma. In short, institutions provide a point of common reference for leaders trying to struggle with turmoil and uncertainty.

In contrast to the situation in the west, eastern Europe after the Soviet withdrawal was virtually bereft of strong institutions. The Warsaw Treaty Organization (WTO) and the Council for Mutual Economic Assistance (CMEA) were obsolete, no longer reflecting the interests of most of their members. Both the WTO and the CMEA were formally dissolved after 1989. The Conference on Security and Cooperation in Europe (CSCE), whose origins lay in the détente of the 1970s, included both east and west; but the rules of this institution were weak; it acted only by unanimity; and it was only beginning to acquire a rudimentary organizational structure. Despite appeals from east European governments to become affiliated with NATO or the EC, these institutions were not expanded to include the east. The western powers sought to extend their individual and collective influence without extending EC or NATO privileges and guarantees. Nevertheless, east European governments sought to join multilateral organizations, strengthen promising bilateral links, and persuade or cajole their putative western partners into pursuing more favorable policies toward them. Some of these policies succeeded: IMF membership was offered even to the states that emerged from the Soviet Union, and quite substantial assistance was selectively provided, most generously to Poland.

This volume's approach to the international relations of Europe can be broadly characterized as institutionalist. This institutionalist perspective can be located in the field of international relations by comparing it to the two classic approaches, realism and liberalism. To summarize briefly, realists focus on the structure of the international system and the incentives it creates for conflict. They argue that in an "anarchic" state system—anarchic not because it is necessarily chaotic but because it lacks common government—

states will use force and guile to preserve their independence, secure their people, and if possible gain additional power. Expansionist states will seek to gain resources at the expense of their neighbors; their conservative rivals will form alliances to balance the power of the apparently strongest or most threatening state or coalition. In a pure realist story, international organizations and the rules to which states may have committed themselves play little role, being swept aside as ephemeral, or as "scraps of paper," when interests so dictate.

Liberal international relations theory is critical of realism's emphasis on the anarchy of relations among states. Liberals stress that states are not all alike: they differ in their institutions, policy networks, and dominant political coalitions. Interests are constructed, not given; they derive not only from considerations of geopolitical position but from both material interests and conceptions of principle as interpreted through varying domestic political structures. In particular, liberal democracies behave differently toward one another than they do toward autocracies, or than autocracies behave toward other autocracies, in two ways: first, depending on how "liberal democracies" are defined, they rarely or never fight wars against one another; and second, their interactions involve complex patterns of transnational relations, which create patterns of social and economic interdependence.[2] Among democracies state structure matters: to understand the policies of Sweden, the United States, France, or Japan, one needs to understand the distinctive features of their institutions and policy networks.[3]

Institutionalist arguments focus neither on the structure of the international system, emphasized by realism, nor on the interactions between domestic politics and international relations, on which liberalism focuses. The principal focus of institutionalists is on international political processes. Institutionalists note that there is variation across time and space in the ability of states to communicate and cooperate with one another, and that increases in the ability to communicate and cooperate can provide opportunities for redefining interests and for pursuing different strategies.[4] Institutionalist analysis makes a distinctive claim of its own: that despite the lack of common government in international politics, sustained cooperation is possible under some fairly well defined conditions. These conditions include the existence of mutual interests that make joint (Pareto-improving) gains from cooperation possible; long-term relationships among a relatively small number of actors; and the practice of reciprocity according to agreed-upon standards of appropriate behavior.[5] Such cooperation is not the antithesis of conflict but constitutes a process for the management of conflict. International institutions can facilitate such a process of cooperation by providing opportunities for negotiations, reducing uncertainty about others' policies, and by affecting leaders' expectations about the future. Thus, international institutions can affect the strategies states choose and the decisions they make.

Institutionalist analysis is consistent with elements of both realism and liberalism. It is consistent with aspects of realism since states are viewed, in both approaches, as the principal actors in world politics, and their relative power capabilities are considered to be crucial determinants of their behavior. States pursue self-interested goals, which are defined at least partially in terms of relative power and autonomy. However, institutionalists recognize, with liberals, that states are not the sole significant actors in world politics: relationships of economic and ecological interdependence, and the nongovernmental activities associated with them, also affect patterns of cooperation and the impact of international institutions. Interdependence poses problems of coordination, creates interests within countries, and generates transnational coalitions whose activities are often closely linked to those of intergovernmental institutions.

International institutions do not call into question the core of the realist model of anarchy, since they do not have the power to enforce their rules on strong states. But they may challenge some of the implications of anarchy for state behavior, making less likely the competitive, worst-case behavior that realists predict.[6] To the extent that international institutions provide information and coordinate actors' expectations, the security dilemma that states face may be less stark, and doctrinaire realist predictions of state behavior may be off the mark. International cooperation will be affected by the richness and appropriateness of available international institutions. Interstate conflicts of interest prompted by concern about relative power and threat (stressed by realism) and transnational and interstate conflicts resulting from domestic and transnational coalitions of political and economic interests (as emphasized by liberalism) are both important determinants of state policy; but international institutions are significant as well.

Since west Europe was densely institutionalized when the Cold War came to an end, institutionalists anticipate more cooperation in Europe than would be expected if international institutions were insignificant, or merely reflected structural forces in world politics. Institutionalists agree with liberals that common or complementary interests can support cooperation, and that international institutions depend for their success on such patterns of complementary interests. Hence it is natural that liberal and institution-alist approaches are often grouped together as a single liberal-institutionalist view; indeed, that association is often made in the succeeding chapters. It is important to recognize, however, that institutionalists have a distinctive argument: institutions can help promote cooperation.

Institutionalist approaches are not uniformly optimistic about world poli-tics. In the first place, international institutions are not necessarily benign: their rules may impose adjustment costs on countries that are weak or have policy preferences that diverge from those of powerful states, and they can foster collusion against adversaries as well as mutually beneficial agree-ments. Second, since institutionalists see cooperation as dependent on com-plementary interests, they are not sanguine about cooperation where such interests do not exist, or are not recognized by those in power. Finally, they suggest that the absence of effective international institutions, as in the former Soviet Union and much of Asia, itself contributes to instability and conflict. The dependence of cooperation on interests and institutions means that institutionalists should expect pacific relationships to sustain themselves in some areas of the world while intense conflict persists in others. Powerful self-reinforcing dynamics are likely to operate in both the western "zone of peace" and the zone of conflict to the east; and it will be impossible to characterize world politics as a whole either as a jungle of unrelenting conflict or as a reflection of patterns of complex interdependence and institutionalized cooperation.[7]

Thus, institutionalist expectations are more complex than the projections of some realists, such as John J. Mearsheimer, who expects west European states to begin "viewing each other with greater fear and suspicion, as they did for centuries before the onset of the Cold War," and to worry "about the imbalances in gains as well as the loss of autonomy that results from coop-eration."[8] Mearsheimer's premonitions of renewed interstate conflict are more likely to be realized in eastern Europe and central Asia than in central and western Europe. One of the most vexing questions in Europe today is where the frontier between the west European zone of peace and the Eurasian zone of conflict will be. For instance, will Hungary, the separate Czech and Slovak republics, Poland, and the Baltic states be incorporated into western-oriented institutions and manage their international relations peacefully? East Asia is another ambiguous area, since it is more marked by relationships of mutually beneficial interdependence than the former USSR or the Middle East but is weakly institutionalized compared to the European-Atlantic area.

Institutionalist arguments resonate with much of what is happening in Europe, but neither they nor realist approaches are sufficiently precisely formulated to permit rigorous testing of hypotheses, and we do not possess an experimental laboratory in which the effects of institutions can be measured, controlling for all other factors. This volume therefore takes a different approach, seeking to examine in detail processes of policy-making and bargaining, to determine the roles that international institutions have played in affecting state strategies and the outcomes of interstate negotiations. Like all attempts at international relations theory, institutionalist arguments have value only insofar as they facilitate more sophisticated empirical investigations. Theories help us devise frameworks of analysis, using "theory as a set of questions," as Stanley Hoffmann has put it.[9] In this volume we apply a general scheme, focusing on the nexus between international institutions and state strategies, which is applied to both analysis of state strategies in Part I and issue areas in Part II. The contributors to this volume examine evidence drawn from contemporary reporting of events, and most of them rely as well on interviews and primary sources carried out and collected in Europe during 1991. They attempt to use questions posed by theory to aid in the collection of perishable information: data on perceptions and attitudes that would not be available unless amassed during the period of immediate transition, and that may therefore be useful to future historians. The contributors find considerable evidence that international institutions play a number of roles that are valuable for governments, suggesting that patterns of cooperation in central and western Europe may well continue. International institutions facilitate policy coordination among powerful states and reduce the likelihood of mutually harmful competition among them for spheres of influence; they therefore serve these states' interests.[10]

Research Design

Our research design is based on an empirical observation and a theoretical claim, both of which were referred to earlier. The observation is that the revolutionary changes of 1989–1991 occurred in an environment that was already rich in international institutions. The theoretical claim is that such institutions are important determinants of state policy. They affect states' interests by creating both opportunities and constraints, and by legitimating collective norms and rules, which may then be taken for granted by governments. This is not to say that international institutions are more important than domestic politics or the international distribution of capabilities; but they are important enough that it is necessary to understand the degree of institutionalization in a problem area before one can understand state strategies. Our focus is not on international institutions per se, but on the connections between international institutions and state strategies. We have therefore sought to devise a set of analytical questions that would illuminate the institutions-strategy nexus.

Although the contributors to this volume share a belief in the significance of international institutions, we do not hold that such institutions are typically strong (indeed, we believe that in comparison to states they are usually quite weak) nor that they are equally significant in different issue areas or for different countries. On the contrary, we assume that the role and significance of international institutions vary across issue areas and countries, and in this volume we try to understand the sources of such variation. Our focus on the nexus between state strategies and international institutions, and our concern with variation both from state to state and by issue area, led us to design a dual framework of analysis. We maintain a common focus on state strategies and institutions, emphasizing the policies of particular states in Part I and institutional configurations by issue area in Part II.

In both Parts I and II the authors pay attention to the choice of institutional options. We ask which institutions are favored by a particular state or are granted responsibility for dealing with a specific issue. Are they bilateral, regional, or global? Why are other institutions or institutional options opposed or rejected? The chapters in both parts of this volume consider institutional functions, asking about the mandate of each institution and the means and authority placed at its disposal. By what rules and procedures are decisions made? Who influences decisions? How do particular states attempt to influence these institutional mandates and decision-making processes? Finally, we ask who benefits and who pays, whether bargaining is accompanied by side payments, and how states calculate the trade-offs involved in these transfers. Throughout the volume the contributors emphasize how institutions help to define choices facing states, affect the processes by which influence is exercised and the resources that confer influence on actors, and contribute to the implementation of decisions.

With respect to the strategies of the major European powers, discussed in Part I, our framework focuses on the impact of institutional configurations on the strategic choices made by leaders of states. We are interested not only in whether states seek to use international institutions but in how they do so. At the broadest level the issue is whether states view institutions purely instrumentally—as means to given ends—or whether they come to redefine their own interests in light of the rules or practices of the institutions. We expected that instrumental uses of institutions would predominate, as indeed they have. But we also found, as the conclusion discusses further, some interesting instances of institutions' helping to define state preferences, particularly with respect to the Federal Republic of Germany. Beyond the question of the instrumental or intrinsic significance of institutions, we ask how strategies are revised as a result of new information from external events or the negotiating process, and about the variety of roles that international institutions play for states.

The studies of issue areas in Part II are all structured around a temporal sequence of action. Interdependence creates *adjustment problems,* which states seek to manage by formulating *appropriate strategies.* These strategies may include multilateral collaboration as well as bilateral and unilateral initiatives. Any cooperation is conditional on a process of *interstate bargaining* on the basis of state interests; finally, these bargains have to be *implemented.* By analyzing in each case the central bargain at the heart of the issue area, the chapters in Part II seek to apply a common political framework to the disparate events that they discuss.

It is important to emphasize that although the analytical lenses of this volume are useful in focusing attention, our principal purpose is descriptive and interpretive. We seek to clarify the connections between international institutions and state strategies, but events as we view them appear too complex for us to be able to make reliable causal inferences. Within a few years the institutional shape of Europe may be much clearer, and both the victors and the vanquished in the institutional struggle may be inclined to rewrite history to show that they had understood the underlying trends all along. Only by interviewing policymakers now, when uncertainty is rife, and trying to reconstruct their actions can we make it possible for future scholars to construct coherent explanations. Without an accurate assessment of what has happened, attempts at explanation are misleading or meaningless.

Organization of This Volume

If international institutions reshape expectations, provide opportunities for action, or constrain state strategies, these effects should be observable in the behavior of states and international organizations. The chapters that follow ask a common set of questions about both state strategies and the roles played by international institutions.

Part I examines the strategies chosen by the major powers in adjusting to the end of the Cold War. In Chapter 1, "Mars or Minerva?" Jeffrey Anderson and John Goodman look at the central actor, Germany, whose policies were closely linked to international institutions. They point out the instrumental value of these institutions to a German policy that depended on reassuring both the Soviet Union and Germany's allies. As Chancellor Helmut Kohl sought to guide German unification, he used German support for NATO to reassure the United States, German membership in the EC to reassure France and Britain, and German support for a strengthened CSCE to allay the worst Soviet fears. But there was more to institutions than international reassurance. Germany's use of international institutions also played a role in mobilizing domestic support and reassuring public opinion and opposition politicians. Anderson and Goodman argue that "West Germany's reliance on a web of international institutions to achieve its foreign policy goals, born of an instrumental choice among painfully few alternatives, was so complete as to cause these institutions to become embedded in the very definition of state interests and strategies." That is, Germany had become reflexively institutionalist: its institutional ties were viewed as intrinsic to the Germans' views of themselves.

The Soviet Union's strategy, according to Celeste Wallander and Jane Prokop in Chapter 2, "Soviet Security Strategies toward Europe," was significantly affected by the existence of international institutions in Europe, but the Soviets perceived institutions as being threats as much as opportunities: indeed, "the Soviet leadership saw any capable, successful institution in which it was not a member as a potential threat." At first, Mikhail Gorbachev resisted any suggestion of German unification within NATO. As he found his position in eastern Europe eroding in 1989, he proposed an alliance between NATO and the Warsaw Treaty Organization (WTO), but the United States refused to provide such an institutional pillar of support. The Soviets then turned to the idea of a strengthened CSCE as an institutional framework for reassurance, a position the United States accepted when the membership of a united Germany in NATO was accepted by the USSR. Soviet policy was different toward economic than toward military institutions: the USSR sought to shape military institutions, but merely to join the economic ones, if it could thereby reap material benefits. In the end, Soviet policy was unsuccessful either in maintaining Soviet influence in eastern Europe or in securing significant resources from the west (except from Germany) before the demise of the Soviet Union itself. Nonetheless, the prospects of a strengthened CSCE and membership in western economic institutions helped cover the Soviet retreat and save face in domestic and foreign opinion.

The three Atlantic powers—the United States, France, and Britain—faced less severe dilemmas than did Germany and the Soviet Union, and their behavior is more easily described. In Chapter 3, "The United States and International Institutions in Europe after the Cold War," we argue that although international institutions did not themselves define U.S. strategy, and were not intrinsically as important as for Germany, the existence and invention of international institutions provided critical signposts to define the national interest as well as useful instruments to implement it. In principle, the United States might have used the collapse of bipolarity to examine a wide range of options such as disengagement or balancing against Germany in Europe. But public and elite support for NATO and the EC meant that such options were not even considered. Instead, the United States sought to adapt NATO in order to maintain it as a source of American influence, and to continue support for the EC as a stabilizing force in western Europe and a magnet for democratic change in eastern Europe. In addition, it used the CSCE as well as global institutions such as GATT and the IMF for tactical bargaining with its former adversaries as well as its allies.

Stanley Hoffmann in Chapter 4, "French Dilemmas and Strategies in the New Europe," emphasizes the confusions and ambiguities of French policy, which sought to cope with the unwelcome prospect of German unification both by tying Germany more tightly to the European Community and by seeking to limit its influence within the Community. Because of French resistance to American influence in NATO, France was loath to strengthen this institution to constrain Germany. Instead, it sought to use Community institutions to achieve its purposes, but the contradictions inherent in its desire to preserve a margin of independence for itself rendered this task a difficult one indeed. France was able to decide on the priority of deepening the EC over widening it, but when François Mitterrand sought in 1991 to make concessions to east European democracies without supporting their membership in the European Community, he was unable to make his institutional alternative to widening, a "Confederation of Europe," appear attractive to anyone.

Like France, Britain sought to promote its distinctively national interests in an institutionally dense environment. As Louise Richardson shows in Chapter 5, "British State Strategies after the Cold War," institutions constrained British policy: the EC played a particularly important constraining role during this period. Institutions also affected the capabilities at Britain's disposal. Indeed, Richardson argues that much of Britain's enthusiasm for the WEU can be explained as an effort to use it to undermine the EC. Britain essentially adopted "an institutional strategy—support for the WEU—to defend an anti-institutionalist position." At the same time, British support for NATO and its own vision of an enlarged, decentralized, and liberal EC helped alleviate its concern about the reunification of Germany.

Part II begins with Chapter 6, "Integrating the Two Halves of Europe," a joint introduction by the authors of the issue-area chapters outlining the sequence of action from adjustment through strategies, bargaining, and implementation that is crucial to their research design. In applying this framework, they find that the east European states have simultaneously used bilateral and multilateral strategies, "a kind of all-fronts blitz," to construct political and economic ties with the west. More surprisingly, they uncover a pattern of *unilateral* strategy that they label "anticipatory adaptation," by which east European governments adopt norms associated with western-led international institutions. Bargaining outcomes between the weak eastern countries and the western nations reflect power, as anyone would expect; but they cannot thoroughly be understood without an understanding of the institutional rules and obligations that affect the conditions under which the east European countries can affiliate with the west, and under which they can receive western resources.

Whether these institutional bargains can be sustained is another matter. International institutions have very little strength of their own: to be successful, they must help states attain their interests. Those interests are by no means entirely determined by geopolitics; they reflect domestic political institutions and the configuration of domestic coalitions. But domestic politics are also affected by international institutional action, as the effects of IMF programs on the politics of developing countries and east European countries such as Poland, Hungary, and Czechoslovakia indicate.

Each issue-area chapter in Part II develops a distinctive argument of its own, linked to the themes developed in the joint introduction and to the strategies-institutions nexus that is the focus of this volume as a whole. In Chapter 7, "East European Trade in the Aftermath of 1989," Kalypso Nicolaïdis shows that east European countries sought in the long term to achieve economic integration with the west, and in the short term to facilitate structural adjustment and to manage balance-of-payments crises. Western responses to eastern demands for cooperation were severely constrained both by the domestic politics of protectionism in the west and by the preexisting western institutional agendas of completing the GATT's Uruguay Round and further expanding and strengthening the European Community. East European negotiators had to learn quickly to devise bilateral and multilateral negotiating strategies that were appropriate to an issue area in which specific sectoral interests were so important. Since in the long term east European governments sought membership in the EC, unilateral adaptation was a key element of their strategies, that is, adopting domestic laws and practices to fit Community standards.

In Chapter 8, "The Political Economy of Financial Assistance to Eastern Europe, 1989–1991," Stephan Haggard and Andrew Moravcsik discuss the creation of the European Bank for Reconstruction and Development (EBRD) and other ad hoc negotiating forums such as the G-7 and G-24 groups, but they argue that their tasks were secondary. The most important aid tasks were carried out bilaterally by governments and multilaterally through the international financial institutions (IFIs). Bilateral aid programs reflect distinctive national interests not conducive to multilateral arrangements. Moreover, systematic coordination of such aid was not essential, since the western countries basically agreed on the conditions for and purposes of public aid. Where systematic coordination among the donors was necessary, the traditional IFIs, particularly the IMF and the World Bank, played critical roles: as quick reactors, gatekeepers, sources of technical expertise, and agents of monitoring. In the end, of course, the success of the strategy of conditionality requires both sufficient credibility in the recipient country—possessed by Lech Walesa's Poland but not by Ion Iliescu's Romania—to acquire western aid, and the political capacity to implement tough adjustment measures at home. If it remained unclear at the end of 1991 whether Poland and the other democratizing east European countries could keep their parts of the "conditionality bargain," it was equally unclear whether countries such as Romania would be able to strike such a bargain at all.

Debora Spar, in Chapter 9, "Foreign Direct Investment in Eastern Europe," highlights an intriguing puzzle. To obtain foreign direct investment, east European governments need to commit themselves to western standards of investment protection. Since clarity and commitment are necessary, international institutions should, according to institutionalist theory, play a key role in providing arenas for negotiation, exchanging information about intentions, and codifying rules. Yet most of the activity with respect to foreign direct investment has been unilateral or bilateral: there has been no delineation of institutional authority, and international organizations in this issue area are weak compared to those in trade and finance. The answer to this puzzle, according to Spar, is consistent with institutionalist theory, since it lies in the prior *lack* of international institutions in this area. There is no GATT for investment because (consistent with liberal analysis) conflicts of interest between investors and host countries have been too sharp to permit such an agreement. Since the Havana Conference of 1948 and the defeat of the charter for an International Trade Organization which arose from it, no consensus on an international investment institution has emerged. As Spar argues: "In an environment that is not richly endowed with international institutions, it is not surprising that countries should define their strategies primarily in terms of noninstitutional options."

It is now well known that socialism in eastern Europe was disastrous for the natural environment of the region. As Marc Levy shows in Chapter 10, "East-West Environmental Politics after 1989," the collapse of these regimes has led to attempts by the new governments in countries such as Poland and Czechoslovakia to adopt tough environmental standards, to gain credibility for their commitments in international institutions, and to acquire resources to support their actions. Thus, in some respects the nature of the bargain in this area is similar to that in others: resources from the west conditional on credible commitments from the new eastern democracies. However, the institutional setting is quite distinctive, since a number of intergovernmental institutions are active in European environmental politics, although none has achieved a position as preeminent as that of the European Community in trade or the International Monetary Fund or World Bank in public finance. The list of agencies with significant involvement is an institutionalist's alphabet soup, including the UN Economic Commission for Europe (ECE), the CSCE, the EC, the Organization for Economic Cooperation and Development (OECD), the EBRD, and the G-24. A great deal has been happening, but clear institutional delineation of functions has not yet occurred.

After the Soviet withdrawal, the new east European governments had to devise ways to provide for their security. Richard Weitz in Chapter 11, "Pursuing Military Security in Eastern Europe," discusses how the institutions that had linked them together under Soviet auspices rapidly collapsed, and they first looked west—toward NATO above all—for protection. Lacking invitations to join NATO, they sought to use the CSCE, although its procedures were cumbersome and its ability to act coherently against a determined threat virtually nonexistent. The east European governments reacted differently to the lack of reassurance provided by international institutions: Czechoslovakia, for instance, sought to tie itself to these institutions, while Poland relied more heavily on unilateral and bilateral strategies. Yet, despite the weakness of security institutions relevant to eastern Europe, NATO and the CSCE structured the situation and fostered state attempts to meet their standards in order to avoid exclusion and isolation. Furthermore, east European states used international institutions instrumentally, to signal intentions, legitimize behavior, and strike favorable bargains for themselves.

The conclusion of this volume, by Robert O. Keohane and Stanley Hoffmann, argues that governments' reactions to the end of the Cold War in Europe were deeply affected by the existence of international institutions. International regimes and organizations were significant not because they controlled state policies but because they were useful to states, and in the process constrained the choices that governments could make. The European Community as the leading European international institution was particularly significant. Its presence, increasing coherence, and economic strength led Germany and the Soviet Union to pursue regime-oriented strategies toward the Community, rather than balancing against potential rival states. France and Britain, despite their ambivalence, could hardly diminish their links to the Community, and the United States found it expedient to pursue a strategy of institutional cooperation toward Europe.

The conclusion formulates the collective answers of the contributors to the question of how international institutions have affected state strategies in Europe since 1989. Realists will not be surprised that international institutions are used by states as arenas for the exercise of influence, or that governments have sought on occasion to use one institution to thwart attempts to strengthen another. As institutionalist theory anticipates, the rules of institutions constrain the bargaining strategies of states and therefore make their actions more predictable. Predictability is also enhanced when governments use institutions to signal their intentions in times of uncertainty. We also observe two roles of institutions that extend beyond either realist or conventional institutionalist theory. Western governments used institutions, including the International Monetary Fund and the European Community, to *coopt* eastern countries into their system of partially managed capitalism. Eager to receive credits and eventually to join the west, the governments of Czechoslovakia, Hungary, and Poland sought to adapt their policies in advance to those of the west. Finally, in some cases, such as that of Germany, international institutions seem to have affected how governments view their own interests: that is, institutionalization can affect *preferences*. These roles of international institutions can be observed to various degrees throughout this volume, and are discussed in more detail in the conclusion.

Institutions at the End of the Cold War in Historical Context

In the course of writing our contributions to this volume, we thought of the period between 1989 and 1991 as constituting at least the first stage of the "post–Cold War settlement" which we believed was taking place in Europe. We recognized that this "settlement" was only incipient, and subject to further changes, yet we found it useful to think about it in historical terms, drawing an analogy to the early stages of previous political settlements after the Napoleonic Wars and World Wars I and II. In each of the earlier cases, defeat in war led to a drastic reduction in the power of a major state and the construction of new international institutions based on a fundamental coalitional realignment. It is too soon since the disintegration of the Soviet Union to assess its long-term effects on war and peace, and hence one must be cautious about the applicability of the analogy. But one can compare the types of institutions that existed during these four instances of fundamental change in the structure of world politics. Perhaps some insights can be drawn from an analysis of the fate of institutions established in the three previous settlements.

In 1815 the Congress of Vienna codified the end of Napoleon's efforts at hegemony and incorporated France into a multipolar Concert of Europe, with a limited but significant degree of institutionalization. The Concert regulated conflict quite explicitly between 1815 and 1823 and to some extent until the Crimean War.[11] Peace in Europe and the security provided overseas by the British navy provided the political basis for a rapid growth of world trade and investment. Yet the institutions of the Concert were informal and weak, and became eroded by ideological contention, colonial quarrels, and struggles for influence among the great powers. Eventually the growth of German power during the second half of the century created the conditions for the next great conflict.

The last two years of World War I were fateful not only for Germany but also for Russia, as the revolution that Lenin and his comrades made in 1917 shook the world. Partly as a result of that revolution, the postwar settlement agreed upon at Versailles in 1919 and the institutions that came out of it were never strongly rooted in the realities of power: the Soviet Union did not support the status quo created by the western allies. Equally important, the

United States, which had tipped the European balance of power in the war, withdrew to its traditional political and military isolationism. When the United States refused to join the League of Nations, the League was unable to become strong enough for states to orient their security strategies around it. Britain paid only lip service to the League, and France turned to a set of fragile alliances with weak east European states against a future German resurgence. Germany, whose people were convinced neither of the necessity of defeat nor of the justice of the peace settlement, saw little reason, even under the democratic Weimar regime, not to try to undermine the settlement where possible. French actions in occupying the Ruhr in 1923 further eroded the legitimacy of the peace. The League, unable to attain effective legitimacy, was not relied upon by the western powers in the crises over Manchuria (1931) and Ethiopia (1935). Ironically, France chose a strategy of confrontation toward Germany in the 1920s when appeasement might have helped, and a strategy of appeasement in the 1930s when confrontation and deterrence would have been more appropriate. Yet without the weight of the United States and the Soviet Union in the balance, it is difficult to see how France and Britain could have withstood the German challenge once the depression had propelled Hitler into power.

If the League was weak, the 1920s were also marked by a lack of strong international economic institutions, except for the gold standard, which was restored with Britain's return to the pound at prewar parity in 1925. The gold standard was not managed by an international organization, but it did involve a rigid set of rules. These rules operated quite differently in different areas of the world, required confidence in the key currency country to be maintained, and contained no built-in device to provide liquidity in a crisis. Hence, they were adequate only when managed by one or a few economically strong and politically coherent countries committed to the gold standard. Such management was facilitated by stable underlying political relationships of dominance and subordination and a sustainable pattern of international flows of capital.

These conditions were not met after World War I. The United States demanded that Britain and France service their war debt, and France required Germany to pay war reparations; but the U.S. trade surplus meant that only so long as American capital flowed to Europe was the international monetary system in equilibrium. Britain, which sought leadership in the system, was weak, and France, once the strength of its currency had been restored, was less than fully supportive of British leadership—seeking in 1927, for example, to convert an awkward amount of sterling into gold. Only America, which shunned a leadership role, had the economic capacity to provide it. When the flow of American private capital to Europe dried up, economic distress could not be avoided, and rather than ameliorating the situation, the institution of the gold standard inhibited creative responses to the crisis of the 1930s.[12] The period after World War II was much richer in international institutions, principally because the United States exercised consistent and sustained leadership, partly in reaction to the failure of its policy after World War I. American wartime planning emphasized the significance of establishing new organizations for the provision and regulation of international finance, such as the International Monetary Fund (IMF) and the World Bank, the basis of which was negotiated at Bretton Woods in 1944. Although efforts to set up an international trade organization failed, the General Agreement on Tariffs and Trade provided a framework of rules, albeit with exceptions for agriculture, no provisions for investment or services, and little organizational structure. On the security side, NATO, founded in 1949, was the key initiative. Incentives provided by the United States helped lead France to seek in the Schuman Plan of 1950 and subsequent policy to incorporate West Germany in a web of economic and institutional ties rather than to prevent it from recovering its strength. These agreements and organizations eventually grew into the European Community, which by 1989 had twelve member states with a population of 340 million people. Altogether, the political and economic institutions created in the 1940s and 1950s provided the basis for unprecedented economic growth and the extension of pluralist capitalist society throughout the Atlantic area.

These postwar settlements suggest one broad comparative generalization and point to one major difference between the current attempted settlement and the previous ones—apart from the difference between a collapsed Cold War and a brutal, destructive war fought to a bloody and decisive end. The generalization, familiar to students of international relations, is that successful international institutions need to be promoted by the most powerful states of their day, which view these institutions as in their interests. The Concert of Europe until 1823 and the American-led system of postwar international regimes met these conditions; the Concert in its later days and the League of Nations—because of the absence of the United States—did not. With respect to the contemporary situation in Europe, the chapters in this volume show a remarkable congruence between institutions and the realities of power: the rich and powerful western states have set the institutional terms for inclusion and the benefits that ensue from it; weak, aspiring countries in the east have to adjust their policies to meet these standards. Hence, as long as the western states remain cohesive and strong, and the United States continues to be involved in European politics, the institutions that serve their interests are likely to persist.

The key institutional difference between the past settlements and the current one is that in the earlier cases international institutions had to be created *de novo,* whereas the key institutions of the post-1989 settlement in Europe have a continuous history since the 1940s and 1950s, and have been consistently supported by the most powerful states during that time. The EC, NATO, GATT, and the IMF all benefit not merely from inertia and the fact that costs of organization have already been paid, but also from fear of the uncertainty that would ensue in the event of their collapse. In general, it seems easier to maintain and adapt existing institutions than to create new ones. Europe in 1815, 1919, and 1945 needed architects and master builders, whereas in 1989 carpenters with some flair for improvisation and modification sufficed. Whether this remodeling will last, of course, remains to be seen.

The authors of this book seek to apply an institutionalist perspective, which draws on both realist and liberal theories of international relations, to events in Europe between November 1989 and August 1991. We explore how international institutions affected state strategies and patterns of cooperation in the wake of the collapse of the Soviet empire in eastern Europe. We are reluctant to draw grandiose or far-reaching theoretical conclusions from such a brief period in which so many unexpected events took place. However, by looking carefully at what strategies states chose at the end of the Cold War and how they worked through established institutions, we show the variety of ways in which these institutions affected these strategies, both on issues of "high politics" and on economic questions. In so doing we provide evidence that may help toward an understanding of a contemporary revolution in world affairs by highlighting the significance for state strategies of international institutions and the variety of roles that such institutions played. The research reported in this volume should also prove useful as future scholars, with greater distance, try to understand what happened in Europe when the bipolar structure of world politics collapsed between 1989 and 1991. In turn, that information can be brought to bear on the grand theories that provide our deepest presumptions, and thus shape our understanding of the changing nature of world politics.

I

Strategies of Major Powers

Chapter 1

Mars or Minerva?
A United Germany in a
Post–Cold War Europe

Jeffrey J. Anderson

John B. Goodman

The reunification of Germany on October 3, 1990, sounded the death knell for the Cold War. This event, unimaginable only years earlier, redefined the German question and recast the debate over the continent's future. Would Europe remain a locus of stability or disintegrate into a cycle of conflict? And what role would a united Germany play in the eventual outcome? In this chapter we seek to shed new light on these questions by analyzing the impact of the end of the Cold War on Germany. We focus on how German elites defined their economic and security interests and strategies in the critical period between the breaching of the Berlin Wall in November 1989 and the fall of 1991. In particular, we examine whether and how this process was influenced by the thick web of international institutions in which West Germany had participated since its inception as a state in 1949.

The most striking feature about West Germany in the Cold War period was the weight attached by its leaders to international institutions such as the North Atlantic Treaty Organization (NATO) and the European Community (EC). Membership provided instruments for the conduct of West German state strategies; that is, institutions enabled West Germany to pursue its economic and political interests, and were valued accordingly. Yet, institutions also restructured and ultimately remolded German interests, so that, in the eyes of German political elites, institutional memberships were not merely instruments of policy but also normative frameworks for policy-making. The development of reflexive support for institutions in the Federal Republic is one of the principal legacies of the Cold War period, and one that has played an important role in shaping German interests since unification.

The origins of Germany's institutional commitments lay in its unique position in the postwar period. Precisely because the Federal Republic was a semi-sovereign state operating within a bipolar system, the country was forced to rely almost entirely on international institutions to achieve its objectives.[1] The country's strategy of export-led growth, for example, rested on the benefits of membership in the European Community. Guaranteed access to a large European market helped German firms achieve scale econo-mies and successfully penetrate international markets.[2] The EC also helped Germany's economy by securing a zone of monetary stability through trade. The EC proved no less important to the Federal Republic in the realm of foreign policy. For obvious reasons, postwar German governments could not aspire to an international role commensurate with their country's economic power. The EC thus served as a legitimate vehicle for West German integra-tion into the international community.[3] Much the same can be said for German membership in NATO. Konrad Adenauer viewed rearmament within NATO as an essential deterrent to Soviet aggression and as a counterweight to Soviet pressure. NATO membership also served to integrate the Federal Republic in the western alliance as a contributing partner, and secured long-term leverage to effect the reunification of Germany (the "policy of strength"). In the realms of both economics and defense, therefore, a web of interlocking institutions defined the range within which the Federal Republic developed its foreign policy.

This is not to suggest that West Germany refrained from unilateral action or that its commitments to international institutions were entirely free of contradiction or internal tension. Bonn's efforts to keep the goal of reunifica-tion simmering, if not at full boil, on the international agenda created tensions with its western allies. Ostpolitik, too, raised international doubts about the strength of Germany's ties to the west.[4] And once Ostpolitik proved success-ful, West German officials became more assertive in the pursuit of their national interests, which translated into a greater reluctance to play the role of Community paymaster or to sacrifice détente during frigid periods in U.S.-Soviet relations.[5] However, the intense debates unleashed within Ger-many by these unilateral initiatives suggested just how firmly the country's conception of its own interests in the Cold War period was shaped by the broader institutional environment.

Given this almost exaggerated reliance on institutions, Germany represents a critical case for examining the relationship between domestic politics, state strategies, and international institutions in the midst of a changing international structure. Germany was the only country in western Europe during this period to sustain a marked transformation of its domestic political system as a result of the passing of the Cold War. The augmentation of domestic resources brought about by unification has combined with changes in the international system to make Germany the most powerful state in western and central Europe. With unification regained in the context of an increasingly multipolar Europe, will Germany continue to pursue its objectives through the EC and NATO? Or will its leaders, freed from the constraints of bipolarity, return to older patterns of autarkic behavior? Plausible arguments can be constructed for either outcome.

German policymakers at the helm of a substantially more powerful state might feel sufficiently capable of pursuing unilateral and bilateral diplomatic strategies. Indeed, Bonn might well be compelled to make use of such options, since the prospects for a return to the pre-1945 geopolitical configuration, in which Germany occupied a tenuous position as "the country in the middle," have increased.[6] Even if multilateral strategies should continue to hold some attraction for Germany, the collapse of bipolarity removes the constraints on conflict in the economic sphere and introduces powerful strains on its relations with EC partners and the United States, thus jeopardizing the foundation on which institutionalized cooperation has been based.[7] In sum, it could be argued that Germany's reliance on international institutions such as the EC and NATO would decline, perhaps precipitously.

One could also argue that Germany confronts strong, if not strengthened, incentives to remain embedded within its web of international institutions. Despite the change in the distribution of capabilities in the international system, institutional memberships should still be attractive to German foreign policymakers. Participation in NATO and other institutions such as the Conference on Security and Cooperation in Europe (CSCE) should continue to satisfy the country's evolving defense needs in very uncertain times while reassuring both allies and (former) adversaries of the benign intentions of a united Germany. The alternative—a renationalization of military security policy—would be prohibitively expensive and in all likelihood lead to balancing behavior by other states. EC membership would provide Germany with the same economic advantages that had accrued to it in the past.[8] Moreover, German governments only recently entered into ongoing, parallel processes of institutional change in the EC, including the completion of the internal market, Economic and Monetary Union (EMU), and a common foreign and defense policy.[9] From a purely instrumental standpoint, strong German commitments to these initiatives should carry into the postunification period for two reasons: first, the factors that gave rise to these initiatives are still operative; and second, any effort by Germany to renege on these commitments would elicit not just negative economic consequences but the very real possibility of economic and political isolation. In short, a united Germany could be expected to seek changes in, or accord different priorities to, the international institutions to which it belongs, but its foreign policy will continue to be shaped by strong, multilateral ties for the foreseeable future.

In addressing these complex questions, we confront a thorny methodological problem: the insufficient passage of time as of this writing. Three years down the road from the breaching of the Berlin Wall and just two from the formal unification of the German state is not, in all probability, enough time to produce definitive changes in state strategies, let alone definitive outcomes. Even if German elites ultimately pursue more self-reliant strategies, the process is likely to take years, if not decades. How to guard against mistaking the inertia that maintains existing state strategies in the short run for a long-term outcome?

Our approach is *not* to look for outcomes or new state strategies in full swing; rather, we examine the way in which German political elites were defining their foreign economic and defense interests, and the extent to which international institutions played a role in the definition process. We explore whether policymakers in a united Germany consciously adopted or eschewed the pursuit of autarkic strategies, and whether they defined their relevant strategic options wholly or partly in terms of institutional solutions. Using pre-1989 state strategies as a benchmark, we focus on two distinct periods in recent German history: the period of unification, which lasted from November 9, 1989, to October 3, 1990, and the postunification period from October 1980 to the fall of 1991. Patterns of continuity and change across these periods are of particular importance in estimating the impact of institutions on emerging German state strategies.

This chapter consists of three sections. The first analyzes the events leading up to unification and their effect on the internal debate in Germany over its foreign economic and defense policies. The second explores the conduct of German foreign policy since unification. The third then draws the implications of our analysis for the ongoing debates about the relationship between domestic politics, institutions, and foreign policy.

The Path to Unification

When the East German government opened its borders with the Federal Republic on November 9, 1989, bowing to the weight of peaceful mass demonstrations, the stunning exodus of its citizenry through adjacent east European countries, and the refusal of its Soviet patron to implement the Brezhnev doctrine, few suspected that unification was a mere eleven months away. To be sure, prospects had risen dramatically; but seasoned observers were speaking in terms of decades before a national reunion could take place. The sequence of events that led to economic and monetary union on July 1, 1990, and to full political union on October 3 are well documented;[10] what concerns us here are the legacies of the unification process for postunification state strategies. The bargains that policymakers pursued, the commitments they made or broke, and the prices they were willing to pay to achieve unification can provide us with reliable indicators of their perceptions of the international environment and the institutional limits within which they formulated the nation's foreign policies. The unification period can also shed light on the basis of German commitments to international institutions. Major stock taking on the part of political elites, even if this resulted in a continuation of preunification strategies, would suggest an instrumental approach to international institutions. The absence of public reappraisals, by way of contrast, would imply that the country's institutional commitments had become part and parcel of German conceptions of state interests.

The loosening of constraints on unification originated outside the territory of the two Germanys. The accelerating drive for unification, however, came from within; the Monday demonstrations in Leipzig turned increasingly into unification rallies; the direct exodus from East to West Germany quickly reached crisis proportions; and the East German economy teetered on the brink of total economic collapse. The sober path to unification soon became a speedway, as politicians in the West raced against the clock and against one another.[11] Along the way, a number of consequential debates and decisions occurred, some of which proved to be of importance to postunification state strategies.

By far the greatest controversy surrounded the issue of German economic and monetary union, which was announced as a goal by Helmut Kohl in early February 1990 and implemented with amazing rapidity on July 1. To characterize it as a controversy is perhaps to force an unwarranted degree of order on the debate, which actually consisted of a bewildering number of competing positions that pitted government against the opposition, ministry against ministry, coalition partner against coalition partner, and region against region. On the major points of contention, the position backed by the chancellor prevailed. For example, the government's intention to rely on *Ordungs-politik*—"the free play of market forces within a secure, unobtrusive, and well-understood institutional and financial framework"[12]—to effect the transformation of the former German Democratic Republic's economy was challenged vigorously but unsuccessfully by the Social Democratic party (SPD), which argued for greater state interventionism. As to the timing and terms of German monetary union, which featured the Bundesbank and the federal government in a public and not entirely restrained debate, the government's position prevailed again: rapid unification on terms much more favorable to wage earners and pensioners in the East.[13] The coalition government, facing an imminent national election, also chose to finance the increasing costs of unification by borrowing instead of increasing taxes, again contrary to the recommendations of the Bundesbank. In short, straightforward political considerations, some justifiable, some perhaps less so, trumped the economic counsel of the custodian of the country's monetary system.

These and other controversies associated with the extension of the West German financial and economic framework to the East—the debate between the eleven western Länder and the government over the financial burden sharing in the GDR bailout; the conflict between the trade unions and the SPD on the one hand and the government and the Bundesbank on the other over wage policies in the East; squabbling in the governing coalition over tax policy in the East—unfolded within reference points established by domestic politics. Nevertheless, the resolution of these conflicts and the ultimate form of German monetary union were also shaped by the country's international commitments. For example, the government's decision to apply the precepts of the social market economy to East Germany was strengthened by perceptions that any weakening of its commitment to market principles and free trade would sour relations with EC partners by calling into question its long-standing positions on these matters at the supranational level. The massive financial costs associated with German monetary union also had international implications.[14] The Bundesbank intensified its commitment to safeguard price stability through a policy of high interest rates, not just to rein in incipient inflationary tendencies touched off by monetary union but also to signal to its partners in the European Monetary System (EMS) that the anchor function of the deutsche mark within the EMS was not in jeopardy despite the difficult economic times.[15] This placed the bank in apparent opposition to government objectives, both domestic and international, and to the expectations of Germany's trading partners in Europe and in North America. Moreover, the rapid snowballing of fiscal burdens promised to constrain Germany's ability to meet the requests for assistance from the poorer members of the EC and from the countries of east Europe.

The security ramifications of German unification were far more consequential, yet in the end they generated much less domestic controversy than the economic dimension. The restoration of full German sovereignty raised issues involving territorial borders, the residual yet legally and symbolically important prerogatives of the Four Powers, and the country's alliance status. The "two-plus-four" talks provided the vehicle for resolving some of the most difficult issues associated with unification. At U.S. insistence, and over the muted objections of France, Britain, and the Soviet Union, the negotiating framework was structured in such a way as to ensure that the restoration of full German sovereignty and unification of the two Germanys remained coupled. Under "two plus four," the two German states formulated a common position on the external aspects of unification, which was then conveyed to the Four Powers. According to Karl Kaiser, this formula "ensured respect for Germany's right to self-determination as well as its established relationship of cooperation with the West. The formula, moreover, implied that Germany's unification was to be achieved not as the result of a peace conference but in the form of what would eventually become the Treaty on the Final Settlement, signed by the six parties on September 12, 1990, in Moscow."[16]

Germany's alliance status and, by implication, its relation to the Soviet Union presented a number of difficult obstacles for the parties involved. For the vast majority of German political elites and their western allies, continued membership in NATO was considered essential to the stability of a post–Cold War Europe.[17] Indeed, there is no evidence of elite reappraisal of Germany's membership in NATO; the question posed by German politicians was not *whether* to remain in the Atlantic Alliance but rather *how to adapt* the alliance, with due regard for the interests of other members, to the rapidly changing circumstances on the continent. The ability of the western alliance to prevail over the initial objections of the Soviet Union can be attributed to several factors.[18] First, internal debates within the Kremlin, which generated a swirl of competing and often contradictory public positions on Germany's future alliance status, eventually centered on the conditional acceptability of what had historically been viewed as unacceptable. Second, the post-1989 NATO was not the NATO of old. An ongoing reform process, sparked by the events of the previous year, had led to public pronouncements such as the June 1990 Message from Turnberry and the London Declaration of July which redefined the Atlantic Alliance. By moving away from the traditional doctrines of "flexible response" and "forward defense," NATO made continued German membership palatable not only to the Soviet Union but also to the German public, in both West and East. Third, additional German assurances to the Soviets sealed agreement on the matter. In a July 1990 meeting between Chancellor Kohl and Soviet President Mikhail Gorbachev, Kohl pledged to limit German troop levels to 370,000 soldiers and to establish a special military status for the former GDR.[19] Bonn also reaffirmed its commitment to the Treaty on the Nonproliferation of Nuclear Weapons; its intention never to engage in the manufacture, possession, and control of nuclear, biological, and chemical weapons; and its desire to deepen consultation procedures within the CSCE. Outside the two-plus-four negotiations, Bonn and Moscow agreed on the terms of a bilateral treaty that sought to deepen consultative relations and provide for economic aid and technical assistance for the faltering Soviet economy; final ratification took place in the first few months of 1991.

Also embedded within the two-plus-four talks was the issue of Germany's eastern border with Poland. Historically, the Christian Democratic Union (CDU) and its sister party the Christian Socialist Union (CSU) had refused to acknowledge the Oder-Neisse line as the permanent border with Poland in order to preserve Bonn's legal right to represent Germany in its pre-1937 borders at any future peace conference at which reunification would be discussed.[20] The chancellor's less than forthright affirmation of the Oder-Neisse border, made largely with domestic electoral considerations in mind, generated a great deal of tension in German-Polish relations and growing unease in the international community. The government's concern to secure the rights of Poland's ethnic minorities of German heritage deepened worries about German irredentism. It should be pointed out that with the exception of a small minority of expellees, refugees, and neofascists, the vast majority of Germans in the West (and, so it would appear, in the East) entertained no thoughts of reestablishing the prewar borders of the Third Reich.[21] With unification completed, they fully expected that a finalization of the border issue would follow as a matter of course. And indeed it did. The final settlement produced by two-plus-four outlined the borders of a united Germany. It also stipulated that Germany and Poland confirm their common border with a treaty and, in an initiative aimed at the constitutional process unfolding in Germany, that Bonn remove all language from the Basic Law that could be interpreted as calling into question the country's borders.[22] In sum, two-plus-four proved to be a flexible vehicle for resolving the difficult questions relating to the sovereignty, alliance status, and territorial borders of a uniting Germany. Thus, in the area of defense the unification process was structured by and ultimately completed within the international institutions to which Germany belonged.

On the economic front, unification raised concerns about Germany's commitments to the European Community. Here, two issues stood out for what they signaled about German intentions and longer-term strategies: first, the terms of East Germany's accession to the EC; and second, the future of European economic and political integration. As a rapid merger of the two Germanys became increasingly likely, the Community faced difficult questions regarding the accession of East Germany. The twelve members and the European Commission were eager to avoid an accession treaty for the GDR or for a newly constituted German state, since either would have required a renegotiation of the Treaty of Rome in the midst of difficult ongoing talks over the implementation of the Single European Act, not to mention EMU and political union. Since German unification proceeded by way of Article 23 of the Basic Law, which provided for the absorption of the five new Länder by the Federal Republic, the treaty of accession route proved unnecessary. Nevertheless, potentially contentious issues remained.

First, it was unclear how quickly and to what extent East Germany would have to accept the *acquis communautaire;* the strictures of competition policy, environmental regulations, taxation, and technical standards would have placed severe burdens on the collapsing regional economy. Many expected Germany to request long grace periods, which heightened concern among other EC members that subsidies and environmental dispensations would give East German industries a competitive advantage and that substandard, even dangerous products from the former GDR would find their way onto Community markets.[23] Second, it was conceivable that East Germany would be entitled to massive assistance from the EC's structural funds, particularly the European Regional Development Fund and the European Social Fund. Its decrepit industry, crumbling infrastructure, polluted landscape, and idled work force made it a prime candidate for transfers from Brussels. Southern members such as Spain, Portugal, and Greece viewed this new competitor for EC largesse with growing alarm.

If the negotiations over the terms of East Germany's accession turned ugly, long-term negative consequences for the Community could result; Germany, bitter over the outcome, would cool to the post-1992 package of reforms, and could even reevaluate its role as financier of the status quo. The German strategy, which took shape during the first half of 1990, dispelled many of these fears. At the Dublin summit in April, Chancellor Kohl announced his government's willingness to waive Community structural fund assistance for the soon-to-be former GDR, and offered to undertake the rehabilitation of the five new Länder on the basis of domestic initiatives consistent with Community law. In this manner Bonn hoped to quell the anxieties of southern members *and* to minimize the European Commission's regulatory control over certain domestic components of the unification process; reforms to the structural funds, dating from the early 1980s, had enabled the commission to intervene directly in the regional policy-making process of member states.[24]

The final terms of accession for East Germany emerged rather painlessly and left no discernible legacy for future relations between Germany and its EC partners. The Community refused to accept Germany's refusal of structural funds assistance; in August 1990 the European Commission committed ECU (European Currency Unit) 3 billion in regional assistance to the former GDR for the period 1991–1993.[25] The agreement also stipulated that fully 80 percent of the single market's rules, including those dealing with financial services, mergers, and the free movement of people and capital, would apply immediately upon unification. Standards for nuclear safety would also apply immediately. On other issues such as agriculture and pollution standards, the agreement provided for grace periods of varying lengths.

With regard to the future of EMU and political union, two complementary forces were at work: first, the desire of Jacques Delors, president of the EC Commission, and of key EC members such as France to secure from Germany an early and irreversible affirmation of the goals and process of integration; and second, the concern of Chancellor Kohl and Foreign Minister Hans-Dietrich Genscher to establish the new Germany's credentials as a pro-European member. In March 1990 Kohl announced his government's unwavering support for EMU, subject to long-standing German concerns about its organization. In April he and French President François Mitterrand called for a December intergovernmental conference on political union, to run parallel to that dealing with EMU, which would chart a course toward a stronger, more democratic Community and a common foreign and defense policy. In the face of domestic concerns about the dangers and risks of EMU, voiced principally by the Bundesbank and the Ministry of Finance, the chancellor committed his country to accelerated progress toward the twin and, as he maintained, inseparable objectives of economic and political reform in the EC. In Kohl's view any German hesitation on these issues, however justified, would be interpreted in EC capitals as foot-dragging by the new colossus. To continue to influence the debate over the future of the EC, Germany had to declare itself ready to lead the reform movement in conjunction with France and other EC partners.

Thus, on October 3, 1990, Germany left the period of "two states, one nation" in possession of the same institutional commitments it had held since 1949. The deepening of its support for NATO and the EC, along with the intense bilateral diplomacy directed at the east bloc countries, was virtually reflexive; reassessments and reappraisals were simply nowhere to be seen. Germany, certain of the economic and security benefits derived from multi-lateralism in the past, sought above all else to allay the doubts of its allies in the west and its (former) adversaries in the east. Many of its actions were directed at one or the other audience, as in the case of its affirmation of German support for EMU and political union. Other actions reached both audiences; for example, its resolute commitment to NATO coupled with self-imposed limits on troop levels and military capabilities reassured not only the Soviet Union and the fledgling democracies in eastern Europe but also its allies in the west. As Karl Kaiser argues, these actions "were meant to create in the eyes of the other powers a reasonable certainty that, even if political circumstances changed, Germany would not be able to reestablish itself as a great military power."[26]

Postunification German State Strategies

The domestic and international terms on which unification took place created strong incentives for continuity in the foreign economic and military security strategies of the German government. Continuity does not connote the absence of change. In fact, the political leadership in government and in the main opposition party supported active adjustment precisely in order to ensure continuity. Several objectives guided their actions: first, to ensure a speedy, collective appraisal of the radically new military situation on the European continent, which had far-ranging implications for German foreign policy; second, to allay the concerns of allies and adversaries about the economic and military intentions of a united Germany; and third, to promote the adaptation of existing international institutions in order to bring them into line with changed circumstances and with evolving German interests.

These objectives resulted in a continuation of the drive to embed Germany in an interlocking network of international institutions. It should be pointed out that the compatibility of Germany's intensified institutional commitments was not self-evident. But on the whole, Germany, of all the states in Europe, continued to promote its economic and military security almost exclusively through multilateral action. State strategies during this period are difficult to explain solely in terms of the pursuit of instrumental interests. To be sure, German policymakers employed institutions and, in some cases, proposed extensive reforms in their structure and goals to achieve concrete national objectives. Yet bedrock institutional commitments were never called into question, and many reform proposals, notably in connection with the EC, aimed to strengthen international institutions at the expense of the national sovereignties of member states, including, of course, Germany itself.

Changes in German State Interests since Unification

The most sweeping changes in German foreign policy occurred in the realm of military security. The principles that guide Germany's foreign economic policy showed fewer signs of change, although the conditions required for their successful implementation altered visibly. These in turn led to clear, conscious strategic choices by German elites, the bulk of which involve international institutions.

The Military Threat and Germany's Evolving Security Needs   For forty years the threat to the Federal Republic emanated from a single adversary—the Soviet Union and its Warsaw Treaty Organization (WTO) allies. Conventional and especially nuclear deterrence were indispensable to the survival of this front-line state. To German policymakers the stakes seemed extraordinarily high; successful deterrence generated at best an uneasy peace, whereas failure would mean the instant transformation of both Germanys into a conventional and, in all likelihood, nuclear battlefield. Thus, the unfolding situation in post–Cold War Europe cannot in truth be represented simply as an easing of east-west tensions. This is far too timid a description. Almost overnight the military situation was transformed, and no other country experienced the change as intensely as Germany. The threat, at least in its Cold War incarnation, expired, and the country faced a completely new risk scenario. Ministries and political parties grappled with the definition of the threat, and their answers provided the basis not only for Germany's defense policies but also for the international role that the country hoped to assume. The Persian Gulf War and the Yugoslavian crisis played important parts in spurring a domestic reappraisal. Although there remained *i*'s to be dotted and *t*'s to be crossed, firm answers to Germany's military security needs and postures began to take shape during this period.

The Ministry of Defense identified at least four types of military threats confronting a unified Germany. The most dangerous threat, but also the least likely to occur, was an attack by the USSR and any loyal remnants of the WTO alliance forces. Officials noted that the Soviet Union, even after the implementation of the Conventional Forces in Europe (CFE) agreement and the START (Strategic Arms Reduction) treaty, would remain the largest conventional power, and the only nuclear superpower, on the continent. Second, the ministry saw new risks stemming from internal instability and fragmentation in east Europe and the Soviet Union. As one official observed, "A wounded bear can be dangerous, and rather incalculable." Third, Germany had to take account of risks emanating from outside the NATO area, particularly to the south, that had the potential to spill over into NATO's traditional area of operations. Finally, Germany had to cope with the possibility of large flows of immigrants fleeing economic deprivation in the south or instability in the east. This latter category of threat, ministry officials freely admitted, could not easily be brought under the traditional rubric of military security, and would necessitate new mechanisms of coordination with the Foreign Ministry. Taken together, these four threats constituted a complete change in the security landscape facing a united Germany.

In general, German officials concurred in at least three respects regarding the threats now facing the country. First, the principal threat from the Soviet Union receded both in intensity and in immediacy. The presence of Soviet troops in East Germany and several former WTO countries notwithstanding, officials argued that with the loss of its glacis, the Soviet Union was no longer poised at the borders of the Federal Republic. Second, perhaps not surprisingly, the threat facing Germany grew more diffuse and less calculable. As an official of the Free Democratic Party (FDP) put it, "We have faith in

Gorbachev, but who knows what comes after him?" A menacing adversary, of known quantity and situated in the center region, gave way to a more complex, less familiar set of hazards. And finally, elites acknowledged that this ongoing reassessment had thus far been a wrenching experience for Germany. Obsessed with regional security since its emergence as a state, the country was unaccustomed to thinking in global terms.

The transformation of the threat scenario had an impact on German perceptions of the country's nuclear and conventional requirements. Although German support for short-range nuclear weapons declined dramatically with the retreat of Soviet power, the risk posed by the large Soviet arsenal, as well as the uncertain risk of nuclear proliferation in the Third World, led elites in both government and opposition to attach great weight to the benefits of the American nuclear umbrella. Indeed, German officials stated that they would not feel comfortable being protected solely by the French and British nuclear deterrents.

Nevertheless, a debate did take shape between the government and the SPD opposition over the necessity of maintaining a land-based nuclear deterrent on German soil. Both agreed on the acceptability of a sea-based deterrent, but here the SPD drew the line. According to the Social Democrats, the presence on German soil of aircraft capable of launching cruise missiles posed a controversial question in times of peace. The party argued that with sufficient warning, it would be possible to "renuclearize" Germany in a time of crisis; indeed, this could function as a deliberate escalatory step. The Ministry of Defense countered that extended deterrence required the stationing of nuclear weapons on land, and it maintained this position during the NATO review. Arguing that NATO members had to share both the benefits and risks of the nuclear deterrent, the ministry maintained that Bonn had to be willing to provide the launchers and aircraft, and station them on German territory.

Regarding Germany's conventional needs the picture was less clear. Estimating minimum force requirements and their composition is not an exact science even in the best of times, and it becomes more difficult in the absence of a well-defined front and the presence of a less distinct threat and an ongoing debate over the missions of NATO, the WEU, and the CSCE. In the run-up to the summit with Gorbachev in July 1990 and at Chancellor Kohl's request, the Ministry of Defense undertook a review of Germany's minimum force requirements. To meet its current obligations to the Atlantic Alliance and any future obligations in the EC (consistent with arms control objectives under CFE), the ministry generated an acceptable minimum force level of between 350,000 and 370,000—the figure agreed to by Kohl and Gorbachev in July 1990.

Thus, there appears to be an ongoing interaction between changes in the structure of the international system on the one hand and changing perceptions of the threat facing the country and of the country's military security requirements on the other. The country faced old threats of substantially diminished magnitude and new threats that were difficult to evaluate precisely. Unlike in the days when NATO and the Warsaw Pact squared off against each other, now the considerations that impinged upon German defense planning were considerably broader. Nevertheless, hardheaded realism continued to permeate German appraisals of Soviet foreign policy; even if a fully articulated cooperative security structure that included the Soviets were eventually formed under CSCE auspices, German defense specialists maintained that the USSR's considerable conventional and strategic options had to be balanced. However, they also insisted that coping with the residual risk from the east required Germany and its allies to take into account the divergent security concerns of the Soviet Union and its former satellites, and to promote actively the region's economic and political stabilization.

German Foreign Economic Policy Objectives Here, continuity with the pre-1989 period was unmistakable. To many officials the economic landscape surrounding a united Germany remained largely unchanged. Thus, despite the mounting costs of restructuring the eastern Länder and the government's occasional departures from the canons of the *Sozialemarktwirtschaft,* they adhered to the overarching objectives of price stability, free trade, and export-led growth. They also assigned a high priority to the expansion of trade links with east Europe and the USSR, which would augment German prosperity and, at the same time, promote stable economic and political liberalization in these countries. Thus, Germany's military and economic security concerns dovetailed in a way that had been inconceivable during the Cold War. Domestic economic objectives played a part in this revised version of Ostpolitik; one of the most direct ways of rejuvenating the East German regional economy was to establish vibrant economic ties to the eastern bloc.

Despite the seismic changes on the domestic scene since November 1989, the politico-economic coalition underpinning export-led growth remained intact in a united Germany. Producer groups were quick to organize in the East, but they exerted no noticeable influence on the broader contours of Germany's foreign economic policy. For the most part they remained vocal yet passive recipients of federal largesse and of the cautious investment initiatives of West German firms. Coupled with the widespread concern in Bonn about the potential for an East German version of Italy's Mezzogiorno, these factors explain the government's drive to effect a short, sharp transition to a competitive economy in the five new Länder and its resolve to ignore the more extreme protectionist demands of local and regional actors in East Germany.

Two new and closely interrelated objectives, which entailed costly financial commitments for the united German state, reinforced the predilection for free trade. On the domestic side, Bonn needed to come up with substantial outlays over the short to medium term to convert the East German regional economy from socialism to capitalism. In addition to the costs of economic modernization, there loomed anticipated expenditures on environmental clean-up, infrastructure, housing, the transfer of the seat of government from Bonn to Berlin, and the gradual withdrawal of Soviet troops. The bill for these huge tasks, estimated at approximately DM 500 billion over the next decade, would in all likelihood be paid with proceeds from the West German economy, which reinforced the value of the perennial cash cow for (West) German industry: free trade on international markets.

The second objective, which promised to be far more expensive and about which German officials were palpably less sanguine, concerned the future of political and economic reform in eastern Europe and the Soviet Union. With the Cold War over and unification complete, there emerged in Bonn a widespread consensus about the obligations of the new Germany to expand its commitments vis-à-vis the East. Germany's proximity to these areas presented an obvious rationale; according to a civil servant in the Foreign Ministry: "In terms of our political geography, we are bound to be pioneers in Ostpolitik . . . We have no interest in building fences." The logic was straightforward. Large amounts of technical and financial assistance would be needed to effect reasonably smooth transitions to a market economy; to make these countries more export-capable so as to increase their earnings of hard currency; and to secure minimum levels of prosperity, which in turn would dampen antidemocratic unrest, regional conflicts, and westward mass migration. Politicians and civil servants alike acknowledged that they enjoyed the least influence in precisely that country most vital to German security: the Soviet Union. Nevertheless, they firmly believed in the need to undertake actions, both unilaterally and multilaterally, that would prevent the political or economic isolation of the USSR.

German officials also viewed the economic and political liberalization process in the eastern bloc as a vital step in the rejuvenation of the five new Länder, which would in turn provide a broader foundation for the country's export-led growth strategy. Comecon's decision in 1990 to shift to trade based on convertible currency, when added to the fall-off in demand for imports from key countries such as the USSR, contributed immensely to the collapse in industrial production in the former GDR. Any reestablishment of trade relations between East Germany and the eastern bloc countries, however, was predicated in large part on providing a jump start to these former command economies in the midst of transition. Once again, the prospect of large, long-term financial commitments strengthened the resolve of German policymakers to maintain Germany's access to international markets. This resolve carried with it consequential implications for the scope of unilateral action on the part of Germany, as well as its role within key international institutions such as the EC and GATT (General Agreement on Tariffs and Trade).

International Institutions and German State Strategies

During this period, international institutions served as the vehicles of choice for the pursuit of the preceding economic and military security objectives, although German foreign policymakers employed bilateral diplomacy on a selective basis.

The Scope for Bilateral Diplomacy and Unilateral Action The bulk of German bilateral diplomacy during this period was directed at the USSR and eastern Europe. After unification Germany sought to conclude bilateral treaties with the Soviet Union and several eastern European countries. The purpose of these treaties was to signal Germany's peaceful intentions to its eastern neighbors and to create the basis for future cooperation in the areas of cultural exchange, the environment, and trade relations.[27] In its "neighbor treaties" with Poland, Hungary, and Czechoslovakia, the German government gave assurances that it would support association with and eventual membership in the European Community. Bonn also sought to guarantee the cultural and political rights of ethnic Germans living in these countries.[28]

The use of bilateral diplomacy arose out of several factors. In the first place, the substance of the negotiations involved issues of a largely bilateral relevance; in other words, these matters could not be addressed through multilateral frameworks such as the EC or CSCE. Second, Bonn policymakers believed that the reestablishment of sound trading relations with these countries could not wait for the cumbersome assembly of multilateral aid packages. Although Germany pressed consistently for multilateral aid to the USSR and the new democracies in eastern Europe, it encountered resistance from the United States, Britain, and Japan, which evaluated such proposals on the basis of commercial criteria. Finally, certain issues such as environmental safety and pollution lacked effective multilateral regimes, and the urgency attached to these problems prompted the Germans to pursue bilateral initiatives. Separate agreements with Poland and Czechoslovakia sought to control water pollution in the Elbe and Oder rivers and, most important, to regulate the operation of what the Germans consider dangerously antiquated nuclear power plants. These worries extended beyond straightforward considerations of public health. As a CDU member of the Bundestag told us: "If we had another Chernobyl in one of the eastern bloc countries, it would set off an irrational debate, a panicked debate in this country that would call into question the very foundation of our government's energy policy. We cannot stand idly by and allow this to happen."

Thus, Bonn's bilateral diplomacy targeted issues that either fell outside the current purview of international institutions or generated such a lack of consensus within multilateral frameworks that timely action was precluded. This is not to suggest that by engaging in these various forms of bilateral diplomacy Germany acted without regard to international institutions. Indeed, elites were sensitive to the potential for misunderstanding in the west and remained convinced of the futility of bilateral initiatives that did not rest on a firm multilateral foundation. Bonn policymakers requested approval of a Soviet trade package from the EC and OECD, and were required to scale back the duration of the program, its scope (Germany wished to extend the program to other eastern European countries), and the terms. Moreover, the prevailing opinion in the finance and economics ministries was that the financial limits of bilateral diplomacy had already been reached.[29] They predicted a concerted effort on the part of the Bonn government to arrange multilateral aid packages through the EC and the G-7 mechanism, since domestic budgetary constraints, exacerbated by the Gulf War contribution, had begun to pinch by the middle of 1991.[30] In the area of environmental policy, Germany also stepped up its emphasis on multilateral cooperation. The environment minister, Klaus Töpfer, called in June 1991 for the creation of an institutional framework to develop a Europe-wide environmental and energy policy. The goal was a set of guidelines that would render compatible the economic development of the eastern bloc and the preservation of the environment; the focus would be on concrete programs developed by smaller sets of contiguous states acting within a broader policy context administered by the EC or even the United Nations.[31]

Where unilateralism was concerned, Germany encountered intermittent, often severe criticism from its EC partners, the United States, and Japan for the externalities generated by its economic policy mix. The combination of the government's expansionary fiscal policy and the Bundesbank's restrictive monetary policy produced high interest rates, an unwelcome outcome for Germany's partners whose economies were slipping into recession. Bonn officials, particularly in the Chancellory and the Foreign Ministry, were sensitive to these charges, believing that German economic policy had to be made with an eye to international perceptions in order to quell doubts abroad about the intentions and goals of the enlarged Germany.[32] Thus, international concerns somewhat narrowed the scope for completely unilateral economic action during this period.

International Institutions and German Military Security   Widespread consensus reigned in German political circles about the present and future role of international institutions in Germany's defense policy. NATO, the WEU, and the CSCE were perceived as indispensable and as basically complementary, since each contributed uniquely to Germany's military security needs. Elites were also aware of the potential incompatibilities among the missions of these organizations, particularly the WEU and NATO, as well as the need for these institutions to adapt to changing circumstances if they were to remain relevant. Despite these strong commitments, there was little evidence of German leadership in the reform efforts under way in these three institutions, a situation that contrasted markedly with the country's role in the EC. In short, although policymakers possessed a strong sense of their interests, they saw their role as co-shapers of developments. They believed that the world was not ready for a high German profile in matters of military security, even if the efforts unfolded exclusively within the confines of international institutions.

Perhaps the best-developed consensus among the established parties (CDU/CSU, FDP, SPD) and the bureaucracy related to NATO. Within government circles the rationale was uniform: although reforms were needed, there was no substitute for NATO. As the only organization with an integrated command structure and forces in place, NATO balanced Soviet residual strategic options and stabilized pan-European cooperative frameworks such as the CSCE. NATO also provided the existential transatlantic tie: a continued albeit scaled-down U.S. presence in Germany was seen as essential. And finally, since German forces with offensive capabilities remained wholly integrated into the NATO command structure, NATO provided a guarantee that there would be no critical mass of forces under German control positioned in the center of Europe.[33] The official SPD position was also on balance positive toward the Atlantic Alliance. In addition to the advantages already outlined, the Social Democrats stressed the effect of NATO membership on the German military as an institution. As one SPD official noted: "Our military has profited greatly from participation in an integrated command, which has had a socializing influence. NATO works against any tendencies toward a renationalization of the German military." All parties agreed that NATO could not move in the direction of playing an "out-of-area" role in international crises without risking public support not only in Germany but across Europe, and all agreed that NATO membership should remain fixed for the foreseeable future, given lingering Soviet concerns. As in the immediately preceding period of unification, German reappraisals of NATO were directed not at the issue of membership but rather at the question of institutional adaptations to meet new challenges and risk scenarios. NATO appeared a veritable fixture in German conceptions of state interests and strategies.

A similar though perhaps less concrete consensus existed over the utility of the CSCE. As the only institution that blanketed Europe and bridged the Atlantic, it provided a framework that was appropriate for increasing stability among the countries on the continent and for addressing spillover regional conflicts. The development and extension of confidence-building measures and cooperation could not substitute for an active balancing of the residual Soviet threat, but they worked against any tendencies to isolate this European superpower. Moreover, the CSCE was home to the former WTO countries, whose security concerns were acute and a source of potential instability. Since these countries could not become members of NATO, the conference could provide a security forum. German policymakers acknowledged that this would be a difficult task, since the eastern Europeans are highly skeptical of the institution, having experienced it only under Soviet tutelage. German officials saw the CSCE as a framework within which successor arms control agreements to the CFE could be lodged. Government and opposition members argued that the thirty-five-member body, despite its unique attributes, bore the legacy of its past, a legacy that was ill suited to the changed situation in Europe. For example, the principles of unanimity and noninterference in domestic matters were dysfunctional in relation to the crises the CSCE would certainly face. The CSCE had to adapt its decision-making structure so as to avoid stasis and inefficiency.[34]

As for the Western European Union, the picture of consensus grows somewhat blurred. Whether the WEU turns out to be, in the words of our respondents, "a sleeping beauty" or "a stillborn child" remains an open question. Within government circles, by far the most consistent argument in favor of developing the WEU related to the priority assigned to European political union. Policymakers simply could not conceive of this ambitious goal without a defense component. As one high-placed government official stated: "Prosperity requires [European] unification, which in turn requires a security component." This same official went on to say that the WEU's field of maneuver was much greater with the decline of east-west tensions. It would be developed not against any alliance or state, least of all the United States, but would be "an expression of identity," the foundation of European union, and a bulwark against the renationalization of national security policies among its members. The organization was envisioned as playing a complementary role to that of NATO, finding its niche, for example, in purely European peacekeeping missions. The Ministry of Defense held to the view that WEU troop movements and even intervention in the context of a limited regional crisis in Europe would be far more acceptable to the Soviet Union than would similar actions by NATO.[35]

Furthermore, government officials expressed a desire to see the WEU participate in out-of-area actions under United Nations auspices. Security risks outside the NATO area, emanating from Europe's dependence on raw materials, stable markets, and unimpeded supply routes, could necessitate the development of this capability. Several officials maintained that the WEU could conceivably serve as an interim security refuge for eastern European countries. Officials acknowledged that it would be a delicate task to enable these countries to draw closer to the west without isolating the Soviet Union. This view of the WEU's potential value-added separated more ambitious proponents from supporters who argued that only the CSCE could walk the fine line between providing for the security concerns of eastern Europe and not angering the bear.

Germany's firm commitment to the WEU also stemmed from the need to keep the French in a cooperative mood in the context of difficult negotiations over EMU and political union. The French placed a high value on the WEU, and the Germans felt they had to remain amenable to the idea for the foreseeable future. In any event, if the WEU did not already exist, it would have to be created simply to complete the successor package to the Single European Act. This derivative justification for the WEU may explain the vague and somewhat inarticulate formulations of German policymakers. Indeed, one of the advantages attributed to the WEU was that it provided a relatively clean slate, an empty frame that presented few *immediate* incompatibilities with NATO; officials were able to argue with conviction that the WEU could be adapted to the as yet undetermined defense requirements of European union while remaining in harmony with the Atlantic Alliance. German officials appear to have given little thought to the ramifications of the non-overlapping memberships of the EC, the WEU, and NATO. In fact, a special attraction of the WEU was the fact that France is a full-fledged member. As a Foreign Ministry official explained: "We have to devise ways and means to bring the French back into the fold regarding the developing security picture."

In the broader debate about security architecture in western Europe, Germany occupied the middle ground between the United States and Britain, which envisioned the WEU as wholly subordinate to NATO, and France, which hoped to see the EC incorporate the WEU and replace NATO as the guarantor of European security.[36] The unalloyed allegiance to NATO that came through in public and private statements would seem to place the Germans much closer to the U.S.-U.K. pole. Policymakers argued that as long as nuclear weapons remained essential to Germany's security, and as long as the Americans were willing to maintain a presence in Europe, NATO would provide something the WEU could not. Indeed, an SPD official pointed out that the main threat to NATO comes not from the WEU but from the American Congress. If the troops were called home, the WEU would have to step in to fill NATO's shoes as a matter of course. Even a diminished U.S. presence in Europe would require considerable adjustment on the part of the Americans if tensions were to be avoided. A Chancellory official remarked that Washington would have to realize that the role it would play in Europe with 75,000 troops is not the same as the one it had played with 450,000. German government officials pointed out that as European union developed, EC foreign ministers would discuss security issues such as arms control with greater frequency, inaugurating an institutionalization of the European security realm. Should this occur, American attitudes toward the WEU as "the

European pillar in NATO" would require even more flexibility in the long run. Although the hardware and defense structures would remain with NATO, the Americans would have to accept that in many areas Europe would make up its own mind. Yet the Germans viewed this as entirely natural. As Chancellor Kohl stated in a speech in mid-May 1990: "Our defensive alliance is not an end in itself, but a mirror of the political situation. As this changes, so too must the alliance. The alliance of tomorrow, with a united Germany, will therefore have to be a different one than the one we know today."[37] The goal was cast in terms of a firm partnership between the United States and a united Europe; the WEU would cement this new partnership.

The Impact of International Crises   Karl Lamers, foreign policy spokesman for the CDU/CSU parliamentary caucus, aptly characterized the impact of the Gulf War on German politics as cathartic.[38] To say that the crisis caught the German political elite unawares understates the rapidity with which this issue took command of the public agenda. The period between the Iraqi invasion of Kuwait on August 2, 1990, and the commencement of the allied air war on January 16, 1991, was not an uneventful time in Germany; the spiraling costs of unification, as well as the campaign for and consequences of the first all-German elections since 1933, generated enough heat and light to occupy even the most inattentive of politicians. Yet, international perceptions of German dithering during the crisis wrenched the elites away from their preoccupation with internal matters. Well before anyone imagined, the country was forced to address difficult questions attached to Germany's international role. Although the debate had yet to achieve closure by the end of 1991, the outlines of a resolution were already apparent.

As a peaceful resolution to the crisis grew increasingly unlikely, the Bonn debate was touched off by German reluctance, led principally by the Foreign Ministry, to approve NATO's response to a Turkish request for protection against an Iraqi attack, which involved the dispatch of three air wings (an Italian, a Belgian, and a German) from the Allied Mobile Force. Although the NATO decision was carried out in early January 1991 with Germany on board, the new year ushered in a mixture of silence and hesitation on the part of government officials and outright opposition on the part of the SPD. For their part, the Social Democrats declared the decision contrary to the NATO charter. They accused NATO of installing a force with offensive capabilities and argued that NATO, as a purely defensive alliance, could not position forces where they would be drawn into a conflict; party officials pointed to the presence of American bombers at Incirlik in southern Turkey, which if used would constitute a casus belli for Iraq. In these circumstances, so maintained the Social Democrats, Germany's treaty obligation to come to the aid of its ally would not apply. The SPD also argued that Bonn's acquiescence in the stationing of the Allied Mobile Force in Turkey ran counter to the German Basic Law. Two members of the SPD presidium maintained that sending German troops into Turkey required two-thirds majority approval of the Bundestag, which had not been consulted by the Bonn government. They expressed serious doubts as to whether the Bundestag would deliver this approval, since efforts to find a peaceful solution to the crisis had not yet been exhausted. On January 22 leading SPD figures called for the withdrawal of the German air wing from Turkey.

On the government side, official statements stressed the defensive nature of the Allied Mobile Force and even cast some doubt as to the automaticity of Bonn's alliance obligations should fighting break out between Iraq and Turkey. One spokesman seemed to suggest that only a clear, unprovoked attack by Iraq would activate the mutual defense obligations of the NATO charter and would be consistent with Germany's constitution, which limited military operations to defensive purposes.[39] The government appeared eager to assure the public that the German component of the Allied Mobile Force represented the absolute limit of German military participation in the Gulf crisis; Chancellor Kohl declared two days after the start of the air campaign that owing to constitutional obstacles, no German troops would be sent to the Gulf. In addition to a succession of large peace demonstrations in major cities across the country, many of which struck a distinctly anti-American tone,[40] German politicians soon found themselves confronted with sharp negative reactions from the international community. The British and American press expressed dismay at the legalistic tone of government statements, pointed out the unseemly role of German firms in providing Iraq with the technology to equip its Scud missiles to reach Israeli territory, and questioned whether incipient pacifism and neutralism were appropriate compensation for the staunch support their countries had provided at critical junctures in the unification process. Many German officials felt the international reaction was overdone.[41] Regardless of the justness of international criticism, the impact on the domestic German debate was immediate.

Stung by the criticism, the government sought to repair its battered image by sending Foreign Minister Genscher on a flurry of trips to the Middle East and western capitals. Far more significant, the feeling that Germany had managed to isolate itself from its principal allies prompted a reassessment within the major parties, including the SPD. The contours of the ensuing debate—specifically, whether German troops should be able to participate in military actions under UN and/or other collective auspices—can be traced to the period during and immediately after the Gulf War.

Unalloyed arguments in favor of a broader international role for Germany came primarily from the CDU/CSU, which had supported a stronger German profile in the Gulf crisis from the beginning. On January 22 Volker Rühe, party chairman of the CDU, warned that Germany's reluctance to play an active role in collective security would threaten the overarching objective of European union. The subsequent clarification of the chancellor's position owed a great deal to the pressure exerted on him by his own party. On January 30 Kohl announced to the Bundestag: "There is for us Germans no niche in world politics, and there can be no flight from responsibility; we intend to make a contribution to a world of peace, freedom, and justice." The chancellor called for a national debate about the creation of a constitutional foundation for German participation in UN security actions.[42] This speech inaugurated a new phase in the debate, which centered on two basic issues.

The first concerned the scope of German participation in military actions outside the NATO area. CDU and CSU members supported a German presence in all UN- and European-sanctioned missions, while the FDP, in general agreement with the union parties, sought to limit German participation exclusively to UN actions. The official SPD position was to confine participation to UN peacekeeping ("blue helmet") missions. The Greens and the Party of Democratic Socialism (the erstwhile ruling Communist party of the GDR) opposed out-of-area actions under any circumstances.

The second issue addressed the need for an amendment to the Basic Law to permit German participation. The chancellor and the CDU/CSU stated that they would seek a constitutional amendment in order to cement a consensus within the country, although they believed that Germany's Basic Law in its present form did not preclude participation under UN auspices. The FDP believed that a constitutional amendment was both necessary and desirable, whereas the SPD supported an amendment that would limit German participation to UN blue helmet missions.[43] Kohl publicly rejected the SPD's position; in light of his party's interpretation of the Basic Law, the SPD proposal represented a retrograde step. Despite the absence of consensus, points of agreement emerged. The government parties wished to commit Germany to more than peacekeeping missions. The FDP and SPD agreed that the issue required constitutional clarification and, perhaps more significant, that UN-sanctioned missions should be the sole occasion for German actions out of area. Each major political party held that Germany's new international role had to be defined in terms of multilateral, collective frameworks of action established by one or more international institutions. Nevertheless, deadlock prevailed within the Bundestag, since no position commanded the two-thirds majority necessary to approve a constitutional amendment.

Government officials expressed confidence that they would be able to create a set of facts within a few years that would restore consensus in German foreign policy on their terms. Kohl's decision to send minesweepers to the Gulf and German units to Iran for the purpose of constructing camps and infirmaries for Iraqi refugees was designed to create precedents that future governments, even one led by the SPD, would find difficult to ignore.[44] The government's objective was to confront the Social Democrats with a transformed constitutional reality by 1994, the date of the next federal elections. A Chancellory official remarked that, given the depth of consensus over European union within Germany, a move to cement a German out-of-area commitment at the European level would create a fait accompli for the SPD.

This debate mirrored faithfully the breadth of opinion within Germany over the proper lessons of its past and its future place in the world. On one side were those who pointed to the burden of German history and the clear mission of home defense anchored in the constitution. On the other side were those who believed that as a stable democracy, Germany should meet additional international obligations commensurate with its enhanced size and economic power. In the words of the CDU politician Karl Lamers: "Responsibility is contingent upon power; power is contingent upon responsibility . . . If Germany acts as if it has no power, it will awaken only mistrust among its neighbors. Germany must therefore acknowledge its power . . . Without forgetting its history, Germany must become as normal as possible."[45] A pledge to participate in out-of-area actions under a UN or European banner, whether in the Middle East or in European regional conflicts, was seen by the chancellor and his supporters as a domestic prerequisite to German, indeed European, ambitions in the field of European union and a common defense policy. As a CDU member stated: "There is no part-time integration in this world anymore."

The critical dividing line in this national debate appeared to run straight through the SPD; of the major parties it was the most deeply split on the international role of a united Germany. Many of the assumptions that underpinned the SPD's Ostpolitik and security policy no longer held, and the party faced a difficult period of adjustment, particularly given the clear intentions of the government. Whether the observed rifts would have electoral ramifications comparable to those of the 1950s, when the party found itself politically isolated on a variety of domestic and foreign policy issues,[46] remained in large part contingent on future international crises, which could expose the party's internal divisions and the government's ability to use the issue effectively in 1994.

There was a profound connection between this domestic debate and Germany's broader international commitments and objectives. The repercussions of the Gulf War gave a significant push to the German commitment to a common EC foreign policy. The failure to secure a coordinated response to the crisis, for which Germany certainly bore a fair share of the responsibility, led to intensified efforts on the part of Germany, France, and the European Commission to move the Community beyond the tepid and ineffectual framework of European Political Cooperation.

In the midst of these deliberations, the Yugoslavian crisis erupted at the southern doorstep of the Community. Casting a nervous eye on the Soviet Union and the Baltic republics, Brussels emphasized the desirability of a peaceful resolution to the conflict and the preservation of national unity. The EC offered its services as a broker between the central government and breakaway republics, sending a delegation of three foreign ministers repeatedly to mediate the conflict. With the cooperation of the United States, the Community of Twelve also activated the CSCE crisis consultation mechanism established earlier in 1991.

A crack appeared in the EC's common front during the first week of July, when the German government signaled that the Community would have to consider accepting the independence of Slovenia and Croatia if the strife continued to worsen and mediation efforts proved ineffectual.[47] Germany pointed to the universally supported principle of self-determination for national and ethnic groups. Although this represented a clear break with the EC's declared position, the Germans reiterated their pledge to work with other Community members to effect what they saw as potentially necessary adjustments. The French foreign minister indicated the unfortunate precedent that any softening of Brussels's position could have on the volatile situation among eastern European ethnic minorities.[48] EC members with separatist problems of their own, such as Britain, Spain, and France, were especially keen to maintain the territorial integrity of Yugoslavia. Nevertheless, the majority of EC countries signaled their intention to reconsider their support for Yugoslav unity if fresh violence occurred. On July 8 an accord was struck between the Yugoslav central government and the republics, with the Europeans assisting in the process. Slovenia and Croatia agreed to suspend the implementation of their declarations of independence for three months, during which the Yugoslav federation would be reorganized in negotiations mediated by the EC. The pledge to maintain a cease-fire was to be overseen by a contingent of 150 unarmed civilians acting under EC auspices.

While the agreement held in Slovenia, the situation in Croatia quickly degenerated into a vicious cycle of violence and exposed along the way the limits of effective EC intervention. European efforts to mediate the conflict failed in early August, and Brussels turned to the CSCE for support. The French raised the possibility of sending in an armed buffer force organized by the WEU to separate the insurgents in Croatia, which drew an ominous response from the Soviets.[49] Germany, ever sensitive to Soviet objections, pushed for a solution involving peacekeeping forces under CSCE auspices. Bonn also threatened Serbia with economic sanctions if it continued to block progress on a settlement.[50] On August 8 Yugoslavia agreed to accept additional international observers, both from the EC and from other CSCE member countries, who were to monitor any accord reached between Croatia and Serbia. These arrangements were quickly swept aside by fresh rounds of violence.

Within a few short days of the December 1991 Maastricht summit, Bonn announced that it would formally recognize Slovenia and Croatia by year's end, even if this meant breaking ranks with the UN, the United States, and the majority of its EC partners. Ultimately, this display of foreign policy muscle pulled the EC in its wake; however, the appearance of unity in Brussels was purchased at a high price, as Bonn's solo left a bitter aftertaste in the mouths of many Community members. While Germany's decision did not violate the text produced at Maastricht, it was interpreted by many both in and outside of Germany as violating the spirit of the accords. German politicians were motivated largely by domestic political factors. They believed that the diplomatic isolation of Serbia would stem the flood of Yugoslavian refugees into Germany, which had tripled in 1991 over the previous year. The government was also under intense public pressure to act in a decisive manner on behalf of Croatia, and policymakers felt that diplomatic failures by the EC, the UN, and the CSCE were undermining the domestic support for these institutions and for Germany's pledge to work within them to achieve a solution to the crisis.

Events in the aftermath of the failed August 1991 coup in the USSR provide an interesting postscript to the preceding arguments about German security and international institutions. Once the breakup of the Soviet Union became inevitable, German concerns centered on the security of the former Soviet nuclear deterrent, the observance of existing treaties such as the CSCE and arms control agreements, the servicing of the Soviet foreign debt, and measures to ease the process of economic and political liberalization. While Bonn was quick to establish bilateral contacts with the increasingly assertive and independent republics, above all Russia,[51] it relied heavily on international institutions to manage what it interpreted as positive though not entirely risk-free developments. Germany reaffirmed the indispensability of the "political parallelogram" consisting of NATO, the CSCE, the EC, and the WEU. It even proposed the creation of joint embassies for EC members in each country of the Commonwealth of Independent States (CIS).[52] Important figures within the foreign policy establishment also called on international institutions to adapt to the rapidly changing circumstances on the continent. Foreign Minister Genscher pushed successfully for the inclusion of all CIS states, including those in Asia, into NATO's North Atlantic Cooperation Council and the CSCE. Genscher also called on the EC to negotiate a treaty with the CIS as well as separate treaties with each of the CIS members, again including those lying wholly in Asia. These proposals, however, touched off a heated debate in the German foreign policy establishment and met with a chilly reception in Brussels.

The Centrality of the European Community To German policymakers the nation's capacity to prosper, to finance its new foreign policy objectives in the east, and to pay the unification bill at home hinged on the completion of the internal market. Officials held that the Community served as an ersatz home market for German export industries. The consensus for keeping European markets open to the international economy remained strong, too. They acknowledged that protectionist rhetoric was on the rise within Europe, yet were confident that a less liberal outcome than that which existed was not in the cards.[53] The German contribution to the collapse of the Uruguay Round at the end of 1990 can be traced to electoral considerations (the government did not wish to alienate the farm vote on the eve of the all-German elections in December) and tactical considerations (the government did not wish to alienate the French with important negotiations over EMU and political union). As a Chancellory official remarked, "We had to salute the tricolor."[54]

Soon thereafter the Chancellory and the economics ministry developed a position that placed Germany in line with the overarching GATT objective of reducing agricultural protectionism. This evolving position on agricultural subsidies underscores the importance of free trade to the German economy and explains Bonn's continued rejection of a "fortress Europe." Officials argued that despite the large proportion of intra-Community trade, Germany could not rely solely on the internal EC market. Germany's partners needed outlets and access to international markets, too—perhaps even more so. Within a fortress Europe they would be completely exposed to German competitiveness, officials point out.

These compelling and, viewed over time, constant economic interests surely explain Germany's unwavering commitment to the Common Market and to the objectives spelled out in the Single European Act. However, they cannot account for the widespread belief in German foreign policy circles that the European status quo was ill suited to meet the challenges facing a postunification Germany and a post–Cold War Europe. Although the Bonn government moved during the course of 1991 to a more sober assessment of the potential pitfalls and risks of Economic and Monetary Union, the consensus over EMU and European union remained strong.

Support for EMU is difficult to account for solely on instrumental grounds. In fact, in economic terms there are probably more disadvantages than advantages in replacing the EMS with EMU. By the end of the 1980s it had become clear that the EMS constituted essentially a deutsche mark zone, in which monetary policy was largely set by the Bundesbank.[55] In this form Europe's monetary policy was set largely by the Bundesbank. EMU, which involves the creation of a single European central bank, with a pan-European board at which the Bundesbank has just one seat at the table, thus represented a potential decline of German influence. Indeed, this is precisely why the French pushed so hard for EMU. To be sure, the effects of this loss of control would be minimized by according the European central bank a high degree of independence, but officials at both the finance ministry and the Bundesbank remained quite cautious. These officials were also suspicious of French intentions, particularly the proposal to create a European central bank at the beginning of stage two with powers and responsibilities that are not clearly defined. Since the transition to stage three is likely to be difficult, given the probable economic divergence among the Twelve, these officials feared that the existence of such an institution might prompt the French to postpone the transition indefinitely and instead recommend additional competence for the

European central bank in a piecemeal fashion that would be inherently open to political influence. This would create an unacceptable confusion of responsibility between the European central bank and the Bundesbank. German central bankers were prepared to recommend that the autonomy of the Bundesbank be absorbed into an autonomous European institution, but they cautioned against entering into ambiguous agreements that would allow for outcomes that contravene the widespread domestic consensus on the need for a politically independent central bank.[56]

Officials in the Chancellory and the Foreign Ministry shared the Bundesbank's concern for retaining an independent central bank but were eager to maintain momentum within the intergovernmental conference because they viewed Economic and Monetary Union as a necessary step on the way to a more ambitious goal: European union. The main target was France; Germany wanted concessions on the issue of political union, whereas France's concerns revolved around Economic and Monetary Union. German support for progress toward both objectives had become a question of national credibility; member governments *and* the German political leadership considered it a litmus test of Germany's commitment to European integration.

In other words, politics, not economics, drove German support for Economic and Monetary Union. Although the long-term benefits of EMU were clear if somewhat remote, rapid progress toward it entailed considerable economic risks, not to mention political conflicts. Even if Germany were successful in realizing its vision of EMU, there could be no guarantee that these institutional arrangements would perform as smoothly and as beneficially for Germany as its domestic arrangements have. Thus, even in the best of all possible worlds EMU contained a strong element of uncertainty. Yet, the political leadership in Bonn took these risks in stride because of the overwhelming importance assigned to political union, a goal that entailed few if any immediate economic advantages. As a Bundesbank official explained: "The dominant voices in the domestic debate over EMU are coming from the political side. We want to show and to fix now that we are . . . the driving force of European integration."

During the period of study, the German position on political union consisted of several elements. First, Germany sought to strengthen the European Parliament by giving it additional competencies, including the right to present legislative proposals on its own initiative. Germany also supported the development of a common foreign and defense policy, as well as interior ministry cooperation on matters of political asylum, visas, and immigration. It favored allotting additional powers to the EC in a host of areas, including energy, the environment, and education. Finally, Germany backed a proposal for a Committee of Regions, which would serve as a point of contact between Brussels and the Community's subnational governments.[57] Alongside the effort to deepen the Community, Germany hoped to widen the EC in the very near future to include eligible eastern European countries, along with Austria, Turkey, and the European Free Trade Area (EFTA) countries; many German officials envisioned a European union of twenty members within ten to fifteen years.[58]

In view of the difficult domestic challenges facing German policymakers, political union—like EMU—must be characterized as a risky objective. Indeed, German officials held anything but a Panglossian view of EC developments. Proposals for a common industrial policy and energy policy, to name just two, could if implemented force unwanted departures from the cherished social market economy. Civil servants in the Ministry of Economics pointed out that Community members, with the possible exception of Britain, were far more interventionist than Germany.

Given these risks, why did Germany, having gained unification and full sovereignty, lead the charge within the Community for the most dramatic initiative since the birth of the EEC in 1957? Members of the Bonn political elite point to Helmut Kohl, who has consistently characterized German unification and European integration as two sides of the same coin. In fact, in early 1991 he went so far as to make the success of EMU negotiations conditional on an agreement on political union. There is certainly something to the argument that had Kohl been more indifferent, progress on European integration would have been much slower. Yet the rationales for political union were sufficiently consistent across political parties and government ministries to suggest that there was more to the German drive for a deeper Community than the chancellor's personal beliefs. The motivations behind German support for political union include the purely instrumental as well as a core belief that to secure prior collective institutional commitments into the future, a deepened and widened Community was absolutely essential.

Officials concede that German initiatives were not driven by naive altruism or a blind fealty to international institutions. Much of the German agenda aimed to bring Community institutions more in line with the country's augmented status and new interests. Although officials still referred to the centrality of the Franco-German axis within the EC and the importance of other large members such as Britain, they spoke of a new balance of power within the Community, with Germany placed on a more nearly equal footing. The source of Germany's power, they contended, would not be procedural. Rather, German influence would derive from its economic strength and its contributions to the EC budget, which would enable it to build winning coalitions in a decision-making framework increasingly dominated by qualified majority voting. In this regard, the widening of the Community to the north and to the east would alter the distribution of interests in the EC to the advantage of current northern members, which of course included Germany. Particularly in the ministries responsible for economic matters, there was a perception that the Community of Twelve tilts toward the Mediterranean. The prospective members would change the regional balance considerably. Officials denied that Kohl was driven by a Machiavellian desire to mobilize bias within the Community; they simply pointed out that this particular ramification of widening was both inevitable and, from the standpoint of German, British, Belgian, and other northern members' interests, desirable. German influence in the EC would also derive from the proven success of its domestic institutional arrangements—federalism and its economic policy-making frameworks—and their compatibility with the incipient European union.

A significant number of officials also pointed to the beneficial impact that the Community had, and that a strengthened Community would have, on the resolution of domestic political conflicts. Since 1990 Brussels had proved itself a significant if unacknowledged ally in the government's drive to reduce expenditures on regional economic assistance, and officials anticipated similar results in the areas of trucking deregulation and agricultural reform.[59] In short, the capacity of Brussels to break intransigent domestic coalitions was of great potential value to the federal government.

Alongside these instrumental calculations, the German push for European integration was motivated by a more reflexive rationale based on the logic of institution building. Officials believed that the EC in its present form was simply not equal to the complex mix of internal and external challenges confronting it. To preserve prior collective commitments and the benefits they generated, an intensification of cooperation was required. At issue were issues such as the spillover effects, existing and anticipated, of the Single European Act and EMU. As the process of economic integration deepened, common problems incuding organized crime, immigration, social incquities, and pollution would begin to confront EC members, and structures were needed to handle them. The new range of responsibilities accruing to the Community also demanded political reform, specifically the elimination of the democratic deficit. To many citizens, groups, and subnational governments, the EC appeared a distributor of costs and a generator of constraints. The national political elite's task of publicizing the very real benefits of Community membership would be all but impossible if public opinion, local officials, and Land governments encountered a remote and insulated European bureaucracy. Moreover, if Germany was expected to continue to bankroll the EC budget, greater accountability to the individual citizen was in order. "No taxation without representation" was a familiar refrain in Bonn's party centrals.

Unification itself also provided a strong justification for European union. Quite simply, the Community was incapable of containing a united Germany to the satisfaction of other member governments or, for that matter, of German officials themselves. Aware of the deeply rooted concern about Germany's status as "das Land der Mitte" and as a potential economic juggernaut, policymakers sought to allay the concerns of EC partners by embedding the nation in a more capable, powerful union. Finally, German officials saw further integration as a means of advancing Europe's, and therefore Germany's, political and economic interests. No European country, including Germany, could achieve its economic objectives and secure domestic prosperity through unilateral action. To survive in an increasingly competitive international economy, Europe had to be strengthened, even if this meant limiting the domestic and foreign policy options available to any one member. Indeed, more than one source pointed out that alone of the larger EC members, Germany had advanced the farthest in leaving behind nineteenth-century principles of national sovereignty and national interests. General agreement reigned that sovereignty was worthless if it carried no influence, and had to be pooled if it were to be effective. In conjunction with France and, common sense willing, Britain, Germany hoped to build a powerful European union that would secure German interests, both directly and, by securing the interests of its partners, indirectly. The fact that a united Germany stood to do stunningly well under the EC status quo lent its offer certain irresistible qualities. As a Foreign Ministry official reasoned: "Europe is a way of taming the German beast. But the beast doesn't exist anymore, so one can't have a framework in which Germany feels discriminated against . . . Germans believe in the political unification of Europe, and [German] unification has not changed this . . . If our partners use this once-in-a-lifetime chance, we can all fulfill the dream."

In diplomacy, however, dreams are shaped by pragmatic considerations. Thus, the results of the Maastricht summit met many, if not all, of Germany's expectations. The summit did provide for a significant deepening of the European Community. The agreement on EMU generally followed the German design, although Kohl was forced to accept inter alia the creation of a "cohesion fund" to assist poorer member countries. On the political side, Germany achieved most but by no means all of its objectives, falling substantially short of its stated objectives vis-à-vis the European Parliament. On the domestic front, Kohl was roundly criticized for failing to insist on linkage between EMU and political union. General public opinion and voices in the business community expressed concern that the deutsche mark had been sold too cheaply. Still, on balance, Germany's role during the negotiations was consistent with the patterns we have outlined. The Bonn delegation defended long-standing positions at the summit, but not to the point of jeopardizing final agreement; indeed, were it not for Kohl's backtracking on parliamentary reform and the part he played in engineering a key compromise on social policy, the summit might well have unraveled.

German policymakers did not remain passive in the face of the changes wrought by the collapse of the Berlin Wall. New or modified German interests, primarily in the realm of military security but also in foreign economic policy, led to discernible shifts in strategies. One of the more remarkable changes, for example, involved Ostpolitik. Policymakers linked the social, political, and economic stability of a united Germany—indeed, of western Europe itself—to the relative success of the transformations under way in the east, and a host of bilateral and multilateral initiatives followed. Whether they implied change or continuity, however, German state strategies during this period developed wholly within the limits set by international institutions. Foreign policymakers sought to employ long-standing institutional memberships to meet new challenges and to secure perennial interests; moreover, they encouraged the adaptation of institutions such as NATO and the EC so as to align them with changing international circumstances and evolving German interests.

On the basis of the preceding analysis, we are in a position to address several questions regarding the sources of German state strategies and their likely paths of development. For example, what was the overall impact of domestic politics on state strategies? On paper and in practice unification produced considerable changes. Yet new borders, new populations, and new problems exercised little observable impact on the formulation and implementation of foreign economic policy. The Federal Republic inherited a huge stock of inefficient, outdated, and environmentally unsafe enterprises, yet its external policy of free trade remained unchanged. The massive regional, agricultural, and environmental problems in the five new Länder cried out for substantial public subsidies, yet the government refused to elbow its way to the front of the structural fund queue in Brussels. This is not to suggest that domestic politics was irrelevant; foreign economic policy continued to be "Made in Germany." Rather, the *change* in domestic German politics placed an almost imperceptible imprint on the country's foreign economic objectives.[60] Continuity reflected the capacity of long-established domestic coalitions and government ministries in Bonn to ignore new interests and new demands emanating from the eastern Länder.

Matters were scarcely different in the realm of defense policy, where fierce external constraints on the domestic debate remained operative. The passing of the Cold War silenced the once powerful German peace movement, thereby removing an organized source of support for radical change in German foreign policy. Despite strong public support in the former GDR for a nonaligned Germany, a position shared by a large segment of West German public opinion,[61] Bonn never questioned its NATO commitments, and led the push, along with France, for a common European foreign and defense policy. In the party political arena, the abortive debate on NATO and the controversy sparked by the Gulf War revealed how difficult it is for an established party to maintain a distinctive, politically viable profile on foreign policy. The SPD's acceptance of continued German membership in a reforming NATO and its internal agonizing over the question of out-of-area actions emerged in response to international expectations, not to domestic constituency pressures. The "intractability of the international system" identified by Wolfram Hanrieder, which makes foreign policy alternatives especially difficult to formulate, was as much a factor in this period as it had been during the years of the West German republic.[62]

In assessing the impact of domestic politics, we must again confront the temporal question: Can we extrapolate from this brief period and conclude that the changes in domestic politics introduced after 1989 will remain of little or no consequence to German foreign policy? Contending models of the interplay between domestic and international politics lead us to interpret such a conclusion as rash. From the standpoint of "the second image reversed," or the metaphor of the two-level bargaining game, one can argue that the process

of political institutionalization and electoral mobilization in the eastern Länder has yet to reach equilibrium.[63] Moreover, the sudden appearance post-
Maastricht of an inchoate public angst about the implications of EMU offers
many possibilities for a domestic politicization of EC issues. In short, domestic pressures that could effect changes in German state strategies are likely to
grow. It is unlikely, however, that these pressures will threaten the institutional foundations of the country's foreign policy.

How durable are the new Germany's international institutional commitments? One could argue that, given Germany's past, it could do little in the
aftermath of unification other than to pledge its loyalty to the web of institutions that had served it so well during the postwar period. Once the rever-
berations generated by unification pass, however, a major reevaluation of
Germany's alliance partnerships will commence. At an existential level, of
course, this position can never be refuted. Yet there are good reasons to
conclude that, barring unforeseen economic or security upheavals on the
continent, German policymakers are unlikely to undertake an extensive stock
taking of the country's institutional memberships in the foreseeable future.
These reasons go to the very heart of German interests in international
institutions and multilateral strategies.

Instrumentalism has always characterized German approaches to international institutions. The period between November 1989 and August 1991
was no exception. Participation in NATO, the CSCE, the EC, and the WEU,
with all the privileges *and* obligations it entailed, served elemental economic
and military security interests insofar as it provided efficient mechanisms for
securing prosperity, coping with uncertainty, and sharing burdens. Such
instrumentalism did not distinguish Germany from its alliance partners; nor
is it likely to distinguish Germany in the future. Surely the *magnitude* of
Germany's reliance on international institutions to quell unease and to reduce
uncertainty about its own intentions was and is unique. Germany conceived
its security in part as making other countries less uncertain about itself, and
employed different institutions to reach overlapping yet distinct audiences.
The desire to reach these audiences—or put a different way, not to ignore
any potentially relevant audiences—may explain the tendency of the German
government to "buy into" all the major institutions operating in Europe.
Moreover, the means by which Germany sought to convince these audiences
involved nontrivial concessions, including the pooling of national sovereignty in the realm of economic policy-making and self-imposed limits on its
military capabilities.[64]

Institutional membership based purely on instrumental rationality implies the possibility of rapid changes, even outright reversals, in behavior; what was rational yesterday becomes decidedly irrational today in light of changed circumstances. No one can reasonably rule out the possibility that Germany might at some future date reduce its international commitments, or even opt out of some or all of them as part of a rational defense of its interests. One might look to contradictions in Germany's overlapping institutional memberships as a possible precipitating factor; for example, actual and potential tradeoffs abound in the field of defense. German membership in NATO and in a strengthened WEU may not be compatible in the long run, if only because France and the United States may require Bonn or Berlin ultimately to choose. If pressed, Germany would in all likelihood plump for Europe, since to do otherwise would pose an insurmountable obstacle to the cherished goal of European union. The disintegration of NATO would surely represent a setback for American interests, but it is important to specify the aftermath: a Europe organized by the WEU and participating as a unified block in CSCE, with Germany safely and voluntarily embedded in both. Architecture, not rubble, will continue to blanket the European security landscape.

Yet we believe there is more to German participation in international institutions than instrumentalism. Indeed, an implicit argument of this chapter is that the very essence of these institutions would have to change before Germany reevaluated its commitments. During this period of momentous change in Europe, the formulation of state objectives and interests in Germany not only took institutions into account but accorded value to these institutions as such; they remained, in the words of Rudolf Hrbek and Wolfgang Wessels, "an essential part of 'the reason of state.'"[65] Over the course of forty years, West Germany's reliance on a web of international institutions to achieve its foreign policy goals, born of an instrumental choice among painfully few alternatives, became so complete as to cause these institutions to become embedded in the very definition of state interests and strategies. In effect, this is what we mean when we describe Germany's institutional commitments in the post-1989 period as reflexive; they have become ingrained, even assumed.[66]

One of the more fascinating results of our investigations into this period is the virtual absence of any serious reassessments of German institutional obligations in light of changing circumstances, a few fringe groups on either end of the political spectrum excepted. To the extent that Germany's institutional commitments became the subject of domestic debate, the chief questions centered not on whether Germany ought to act through institutions, but on which ones should be employed and whether any adjustments in their structure and/or brief were required. Social Democratic opposition to the stationing of German NATO forces in Turkey was based on the party's interpretation of NATO's functions; as a self-described defensive alliance, it could not be used in offensive out-of-area missions without undercutting the domestic consensus on which it rested. The domestic debate over EMU was resolved in favor of the Chancellory and the Foreign Ministry on the basis of maintaining a leadership role in the EC's political project; international institutional commitments trumped very real and widely held domestic economic reservations. Was the SPD's interpretation of the NATO charter accurate? Was the decision to take on the risks of EMU for the sake of political union advisable? Such questions, while valid, are beside the point. Rather, these episodes provide evidence of the systematic and profound effects of international institutions on the terms of domestic debate, and suggest that an analysis of German institutional commitments which looked only to an instrumental rationale would be incomplete.

One might just as easily conclude that Germany has every reason, rational or otherwise, to remain firmly ensconced in its institutional web, since it is only a matter of time before it emerges as the new hegemon on the European continent. Just as the United States sought to remake Europe in its own image after 1945, now a unified Germany is doing the same as it reforges international rules and organizations in a manner consistent with its new interests and capabilities. This argument, while intriguing, requires additional theoretical and empirical work. To be sure, the German government, working from domestic recipes for economic prosperity and political stability, set stringent terms for Economic and Monetary Union and pushed a federal agenda in the intergovernmental conference on political union. Furthermore, it stands to be a weighty, perhaps even the weightiest, member of a deepening and widening European Community. These observations, of course, are consistent with our understanding of international institutions. Institutions are rarely neutral; rather, they are shaped by the interests and resources of member states, and consistently privilege some, particularly the more powerful, over others.[67] It is only to be expected that adjustments would take place to reflect the new balance of power among the Twelve.

The question, of course, is whether these adjustments signal a hegemon in the making. In the pursuit of an answer, one fact cannot be overlooked: the fundamental German bargaining position during this period belies the image of a sovereign actor seeking to impose its will on other participants. For if Germany were to realize its vision of Europe, it would emerge as a consequential but *semi-sovereign* member of a supranational authority. In other words, German EC reform objectives were cast in terms of a substantial pooling of national sovereignty, a fact that is difficult to reconcile with conventional hegemonic stability theory.[68] A disastrous prewar history coupled with forty successful years in an interlocking network of international institutions led German leaders away from traditional nineteenth-century conceptions of state sovereignty.

Germany's postmodern conception of sovereignty notwithstanding, recent actions underscore the fact that a united Germany is not averse to acting in what it perceives to be its national interest. The Federal Republic is now as "normal" a state as Britain or France, countries long used to pursuing their national interests even when this entails conflict with friendly nations. Yet even the more unpopular "solo" initiatives are compatible with its bedrock commitment to international institutions. The Bundesbank's policy of high interest rates generated negative externalities for many countries, yet viewed in the context of the stringent admission criteria for EMU, it is a defensible action.[69] The Yugoslavian episode can be interpreted as an exercise in agenda setting. The Maastricht summit established the framework within which a common foreign policy is to be created; what remains to be determined is the content of that foreign policy. With its initiative on Yugoslavia, Germany laid down a marker.

And it is here that the greatest potential for conflict with Germany's partners lies, particularly in the EC but also in NATO. The extension and intensification of Ostpolitik are viewed by German policymakers as a common interest of EC members. Yet these interests are not necessarily shared equally by Germany's various alliance partners. To the extent that these institutions do not adapt sufficiently to take account of what German officials perceive to be their country's unique position straddling eastern and western Europe, Germany may begin to question its place in these institutions. This issue is complicated by the apparent lack of consensus among and within the German political parties as to the desired limits of institutional adaptation and by growing public unease over the ramifications of institutional commitments, above all EMU. It is ironic but perhaps not unexpected that the new Ostpolitik, like its predecessor, will be a source of tension between Germany and the network of partners it joined during the Cold War years. Whether this tension will be creative is up to Germany, its partners, and the institutions to which they belong.

Chapter 2

Soviet Security Strategies toward Europe: After the Wall, with Their Backs up against It

---

Celeste A. Wallander

Jane E. Prokop

The collapse of socialist rule in the east European countries and Soviet accession to that collapse transformed the European postwar order, which had been predicated on the political division of Europe and was organized by respective sets of military and economic institutions: the North Atlantic Treaty Organization (NATO) and the European Community (EC) in the west, and the Warsaw Treaty Organization (WTO) and Council for Mutual Economic Assistance (CMEA) in the east. This transformation of the international system altered nearly all of the basic conditions that had defined European security policies since 1945. In particular, the diminution of Soviet power, the creation of a unified Germany, and the transformation of the Cold War alliance system may affect the political, military, and economic stability of Europe, and thus both create new conditions and pose potential new threats to security. This chapter assesses how the Soviet Union reacted to two related crises: German unification and the collapse of the alliance system it had imposed in eastern Europe. In particular, it investigates the degree to which the Soviet Union acknowledged or utilized international and European institutions in the management of its national security policies from October 1989 to August 1991.[1]

In order to discuss how Soviet decision makers developed Soviet European security strategies, we must also identify and explain the content and sources of Soviet national security interests. We have found that definition of security interests became increasingly bound up with the development of strategies and attempts to respond to the constraints of the international environment in which the country found itself from October 1989 to August 1991. The result is a less theoretically exact but more realistic assessment of the complex and even chaotic process of security policy formation.

We should note that this chapter is based on an analysis of Soviet policy up to mid-August 1991, that is, before the August 18 coup attempt and the enormous political changes that have resulted from its failure. The analysis cannot be, nor does it pretend to be, a precise guide to post-Soviet security policy in the near future—if indeed there will be any unified security policy of the Commonwealth of Independent States at all. Its purpose is limited to two important tasks: to document and explain the sources of Soviet responses to international change in a crucial period of world history; and to suggest in more general terms what was important in this process in ways that might suggest how that process will work in the future, even if the players and the former Soviet Union themselves change substantially.

We first outline the basic issues addressed by our research and explain the theoretical context for the study. The second section provides some background on Soviet foreign policy and explains the role of the "new thinking" in changing Soviet policies, and argues that the sources of that new thinking lie in domestic politics. The changes in Soviet policies and priorities in turn were the catalysts for two crises in European security affairs in 1989–1991: German unification and the disintegration of the Soviet alliance system in eastern Europe. We document Soviet responses to that dual crisis and explain Soviet strategies in terms of the opportunities and constraints presented by European international and regional institutions. And we conclude that in this crucial period of international relations, institutions played a central role in how the Soviet leadership sought to manage and profit from the fundamental changes it faced.

Problem and Theory

From a regional perspective the Soviet Union and its policies in Europe were a fundamental cause of the security problem in Europe, and by the same token, the single most important cause of the crises of 1989–1991 was the change in Soviet foreign policy known as "new thinking." Therefore, it is important to keep in mind that while we look at Soviet responses to German unification and changes in eastern Europe, more than most of the participants, the Soviet leaders themselves were not only responders to change but its principal agents. Other than Germany, no country faced so fundamental an alteration in its international security condition as the Soviet Union. This should seem somewhat paradoxical. Why would national leaders choose to pursue policies that risked reduced international influence and encouraged competing centers of power in Europe? The only explanation that makes sense is the extreme nature of the domestic economic crisis and the demands that crisis placed on Soviet relations with the outside world. New thinking was predominantly a pragmatic response to the internal economic crisis brought on by systemic factors in the planned economic system, which placed serious constraints on Soviet technological and arms production capabilities. Although changes in policies entailed high costs and risks, they were seen as less costly and risky than the previous policies by a substantial portion of the Soviet leadership, led by Mikhail Gorbachev after March 1985.

These altered domestic priorities and their impact on basic foreign policy were relatively straightforward, but they did not offer a blueprint for Soviet responses to German unification and the terms of Soviet withdrawal from eastern Europe. Although certain basic Soviet interests had changed, several alternative strategies for coping with the crises could be imagined. Western international relations theory directs our attention to two broad possibilities. In the traditional realist view, states operating under systemic conditions of uncertainty, complexity, and multiple sources of power may turn to balancing against other powerful states. They may make alliances and join with other less powerful states to balance against threatening states. But state strategies will be distinctive in two respects: states will be predominantly power-oriented in their calculations, and any attempts to work with other states will be limited to the minimum necessary to balance in this manner. In the new Europe states are more nearly equal in their relative power capabilities, so they will be less likely to commit themselves to alliances and institutions for fear of being exploited (that is, cooperating while other states do not) because there are more potential exploiters, and because the costs of being exploited are greater than before. Consequently, these multiple potential threats will lead to more flexible, ad hoc balancing attempts.[2]

Institutionalists concede the importance of power in states' security policies. They also agree on the change in systemic features in post–Cold War Europe, but because they have an alternative view of how the international system works, they expect different outcomes. Institutionalists predict that

European states will be less likely to rely solely on balancing and more likely to seek to utilize institutional arrangements to manage threats.[3] They focus on conditions in which states have a mix of common and conflicting interests in a set of choices and outcomes. Theorists do not assume that states can be forced by institutions to act against their own interests. Instead, they predict that under conditions of interdependence, as is the case in post–Cold War Europe, institutions can be used more effectively than self-reliant strategies to secure state interests, despite the structural constraints of anarchy.[4] They argue that states may use institutions to manage uncertainty because decision makers are less concerned with the power they can amass than with the value of institutional mechanisms for maintaining repeated interactions, providing information, and increasing transparency. They predict that states, acting in their rational self-interest, will not abandon existing international institutions, but will attempt to use and perhaps modify these institutions to identify and manage their security strategies.

Alliances are institutions, and in this respect there is potentially considerable overlap in the expectations of realist and institutionalist theory regarding state strategies. Both theoretical approaches expect that states will be concerned with interests and power, and both expect that states may engage in a wide variety of cooperative activities in order to pursue their self-interests. The difference is largely one of emphasis, but it can be a substantial difference nonetheless. The institutionalist would not be surprised to learn that states in the new Europe are concerned with military power, but she might not expect to find states avoiding arms control commitments that increased constraints on and information about other states' military capabilities. Similarly, realists might expect the United States to support NATO, but they would not expect Germany to avoid an enhanced role in military operations commensurate with its increased power. This chapter cannot and does not set out to falsify one or both of these theories; rather, we mean to investigate the relative importance of institutional factors in Soviet responses to crisis in Europe.

There are a number of questions one could ask about the connection between international institutions and relations among states: How are institutions created? Under what conditions do they change or persist? How can we account for variations in specificity, scope, rules, membership, and effectiveness? But the prior question is whether international institutions matter at all. In setting national security policies, responding to international events, and in interpreting the strategies and actions of other states, do decision makers take into account the existence of international institutions and their functions? This basic question is the focus of this chapter.

Soviet National Security Interests and the Crises in Europe

Prior to 1987 Soviet foreign policy was premised on a Leninist world view, which saw no room for ultimate coexistence of capitalist and socialist systems. Capitalism had to be an international system to survive and could not tolerate the existence of socialism. Therefore, all international interactions were zero-sum. The threat to Soviet national security was consequently the presence of capitalist states. The solution to Soviet security problems was in the long term their disappearance, and in the short term the development of an alternative socialist international system. New thinking altered most of the basic principles of Leninist Soviet foreign policy. Originally it did not abandon the socialist ideal in Soviet domestic matters, but declared that Soviet foreign policy would no longer hold as its basic assumption that the fundamental condition of the international system was class conflict. Instead, "common human values"—such as the avoidance of global nuclear war and peaceful economic development—were declared to be prior to any socialist-capitalist cleavages. Therefore, Soviet priorities in foreign affairs would turn toward policies consistent with these common values. The change disengaged Soviet national security from the concerns over the precise nature of internal development of other states and shifted it to more tractable issues of geographic security from external threats and a potentially wide variety of relations with other states.[5] The Soviet Foreign Ministry's review for 1989–90 stated that the advent of political, economic, social, and informational interdependence (vzaimozavisimost) changed the understanding of "national security" so that it is insufficient to define national security simply as the ability to defend oneself from external military threat. Interdependence created new opportunities and potentials for strengthening security, but this meant that security requires "common efforts." Arguing that under interdependence national security no longer meant only the ability to defend oneself from external military threat, it concluded that "the overexaggerated attention given to the buildup of military might in the last decades gave birth to a series of phenomena which brought society to the brink of catastrophe and brought under question its ability to develop in modern terms, to remain a part of world civilization."[6]

While new thinking in traditional security affairs implied larger areas for common interests in traditional security concerns, Gorbachev's limited domestic political and economic reforms remained a significant constraint on the potential for broader, long-term cooperation in Europe. The central government crackdown on Baltic dissent in January 1991 seemed to substantiate claims that Gorbachev had taken a turn away from economic and political reform under heavy pressure from conservatives, including his defense and interior ministers, the head of the KGB, and the Soyuz group in the Supreme Soviet, whose attacks on Eduard Shevardnadze for "losing" eastern Europe have been partly blamed for the foreign minister's resignation in December 1990.[7]

However, the domestic economic crisis continued unabated, creating ever-increasing pressure for further change in Soviet self-defined national security and interests. The transformation of European international conditions made such changes possible. This explains the Soviet Union's redoubled efforts to become part of the international community. In May 1991 there was a renewed effort to propose economic reform programs (not always radical or coherent) to both internal and external audiences. In early May, Soviet Prime Minister Valentin Pavlov called on western leaders to back ruble conversion to prevent the collapse of the Soviet currency in the process. Gorbachev sent Chief of the General Staff Mikhail Moiseyev to Washington to break the impasse on interpreting Conventional Forces in Europe (CFE), and the dispute was resolved. On May 22 Gorbachev called for a western effort on the scale of the Persian Gulf War for aid to the Soviet Union in implementing reform. At the end of the month, Soviet deputy foreign minister Vladimir Scherbakov (head of the former state economic planning agency, Gosplan) and Gorbachev's adviser Yevgeniy Primakov presented new reform plans to U.S. Secretary of State James Baker in Washington.

The focus of these efforts became clear in early June, when Soviet Foreign Minister Aleksandr Bessmertnykh suggested to Baker that Gorbachev be invited to the Group of Seven (G-7) meeting in London. The place this invitation played in Gorbachev's subsequent internal reform and foreign policy strategies was clear in his Nobel Prize speech, delivered in Oslo on June 5, which is worth quoting at length:

We are now approaching what might be the decisive point when the world community and, above all, the states with the greatest potential to influence world development, have to decide on their attitude to the Soviet Union . . . I am convinced that the world needs perestroika no

less than the Soviet Union itself does. Fortunately, the present generation of politicians for the most part are becoming ever more deeply
aware of this interrelationship, and also the fact that now, when perestroika has entered its critical phase, the Soviet Union is entitled to
expect large-scale support to ensure its success. Recently we have been
seriously rethinking the substance and role of our economic cooperation
with other countries, above all the major western nations. We realize, of
course, that we have to carry out measures which would enable us
genuinely to open up to the world economy, to become an organic part
of it. But we have come to a conclusion on the need for a kind of
synchronization of our actions in that plan with the Group of Seven and
the European communities.[8]

By June 1991, then, Gorbachev's view of Soviet national interests had
focused on integration into (not mere participation in) the world economy,
for integration was essential to the success of Soviet domestic economic
reform, the Soviet national priority. His chief complaint was that structures
and institutions created during the Cold War under conditions of confrontation continued to block this integration, even though the confrontation was
over, and he appealed for change in the rules and restrictions of the General
Agreement on Tariffs and Trade (GATT), the International Monetary Fund
(IMF), and the World Bank.

This change in viewpoint was not supported by conservative elements in
Gorbachev's government; indeed, it was opposed by the August coup leaders.
His policy was attacked at a closed Supreme Soviet session by KGB head
Vladimir Kyruchkov, who claimed that the Soviet Union was being manipu-
lated by the west, which did not reciprocate Soviet concessions and which
sought to dictate the terms of perestroika. Criticisms and defenses of Gorbachev's G-7 meeting in the Soviet press also focused on whether Gorbachev
had put himself in the demeaning position of begging for aid from the west.
Former Defense Minister Dmitriy Yazov argued that "the fact remains that
the attainment of military-strategic parity between west and east was the most
important condition allowing the prevention of a new world war, the preservation of peace,"[9] not mutual interests or cooperation. This viewpoint was
not restricted to the Soviet military. A CPSU (Communist Party of the Soviet
Union) Central Committee memorandum published in a German newspaper
in June 1991 criticized Soviet policy toward eastern Europe, and insisted that
western advances in the region threatened Soviet interests. It warned that the

former Soviet allies could not join western military alliances, nor allow their territories to be used for any western military deployments.[10]

Central to these competing views were the academic-sounding but politically charged concepts of the "balance of power" and the "balance of interests." Soviet reformers sought to distinguish between policy based on the "balance of power" (that is, military power and influence) and the "balance of interests" (the pursuit of one's national interests accomplished by taking into account other states' interests).[11] In defending the treaties with Germany, for example, Shevardnadze admitted that the "balance of interests" was not preserved in the "two-plus-four" treaty alone, but in the set of multilateral and bilateral arrangements on the unification and future of Germany. That is, focus on the balance of interests entails use of international institutions in foreign policy, whereas reliance on the balance of power does not. But critics of government policy used this framework as well. The Central Committee memorandum warned that Soviet security must be promoted by a policy of a balance of interests with regard to the countries of eastern Europe. Critics often claimed that the United States and NATO continued to rely on the balance of forces through military power and predominance.

Examples are numerous; the point is relatively simple. First, although official government policy used the term *balance of interests,* it did not define it or give it concrete meaning in terms of strategies, relations, or negotiations. Second, there is some sense that the shift to calculations based on the balance of interests is linked to interdependence and foreign policy strategies based on the use of international institutions, but again this was not clearly spelled out. Third, because the term was important yet ill defined, it was appropriated by critics of the change in the government's definition of Soviet national security and interests. We will go on to discuss one of the concrete examples of this confusion.

As this brief discussion of the broad Soviet definition of its national security interests demonstrates, institutions played a role more fundamental than merely affecting Soviet strategies, in two ways. By summer 1991 a significant portion of the leadership was defining Soviet national interests in terms of the need to participate in international institutions. When a national leadership argues that its internal political and economic priorities require participation in international institutions, it no longer makes sense to think that these institutions affect only strategies. Also, the existence of institutions and their benefits and costs for Soviet interests became part of the internal political debate in 1991. Gorbachev sought to use the rules and requirements of these external phenomena to create pressure for internal market and constitutional reforms. Thus, as in the east European states, Soviet decision makers attempted to use "anticipatory adaptation" to support internal policies.[12]

Crisis and Change in the European Security System

German Unification

Hungary became the first east European state to begin to test the meaning and limits of the Soviet new thinking. By August 1989 the Hungarian government was permitting citizens from the German Democratic Republic to travel to the west via Hungarian territory and the West German embassy in Budapest. The Hungarian policy became a way for refugees from the GDR to bypass the Berlin Wall and the east-west border. When Czechoslovakia and Poland also adopted the new policy by September 1989, one of the basic functions of the Berlin Wall ceased to exist. In early October the new East German leadership under Egon Krenz attempted to stem the flood of emigrants by easing political control, and in early November announced that all GDR citizens would be granted exit visas to travel freely across borders. On November 9 the Berlin Wall itself was opened.

The Gorbachev government was then caught between its need to abide by its new international priorities and respect for free choice *(svoboda vybora)*, and its preferences for the maintenance of a divided Germany and a presence in east Europe. Gorbachev repeatedly claimed in late 1989 that Germany would remain divided. This position immediately began to look problematic, as the GDR began to collapse internally. The USSR stepped back from confrontation on this issue; in February 1990 Gorbachev affirmed that the Soviet position on freedom of choice would apply to the German case, and that the two Germanys should decide the matter of unification themselves. Three days later NATO and WTO foreign ministers meeting in Ottawa announced the "two-plus-four" formula for procedures and negotiations on German unification, thus recognizing both the internal and international aspects of unification. When the Alliance for Germany, which advocated quick unification after the formation of the East German federal states, won the March 1990 elections in the GDR, a rapid unification process was certain.

This victory, however, did not resolve the issue of Germany's international relations and its place in Europe. The western powers called for German membership in NATO and the EC, with possible strengthening of the Conference on Security and Cooperation in Europe (CSCE) as a factor contributing to stability. This was the primary sticking point for the Soviet Union. Gorbachev had accepted a united Germany, but a united Germany in NATO was another matter. Since the internal and international terms were linked in the two-plus-four format, Soviet opposition threatened to hold up German unification. The Soviets were also increasingly constrained by the probable disintegration of the WTO. Hungary had announced its intention to exit from the alliance's military structure in May, despite Soviet troop withdrawals from its territory. In June the Soviet leaders continued to offer different proposals for constraints on the status of German membership in various political and economic institutions, and for the composition and readiness of its military forces, but these were rejected by Germany and/or the other four powers. Meanwhile, German monetary and economic unification was implemented on July 1, and the following day the GDR government agreed to all-German elections in December.

The stalemate caused by Soviet opposition to reunification was finally ended in July. On the sixth of that month NATO leaders issued the London Declaration, which provided for limits on German military forces and declared that NATO would no longer rely on the early first use of nuclear weapons, and also called for political consultation of NATO and WTO members. The London Declaration gave the Soviet leadership an opportunity for graceful retreat from their seemingly intransigent position, and they quickly seized the opportunity. Less than two weeks later Kohl and Gorbachev announced an agreement on Soviet terms for German membership in NATO. The final sticking point— troop levels of the united Germany—was resolved in August when the foreign ministers of the German Democratic Republic and the Federal Republic of Germany agreed that a united Germany's armed forces would not exceed 370,000. On August 31 the two German states signed the treaty setting October 3, 1990, as the official date for reunification.

The Treaty on the Final Settlement of the German Problem—signed at the September two-plus-four meeting—concentrated on military issues. Its main provisions were:

The current borders of Germany were acknowledged to be permanent.
Germany pledged itself to a peaceful future.
Soviet troops would be withdrawn from Germany over a period of three to
    four years as German armed forces were reduced.
Germany would cut its armed forces to 370,000.

Germany renounced the possession of nuclear, chemical, and
 bacteriological weapons.
The eastern part of Germany was granted special military-political status.
 No foreign armed forces or foreign nuclear arms were to be deployed
 there, and German troops were not to have any delivery vehicles for
 nuclear arms.
Germany would not deploy armed forces which had been integrated into
 NATO on the territory of the former GDR until the completion of the
 withdrawal of Soviet troops.
The system of controls and inspections provided for in the CFE treaty, as
 well as other confidence-building measures and the Center for Conflict
 Prevention, would ensure the transparency of military activity in the
 territory of Germany.
Germany guaranteed that the revival of Nazism and its ideology would not
 be permitted.
Germany would support the honoring of active agreements concluded by
 the GDR and FRG with third countries.[13]

A bilateral agreement, the Soviet-German Treaty on Good-Neighborliness, Partnership, and Cooperation, was ultimately signed in Bonn on November 9, and added other military-political guarantees to its more general provisions on political consultation and cooperation in various spheres. Each side agreed to the principles of nonaggression, no first use of armed forces against the other, and refusal to support any aggression directed at the other party.

The economic aspects of German reunification were quietly dealt with in high-level German-Soviet negotiations. An agreement on German aid to finance Soviet troop withdrawal was reached just prior to the final two-plus-four session in September. By September 13 the amount of German aid for troop withdrawal had been set at DM 15 billion. The Transitional Treaty in which these arrangements were embedded was signed November 9 in Bonn. Of the DM 15 billion, a DM 3 billion loan was earmarked for financing the maintenance of troops in GDR territory. DM 1 billion was to help defray the costs of transporting troops back to the Soviet Union. A further DM 7.8 billion was allocated for the construction of housing in the USSR for returning servicemen, and DM 200 million was to go to retraining programs for the servicemen. The remaining DM 3 billion was an interest-free loan for further unspecified expenses for the troop withdrawal.

Thus, for the Soviet Union the problem of Germany was dealt with primarily within the two-plus-four rubric, and once acceptable terms for German membership in NATO had been negotiated along with the development of Soviet-German economic ties (largely in the form of German aid to the USSR), the immediate crisis posed by German unification was over. Soviet strategies for dealing with Germany turned to ways of using the special relation and Germany's special concerns toward the East for gaining economic aid and access to western institutional assets.

The Disintegration of the Soviet Alliance System in Eastern Europe

By the end of 1990 the activities of the WTO and the CMEA had sunk to a negligible level, and the east Europeans were increasingly turning to the west for guidance and cooperation. For its part, the Soviet leadership sought to use the WTO both to balance the NATO threat in classic neorealist terms and to offer it as part of a cooperative framework for the integration of Germany into a new European security structure. However, reliance on the WTO as either a power or an institutional bid became increasingly untenable as the Soviet leadership was faced with negotiating the demise of the military function of the alliance. The process of disintegration had begun in June 1990, when Hungary, Poland, and Czechoslovakia called for the dissolution of WTO military structures during a meeting of the WTO Political Consultative Committee. In December 1990 Czechoslovak Foreign Minister Jiri Dienstbier declared the October 1968 agreement on the stationing of Soviet troops in Czechoslovakia invalid, and by February 26 the two countries had signed an agreement for phased withdrawal of all Soviet troops, to begin immediately and to finish by July 1991. On March 11, 1990, Soviet forces in Hungary began their withdrawal in accordance with an agreement negotiated the previous year: all Soviet forces were out by July 1991. When the Soviet leadership called for transforming the WTO from a primarily military institution to a political one, it simply had no choice. Indeed, even the political function became irrelevant. On July 1, 1991, the end of the WTO as a whole was marked by a final meeting of the Political Consultative Committee in Prague.

Hints of the CMEA's demise also began to appear soon after the east European democratic revolutions of 1989. At the January 1990 session of the CMEA council earlier proposals for reform of the CMEA were rejected as inadequate, and a new study group was set up to formulate more radical reforms.[14] During the course of the year, trade between member countries declined dramatically. The shift to hard currency transactions in January 1991 only exacerbated this tendency, and the January 1991 session of the CMEA executive committee witnessed the decision to terminate the activities of the CMEA. The last meeting of this organization was held only three days before the final WTO session.

The restructuring of east European commitments to the Soviet Union was accompanied by a "turn to the west." Hungary applied for membership in NATO (albeit unsuccessfully), and aspirations in the economic sphere were also reoriented toward western Europe. A system of "European agreements" between the EC and Hungary, Poland, and Czechoslovakia had been decided upon in principle by August 1990, and on December 18 the European Council authorized the EC Commission to negotiate these agreements. They were to be aimed at progressively establishing a free trade area and developing economic, scientific, and technical cooperation. They would also provide the appropriate institutional framework for genuine political dialogue. As the European Council consolidated its negotiating stance in April 1991, it decided that the accession of the three east European countries to the EC as full members would be an ultimate but not an automatic objective. The European Parliament also considered that the countries of central and eastern Europe should negotiate free trade agreements with the European Free Trade Area (EFTA) countries and develop forms of multilateral cooperation among themselves.[15]

To some extent this cooperation began to develop; several subregional groups emerged in eastern Europe. These include the "Danube-Adriatic Association" (Italy, Austria, Hungary, Yugoslavia, Czechoslovakia, and Poland), the Balkan meetings (attended by representatives of Albania, Bulgaria, Greece, Romania, Turkey, and Yugoslavia), and the "trilateral group" (composed of Czechoslovakia, Hungary, and Poland). The last caused some concern on the part of the Soviets, especially insofar as such cooperation reinforced the individual states' bargaining strength vis-à-vis the Soviet Union. The group had begun meeting in 1990, and their second summit meeting in Visegrad in February 1991 was followed by the conclusion of bilateral military cooperation treaties among themselves. The three countries were also said to be collaborating on the negotiation of the military clause in their bilateral treaties with the USSR. Their mutual consultations on military relations with the USSR began as early as September 1990, and the failure to invite Soviet representatives did not escape notice in that country's press.[16]

So by 1991 not only was the Soviet government faced with the loss of military presence, political influence, and economic control in the east, but it saw the development of western penetration and influence in central and eastern Europe—precisely the threat to Soviet security that Stalin had advanced as his reason for occupying the countries of east Europe in the first place. However, so fundamental had the changes in basic Soviet national interests become that not only were old strategies costly or inappropriate, but they would have been entirely contradictory to the new priorities. The Soviet Union's strategies for dealing with its loss of influence and with growing western influence first attempted to reconstitute institutional arrangements, then sought to gain bilateral assurances while controlling or at least slowing western influence, and ultimately abandoned costly relations with the east in favor of developing ties with the west.

Soviet Responses and Strategies

German Unification

The initial Soviet policy response to the prospect of German unification was to stall and attempt to use the weight of the status quo—two alliance systems and Soviet military forces deployed in Germany—to block undesirable outcomes. Despite Gorbachev's enunciation of the principle of *svoboda vybora,* Soviet officials and policymakers at first firmly declared German unification to be impossible. At the U.S.-Soviet summit in Malta in early December 1989, Gorbachev said that "history" had created two German states and implied that there were good reasons for it. The official Soviet line saw the division of Germany and existing alliance structure as necessary for maintaining stability in Europe.[17] The Soviets also suggested that German unification would not fit the existing European institutional order. On the one hand, a unified Germany could not practically maintain its membership and participation in existing institutions, for how could it be a member of both the WTO and NATO, or the CMEA and the EC? On the other hand, the GDR could be absorbed by the FRG, thus joining only the latter two institutions; but such asymmetrical membership was clearly unacceptable for Soviet security and interests.

By January 1990 this approach had clearly become untenable, as demonstrations for unification in the East and the resurgence of migration to the West demonstrated that the citizens of the GDR did not want their separate socialist state. Intransigence on this point would only have raised the specter of the Brezhnev doctrine. Speaking with GDR Premier Hans Modrow in Moscow on

January 30, 1990, Gorbachev accepted German unification in principle. Foreign Minister Shevardnadze suggested the terms of Soviet acceptance of the principle of unification in early February 1990. He explained that "all peoples, particularly the peoples of the Soviet Union, should have the right to a guarantee that German territory should never again be the source of a threat of war." He proposed that this be accomplished by a gradual process in which both Germanys became neutral, while "reliable political, juridical, and material guarantees" would ensure that the new German state would have a clear place in a new, peaceful European order. Similarly, in a *Pravda* interview Gorbachev noted that unification concerned other states besides Germany, and that Germany had no peace treaty with the wartime Allies. He suggested that this external aspect of unification be addressed through the two-plus-four structure. He had a limited view of which structures and institutions could effect this transition: "Violation of the military-strategic balance is impermissible," he declared, meaning that German unification could not alter the NATO-WTO balance, and thus a unified Germany in NATO was unacceptable.[18]

So at the center of Soviet concern in the earliest stages was the nature of the military balance. A leading Soviet policymaker on Germany stated very clearly that "the nucleus of the German problem was and continues to be the military component."[19] Although Soviet analysts spoke in terms of "stability," and the instability arising from a powerful Germany, their objections to a unified Germany in NATO were clearly based not on the potential for general instability in Europe but on the reconstitution and growth of the military threat directed against the Soviet Union by a more powerful NATO. This probably would have been a concern under any circumstances, but it was magnified by the process of disintegration of the WTO. The pact had been the Soviet response to the creation of NATO, and now the "balance" between the blocs was being not simply adjusted but fundamentally altered.

But the strict balance-of-power concern was joined by Soviet worries of an institutional cast. Soviet leaders also expressed their concern that German unification should accompany the various processes of European integration, both actual and potential. Shevardnadze first suggested this approach in February 1990, and it remained a fairly consistent theme through July. Shevardnadze warned that unification was "outdistancing the formation of common European structures that could become a guarantee of stability." A few weeks later Gorbachev offered that if CFE talks continued and a "Helsinki II" were held, NATO and the WTO would "be transformed from military-political organizations into political organizations . . . Then there will be no need for this haggling about where a united Germany will be."[20]

The creation of the two-plus-four structure in early 1990 addressed some of these concerns. In exchange for formal recognition that unification itself was solely an internal matter for the two Germanys, the Soviets achieved several objectives. First, the other major powers accepted and institutionalized the Soviet argument that German unification involved the rights and responsibilities of the four wartime powers. Second, the two-plus-four structure ensured a legitimate role for Soviet participation in the disposition of the postwar European system and in creating the form of the new system.

By March and April 1990 Soviet insistence on German neutrality was going nowhere, so the leadership changed its tune, favoring institutional restraints on Germany as a necessary condition for peace and Soviet security. Pressing for an outcome that ensured the balance of interests rather than the balance of power in Europe, the Soviet official and academic press was filled with alternative proposals and rationales for institutional restraints on Germany. They generally coalesced around three positions. First, some Soviet analysts seemed to decide that institutions were so useful that Germany ought to belong to both NATO and the WTO. This would place maximum constraints on German power and provide maximum information about German intentions, but it would avoid the asymmetry favoring the West that NATO membership alone entailed. Second, some suggested that if institutional constraints were desirable, but the military threat from NATO was unacceptable, NATO could be transformed into a political organization. Finally, more ambitious voices called for the creation of new all-European institutions, or the development of existing common European institutions (particularly the CSCE). At a meeting with Secretary of State Baker in mid-April, Shevardnadze proposed that Germany could have simultaneous membership in both NATO and the WTO, while structures such as a European council of heads of state or a CSCE committee of foreign ministers were developed.[21]

Thus, the two-plus-four talks became for the Soviets a way not to construct (or force) German neutrality but to bargain for alternative institutions in Europe that would serve the security needs of the USSR without either enhancing NATO's power or shutting out Soviet participation. Shevardnadze explicitly discussed the value of the two-plus-four framework as a way "to synchronize the movement toward German unity with the Helsinki process."[22] Having secured a legitimate role in the unification process by means of the two-plus-four talks, the Soviets began to speak in terms of a gradual process in which the two defense organizations could be transformed into purely political institutions. Institutions and overlapping institutional arrangements grew more important as it became clear to the Soviets that Germany would remain in NATO.

However, faced with western immobility on their proposals once again, the Soviets began in June 1990 to push instead for limits on the terms of German membership in NATO. Gorbachev hinted at a key to Soviet terms for a settlement when French President François Mitterrand visited Moscow in May 1990. As a necessary condition for the alliance's evolution toward a political forum, he noted pointedly, "NATO doctrine must be revised."[23] He also called for a "transition period" for military changes in Europe, taking up a proposal by West German Foreign Minister Hans-Dietrich Genscher for a period during which no NATO troops would be deployed in the former GDR and Soviet troops would gradually be withdrawn.

At the Warsaw Treaty meeting June 7 in Moscow, the heads of state issued a declaration that announced the effective end of ideological confrontation between east and west, and expressed the member states' intention to take steps to transform the organization into a democratic treaty of sovereign states with equal rights, emphasizing their political relations and consultations. Lest there be any doubt as to the reason for this declaration, in meetings with British Prime Minister Margaret Thatcher in Moscow on June 8, 1990, Gorbachev stressed the declaration as evidence that the WTO was becoming a political rather than a military organization, and observed that if at its July meeting NATO "undergoes similar changes in its doctrine, structure, contents and functions, with an accent on the political aspect of its activities, then appropriate institutions may emerge which will somehow reflect these changes."[24] The draft Soviet proposal on an international settlement regarding Germany which was submitted by Shevardnadze at the two-plus-four talks in June 1990 reiterated this theme. Whether German NATO membership was viewed as a threat to peace, the document said, would depend on the changes taking place in Europe. The level of armaments in Europe—explicitly including the German military—must be reduced "to the level of defense sufficiency," and the alliances must adopt a declaration of peaceful intentions toward one another.[25]

On July 6 NATO leaders released the London Declaration, which proposed a joint NATO-WTO statement declaring that the two blocs no longer considered each other adversaries, and committed NATO to a revision of strategy such that the first use of nuclear weapons would no longer be contemplated; rather, this would be relied on only as a last resort. The declaration was warmly received in Moscow. Ten days later German Chancellor Helmut Kohl and Gorbachev announced the Soviet-German agreement, effectively settling Soviet policy in the two-plus-four talks as well. Both Gorbachev and Shevardnadze explicitly referred to the NATO declaration as the key to Soviet agreement, the latter stating that the change in NATO "has enabled us to look differently on the role and place of a reformed NATO in Europe" and had given rise to a "qualitatively new military-political situation."[26]

Vadim Zagladin, a foreign policy adviser to Gorbachev, put the Soviet strategy in perspective a few months later. The real problem, he claimed, was the nature of NATO and a united Germany in that alliance. Although the principle of Germany's right to choose whatever alliance it liked was never in doubt, the Soviet task was to negotiate for conditions that would meet its security needs: a lower level of German arms, inviolability of borders, change in NATO doctrine, and movement toward developing European security structures along the lines of the Helsinki Final Act. He acknowledged that the Soviet Union was caught in a bargaining process in which it could not hope to get all it wanted, so it had to stand firm and make stronger demands than were necessary in order to squeeze the best possible deal out of the west. In achieving these objectives, he noted that the two-plus-four talks were a particularly valuable forum for pressing Soviet demands.[27]

While the primary Soviet military and defense concerns with respect to Germany had to do with limiting its defense capabilities and deployments and those of NATO in the former GDR, there was also a less traditional element in Soviet thinking and policy on the nature of a German threat which is somewhat counterintuitive and decidedly institutional. The Soviet Foreign Ministry report concluded that "important components of the system of guarantees lie in the complex of agreements, in the organization of German arms, in the exclusion of the possible renewal by Germany of political and territorial expansion, and in its integration in a *double ring* of all-European and west European institutions." The Soviets even proposed that Germany become the sixth member of the United Nations Security Council. The Soviets were confident that membership in several institutions would not only constrain Germany but enable that country to serve as a link between Soviet security and western security. First, by facilitating the development of market structures in the East, Germany would "prevent the disintegration of the Soviet Union into fifteen nuclear powers . . . [something] which the civilized world should dread." Second, Deputy Minister of Foreign Affairs Yuliy Kvitsinskiy hinted that Soviet-German security treaties (with their non-aggression pledges) would somehow be binding on NATO by virtue of Germany's membership in that organization.[28]

Shevardnadze went even further in emphasizing the centrality of institutional guarantees of security. He posed the problem of Soviet security as not merely one of the armed forces of a united Germany, but as one of a divided Germany and Europe split into armed blocs. The two-plus-four agreement, when combined with the series of bilateral Soviet-German agreements, reduced the probability of mass-scale military confrontation on the European continent, and thus satisfied Soviet security interests.[29] By mid-1990 the evolution of Soviet strategies was complete, and German membership in NATO was praised as a constraint on German policies and a plus for Soviet security.

The question of whether any feasible alternatives were available to Soviet policymakers was evaluated succinctly by Deputy Foreign Minister Kvitsinskiy in a March 1991 interview. He stated bluntly that Soviet refusal to give up occupation of Germany would only put the USSR in the position of relying on force and causing an armed confrontation. Kvitsinskiy echoed Gorbachev's question to Communist party critics in July 1990: if they did not like the withdrawal, what would they have him do—send in the tanks again? Asked why the Soviet government did not achieve the removal of western military forces from Germany, he replied: "There are . . . no ideal solutions in politics. Something always has to be forgone, realizing that what is desired and what is actually attainable are by no means one and the same thing." Since Germany wanted U.S. troops to remain, the Soviet Union could not force them out. What it did manage to negotiate—restrictions on German military forces and the deployment of NATO forces—was better than no constraints at all.[30]

The evolution of Soviet policy on German unification shows that it was not so much a powerful Germany or multipolarity in Europe that the Soviet leadership saw as threatening as the increase of NATO military power directed against the Soviet Union. Furthermore, a major issue in Soviet concerns was not just NATO as a military threat but NATO as an institution that excluded Soviet participation. As long as Gorbachev could go back to his relevant public and claim that the military threat to the Soviet Union was reduced because of the terms of German unification within a reformed NATO, he could live with the post–Cold War existence of the alliance. It is clear that the Gorbachev leadership did not believe that preponderant military power was necessary for Soviet security regardless of other institutional arrangements in Europe. A policy based on reduced reliance on military power was at least acceptable (if not preferred) so long as other institutional arrangements—the form, purpose, and deployment of NATO and the CSCE—underwent parallel revisions.

The Turn toward Economic Issues

Ever since the advent of the new thinking in 1987, the Soviets had conducted negotiations with western countries with the ultimate aim of fashioning closer economic ties—and using these ties to shore up and/or reform their failing economy. Yet for the most part these negotiations on economic matters were very much secondary to events in the political and military spheres. Thus, economic matters received only quiet attention in the months leading up to German unification. Periodic Soviet consultations with the Twelve, the conclusion of the Framework Agreement between the USSR and the EC in April 1990, and the intense negotiations with Germany over the financing of Soviet troop withdrawals and the maintenance of previously existing contracts with GDR enterprises all testify to the level of Soviet concern in this area. However, these issues had taken a back seat to the disputes over security-related aspects of German reunification. Once a satisfactory settlement of those aspects had been reached, economic issues—particularly the question of western aid to the USSR—moved into the foreground.[31]

The dramatic intensification of Soviet efforts in the realm of foreign economic policy is less a part of Soviet strategies to cope with the crisis posed by German unification than a striking example of how the Gorbachev leadership made use of German developments to further its own foreign and domestic policy goals. The "good citizen" image bestowed on the USSR by its acquiescence to German reunification provided Gorbachev with a perfect opportunity to press his claims for western aid and inclusion in the world economy on a more receptive audience. Thus, the "crisis" of German unification made it possible for the Soviet leadership to speed up the process of rapprochement with the west, and improve its chances of receiving western assistance in the process. These goals were pursued through both bilateral and multilateral channels.

Aid   Direct aid from Germany to cover the cost of Soviet troop withdrawal was an integral part of the agreements surrounding German reunification. As time went on, however, it became clear that the Soviets expected more than temporary aid. Initially, continued support from Germany appears to have been perceived as a quid pro quo for Soviet cooperativeness on unification; later it was seen as just compensation for Soviet "losses" related to German unification. These included much higher costs for imports from Germany owing to the introduction of the deutsche mark into East Germany, and reductions in Soviet exports to Germany as previously established trade links with East German enterprises declined. Gorbachev deemphasized this aspect of Soviet-German relations, even when questioned directly about it.[32] Nevertheless, pressure was obviously being exerted, for German Economics Minister Jurgen Möllemann visited Moscow in late May and reached agreement on both the placement of a large Soviet order with eastern German shipyards and the provision of a DM 2 billion "bridging loan" by the German federal government to cover the costs of these Soviet imports. German aid to the Soviets over 1990 (in the form of pledges, loans, or straight payments) amounted to $31 billion.[33] The Soviets also signed separate bilateral treaties of "friendship and cooperation" with several European states during the course of 1990 and 1991 (including France, Italy, and Greece) that provided for financial assistance to their ailing economy.

Not only was Germany the source of much direct aid to the Soviets; it also came to be seen as the key to east-west ties in economic relations. In mid-November 1990 *Pravda* cited a bulletin from the German Chancellory which stated that Kohl would use all his authority in the EC and the international community to ensure that help would be forthcoming to the USSR in the particularly difficult winter months. If that did not work, Germany would supply the food to plug the major gaps in winter supplies.[34] Expectations of assistance from Germany extended to the long-term perspective as well; the official view of the Ministry of Foreign Affairs as stated in December 1990 was that "cooperation with Germany can become one of the fundamental channels for the expansion of business contacts between the USSR and the European communities . . . Germany can also be used to provide for greater compatibility of the USSR's economy with common European and global structures, and also for the inclusion of the Soviet economy in the world economic system."[35]

Germany's influence with other western nations on the USSR's behalf would be most effective in a setting where Germany appeared as a principal actor among the few. This explains the extraordinary emphasis placed by the Soviets on the July Group of Seven (G-7) summit as a principal source of financial support for internal Soviet reforms. According to Deputy Foreign Minister Ernest Obminskiy, the choice of a multilateral forum for the discussion of aid issues was quite deliberate—although he did not mention why this particular multilateral forum was selected. He emphasized the superiority of multilateral over bilateral negotiations for the purpose of "synchronizing the processes taking place in the USSR, the reforms, and the actions of the west in response."[36]

In the months leading up to the summit, the Soviets prepared the ground by arguing over and over again that Soviet well-being and western security were integrally linked. Summing up the stance adopted by Gorbachev toward aid questions, Soviet Foreign Minister Aleksandr Bessmertnykh assured the Council of Europe committee of ministers that "the construction of a new Europe is unthinkable outside the context of success of reforms in the USSR. A united, stable, economically healthy, and politically self-assured Soviet Union is needed no less than a strong and united Europe is needed by the Soviet Union."[37]

What does this argument mean in more concrete terms? A post-summit interview with Deputy Prime Minister Vladimir Scherbakov touched on two specific mechanisms. First, he said, "as soon as our ties [with east European economic enterprises] were broken, these enterprises were thrown into a critical state. And now the western world is compelled to help eastern Europe, because the 'echo' of these unpleasant events is reaching them." Second, he claimed that a chain reaction of payment problems and insolvency among western companies had been touched off by defaults on the part of Soviet firms.[38]

Deputy Foreign Minister Obminskiy offered similar arguments in a radio interview in mid-June. First, he argued, consistent progress on disarmament can be made only if western aid helps the Soviet Union find its way out of the ongoing economic crisis. Second, the Soviet Union's integration into the global economy would mean that the west would gain an immense new trade partner. Finally, the Soviet Union's economic distress could surface in fairly unexpected ways, such as the mass exodus of displaced Soviet workers into western countries, disturbing whatever precarious balances had previously been achieved between labor and management and overwhelming the social service network. The argument that western stability depends on Soviet well-being was perhaps most bluntly explicated, however, by reform economist Leonid Abalkin. In a July interview he argued that "a satisfied country is not inclined to extremist strivings and manifestations of aggression. [The west] has an interest in a sufficiently powerful economic union, too, because the exclusion of a competitor like the USSR is a factor which will slow down the technical quest."[39]

Integration The drive toward integration constituted the second thrust of Soviet foreign economic policy after German reunification. On one level, the goal of integration into the global economy was frequently portrayed in Soviet statements as a natural outgrowth of the new thinking's emphasis on universal human values. On the practical level, however, it served two quite distinct functions—propping up the Soviet Union's economy while internal reforms ran their course, and creating a web of interdependence which would serve to restrain Germany.[40]

Hence, the issues of aid and integration were very closely intertwined. Efforts by Soviet leaders to promote a stabilization fund for ruble convertibility in the periods before and after the July G-7 summit are a prime example. Requests for a stabilization fund appeared repeatedly in official Soviet statements both before and after the summit.[41] As the issue was presented by Soviet spokesmen, the move to ruble convertibility was possible only if backed by a stabilization fund. Convertibility, in turn, was necessary for integration to take place, and the Soviet Union's stability (and thus ultimately the stability of Europe) depended on integration into the western economic system.

The second function of integration, from the Soviet point of view, was restraining Germany. It was all too apparent that German economic strength, once the trauma of unification had been overcome, would make it the most powerful and potentially the most threatening actor on the European continent. The legal bonds and economic interdependence involved in integration promised to provide some restraint on German foreign policy. As the summary of a seminar held by the Institute of the World Economy and International Relations (IMEMO) concluded: "Overall, opinions converged on the idea that the deepening of integration in the EC will facilitate a greater predictability and clarity of the role of united Germany in the future Europe." More generally speaking, Soviet officials repeatedly claimed that security was impossible without *their* integration into the European community of states. In early July Soviet Vice President Gennadiy Yanayev stated that interdependence was to become "a new and more reliable factor of stability than the former mutual fear and at the same time the guarantee of Europe's irreversible transition to a new situation." Gorbachev's statements at the G-7 meeting contained repeated references to the role of integration as the only cement capable of holding together the political accomplishments of the past decade. The USSR's attainment of direct contact with the major industrial powers was, said Gorbachev, the first step toward "creating a material basis for the irreversibility of those fundamental changes in world politics that have taken place over the past few years."[42] The implication was that all-around integration not only would make Germany's role more "transparent" but, more important, would enlarge the pool of common interests shared by the Soviet Union and the western nations.

Not all segments of the Soviet apparatus regarded integration as a desirable development. Conservative critics of Gorbachev's foreign policy pointed out that the cost of integration into the world economy and aid from the west would be external influence (if not control) over internal political economic decisions and conditions. But these voices of restraint represented a minority, and the USSR moved ahead quickly with plans for integration—at least on the diplomatic level. Domestic restructuring to make integration technically feasible was, of course, much slower in the making.

Engagement with International Institutions   As we have seen, the constructive involvement in the process of German reunification provided the USSR with political capital which it immediately put to use in lobbying for western aid and inclusion in the world economic system. A large part of its strategy consisted of putting Germany to work as its "bridge" to the west. But another part of its activities represented a continuation of diplomatic efforts which had been initiated years earlier: formal rapprochement with a number of international institutions.

The USSR's relations with the EC varied with the political currents of the 1970s and early 1980s.[43] Under Gorbachev, however, diplomatic relations with the EC were placed on a firm footing. These relations began to yield fruit when, in 1988, discussions on a comprehensive economic agreement were opened. The agreement went into effect in April 1990, and the benefits were very much in the USSR's favor. For example, the EC provided the USSR with humanitarian aid and technical cooperation, and canceled or suspended a number of quantitative restrictions on Soviet exports.[44]

Soviet attempts to establish relations with GATT also began earlier in the 1980s. The first moves began in 1982, and observer status—for which the USSR first applied in 1986—was finally granted in May 1990. A special commission was created within the Foreign Ministry to conduct negotiations regarding the Soviet Union's participation in the trade organization. The benefits, as seen by the Soviets, were threefold. First, GATT membership would eliminate discriminatory trade policies toward the USSR. Second, the obligations involved in GATT membership would be added incentive for the USSR to bring domestic economic standards into line with those imposed by the organization. Third, in the world trade system as it is, bilateral trade and political relations can serve not as an alternative but only as a supplement to multilateral cooperation. Not only do multilateral ties reduce the negotiating costs that would be required to conclude equivalent bilateral arrangements, but "the contractual character of GATT . . . provides fairly serious possibilities for the defense of national interests against violations of obligations."[45]

In the more recent past the USSR moved to create or strengthen economic ties with other international institutions. At the Bonn conference on economic cooperation in March–April 1990, the CSCE states considered measures to create a macroeconomic environment which would facilitate business cooperation between western and Soviet enterprises. The USSR signed the founding agreement for the European Bank for Reconstruction and Development (EBRD) in May 1990, and in July 1991 it applied for membership in the IMF (International Monetary Fund) and World Bank. As the Foreign Ministry's 1990 annual report stated: "The goal here is the creation—under the aegis of the World Bank and possibly of the IMF—of a new structure of external support for economic reforms in the USSR." Gorbachev assigned to institutions an even broader and more crucial role; when asked what guarantees existed to ensure that decisions taken at the Paris meeting would actually be carried out, he emphasized the role of international institutions—both old and new—in ensuring implementation.[46]

Access to all of these international organizations would obviously be beneficial to the Soviet Union. However, the EC seems both to offer the most gain in the case of Soviet inclusion and to represent the most danger to the USSR if it were to be excluded. Soviet fears of the latter possibility in both the economic and the broader political-security sphere surfaced throughout 1990. In September of that year an article in the Soviet military newspaper stated that "integration is the most powerful factor for security" but at the same time warned against the transformation of the European economy into a "European fortress" which would damage east-west rapprochement. Similarly, an article in *Izvestiya* assessing the CSCE talks noted that the eastern half of the European continent (including the USSR) was threatened by an "economic curtain" and had already earned for itself the title of the "third world" of Europe.[47] It was generally recognized that inclusion in western economic institutions constituted the USSR's best hope for economic recovery. Furthermore, Soviet appeals for western aid and for admittance into western institutions were related in an ominous way: if the USSR did not receive sufficient aid to shift its economy onto a market basis, it would be unable to participate fully in these institutions and would be left behind on the periphery even as the west European states accelerated their processes of integration. The Soviets were well aware of the tenuous quality of the link provided by the EBRD; at the assembly on European confederation held in Prague in June 1991, Gorbachev's adviser Vadim Zagladin complained of a "shortage" of institutions in the economic sphere.[48]

By the G-7 meeting, it had become clear that the immediate priorities of Soviet foreign policy had become financial stabilization and ruble convertibility, and fine points on the distribution of mutual economic benefits through institutions were less important than strategies to make Soviet economic reform possible at acceptable economic and political cost. It was very clear to both Scherbakov and Gorbachev that the Soviet Union faced a critical point in its reform efforts, and their strategies depended on international mechanisms. Gorbachev claimed that the Soviet Union would reform regardless of western responses, but that claim was not likely to be tested. Furthermore, although he asserted, "We have made our choice, we are taking the road of reforms toward a market economy," he also pointed out that "this will not just happen." That is, western countries had to remove the obstacles created during the Cold War. While credits would not save the Soviet Union, and reform must come from within, the process would be easier, more successful, and quicker with international cooperation.[49] Multilateral mechanisms represented the best option for the Soviets, owing to the magnitude, scale, and long-term nature of the assistance they needed for reform. Both the stabilization fund and the provision of huge quantities of consumer goods to the USSR represented measures which the western nations individually could not afford.

Insofar as integration into the world economy would lead the USSR toward dependence on trade ties and/or specific institutions, the Soviet leaders might have been expected to approach full-scale integration with caution. For example, one might have anticipated careful negotiation by the Soviets regarding the specific rules and procedures of any international organization in which they sought membership (for example, the IMF) or in the creation of which they took part (for example, new CSCE organizations).[50] New institutions obviously present greater opportunity for "tailoring" than do established ones. But in Soviet foreign policy strategy, membership in already established organizations such as the EC was clearly better than exclusion. International institutions are costly to create, and the Soviets tacitly acknowledged this in agreeing that NATO and other established institutions should be utilized during the transitional period.

The Soviet Union pursued a mix of bilateral and multilateral avenues in its attempts to obtain western aid and acceptance into international institutions. It took, in effect, a "shotgun approach": it signed bilateral treaties of "friendship and cooperation" with a number of west European countries, applied directly to international institutions for affiliation, and used Germany's influence to lend emphasis to its requests for aid in international forums. Could the USSR have used any other mix of strategies? It seems clear that the goal of integration into the global economy could not be fulfilled in any concrete way unless the Soviets were to gain access to institutions such as GATT. Pursuit of any one of these strategies in isolation would probably not have brought the USSR even the publicity and the limited success it did enjoy.

The Disintegration of the Soviet Alliance System in Eastern Europe
The alliance system in eastern Europe fashioned by the Soviet Union in the early postwar years began to founder after the 1989 "revolutions" in eastern Europe, and by late 1990 it had virtually ceased to function. As other chapters in this volume detail, eastern Europe turned toward the west in a flurry of "anticipatory adaptation." The European Community emerged by late 1990 as the dominant institution on the continent. How did the Soviet Union seek to ensure its military and economic security in the face of this rapid institutional change?

In the economic sphere the USSR hoped at first for the creation of another multilateral organization in the CMEA's stead. In January 1991 *Pravitel'stvennyy Vestnik* carried an optimistic and detailed description of the "new collective forum" that was to be created immediately in the CMEA's wake. The functions of this organization were reduced from planning to "consultation, exchange of information, and discussion," and it was to operate on a strict one-state-one-vote basis. Documents forming the legal base of this organization and stipulating its functions had apparently been drawn up, and as late as May 1991 the Hungarian Minister of International Economic Relations Bela Kadar indicated that a serious debate among CMEA members was continuing over the possible creation of a new multilateral economic organization. Once the debate had been resolved and the CMEA disbanded, of course, *Pravda* carried an article in which the demise of both the CMEA and the WTO was hailed as an opportunity to restructure relations with eastern Europe along "all-European" lines.[51]

Why was this strategy adopted? The USSR's historical experience with the CMEA was hardly a glowing success in terms of integration or Soviet control over its allies' economies. If anything, maintenance of the CMEA (like that of the WTO) was probably disproportionately costly to the USSR.[52] Furthermore, the sketch of the new organization presented in *Pravitel'stvennyy Vestnik* in early 1991 indicated that it was to be purely consultative and thus afford even less "control" over eastern Europe than did the CMEA. Three explanations are possible, none of which is completely satisfactory. First, the fact that the new organization was to operate on market principles may have led the Soviets to believe that it would be more effective at regional integration than the CMEA had been. Second, the central Soviet government might have felt that an organization which held regular consultations would be better able to deal with new developments such as agreements between foreign governments and subnational units of government in the Soviet Union.[53] Third, the drive to establish a multilateral economic organization may have been a last-ditch attempt at jump-starting the stagnant trade relations. By spring it was obvious that the bilateral trade agreements signed between the USSR and its former CMEA partners in late 1990 were not maintaining Soviet–east European trade at anything near its former level. Trade turnover with Poland was down 80 percent over 1990, with Czechoslovakia by 36 percent, and with Hungary by 86 percent. One of the main reasons behind this decline was the changeover (beginning January 1, 1991) to hard currency payments. Neither the USSR nor east European countries had adequate supplies of hard currencies for such transactions.[54]

Hopes for continued multilateral security seem to have vanished fairly quickly. Until November officials had spoken of a WTO transformed into a new cooperative political security institution. But the official statement of the Ministry of Foreign Affairs in December 1990 expressed the intention of "renewing" the legal basis of relations with eastern Europe using, as implicit models, the bilateral Treaties on Friendship, Cooperation, and Mutual Aid concluded with these countries during the 1965–1970 period.[55] In February 1991 Gorbachev reportedly wrote a letter to Lech Walesa in which he expressed the intention to work toward bilateral security guarantees with former WTO members.[56] The pact's military functions ceased on March 31, 1991, and its demise as a political-consultative organization followed only three months later.

The Soviets sought to put the best possible face on the dismantling of the WTO and to use it as an example for NATO. Vice President Yanayev's Prague address at the last WTO meeting in July 1991 was typical. He praised the Soviet Union and east Europe for being fully in step with the times by ending the WTO and discarding the old "bloc" mentality.[57] Foreign Minister Bessmertnykh also trumpeted this logic: with the end of the Cold War and military confrontation, structures built on those conditions should disappear or merge into the CSCE, a more appropriate institution for post-confrontation European security.

> We have links with NATO. We welcome the process of its politicization. What do we not accept? The concept whereby NATO is the cornerstone of all-European stability. NATO was set up during the Cold War, and to this day it is a twelve-country military-political grouping. We have entered a transitional period of European reorganization . . . Unlike the west, we regard NATO as a transitional mechanism. Even if they turn it into a political organization it still cannot be the foundation for an all-European process. Why? Well, because the institutions we are now talking about are the product of one part of Europe and part of Europe believes in them, but for Europe to be united, all those living on the continent, all countries and leaders, must be suffused with all-European ideas born of the European process. A Greater Europe has a chance to transform itself. But if there is a grouping of countries in the center, where is the Europe from the Atlantic to the Urals?[58]

Reading between the lines, we see that it is not only the military capability of NATO that concerned Soviet decision makers. The issue of restricted membership is important here. A fundamental problem in Soviet military-security policy was that the country faced a united and strengthened NATO as the WTO disintegrated. A spokesman for the Ministry of Defense put the problem in rather stark terms: the Soviet Union had lost military sites and infrastructure, was forced to confront NATO one-on-one, and faced the possibility that its former allies would join NATO.[59] These types of calculations probably were the source of Soviet attempts both to reinterpret the CFE limits[60] and to have assurances that the east European countries would not join military-political alliances directed against the USSR written into the bilateral treaties. Defense Minister Yazov had defended the CFE agreement in late November 1990. However, his defense was for the most part based on traditional calculations of balances of forces and arms control criteria, emphasizing minimum defense requirements and the *mutual* nature of the agreement.[61] Soviet military officers were willing to defend the CFE agreement, but on the basis of its precise military balancing value in coping with the WTO's disintegration.

These preoccupations require explanation. When military analysts such as Yazov and Moiseyev argued that military force would not guarantee security, they meant NATO and western security. This was not an argument that the Soviet Union does not have to match opposing military forces one-to-one. Further, when military leaders emphasized that the Soviet Union has made greater and even unilateral military reductions, they meant that equal numbers of military forces do matter. When they defended reductions, they thought in terms of a balance of military forces, not the uselessness of military forces for security. The Soviet military leadership accepted that *offensive* operations and capabilities were not necessary for defense and security, not that a balance of forces was irrelevant.

Official state spokespersons also expressed concern on this score. Foreign Minister Bessmertnykh wrote in a letter to the UN secretary general that although a new system of security could be developed, "the factor of military force remains one of the main means of providing security, both national and international . . . Special importance attaches to multilateral coordination of reliable guarantees in international law on the use of military force exclusively in the interests of maintaining peace and security. Imparting a defensive orientation for the military-force component in the provision of security would meet the attainment of this task."[62]

This issue may help to clarify the confusion surrounding the issue of balance of interests. As we discussed earlier, the balance of force concept and the balance of interest concept originally distinguished arguments that focused on military power and security from those that focused on interdependence and cooperative international negotiation in Soviet foreign policy. But the distinction became blurred by the fact that those arguing for the central (and immediate) importance of defense capabilities also argued for a balance of interests in security affairs, while officials who endorsed an interdependence-based notion of security interests were concerned with military balances and capabilities, and in particular with the continued existence of a powerful NATO.

The analytical source of the overlap was the distinction between offensive and defensive capabilities. Acceptance of the principles of minimum defense and reasonable sufficiency permitted Soviet military leaders (and conservatives in the government and the party as well) to endorse the CFE negotiations and the principle that one does not necessarily increase one's own security by having the offensive capability to threaten others. But they did so by focusing on and guaranteeing the *balance of defensive forces.* However, they did not call this the balance of power, for in Soviet discourse that meant the balance of ability to threaten other countries and force them to accept one's demands. In this context, balance of interests comes to mean a condition in which a state's security cannot be threatened by offensive military capability—a defensive balance.

Acceptance and implementation of the offense-defense distinction and the principle that military security is best maintained when all states have only a defensive capability was a major success of the "new thinking" reformers. Yet it required them to articulate and defend an understanding of security that was ultimately based on the balance of military power.[63] Since a defensive balance could be achieved in Europe only through negotiations and arms control agreements, the balance of interests concept also made its way into reformist discussion of military and defense security. The element common to the otherwise divergent views of traditionalists and new thinkers is the role of the offense-defense distinction in security.

The Soviets expressed their strongest and most consistent support for managing USSR withdrawal from eastern Europe through the Conference on Security and Cooperation in Europe. Soviet support was based on three features of the CSCE: its basis in the Helsinki Final Act, which recognized postwar European borders; its comprehensive membership; and the fact that it was not a product of the Cold War bipolar structure.[64] The CSCE was supported even by conservatives such as Defense Minister Yazov as the best forum for future cooperation in Europe because it was the basis for the existing European order. Soviet officials pointed to the acceptance of European borders and to the sets of rights agreed to under the Helsinki Final Act of 1975 as having made the shift from confrontation to cooperation in Europe possible.[65]

Of course, it was not the mere principle of the privileged role of the CSCE in Europe that drew Soviet support. The real value of the CSCE for the Soviets was that it was the only major existing European institution (other than the twenty-two-nation CFE talks) in which it was a member. Although the government endorsed this as a principle of comprehensive participation,[66] it is clear that it was Soviet participation they were worried about. In the fall 1990 negotiations with east Europe, the Soviets were seeking to make sure their physical withdrawal from eastern Europe was a negotiated one, and intensified their efforts to support CSCE development as a way to prevent Soviet political withdrawal from Europe as well. In theory this could have been accomplished through bilateral agreements, but the Soviet leadership preferred it be accomplished through institutions.

The CSCE also had the advantage (from the Soviet perspective) of being comprehensive in scope. Through the CSCE, by virtue of Soviet military and political standing in Europe, the Soviet Union could play a role in economic, technological, and ecological negotiations as well. Solely on the basis of its capabilities, it is difficult to see how the Soviet Union might have been a major player in defining the future of European relations on these issues. With the CSCE it was at least possible to play a larger role. Shevardnadze consistently pushed the value of the CSCE as the only all-European institution with the scope to address the entire range of European security—as opposed to purely military—policy. He proposed that the Helsinki process be institutionalized, preferably through the creation of permanent CSCE organizations, and identified mechanisms that were adopted in the Paris Charter. In his speech at the Paris summit Gorbachev urged "institutionalization" of the CSCE process and stressed the importance of establishing a center for conflict prevention.[67] All these plainly required a leading Soviet role. Thus, the Soviet leadership sought to press the view that the advantage of the CSCE was its comprehensiveness, unlike most western governments, which saw the CSCE as a very weak and unstable institution.

Therefore, it was not that the Soviet government favored the CSCE because it was a weak institution (although it was). The Gorbachev leadership sought to place it at the center of European security because it was the only important existing institution in which the Soviet Union was a member. With the WTO disintegrating and the major western governments favoring a future based on NATO and/or the EC, the Soviet Union would have no legitimate institutional role in post–Cold War Europe. The CSCE was the only institution in which the Soviets could possibly play a role in defining rules and procedures.

But the primary Soviet theme in support of the CSCE by 1991 was the fact that it was not a product of the Cold War. This was partly an argument for the CSCE, likely to be favorably viewed in much of Europe, but it was primarily an argument against NATO. Nearly all endorsements of the CSCE as a nonbloc security institution contrasted it to NATO in these terms.[68] The argument that old bloc-based institutions are an obstacle to Soviet reform and integration into world society was Gorbachev's primary theme in London. The entire argument rests on the assumption that security in Europe now depends on active Soviet participation in all areas of activity, so that the continent moves "from a bloc-based system to the creation of all-European structures of security in the limits of the CSCE process, by its institutionalization, by formulation of European economic and legal space [*prostranstvo*], construction of a single European peace, and cooperation."[69]

Soviet arguments for the demise of NATO and the development of the CSCE failed for the most part, and Soviet strategies fell back on bilateral negotiations to cope with eastern Europe. Interestingly, the decision to move to bilateral security guarantees with respect to eastern Europe apparently was taken at the highest levels even before the end of 1990. Jerzy Sulek, the head of the Polish Foreign Ministry's Europe department, stated in July 1991 that preparations for the conclusion of a new treaty with the USSR had begun late the previous year. Likewise, Hungarian Defense Minister Lajos Fur stated in the spring of 1991 that Hungary had sent to Moscow in late 1990 drafts on the basis of which they wanted to conclude a bilateral military agreement with the USSR. In both cases, however, actual negotiations did not begin until at least May.[70] One way in which the delay in starting negotiations could be explained is that there was dissent in the Soviet policy-making establishment; namely, parts of the military command opposed the decision to fall back on bilateral ties until sometime in the spring. Indeed, the past has seen recurrent Soviet calls for the simultaneous dissolution of NATO and the WTO, but in the absence of significant change in NATO's structure and objectives it is reasonable to assume that the Soviets would have preferred continued multilateral security arrangements. Only in March 1991 did a military officer writing under the aegis of the defense ministry voice the opinion that the Soviet Union should move toward bilateral security arrangements with its erstwhile "allies," but only because the USSR was not "strong enough to form a completely new defensive union with like-minded states."[71] Moiseyev confirmed the new stance a month later, asserting that Soviet security interests with respect to eastern Europe could be ensured "reliably" through bilateral cooperation.[72]

The bilateral agreements which began to be negotiated that spring were modeled on the treaties of the 1965–1980 period, which constituted the general legal foundation for all Soviet–east European relations. In contrast to the previous generation of bilateral treaties, these were formulated around "respect for sovereignty, noninterference in internal matters, recognition of freedom of choice, and the rights of each people to decide its own destiny"— the new principles of Soviet–east European relations. Nevertheless, the Soviets' attempts to create a fifteen- to twenty-year "contract" with Hungary were hindered by their insistence on a clause according to which each party would agree not to participate in military-political alliances that could be directed against either side. Such alliances would naturally include NATO, and "in theory, the Soviet Union could object to Hungary's or Czechoslovakia's full European Community membership" as well.[73]

By late 1991, only the treaty with Romania had been signed, and even this was not as binding as the USSR would have liked. The Romanian foreign minister asserted that his country retained complete freedom to participate in "defensive alliances" such as NATO. Negotiations on the Hungarian, Czechoslovakian, and Polish treaties with the USSR slowed to a crawl owing to those countries' refusal to allow such a clause to be included at all.[74] Nevertheless, only in the case of Poland did the Soviets delay troop withdrawal; all Soviet troops had been removed from Czechoslovakia and Hungary by June 30, 1991.

The relative lack of concern regarding multiple (that is, multilateral as well as bilateral) security guarantees, as compared with the push for both types of arrangements in the economic sphere, appears to contradict the conventional wisdom on the priority given to military security. This is particularly striking since the Soviets were acutely aware of the rudimentary nature of security arrangements thus far within the framework of the CSCE. It is clear that the east and central European region still carried enormous importance for Soviet foreign policy. Excerpts allegedly taken from a CPSU memorandum on eastern Europe stated: "Under no circumstances can there be a real or potential threat to the military security of the USSR emanating from the east European region . . . It is necessary to act against the accession of our former allies to other military blocs and groups, especially NATO (and in the future possibly the West European Union as well), as well as against involvement in agreements that could lead to the stationing of foreign armed forces on their territory."[75] Moiseyev's April 1991 article in *Izvestiya* echoed almost verbatim some of these declarations, and Deputy Foreign Minister Kvitsinskiy heavily emphasized the strategic significance of the east European states for Soviet foreign policy by virtue of their location on the USSR's western borders.[76] The Soviets' early resignation to bilateralism in the security sphere, then, is a puzzle which cannot yet be resolved; at best we can speculate. First, they were constrained by the public and much-lauded principle of *svoboda vybora*. If the east European countries did not want to join a Soviet military alliance, there was little short of invasion that the Soviet government could do about it.[77] Similarly, even a delay in withdrawing Soviet forces as a pressure tactic would have violated that principle and raised serious international doubts that Soviet foreign policy was truly undergoing reform. The exception of Poland, where the Soviets dragged their feet on negotiating an agreement, may be more acceptable to the west because Poland is the corridor through which Soviet forces in the former GDR would most efficiently and quickly be removed. Finally, unlike in the economic sphere, the east European governments simply saw no mutual interests with the Soviet Union in military affairs, so they were uncompromising in their positions against any need for cooperative military structures (as opposed to nonaggression pledges).[78] In economic affairs the former Soviet allies clearly may gain from reformed trade relations, although their long-term goal is to turn to the west. Therefore, there was something about which to bargain. In Soviet–east European military affairs, there simply was no bargaining space.

An East European Test Case: The Yugoslav Conflict

A major problem for Soviet support of the evocative single "European space" and the conflict resolution and prevention role for the CSCE appeared in Soviet positions on the Yugoslav conflict. Overall, the conflict received relatively light and measured treatment in the Soviet press. Reporting was largely neutral and factual, with events and diverging interpretations systematically reported. A fair amount of attention was given to CSCE and EC efforts to moderate the conflict in generally optimistic terms, but despite Soviet praise for all-European institutions, the Soviet government consistently supported the basic right of Yugoslavians to settle their own internal matters, and clearly came out against direct institutional involvement in the Yugoslav civil conflict. Gorbachev expressed these preferences in a note to Yugoslav President Stepan Mesich: "[The USSR] wishes that all the people of Yugoslavia will come to an agreement on peaceful democratic methods for resolving the crisis situation, and will preserve the unity of the common state." The comparison to conflict in the Soviet Union was obvious, and dominated Soviet positions. An editorial in *Pravda* observed that Yugoslavia's "multinational federal state has been hit by the virus of separatism," and claimed that western leaders who encouraged Baltic nationalism might be one source of the Yugoslav conflict. The Soviets endorsed CSCE and EC mediation efforts, and accepted cease-fire monitors as long as they were accepted by the Yugoslav government. But the official position balked at two developments: the right of international institutions to intervene in internal matters, and any western military presence—NATO, Western European Union (WEU), or ad hoc—in Yugoslavia.[79]

This points to two fundamental problems in Soviet policies on European security with respect to institutions. First, the institutions the Soviet Union most opposed are those that may be most effective, and the one that the Soviets supported—the CSCE—has been least capable of responding to the conflict (hence western attempts to rely on the EC or the WEU instead); furthermore, the source of the CSCE's ineffectiveness may be the very features the Soviets valued in it—comprehensiveness with respect to both membership and issues. Second, the very interdependence of security (military, economic, political, and so on) in Europe which lay behind Soviet calls for a "European space" contradicted the notion that the Yugoslav conflict was an "internal" matter. It was not merely a question of principle; armed conflict within that country might produce international conflict. In order to have a consistent policy on interdependence and security in Europe, the Soviet Union would have had to open its domestic political affairs to potential international influence.

Gorbachev himself declared in Germany in November 1990 that the "absolutization of sovereignty means the isolation from historical and modern realities, an isolation that may cost dearly. Such absolutization is already disproved by the attainments of west European integration. Sovereign peoples need organic cooperation."[80] This would seem to be in line with the heralded transformation of Soviet national security interests from calculations of the balance of power to preservation of the balance of interests and integration into the international system—economically and politically. But the Yugoslav crisis demonstrated that traditional concepts of sovereignty and calculations of military capability and threat continued to form the minimal requirements for the Soviet Union's European security policy.

The Soviet position on Yugoslavia lent credibility to the purported CPSU Central Committee memorandum on east Europe cited earlier, which stated that eastern Europe must be kept free of foreign military bases and armed forces. The position in this memo, and Soviet policy on the Yugoslavian civil conflict, indicated that while the creation of a cooperative, mutually beneficial economic, technological, cultural, and ecological "space" in Europe may have been considered necessary for Soviet security, it was not a substitute for the proper balance of military forces and capabilities.

One analyst of Soviet security policy has written that the Soviets have reason to prefer that European institutions fail and Europe returns to the old multilateral balance of power system because east European countries would become dependent on the Soviets to balance against Germany, and Soviet power would be important again.[81] The course of Soviet policy responses to the changed structure of Europe provides strong evidence that Soviet strategy was substantially affected by the existence of institutions in Europe, and it relied at least in part on institutional restraints and opportunities in calculating policies. However, Soviet attitudes toward institutions were not undifferentiated, and a comparison of these attitudes aids in understanding how institutions affected Soviet calculations.

The Soviet definition of its national security interests in post–Cold War Europe included strong traditional elements. The Soviet government was concerned at a minimum with the capabilities of other states in Europe (including the United States), and identified the Soviet Union's ability to defend itself from military attack as the basic condition of national security. Its primary concerns were the military capability of NATO and Germany. In this respect, uncertainty about the ability and intentions of other states increased with the disappearance of a bipolar Europe.

However, the Soviet Union responded to heightened uncertainty by intensifying its reliance on institutions for calculating and managing power balances. Furthermore, the Soviet leadership was concerned not only with power but also with intentions as a measure of security threat. NATO's doctrinal revisions and development of political consultation with its former adversaries notably dampened Soviet complaints about NATO's future role. Similarly, rather than abandon the WTO as a useless artifact of bipolarity, it first sought to "transform" the pact into a political alliance. The pattern is even stronger in the case of the CMEA: Soviet officials made repeated efforts to preserve or replace it with a new multilateral agreement. Furthermore, while the Soviet leadership was centrally concerned with the balance of defensive military capabilities in Europe, its response to uncertainty and structural change (notably the demise of the WTO as "balance" to NATO) was to press for completion and implementation of the CFE agreement.

In understanding Soviet strategies, we must keep in mind that the leadership saw institutions as being as much a potential source of threat as a source of opportunity. NATO was the obvious example, but the Soviet leadership feared that the WEU, the EC, a central European security alliance, and other sub-European groupings would threaten Soviet interests as well. Some west European leaders advocated a security component for the EC or advanced the "European pillar" of the WEU with the argument that, since those institutions did not include the United States, they would be perceived as nonthreatening to the Soviets. This reasoning was not borne out. The Soviet leadership saw any capable, successful institution in which it was not a member as a potential threat.

This fear of exclusion can be explained very simply: economic reform and development rose in the hierarchy of Soviet national security interests and calculations. While military defense remained the basic element of Soviet security calculations, it was seen as only the minimal condition for security, *and* the tradeoffs between military predominance and economic well-being played a more important role in strategy. The internal tradeoffs between military spending and Soviet economic reform are well known. In 1991, however, the external aspects of this tradeoff became important in Soviet strategy. The Soviet Union had to be a good, cooperative, nonthreatening European citizen if it hoped to live in the European economic home. Because perestroika depended on Soviet integration in the world economy, Soviet economic integration was a central component of Soviet security policy, second only to maintaining the minimum conditions for defense.

The Gorbachev leadership was eager to join institutions to deal with two immediate problems: the painful process toward ruble convertibility and the need to create some rational, secure framework for foreign investment in the Soviet economy. International institutions are not merely efficient mechanisms for coordination with foreign countries. They are powerful assets for domestic economic reform. Access to such assets entails costs, including some loss of control over domestic political economic conditions and vulnerability to the downswings of the international economy. In this conservative critics were correct in claiming that the leadership permitted outside influences to affect Soviet policies. But Gorbachev's definition of national security and national interests deemed such costs acceptable when compared to the costs of autarky.

An important aspect of Soviet strategy was the attempt to reassure other states about Soviet intentions. In the political and military arena this meant transparency in military affairs, real reductions of military capability, a resolution of the CFE dispute, and implementation of the policy of *svoboda vybora* despite considerable loss of power and influence in eastern Europe. In economic affairs this meant cooperation with institutions such as the IMF and the World Bank in adjusting Soviet economic policies and conditions. In this respect Soviet participation in military and economic institutions in Europe became not only a way to manage uncertainty regarding others' intentions and capabilities but also a way to reduce some forms of uncertainty about Soviet intentions and capabilities. There was considerable variation in Soviet willingness to use institutions to reassure other European states—for example, the Soviet leadership did not wish to join NATO, nor did it wish the CSCE to contribute to European stability by dealing with ethnic conflicts.

The Soviet leadership was not particularly predisposed to new or existing institutions—they seemed to favor whatever worked—but an important difference appears when we compare military-defense institutions to economic institutions. In military and defense areas the leadership favored the creation of new multilateral forums or the development of the weak CSCE structures, whereas in economic areas it favored existing efficient institutions such as GATT, the IMF, and the EC (the exception is the Coordinating Committee, COCOM). The reason is relatively straightforward: in military and defense areas the Soviets valued very highly their participation in determining the rules and procedures of any important institution. They did not want merely to join existing institutions, no matter how efficient (such as NATO); they wanted to define those institutions. In economic areas the Soviet government wanted to join whatever worked, as long as the rules were not exclusionary.

In all these respects Germany remained central to Soviet calculations in both positive and negative terms. Germany as a member of NATO and as a location of NATO forces and nuclear capability continued to be a concern in Soviet defense calculations. But Germany played a leading role in easing the costs of transition to the post–Cold War Europe. This is in part very concrete: Germany paid for Soviet military withdrawal, and guaranteed former GDR–Soviet economic relations. But the special Soviet-German relationship demonstrated in the numerous meetings between their highest officials gave the Soviet Union a less direct advantage as well. As an actor more sympathetic to Soviet concerns than other western states and as one of the leading western powers, the Germans on several occasions gained the Soviets better terms from other western states than they could have gotten bilaterally. The two-plus-four agreement and Gorbachev's invitation to the G-7 meeting were two notable examples. This may explain why the Soviets strongly favored multi-lateralism in economic affairs. As long as Germany was a member of those organizations, it pulled along the more reluctant members toward policies more in line with Soviet strategies.

Our analysis was concluded in August 1991, with the end of the era of *Soviet* foreign policy. The creation of the Commonwealth of Independent States and the shift to republic-level foreign policy–making has introduced striking differences that are worth noting, but also some important continuities. Perhaps the largest difference is the republics' attitude toward NATO, which they no longer see as a source of threat. Indeed, President Boris Yeltsin has declared Russia's intention to join NATO eventually. This diminished sense of a military threat from the west is accompanied by a heightened sense of the importance of interrepublic military balances and the emergence of political disputes among the republics. Another important difference, not surprisingly, is that the republics did not offer objections to Germany's swift recognition of Slovenia and Croatia. All is not harmonious in post-Soviet east European relations, however. Russia has failed to supply Poland with the natural gas agreed to in a barter for credits to purchase Polish goods. The Russian government is rumored to be seeking hard currency or a better exchange for its fuel exports.

Certain continuities should be noted. Economic reform and the role of international institutions remain the primary factors in post-Soviet strategies. The price increases of January 1992 were implemented to follow the IMF's "shock therapy" program for reform and stabilization. The post-Soviet leadership still finds itself constrained by institutions and by its desperate need for aid. One official of the Russian Foreign Ministry said in an interview that the post-Soviet republics know they must observe the CFE limits and make progress toward a CFE1A agreement "or you [the west] will simply not believe us anymore." Similarly, another official argued very strongly that COCOM restrictions must be lifted if post-Soviet industry is to reform and compete in the international consumer (rather than military) market. More recently, the German government limited future export credits for Russia in response to Yeltsin's retreat on promises of autonomy for the Volga Germans.

Thus, post-Soviet European security relations may be less confrontational and less dominated by the prospect of global military conflict, but they are developing their own complexities. It is too early to conclude how these patterns will develop, but one interesting distinction is relatively clear. Where international institutions exist (NATO, the EC, IMF, and UN) the post-Soviet leadership attempts to use them to gain access to resources and help stabilize their tumultuous political and economic relations. Where international institutions are lacking (in interrepublic and east European relations), political, economic, and even military conflicts are emerging almost daily and are not being managed very well. The source of future conflict in Europe may lie within the east rather than between east and west if the pace of institution building in the east continues to fall so far behind the development of serious disputes.

Chapter 3

The United States and International Institutions in Europe after the Cold War

Joseph S. Nye

Robert O. Keohane

The United States had a relatively consistent grand strategy during the Cold War to contain Soviet power and to maintain an open international economy. As George Kennan observed shortly after World War II, the global balance of power would be affected by five significant regions of industrial and technological potential, namely, the United States, the Soviet Union, Japan, Britain, and the European continent. United States alliances with Europe and Japan were geopolitically critical to containing Soviet power in the center of the Eurasian landmass. Twice before in the century the United States had been drawn into European conflicts after thinking it could ignore the continent. In the bipolar world of the Cold War, the United States could not afford to ignore a weakened Europe. Structural changes wrought by World War II go a long way toward explaining the new definition of American interests, but international institutions such as the North Atlantic Treaty Organization (NATO) and the European Community (EC) were essential instruments in the implementation of that strategy.

Four decades later, at the end of the Cold War, the structure of world politics changed fundamentally with the retreat, and then the collapse, of the Soviet Union. By the end of 1990 the world was no longer bipolar in a politically meaningful sense. The Soviet threat to west European and American interests collapsed equally rapidly, to be replaced by less focused fears of economic and political disruption in eastern Europe, leading to flows of refugees or migrants to the west. One might have thought, on the basis of either "balance of power" or "balance of threat" theory, that European alignments with the United States would have weakened more than they did in the early post–Cold War period. Signs of tensions between the United States and its European allies over trade, the role of the European Community, and relations with the east had begun to mount in the later years of the Reagan administration. In 1989 and 1990 many Europeans, including President Vaclav Havel of Czechoslovakia, were calling for the dissolution of the Warsaw Pact and NATO. Two years later, however, Havel was speaking about joining NATO. Paradoxically, from a realist perspective, American influence was greater in the early 1990s than during the mid-1980s.

One must be careful, of course, about reading too much into this paradox. As we explained in the introduction to this volume, realism and liberal institutionalism are too loosely specified as theories to be subjected to rigorous tests. Moreover, as we shall see in this chapter and in the conclusions to the volume, institutions can be used for realist as well as liberal strategies. And two years is too brief a period from which to draw conclusions about the longer term. Nonetheless, from the perspective of this volume, it is interesting that the changes that occurred in the early postwar period were not in the direction of erosion, as the structural factors would have predicted. Equally interesting was the extent to which American strategy relied on international institutions. Of course, it is not surprising that the United States would rely on institutions that it had created, but as we shall see, there were other conceivable strategies available.

The United States successfully sought to prevent a loss of influence by using international institutions to maintain a congenial political-economic order in Europe. Institutions that have been successful tend to create interests that support them: even if NATO and the General Agreement on Tariffs and Trade (GATT) could not have been formed *de novo* under the conditions of 1990, they were able to persist under those new conditions. The Soviet Union sought to cover its retreat from Europe by using the rhetoric of international institutions; Germany sought to use institutions to reassure its neighbors as it regained a central role in Europe; and Britain tried to retain institutions such as NATO that magnified its influence. Somewhat like Britain but on a larger scale, the United States sought to maintain a complex of interests that had formed around institutions that it had itself created.

The American interests were shaped, as were those of other major states, by history. The United States had played a key role in constructing the institutions in place in 1989: they reflected not merely United States interests but also the character of American society and Americans' conception of their role in the world. To understand American interests as viewed by the Bush administration in early 1989, therefore, we need briefly to examine the decisions that had created major international institutions, and the evolution of policy with respect to them. The first part of this chapter is devoted to that task. We then turn to the new opportunities and problems created by the sudden end of the Cold War: the reunification of Germany and the agreed-upon withdrawal of Soviet troops from eastern Europe. The third section addresses the question of U.S. policies after 1989: How did the United States define its interests and seek to use institutions to attain its objectives? In the conclusion we ask about possible alternative strategies.

The Situation in 1989

At the beginning of the Bush administration, America's foreign policy leaders could look back with satisfaction. The most important goals of the United States with respect to Europe had been achieved. The contentious states of western Europe were tied together in an economic community. They were governed by democratic regimes, presiding over market-oriented economies. Europe's alliance with the United States had provided a strong defense and had built enduring political ties; and Europe was also closely linked to the United States economically, under predominantly liberal rules governing international trade and investment. Although particular aspects of the U.S.-European relationship had often been disputed, none of these disputes had threatened the strong underlying basis of the alliance. NATO in 1989 was the most successful multilateral alliance in history; and the world had never experienced an institutionalized international regime for the governance of trade, investment, and monetary issues as enduring as that constructed through GATT, the World Bank and International Monetary Fund, and the Group of Seven.

The security and economic systems in place in 1989 were distinguished not merely for their success but for two other features: they were *multilateral* and highly *institutionalized*. John Ruggie has defined multilateralism as "an institutional form which coordinates relations among three or more states on the basis of generalized principles of conduct."[1] NATO was predicated on the indivisibility of threats to the collectivity; GATT rested on the unconditional most favored nation principle. The arrangements were also highly institutionalized, characterized by explicit rules, and speckled with international organizations ranging from the small secretariat of GATT to the larger bureaucracies of NATO and the European Community.

The multilateral and institutionalized quality of the ties between the United States and Europe also affected their relations with the rest of the world. The EC had acted as a "magnet" for former dictatorships on the periphery of Europe—for Greece, Portugal, and Spain in the 1970s and 1980s. Cooperation between the United States and Europe had led to joint action through the World Bank (always run by an American) and the International Monetary Fund (always led by a European). Somewhat more tenuous but still institutionalized cooperation on economic issues had taken place since the 1950s in the Organization for European Economic Cooperation (OEEC) and its successor, the Organization for Economic Cooperation and Development (OECD). Since 1974 Europe and the United States had cooperated, along with Japan and a few other industrialized countries, on energy issues in the International Energy Agency (IEA), securing some degree of insurance against embargoes directed against one or a few of them.

Throughout the Cold War both NATO and the economic regimes of the west rested on a firm basis of common interests. NATO drew much of its strength from continuing Soviet pressure, repeatedly evidenced in threatening Soviet policies ranging from the Berlin blockade of 1948–49 to the Euromissile affair of the early 1980s. Military bipolarity meant that Europe needed American protection, and that the United States needed European support to reinforce its power position. Alleged "crises" in NATO, as Glenn Snyder pointed out in 1984, were not serious: crises persisted "because the alliance *cannot* break up. Since NATO is a product of the bipolar structure of the system, it cannot collapse or change basically until that structure changes."[2]

The stability of NATO was reinforced by the consistency of American policy toward Europe, and by stronger European-American economic ties. In 1983, for instance, industrial Europe accounted for 26.6 percent of all U.S. exports and 17.7 percent of all U.S. imports.[3] Investment grew rapidly in both directions: first U.S. investment in Europe in the 1950s and 1960s, later a reverse flow of European investment in the United States. And successful institutions, providing information and facilitating cooperation, tended to reinforce themselves.[4]

Despite the worries of generations of American and European commentators, the openness of the United States' domestic structure seems to have been an asset. Its partners gained access to a steady flow of knowledge about American preferences and internal arguments, which provided them with information and thus made the United States more attractive than a closed society as an alliance and regime leader. The transnational and transgovernmental flow of internal memos from the American bureaucracy to the press and diplomats of friendly countries gave some protection to European governments against unpleasant surprises.[5]

Throughout the forty years between the formation of NATO and 1989, two rather continuous sources of stress affected European-American relations. One involved controversies over the defense of Europe, focused on the adequacy of European contributions to their own defense, on the credibility of the American nuclear commitment, and on the relation of European defense to conflicts arising outside the NATO area. The other source of stress involved links between economic and security issues.

NATO Issues

During 1945–46, the U.S. government was slow to adapt to the new structure created by the end of Word War II and the division of Germany. During that time President Harry Truman sought to implement Franklin Roosevelt's strategic design for postwar accommodation with the Soviet Union and reliance on universal institutions. Security was to be provided by the collective security provisions of the United Nations charter based on an expectation of a multipolar world in which Britain and France would be two of the five world policemen with vetoes on the Security Council. The lag in the adjustment of American policy to the new structure was caused in part by domestic politics, in part by uncertainty about Soviet intentions, and in part by the commitment to Roosevelt's global institutional design. The inability of a weakened Britain to balance power in the eastern Mediterranean, the threat of communism in French and Italian domestic politics, and the increased Soviet control in eastern Europe led to the redefinition of American interests and the hardening of Cold War attitudes after 1947, with the Truman doctrine and the Marshall Plan.

With the new definition of interests came new institutional frameworks. The universal institutions were not discarded but were held in abeyance or given a secondary priority. The United States first encouraged European defense cooperation in the Brussels Pact of 1948, then moved to create NATO, which was justified under Article 51 of the UN charter as a framework for self-defense. In short, the selective security of an alliance now supplemented and largely replaced the collective security of the UN charter. By 1955, after the French parliament's refusal to ratify plans for a European Defense Community (EDC), a rearmed Federal Republic of Germany was incorporated within the alliance.

In the 1950s the acquisition of nuclear weapons and strategic delivery capacity by the Soviet Union created the possibility of an atomic attack on the United States as part of a European war. Europeans such as French President Charles de Gaulle questioned the credibility of the American nuclear commitment. The United States responded by intensifying its declared policy of support for European security, being willing to engage in potentially dangerous confrontations with the Soviet Union in Berlin in order to preserve its credibility as a guarantor.

Although the United States had supported stronger European defense cooperation since the days of the ill-fated European Defense Community, American practice often varied from declared policy. In the early 1960s the Kennedy administration's "grand design" spoke of twin pillars or a dumbbell structure for the Atlantic Alliance. British entry into the Common Market was to strengthen the security structure as well as economic integration. The United States sought both to preserve its leading role in European defense and to strengthen European defenses, but these objectives were not always entirely consistent with each other. American efforts to halt the development of French nuclear weapons and to resist demands for a greater French role in security matters, combined with continuing U.S. support for Britain's nuclear deterrence, led to friction which contributed to De Gaulle's veto of British entry into the Common Market and later to French withdrawal from the integrated NATO structure. American efforts to head off Germany's interest in developing nuclear weapons led to the institutional proposal of a multilateral force within NATO and, when that failed, to the global institutional framework of the nonproliferation treaty which Germany eventually signed on assurance that the United States would continue to use its nuclear weapons to deter any attack against the Federal Republic. Franco-German differences over American security guarantees contributed to slowing European integration. Nonetheless, through quiet diplomacy France remained informally integrated in NATO defenses in important areas such as control of air space, coordination of navies, and secret nuclear cooperation.

In the latter half of the 1970s, both Europeans and Americans were torn internally over conflicting interpretations of increased Soviet defense expenditure and missile deployments. Europeans were caught between their traditional fear of being trapped in a war by the American security guarantee or alternatively of being abandoned by the United States and having to face the Soviet Union alone. President Jimmy Carter's decision to deploy intermediate-range nuclear forces (INF) within the NATO context on the continent of Europe was designed to allay such fears. While bitter divisions persisted in Europe after the Soviet invasion of Afghanistan and the advent of the Reagan administration, the ability of European parliaments to agree to the NATO deployment in 1983 was a critical symbolic as well as military response to the Soviet Union in the mini–Cold War that marked the beginning of the 1980s. NATO gained increasing importance, both as a symbol and as a forum for alliance decisions in the early 1980s, but this did not extend to out-of-area conflicts. A number of European states refused to give the United States overflight permission for the attack on Libya in 1986, and U.S.-European differences over the Middle East which emerged in 1973 continued in the United Nations.

In sum, by the closing days of the Cold War, the United States' commitment to European security had been reinforced. Friction over some issues continued; but this had been a continual feature of the alliance, more an indication of stability (as Snyder had argued) than of underlying difficulty.[6] There were difficulties over out-of-area conflicts as well as increasing concern in American domestic politics over burden sharing and arguments with the allies about how to measure it. In this regard, while the United States officially welcomed efforts to reinvigorate the Western European Union (WEU) in the mid-1980s, there was little fear that it would be more than, as diplomatic jokes put it, a place to put retired Italian admirals. And the Conference on Security and Cooperation in Europe (CSCE) was regarded primarily as an instrument for waging ideological warfare and putting pressure on the Soviet Union regarding human rights.

At the beginning of the period under examination NATO was central to the American strategy for remaining the most influential state in the world. As Deputy Secretary of State Lawrence Eagleburger said in testimony before the Senate Foreign Relations Committee:

We continue to see NATO as the appropriate forum for discussions affecting our security interests. Some argue the growing clout of Europe warrants a reassessment of the U.S. role in Europe. We could not disagree more strongly. Regardless of how big the EC gets, or what issues European governments devolve to common decisionmaking, the need for a strong American voice in Western affairs will not be diminished . . . While we expect Europe to shoulder more of the burden for the West's defense and while Europe will be more forceful in asserting its own needs and ideas, the President will remain the pre-eminent spokesman for the free world in the decade ahead.[7]

Early in 1989 the United States placed primary emphasis on NATO, consistent with its position throughout the Cold War years, and combined it with a mild tolerance of European (especially French) efforts to invigorate the WEU and a willingness to use the CSCE primarily as an ideological and human rights institution.

Economics and Security

Since institutions often reflect the conditions of their origin, it is helpful to understand those origins, to undertake a sort of archaeology of institutions.[8] It might be thought, for instance, that the end of the Cold War would put more stress on institutions that developed as a result of a perceived Soviet threat than on those that predated that threat. Obviously the formation of the WEU (1948) and NATO (1949) were coterminous with the beginning of the Cold War, and the formation of the European Common Market was strongly influenced by it.

With the exception of the OECD and International Energy Agency, however, the global economic organizations that were prominent in 1989 all originated before the Cold War began. GATT is the residual agreement left over from the proposed International Trade Organization (ITO) planned in 1943, finally negotiated in 1947–48 but never ratified by the Senate. Arguments that the ITO should be ratified as part of a broad anti-Soviet strategy were not effective in 1949.[9] The "Bretton Woods Twins," the IMF and World Bank, were agreed on in 1944; the Marshall Plan temporarily put them into subordinate status. The United States and Britain did not seek universalism in oil issues in 1944 but rather an Anglo-American condominium; when this plan was thwarted by resistance in the United States Senate, oil issues were left up to the major companies, in conjunction with the U.S. and British governments, until the formation of the International Energy Agency in 1974.

When the global international economic organizations were founded, American policymakers hoped for a liberal world order based on nondiscriminatory trade and convertible currencies. The Cold War changed American priorities. After the announcement of the Marshall Plan in 1947, the United States dropped the universalism of the Bretton Woods approach and allowed discrimination against the dollar and against U.S. goods. It also eased up on its pressure against European colonial preference systems. The Americans supported a process of European economic integration, beginning in 1950 with the Schuman Plan, which created the European Coal and Steel Community, and culminating with the Treaty of Rome in 1957. American encouragement for these organizations was based on both economic and security rationales. The United States acquiesced in a less liberal Europe than American leaders would have preferred because it believed that an economically integrated Europe would be better able to combat communist subversion and deter Soviet aggression.

European bargaining strength was enhanced by the bipolar structure of the balance of power. The United States' first priority was to balance Soviet power rather than maximize economic gain. The politics of security and long-term economic cooperation prevailed over pressures for immediate liberalization (which could have driven European governments away from the American embrace) or immediate economic gain. In the face of European resistance to its ambitious plans, the United States had to make compromises; so the shape of the institutional arrangements of the OEEC, the European Payments Union, and the European Community owed at least as much to European as to U.S. preferences. Yet the United States, although often losing tactical struggles, achieved its overall objectives: multilateral trade, close political and economic association between the United States and Europe, and prosperity. Finding its plans resisted or whittled down, the United States kept coming back with new plans and eventually achieved a great deal.[10] After all, a European Community, along with NATO, was one of its two primary institutional instruments for waging the Cold War in Europe. But there was a difference: in the security area the United States was a member of the key institutional instrument in Europe, while in the economic area it was not.

After formal convertibility of major European currencies was achieved in 1958, the United States sought again to institutionalize the principles of Bretton Woods, and to couple them with its support for European integration as desirable in itself (reflecting the American experience) and as a means of balancing Soviet power. As President John F. Kennedy put it when launching the GATT round in 1962: "An integrated western Europe, joined in trading partnership with the United States, will . . . further shift the world balance of power to the side of freedom."[11]

Kennedy's grand design aimed to reconcile global and regional systems by encouraging a larger integrated Europe of which Britain would be a member while at the same time reducing tariffs globally within GATT. British entry into the Common Market would strengthen the security structure as well as the economic integration of Europe. In addition, the OEEC gained a more global focus by including Japan and was transformed into the OECD. As Secretary of State Dean Rusk expressed the American position in 1964: "The Kennedy Round embodies two long-standing and basic lines of American foreign policy. One is the drive for freer trade . . . the other is our support for a strong and united western Europe, capable of acting in partnership with the United States in the great enterprises that lie before us."[12]

By 1970 the artificially high American share of world product had returned to nearly its prewar levels. In addition, détente had moderated the American relationship with the Soviet Union, and the United States was distracted from Europe by the war in Vietnam. Major adjustments occurred in American policy. In 1971 the United States ended the convertibility of the dollar into gold, thus backing away from one of the aspects of the Bretton Woods system. At the end of 1972 it finally disengaged its forces from Vietnam, although the civil war continued until the North Vietnamese victory in 1975. With the Middle East crisis of 1973 and the OPEC oil embargo, the United States was unable to play its previous role as the supplier of last resort in world oil markets.

Henry Kissinger proclaimed 1973 the Year of Europe to symbolize returning to alliance relationships from the preoccupation with the Vietnam War, but it turned out to be the Year of the Middle East, in which Europe and the United States divided on responses to events outside Europe. The United States, however, took the lead in establishing the IEA, a global institution designed to respond to energy crises. The Year of Europe was lost, but the American concern to tighten the link between security and economic affairs was not. In the words of Secretary of State Henry Kissinger: "Economic rivalry, if carried on without restraint, will in the end damage other relationships."[13] A British scholar described the Year of Europe as "a deliberate attempt to force a tradeoff between trans-Atlantic economic and financial relations—which the Nixon administration now saw as biased in Europe's favor—and military and security obligations."[14]

During the 1980s the European Community emerged from its "Euro-sclerosis," adding Greece (1981), Portugal (1986), and Spain (1986) to its membership, and concluding the Single European Act, negotiated in 1984–85, signed in 1986, and finally ratified by 1987. This act called for a genuine internal market by the end of 1992, and sharply improved the coherence and speed of EC decision making by providing for qualified majority voting on issues concerning the internal market.[15] By 1989 Europe was substantially larger in population than the United States and of comparable economic size.

Since pursuing a joint foreign economic policy, the European Community has become a much more difficult negotiating partner for the United States. Indeed, even before the end of the Cold War, between the conclusion of the Tokyo Round and 1989, trade relations between Europe and America had often been quite acrimonious. A low point occurred at a meeting in Montreal in 1982, which resulted in little agreement other than a statement that "pressures for the adoption of protectionist measures have intensified" and "threaten to fragment the world economy."[16] In 1986 a new negotiating round, the Uruguay Round, was launched, although even in 1988 it appeared to be in trouble, and had not yet reached agreement by the summer of 1992. Indeed, the failure to reach agreement by the initial deadline of December 1990 was principally due to U.S.-European deadlock on the issue of demands from the United States and other countries for drastic cuts in agricultural subsidies.

Thus, at the end of the Cold War the United States maintained its commitment to a united Europe as a bulwark against Soviet power, but was concerned about the relationship between the regional economic institutions, global economic regimes, and specific American economic interests to a greater degree than it had been in the early days of the Cold War. The United States still supported the European Community, but there were growing concerns about what was colloquially termed the dangers of a "fortress Europe." With Europe stronger than it had formerly been, the difficulties of managing the trans-Atlantic economic relationship, and keeping it from disrupting security ties, seemed to be more severe than ever. Senior U.S. officials warned that some Europeans sought to erect a "protective curtain" around their market and that it would require "continuous pressure to get them to write the rules to keep their markets as open as we have ours."[17] Yet U.S.-European economic ties were less tense than those between the United States and Japan. In May 1989 the Bush administration listed a number of alleged unfair European trade practices, but omitted the EC from the list of unfair traders that was mandated by the Trade Act of 1988. Only Brazil, India, and Japan were named.[18]

In his testimony in 1989, Deputy Secretary of State Eagleburger declared that "the next ten years in our relationship with Europe will be a transitional period in which the patterns of the postwar era undergo significant adjustment in the face of change in the East and the political and economic growth of western Europe itself. U.S. relations with Europe will become more complicated as Europeans formulate their own responses to Soviet initiatives, seek a more coherent political and economic identity, and generally adopt more assertive postures in dealing with the United States."[19] He went on to express support for the 1992 initiative and argued that global developments such as Third World debt, environmental degradation, and transformations under way in communist countries would require increased cooperation among all industrialized countries. Or in President Bush's words at Leiden in July 1989: "A stronger Europe, a more united Europe, is good for the United States of America."[20]

The End of the Cold War and New Challenges

The rapidity of the collapse of the Soviet empire in 1989 caught almost everyone by surprise, including the Bush administration. While there was a degree of uncertainty and division, the most impressive feature of its response was its relative coherence, consistent with the definition of U.S. interests during the Cold War. After a somewhat slow reaction to the new realities in eastern Europe and their effects on NATO in early 1989, the administration responded quickly after the revolutions in the fall of that year. Over the course of the next two years it was by and large able to keep its policy and institutional preferences intact. Before we analyze the rationale of administration policy and its pattern, it is worthwhile to look at the remarkable absence of domestic political constraints on administration reactions.

Domestic Constraints

For the most part the public and domestic situation was very permissive, allowing political leaders to establish any definition of national interest without strong pressure from below. For example, an EC poll found in 1988 that while only 29 percent of Americans knew about the EC, 90 percent of those who knew about it had a favorable opinion.[21] A 1990 Gallup Poll showed awareness of the EC increasing from 29 percent in 1987 to 47 percent in 1990, but of those, 71 percent had a favorable attitude.[22] A 1990 poll of several hundred American executives showed that a majority believed that the European program for a single market by 1992 would have a positive impact on the United States, 70 percent thought it would have a positive impact on their own industries in the EC, and 65 percent were planning to expand or had expanded their production in Europe.[23]

With regard to NATO, nearly three quarters of the American public had heard of it, roughly double the number who had heard of the EC. In 1990 a Chicago Council on Foreign Relations poll found that 56 percent of the public favored maintaining the same level of commitment to NATO, while 22 percent wanted to reduce it, the latter an 11 percent increase over 1986 responses. Only 12 percent of the public and 10 percent of the leaders polled favored a complete troop withdrawal from Europe.[24] In an early 1990 poll on U.S. responses to a changing Europe, a Gallup Poll found that 45 percent of the public believed that gradual U.S. withdrawal from involvement in European affairs was a good idea, and 43 percent thought it a bad idea, but by a large majority (75 percent to 12 percent) respondents believed that the United States should have a special relationship with the EC.[25]

These attitudes affected both major political parties. Whereas the Democrats were more responsive to labor constituencies, candidates with protectionist appeals were not successful in the 1988 presidential primaries. And in the general election, despite the impending end of the Cold War, commitment to NATO was a common strand in both political parties. While the Democratic-controlled Congress often pressed particular protectionist issues and called for more burden sharing in NATO, these were marginal rather than central dissents. Thus, the administration enjoyed a relatively free hand in adjusting its policies toward Europe in the aftermath of the revolutions of 1989.

Interests and Opportunities

Relatively unconstrained by domestic opinion, the Bush administration could construct its own conception of American interests in Europe. Here continuity prevailed. Three principal objectives remained as they had been for forty years: to maintain a strong European defense capacity, led by the United States; to encourage a European integration that remained open to the rest of the world; and to continue global liberalization of trade and investment on terms favorable to American interests. To attain all three objectives the United States had to maintain a strong influence in Europe, and either cooperation on economic and security issues had to be mutually reinforcing or, at worst, conflicts in one area (especially economic) had to be prevented from contaminating relations in the other. The ancillary objectives of American policy in Europe also displayed continuity: to secure European support, where possible, for American actions outside Europe, and to avoid acceptance of increased financial or military obligations on the continent. Fiscal pressures in the United States made the latter objective more important than it had previously been and reinforced American interest in European initiatives for greater burden sharing in defense.

The collapse of the Soviet empire in August 1989 posed three new challenges to these American objectives: German unification, the collapse of communist governments in eastern Europe, and a diminished Soviet threat. American policy during the Cold War had been premised on a continuing Soviet threat to western Europe, the de facto division of Germany, and effective Soviet stabilization of eastern Europe. The repression of both civil society and international conflict in that region meant that the United States was unable to exert much political influence in eastern Europe or to extend western institutions beyond the center of Europe. During the "revolution of 1989," all three of these policy assumptions changed radically; and the collapse of each assumption created a major issue in American policy toward Europe. As these assumptions changed, new implications for economic relations between Europe and the United States emerged.

We first consider American policy toward Germany, since breaches in the Berlin Wall and rapid movement toward German reunification set the revolutionary process into irrevocable motion and fundamentally changed the nature of the Soviet threat to western Europe as well as the eastern European scene.

The German Question

For many decades the United States, like other countries, had worried that reunification of Germany might disrupt European security. Although it nominally favored reunification, American policymakers were not unhappy with a stable and divided Germany with the larger part firmly anchored to the west by the EC and NATO. At the same time, the United States was less frightened by Germany than were its neighbors, and more willing to accommodate rising German strength. President George Bush emphasized German leadership in NATO in May 1989, to the dismay of British Prime Minister Margaret Thatcher.[26] In September 1989 he stated: "I think there is in some quarters a feeling—well, a reunified Germany would be detrimental to the peace of Europe, of western Europe, in some way; and I don't accept that at all, simply don't."[27] Shortly after the wall came down in November 1989, Helmut Kohl announced a ten-point plan for German reunification. Significant in its omission was any mention of NATO; thus, despite the good will which the Bush administration had engendered, it still faced a difficult situation. It feared that the Soviet Union would offer Germany a deal for reunification on the condition that Germany leave NATO.

In January 1990 the Soviets proposed to activate the four-power rights of Britain, France, the United States, and the Soviet Union that went back to World War II. The United States countered with a proposal known as "two plus four," which left internal affairs to the Germans and external affairs to the four Allied victor powers. This multilateral formula avoided offending the Germans as well as reduced the danger of a separate bilateral deals. With the pressure of three against one, the Soviet Union was in a difficult position if it wished to avoid being blamed for the delay of German unity.

In March the Soviets were still opposing German membership in NATO, but the Americans countered with arguments that a neutral Germany might be more likely to develop its own nuclear weapons and that the U.S. military presence in Europe had a stabilizing effect. The Soviets were reluctant to move on the issue, however, so long as there was no larger pan-European security structure. The United States gave enough ground on the CSCE to allow Mikhail Gorbachev some leverage with which to sell the change in policy back home. In addition, the Americans agreed to limits on American manpower in the conventional force negotiations (though these later became obsolete). The United States, however, made a CSCE agreement contingent on conclusion of the negotiations on conventional forces in Europe.

Equally important was the July 1990 NATO meeting in London in which the Bush administration overcame reluctance on the part of Prime Minister Thatcher and persuaded NATO to declare that the Warsaw Treaty Organization (WTO) was not the enemy, agreed to review its strategy so that nuclear weapons would be used only as a last resort, and agreed to a joint declaration with the WTO as well as talks over short-range nuclear forces in Europe. In taking these steps NATO not only decided on a new strategy but signaled the Soviet Union its willingness to forgo any short-run advantage from Soviet acceptance of reunified German membership in NATO. Soon thereafter Gorbachev and Helmut Kohl were able to meet and agree on terms for German reunification that included German membership in NATO. Such an outcome was fully consistent with American security objectives but would have seemed highly unlikely less than a year before.

European Defense and U.S. Influence

A second major issue was the organization of European defense in the face of a diminished Soviet threat. With the collapse of the Soviet empire in eastern Europe in 1989, the withdrawal of Soviet troops from Hungary and Czechoslovakia in 1990, and the formal termination of the Warsaw Treaty Organization in 1991, the ability of the Soviet Union to mount a short-warning attack essentially vanished, and with it the need for NATO to maintain a doctrine of first use of nuclear weapons as well as massive forward-based troop deployments. Under strong congressional pressure to cut the defense budget in the spring of 1990, the Bush administration agreed to a 25 percent reduction in the American force structure, including a sharp drawdown of American troops in Europe. Nonetheless, the United States wished to maintain the centrality of NATO in European defense, albeit at lower force levels. At the same time, some Europeans were interested in reducing the centrality of NATO. As French Defense Minister Jean-Pierre Chevènement put it in February 1989: "International events are encouraging us to take our own security into our own hands, at the same time as offering us new possibilities to do so."[28]

American attitudes toward increased European defense cooperation had always been ambivalent, with the United States willing to see greater cooperation in order to reduce the American burden, but not to the point of undercutting NATO. A standard position was expressed by Stephen Ledogar, the American permanent deputy representative to NATO in 1986: "There is no way that I can discern that a subcaucus of western European NATO Allies could proceed beyond discussion to take up a rigid position vis-à-vis the East on arms control matters—departing significantly from that agreed in NATO—without violating the security rights of the US and other nonparticipating NATO Allies."[29]

As the Cold War ebbed, American officials tried to find a variety of ways to bolster NATO. In June 1989 Secretary of State James Baker referred to environmental roles for NATO, in November to new diplomatic roles. In June 1990 President Bush stressed that NATO related to basic values, not just military tasks, and Baker suggested that NATO reach out diplomatically to all of Europe, including eastern Europe. The French replied that contacts were all right, but there should be no institutional links between NATO and eastern Europe.

In December 1990 Helmut Kohl and François Mitterrand issued a statement suggesting that the Western European Union evolve into a European defense capability which would be folded into the European Community in five or six years. In February 1991 the State Department sent a letter signed by an undersecretary to all west European capitals expressing concern about the development of a separate WEU caucus within NATO; but in March, President Bush referred to such concerns as manageable differences and nuances, and the American government responded calmly to a further Kohl-Mitterrand announcement of an integrated force in October 1991. Similarly, the United States was not displeased by the language on defense at the December 1991 Maastricht summit which left WEU subordinate to NATO.

The inability of the European Community to develop a common position on the Gulf crisis and the de facto effective cooperation of the United States, Britain, and France in the Gulf War somewhat diminished the degree of American concern about NATO's role even though it played no official part in out-of-area crises. NATO's announcement in June 1990 of a mobile force structure had as much to do with keeping British and American troops involved at lower numbers as it did with any out-of-area capabilities. Subordinating American troops to multinational operational command also reduced their separate national identity. By adapting NATO doctrine and structure, and by fending off French efforts to replace it as the central focus for the organization of defense, the United States was able to maintain its long-standing interest in NATO as the central focus for European defense, and thus to maintain its own influence as a central participant in that defense.

Politics and Economics in Eastern Europe

While there had been modest efforts earlier, after 1989 eastern Europe became a significant arena in which American policy could operate. The Bush administration made it clear from the outset that it would not attempt to move NATO eastward to Poland, Hungary, and Czechoslovakia, much less other former communist countries of the region. But it faced the problem of how to contribute to both international stability in eastern Europe—stability that was seen as resting in the long run on progress toward prosperous democratic, market-oriented societies in these countries, but in the short run requiring international conflict resolution mechanisms to replace the defunct Soviet empire. Despite French reservations, the United States led NATO to accept the presence of east European and former Soviet liaison teams and observers at NATO headquarters and at a number of committee meetings, thus increasing NATO's political role. This North Atlantic Cooperation Council symbolized a NATO interest in east European security.

From the outset, however, the Bush administration was happy to have the European Community take the lead in organizing economic assistance within the larger group of twenty-four that was loosely related to the OECD. At the Paris summit of July 1989 President Bush made this point abundantly clear.[30] The United States also went along with a French proposal for a European Bank for Reconstruction and Development (EBRD), which included the Soviet Union but limited Soviet borrowing to the equivalent of its contributed capital. Here again, although the United States was the largest country, it was willing to see the preponderance of votes in the bank as well as the presidency go to the west Europeans.

With respect to aid to the Soviet Union itself, American policy started out adamantly opposed in 1987, then underwent a gradual evolution. In March 1987 James Baker, then secretary of the treasury, announced that he was unqualifiedly opposed to Soviet membership in GATT or the IMF. By January 1988 President Ronald Reagan had opened the door to the possibility of Soviet participation in such institutions provided there was serious economic reform in the Soviet Union. In October 1989 Baker, now secretary of state, announced that Soviet membership in the international institutions was still premature, but by December 1990 President Bush was willing to contemplate the idea of special association for the Soviet Union. When the Group of Seven met in Houston in July 1990, they turned the question of Soviet economic reform over to a task force of officials from the secretariat of the international financial institution headed by the IMF. That group prepared a report on the problems of the Soviet economy which established a common point of reference for the discussions at the G-7 meeting in London a year later.

When Gorbachev appeared in London in the summer of 1991, he requested membership in the institutions but was offered association until the Soviet reforms progressed further. After the abortive August coup, events accelerated: the Soviet economy disintegrated more rapidly, and the industrialized countries moved more quickly to provide aid. In October the Group of Seven agreed to provide large-scale help to the Soviet Union in the event of an external financial crisis,[31] and after the demise of the Soviet government in December, the World Bank and the IMF played significant roles in organizing technical assistance for the successor states.

U.S. policy also evolved toward security institutions in eastern Europe. Although the United States had treated the CSCE primarily as a human rights organization during the 1980s, it began to see a potential for a greater role for the CSCE in dampening conflicts within Europe. After the collapse of the

Berlin Wall, there was considerable concern in some parts of the United States government that the CSCE might become a rival to NATO for the organization of European security. In early 1990 the United States successfully resisted Soviet efforts for a general European conference. Only after the resolution of the German unification question on American terms and a reduction of concerns about damage to NATO's role did the American position change.

The United States joined in the November 1990 Paris joint declaration which envisioned a larger role for the CSCE and the February 1991 agreement on establishing dispute resolution mechanisms. The United States showed interest in having the CSCE institutions located in eastern Europe as a means of tying eastern Europeans into a larger security framework and using CSCE to encourage democracy and supervise elections. In May 1990 Secretary of State Baker referred to the CSCE as the "conscience of the continent" but pointed out that NATO guaranteed the new peace.[32] By June 1991 Baker was suggesting a procedure for calling emergency meetings of CSCE officials at the subministerial level and strengthening the conflict prevention center.[33] In practice, however, the CSCE was hindered by its structure as an intergovernmental conference requiring unanimity. The CSCE was invoked in the Yugoslav crisis during the summer of 1991, but it failed to accomplish anything. Later the EC and then the UN took the lead in mediation and peacekeeping efforts, none of which had succeeded by mid-1992.

Trade and Investment

Trade issues in GATT were not directly affected by the end of the Cold War, since the issues had always principally involved the United States, the EC, and Japan, with other countries, industrialized and developing, playing roles of greater or lesser significance depending on the issue. Stalemate on trade issues was already visible in 1988, and in December 1990 the Uruguay Round negotiations broke down over the issue of agricultural subsidies.

While there were a number of contentious issues in U.S.-European trade relations, cooperation between the two huge markets was supported by both economic logic and interests. Transnational corporations represented a strong lobby against any breakdown in EC-U.S. trade and investment relations; and in both regions these firms were influential—institutionalized in an elaborate advisory committee process in the United States, less formal but no less effective in Europe.[34]

During the Cold War, trade and security issues were handled on separate tracks.[35] In general, the United States tended to subordinate its trade interests to its security interests. With the end of the Cold War many observers predicted that trade frictions would disrupt security relations. In the early post–Cold War period this did not happen. One reason why the conflicts were controlled is that U.S.-European trade was clearly mutually beneficial. However, security ties helped reinforce the relationship: Europeans still wanted an American security guarantee, and the United States still saw the EC as crucial to European stability.

Thus, the removal of the security blanket which often led the Americans to make concessions during the Cold War period did not have as strong an effect in U.S.-EC relations as in U.S.-Japan relations. The American interest in having the EC reach out to eastern Europe and become a magnet to draw the eastern European countries toward a democratic orientation gave the United States an incentive to cooperate effectively with Europe rather than to sharpen trade conflicts with it. And Germany, if not France, had a strong incentive not to antagonize the United States over issues such as agricultural subsidies that were actually peripheral to its most fundamental interests.

The most remarkable feature about the American position over the revolutionary years of 1989 to 1991 was the degree of consistency in the definition of national interest and the ability to preserve those interests despite political turmoil. Yet, while the headlines of this story stress continuity, there were changes in the fine print. A number of details in doctrine and position were altered, but the overall strategy was one of continuity despite revolutionary times.

What role did international institutions play in this definition of national interest and strategy? Since institutions represent the shadow of the past, it is not surprising to find the status quo powers turning to them, but there is a more general point that as leaders struggle with turmoil and uncertainty, institutions provide a point of common reference.

Secretariats of institutions sometimes took initiatives: for example, efforts by the WEU secretariat to carve out a larger role, or efforts by the European Community Commission to establish a common position on foreign policy, or efforts by the NATO secretary general to bring about adaptations in NATO doctrine. But except for the role of the EC Commission, the roles of the secretariats were secondary. The key initiatives came from member states, particularly the United States. Nonetheless, the institutions were instrumental in terms of signaling, either individually or collectively. For example,

Germany's statements of loyalty to the EC in early 1990 as reunification negotiations took place provided an important signal of reassurance to its partners, including the United States. Similarly, NATO's June 1990 decision to change its doctrine was an important collective signal to the Soviet Union about the future structure of European security. And the creation of the North Atlantic Cooperation Council and the acceptance of eastern observers at NATO meetings and headquarters signaled a concern for security beyond NATO's traditional boundaries.

In terms of the roles outlined in the introduction and conclusion of this volume, institutions were important for American strategy in all categories. As arenas for *exercising influence,* both NATO and GATT were central to American strategy. Indeed, GATT was used to constrain European Community bargaining tactics in trade, and NATO was used to set limits on French tactics of developing the Western European Union in defense. NATO was used to *combat other institutions* such as the CSCE, although once it became clear that the plans of some Europeans to replace NATO with the CSCE would not materialize, the two organizations were treated as complementary. By early 1992 American officials were even speaking of NATO peace-keeping operations' being requested and legitimized in eastern Europe by the CSCE. Similarly, the London changes in NATO doctrines and the Copenhagen declaration on the security of eastern Europe were important means of *signaling government intentions.* The subsequent creation of the North Atlantic Cooperation Council was a good example of *cooptation.* And back home, institutional symbols muted public debate about alternatives, forestalling any agonizing reappraisal, and thus helped in *affecting preferences.*

The key question, however, is the counterfactual one: How might U.S. strategy and European outcomes have differed if institutions had not existed? The overall counterfactual is difficult to develop because American national interests had become so heavily institutionalized during the entire Cold War period that such alternatives were never considered. Instead, institutions had an important effect. Without NATO and the EC, German unification would have appeared much more threatening than it did after 1989. Without the preexisting commitments to GATT, the United States might have had a more difficult time trying to persuade the European Community to reduce tariff barriers as it pursued its economic integration. Without the CSCE, the Americans might have had a harder time persuading Gorbachev to accede to the unification of Germany within the framework of NATO. Without the G-7 summits, it might have been harder to coordinate economic policy toward the

Soviet Union; and without the secretariats of the international financial institutions, it might have been harder to come to a common position of understanding the Soviet economy.

In principle, however, one could imagine quite a different choice of American strategies at the end of the Cold War. On a realist explanation, American grand strategy toward Europe in this century was designed to prevent any one country from dominating the continent. That explains 1917, 1941, and continued American involvement during the four decades of the Cold War. With the collapse of the Soviet empire and the end of bipolarity after 1989, neither Russia nor Germany was likely to dominate Europe. From a simple balance-of-power perspective, the United States could have chosen a strategy of unilateral withdrawal. This would have been consistent with portraits of a declining and imperially overstretched America that were popular in 1989, as well as with the domestic politics of the federal budget deficit and resistance to raising taxes.[36] In the security area, the United States could have chosen to withdraw from NATO or let it erode, signed a few bilateral defense and base agreements to ensure a global presence, and eschewed any interest in the CSCE. In economics, it could have tried to fragment the EC by playing countries off against one another, or accepted the idea of a world divided into large trading blocs.

In either event, the end of the Cold War would probably have taken a different shape. Germany might have purchased its reunification through a bilateral arrangement with the Soviet Union, and west European defense unity might have been stimulated. It is equally likely, however, that EC members might have cast about for separate alliances and reassurance, and east European societies would have been less drawn to a western magnet of security represented by NATO and prosperity represented by the EC.

In short, institutions are the shadows of the past that shape visions and choices about the future. Without institutional signposts and multilateral procedures, American leaders might have examined a wider range of strategies. It would have been much more difficult to maintain steady and common positions during a period of revolutionary change in the structure of the international system. The existence and invention of international institutions provided critical signposts to define the national interest as well as useful instruments to implement it. While the institutions did not in themselves determine the national strategy, in a period of rapid change strategy might have evolved quite differently without them. Of the three new issues at the end of the Cold War, it is worth noting the greater success in the areas which were well endowed with institutional instruments (German unification, European defense) and the more uncertain performance in the area of eastern Europe, where institutions were weak.

Looking ahead, there are two major challenges to the continued success of this post–Cold War strategy: institutionalizing western security and preventing instability in the east from unraveling stability in the west. Instability in parts of eastern Europe may spill over into and destabilize western Europe. The familiar checkerboard pattern of power balances could spread. Ukraine, next to Russia, feels it needs a significant army, but such an army could frighten Poland or Romania, which could turn westward for support. Such patterns could be exacerbated if the disintegration in the east further stimulates the hypernationalism tamed by forty years of institutional integration in the west.

In the eyes of American leaders at the end of the Cold War, the best prospect for avoiding such a future was adapting existing institutions to the post–Cold War world. Continuing integration ("deepening") of the EC was a means of preserving the successful solution of the German problem that plagued Europe from the days of Bismarck until those of Adenauer. A deepened Community could prevent the checkerboard spread of alliances from unraveling progress in the west. And, given the uncertainties of the second Russian revolution, NATO would play a role in political reassurance. Since the United States wished the Europeans to share more of the burden for promoting security in Europe, a greater European role was not seen as inconsistent with the role of NATO.

For the four decades of the Cold War the United States pursued its interests in Europe with these institutional instruments. They proved more robust in the early post–Cold War period than a simple structural realist analysis would have predicted. But two years is too brief a period for a real test. What we have tried to do in this chapter is to provide a snapshot of the difference that institutions made so as to suggest a richer set of hypotheses for further investigation. The real test is the future.

Chapter 4

French Dilemmas and Strategies in the New Europe

Stanley Hoffmann

The sudden end of the Cold War in Europe, the collapse of the Soviet empire in the eastern half of the continent, and the fall of the Berlin Wall put the French government in an awkward and paradoxical situation. It was awkward because France had been concentrating its attention on western Europe—on the progress of the European Community. The momentous events in the east risked changing the priorities and delaying the "deepening" of the Community. The *relance* of 1984–1988 had committed France to the ambitious agenda of the Single Market, which meant nothing less than an accelerated dismantling of the neomercantilist policies, price controls, and *dirigiste* regulations that had characterized France's economic strategies and the relations between government and business since Liberation. It also meant a vast reorganization of private enterprises and a search for corporate partners abroad. Moreover, in the spring of 1989 the EC Council had endorsed the first phase of the plan for a European monetary union, prepared by Jacques Delors, and the idea of two intergovernmental conferences that would set up the Economic and Monetary Union (EMU) and modify the political institutions. All of these pushes could be jeopardized by the pull of the events in the east.

Reaching the Goal but Not Liking the Landscape

The paradox was stark. For almost forty-five years France had denounced the division of Europe, what French leaders from Charles de Gaulle to François Mitterrand had called the "order of Yalta"—where, in French mythology, two external superpowers had partitioned the continent and ensured their hegemony over its respective halves. And yet, now that the partitions had fallen, French authorities, elites, and publics seemed dazed. Not only had the revolutions in the east been unexpected, but the conditions under which Europe was being reunified were quite different from those French leaders had expected. Nobody—not even De Gaulle, the prophet of nationalism's victory over communism—had expected the disintegration of Soviet power and such a smashing triumph of the United States (and the west) over communism. Those who, like De Gaulle, had deemed German unification likely in a world that would have overcome the Cold War expected it to result from an orderly process firmly controlled by Germany's neighbors and by the major powers. The working hypotheses or imperatives of French diplomacy, which had been remarkably stable (despite secondary changes) throughout the Fifth Republic, had all turned out to be false or misleading, and this explains why, having apparently obtained what French diplomacy had called and worked for, France woke up with a massive malaise.

There had been three imperatives. The first was to maintain a will to independence in French diplomacy. But independence and effectiveness had not come together. Effectiveness would have required an international system in which military might mattered more than economic power, and in which France would have been a major military actor. But in a world, and especially a continent, where the superpowers' arsenals and forces neutralized one another, the opportunities for French armored might were few; and the fact that France had put so much of its defense money into the nuclear *force de frappe,* and comparatively little into conventional forces, resulted in providing the nation with an insurance policy in case of a bipolar collision that fortunately never came, and only very little else. Effectiveness, alternatively, would have required great economic power. But in this realm, even though successive presidents had declared that their goal was to catch up with the Federal Republic, France had remained far behind on practically every count. From the viewpoint of effectiveness, by the end of the Cold War France's strategy of independence, markedly in the military realm (the exit from

NATO, the nuclear force) had not paid off better than the very different strategy of West Germany, or the British one.

A second imperative had been the construction of a west European entity owing to which many of the national objectives France could no longer reach by itself could be met; as one of the most pro-European French foreign ministers put it (sitting next to his Belgian counterpart at an anniversary conference of the Institut Français des Relations Internationales), for France Europe was "a means." It was expected that French influence would be, if not hegemonic, at least superior to anyone else's in that entity—not only because of France's geographic position in the Europe first of the Six, later of the Twelve, but also because of the handicaps that affected the other "Big Three" of the Community. The Federal Republic was burdened by its past, by its location, and by its division: all three required singular prudence, and the latter two made it deeply dependent on American protection and diplomacy, something which exasperated French officials yet in fact served their interest in being *primi inter* (not quite) *pares* in the EC. Britain was handicapped by the time it had lost fighting rather than joining European integration, and fighting it for ten more years even after the French had finally allowed London to join. Italy—well, it was Italy, hampered, despite its economic performance, by the weakness of its bureaucracy, the paralysis of its eternal yet fluctuating governmental coalition, and its remarkable absence of diplomatic ambition. It is because of these relative advantages that French presidents, whether they were distrustful or not of the traps of "supranationality," saw no necessary contradiction between a European entity that fell well short of federalism and the will to national independence. But there was an implicit precondition: the continuing division of Germany (and Europe).

A third imperative was the preservation of a sphere of French influence abroad—in North Africa, in the Middle East, in black Africa, primarily but not exclusively in areas such as Lebanon or Algeria which had been under French control and with which strong cultural ties had been kept. But this influence had eroded because of the increasing marginalization of Africa in world politics (as well as increasing doubts in France about the cost of supporting often very unattractive regimes) as well as because of the increasing difficulties encountered by France in the Islamic world. Among western powers it was not the one most capable of providing economic assistance or investments, or most useful for diplomatic leverage on Israel; and all western powers found it hard to cope with nationalism and fundamentalism in this part of the world.

It is therefore not surprising that French foreign policy should have appeared somewhat erratic between the middle of 1989 and the summer of 1991. This was so, first, because the French president seemed initially disturbed by the change in the distribution of power between France and Germany. He "recovered" after a few months, and decided that the deepening of the EC would be the best way of coping with a united Germany. But tensions between the priority given to the Community of the Twelve and the old French quest for independence have remained, and new strains have appeared, between that priority and the French desire to meet the aspirations of east European countries so as not to leave Germany the dominant player there.

A Period of Trouble

In the fall of 1989 observers noticed certain signs of trouble. First, there was the bewildered and bewildering reaction of Mitterrand to the prospect of rapid German unification. In the beginning he and his foreign minister argued that this was still far in the future, and Mitterrand even paid a visit, late in 1989, to the fatally ill post-Ulbricht communist regime of the German Democratic Republic. His concern about the rights of the four victors of World War II, and his shock when Chancellor Helmut Kohl announced, out of the blue, on November 28, 1989, his own plan for a speedy reunification, led him to Kiev on December 9 for a joint discussion of the issues with Mikhail Gorbachev— a visit that could not but evoke the ghosts of Franco-Russian alliances against the German danger and of German obsessions about encirclement. On television, after his return, he even talked about the centuries-old role played by Russia and France in preserving stability in Europe. Mitterrand also went to London to consult with the Iron Lady, who had done so much to thwart Franco-German designs for west European integration, but who was even more, and more openly, upset about a reunified Germany. It was not until April 1990 that Mitterrand realized—after the elections that swept the communists out of power in the GDR—that German unity was a fait accompli for all practical purposes; the problem for France was accommodation, not prevention.

Second, major uncertainties and hesitations appeared in French diplomacy. While celebrating the end of the Cold War and the new foreign and defense policies of Moscow, Mitterrand maintained France's preference for a deterrence strategy that relies on the threat of an early use of nuclear weapons, and dissociated France from NATO's decision in July 1990 to treat these weapons as "arms of final recourse." But planning for the future of the *force de frappe* turned somewhat erratic; the president vetoed the construction of mobile ground launchers for strategic nuclear weapons, although not for short-range "prestrategic" systems. In the Gulf War he tried to be altogether a good ally of the United States, a rigorous defender of the primary role of the Security Council, and a preserver of France's independent "difference" (through a number of peace initiatives up to January 15, 1991), an acrobatic exercise that often created more bafflement than admiration abroad. In the Yugoslav tragedy France switched from a strong profederation stance to a call for a European force of interposition, which the sole beneficiaries of the federal state, the Serbs, denounced as a potential enemy army.

Third, there were sharp contradictions. Thus, while in Mitterrand's European policy the language used about the reform of EC institutions—especially in Franco-German communiqués—was often federalist, the French proposals at the Intergovernmental Conference on Political Cooperation were decidedly not. And there was a similar contradiction between the calls for a reenforcement of the Western European Union (WEU) as the EC's pillar of a European security system and the preservation of French military independence. In Mitterrand's policy toward the United States the unprecedented military cooperation in the Gulf War, with French forces under U.S. command, and French participation in the bombing and invasion of Iraq (despite the defense minister's objections to any role for French forces outside of Kuwait) was preceded and quickly followed by the usual French exasperation at and attacks on America's defense and political activities as a self-appointed European power. All these contradictions could be explained, as often in the past, but they added to the sense of unsteadiness.

Fourth, and more serious, were some failures. Like many failures in diplomacy, these may turn out to have been temporary or reversible; but as of this writing they remain on the books. In the quasi-theological debate between the primacy of NATO and an independent role for the WEU, Mitterrand appears to have, during the winter of 1990–91, rejected opportunities for a compromise. He thus allowed the United States to rally both England *and* Germany behind the reform of the force structure of NATO which was endorsed by the NATO allies in June 1991. French participation in the Gulf War was justified by Mitterrand both in moral-legal terms and in power-political ones: France had to fight so as to be a party, after the war, to all the coming settlements (an argument used by De Gaulle, Mitterrand's lifelong nemesis and model, in 1944–45). But if France went into battle in order to make its weight felt in peacemaking, it was conspicuously ignored after the war ended. A third fiasco was Mitterrand's project of a confederation, his attempt to square the circle of "deepening" versus "opening," and to persuade the east Europeans to accept a halfway house for many years to come. Both in this fiasco (at a meeting in Prague in June 1991) and in the NATO versus WEU affair a few months earlier, failure resulted in part from an unwillingness to listen to the grievances or desires of others.

These four signs of confusion are not difficult to explain. Partly they express the felt need to navigate (biaiser) among options none of which is very satisfactory, and therefore to adopt some elements of each—thus, inevitably, with the risk of tensions, contradictions, setbacks. A policy of strict independence tous azimuts is clearly not tenable: not even De Gaulle, the champion of common policies for the EC, had believed it possible. In the world of 1990–91 independence for France could not but license full independence for Germany. A policy of European federalism means trouble for France's residues of independence in defense and abroad, and a risk of German predominance in the federation. A policy of enlargement, toward a "grande Europe," risked jeopardizing years of efforts toward "deepening," turning the enlarged Community into a mere free trade area (something France had always resisted and Britain always desired) and into an amorphous entity where French influence might be irreparably diluted.

Another part of the explanation lies in French foreign policy-making. There is no need for complex theories of decision, for Graham Allison's models II and III here. French foreign and defense policy is the president's domain. It was so, despite the prime minister's attempts at power sharing, even during the two years of "cohabitation" between a socialist president and a neo-Gaullist premier. It was a fortiori more so in 1988–1991, when Mitterrand, assured of a majority in the National Assembly (where the socialists, just short of majority, could find the handful of votes necessary to survive motions of no confidence), chose prime ministers who understood that the president's domain was untouchable. Parties might offer dissents; nationalist socialists (such as former Defense Minister Jean-Pierre Chevènement) or neo-Gaullists might demand a different kind of Europe; centrists might plead for tighter federal integration: it did not seem to matter much, except insofar as Mitterrand liked to appear, from time to time, as if he had heard this or that domestic claim. And yet to speak only about the constitutional prerogative of the president is not enough.

The parliamentary debate in June 1991 on the ratification of the Schengen agreements abolishing border controls among its six members ended in a lopsided vote for the government: 495 to 61 (including the 26 communists) in the National Assembly; and the Constitutional Council later declared that the treaty did not clash with the French constitution because it entailed no transfer of sovereignty. It is impossible to understand the course of French foreign policy if one does not focus on the interplay between two factors: the personality of the president and what could be called the French situation. For the president, who enjoys unshared power, does not have unlimited power at all.

What is the French situation? It is in part the product of the structure of the international, and especially the European, system, in the Waltzian meaning of the term *structure*—that is, the distribution of power among competing units, or in the Waltzian conception the alignments formed against threats. France's concern for the balance of power in a continent dominated by the superpowers, or for the reduction of the (very different kinds of) threats represented by them, certainly dictated the mix of search for independence and reliance on institutions capable of providing security from the Soviet threat characteristic of both the Fourth and the Fifth Republics. After the failure of the repressive policy of 1945–1949, which nobody else supported, the permanent worry about German power led to the highly original strategy of west European integration, which I have elsewhere described as balancing through bandwagoning.[1] Another part of the situation was the legacy of the past—a heavy baggage in the French case. Bitter memories of the 1930s, when France behaved as a dependent of Britain, exacerbated the desire for independence, and the humiliations of World War II and of forced decolonization exacerbated the desire for activism, for a sphere of influence, as well as resentment aimed at the superpowers.

It was not only the weight of past disasters; it was also that of past choices. The rails that De Gaulle had put down, and on which he placed and drove the train of French policy, have proved extraordinarily durable; the policy mix he devised seemed—because of its ambiguities, which left much room for tactical maneuver—to serve most French interests well, and to preserve what was so dear to so many of the French: French distinctiveness. These ambiguities and that flexibility had allowed for a vague yet potent national consensus, a benefit that had eluded the Fourth Republic.

De Gaulle, despite opposition from communists and from orthodox Atlanticists and champions of a supranational European Community, was able to impose his shrewd mix on an often reluctant parliament because of the tools his constitution provides to the executive, the division of his opponents, and his popularity in "La France profonde." De Gaulle's successors could depart from Gaullist orthodoxy in minor ways: Pompidou could lift the General's veto on Britain, Giscard agree to a popular election for the European Parliament, Mitterrand embrace qualified majority voting in the Single Act. But the central tenets stood, both because they seemed apt to the situation of France in the Cold War and because they were supported by the public. Now their adequacy to the new world was questionable, but the consensus was still there—and no president could, by breaking it, undermine his own position or effectiveness, unless he was able to build a new one around a new set of tenets and "sell" it to the public, if not to parliament. The political cost of leaving the safe (if increasingly shallow) harbor for the high seas would be too high for the pilot, unless he could point convincingly to a better harbor and a safe journey.

Mitterrand, however, was not the man for such a task: to revert to my earlier metaphor, he was better at driving on old tracks, or at moving them just a shade, than at setting down new ones in new directions. He had, in his slow march to the presidency, shifted from a left-wing utopia to an unacknowledged acceptance of Gaullism (in foreign as well as in constitutional affairs). He was better at proceeding by small touches, oblique statements, contradictory advances and retreats than at the bold strokes and grand designs of his august predecessor. Foreign policy had not been his priority before his election in 1981 and in 1981–1983. It became his preferred field of action after the fiasco of his socialist economic program, when the preservation and development of the western European Community served both as a rationale for domestic policy retreat and as the domain in which he could now make his mark. The earthquake of 1989–90 upset his expectations and calculations; he had to improvise, and it showed. When one writes about a certain marginalization of France in the new European order,[2] one refers not only to the new situation, in which France, having satisfied old anti-Yalta desires, discovered that the hated status quo ante 1989 had been highly advantageous. One refers also to the steps and missteps of a president who simply did not have the General's ability to make the best of a bad deal, to play even poor cards with a bravado that gave the French the illusion of being the chief actors in the play and made France's partners wonder, more or less angrily, whether that supposedly fading former great power did not exert, if only by obstruction, far more influence than its resources should have allowed. De Gaulle's deliberate ambiguities gave France some freedom for maneuver. Mitterrand's ambiguities appeared to be the products of embarrassment, and to restrict this freedom.

Integration and Independence

It has been said, by Clausewitz and Aron among others, that the state can be analyzed as a rational intelligence. What follows is an attempt, ex post, to uncover the threads and calculations of a policy whose author has rarely seen fit to present it as a whole.

Since the end of 1989 Mitterrand's policy appears to have been dominated by two concerns. The first is the "German question," acutely revived. A unified Germany, even if its energies and resources were going to be temporarily absorbed by the rehabilitation of the former GDR, broke by its very existence the "balance of imbalances" that had existed among the big three (or four) of western Europe. The reunification of the continent put Germany, not France, at the center. This was obvious. But the anxieties about Germany were contradictory.

First, French elites worried that a united Germany might embrace the heady virtues of independence (or renationalization) and wanted to remove or reduce the restraints which the institutions and rules of the EC had put on Germany's "operational sovereignty" (De Gaulle, after all, had tried to do just this between 1958 and 1966). The nightmare of an unfettered Germany rediscovering Bismarck's *Schaukelpolitik*, moving away from the West and toward the East, agitated French conversations (as well as Henry Kissinger's columns) throughout the first half of 1990. French policy in those months aimed at "smoking out" Bonn, at probing and prodding in order to find out whether the constraints of NATO and, above all, of the EC were still acceptable to the Federal Republic, and indeed whether Chancellor Kohl was willing to tighten the bonds to the Community and to dismiss any deal that would have loosened the Federal Republic's ties to NATO in exchange for a guaranteed Soviet exit from the GDR and formal Soviet acceptance of German unity. The Franco-German joint message of April 19, 1990, asking the members of the EC to hasten work on the Intergovernmental Conference for monetary union and to begin serious work on the IGC for political union, provided partial reassurance.

The negotiation between Kohl—backed by George Bush—and Mikhail Gorbachev on the issue of Germany's right to stay in NATO evoked more mixed feelings in France: the outcome was greeted with relief; but the way in which Kohl dealt directly with Moscow, and treated German unification as a matter for Germans alone, whatever rights Britain and France might still have had in Berlin, worried Paris, both because it was so unilateral and because it seemed to make of Bonn the privileged partner, and provider, of Moscow. The fear of giving Germany a cause or pretext for renationalization explains the French decision, announced in the summer of 1990, to withdraw France's troops from German soil, thus depriving Bonn of any reason for asking that they be removed. But this was something Bonn had no intention of doing. The French misstep was in turn misinterpreted in Germany as evidence of France's inveterate nationalism and uncooperativeness in matters of defense.

Second, these relatively good German dispositions, however, fed another fear: that the new Germany might dominate the institutions aimed at containing it. The Federal Republic would have even more economic and financial power in the Community after the absorption of the GDR; and in a NATO from which American forces and weapons might be partly removed, German influence might rise, even if the limits placed on German forces by agreement with the Soviets were respected. As for the Conference on Security and Cooperation in Europe (CSCE), which was to be given new importance and functions in the Paris meeting of November 1990, the French had appreciated its usefulness before the earthquake of 1989 because (unlike the Mutual Balanced Force Reductions talks) it was not just a confrontation of the two military blocs, and because its existence and the principles of Helsinki gave hope to dissidents in the East. But now France became somewhat apprehensive: this large and amorphous organization simply did not have the potential for containing Germany that still existed in NATO and would persist in a deepening Community. Hans-Dietrich Genscher's enthusiasm for the CSCE, and its very composition, suggested that Germany might want to serve as a kind of go-between for the superpowers in European affairs; moreover, the weakness of the CSCE's powers seemed to explain why German "renationalizers" might prefer it to other forums. There was little France could do in the short run about NATO and the CSCE. But in the long run France could try to prod the Federal Republic away from a NATO Germany might dominate toward a European security system in which France and Britain would prevent any such outcome; and in the short or middle run France could press for the kind of European monetary union in which the central bank would be under joint management by the members, rather than having a European

Monetary System dominated by the Bundesbank, and therefore by purely German domestic financial considerations and interests: after all, why should French interest rates be determined by the Bundesbank?

Third, the Persian Gulf crisis made the French acutely aware of a contradiction between their preferred strategy for the containment of German power—the reenforcement and extension of scope of the EC—and France's push for an active diplomatic role for the EC. Such a role, to be sure, was desired in part as a way of preventing German independent activism in eastern Europe; but Germany's unwillingness to play any role in extra-European crises that could entail the sending of forces abroad, even under a United Nations flag, risked paralyzing the delicate machinery of European foreign policy cooperation. Germany's lack of enthusiasm for a *Weltpolitik* reassured the first of France's anxieties about its neighbor, but was lamented insofar as it risked paralyzing the European "container" of Germany in the crucial domain of "out-of-area" security and diplomacy. A year later, during the Yugoslav crisis, Genscher's initial statements in favor of Slovenia and Croatia revived French fears of uncontrolled German initiatives; but when Germany temporarily abandoned both such attempts and the effort to have the CSCE play a major role in the drama, and agreed to have it played by the EC, Franco-German (and Franco-British) divergences about the policies the EC ought to follow made the Community look even more impotent than the situation on the ground obliged it to be. France was reluctant but Germany eager to acknowledge the breakup of Yugoslavia; France proposed to send a European force, but Britain opposed the idea so long as no cease-fire lasted more than a few hours.

Against such Community paralysis there was only one recourse: independent French action. Precisely the second major concern of French policy was the preservation of a margin of independence. I have explained why this has not made for maximum effectiveness. But the quest was intensified rather than reduced; and this was caused by the change in the world balance of power. Yesterday independence and activism were presented as necessary to save a margin of maneuver between, and to weaken the grip of, the "two hegemonies." Now they were justified as indispensable to safeguarding French interests in a "unipolar" world dominated by the winner of the Cold War. Someday a united Europe might inherit and carry out this concern for autonomy and play the role, evoked by Foreign Minister Roland Dumas at a Socialist party meeting, of "balancer" of U.S. might, but that was in the future; today it was up to France.

This concern became especially visible in two cases. One was the Gulf crisis. France (like Britain) wanted to play a role, as a former Middle Eastern power with memories and interests; but (unlike Britain) it did not want to play this role as a NATO member, and to grant to NATO what Paris had consistently refused to accept from Washington: the idea that NATO could legitimately intervene out of area. The solution was to demand that every move toward war be approved by the Security Council: the UN appeared as a kind of welcome substitute for NATO. In reality the Security Council turned out to be as dominated by the United States as NATO. But it is an intergovernmental, not an "integrated," organization, and thus the appearance of French independence was preserved. During the period of the Gulf War, Mitterrand, for once prodigal in explaining French policy, emphasized France's world role but rarely mentioned Europe.

The other case is the issue of nuclear reductions, which—after the Strategic Arms Reduction Talks (START) and the unilateral cuts announced by Washington and Moscow—might affect the independent forces of third parties. Here Paris wanted neither superpower deals at its expense nor too much of a role for a UN that had traditionally been antinuclear; Mitterrand proposed talks by four of the Security Council's permanent members: those with nuclear forces in Europe (another way of leaving Germany out).

It is the difficult combination of anxiety about Germany and worry about French independence which explains the subtleties and contradictions of France's European policy. The will to harness Germany and to tie it as tightly as possible to France so as to give a now relatively weaker France a hold on its united neighbor explains the strong emphasis on deepening characteristic of French diplomacy and the rejection by the French president of the suggestion, made by some leaders of the French Gaullist party and by members of the nationalist (Chevènement) wing of his own Socialist party, that the new situation in Europe required a looser confederation of states that would include eastern Europe, so as not to leave those countries isolated nor tie France to a Community Germany might dominate. The compromise that was worked out, during the Dutch presidency, about EMU is above all a compromise between French insistence on a full and genuine monetary union, with a central bank and a single currency, and German insistence on a prior rapprochement of economic policies, on an independent bank, and on some institutional reform. The Kohl-Mitterrand letters of December 6, 1990, and October 14, 1991, reflect the French objective of extending the functions of the Community, especially in foreign affairs and in security policy.

The old French concern for a "European Europe"—that is, a Europe that would not be dominated by the United States—accounts not only for France's intransigent stance over agriculture (and Airbus) at the General Agreement on Tariffs and Trade (GATT) meetings at the end of 1990 and throughout 1991, but also for France's refusal to make of the WEU a "link" between the EC and NATO, or a subordinate of NATO, as in the British proposals. France wants an "organic link" between the WEU and the EC (a notion endorsed by Kohl in the joint letter of October 14, 1991), and a "European force" of WEU members that would somehow be distinct from NATO's forces, and could be used out of area (that is, outside Europe or in eastern and southeastern Europe) without NATO's consent, beyond NATO's mandate. The British plan that prevailed within NATO last June increased the role of the Europeans (minus France) *within* NATO, especially through the creation of a rapid reaction force of Europeans, integrated in NATO's command structure. France's plan would strengthen ties between Germany and France in the military realm, and thus alleviate two very different fears: that within post–Cold War NATO Germany might become more autonomous (or predominant), *and* that Germany would put security and defense at the bottom of its list of priorities and become entirely self-absorbed.

Whether Germany's apparent shift between the NATO council meeting in Copenhagen in June 1991 and the Kohl-Mitterrand letter of October 14 reflects a genuine evolution or a tactical adjustment facilitated by French acceptance, in the letter, of language favorable to the reenforcement of the Atlantic Alliance remains unclear. What is clear is that each of the two partners is trying to pull the other. Bonn is trying to push France a little closer to NATO, and France is trying to move Germany closer to the French view of a European autonomous defense system. What has kept Germany from "choosing" the WEU-EC way over NATO's is not only the stabilizing role played by NATO in Europe (and acknowledged by the east European governments which have been eager to cooperate with, and in some cases even to join, NATO, an organization in which Germany is a major force), but also France's own reluctance to abandon its cherished military autonomy, conventional as well as nuclear. The French, in return, explain that they cannot give it up if this would merely reenforce America's grip on European security, as long as France's main partners, Britain and Germany, remain satisfied with American predominance in this area. This dialogue of the deaf has been going on ad infinitum and ad nauseam. The compromise formula adopted about WEU at Maastricht remains profoundly ambiguous.

Worry about Germany also explains a great deal of France's policy toward eastern Europe. I have already referred to the Yugoslav crisis and to France's efforts to make it an EC affair, rather than having Germany or the CSCE play major roles. But it appears that Mitterrand's opposition to any quick enlargement of the Community, and even to a statement of policy that would guarantee the entry of Poland, Czechoslovakia, and Hungary into the EC by a certain date or if specific conditions are met, is caused by the obsession with German power. A deepened (but not enlarged) EC could take the initiative of aid to the east away from German industry and German public assistance. In this view an enlarged Community, with new members from northern and eastern Europe, would have its center of gravity in Germany, and would strengthen the tendency in the eastern countries to see in the Federal Republic both an economic model and the political model of a successful transition from totalitarianism to democracy.[3] Here we find again the fear of German domination (such a Community would be so heterogeneous as to be little more than a free trade area), the fear of an unfettered Germany. Whether the Federal Republic's influence east of its borders is not actually greater when the three former communist candidates for membership are left out, face to face with German economic power and political influence, rather than brought in so as to join with countries just as unenthusiastic about German predominance as they are, has not really been openly debated.

Mitterrand's attempts at squaring the circle—at showing French and west European concern for the fate of the east Europeans without, however, fully opening the EC's doors—have been numerous. He got his partners to establish, in London, the European Bank for Reconstruction and Development (EBRD), an initiative of his adviser Jacques Attali, and to accept Attali as its head: a Franco-British deal that seemed to move at least part of the effort to help the east away from Bonn. He accepted the negotiation of a "European economic space" with the European Free Trade Area (EFTA) and of association agreements with the three former communist states. He proposed a "confederation" that would have included the USSR (but not the United States and Canada) and dealt with issues such as energy, transportation systems, the environment, the free circulation of people, and culture. But none of this has really been enough to stop Poland, Czechoslovakia, and Hungary from knocking at the door, or many voices in Britain and Germany from asking that it be quickly opened. The EBRD's means are limited. The association agreements hit a French snag over imports of meat from the east—a small issue, but of symbolic import—before a final compromise was reached, but they are a poor substitute for membership.

As for the confederation, Mitterrand himself undercut it by objecting to America's presence, and by declaring shortly before flying to Prague (only for the final session—that is, for his own speech—of a three-day meeting he had more or less imposed on Vaclav Havel) that it would take dozens of years before the east European states could become members of the EC. Their viewpoint was perfectly expressed by Havel in his opening speech: nothing without the United States (especially if the enterprise includes the USSR; but then if it includes both, it is the CSCE); technical issues could be dealt with by existing organizations (such as the Council of Europe, or the Economic Commission for Europe of the UN, and so on); and no halfway house. The fact that the official part of the French delegation failed to get Havel's rather blunt point, and that it did not want to acknowledge the evident opposition of the great majority of the members of the political committee of the conference to the French plan, revealed a disturbing degree of high-handedness and insensitivity.[4] France has signed treaties of cooperation with Poland, Hungary, and Czechoslovakia, and these treaties contain a promise to support the eventual entry of these countries into the EC. But there has been little private French investment in them, and public efforts have tended to concentrate on Romania because of old cultural ties; a treaty of cooperation with Romania (but without any mention of the EC) was signed in November 1991, despite Romania's shaky democratic credentials.

Where the concern for French independence and the desire to tighten the knots on Germany evidently clash is in French policy on institutional reform of the EC. The Kohl-Mitterrand letter of December 6, 1990, which dealt with the Community's "democratic legitimacy," clearly indicated that diplomacy and security would remain matters to be decided by unanimity; it also mentioned the possibility of qualified majority rule for enforcement measures, but France has shown little enthusiasm for this. France's preference for the intergovernmental method characteristic of the Fouchet plan of 1961–62 means accepting the risk of a more assertive and unconstrained Germany in this realm. Paradoxically, in the Yugoslav crisis this method allowed Germany both to bludgeon its partners into endorsing its position in order to avert an ugly split *and* to jump the gun on them by recognizing Slovenia and Croatia before anyone else, despite the common agreement.

France hinted at a move toward a power of "co-decision" for the European Parliament, but French proposals have been distrustful of the Parliament, and reluctant to grant a significant role to the Commission in the realms of defense and diplomacy. Maastricht settled for a point close to the French position. In thus braking the strengthening of the more "supranational" among the Community's political institutions, France has been—for once—Britain's ally. Britain's argument is the "sovereignty" of the British Parliament; Mitterrand's concern is both for protecting French autonomy in essential matters, and for protecting his own power: in this affair Jacques Delors has been closer to the German position than to the French one. There is a clear contradiction between the stand of the French president and his willingness to assert, in the draft of the new treaty on political union, that the union has a "federal calling"—a sentence that London rejected and that ended up on the cutting-room floor. The fact that Germany would soon have more representatives than Britain or France in the European Parliament did not, of course, do much to increase Mitterrand's enthusiasm for this body: here, anxiety about German influence supersedes the fear of an unfettered Germany.

The Role of International Institutions

This account has been written pretty much in "realist" terms: that is, in terms of a national strategy by a unified actor who defines interests in terms of power, and whose goals and preferences come from his position in the structure, from past experiences and past choices. What about the role of international institutions in this story? Four points need to be made about their importance.

First, as I have tried to show, they matter greatly to France as precious instruments, as often indispensable means toward goals, as necessary fields of action. France is engaged in complex games with the United States, the Soviets and now the Russians (whom Mitterrand is determined not to leave in too much of a tête-à-tête with Germany), the British, the Germans, and many others. International organizations are the arenas in which these games are usually played, for they carry out the varied functions of containment, reassurance, assistance, and attraction France wants them to perform. The confederation was supposed to serve as a reassurance to those excluded from the EC; the EC and the EBRD as assistance agencies while these countries wait; the EC, most important of all in French strategy, as a tamer of German power, a pole of resistance to American economic pressures, and a magnet for eastern Europe. Indeed, the EC has become the instrument France needs to exert influence in the directions Paris has set, whenever France needs the support of others in order to be able to move in those directions. The consent of Germany and Britain is necessary to build a European defense system that will remove the continent from under American tutelage; hence the French emphasis on the WEU and on making of it a branch of the EC. In the Balkans, where the French want both to regain influence and to contain Germany, Mitterrand has pushed for the involvement of the EC in the Yugoslav conflict, even though, on balance, there was little the EC could gain from plunging into the maelstrom, and a strong probability that even a less divided Community would find the Serbs intractable and the war hard to stop.

Second, much of French diplomacy focuses, as a consequence, on two issues: on choosing among the existing international and regional institutions in a given field the one most likely to serve French purposes, and on the internal politics of the preferred organizations. For instance, concerning the first issue, Mitterrand has resisted the tendency of the Group of Seven to deal not only with economic but also with security issues; he has resisted any extension of NATO's functions, especially toward the east; he has opted for the WEU over NATO and preferred to have the EC and the UN Security Council deal with Yugoslavia rather than the CSCE or NATO; he has not had much use for the CSCE, and has clearly put the development of the EC as a "hegemonic bloc" (through the creation of the European economic space and through a network of association agreements) far ahead of GATT. He obtained Bush's consent to entrusting the Community and the EBRD, rather than "Americanized" institutions such as NATO and the World Bank or largely non-European ones such as the Organization for Economic Cooperation and Development (OECD), with economic help to eastern Europe.

As for the internal politics of international institutions, French strategy is most visible in the one that matters most: the EC. It aims at maximizing the influence of France in it, and at minimizing the risk of France's being controlled by it. Delors would not forever be head of the Commission; it might soon be Germany's turn. In the council French diplomacy, and in the galaxy of committees around the council French bureaucracy, have often exerted leadership: French proposals on the institutions of the future union reflect these facts. French views on the EMU follow from this consideration; here the purpose is to minimize Bundesbank domination and to have a say in the future central bank's decisions. Since France has little chance of weighing much in NATO, even if it returned to it (and in no case would Paris assign its nuclear forces to it), French policy has been to minimize NATO's grip on French defense by staying out and by refusing any subordination of the WEU to NATO. In the UN the French have been understandably cool to the suggestion that France and Britain should transfer their permanent seats to the EC, or that Germany should join, along with Japan, the original Big Five.

My first two points view the institutions as instruments of policy—another "realist" perspective. But my third and fourth points are "institutionalist." Indispensable as arenas and tools, the institutions the French need most—those of the EC—have been nurtured even when they fail to move in directions the French leaders would like (such as social and industrial policy) or act in ways they deplore (as in the case of the Commission's tough antitrust and procompetition policy). Moreover, unavoidable as means, international institutions also affect the way in which the French now conceive of their objectives. These are still, in large part, national; but they tend increasingly to be defined in ways that require external participation, support, or consent, and therefore accommodation. This has been most clearly understood by the French administrative and industrial elites. For a Colbertiste bureaucracy and a business community largely dependent on crutches provided by the state, to endorse the notion of a single deregulated economic market was a real revolution. French monetary policy, applauded by the OECD, clearly put the EMS (ever since 1983) and now the EMU above the interests and clamors of those who, in France, denounce anti-inflationary fiscal rigor as a brake on industrial growth, employment, and social policy. The Schengen agreement, opposed in parliament by the last defenders of an intransigent conception of sovereignty, was declared by the Constitutional Council not to be unconstitutional because it does not "transfer" sovereignty to a non-French institution; but it certainly entails a "pooling" of national powers in vital matters such as border controls. The Franco-German list of new areas that the political union should cover (environment, health, energy, technology, immigration, and so on) shows that this concept of pooled sovereignty prevails increasingly over older notions of independence. The still fragile signs of evolution in French agricultural policy—a somewhat diminished unwillingness to accept a Community plan that would drastically revise the Common Agricultural Policy and amount to an income policy for farmers instead of a subsidy policy at the consumers' expense—are significant: here the long-term interest of France coincides with the preferences of most of France's partners (even Germany has now seen the light) as against the short-term demands of politically potent French peasants.

It is in diplomatic and national security affairs that the clash between the old and the new way of defining the national interest still goes on most vigorously, as we have seen. But even there an evolution has begun. During the Gulf crisis the old way prevailed; France acted as an independent former great power, but all the alternatives were bad: subordination to a NATO extended out of area (an old French taboo) or EC paralysis. The French managed to conciliate their own engagement with a management role entrusted to the WEU, which coordinated the Europeans' sanctions. In the Yugoslav crisis French temptations to national diplomatic activism were subordinated to EC moves (and the EC ministers did send the head of France's Constitutional Council, Mitterrand's friend Badinter, on an arbitration mission). The French insistence on making of the WEU the center of a European security system (and Mitterrand's new willingness, after the fiasco of winter 1990–91, to find a formula acceptable to Britain, and to the United States, in order to rescue the EC summit at Maastricht from deadlock) could not but gradually erode the old shibboleth of national military autonomy. The call for an expansion of the Franco-German brigade, and for other members of the WEU to join in a "corps" that could become "the model of a tighter military cooperation among them"—a call Mitterrand inserted into the Franco-German initiative of October 14, 1991—was a small first step in this direction. In January 1992 a second step was taken with his call for a "reflection" on a common European nuclear doctrine.

Past and Future

The evolution in the definition of French interests and objectives has been proceeding step by step, more through actions than through public discussion (which the ratification of the Maastricht treaties now imposes). There are, in the political class, enough Jacobin nationalists on the left and among Gaullists to impose caution on an already innately stealthy president, and the French elites prefer technocracy to democracy anyhow. Moreover, the French assertion of independence, which has proved so irritating to France's neighbors and partners, has had three functions they rarely understood. One was to exorcise a troubled past (this was De Gaulle's great achievement). The second was to resist external domination, and particularly that of the superpower whose protection was needed—the United States—at a time when the idea of a "European Europe" able and willing to resist American pressures was merely a hope and a distant objective. The third function of France's self-assertion was a kind of *tous azimuts* insurance policy against future perils (this was how De Gaulle presented the *force de frappe*). Today the first function is probably played out. As for resistance to the United States, as America's role as a tutor of Europe shrinks, as its weight in NATO decreases, as its priorities shift to its own internal problems, this function too will dwindle. This does not mean that the French desire for distinctiveness will disappear quickly. America's resources for external action still exceed those of all other powers; the American role in Europe, America's noisy pride in being number one and its habit of treating partners as junior associates, may remain sufficiently in evidence to arouse the French instinct of resistance.

Moreover, the third function is far from being seen as obsolete. A volatile electorate and a political class in which the two extremes are "anti-European," and both the ecologists and the two large "management coalitions" that have ruled France under the Fifth Republic (the socialists and their allies on the left, the Gaullists and centrists on the right) are divided on the issue of further European integration, continue to harbor a fear of external threats requiring French self-defense. Current fears about French national identity focus not only on what Valéry Giscard d'Estaing shamelessly called an "invasion" of immigrants, but also on a European Community which—as in a 1991 Commission decision preventing a Franco-Italian conglomerate from acquiring a British firm—often decides against French interests, which moves toward a concept of European citizenship that goes against the Jacobin strain (and the constitution of the Fifth Republic) by dissociating citizenship from nationality,[5] and whose institutional system is far closer to the German federal model than to the French unitary one. And a fear of German domination of the Community is occasionally expressed by those who point to the Federal Republic's monetary and interest rate policies and to its new assertiveness in eastern and southeastern Europe.

So far no policy other than the current uneasy mix of "Europeanism" and independence seems able to obtain a broad popular consensus, and we all know that even obsolete policies and institutions hang on when no replacement is in sight.

However, in the long run the changes in France's outlook are likely to continue, unless one or more of three things happen. First, the increasingly complex Community might fail in coping with its new functions and its probable enlargement. Second, Germany might behave tactlessly within the Community and/or renationalize its policy. In the past the EC had provided a field and a shelter for a West German state that was only half a nation. In the new EC Germany is again a national state. If the French were faced, in the Community, with the paradox of a Germany that begins to behave like one (and no longer like a "postnational" state that pools its sovereignty with its partners and transfers some of it to the common institutions while France's traditional independence fades away), there could be a strong nationalist reaction. Third (as in the sad case of the European Defense Community in the 1950s), the debate on the ratification of the Maastricht treaties and on the constitutional revision they require could get entangled in the domestic discontent with Mitterrand's failing leadership and with a declining Socialist government and party. These are big "ifs." And yet even now the foreign "invasion" can be checked only by a common or coordinated European policy, and a "purely French" national identity today means an isolated and xenophobic France. A "return to the past," rashly forecast by some neorealists, would, on balance, be more advantageous to an unfettered Germany than to France. It is through international institutions—so often treated with contempt or little studied in France—that France can best hope to exert political influence, to promote its economic interests, and to exploit its one military asset, a nuclear force that could serve European deterrent purposes. The malaise about identity results more from domestic politics, and from Mitterrand's failure to articulate clearly enough the new conditions of French action abroad and the new definition of the national interest. Over time the French search for distinctiveness and autonomy may transfer its focus from France to a Europe in which France will continue to play an important role. Thus, France would at last become an "ordinary" European nation, encased in a highly original Community: an unromantic prospect, but a likely fate.[6]

Chapter 5

British State Strategies
after the Cold War

Louise Richardson

Britain was on the winning side of the Cold War, a fact that would not easily be gleaned from a comparison between British power at the beginning and the end of the period. Whereas in the 1940s Britain was one of the chief architects of the postwar order that became the context for the Cold War, by 1989 Britain was largely reduced to the status of observer of the transformation of its security environment. The grace and skill which, with rare exceptions, marked the British postwar adjustment to its reduced circumstances have been the subject of much admiration. This chapter reflects an attempt to examine the application of those skills to the adjustment to the new, as yet unnamed order.[1]

At the end of the Cold War Britain found itself not in the anarchic world of the realist vision but in a world full of institutions.[2] In this world of institutions to which it was, to one degree or another, connected, Britain simply did not have the option to pursue a self-reliant strategy, as a realist analysis might posit.[3] Britain had helped create some of these institutions, some it had joined, and some it opposed. Those it opposed, such as the Council for Mutual Economic Assistance (CMEA) and the Warsaw Pact, were disintegrating at startling speed. Those it had helped create, such as the North Atlantic Treaty Organization (NATO) and the Western European Union (WEU), it clung to like a life raft in a stormy sea. Those it had joined, most significantly the European Community (EC), became the scene of bitter battles over competing visions of the emerging order.

The dramatic transformation of Europe since 1989 provides a rare and irresistible opportunity for political scientists, and especially international relations theorists, to test core hypotheses of the discipline. In particular, the events have been seen as providing, in effect, a test case for assessing the rival claims of neorealist and institutionalist theories. The revolution of 1989 (among more tangible accomplishments) provided a transfusion to the ongoing neorealist-institutionalist debate in international relations, precisely because both sets of theories seem to predict very different outcomes.

The strategies of adjustment adopted by British decision makers, however, do not fit neatly into either camp. Britain instead pursued a range of strategies. Given the pervasiveness of international institutions in the security and economic scenes in Europe, these strategies necessarily had to be implemented through institutions such as NATO and the EC. As a realist might predict, Britain chose NATO, an organization within which it exercised considerable influence, to balance against threats to its security, just as it had always done. Yet, as an institutionalist might predict, the persistent progress toward economic and even political union being forged by the EC forced Britain reluctantly to make concessions on these issues for fear of being marginalized. Finally, in a fusion of realist and institutionalist tactics, Britain rediscovered the WEU and used it to prevent the EC Commission from gaining control over European defense. In effect, therefore, Britain used an institutional strategy to defend an anti-institutionalist position; it used one institution to balance against another.

The nuances of strategy, therefore, suggest the need for a more sophisticated theoretical analysis than is provided by a duel between neorealists and institutionalists. In this chapter I attempt to provide the empirical basis for such an analysis by examining British state strategies in the first two years after the end of the Cold War.

British Response to German Unification

While German unification did not pose fundamental dilemmas for Britain to the extent that it did for France,[4] it nevertheless confronted the British leadership with the reality of its own weakness. Most British officials had long since lost any delusions of grandeur they might once have entertained about Britain's role in the world. Indeed, most of the younger generation, represented by John Major, never suffered from such delusions. Nonetheless, throughout the Cold War Britain had managed to play a larger role and exercise more influence internationally than was warranted by its power position. There were many reasons for this: the pervasiveness of the English language, the legacy of empire, the professionalism of British diplomats and soldiers, the (at least nominally) independent nuclear deterrent, and most of all Britain's very close relationship with the United States.

Britain perceived German unification as a threat both to its position in Europe and to its relationship with the United States. It had been a guiding principle of British foreign policy since the Suez crisis to keep its policies as closely in line with those of the United States as possible. This principle, however, now came in conflict with another principle of British foreign policy, and one of even longer standing: the need to prevent the domination of Europe by a single power. For the United States the unification of Germany presented the prospect of victory in the Cold War; for Britain it presented the prospect of accommodating another great power in Europe.

Britain responded in its traditional way. It tried to serve as sage counsellor to the impetuous Americans, but this did not work. Whereas Britain persistently tried to slow down the process toward unification, the Americans (not to mention the Germans) were determined to seize the moment. Whatever the private misgivings of the British leadership (and they often did not remain very private), as an ally in the western alliance Britain had little option but to endorse formally Germany's right to unify. Nevertheless, Britain's discomfiture was evident. Margaret Thatcher consistently argued that the issue of German unification had to be placed in the context of broader security arrangements in Europe. Displaying a rare concern for the EC, Thatcher argued at one point that the integration of East Germany into the Community might undermine it. She wanted as little change in NATO as possible and insisted throughout that the new Germany would have to be a member of NATO.[5]

For many years the British foreign policy establishment had been concerned by the rise of the successor generation in the United States. It was feared that as this generation of men (and they were, of course, almost always men) who had no personal memory of the wartime Anglo-American collaboration and few personal ties to Britain came to power, they would be less interested in continuing the "special relationship" with the United Kingdom. Germany had always been best placed to dislodge Britain as America's closest friend in Europe, and in the process of adjustment to German unification seemed to be doing just that. British leaders did not, for example, take kindly to occupying what was essentially observer status at the "two-plus-four" talks. This may have contributed to the last-minute difficulties Britain created at the talks over military maneuvers in East Germany.[6]

British apprehensions were confirmed by George Bush's offer to Germany of a "partnership in leadership" in May 1989. Britain was usually the occupant of that role (though it could, of course, be argued that the EC rather than any particular country was the more appropriate partner). Whatever its misgivings, however, Britain had little option but to respect the German right to unify and accede, like everyone else, to the fait accompli. The early debates within the elite about how best to fit a united Germany into Europe, therefore, were all superseded by events.

Britain, moreover, even found itself sidelined in its own capital. The London summit was very much a U.S.-German affair. Thatcher's cautionary remarks and emphasis on the need for NATO to keep up its defenses in the face of the still formidable Soviet arsenal had little impact. At one point she threatened not to sign the declaration if Bush's favored "last resort" language were included. She eventually did sign, but only after ensuring the inclusion of a qualifying paragraph. The differences of emphasis at the closing press conferences were striking, with Thatcher alone insisting that the new formula for using nuclear weapons as a last resort in no way altered NATO's deterrent posture.[7]

Britain felt threatened by the pace of events in Europe and was far from enthusiastic about the prospect of a united Germany. Anglo-German relations had never been particularly close and had become even more distant after the Heath-Brandt years of relative amity. At a technical level, however, Britain and Germany had cooperated successfully, particularly in security and defense matters. This cooperation was nonetheless overshadowed over the years by disputes centering on the European Community, with Britain self-consciously assuming the role of brake to the German, and later Franco-German, engine. Relations improved dramatically once Prime Minister Thatcher was replaced by John Major, but the honeymoon was short-lived. Although Major, unlike his predecessor, immediately established warm personal relations with Chancellor Helmut Kohl, the differences between the two governments did not pass with Thatcher. Major immediately took up the baton by trying (albeit with more grace than his mentor) to dilute German proposals for political and monetary union.

The close personal ties that were established between Kohl and Major provide yet another example of the interplay of domestic and international affairs that is an outgrowth of increasing interdependence and institutional activity. Kohl knew that his plans for the EC would be affected by the result of the anticipated British election. He believed that they would best be served with Major as prime minister rather than the Labour leader, Neil Kinnock. Kohl, therefore, was anxious to make a deal with Britain at Maastricht that would not impair Major's electoral chances. (It would, of course, be easy to overstate this point, as Kohl's preference for a Conservative victory in Britain was just one of a myriad of considerations that he had to take into account in formulating his negotiating position at Maastricht.)

While the British government was primarily concerned with the implications of German unification for Britain's place in Europe and the world, the public discussion concentrated on British attitudes toward Germany and the Germans. Here the British position on the German question was overshadowed by the infamous Ridley affair.[8] Nicholas Ridley, the secretary of state for industry, and a close colleague and confidant of Prime Minister Thatcher, denounced Germany and accused the Germans of attempting to take over Europe. In an interview published in the *Spectator,* Ridley, among other impolitic phrases, compared Chancellor Kohl to Hitler. The incident is something of a caricature of the British perspective on Germany. That said, there can be little doubt that his views found some sympathy in Downing Street, although even Mrs. Thatcher would have been more diplomatic in expressing them. Ridley was one of Thatcher's closest advisers and would hardly have felt free to state such views unless he knew them to be shared. Moreover, Mrs. Thatcher's delay in sacking him indicated that she was deeply reluctant to do so and did not perceive the interview as a firing offense.[9] That said, Ridley was after all forced to resign, an outcome that suggests an elite and public consensus that his views were inappropriate.

Public opinion polls do not indicate widespread support for his position. Asked whether they agreed with Ridley that there was a "German racket designed to take over the whole of Europe," 53 percent of the British public disagreed and 31 percent agreed. Interestingly, of the 18–34 age group, 67 percent disagreed and only 16 percent agreed. Asked whether they thought that a united Germany would pose a threat to European peace, 29 percent answered yes and 62 percent answered no. Again the generational difference was manifest, with those having memories of the war more suspicious of Germany than the more politically significant youth. In the 18–34 age group, 20 percent answered yes and 70 percent answered no. The figures for the over-55 age group were 37 percent and 53 percent. Even in this group, however, the majority did not perceive German unification as a threat to European peace.[10]

The Chequers meeting of March 24, 1990, which again has been misrepresented as confirming that Ridley's views were widely shared in the foreign policy establishment, actually indicates only that the prime minister was genuinely trying to grapple with the implications for Britain of a united Germany. At the meeting, which was supposed to be private, the prime minister and some of her colleagues consulted with prominent academics about the implications for Britain of German unification. The minutes of the meeting were leaked to the press, where the emphasis was placed on some crude characterizations of Germans. The minutes suggest, however, that the discussions were altogether more measured, and the conclusion drawn was that "we should be nice to the Germans."[11]

German unification brought to light at least two new strands in the perennial British debate on Europe. The first was the fear of German economic domination in the EC. This was really the point Ridley was making in his notorious interview. His diatribe was directed far more at current German economic power than at any potential German military power. The minutes of the Chequers meeting indicated that this was also the primary concern of those present.[12] The other fear was to be found among pro-Europe officials and in intellectual circles. It was the fear that Germany would turn in on itself and in the process would bring Europe in on itself too.[13] Support for these fears was found in the irresponsible handling of the GATT (General Agreement on Tariffs and Trade) negotiations, in the insipid EC response to the Gulf War, and in the paltry sums offered as aid to eastern Europe.

British Response to the End of the Cold War

German unification did not in itself constitute the end of the Cold War; the other critical dimension was the collapse of communism in the Soviet Union and eastern Europe and the disintegration of the Warsaw Pact. While German unification was perceived as a threat to Britain's position in Europe and its relationship with the United States, events in eastern Europe were watched with bemusement and later delight and seen as a confirmation of British principles. The new strategic context provoked pressure in Britain, as elsewhere, for a peace dividend. This coincided with a collapse of service morale in the face of widespread uncertainty. Responding in part to these domestic pressures and in part to the realization that Britain would need to be clear about its own interests and preferences in order to influence the forthcoming debates within NATO, the government launched a defense review. (Given the opprobrium that usually attaches to defense reviews, this one was coyly termed "Options for Change.")

A senior working group within the Ministry of Defence was established to review the implications of events in Europe for British defense policy. The secretary of defense and the cabinet, however, took the critical decisions out of the hands of the working group by insisting that each of Britain's four basic defense commitments be maintained. These were specified as: maintenance of nuclear forces, the defense of the United Kingdom, the defense of the European mainland, and maintenance of maritime forces.[14]

The proposals announced in July 1990 were not at all as radical as had been feared by the services or hoped by the treasury and the opposition. The government proposed a "smaller but better" defense system but one that essentially fulfilled the same functions.[15] The much delayed defense white paper was finally announced in July 1991. In making the announcement, defense secretary Tom King declared that it reflected the most momentous change in British defense policy since the Second World War.[16] The white paper, in proposing to eliminate one sixth of the armed services, would leave Britain with a smaller army than it had had since 1885. As a result, British defense spending, which was over 5 percent of gross domestic product (GDP) in the early 1980s (5.7 percent in 1985), would fall to 3.4 percent by 1993–94, its lowest share since the 1930s. These figures elicited concern among Tory backbenchers, and even King's predecessor, that the cuts went too far. Of even more concern was King's proposal to reduce the number of regiments in the army. Elimination of historic, locally recruited regiments arouses passions like few other issues among Tories and threatened to derail the defense proposals.

Secretary King's hyperbole and backbench Tory anxieties notwithstanding, when considered against the background of the veritable revolution in eastern Europe, the defense white paper was far from radical. Indeed, the review was not really a review at all. It certainly failed to seize the opportunity for a strategic review of Britain's defense commitments and capabilities. In domestic political terms it is not difficult to see why a thoroughgoing debate was avoided. Tories had nothing to gain by drawing attention to the fact that they were enforcing cuts on their natural supporters. As for the Labour party, having seriously impaired its electoral prospects over the years by a policy of unilateral disarmament, and unwilling to appear to be in favor of eliminating jobs, it saw itself as politically vulnerable on the defense issue and therefore acquiesced to the avoidance of a defense debate.

In effect, the white paper called for the adoption of a comprehensive insurance policy against all unforeseeable threats. But that is not the only approach that might have been adopted. In light of the seriousness of treasury constraints, rather than engage in an exercise in "salami slicing" by reducing each part of the forces, the government might have dropped one of Britain's defense roles. There were advocates for such a radical approach. Alan Clark, King's junior minister, for example, argued for abandoning the European commitment altogether and instead adopting a maritime strategy based on mobile forces capable of rapid deployment anywhere. Others in the ministry argued for dramatic cuts in naval forces, pointing out that the threat of a Soviet naval blockade had diminished at least as much as the threat of invasion across the central front and that, therefore, Britain no longer needed a navy which was the largest in Europe and the fourth largest in the world.

The new defense policy could be construed as consistent with either a neorealist or an institutionalist interpretation (though to be fair to system theorists, it should be pointed out that they do not claim to predict state preferences but rather predict the conditions under which states will pursue particular lines of policy). The experience and professionalism of the British armed forces had undoubtedly been an asset to successive British governments in their efforts to retain what in Britain is called a seat at the top table. That Britain chose to maintain at least the semblance of an army worthy of a global power is consistent with a realist interpretation of the national interest. Britain needed an army with global commitments, if not quite global capabilities, in order to exercise influence globally. But Britain's involvement in a network of defense organizations in which it fulfilled diverse defense roles substantially increased the costs of adopting a radically new defense posture, such as the maritime posture proposed by Clark. The other point to be borne in mind, and one that both neorealists and institutionalists often find difficult to accommodate, is the power of domestic politics. In the various parliamentary debates on the defense proposals, the issue that dominated discussion was not that of international status or institutional obligations nor even national issues of defense posture but rather the local, even parochial issue of regimental recruitment.[17] That said, the government did withstand fierce bipartisan, loud public, quiet military, and even discreet royal opposition to the defense cuts.

In addition to the requirement to reorient Britain's defense posture, the disintegration of eastern Europe raised the need to integrate east European countries into the western economy. There were not many issues on which the Tory government and the Labour opposition were in agreement in the latter years of the Thatcher premiership, but Britain's responsibilities toward eastern Europe (or the absence thereof) was one of them. There was no particular pressure from political or domestic sources for Britain to take a lead in integrating eastern Europe into the west.[18] Moreover, there was determined opposition to the expenditure of large sums overseas no matter what the cause.

Domestically the Thatcherite view of government, the power of the market, and the need to privatize state ownership seemed to be confirmed by events in the east. Indeed, government ministers, on their many trips east, often appeared more intent on sharing the secrets of the British political system than on sharing their resources. This led Labour spokesmen to complain that the government seemed to be more eager to export ideology than goods. As far as the government was concerned, however, the task of exporting goods should be left to the private sector. The amount of British assistance, therefore, was small both in comparison with that offered by other European countries and in relation to the overall budget for foreign aid. In 1990 that assistance was listed as £225 million, though of course Britain also incurred contingent liabilities through membership in the International Monetary Fund (IMF) and the World Bank.[19]

The government insisted that any assistance given would only be in response to democratic reforms. Moreover, in Britain's domestic version of subsidiarity, the public sector would do nothing that the private sector could do. The role of the British government, therefore, was to facilitate the private sector in exploiting the economic opportunities proffered by the collapse of communism. The chancellor of the exchequer stated this succinctly in his budget speech: "The whole of eastern Europe has opened up in the most dramatic way. We need to make sure that British business can take advantage of these changes."[20] Far from Britain's taking the lead and acting as architect of the new economic order, therefore, the British response, such as it was, was largely short-term and self-interested.

One of the most successful, creative, and uniquely British responses to events in eastern Europe (albeit not the most generous) was the Know-How Fund. The fund was started with £25 million and subsequently expanded to £75. The idea was to make funds available to eastern countries as they abandoned communism. The plan was to enable the governments to acquire the skills they needed to run a market economy in a pluralist democracy. Funds were therefore made available for training in areas such as banking, financial services, and the management of the process of privatization.

As with so many of its other projects in different areas, the Foreign Office managed to derive considerable diplomatic benefits from a very small expenditure. British diplomats delighted in expounding on the unique virtues of the fund. In its first two years the Know-How Fund financed two hundred projects at a cost of £18 million, not the kind of spending likely to have a dramatic impact on the reconstruction of the east European economies. The fund, however, reflected very well the attitude of the British government toward western assistance to eastern Europe: first, economic assistance should be directly linked to political and economic reforms; second, assistance should serve British business interests; third, the private sector should be the medium of assistance.

The same themes were in evidence in the British government's support for the establishment of the European Bank for Reconstruction and Development (EBRD).[21] The focus of the bank on the transition from centrally planned economies to market economies, privatization, and the emphasis on lending to the private sector were fully in keeping with the British approach. There was nevertheless widespread skepticism as to the need for the bank, particularly in light of the fact that several private investment funds for eastern Europe seemed to be experiencing more difficulties in finding eligible borrowers than in raising capital. The British government was determined that, whatever the weaknesses of the bank, once it was created it must be headquartered in London. The government argued that, as Europe's premier financial center, possessing unrivaled experience in the privatization of state enterprises, London was the most appropriate home for the bank. After agreeing to a French president for the bank, the mercurial Jacques Attali, the British won their claim. Whatever the shortcomings of the bank as a multilateral institution, therefore, it served the British interest by bolstering London's position as the financial hub of Europe.

For all the talk of finance and know-how, the British private sector was very cautious about getting involved in eastern Europe. Only one of the top twenty investors in the region was British.[22] Britain ranked behind Germany, the United States, Austria, France, and Italy in the number of retail operations in eastern Europe.[23] The poor performance even elicited criticism from the Bank of England[24] and from the Confederation of British Industry.[25] Part of the difficulty was that most British firms had very little experience dealing with eastern Europe. In 1989 eastern Europe took only about 1 percent of British exports.[26] There was little concerted effort to redress this.

Through its membership in a number of international institutions Britain did participate in multilateral efforts to assist eastern Europe. During this initial period, however, of the £225 million Britain offered to eastern Europe, £150 million was in bilateral assistance.[27] British officials, however, often argued for a multilateral response to the problem and supported the efforts of the EC to coordinate western assistance. The Foreign Office also tried to influence the distribution of EC assistance by insisting on the link between assistance and reform, and on a country-by-country rather than a regional approach.[28] The Foreign Office also pushed for a closer institutional link between eastern Europe and the EC.[29]

Prime Minister Thatcher went so far as to raise the issue of membership in the EC for eastern European countries. At her speech to the Aspen Institute in August 1990, she called on the EC to give an unequivocal commitment to offer membership to the emerging democracies. This proposal should be interpreted as a demonstration less of the prime minister's commitment either to eastern Europe or to the EC than of her determination to dilute the latter. In effect it reflected a sophisticated effort to balance against the EC by facilitating the efforts of the eastern Europeans to bandwagon with the EC. A European Community which included the emerging democracies of eastern Europe could not hope to effect the type of monetary and political union to which she was opposed.

Britain and Europe's Institutions

In formulating their response to the revolution of 1989, British decision makers confronted a new security environment. Several international institutions were very much a part of that environment. In this respect the neorealist concept of anarchy is not very useful. Owing to the peaceful nature of the end of the Cold War, the preexisting institutions were not swept away with the war (which is not to say that some will not in time be swept away). The two institutions of central importance to Britain's place in the world during the Cold War, and hence to British strategy after it, were NATO and the EC.

NATO
Historically an enthusiast for NATO, Britain perceived NATO as the sine qua non of the post–Cold War settlement. Britain insisted throughout the nego-

tiations on unity that the new Germany would have to be a member of NATO. Having achieved that, Britain insisted that NATO must remain the linchpin of European security. Throughout the conduct of the Cold War, British defense policy had become so integrated with NATO policy that it was difficult to separate the two. When the Defence Committee of the House of Commons sought the advice of Lord Lewin, chief of the defense staff from 1979 to 1982, he told them: "I have always found it very difficult, when we have been so completely supportive of NATO, to recognise an independent UK defence policy. There really has been no such thing. We have been completely committed to NATO and our forces have been structured to contribute to NATO. I believe our first effort should be to discuss with our NATO allies how then to meet these changing circumstances and not to go off on our own and try to make changes in our own force structures which may not match with what our allies feel."[30] The secretary of defense, in speaking to the committee, was equally adamant that any change in British defense policy must take place within the NATO context.[31] The bipartisan committee, in its final report, fully concurred. Dismissing suggestions that NATO had been rendered obsolete, the committee argued instead that "the fundamental principles of the North Atlantic Treaty which are the foundation of NATO are as relevant now as they were in 1949."[32] As the institutionalists would predict, therefore, British decision makers realized that they could not formulate their strategies, much less secure their objectives, without taking into account the strategies of other states.

The British government fully conceded that NATO would have to undergo some adjustments. Britain was prepared to welcome a more political role for NATO, unlike France, which had always rejected this, and for similar reasons. The French had sought to avoid American domination, and the British had sought to ensure American involvement in European security. The British strategy of securing American involvement had served the security goals of balancing the Soviets and anchoring the Germans—goals which Britain could not have achieved on its own, and which appear to be surviving the current changes in Europe. The British, while concerned that "more political" might mean "less military," nevertheless wholeheartedly endorsed that part of the London declaration which expressed NATO's intention to enhance the political component of the alliance as provided for by Article 2 of the treaty.

In the NATO review in 1991 Britain lobbied successfully for the lead role in the new Rapid Reaction Corps. This new position would give the British army experience of higher allied command and provide a role for the reduced forces for which it was planning. More important, the position combined the practical benefit of reducing the need for further army cuts with the symbolic benefit of demonstrating British military prowess. Both points again demonstrate the interdependence of international institutions and domestic politics. (It also demonstrates British diplomatic skill in exploiting what a defense official cynically described as the "halo effect" after the Gulf War.) The 1991 defense white paper proudly points to Britain's new leadership role in NATO: "The fact that we have been invited to lead the Rapid Reaction Corps is a considerable achievement for the United Kingdom. It is evidence of the high regard in which our professional forces are held by our allies."[33] (A NATO official was more cynical, pointing out that as the Germans could not, and the French would not, there really was no other choice.)

The white paper went on to reiterate British insistence on NATO as the cornerstone of western security and to spell out some of the reasons for the British position: "Fundamental to our perception is the conviction that the NATO Alliance remains the essential framework for safe-guarding the freedom and security of its members. No other institution can provide deterrence and defence against all threats of aggression; can preserve a strategic balance in Europe, bearing in mind the power of the Soviet Union; or can ensure a full role for the United States and Canada in the defence of Europe."[34]

The explanation for British enthusiasm for NATO is the same as it has always been: NATO is the means for ensuring an American commitment to European defense. This was evident in Foreign Secretary Douglas Hurd's remarks to a press conference in Berlin: "So this Alliance is an asset which we simply cannot allow to evaporate or disappear. European security without the United States simply does not make sense. If we were ever foolish enough to try it, we would soon realise what nonsense it is."[35]

Lord Carrington, former foreign secretary and former secretary general of NATO, gave a slightly different twist, and one of particular interest to institutionalists, in speaking to the defense committee. Carrington also believed in the centrality of the American commitment to Europe and in the need to bolster the European side of the alliance. He argued that one could not have another organization which would displace NATO: "I think that it would be very dangerous to supersede NATO in the foreseeable future because I do not believe that American public opinion and the American Congress—they know NATO, understand it and know the reason for it— would be prepared to have some kind of new set up that superseded NATO in the current circumstances. Therefore I think that there has to be an evolution of NATO. You have to call it NATO. You have to make the Americans think that it is still NATO. But it has to evolve into something slightly different."[36] The British government fears that as the Soviet threat recedes and the Soviet Union disintegrates just as the European Community members become more united and more wealthy, the U.S. public will lose interest in NATO and refuse to underwrite it. This would undermine the influential position Britain has assiduously cultivated over the years. NATO is the forum through which Britain has demonstrated its loyalty to the Atlantic Alliance and has exercised its role as first lieutenant.

The British government determined, therefore, not only to work within NATO but to oppose any European defense proposals which might threaten to undermine it. At the NATO summit in Rome in November 1991, Britain firmly placed itself on the side of the United States in asserting that any European defense efforts would strengthen rather than undermine NATO. The prime minister reassured the American president that Britain would not support the creation of a European army subordinate to the European Council.[37]

The British government was determined that NATO would play a crucial role in the post–Cold War settlement. The constant refrain from the Ministry of Defence was that it was premature to relax, that there were many possible outcomes to events in the Soviet Union, "not all of them comfortable," and that therefore a strong defense was needed as an insurance policy. The August 1991 coup in the Soviet Union won more adherents to this particular argument. In spite of the many radical changes in the strategic context of post–Cold War Europe, the British attitude toward NATO remained fundamentally the same as it had been throughout the Cold War period: NATO ensured Britain's position in the west and defended against threats from the east.

WEU

Britain chose the WEU to be the mechanism for building up the European defense pillar. And Britain rejected the notion of a new Western European Treaty Organization (WETO) out of fear that it would be dominated by the Germans, would be provocative to the Soviets, and might drive the United States out of Europe. Instead, the British Foreign Office rediscovered the Western European Union.[38]

Foreign Secretary Hurd repeatedly stated that the WEU was the obvious instrument to serve as the "bridge" between NATO and the EC and to give an impetus to Europe to take a greater share in its own defense. Hurd argued that there was a strong legal basis for this role in the modified Brussels Treaty of 1954, and that the WEU had the flexibility to take on the challenge. The fact that the WEU membership differed from that of the EC was a definite advantage from a British perspective in that it facilitated keeping both organizations separate and excluded the three EC members with the most awkward defense postures: Ireland, Greece, and Denmark. Not everyone was as sanguine as the foreign secretary about the prospects for yet another revitalization of the WEU. The metaphor repeatedly invoked by officials to describe the WEU was that of a sleeping beauty who keeps being kissed by a handsome prince but never quite manages to wake up.

It is quite clear that the relatively unknown WEU was seized upon by British officials as a tool for the pursuit of their policies. One senior Ministry of Defence official emerged from a conversation with the secretary of state for defense as late as November 1989 saying: "We've been talking about the WEU, it's a rum old thing, we must find out more about it." Another defense official argued: "If the WEU didn't exist it would have been necessary to invent it. There were other possibilities, such as the EuroGroup, but that was ruled out early on because of the French." Neither neorealists nor institutionalists are very good at telling us why a state will choose a particular institution. It is clear that in this case, as the realists would suggest, Britain chose the WEU as an instrument of its policy, but it is also clear that the existence of a number of institutions constrained the options and that the nature of those institutions influenced the operation of the policy.

The 1991 defense white paper was very clear on the importance attached by Britain to the WEU:

> To thrive, NATO needs a strong European pillar. In building this we see a central role for the WEU, which has been a clear existing defence commitment binding its members together.
>
> In the British view the WEU can serve as a bridge between the transatlantic security and defence structures of NATO and the developing political and security policies of the Twelve . . . Building totally distinct Western European Defence entities, involving the eventual absorption of the WEU by the Twelve, would be disruptive of NATO. It would result in two classes of European state and erode the principle of equal security for all . . . Because there is already one neutral country within the Twelve, and others may join, a defence organization based on

the Twelve would need to set up its own separate defence structures. To follow this route would be to invite confusion and a less reliable defence than we have enjoyed over the last 40 years.[39]

Ministry of Defence and Foreign Office officials were quite happy to state explicitly what the white paper suggested implicitly—that British enthusiasm for the WEU as the defense arm of Europe was largely due to its determination to keep defense out of the hands of the EC Commission. In private, Ministry of Defence officials were less effusive about the WEU. As one official phrased it: "It is the NATO alliance and nothing more which gives us our security. WEU is just a talking shop." That said, the existence of the WEU gave Britain a weapon in its battle against the European Commission over a common defense policy. It was not, however, a cost-free weapon and entailed a price of its own. The price was supporting the development of a WEU role in European defense instead of increased European contributions to NATO.

While France seized on the EC to exert some control over events, Britain seized on the Gulf War to confirm all its worst suspicions about the EC. The war in the Gulf was the perfect opportunity for Britain to reaffirm its Cold War relationship with the United States. During the war Britain enthusiastically assumed its familiar role as loyal ally and junior partner to the United States. British traditionalists could not resist pointing out to their American allies that the war proved what they had been saying all along: that Germany could not be counted on, was not a loyal ally, and could never replace Britain as America's closest ally. British politicians, columnists, and editorial writers delighted in contrasting their own moral fortitude to the cowardice of their EC partners, who, in Alan Clark's memorable phrase, "took to their cellars."

British cabinet ministers were unanimous in insisting that the EC was not going to move in the direction of a common defense and security policy, and used the Gulf War to illustrate the point. The constant refrain of the foreign secretary was that the EC could not be "catapulted" into being a defense community.[40] At Maastricht the wording of the final treaty was such as to allow both the British and Italians, who had one defense proposal, and the French and Germans, who had a very different one, to claim success. At French insistence there will be a review of defense arrangements in 1996. At British insistence the treaty stipulates that these arrangements will be compatible with NATO.

There was a real difference between the public rhetoric and the private sentiments of British officials with respect to the WEU. Both neorealist and institutionalist interpretations converge in explaining the sudden British conversion to the WEU. Realists would point to the fact that Britain was quite happy with its place in the Cold War security structure. By participating in NATO, the United Kingdom cemented its close military ties with the United States and exercised a leadership role in the western alliance. Taking only its immediate interests into account, Britain would be perfectly happy with a continuation of NATO. However, as the British leadership sees it, the threat to NATO no longer comes simply from the Soviet Union but rather from a disintegrating Soviet empire, the American Congress, and European complacency. Britain therefore seized on the WEU to be the European pillar of NATO, that is, to be the mechanism for Europeans to assume a greater share of their own defense costs without undermining NATO. While this explanation is plausible as far as it goes, the same ends could have been achieved without the WEU, simply by arguing for greater coordination and expenditures among the Europeans in NATO. The WEU provided Britain with an opportunity to pursue its goal of supporting NATO, but in doing so it embroiled Britain far deeper in the debate on European defense than the leadership would have preferred.

Institutionalist analysis takes the explanation somewhat further. Britain essentially adopted an institutional strategy—support for the WEU—to defend an anti-institutionalist position—curtailment of the EC Commission. Whereas twenty years previously Britain might simply have said that British interests were served by the present structure, that NATO sufficed to defend European security, and that the EC had no business meddling in matters of defense, by 1990 Britain felt compelled to pose as a champion of the WEU, though of course of a very British variant of the WEU. This suggests an acceptance of the pervasiveness of international institutions as well as a recognition of the extent of their bearing on British foreign policy. The traditional argument that Britain could go it alone without its European counterparts, while occasionally heard on the fringes of the political parties, was no longer in the mainstream of political discourse. The culture of international institutions was so pervasive in the Europe of 1990 that to be considered a serious player, one had to be seen to work through at least some of them.

EC

The saga of British relations with the EC since 1957 has been told many times and does not need to be repeated here. Essentially it is a litany of missed opportunities. This was another. Whereas France used the occasion of German unification to extract concessions on monetary union from Germany and sought to use the EC to anchor Germany to the west, Britain demonstrated considerable reticence in exploiting the opportunities of EC membership. (Britain might, for example, have used the opportunity to wrest concessions on agriculture in return for acceding to the inevitable.)

The disputes, both within the Tory party and indeed within the Labour party, on the subject of the EC are well known, as is Britain's grudging membership in the organization. Each of the major parties in Britain had, at one time or another, split on the issue of the EC. All had failed to build a domestic consensus behind British membership. The consensus nevertheless began to emerge. The younger generation, spared the historical baggage of their parents and with unprecedented opportunities for European travel, possessed fewer reservations about EC membership. Much of the official and business world, by dint of the scale of their interactions with European counterparts, also came to take EC membership for granted.

Many of the reservations about membership were deep-seated and were openly debated within Tory ranks in the run-up to the Maastricht summit. Britain particularly objected to the supranational aspects of the EC as represented by the EC Commission. British officials in all ministries perceived themselves as permanently on the lookout for evidence of "creeping competence," as the extension of the jurisdiction of the Commission was termed. The fact that the president of the EC Commission was a French socialist did nothing to endear the body to British Tories. It should be pointed out, however, that when Roy Jenkins was president of the Commission, his own government sought to have him excluded from meetings of the newly formed European Council.

The EC was perceived by Prime Minister Thatcher and many of her colleagues as a threat to the sovereignty of the British Parliament. The sovereignty issue raised both practical and symbolic issues. On the one hand, it reflected a very real concern about the difficulty of exercising scrutiny over directly binding EC law. The absence of a written constitution made it very difficult for Britain to clarify the practical implications of the pooling, or cession, of sovereignty to Brussels. On the other hand, it also reflected a sense of the superiority of British parliamentary institutions as compared to those on the continent. Mrs. Thatcher never tired of invoking "seven hundred years of the British Parliament" in implicit contrast to the rather less glorious continental experience.

The concept of federalism, which carried such benign connotations to

German and American ears, soon became the *f*-word in the politics of the unitary United Kingdom. British insistence ensured that the word was dropped at Maastricht and replaced with the more anemic term "ever closer union." These views on federalism and parliamentary sovereignty were by no means peculiar to Thatcher. Her intransigence on Europe was undoubtedly one of the main reasons for her downfall. Nevertheless, her replacement was not the avowedly pro-Europe Michael Heseltine but rather her personal choice, John Major. Although Major eventually faced down the anti-Europe wing of his party on the eve of the Maastricht summit, he nonetheless shared many of their views.

Major, like Thatcher, was determined to ensure that the EC would not become a mechanism for introducing socialism into Britain "through the back door." At the end of the summit Major declared: "I would not accept a text that would allow the Community to adopt measures that would drive a coach and horses through the trade union reforms we have won over the last decade."[41] In what can only be described as a latter-day equivalent of the infamous *Times* headline which read "Channel Storms, Continent Isolated," the eleven other members of the EC "opted out" of the social charter.

In spite of these many reservations, the inexorable pull on British policy exercised by the EC can be seen in a number of areas. One was articulated in 1962 by Harold Macmillan. He wrote: "If we remain outside the European Community, it seems to me inevitable that the realities of power would compel our American friends to attach increasing weight to the views and interests of the Community, and to pay less attention to our own. We would find the United States and the Community concerting policy together on major issues, with much less incentive than now to secure our agreement or even consult our opinion. To lose influence both in Europe and Washington, as this must mean, would seriously undermine our international position."[42] Macmillan feared that if Britain remained outside the EC, Britain's global position would be undermined. This same argument was used again and again by advocates of closer British integration with Europe. They also argued that by not signing the Treaty of Rome in 1957, Britain lost the opportunity to influence the evolution of the Community, and that by failing to participate fully in the EC in the 1980s, Britain was continuing and compounding the earlier error.

A related argument was the fear expressed by advocates of closer integration that if Britain failed to play a full role in the EC, it would be marginalized, relegated to second-class status in Europe, for the process of integration would proceed whether or not Britain participated. This was the point made with a rare and devastating display of passion by Geoffrey Howe in his speech resigning from Thatcher's cabinet in November 1990.[43] Helmut Schmidt made a similar point when he reminded the Oxbridge-trained classicists of their Seneca: "Ducunt volentem fata, nolentem trahunt."[44]

This desire not to be left behind was a powerful incentive for Britain to reach agreement with its EC partners at Maastricht. While Britain did successfully dilute the overall arrangement and managed an opt-out clause for itself on monetary union, it was widely perceived that Britain would eventually have no option but to go along with monetary union. As the institutionalists would argue, the EC seriously constrained the options open to Britain.

The traumatic events of 1989–90 did not, therefore, succeed in transforming the British attitude toward the EC. Indeed, the Gulf War may actually have further strengthened these attitudes. The experience of the Exchange Rate Mechanism (ERM), however, suggests the inexorable pull of economic forces which are likely to draw Britain, albeit reluctantly, closer to the EC. In the language of the institutionalists, the longer Britain remains a member of the EC, the greater the opportunity costs of not coordinating policy compared to the costs in diminished sovereignty as a result of complying with binding agreements. The option of pulling out of the EC altogether has become unthinkable.

There were, of course, any number of other institutions to which Britain belonged, but these did not loom large in Britain's strategy of adjusting to the end of the Cold War. For example, Britain had little faith in the prospect that the Conference on Security and Cooperation in Europe (CSCE), the only pan-European security organization, would be in a position to provide a security guarantee. Nor, given the unwieldiness of the organization and the commensurate difficulty of exercising influence within it, was there much interest in investing in the organization. Britain was happy to tolerate the CSCE as an inoffensive and largely ineffectual body and to go along with the plans announced at the November summit in Paris to strengthen it, but was unwilling to invest any great energy, or any great hope, in the organization.

There was little official discussion in Britain about creating new European security institutions in Europe. (Academics, of course, engaged in these discussions all the time.) Any new organization would have to meet at least four objectives: anchor a united Germany to Europe; engage both the United States and the former USSR; prevent isolationism and contain nationalism in eastern Europe; and meet eastern concerns about a united Germany. At the end of 1991 NATO, augmented by a revitalized WEU, was the institution of choice for Britain to obtain these objectives.

Throughout this two-year period of extraordinary political change, Britain continued to conceive of security in entirely traditional terms. The overwhelming concern of British decision makers was with the scale of military power that might pose a threat to British national security. (It was even suggested that traditional thinking was so entrenched in Britain that it failed to make adjustments commensurate with the reduced threat it faced.) The British case suggests, as the classical realists would argue (and as British decision makers insist) that Britain calculates strategically. Although emphasis on economic ties and mutual interests arising from interdependence figure prominently in political rhetoric, decision makers clearly did not see such factors as playing a significant role in the definition of security or in the way the European system would affect the nature of the threat. Indeed, in Britain, unlike in other countries such as France, there was very little linkage between the economic and security debates. It is quite clear from the account I have given that Britain was primarily concerned with power and interest and defined threat in much the same way it has always done. This would appear to confirm neorealist predictions, as would Britain's attachment to NATO, which was clearly an effort to balance the threats arrayed against it.

Nevertheless, it is also clear from this account that institutions, and the structures and procedures of those institutions, affected British strategy. Institutions served as both capability and constraint. As capability, institutions such as NATO served to enhance British power and diplomatic influence, facilitated the coordination of defense policies, and created incentives for other states to cooperate in pursuing security goals shared by Britain. Institutions also constrained British national security policy by making demands on the disposition of forces and impeding the implementation of preferred policies. By defining the context of European discourse, they also drew Britain away from many of its more isolationist predilections. The EC acted as a very powerful constraint on many facets of British policy throughout this period. The fear of being marginalized by the ongoing process of European unification seriously constrained the options available to Britain. The ability of the EC to pull Britain reluctantly behind it was a striking feature of this period.

Of course, different institutions offered different constraints and capabilities; the precise nature of these depended on the nature of the institution itself and the interests of the member states. My account describes the manner in which, as institutionalists would predict, Britain chose institutions such as NATO and the WEU to fashion its response to the end of the Cold War. Britain, however, chose not to use the EC, which suggests that other factors (in this instance the intergovernmentalism of NATO and the supranationalism of the EC), largely unexplored by institutionalists, influence the choice of institutional forum. It is also clear from this account that the degree of enthusiasm for an institution correlates closely to the degree of influence exercised within it.

What we see in the British case is a policy of balancing through institutions, a fusion of institutionalist tactics and realist strategy. Britain used and modified existing institutions, as the institutionalists would predict, in order to balance against traditional threats, as the neorealists would predict. Institutions are not, therefore, as institutionalist analysis sometimes implies, always mechanisms for benign cooperation; rather, they can be used against other institutions (as in the British use of the WEU against the EC) and against other states, both inside and outside the institution.

II

Adjustment and Adaptation in Eastern Europe

Chapter 6

Integrating the Two Halves of Europe: Theories of Interests, Bargaining, and Institutions

Stephan Haggard

Marc A. Levy

Andrew Moravcsik

Kalypso Nicolaïdis

The chapters in Part I of this volume examined the strategies of the major powers in response to the political problems posed by the end of the Cold War, focusing particularly on the role of international institutions in shaping strategic calculations. The chapters that follow perform a complementary task. The theoretical concern is the same: ascertaining and explaining the extent to which, during the first two years of the post–Cold War era, the relationship between eastern and western Europe was mediated by international institutions, as distinct from underlying patterns of state preferences and power. The method, however, is different. Rather than examining the policies of individual governments, the authors of these chapters explore how governments collectively managed five specific issue areas in the emerging relations between eastern Europe and the major western powers: the liberalization of trade, the coordination of public financial flows, the regulation of direct foreign investment, the reduction of transborder pollution, and the provision of national security.

The Framework of Analysis

In each of the following chapters the authors set themselves two tasks, one descriptive and one analytical. The descriptive task consists of recording the bargaining process through which agreements in each issue area took place. The empirical material within each issue area is organized according to a four-stage bargaining sequence, which characterizes political responses to regional integration. Accordingly, each chapter provides empirical answers to four questions: What challenges were created by new patterns of interdependence? What strategies did states pursue to manage this interdependence? How did they reach intergovernmental bargains—both among western nations and between east and west—on issues of common concern? Finally, is compliance with these bargains stable, given the constraints of domestic politics?

Viewed together these questions constitute a temporal sequence that, we maintain, characterizes any process of international cooperation. First, states confront adjustment problems associated with existing or anticipated interdependence. This starting point marks our approach to cooperation as broadly functionalist, yet we do not assume that the existence of a common problem necessarily produces a cooperative outcome. Second, states develop strategies to manage those functional problems, which may include multilateral international cooperation but are certainly not limited to it; bilateralism and unilateral adjustment are also options. To the extent that these strategies do involve cooperation, a third stage ensues, a process of interstate negotiation, the outcomes of which must be explained through interests, power, and institutions. In the fourth and final stage, states face the political task of implementing and complying with the bargains through mutual policy adjustment.[1] By disaggregating the process of international cooperation into these four stages, we isolate intermediate or process variables that permit more precise prediction and evaluation of state behavior.

The analytical task performed by each of the authors is to identify puzzling outcomes worthy of scholarly debate and additional inquiry. Our objective is to ascertain the precise ways in which international institutions shaped state responses to the end of the Cold War in Europe. Were state strategies influenced by preexisting international institutions, or did they, while perhaps employing institutions as means, simply reflect underlying patterns of state preference and power?

In order to isolate the independent role of international institutions from other social and political factors, we organized our analysis of the cases around three competing analytical approaches. These three approaches are drawn from the institutionalist, liberal, and realist traditions. Institutionalists argue that international institutions can affect outcomes, within a context shaped by state power and preferences.[2] Pure liberals and pure realists, each for a very different reason, argue that variations in preexisting institutional circumstances contribute only in minor ways, if at all, to the pattern of collective outcomes. These three approaches are not in all cases mutually exclusive.[3] Moreover, devising clear tests is difficult given the variety of factors that affected east-west relations during the tumultuous 1989–1991 period. Nonetheless, they do suggest different emphases and hypotheses that help provide a common structure for the analysis of our five issue areas.[4]

In the institutionalist view, patterns of cooperation cannot be predicted from preferences alone because of the ubiquity of collective action problems: preferences may converge, but cooperation will not be forthcoming because of the problem of the free rider, the inefficiency of bargaining, or high levels of uncertainty as to the intentions of other states. The power structure is also a weak predictor of state action, since interests cannot be derived from power alone and because interstate relations are typically mediated by existing norms and institutional structures. Institutions reduce the transaction costs of bargaining, provide opportunities for linking issues, inform governments about their alternatives, and mitigate fears of uncoordinated or exploitive strategies by stabilizing expectations about future state behavior.[5] In this model international institutions do more than reflect patterns of interest and power; they help define cooperative solutions that might not otherwise emerge.

The second approach, derived primarily from the liberal tradition, focuses on the underlying convergence or divergence of state policy preferences, which in turn are traced to the interests of domestic groups and coalitions as shaped by patterns of interdependence.[6] Security threats stem from the aggressive goals of governments as much as from their power. Interest-based interstate bargaining, according to this view, determines collective outcomes; institutions tend to reflect rather than shape the underlying interests. Where the interests of influential private groups converge across countries, cooperation is relatively unproblematic; relative power becomes secondary, and the demand for international institutions creates its own supply. Where interests conflict, there tends to be lower demand for institutions, and they play a less important role. The interests of countries tend to clash when interdependence creates distributional conflict within societies. In such cases influential private groups may "capture" state policy for their particular purposes, as in the classic interest group explanation of trade protection. Liberals do not deny that international institutions may perform important and necessary functions, but they believe that the supply of international institutions is generally flexible and can be altered to fit new patterns of demand.

The third approach, derived primarily from realism, emphasizes the continuing role of state power. In this view state behavior is primarily influenced by the distribution of strategic capabilities and threats rather than the pattern of state preferences or international institutions.[7] Powerful countries generally seek to maintain a maximum degree of flexibility and autonomy and avoid situations that tie their hands; weak states, by contrast, are "regime takers." In 1989–1991, for example, the balance of bargaining power clearly favored the west European countries over their eastern European counterparts and, secondarily, large west European countries over their smaller western neighbors. Cooperative arrangements, including those undertaken through international institutions, should "reflect" this distribution of power. As with liberalism, this approach explains collective outcomes in terms of forces which are seen as more fundamental than international institutions, which often reflect such power but seldom counteract it.

Empirical Findings and Theoretical Evaluation

In this section we employ the four-stage descriptive model to structure a comparison of the process in each issue area. In each section the comparisons are analyzed according to the three approaches introduced in the previous section.

The Bargaining Space: Interdependence and Adjustment

In each issue area the political events of 1989–1991 either created new patterns of interdependence between eastern Europe and the west or created new political opportunities for managing preexisting patterns of interdependence.[8] This in turn defined a new "bargaining space" in which agreements between eastern Europe and the west could be reached.

Initially, in both east and west a number of broad interests converged in managing trade and financial, environmental, and military problems in a cooperative fashion; it is therefore difficult to isolate one causal factor as paramount. For east European governments, economic concerns were arguably most salient. Rapid transition to democratic capitalism demanded close association with the west in general, and with the European Community (EC) in particular. It was hoped that access to markets and finance would offset the high short-term costs associated with the transition to market-oriented policies and the collapse of the Soviet empire, providing a political as well as economic anchor for economic reform efforts. Nonetheless, the rapid shift in foreign policy away from the Soviet Union and toward the west initially created high uncertainty and great concern for security, which led to an interest in establishing a variety of political and economic linkages to counterbalance Soviet influence.

Among western governments there was initially a widespread perception that it was in the general ideological and politico-military interest of the west to assist the "dual transitions" to democracy and the market. Economic interests naturally came into play, particularly in Germany, which was clearly best positioned to exploit the economic opportunities of closer integration. But the major concern in 1989 appears to have been the strategic one of reducing the risks that would result from political and economic destabilization in eastern Europe. These included a need to balance uncertain Soviet behavior and to deter the massive migration that was widely expected to occur in the wake of political and economic collapse or the outbreak of new inter- or intrastate rivalries. For Germany in particular, the goal of ensuring Soviet acquiescence in reunification was apparently paramount.

Although this strategic motivation may have been important at the outset, perceptions of interests changed swiftly. The problems of the economic transition proved far more daunting than was originally thought, and necessarily entailed economic concessions on the part of western European countries and wrenching adjustments for the east European countries themselves. Moreover, once it became clear that fundamental changes within the Soviet Union prevented the restoration of a cohesive communist bloc, geopolitical motivations receded in significance. Finally, the specter of massive westward migration remained a concern and affected domestic politics, particularly in Germany. But here too, initial fears about the magnitude of the phenomenon soon appeared to have been exaggerated.

By late 1990 the interest of western states in facilitating a smooth transition in eastern Europe was increasingly guided by the *specific* national interest of individual countries in ensuring desirable economic transactions. Concern about securing trade and investment opportunities in the east and preventing economic collapse and westward migration varied greatly across western countries and issues, reflecting economic and domestic political interests. In general, Germany favored strong commitment, other continental countries somewhat weaker commitment, and the United Kingdom, United States, and Japan even weaker commitment.

Differences in national commitment to the reconstruction of eastern Europe can be traced through the various issue areas (Table 6.1). In trade policy the core bargaining took place over the terms of liberalization: in which sectors and at what rate would east-west trade be liberalized? The eastern countries shared an interest in rapid liberalization across all sectors in their western markets, displaying a remarkable commitment to liberalize their own markets in return. Western governments, by contrast, faced stiff resistance from sheltered sectors in which the east had a potential competitive advantage, including steel, agriculture, and textiles. The policy coordination problem facing western countries has been compounded by the distribution of import pressure and export opportunities, with the import pressure primarily directed against the traditional industrial and agricultural sectors of France and southern Europe, while the export opportunities are enjoyed disproportionately by the German capital and consumer goods sectors.

In the area of public aid two issues were preeminent: how much aid to give

Table 6.1. Bargaining Dynamics in Post–Cold War Europe

Issue Area	Central Bargain	Important Conflicts
Trade	Mutual reduction of trade barriers	Protected sectors in western vs. eastern governments
Aid	Western aid in exchange for eastern adjustments	Fast vs. slow advocates in east; different levels of commitment in the west
Investment	Western investment in exchange for stable property rights	No serious conflicts of interest
Environment	Western aid in exchange for environmental protection	No serious conflicts of interest
Security	Mutual commitment to respect national integrity, respond to regional violence	Eastern advocates of NATO membership vs. eastern and western proponents of eastern neutrality

and what political and economic conditions to impose. The level of aid depended primarily on the level of western commitment, while conditionality had to be negotiated between east and west. In the west, different trade and investment linkages, as well as different political interests, resulted in a varying commitment to aid. Germany was inclined to be generous, others more selective. There was general agreement in the west on the imposition of political and economic conditionality: recipients were required to maintain democratic institutions and adopt the structural adjustment programs of the International Monetary Fund (IMF) and World Bank. Initially this did not appear to constitute an area of east-west conflict either, since the interest in the eastern European countries in advancing toward market-oriented economies appeared nearly universal. As the true costs of the transition become clear, compliance with external conditionality became more problematic, and economic policy became an increasingly divisive issue.

In two areas, investment and the environment, interests converged to an even greater extent. East European elites were united behind the goal of harmonizing environmental regulations with western standards and complying with international environmental norms that their communist predecessors had openly flouted. Western countries were willing to fund specific cleanup projects as well as broader efforts to increase policy-making capacity. In terms of investment, western firms were, in principle, interested; east European governments wanted to encourage investment by establishing the legal and economic framework that would make investment attractive. The key constraint on cooperation in both issue areas was thus domestic rather than international: the extent to which the eastern European countries themselves were capable of taking the actions required to cooperate.

The central military security bargain in Europe was not disputed: both the west and the former members of the Warsaw Treaty Organization accepted the mutual commitment to respect existing borders and to respond collectively to the threat of regional violence. But as the Yugoslav civil war painfully demonstrated, there were key differences over the institutional form through which this cooperation could be achieved and severe limitations on the ability of existing institutions to respond. Once again, the major constraint was the weakness of the western commitment to intervention, far below what some east European countries would have preferred.

This brief review suggests that the bargaining space was initially shaped to some extent by strategic considerations and ideological solidarity, but more fundamentally by *domestic* constraints on economic adjustment and specific economic interests. The tendency among western countries to view relations with eastern Europe through the lens of their broader relations with the Soviet Union quickly faded. The main factors defining the bargaining space were the convergence or divergence of underlying social interests in interdependence, as best predicted by liberals. Within the west, all major governments favored broadly similar outcomes, but were willing to incur different levels of cost to attain them. In east Europe the willingness to comply with western norms, particularly EC norms, was greater than interstate agreements required—a stance (discussed in the next section) which we term *anticipatory adaptation*. In the area of environmental protection, eastern convergence to western norms appears to have been unexpectedly swift, paralleled by the broader embrace of liberal norms regarding trade and investment. It still remains to be seen, however, how these state interests were translated into institutional strategies, a topic to which we now turn.

Unilateral, Bilateral, or Multilateral Strategies?

In confronting functional problems within a political bargaining space, governments face a range of possible institutional strategies, which can be broadly stated as unilateralism, bilateralism, and multilateralism. In addition, they may choose to act through preexisting institutions or to create new ones. It is difficult to deduce institutional strategies from institutionalism, liberalism, or realism, but some general expectations can be established.[9]

Realists have traditionally been skeptical of international institutions, particularly multilateral ones. They expect states to prefer unilateralism or bilateralism, an approach realists term a strategy of *self-help*. Powerful states are particularly apt to pursue self-help strategies since they are capable of achieving security in this way. For liberals, in contrast, self-help strategies may simply reflect the unwillingness of rich states to aid weaker countries, which are therefore thrown back on their own resources.

Institutionalists advance two other, more specific predictions, namely, that multilateralism will dominate unilateralism and bilateralism when "issue density" is high, and when preexisting multilateral organizations exist.[10] The first prediction, concerning issue density, rests on the argument that multilateralism tends to entail lower transaction and information costs than bilateralism and unilateralism, particularly in areas of high issue density—a situation in which greater numbers of issues (or the most important issues) arise within the same policy space. The logic of this argument, which shares much with liberal accounts, is that "where issue density is high . . . one substantive objective may well impinge on another and regimes will achieve economies of scale, for instance in establishing negotiating procedures that are applicable to a variety of potential agreements within similar substantive areas of activity."[11] So underlying linkages among issues may lead multi-lateral organizations to form or expand.

A second institutionalist prediction is that existing international arrange-ments will occupy a privileged position in determining future patterns of cooperation. This bias in favor of the multilateral status quo stems from the presumption that costs of creating new institutions are high, measured in terms of time and resources expended on negotiation, institutional consolida-tion, and social adjustment.[12] The quickest and least expensive method of coping with a new and uncertain environment is to extend existing rules. The more complex and detailed the rules embodied in institutions, the stronger this effect should be. In this view bilateralism and unilateralism are default strategies in the face of failed attempts at cooperation in an underinstitution-alized environment.

Realists, liberals, and institutionalists agree in their prediction that the east European countries would support multilateral cooperation. Realists might see such cooperation as a defense against bilateral exploitation by more powerful western countries and the threat from the east. From the institution-alist perspective such institutions provide a means of reducing bargaining costs. Institutionalists might predict the maintenance of the Warsaw Pact institutions but a shift in their purposes.[13] Liberals would also view east-west institutions as means of integrating east European economies into the west, although as a result of the underlying convergence of their domestic institu-tions and norms toward the west. Liberals might also point out, however, that the political and economic situation varies widely among east European countries. To the extent that east European policies were converging with the west unilaterally, no new institutions would be needed.

What do the cases show? East European countries simultaneously pur-sued multilateral as well as bilateral strategies, a kind of all-fronts blitz aimed at building political as well as economic ties with the west. The multilateral strategy—essentially: join every western institution, leave every eastern one—had considerable symbolic importance (representing the political closure of the communist era), was consistent with a grand strategy of breaking all links with the former Soviet empire while balancing against continued uncertainty there, and promised to facilitate the domestic restructuring eastern elites favored by providing resources and assistance.

Neither was there any attempt to reform existing CMEA (Council for Mutual Economic Assistance) institutions, nor much attempt to create new eastern institutions.

Particularly striking—and most consistent with liberal theory—was the extent to which the countries of eastern Europe also moved beyond both multilateral *and* bilateral strategies to unilateral ones. We call this policy pattern *anticipatory adaptation:* a country's unilateral adoption of a set of norms associated with membership in an organization prior to its actually being accorded full status in that organization, or even receiving guarantees of entry. Although significant convergence took place without any international institutional link, the precise form, institutional and substantive, of the policies that are being adopted conformed closely with preexisting European Community norms. Chapters 7 and 10 in this volume, by Kalypso Nicolaïdis and Marc Levy, respectively, show this very clearly. In addition to the material support that international institutions offer to the east, therefore, one of the most important functions they have performed has been to transfer information and norms.[14] Institutions, particularly those of the European Community, are therefore as much instruments of cooptation and socialization as they are tools of regulation.

Since east European support for closer integration with the west was overdetermined, the fundamental constraints on the willingness to promote east-west institutional development were imposed by the west. In principle, the western governments have faced the same array of choices for managing new interdependencies as the east, namely, unilateral, bilateral, and multilateral strategies. Yet the willingness of western governments to adjust to the new situation by providing trading opportunities and aid to the east, as we have seen, was limited. The United States and Japan did relatively little. The policy of the EC, while on balance slightly more positive, was nonetheless fundamentally ambivalent, both promoting and blocking east-west political and economic integration.[15]

In trade policy the European Community did offer to negotiate "association agreements," which foresaw a transition to free trade in goods within ten years and progressive liberalization for services and factors of production, rather than "trade and cooperation agreements" of the kind commonly offered to less developed countries (LDCs). This implied a closer, multilaterally sanctioned relationship. Yet Brussels simultaneously opposed mention of future membership in the agreements. The eventual inclusion of such language represented a negotiating victory for eastern countries (aided by the European Parliament), although one limited to the symbolic language of the preambles.

On concrete trade issues negotiating victories were harder to come by. In the short term the willingness of the EC to contemplate rapid adjustment in sensitive sectors such as textiles, steel, and chemicals proved quite limited, at least in comparison with eastern Europeans' initial expectations. The treaties have exceptionally extensive safeguard provisions. Agriculture is excluded from the Community's commitment to move toward a free trade area. No attempt was made to further east European regional trade through a post–Cold War version of the Marshall Plan.[16] At least in the short run, then, the major effect of the preexisting multilateral institutions of the European Community was less to promote aggregate trade liberalization than to smooth out the differences among western countries.[17] In a bilateralist world, without the EC's Common Commercial Policy one would expect more protectionist trade agreements by France and more liberal ones by Germany. The joint EC policy preempted such bilateral trade strategies by west European states.

The most fundamental reason for the stability of preexisting EC arrangements in trade in the face of divergent interests is not simply the transaction costs of negotiating bilateral trade agreements, since the negotiation of association agreements was in any case an ad hoc process involving high coordination costs among the EC countries. A more plausible reason was the existence of a strong legal precedent whereby EC trade policy preempts member state policies in nearly all areas.[18] Yet it is important to remember that this legal precedent itself rests on the logic of linkage. Bilateral trade negotiations threaten the integrity of the Common Market *within* the EC. In areas where this linkage was not present, as in the provision of subsidized export finance, bilateralism reasserted itself. This suggests that underlying linkages between issues provide one reason for the stability of multilateral institutions in the face of new issues—a finding that supports the institutionalist argument about issue density.[19]

The aid offered by international institutions to east Europe seemed inadequate to the fragile new governments, as well as to some western critics. While the French and British governments may in principle have preferred multilateral aid strategies as a means of curbing German influence in the region, they were willing to dedicate few financial resources to the realization of this geopolitical aim. Accordingly, as Stephan Haggard and Andrew Moravcsik chronicle in Chapter 8, the European Bank for Reconstruction and Development (EBRD) was launched with much fanfare, but commitments of capital for the new bank represented a modest sum—no more than a pale reflection of the Marshall Plan. This was, to be sure, a multilateral strategy, but without strong financial support.

In contrast to trade policy, the case of aid (including debt relief) is one in which bilateralism has coexisted with multilateralism and is assuming increased importance. This finding calls into question the institutionalist presumption that multilateral institutions will arise in areas of high issue density. As the Uruguay Round suggests, multilateralism can be unwieldy and involve high negotiation costs as well. Bilateral solutions can often be negotiated and implemented more quickly than multilateral ones. Moreover, bilateralism has further advantages that go beyond the question of transaction costs. As both realists and liberals remind us, the rules associated with multilateralism may constitute a constraint rather than an advantage for more powerful states or states with a relatively greater interest in an issue area. Bilateralism affords governments the flexibility to tailor precise arrangements that exploit their particular advantages. States with less interest in an issue area may prefer "exit" from an institution over "voice" regarding the implementation of a policy in which they have little interest. The use of existing regional or multilateral international organizations or the formation of new ones thus emerges as only one possible component of any national strategy. Judging the influence of international institutions demands that we weigh the efficiency gains of multilateralism against the flexibility advantages of unilateral and bilateral options.

Public aid policy suggests that we need to specify institutionalist theories more precisely in order to predict under what conditions institutions will persist. In particular, it suggests two reasons why multilateral institutions may be stable in the face of changing external circumstances: the need to form a common front in negotiations with third parties and the efficient provision of certain technical or administrative functions. It is the ability to serve as a negotiating agent of western governments, to provide administrative and technical expertise, and to provide finance quickly that accounts for the importance of the Bretton Woods institutions in the first years of the transition. The IMF, World Bank, and EC, as well as the EBRD, played leading roles as sources of immediate finance and expertise, and as what Haggard and Moravcsik in Chapter 8 term "gatekeepers," coordinating the implementation of western economic conditionality. The need to respond quickly to events in eastern Europe gave an advantage to established multilateral organizations; and because of the high levels of expertise and coordination required to impose effective conditionality, none of these functions would have been easy to coordinate bilaterally.

Where such specific rationales for multilateralism were absent, the major western powers appeared to favor bilateral approaches. In foreign aid, both aid linked to environmental commitments and more traditional assistance, western countries continued to channel a substantial portion of total assistance bilaterally despite the existence of a coordinating mechanism through the Group of Twenty-Four (G-24). Much "aid" has taken the form of trade credits, designed not only to secure particularistic benefits but also to create longer-term commercial relationships. Similarly with reference to foreign direct investment, where codified international norms are weak, bilateral investment codes of conduct have played an important role, in large part because western firms place more faith in commitments backed up by their home governments than they do in multilateral agreements housed in weak institutions. In particular, the "pure" coordination of aid, heralded in the policy statements of the Commission of the European Communities, remained of secondary utility.[20] Much international coordination was carried out through ad hoc organizations such as the G-7 and G-24, which suggests that there was no "market failure" for which the reduction of uncertainty through explicit norms and procedures was an efficient solution. Moreover, new multilateral organizations, such as the EBRD and the EC PHARE (Poland/Hungary Aid for Restructuring Economies) program, were created at relatively little cost—posing a direct challenge to the logic of institutionalist theory.

On balance, these findings most strongly support liberal and institutionalist theory. In both east and west, the choice of a strategy of multilateralism through preexisting international institutions was in most cases circumscribed by the preferences of western governments—suggesting that institutionalist theories need to be set even more firmly in the context of the underlying structure of social interests.[21] A clear statement of the precise functions that an institution serves greatly strengthens the explanatory power of institutionalist theory.

In the east, preexisting multilateral institutions constrained state behavior primarily by creating a normative focal point for domestic adjustment efforts, often in advance of participation in existing organizations or western demands. Initially such adjustments were, to a great extent, in line with what these countries would have wanted to do regardless of international diktats, so they do not constitute strong evidence for the autonomous impact of international institutions; as we will argue, compliance became more problematic as the costs of a wholesale embrace of western norms became apparent.

In the west, preexisting multilateral institutions presented a decisive constraint on the behavior of western countries in those areas, such as trade, in which one or more of three conditions were fulfilled: (1) the issue in question was linked to another multilaterally regulated issue; (2) institutional officials acted as bargaining agents for states; or (3) institutions provided technical services, such as expertise or rapid finance. The first two factors dominated in trade policy; the latter two constituted the "gatekeeping" function in aid policy and contributed to environmental policy formulation as well, although in both areas widely divergent levels of commitment across western governments meant that bilateralism emerged as the dominant strategy, with centralized expertise fulfilling complementary functions. In the security area multilateral institutions offered forums for negotiation, but there is little evidence that they constrained state behavior in an essential way. Finally, in the area of investment, multilateral institutions were weak and unilateralism and bilateralism were from the start preferred solutions.

A first glance might have suggested that the areas in which bilateralism has been most evident are precisely those in which either international institutions are weak, as in the case of foreign direct investment, or bilateral strategies complement multilateral ones in key ways, as is the case with reference to foreign assistance. Yet, even when they should have been prominent, not all multilateral institutions persisted. Some international institutions proved highly durable, exerting a significant influence on many aspects of the post–Cold War settlement. The major European countries are bound by the decision-making structures and procedures of the EC, including its common commercial policy and, to a lesser extent, its implicit commitment to consider requests for membership on the part of "worthy" candidates. Similar arguments could be made for institutions such as GATT and the IMF, which provide unique functions of use to the western powers in managing the integration of the eastern European countries. In contrast, many issues, such as political conditionality, the future status of Germany, and the creation (as well as the operation) of the EBRD, were handled through new, ad hoc, or relatively non–rule-bound institutions, such as the G-7, the G-24, the Franco-German summit process, and the "two-plus-four" arrangement.

A more plausible explanation for the pattern therefore embeds institutionalist theory in noninstitutionalist approaches. It is the pattern of underlying interests *or* the provision of specific technical or management services, rather than the stability of multilateral institutions per se, that seems to account for the stability of EC institutions. Liberal and institutionalist approaches are the most important parts of the analysis. Nonetheless, realist theory helps us understand that institutions can reflect disparities of power and information as well as common interests and the institutional landscape. This is most obvious in the area of trade, where policy coordination necessarily reflects, in the first instance, the "domestic" compromises worked out within the Community, and enables the western European countries to act in a relatively concerted fashion against their weak eastern European interlocutors. Similarly, in the area of public aid, multilateral institutions such as the IMF served to impose western conditions on the east. As conditionality increased in political salience between 1989 and 1991, the conflicts between donors and aid recipients also increased.

International Bargaining

After examining the preferences and strategies of the major governments, each of the case studies looks at the process leading to the particular bargaining outcomes in its issue area. These outcomes include not only the substantive agreements reached but the roles assigned to international institutions in the area: their mandate, level of resources and authority, and rules and procedures for decision making. For clarity of presentation it is possible to distinguish between negotiations between the major western powers and the eastern European countries and negotiations among the western European countries about their stance vis-à-vis the east; on most issues, significantly, "east-east" cooperation has been limited.

Here realism is on its home ground. The most obvious starting point for analyzing east-west negotiations is the clear power differential between the two sides. First, considerations of grand strategy and power balancing were not eliminated by the disappearance of the Soviet empire. East Europe's quest for integration with the west, including not only the EC but the aborted efforts to enter NATO, can be seen as a counter to the continuing uncertainties associated with proximity first to the Soviet Union, then to the post-Soviet republics.

Second, the east European countries were impelled to seek close association with the west in the search for resources to overcome daunting economic problems. These adjustment problems included not only the uncharted task of forging market economies out of planned systems but also a series of conjunctural difficulties: continuing problems of external indebtedness, severe macroeconomic imbalances, and the pressing need to diversify economic ties away from a collapsing Soviet Union. These economic difficulties further weakened eastern bargaining power.

Third, the east European countries lacked the technical expertise to design their own strategies. Naively optimistic prognoses about a smooth transition to capitalism and imminent admission to the EC abounded. Whereas in the 1950s the west European states had been able—indeed, they were encouraged—to turn Marshall Plan aid to their own purposes, in the 1990s the east European countries found themselves in no position to do likewise.[22]

On this basis, realists would predict that, on balance, the eastern European countries would be "regime takers" in their negotiations with the west. Indeed, the cases show that the western European countries have not fundamentally modified existing institutions to accommodate the eastern European countries; rather, the expectation is that the east will adapt to existing norms. Yet if the exercise of power is conceived in terms of getting the east European countries to do what they would not do otherwise, the realist interpretation of the findings is flawed in several respects.

First, the epochal regime changes of 1989 and the phenomenon of anticipatory adaptation suggest that power is of less significance than the fundamental internal political changes in the eastern European countries themselves. This "convergence" explanation, most consistent with a liberal approach, stresses the willingness of the east European states to conform to western expectations quite apart from the exercise of influence. Although the weakness of the eastern European countries is manifest, the case studies provide substantial support for the claim that the domestic political changes in the eastern European countries themselves constituted a crucial explanation of their policy choices. Although the Romanian case is a reminder that these political changes have been far from uniform, they have in general installed governments that are ideologically, politically, and economically inclined toward the west. Ironically, anticipatory adaptation may have further contributed to eastern European bargaining weakness in that it effectively involves making concessions prior to securing any quid pro quo. Marc Levy in Chapter 10 finds, for example, that in negotiating new pan-European air pollution standards in 1991, east European governments steadfastly eschewed the logical tactic of linking their cooperation to financial assistance from the west. And in Chapter 7 Kalypso Nicolaïdis describes the radical tariff cuts undertaken by central European governments prior to entering trade negotiations with the EC. Changed preferences rather than power asymmetries are the most fundamental variable in explaining bargaining outcomes.

Second, the weight that realists give to power in determining bargaining outcomes once again overlooks the intervening role that international institutions play in structuring the precise terms of new bargains. Our studies find that the nature of this bargain reflects to a large extent the existence of international institutional norms, rules, and procedures that provide "templates" not only for the western response but also for essential aspects of eastern Europe's foreign policy.[23]

Third, the existing matrix of international rules does not necessarily imply that the costs of adjustment will be borne asymmetrically. To a surprising extent, existing institutions and rules imply obligations on the part of the west to provide certain public goods to the east, regardless of the short-term costs. Thus, once the eastern European countries sought membership in the universal international organizations, GATT, the IMF, and the World Bank, they became beneficiaries. Even in the area of trade with the EC, one of the most contentious areas, the long-standing practice of negotiating association agreements with potential members has constrained the EC's ability to design trade packages in response to pressures from national-level constituencies, or even from negatively affected members.

Of course, the extension of institutional rules to east European countries implies that western countries see some advantage in doing so. In areas where this was not so, as in certain aspects of the trade negotiations, multilateral institutions were not expanded. This would lead us to expect certain parallels between the west's stance toward eastern Europe after 1989 and the U.S. stance toward Europe in the early Cold War period. Western power must be balanced against the general western interest in maintaining the stability of eastern Europe, independent of its position in the global balance of power. In addition to ideological, economic, and political interests in advancing the cause of democracy, the western European powers rightly fear that economic and political collapse would have profound social consequences for Europe, including migration and, as the Yugoslav civil war has shown, the spread of civil violence—a set of concerns of special interest to Germany. In this sense the eastern European countries have a sort of countervailing bargaining leverage, though one that is not easy to manipulate and exploit. Rather than using superior power to extract concessions, the nature of "hegemony" was rather to provide public goods and assistance in the knowledge that a restructured international system was in the long-run interest of the hegemon even if it entailed certain short-term concessions.

As we have seen, however, this threat of collapse was less credible (or potentially costly) to the west in 1990 than to the United States in 1948. For the provision of public goods to take place, there must be a compelling danger. The result is that eastern bargaining power—if we are to call it that—was low. Aid flows reflected specific national interests rather than common interests. Realists might argue that it was the lack of a hegemon that limited aid flows, but the EC could have assumed that role had the political will existed. There is instead a more profound realist insight here, namely, that in the absence of a security threat, it is difficult to mobilize support for generous foreign aid or trade concessions.[24]

Domestic Politics and Sustainability

The completion of an international negotiation does not signal the end of the cooperation effort, for international bargains, as Robert Putnam has cogently argued, are embedded in a "two-level game."[25] The existence of domestic opposition to internationally negotiated outcomes may lead to "involuntary defection." Even where political leaders both east and west have expressed an interest in abiding by commitments to multilateral agreements, we must determine the extent to which they are—or will be—capable of compliance. In the chapters that follow, the authors address the possibility that the east European countries have negotiated agreements that are unsustainable domestically.

At the beginning of the political and economic transition, there was a widespread conviction, bordering on the euphoric, that the transition from planned economies dominated by communist parties to capitalist democracies would be relatively smooth, at least in the more advanced "northern tier" countries of Hungary, Poland, and Czechoslovakia. This expectation proved to be based on a profound naïveté across eastern Europe, as evidenced by the widespread belief in the imminence of EC membership. Our case studies repeatedly emphasize the domestic political and institutional difficulties of abiding by international norms, even where there are good intentions to do so. In the area of trade and aid the difficulties of implementing wide-ranging structural adjustment measures became increasingly apparent during the 1989–1991 period, giving rise to political forces that either rejected liberalization or called for more gradual social democratic alternatives. In the areas of the environment and investment, as we have already noted, similar difficulties arose because of the domestic political difficulties of developing an adequate policy environment.

This problem is related to the domestic foundations of the liberal multilateral order that has evolved in the west. The international norms of the present era are not analogous to the gold standard of the nineteenth century; rather, they embed a series of political compromises designed to protect the welfare state. These compromises were developed gradually—during the interwar years in some cases and during the postwar period in others.[26]

The liberal international order that the United States helped to construct in the postwar period had a key role itself in nurturing these social democratic experiments, as did more direct forms of assistance. It is certainly not impossible, as we have suggested, that a new period of broader western hegemony would contribute to the political as well as economic reconstruction and reintegration of the eastern European countries. But it is important to remember that liberal norms cannot necessarily be adopted off the shelf and applied successfully in any domestic context. The fragility of the experiment in rapid political and economic change, particularly in light of the harsh international financial environment, serves as a caveat concerning the stability of existing international bargains, but also a reminder of the need for western support.

Empirical Findings and Theoretical Implications

The case studies suggest that state strategies in the immediate aftermath of the events of 1989 were primarily defined in terms of specific national interests, which in turn reflected domestic political calculations of the effects of interdependence. Concrete economic interests and, secondarily, proximity to potentially disruptive flows of immigrants were better predictors of western commitment to institutionalized cooperation than idealism or security concerns. Strategies reflected a keen calculation of interest. Where underlying linkages, principal-agent problems, or institutional expertise existed, institutions were influential; elsewhere, bilateralism or unilateralism dominated. In bargaining, western countries were regime makers, eastern countries regime takers. To be sure, the outcome of distributional issues, such as membership in the EC, the content of trade agreements, or the level of public aid reflected power differentials, but more fundamental to the bargains was the convergence of interest between the two halves of Europe. Finally, east European compliance with western norms has been enforced by external bargains, but the future stability of those bargains remains uncertain.

The theoretical significance of these findings can best be summarized by returning to the three competing approaches. In the first instance, realist theory would point to the strategic interest in both east and west in avoiding the reconstitution of the Soviet bloc and in continuing to balance Soviet power. Yet the cases suggest that this concern was relatively insignificant in the actual bargains struck in these issue areas. The extent of linkage to security concerns was surprisingly weak. For example, if strategic concerns had been important, we might have expected a much more vigorous and rapid response with reference to trade, aid, and investment guarantees; in fact, developments followed an autonomous logic related to the dictates of those specific issue areas.

Realism also alerts us to the bargaining disparities across the two sides. Indeed, in all of our issue areas bargains were struck along the terms imposed by the west. But we have argued that power differentials proved somewhat less important than the evidence suggests. Western power was not fully exploited, and in any case the eastern European countries were independently willing to conform to western norms. The most compelling realist prediction concerned the relative weight of multilateral and bilateral strategies of adoption, and even here, much hinges on prior expectations. While the cases show that international institutions did in fact play a substantial and significant role in structuring patterns of integration in the post–Cold War period, it is also true that the major powers, but the eastern European countries as well, maintained bilateral options, and that these options reflected a concern with particularistic interests and the maintenance of strategic flexibility.

Institutionalism also provided some insights, yet as with realism, these needed qualification. The least surprising functions which international institutions bring to bear on the problems raised by the end of the Cold War are those relating to collective and interactive decision making. Institutions are used as forums in which to strike bargains and as sources of information about others' behavior and intentions. The very existence of western institutions with a mandate to integrate eastern Europe has meant that the events of 1989 were swiftly followed by the deepening or initiation of negotiations in each of their functional realms. Also, as bargaining forums, institutions serve to increase the visibility of noncooperative behavior and to diffuse resistance to agreement in isolated states. For instance, during the negotiation of the EC association agreements, France and Spain were pressured by the other member states into accepting concessions they might not otherwise have made.

The interactive functions are more clearly important in the area of public finance and debt, though it is necessary to specify them clearly. Despite loose coordination through the G-24, it is not so much the locus of bargaining that is important as the *monitoring* functions provided by the IMF and the World Bank. These are highly valued by western governments and private lenders, though in the future they could very well be viewed as an imposition from the perspective of the eastern European countries.

Why are interactive functions of less apparent significance in trade, foreign direct investment (FDI), and environment than they are for public finance and debt? The answer seems to lie in the degree of conflict of interest between east and west. Where interests are the most conflictual (as in trade liberalization), communication dilemmas may be less profound than has been thought. Conversely, where interests are more or less harmonious (as in environmental norms, as of this writing) bargaining forums are of lower priority because they have less to offer. Only in cases where interests are mixed, where there are strong imperatives to cooperate but equally strong incentives to shirk, are interactive functions high on governments' agendas. This is the case for the provision of public aid.

Yet on balance we find that these bargaining forum (or transaction cost-reducing) functions are of fairly low importance, in spite of the emphasis in the theoretical literature. We find that states create new institutions even where existing ones appear to suffice (for example, the EBRD), that the presence of efficient bargaining forums does not appreciably contribute to new bargains, and that, when institutions do help craft new bargains, these do not significantly override blocking domestic interests (for instance, trade). More generally, we find that international institutions are plagued with a certain dose of inertia which does not allow them to respond innovatively to new demands in a time of crisis.

We have argued that the most fundamental factor in each of our four stages—the definition of the bargaining space, the strategies nations adopt, the outcomes of international bargaining, and eventual compliance with the agreements—is the socioeconomic interests of national societies as reflected through political systems, an insight broadly in line with liberal approaches to international cooperation as we have defined them. This has notable implications for the study of cooperation. Realist and institutionalist approaches that emphasize the international level of analysis clearly need to be supplemented by analyses of the domestic interests that have driven foreign economic policies. In the eastern European cases, the most fundamental factor affecting national strategies was the collapse of communism and the embrace of democratic capitalism as an objective. This was the basic factor shaping decisions concerning cooperation, and the maintenance of that consensus will be crucial to guaranteeing the stability of the agreements reached.

None of the effects we observe constitute definitive "tests" of the three theoretical approaches; for some phenomena there is supporting evidence for more than one approach. Our analysis leads us to conclude that international institutions play a variety of influential roles, in some instances much more profound than the theoretical debate on institutions would lead one to expect, and in other instances surprisingly peripheral to state strategies and bargaining outcomes.

Where institutions had the most profound effect in integrating eastern and western Europe, they have done so by virtue of the underlying social and political norms and interests that they codified. Such an effect can be understood only with reference to institutionalist and liberal approaches. In the first instance, they served as focal points for policy-making in both the east and the west. When the new regimes of 1989–1991 looked westward to plot their return to global society, they faced a powerful array of norms embodied in international institutions and the practices of western governments. When western nations looked east, they were constrained by a variety of obligations embedded in the postwar international institutions they had created. These institutions—taken in the broadest sense—served as templates that guided policy choices in both east and west, and it is this process that we feel constitutes the primary role of international institutions in post–Cold War Europe. But whereas the functional role these institutions played can be understood only with reference to institutionalist theory, the content of the norms they embodied can be understood only in terms of liberal theory. The international institutions which provoked anticipatory adaptation in the east and serious cooperation in the west reflected the social and political consensus of western societies; institutions based on a different set of norms rooted in a different social consensus would have had different effects.

What empirical patterns do we observe which seem especially significant and worthy of further debate and scholarship? We have stressed in the foregoing analysis two particular findings that we think should be significant to a range of scholars.

First, the policy pattern in east Europe which we have called anticipatory adaptation deserves further consideration. We have offered a descriptive account centered on the magnetic pull of the European Community, and an explanation that favors domestic interests over interstate power differences. Yet we welcome alternative interpretations and competing explanations. It could be, for example, that we have exaggerated the pull of the EC, and that a more central force was the political struggles between competing factions in the east—between those favoring rapid liberalization and those favoring a more gradual approach.

The other empirical pattern clearly worthy of further analysis is the extent to which the understanding of institutionalized cooperation must be grounded in strong theories and close empirical observation of state preferences. We have described the west's cooperation with the east as having gone further than simple calculations of interest dictated, and argued that this can be explained by the obligations embedded in the international institutions created by the west. Yet we have also maintained that such institutional effects take place under particular limited conditions. It cannot be assumed, even in economic relations among developed western countries, that underlying preferences, whether over outcomes or strategies, converge. Often bilateralism or unilateralism may be an optimal strategy.

These cases suggest that patterns of cooperation between the two halves of Europe in 1989–1991 were above all determined by the degree and nature of the conflicts of interest between these countries. In turn, the leading cause of conflicting interests and, more important for explanatory purposes, of *variance* in the levels of such conflict does not lie in the bargaining process, as realists argue, or in the level of preexisting institutional public goods, as institutionalists maintain. Instead, it lies in domestic distributional conflicts and patterns of international interdependence. Without precise specification of the social preconditions for cooperation, grounded in a liberal theory of international relations, generalizations about the role of institutions are likely to be unreliable guides to the analysis of international politics.

Chapter 7

East European Trade in the Aftermath of 1989: Did International Institutions Matter?

Kalypso Nicolaïdis

The end of the Cold War spelled the promise of a new Europe. More immediately, it created a new bargaining space for relations between eastern Europe and the west.[1] This chapter examines the strategies of eastern and western European states in the field of trade in the aftermath of the 1989 revolutions. The aim is neither to evaluate these strategies nor to predict their evolution but rather to capture them "in the making" during the crucial transition period from 1989 to 1991. As with the other contributions to this volume, this chapter seeks to provide data on the perceptions and attitudes of decision makers at the time, with a conceptual focus on the role of international institutions and international political processes in shaping cooperative outcomes.[2] Thus, I will explore how actors sought to use, and were constrained by, international institutions in devising new trade relations between east and west. Given the role of the European Community (EC) as the main partner for the new eastern European governments, and the fact that Czechoslovakia, Hungary, and Poland were the first eastern countries to institutionalize their trade relations with the west, the chapter focuses mainly on the European Community and its relations with these three countries.

East-west trade relations in 1989–1991 speak to both the importance and the limits of institutions in a period of profound reshaping of the international system. On the one hand, international institutions have already played and are likely to continue to play a decisive role in the integration of eastern Europe into the international trading system. During the Cold War the participation of eastern European countries in GATT (General Agreement on Tariffs and Trade) and in negotiations with the EC had been made virtually impossible by the inherent incompatibility of planned economies with the liberal presumptions underlying the multilateral trading system. Moreover, the existence of an alternative regional trading organization, the Council of Mutual Economic Assistance (CMEA, or Comecon), prevented individual eastern European countries from pursuing bilateral relations with their western counterparts.

The political changes of 1989 alleviated both of these constraints, albeit more gradually with reference to the first than to the second. International institutions, in particular GATT and the EC, have served as the main locus for renewed trade negotiations between eastern European countries and the west, and arguably have helped western governments respond more rapidly to the initial changes in eastern Europe than they might otherwise have done. Indeed, the attractiveness of western institutions inherited from the Cold War has led eastern Europeans to engage in unilateral adaptation with regard both to their trade policies per se and to their domestic laws and regulations bearing on trade: anticipating future membership, east European countries sought to conform to the norms embodied in these institutions, irrespective of western demands to do so. This pattern of "anticipatory adaptation" can be observed in all of the issue areas examined in this volume, albeit to different degrees. By making western institutions the sole locus of trade cooperation and beacons for eastern Europe, the end of the Cold War has reinforced their influence but has also underscored the necessity for western states to strengthen their institutions in order to accommodate the eastern European demands.

On the other hand, however, the capacity of international institutions to affect trade bargains has been severely constrained by the traditional features of trade politics. In the aftermath of the 1989 revolutions, the decisive shift westward on the part of eastern European countries was met by a strong pledge of support on the part of the west, as both sides shared an overriding interest in strengthening the democratization process and ensuring these countries' successful transition to market economies. Yet the next two years exposed a sizable gap in the sense of urgency between the two sides.

For eastern governments, increased access to western European markets was seen as one of the most crucial ingredients for the viability of radical economic reforms. In the medium run, trade opportunities were to provide incentives for foreign direct investment (FDI) and to sustain production as domestic income fell. In the short run, the demands for market access were given greater urgency by the need to make up for the sudden collapse of trade with the Soviet Union in 1991, and to ease the pain of adjustment before the closing of a relatively short-lived "window of opportunity" when the citizens of these countries were prepared to bear the costs of radical opening to the west.

For the west, on the benefit side, eastern countries represented potentially valuable markets of consumers starved for western goods. In the short term, however, given the low absorption capacity of these countries, export opportunities appeared rather limited. On the cost side, trade concessions to the east needed to be weighed against existing or potential benefits granted to other trading partners, in particular developing countries. More generally, western countries were concerned that their new trade relations with eastern Europe should not jeopardize their preexisting agenda of completing the Uruguay Round, as well as of the EC's Single Market and the European Economic Space which was being set up at the same time by the EC and the European Free Trade Association (EFTA).[3] Yet, managing external fears of diversion was less of a constraint than dealing with domestic opposition. The conflictual nature of the "trade bargain" was heightened by the geographically and sectorally concentrated nature of eastern demands: the European Community was by far the main market for these countries, and producers in so-called sensitive sectors in Europe (agriculture, textiles, and steel) stood to lose most from the immediate granting of concessions to eastern Europeans. In part, alleviating resistance to market access on the part of western producers depended on the pace at which eastern European economies were to diversify away from these sensitive sectors. In the short run, however, negotiations conducted within international institutions on market access could mitigate but not override sectoral interests. Moreover, and to the disappointment of eastern Europeans, western states and institutions were either unable or unwilling to set up mechanisms such as those associated with the post–World War II Marshall Plan that would have eased the conversion away from intra-eastern trade.

The first section of this chapter, "Shifting to the West," examines the underlying motivations and ensuing strategies of eastern Europeans in 1989–1991. The section titled "Dealing with the West" then describes the western response and bargaining outcomes, with a focus on the European Community. In "Learning from the West" I move on to an examination of some of the lessons that can be drawn from the negotiation of the association agreements between the EC and the three central European countries. I conclude by drawing on the historical narrative to address some of the core questions posed by the institutionalist theoretical agenda.

Shifting to the West: Choice and Necessity

Strengthening economic ties to the west was obviously a core objective for the new governments in power in eastern Europe during the transition years of 1989 to 1991. In the short term this translated into immediate demands for financial and technical public assistance as well as public investment, to be implemented both bilaterally and through existing or new multilateral institutions such as the International Monetary Fund (IMF), the World Bank, the European Investment Bank (EIB), the European Bank for Reconstruction and Development (EBRD), and the EC PHARE (Poland/Hungary Aid for Restructuring Economies) program.

It was clear, however, that both the short-term viability of market-oriented economic reforms and long-term restructuring would ultimately depend on changes in the incentives and environment faced by domestic and foreign investors and producers. In this light, trade policy was to play a decisive role at three levels. For the long run, eastern European governments unequivocally subscribed to the liberal view that trade is the linchpin of political integration and thus the key to their reintegration into the "community of nations." This perspective translated not only into a long-term vision but also into an eagerness to participate as soon as possible in all realms of international trade cooperation. Second, trade liberalization was at the core of structural economic reform. Finally, eastern European governments faced a short-term crisis as a result of large-scale collapse of eastern trade with a devastating impact on their economies. In a nutshell, the trade goals and policies of eastern European countries in 1990–91 were both proactive and reactive, driven by an uneasy mix of grand long-term goals and very short-term measures spurred by urgency. Consistently, however, trade relations with the European Community were central at each of these three levels. Before examining each one in greater detail, let us turn to the trade situation in which eastern European countries found themselves in 1989.

The Legacy of the CMEA: Closing the Parenthesis

For the newly elected governments in the east there was no doubt that the postwar decades had constituted a parenthesis which had to be closed. The CMEA had been created in October 1949 as a supranational planning institution, setting the long-term basis for a "socialist division of labor" according to fixed allocation and transnational supply rules and procedures, based on the "coordination of national plans." Trade with non-CMEA members consisted of only residual production and was greatly impeded by the monopoly structure of foreign trade organizations and the central management of scarce foreign exchange. One result of the induced bias toward self-sufficiency was that the overall openness and extent of trade significantly decreased, even within the CMEA.[4] The other was a forced redirection of trade from west to east, in particular between eastern European countries and the Soviet Union. Hence, for instance, whereas in the prewar period Poland's imports from the Soviet Union had constituted less than 3 percent of its total imports and its exports to the Soviet Union less than 6 percent, by 1985 one third of Poland's trade was with the Soviet Union. Similarly, the Soviet Union accounted for only 5 to 10 percent of Czechoslovakia's trade in the prewar period but for more than two thirds by the mid-1980s (Table 7.1).

In addition to the features of the CMEA, western policies themselves contributed to such redirection of trade. After World War II, most western

Table 7.1. Share of CMEA in Total Trade of Member Countries, 1988

Countries	Exports (%)	Imports (%)
Bulgaria	80.8	73.8
Czechoslovakia	73.1	72.6
East Germany	60.9	62.0
Hungary	44.6	43.8
Poland	40.7	40.6
Romania	40.9	58.4
Soviet Union	48.9	54.1
Average for EE	60.4	61.9

Source: Economic Commission for Europe.

European countries introduced stringent quantitative restrictions against east European exports, and in 1972 the EC instituted a system of specific quantitative restrictions against state trading countries (countries where trade flows are controlled by the state), which further reduced trade with these countries. Despite existing differences in their respective trade policies, all CMEA countries were treated in roughly the same way. The Community's promise that such restrictions would be progressively eliminated was never fulfilled; the CMEA and the EC continued to dispute until the mid-1980s. Similarly, these countries either were not members of GATT, or, when they were (for example, Poland, Romania, Czechoslovakia, and Hungary), they did not benefit from most favored nation treatment.[5]

In the wake of the revolutions of 1989, one of the first decisions of east European governments was to scrap past patterns of cooperation. Accordingly, in January 1990 they voted unanimously to do away with the CMEA, and it was dissolved on June 28, 1991. The general feeling was that trying to reform the institution would be a waste of time. In the words of a Polish official: "We had been treating the CMEA as a bureaucratic institution in which we had to participate. But it didn't make economic sense." Analysts in the trade ministries usually concurred in viewing the trade patterns created by the CMEA as artificial deviations from those that would have been created by their "natural" comparative advantage. Prewar patterns of trade were foremost in their minds as evidence of such "natural" trading patterns and of the "abnormal" character of current ones: "closing the parenthesis" of the communist era meant reverting to prewar patterns of trade. In a 1991 econometric study, two Harvard economists provide a systematic forecast based on such assumptions, using as indicators of likely future patterns of trade both prewar figures and the performance of what are identified as "comparator" countries.[6] Table 7.2 combines figures on trade flows and these authors' prediction for the central European states.

It is clear that the trade relations of eastern Europe in the long term were bound to revert to the Eurocentric patterns of the prewar period. Indeed, after 1989 government officials in Czechoslovakia, Hungary, and Poland operated on the assumption that in the course of a few years they would be conducting about half of their trade with the EC. Already over the 1988–1990 period, Poland's exports to the EC had risen by 53 percent, Hungary's by 27 percent, and Czechoslovakia's by 22 percent; while Poland's imports from the EC increased by 59 percent, Hungary's 22 percent, and Czechoslovakia's 17

Table 7.2. Share of Imports as a Percentage of Total Imports for Czechoslovakia, Hungary, and Poland, 1928–Present

Country	1928[a]	1984	1989	1990	Predicted[a, b]
Czechoslovakia					
EC	55	23	15.3	31	55
United States	6	0.4	0.3	0.5	3
Soviet Union	1	40	45.5	40	10.2
Eastern Europe	17	17	16.6	20	9
Hungary					
EC	32	20	30.9	30	47
United States	3.6	2.3	1.6	2.4	3
Soviet Union	0.3	30	24.2	20	15
Eastern Europe	40	16.7	14.2	10	12
Poland					
EC	54	18	27.7	46	56
United States	13.9	1.6	1.7	2.3	5.4
Soviet Union	1	37	26.1	20	9
Eastern Europe	9	16	13.4	10	6

Source: IMF, *Direction of Trade Statistics Yearbook,* 1991.

a. Collins and Rodrick, 1991 (figures to the round number).

b. The predicted figures refer to what the authors call the post-transition phase, varying in length according to different scenarios.

percent. The figures are even higher when countries in the European Free Trade Association are included.

It must be noted, however, that de facto disintegration of the CMEA had started before 1989 in the context of détente. Indeed, as of the mid-1980s trade with the west had already begun to rise.[7] The institutional dismantling of CMEA procedures greatly accelerated an already existing trend, as Table 7.3 illustrates for Poland and Hungary.

To be sure, a distinction must be drawn between the sudden and almost total collapse of the CMEA as a formal institution on the one hand and sustained economic and trade ties among its member countries on the other. Underlying patterns of trade were likely, by necessity, to survive for an extended period of time despite the demise of the institutions that fostered them in the first place. The resilience of past patterns of cooperation stems from both supply and demand factors. On the supply side, more than four

Table 7.3. Shifts in Direction of Trade in Poland and Hungary, 1984–1990

Country	1984	1985	1986	1987	1988	1989	1990
Hungary							
Industrial countries							
Exports	28.7	27.9	29.4	33.3	37.2	40.4	49.5
Imports	33.1	37.1	36.3	39.5	41.4	46.4	51.2
Developing countries							
Exports	12.4	12.3	10.3	9.8	11.4	9.0	8.3
Imports	12.3	8.1	8.4	8.8	9.2	6.9	10.0
USSR/nie[a]							
Exports	38.6	42.2	42.7	40.8	35.0	32.0	24.3
Imports	37.5	38.5	39.4	36.6	35.5	29.5	26.0
Other CMEA							
Exports	20.3	17.7	17.5	16.1	16.4	15.7	13.6
Imports	16.7	16.3	15.9	15.0	15.9	14.8	10.5
Poland							
Industrial countries							
Exports	33.4	33.4	31.6	39.0	44.7	45.5	48.2
Imports	29.0	30.7	30.1	36.2	43.9	44.7	60.6
Developing countries							
Exports	9.3	9.6	11.5	9.3	9.7	8.4	9.4
Imports	7.4	7.5	10.2	9.0	8.2	8.5	7.3
USSR/nie							
Exports	36.9	31.2	30.0	27.1	32.1	31.9	27.4
Imports	44.9	37.7	36.3	32.0	34.5	33.3	21.9
Other CMEA							
Exports	15.7	14.5	13.2	12.2	13.5	13.0	15.1
Imports	16.0	14.5	14.1	13.2	13.5	13.5	10.1

Source: IMF, *Direction of Trade Statistics Yearbook,* 1991.

a. USSR/nie figures include non-European CMEA partners.

decades of division of labor among these countries had created production complementarities, and the fact that, albeit artificially, eastern European firms were used to dealing with one another meant that trade based on such complementarities would persist until installed capital was amortized. On the demand side, goods designed for eastern markets, such as machinery or consumer products, could never find buyers in the west. Even while engaging in swift conversion, eastern firms could not fit western consumption patterns overnight. Thus, notwithstanding short-term disruptions, intra-eastern trade relations were likely to continue playing a larger role than prewar patterns would have suggested.

The Collapse of CMEA Trade and the Limits of Intraregional Solutions
On January 1, 1991, the former CMEA partners switched to a dollar clearing system, which meant that imports from the Soviet Union, in particular oil, were to be paid for in hard currency at a nonsubsidized rate. As a result of the abolition of the CMEA, the introduction of hard currency payment, and the overall deterioration of the Soviet economy, trade between the Soviet Union and its former east European partners started to decline at the end of 1990 and collapsed abruptly in 1991. Exports to the Soviet Union plummeted as a result of its inability to pay in hard currency.[8] The markets of the former German Democratic Republic (GDR) collapsed at the same time as a result of its swift absorption into the western system. Combined with the abrupt rise in world prices of oil because of the Gulf War and increased competition from the west, the collapse of trade with the Soviet Union turned out to be a major and largely unforeseen shock for east European producers. Many companies whose sole outlet had traditionally been the Soviet market were unable to switch to alternative markets in such a short time and were forced to lay off a large proportion of their work force.[9]

Trade among the eastern European countries themselves was diversely affected by the dismantling of the CMEA. Trade between Poland, Romania, and Bulgaria virtually disappeared, while trade between the three central European countries was in great part restored by the end of 1991 after a temporary drop. According to the Central European Research Center, a Budapest-based economic institute, Czechoslovakia's exports to former Comecon countries fell by 24 percent in 1991, Hungary's by 26 percent, and Poland's by 10 percent. The crisis both provided the necessary momentum for reconsidering intraregional institutional cooperation and highlighted the limits of intraregional solutions.

In early 1991 the three central European governments agreed on the creation of an Organization for European Cooperation whose aim would be to exchange views on economic reform and to channel economic ideas. In March 1991 they issued a declaration in Vichegrad, committing to holding a yearly tripartite summit. (In the atmosphere of cooperation, Poland even proposed that Prague be the venue for these meetings.)[10] During this period they also envisaged the creation of a Payment Union along the lines of the

European Payment Union of the 1950s, which would eventually be integrated into the EC's European Monetary Union (EMU).[11] The short-term aim was clearly to avoid further collapse of trade among themselves. However, it also quickly became clear that engaging in such a venture would require the support of western governments. If the ultimate goal was to be integration into the EMU, the creation of an "ECU zone" in central Europe would require setting up a stabilization fund and standby credit on the part of the EC in order to back up currency stability within the zone. By the end of 1991 there was little prospect for such a mechanism.

The longer-term issue was whether the creation of a free trade area in central Europe should be envisaged, even if in practice it would resemble an eastern OECD more than it would the EC.[12] In this vein the major question for central European governments was what effect intraregional cooperation would have on prospects for cooperation with the EC. On the one hand, some thought that the way to integration within the EC could be hastened through preliminary subregional integration. A Czech official stated: "Our ability to cooperate on a regional scale can be a compelling argument for our ability to integrate with the EC. The more we are perceived as one region, the more positive the western response will be toward us. This is the reason—in addition to our higher level of development—that the west is more forth-coming toward us than toward Romania and Bulgaria."[13] Central European governments had been particularly sensitive to the lessons emerging from the negotiations between EFTA countries and the EC over the creation of a European Economic Space, whereby the strengthening of cooperation among EFTA countries had been a prerequisite to the negotiations. On the other hand, central Europeans were wary that their internal dealings would create a diversion from their dealings with the EC. As a Polish analyst remarked: "We still have the obsession that anything we do at the regional level will create barriers to integration with the EC."[14] In effect, intraregional coopera-tion projects were generally not envisaged independently from the broader, long-term strategy of integration in the EC.[15]

Integration through Trade: The Return to Europe

The policy goals of the new democratic eastern governments in the realm of trade must be analyzed against the structural backdrop of "natural" trade patterns and relative comparative advantage on the one hand and the fluctuation of market conditions on the other. The trade figures mentioned earlier for observed short-term trade patterns and long-term predictions do suggest that regardless of the specifics of western and eastern strategies and the efficiency of western institutions in accompanying this shift, the redirection of trade from east to west was unavoidable. Nevertheless, the policies adopted by eastern and western governments could certainly make a great difference in determining the pace of such a shift, as well as the distribution of costs and benefits between and within these countries. While such policy choices could fluctuate according to prevailing economic or political circumstances, there was a widely shared notion among eastern European policymakers of what their long-term objectives should be.

What eastern governments clearly consider an overriding long-term objective is to be able, as soon as possible, to become full-fledged participants in the international trading system and play by the "rules of the game." At the multilateral level all eastern European countries were, to varying degrees, associated with GATT by 1991 and sought to play a constructive role in the Uruguay Round negotiations. Most also applied for membership in the Organization for Economic Cooperation and Development (OECD).

However, the institutionalization of their political and economic relationships with the European Community was clearly their top priority. Central Europeans in particular did not doubt their "vocation" to be part of the Community. "Return to Europe" was the main slogan used by Czechoslovakia's civic forum in the first democratic election that country had held in more than forty years. As a Polish official put it: "People realize they will have to suffer, but they need at least to see a light at the end of the tunnel: that is the EC."[16] Spain, Greece, and Portugal, which all joined the EC in the early 1980s, were often cited as inspiring examples of countries with comparable levels of development whose transition to democracy had been sustained by prospective membership in the Community.

This Eurocentric attitude was not seen as contradictory to the necessity of American involvement in European affairs. Eastern Europeans had not had the luxury to forget that, when left to themselves, Europeans were more likely than not to enter into conflicts or at least competitive behavior. According to a Polish official: "The United States in a way is our closest ally, but it is difficult to state this officially for political reasons. The EC and the USSR, our core partners, each want us to distance ourselves from the United States for different and obvious reasons. Therefore, we coordinate very closely with the United States, but we are very careful about the institutional character of this cooperation."[17] At a time when east Europeans were engaged in an all-out diplomatic effort to accelerate their reinsertion into a global economy, an exclusive focus on the EC could well appear somewhat parochial: "Our commission for administrative reform argued against regionalism within Poland. In the long term, EC is regionalism too, isn't it?" asked a Polish official. Concretely, central Europeans were above all eager to help alleviate actual or potential tensions between the EC and the United States and "to play a central role in Euro-Atlantic relations," if necessary mediating any trade conflicts that emerged between the two.[18] Ultimately, however, the United States was only a marginal trade partner, and eastern governments were well aware of the requirements imposed by their own European ambitions. In particular, it was clear that their European vocation might lead them to take sides at the international level.[19]

In the course of 1990, with no opposing voice from anywhere in the political spectrum, all postcommunist eastern European governments promptly announced their willingness to join the European Community. To be sure, in early 1990 the central European states actively considered applying to EFTA (Hungary submitted a formal application), through which they would be able to apply for membership in the European Economic Space, which extends to EFTA countries the benefits of the Community's single market in goods, services, capital, and labor.[20] But as EFTA members decided one after the other to apply for full membership in the EC, this strategy started losing its appeal. "In the abstract we can ask ourselves which part of Europe we should associate ourselves with," commented a Czechoslovak diplomat. "In practice, the only option for us is to move as close as possible to the EC: it has by far the largest, closest, and most developed market available to us. Other existing groupings such as EFTA will disappear."[21]

These overall considerations were reinforced by a concern on the part of many eastern Europeans, especially in Poland and Czechoslovakia, about a potential resurgence of German hegemony in the region. The Czechoslovaks remembered with a mixture of pride and fear Bismarck's dictum that "who controls Prague controls Europe." To be sure, they could not but welcome a high degree of trade interaction with Germany, which absorbed a third of their trade with the EC. Yet they typically feared the prospect of replacing the former Soviet dependency with another. In this light, eastern Europeans and, even more, central Europeans argued that they preferred dealing with the Community as a whole to dealing with Germany alone and that speedy enlargement of the Community would contribute to the "containment" of Germany.[22]

Assessments of the desirable pace of accession to the EC varied among the three central European countries. Many Poles felt that they had "lost thirty years, and don't have time to go through years of lectures." Underlying this sense of urgency was the perception that short of a firm prospect of membership, the economic gap between east and west would widen rather than close. Yet there was also a feeling that "to be absorbed too quickly in the EC is to be deprived of our own development."[23] Czechoslovakia's approach was generally more cautious than Poland's: "We see this as a step-by-step development. We are not in a position to apply for membership now. Our economy is in such a state that we could not withstand competition."[24] Hungary shared Poland's eagerness but was less willing to give up autonomy as a price for accession. Developments in the former GDR in particular, which was the most advanced among CMEA countries and also benefited from an enormous amount of aid and investment from West Germany, were considered indicators of the desirability—or the lack thereof—of attaining membership quickly.

Eastern Europeans also often displayed a certain amount of ironic realism in assessing their position vis-à-vis the EC. A Polish official, deeply involved in the day-to-day technicalities of negotiating with the EC, remarked that "the Polish parliament is dominated by intellectuals who believe in words; and with great arrogance, they say: 'We are Europeans!'" Another recalled that "when Mazowiecki became prime minister he sent a trial balloon regarding EC application. We were positively astonished that the response was not negative! Could we, humble Poles, eventually be like France? Well at least we could be like Greece, with our shipping industry and our backward agriculture."[25] And yet another: "What can we offer besides good will and being a burden!" One Polish official summed it up thus: "Surely the EC doesn't like us in this shape, and they are right!"[26]

While for the long run the EC was to serve as a political and economic anchor with membership as a long-term goal, in the meantime it would serve as "partner in transition," helping its eastern neighbors get in shape. During 1990 and 1991 these countries' short-term priority was not negotiation to enter the EC but negotiation to strike a bargain with it through association agreements, guaranteeing short-term market access.

Rapidly obtaining increased market access in the west and in particular in the EC was the core objective of economic policymakers in post-1989 eastern Europe. As we will see, the bold and unconditional character of trade liberalization in these countries, combined with the collapse of intra-eastern trade, greatly accelerated the need to shift exports to the west in order to prevent a rapid collapse in domestic production. Moreover, in spite of the assistance and rescheduling engineered by the World Bank and the IMF, exports were crucial to servicing external debt.[27] In short, "trade not aid" was a slogan often heard in eastern Europe at that point.[28]

Also, market access in the west was seen as central in the context of the argument for structural efficiency: exports would allow imports of technology, which in turn would facilitate domestic investment. But the strategies of modernization through trade could be seen as a vicious circle: exports were necessary for increasing investment, but investment was necessary for competitive exports. This is why these countries first needed to exploit the remaining components of their rapidly eroding competitive advantage and were eager in the short run to obtain access for steel, textiles, footwear, or agricultural products as well as more generally to be able to increase their qualified labor-intensive exports. In the longer run, eastern Europeans looked forward to upgrading the value-added of their exports and to benefiting from the flow of ideas and people expected to ensue from the deepening of relations with the EC.

Most important, the perception in the east was that only the prospect of market access in the west could lure western investors. Indeed, in light of initial expectations, the level of foreign direct investment in response to initial domestic reform had been disappointing, owing to a combination of factors including continuing political uncertainties.[29] Trade concessions were a prerequisite to FDI. "Given our small internal market," said a Czechoslovak diplomat, "there will be no investment in our countries without good access to the EC market."[30] In turn, the ability to take advantage of access granted by western partners was seen as highly dependent on foreign investment. Henceforth, access concessions from the west would create a beneficial cycle in which exports and capital inflows would reinforce each other. (Bela Kadar, the Hungarian minister for international economic relations, calculated that FDI, which had reached close to $3 billion in Hungary by the end of 1991, produced half that amount annually in additional exports.) However, in the context of the overall transition to market economics, the immediate steps for trade policy reforms clearly needed to be taken unilaterally.

Modernization through Trade: Unilateral Liberalization

Undertaking trade commitments with the west could provide leverage for reform at home and, perhaps more important, given the foreseeable political instability in these countries, a means to "lock in" these reforms. The implementation of new trade policies in the east in 1990 and 1991 was above all, however, an exercise in unilateral liberalization. Trade liberalization was an integral part of economic reforms aimed at introducing market competition in the east through the liberalization of prices, elimination of subsidies, and privatization of state-owned industries. In this overall framework every eastern European government was committed to abolishing the structural impediments inherited from the CMEA years, eliminating import licenses, de-monopolizing trade, removing quantitative restrictions of all sorts, and introducing currency convertibility.

Such plans for "structural liberalization" were truly radical. The markets of CMEA member countries had not had to be protected through western-type tariffs and quotas: the CMEA's elaborate system of preestablished cross-border exchange of intermediary or final products had provided for an ironclad protection before 1989. Firms or individuals were simply not allowed to import outside the framework of the planning system. With the dismantling of their administrative measures, these countries abruptly found themselves with very low levels of protection in the form of tariffs or nontariff barriers, and more open and vulnerable than their western trading partners. Given the scarcity of budgetary resources available for export subsidies and the undeveloped state of their new legal and regulatory system, eastern producers could not count on western-style nontariff protection; and tariff policies had to be virtually reinvented as an integral part of the transition to market economies.

To be sure, eastern Europeans did face different international tariff commitments as legacies of their respective pre-1989 policies. Czechoslovakia had been a founding member of GATT. In 1990, 96 percent of its tariff rates were thus bound under GATT agreements and could not be raised unilaterally. In 1989 its average weighted protection of 5 percent was lower than that of the EC. But in effect, given that its trade had stayed under strict central control, Czechoslovakia's GATT membership had been frozen. As a Czechoslovak trade official summarized: "We never left GATT, but our activity in it was limited and to a great extent formal and insufficient. Under the communist regime, one of the areas in which we could show our active partnership in the GATT was tariffs: we were therefore giving away our already very low customs tariff protection. This was easy since tariffs played no role in determining our trade patterns!"[31] For its part, Hungary had become a member of GATT in 1973 and since then had progressively implemented a tariff policy. In 1990, 60 percent of its tariffs were bound. In

1989 Hungary was considered the most liberal of the central European countries, given both its advanced shift to tarification and the higher degree of internal liberalization prevailing in that country, which effectively enabled imports to penetrate its markets. In contrast, upon acceding to GATT in 1967, Poland had undertaken only quantitative import commitments (a 7 percent annual increase from GATT's contracting parties). As a result, most Polish tariffs were unbound in 1989. All eastern countries, however, faced the same situation in that trade policy decisions had to be made prior to negotiating or renegotiating their terms of membership in GATT (see note 39).

In this context most of the decisions faced by eastern trade officials early on had to do with the pace of unilateral liberalization. There was a great divergence of views as to the optimal pace for such liberalization both among and within eastern European countries. Initially trade analysts in the east and in the west engaged in complex debates over the question of optimal sequencing between trade policy and other dimensions of economic reform. In practice, however, the pace of trade liberalization depended on the overall policy choice between the "big bang" and the "gradual" approach to economic reforms.

Proponents of the first approach—the shock therapists—argued that the introduction of free trade would be the quickest way to introduce competition in their country, forcing a realignment of the domestic price structure to world prices and providing sharp incentives for increased competitiveness. Strong external pressure was seen as the most efficient means of forcing managers to change and industries to restructure. In this view, industries that could not restructure within a few years should not be helped to survive anyway.

Proponents of the second approach—the gradualists—argued that in their current state of competitiveness local firms would simply not be able to face the sudden introduction of foreign competition. In their view it was "easy" just to decide to open, but unfortunately they had no industry which could survive. The political consequences of the ensuing massive unemployment could be lethal to their still fragile political systems. This cautious attitude did not necessarily imply adopting differential tariff structures along the lines of the classic infant industry argument, since, in economies in which the price structure had been shaped by decades of central planning, seldom reflecting relative costs, distortions were present across the board. Hence, protection was to be not an end in itself but a means to reallocate resources, and a means of giving firms a breathing space while converting their production to the requirements of western standards. The strongest advocates of this second approach argued that trade policy needed to be thought of as part of a broader industrial policy.

In the early phase of liberalization, the "big bang" approach seemed to command intellectual hegemony throughout central Europe, but only in Poland did this carry over in its pure form to the field of trade. Indeed, Poland implemented by far the most radical program, opening its economy to foreign trade overnight on January 1, 1990. During 1990 it dropped its tariffs to one of the lowest levels in the world, reaching by early 1991 an average tariff protection of 4 percent. To be sure, in 1990 all three central European countries eliminated most of their import quotas and allowed their domestic firms to manage their trade deals directly. Full internal convertibility was introduced by the beginning of 1991. But Czechoslovakia and Hungary took a more gradual approach than Poland, keeping higher tariffs on imports that competed directly with local production.[32] While both countries introduced internal convertibility, companies still could not hold foreign exchange balances or borrow from foreign banks, and capital movement was strictly controlled. Notwithstanding these remaining constraints, radical structural liberalization measures were taken in both countries during the course of 1990–91.[33] Albeit more gradually, Bulgaria, Romania, and Albania followed in the footsteps of their central European neighbors.[34]

The initial impact of these early trade liberalization policies was mixed. Overall, most eastern European countries experienced a deterioration in their trade balance as a result of the rapidity of the opening to imports from the west and the concurrent loss of market in the east. Yet the early impact of structural adjustment in these countries also contributed to a sharp decrease in their capacity to absorb imports.[35] Thus, because of depressed demand at home and a decisive shift to western markets, Poland, and to a lesser degree Hungary, actually managed to achieve significant trade surpluses in 1990 (in a single year Poland accumulated a surplus of $3.5 billion, with exports growing by 11 percent and imports by 9 percent). By 1991, however, both Hungary and Poland showed a current account deficit. Czechoslovakia, by contrast, saw its trade position deteriorate initially, but managed to achieve a trade surplus in 1991 owing to a 25 percent drop in its imports. Figure 7.1 shows the evolution of the current account positions of these countries through 1991.

In this light, critics of the "big bang" approach to liberalization felt vindicated and argued that there had been overreaching in liberalization, and that "liberal" policymakers were disregarding structural problems.[36] In their

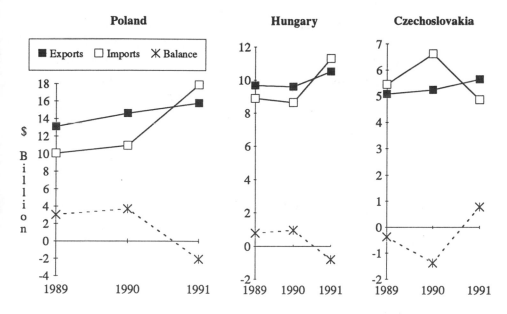

Figure 7.1. Balance of trade of the three central European countries, 1989–1991.
Source: IMF, *Direction of Trade Statistics* (August 1992).

view, initial trade successes were due in large part to exchange rate policies which undervalued local currencies in turn made possible by the implementation of very stringent anti-inflationary policies. Such policies, however, would not be sustainable and, most important, did not create the basis for long-term competitiveness. As a Polish analyst summed up: "How can we restructure our economy without growth? We can't expect the whole trade sector to decrease its costs by 70 percent in a couple of years!"[37]

Whatever the analytical merit of gradualist critics, the sociopolitical effects of trade liberalization quickly became apparent, leading in the fall of 1991 to the beginnings of a protectionist backlash in eastern and central Europe. In October 1991 major agricultural protests took place in Czechoslovakia against competition from cheap EC imports. Similarly, the October election campaign in Poland also featured increased calls for protection, and the new government elected in the fall of 1991 raised tariff levels back to an average of 14 percent, allegedly to protect Polish industries from "unfair competition" from western subsidized products. Foreign investors themselves sometimes became advocates for protection, in order to capture the rents from their early entry into eastern markets. In October 1991, for instance, Hungary raised its tariffs on television set imports to 25 percent in response to demands by foreign joint ventures. In addition, trade tensions were exacerbated by growing regional imbalances. Slovakia was hit particularly hard by the dual trade shock, since its production infrastructure inherited from the communist era was not prone to swift conversion. Its heavy industries were the principal suppliers in Czechoslovakia for the Soviet market and suffered disproportionately from the collapse of CMEA trade.[38]

In this context eastern European governments held a type of bargaining leverage which, though difficult to manipulate, constituted an incentive for the west to consider its demands seriously. The risk for the west in responding halfheartedly to eastern needs was not only the probability of increased protectionism in the east, but also an exacerbation of social and regional conflicts that could compromise the successful implementation of economic reform and lead to a major political crisis and possible reversals in the democratization process. By the end of 1991, however, it seemed that these fears had been overly pessimistic. While the populations of eastern Europe sporadically complained about economic hardship and growing unemployment, there had been no major unrest, and it appeared that expectations of mass migration had been widely exaggerated. Moreover, the spectacular growth of private initiative, in particular in services activities, granted hope for the future. Nevertheless, few ventured to make predictions regarding what remained a highly volatile situation.

The Eastern Demand for Trade Cooperation

In summary, eastern demands for trade cooperation with the west can be analyzed along two dimensions—policy objectives from the eastern viewpoint and policy options available to the west—each of which can be roughly divided into long-term, medium-term, and short-term categories. In Table 7.4 the vertical columns represent the objectives to be fulfilled by east-west cooperation from the east European perspective. In the long run, eastern European governments sought economic integration in the global economy through the development of trade. More immediately, trade with the west was seen as a key ingredient for the success of economic reform and structural adjustment, in particular through its effect on foreign investment. Finally, in the very short run, eastern European governments needed to cope with trade imbalances and the political and social crisis that might result from a further decline in domestic activity.

The horizontal terms represent the policy options available to western

Table 7.4. A Model of Trade Cooperation with Eastern Europe

Objectives for the East	Policy Options for the West		
	Institutional Membership	Granting of Market Access	Support for Intra-East Trade
Long-term economic integration with west	Long-term trade policy and regulatory adaptation	Integration through interdependence	EFTA model of accession
Domestic policies of structural adjustment	Long-term economic expectations	Foreign invest-ment; structural incentives	Resilience of trade patterns
Balance of payment and crisis management	Political signal	Short-term deficit and link to debt	Transitional markets

countries in order to respond to eastern needs. Institutionalized membership in global and regional institutions, especially the EC, was to be the ultimate source and measure of economic integration, in particular by providing a coherent framework for the lowering of trade barriers and the development of compatible laws at the domestic level. Such cooperation could also be indirectly beneficial with regard to shorter-term objectives as a signal of western commitment to domestic economic reform and western solidarity in the event of domestic upheaval. Ad hoc granting of market access was a means to long-term economic integration, a key ingredient in the restructuring of eastern economies, and a means of reducing the stringency of short-term domestic crises. The third policy option for the west was to set up mechanisms to sustain trade among eastern European countries as well as their trade with the Soviet Union. In the long term this could help foster the creation of a more coherent economic zone in central Europe, which in turn could facilitate integration with the European Community, as illustrated by the negotiations between the EC and EFTA over the creation of a European Economic Space. More immediately, sustaining intra-eastern trade could help ease the pain of economic conversion by providing transitional markets for one another's products.

Obviously these categories are interrelated, and action along one of these dimensions can reinforce or undermine the others. As policy dilemmas became sharper both in the west and in the east, tradeoffs became more apparent between types of cooperative options, such as between long-term commitment to institutional cooperation and short-term granting of market access and between the latter and supporting eastern European trading arrangements. Let us now explore how western countries assessed and acted upon these alternative options.

Dealing with the West: Long-Term Vision and Short-Term Caution

The western response to the eastern European set of needs and demands in the first two years of the postcommunist transition was at times greatly encouraging, at times greatly disappointing to eastern European countries. The encouragement came from the rapidity of the initial western response and implementation of short-term trade measures, the disappointment in the gap between initial promises and the capacity of western countries to carry them out. In providing long-term commitment over membership, granting market access to sensitive sectors, and addressing the collapse of CMEA trade, western governments were often perceived in the east as reactive at best, reluctant at worst, and sometimes even counterproductive. From the eastern viewpoint it seemed all that was required was political will and institutional adaptability. Indeed, the increased willingness of EC member states to stand up to trade lobbies after the August 1991 coup in Moscow speaks to a certain degree of responsiveness of western governments when the political implications of their trade policies became highly visible. On the whole, however, trade politics confirmed that political will and institutional adaptability do not always override the constraints of domestic politics.

Balancing Interests in the West

Up to 1990, eastern Europeans had either been kept outside of GATT or, when members, had been placed in a category often referred to as second-class citizenship.[39] Normalization of their relationship with GATT began in early 1990 when Poland submitted a formal request to renegotiate the terms of its accession protocol, asking that its original "entrance fee," a quantitative commitment, be replaced by conventional procedures of tariff negotiations. This was followed a year later by Hungary's request for a review of its own protocol, while in December 1991, Czechoslovakia was granted a waiver by the GATT Council under GATT Article 28 in order to restructure its tariff schedule. Romania, for its part, did not feel ready to put in place a new tariff structure and, by the end of 1991, had not yet formally initiated renegotiations under GATT. Overall, eastern European countries asked that their terms of participation in GATT be the same as those accorded to market economy countries.

Thus, in this transitional phase, in keeping with the new post–Cold War world and its own vow of universalism, GATT was faced with the task of formulating new policies toward countries which had only begun their process of economic transition. More specifically, GATT's institutional functions were twofold: to facilitate bargaining on trade restrictions and to provide the institutional locus for nondiscrimination through the granting of most favored nation (MFN) status. From the east European standpoint this tariff restructuring had two aims: to rationalize tariff structures according to actual needs for differential protection, and to adjust their tariffs to compensate for their rapid structural liberalization. By the end of 1991 Czechoslovakia, Hungary, and Poland had all restructured their overall tariff schedules, leading to average tariffs of 5.7 percent, 13 percent, and 14 percent, respectively. These changes, however, still needed to be formally adopted by GATT working groups.

As to the second function, eastern European countries sought to shift from observer status to full membership status within GATT or, when already members, from exceptional treatment to full most favored nation treatment. This was to depend in part on the pace at which eastern European countries were able to implement their privatization programs and to dismantle state subsidies. As for the issue of MFN treatment, the western countries seem to have had no integrated strategy for extending trade benefits to eastern Europeans. The United States first extended MFN treatment to Czechoslovakia, Hungary, and the Soviet Union, while the European Community took a separate approach. Western states usually did not seek to coordinate their approach to the trade status of eastern European countries even under the common umbrella of GATT. More generally, the early plans in 1990 to revamp GATT in the form of a new "multilateral trade organization" in part to accommodate membership of economies in transition were quickly abandoned. The GATT contracting parties were too busy overcoming trade conflicts among themselves and were not willing to draw resources away from the goal of completing the Uruguay Round (conducted under GATT between 1986 and 1992).

Another international economic organization, the OECD, played an important role during the transitional period. Unlike GATT, the OECD did not impose formally binding commitments on its members, and thus constituted a more flexible "learning environment" for devising means of integrating eastern Europeans into the rules and customs of western trade cooperation. In 1990 the OECD developed the "Partners in Transition" program and a new Center for Central Europe, with the aim of serving as a forum for discussion and for advising eastern European countries on their economic reform. Moreover, OECD members signaled their willingness to consider membership for the three central European countries by the mid-1990s, and, in view of that goal, the secretariat invited these countries to attend some of its general committee meetings. Thus, notwithstanding its limited influence on actual trade policies, the OECD served in part as an antechamber for eastern Europeans prior to their full-fledged participation in institutions such as GATT.

The western countries did acknowledge that they shared a long-term political interest in ensuring that eastern European governments establish sustainable democratic regimes in their countries and forestall regional conflicts. In the short term, however, eastern European markets offered relatively few gains. Their low absorptive capacity, foreign exchange shortages, and exchange rate policies severely limited their ability to import. In 1990 they still constituted only 4 percent of western trade. Moreover, short-term adjustment costs associated with increased imports from the east were concentrated in highly sensitive sectors in Europe (agriculture, textiles, and steel) that—notwithstanding the results of the Uruguay Round—had traditionally been strictly protected. In the long run, however, prosperous economies in eastern Europe would constitute a significant market of 110 million consumers for both capital and consumer goods from the west. Political affinity, geographic proximity, and historical ties ensured that the bulk of eastern European trade would increasingly be conducted with the European Community, which therefore stood to benefit or lose most from future developments.

That the bulk of responsibility in dealing with eastern Europe should be borne by the EC was signaled early on by the United States when it proposed to entrust the EC Commission with the task of channeling western aid to eastern Europe during the Paris summit in July 1989, and later in its acquiescence to the creation and structure of the EBRD. Given the 1 percent average share of the American market for eastern European exports, there was little at stake in the trade relationship between the United States and eastern Europe except in a few concentrated markets such as textiles. But misgivings were not absent from the United States government's stance during this period. It resented the fact that the GATT-based restructuring of eastern European tariffs would be followed by selective reduction in favor of the EC and consistently insisted that any EC–eastern European deal be in conformity with GATT, including in agriculture. In September 1991 President George Bush even launched a "trade enhancement initiative" toward eastern and central European countries. Nevertheless, there was no question that institutionalization of trade relations was to occur through the European Community.[40]

The interests of individual EC member states were not necessarily convergent as they sought to maximize their relative influence in the east or control the impact of post–Cold War developments on internal EC dynamics. France was most explicit in expressing its reservations toward prospective eastern European membership in the Community for fear of seeing the center of gravity of Europe move toward a German hinterland.[41] Under the protective shadow of the French veto, supportive attitudes of other EC members were not without ambivalence. The United Kingdom was suspected by its EC partners of supporting speedy widening for motives that had more to do with dilution than with integration. Italy, while formally supporting ties channeled through the EC, actively pursued its own subregional strategy based on the Pentagonale grouping.[42] Germany, while still pursuing the most open and active policy with eastern Europe, hesitated in taking the lead in the Community's dealings with the eastern states at a time when its own reunification placed strains on internal EC policies.

This broad divergence in strategies was heightened by the geographically concentrated nature of eastern European trade. For the United Kingdom—as for the United States—its relatively scanty trade relations with eastern Europe made a free trade stance much easier. German producers stood to benefit disproportionately from increased European exports to the east.[43] Yet the Mediterranean member states, along with France, feared they had the most to lose in granting broad-ranging market access to eastern European products. France feared increased agricultural imports, Portugal was concerned with textiles, and Spain with the fate of its steel industry. Thus, it was unclear whether those countries that would stand to benefit most from tighter integration with the east would be able to persuade others that would be most hurt to enter into rapid liberalization.

The Immediate Response to the Revolutions in the East

Institutional relationships between the EC and eastern European countries in the field of trade had historically been completely determined by geopolitical considerations. In its efforts to counter the economic hegemony of the Soviet Union in eastern Europe, and to make the point that eastern European CMEA member countries had kept their sovereign rights, the EC had traditionally refused to recognize the CMEA's possession of external competence. This had meant that since the early 1970s, with the implementation of its new trade policy toward state trading countries, and following the expiry of most of the member states' individual trade agreements with eastern Europe by 1974, the EC had consistently demanded to be able to negotiate bilateral agreements with individual eastern European countries. In effect, the Soviet veto of bilateral relations had forced eastern European states to abstain from institutionalized relations with the EC (except for Romania, which had signed a limited agreement with the EC in 1980). By the early 1980s the EC and the CMEA had completely severed relations, with the resultant creation of major strains in the CMEA itself. Hungary, Poland, and Romania were keen on devising their individual "road to Brussels" but were strongly curtailed in their wishes by the Soviet Union, the German Democratic Republic, and Czechoslovakia.

In the wake of perestroika and the initial economic reform under eastern European communist regimes, the EC and the CMEA resumed relations, and the CMEA abandoned its demand to negotiate an agreement with the EC that would regulate substantive matters of trade and economic cooperation. A joint declaration of mutual recognition between the two organizations was signed in parallel with the launching of bilateral negotiations of trade agreements with individual CMEA countries.[44] Bilateral agreements were to eliminate the EC's specific and discriminatory trade restrictions and thus extend MFN treatment to eastern European countries. Following these developments, and in the footsteps of Romania, all eastern European countries expressed their readiness to establish official relations with the EC, even though they differed in the extent to which they were willing to open up. The first agreement on trade and cooperation was concluded with Hungary in September 1988.

The series of trade and cooperation agreements negotiated between the EC and eastern European countries up to the summer of 1990 were therefore merely the end point of a process initiated well before 1989.[45] In effect, however, the swift EC response to the events of 1989 rendered these agreements obsolete by turning their contractual obligations into autonomous measures on the part of the EC, which, in any case, went much further than the former. First, in order to improve access for eastern Europe in the short term, EC markets were immediately opened to "noncompetitive" eastern products, thereby implementing by January 1990 concessions which, in the agreements, had been scheduled to be spread over ten years. More important, the Community went beyond the granting of MFN treatment as negotiated in the agreements by also suspending a host of nondiscriminatory measures applied to eastern imports and including eastern European countries in its Generalized System of Preferences (GSP), a system for giving favorable trade terms to developing countries.[46]

Another set of immediate measures sought to take into account the negative effects of German unification on these countries' trade balances. In this vein the EC Commission filed in October 1990 for a two-year waiver (and possible renewal in 1992) from the GATT MFN clause regarding the transitional measures the EC planned to apply to trade between the former east Germany and its former partners in the CMEA trade bloc.[47] In order to avoid major dislocation effects, the EC decided to apply duty-free tariff quotas for imports to the maximum allowed in east German bilateral agreements, while final consumption of imports from the Comecon countries would be restricted to the former east German territory.[48]

This series of measures testifies to the rapidity of the western response in the immediate aftermath of the events of 1989, owing, to a great extent, to the role of international institutions in providing clear guidelines and available expertise. Partly as a result of these measures, and partly because of the need for eastern producers to find new outlets in the west in the face of the collapse of trade with the Soviet Union, the exports of central European countries to the EC rose by 30 to 60 percent between 1989 and 1991. Overall, the share of the central European countries' exports to the EC almost doubled between 1988 and 1991, while that to their former CMEA partners halved during the same period. By the end of 1991 the EC represented 54 and 44 percent of Poland's total imports and exports, 42 and 42 percent for Hungary, and 32 and 41 percent for Czechoslovakia (see Figure 7.2). In contrast, the share of extra-Community trade accounted for by the six eastern European

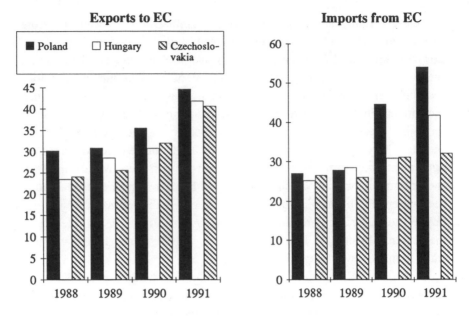

Figure 7.2. Central European trade with the EC (% of total trade), 1988–1991.
Source: IMF, Direction of Trade Statistics (August 1992).

countries rose from 4.5 percent in 1989 to 5.9 percent in 1990, with the three central European countries accounting for 2.6 percent.

But the initial set of measures adopted by the EC were obviously of a short-term nature. The EC's GSP was due for major reform in 1992 in order to bring it in line with the evolution of the global trade regime, making it likely that such preferential schemes would be phased into the more ambitious association agreements. In any case, the central European countries were not eager to have their GSP status extended indefinitely. They wanted full-blown association agreements that would return the autonomous concessions of the EC to a contractual basis. Feeling that they were already reciprocating through their own autonomous liberalization policies, they wanted to establish clearly the reciprocal character of their relationship with the EC.

The New Era: Negotiating Association Agreements with Central Europe
The dawn of a new era required new cooperative initiatives, while institutional connections had to be built from scratch.[49] The EC had traditionally

negotiated association agreements with its neighbors and was now negotiating the creation of a European Economic Space with the EFTA countries. Eastern European countries were the next candidates in line. There again, the preexisting standard operating procedures of the EC as an institution served as the focal point.[50]

In the spring of 1990 Poland issued a memorandum calling for new negotiations with the EC, and in August 1990 Czechoslovakia presented a memorandum to the EC Commission. On August 1, 1990, the Commission published a communication to the Parliament and the Council outlining objectives and requirements for future association agreements with eastern European countries, or so-called Europe agreements. The agreements' overall objective would be to encourage "close political relations which reflect shared values," in order to create a climate of stability favoring economic and political reform. These agreements would be broad-reaching, covering trade and investment as well as financial and cultural cooperation and the free movement of people and capital. They would implement asymmetric trade liberalization along with customs normalization, applying to trade in goods, agricultural products, and services. They would also help to pinpoint the priority areas for assistance and promote a more efficient system for information exchange between eastern European countries and the Community. These association agreements, however, would not provide formally for ultimate accession to the Community, unlike that with Turkey in 1963. To make up for nonmembership, political cooperation or political dialogue would also be institutionalized through the establishment of association councils.[51]

In light of their relatively more advanced economic and political situation, Czechoslovakia, Hungary, and Poland (sometimes referred to as the Troïka) were the first and only eastern European countries to engage in exploratory discussions with the EC. Nothing stood in the way of launching actual negotiations as these countries held free elections, established multiparty systems, and demonstrated their commitment to all other core principles of the Community, the rule of law, respect for human rights, and the introduction of market economies.[52] The negotiations were officially launched in November 1990 with Poland and Hungary and in December 1990 with Czechoslovakia. In contrast with their initial swift response, it had taken EC member states a year to provide the Commission with a clear mandate for negotiating with central Europe. In the following year a round of talks was held approximately every month.

The Free Trade Area: From Principled "Asymmetry" to Sectoral Bargaining

It quickly became evident that reaching agreement over the pace and scope of trade liberalization and the precise nature of the free trade area to be established between the EC and the Troïka would not be easy. Globally, the central Europeans demanded that asymmetry of concessions compensate asymmetry in competitiveness and, more fundamentally, that the structural asymmetry in the underlying risk associated with trade liberalization be taken into account. In any case, in light of their unilateral liberalization policies, central European negotiators argued, asymmetric concessions were not going to lead to great overall imbalances in actual access. In the words of a Polish official: "How can we give concessions to European lobbies when we have no protection to give away?" Indeed, in the spring of 1991 the Community found itself in the rather paradoxical situation of informally suggesting that its negotiation partners raise the tariffs they had so drastically lowered in their initial liberalization drive. A sharp decrease in the tariffs of the EC's partners—justifying in turn concessions by the EC—would be made easier by a preliminary upward leveling. Moreover, the asymmetry the central Europeans demanded was to be temporary, allowing for a transition period during which restructuring would take place.

The Community agreed to, and even promoted, the notion of asymmetry in principle but was not ready to apply it generously in practice. At the core of the tensions between the EC and central Europeans was the correspondence between those sectors in which the latter countries considered that they had the greatest comparative advantage and those for which liberalization was the most sensitive for the EC: agricultural products, textiles, and steel. These sensitive sectors represented roughly 35 percent of Polish exports, 30 percent of Czechoslovak exports, and 40 percent of Hungary's exports. At the same time, Czechoslovakia was the biggest exporter of steel to the Community. Nevertheless, "our arguments," explained a Czechoslovak official, "are based on the assumption that in most products we are not a great exporter to the Community, and in those where our relative share is big, it is still negligible in comparison with total EC production."[53] Moreover, even in nonsensitive sectors the EC wanted to retain certain restrictions.[54]

Early on, all sides agreed to the elimination of most tariffs within five years and agreed on a longer-term framework for "sensitive goods" while bargaining over actual schedules. The Poles were the most insistent that a free trade zone be implemented within five years. Yet, while eastern Europeans argued for immediate elimination of all quotas, the EC sought to maintain its quota restrictions for five years in textiles, steel, and building services. The EC also wanted to maintain price-fixing restrictions for unspecified periods in steel and agricultural products, while eastern Europeans sought a commitment to eliminate these restrictions within ten years.[55] The three central European countries wanted the EC to lift all textile import quotas within five years according to a strict timetable.[56] Under pressure from Portugal, where one job in three is in the textile industry, the Community argued that phasing out all the import quotas on textiles even in six years would set too liberal a standard for world trade negotiations concurrently going on under GATT. In this case the establishment of a linkage between various forums of trade liberalization served as an argument to forestall liberalization. Safeguards and antidumping rules constituted other contentious points, as eastern Europeans feared that these would constitute too easy a means for the EC to stop their exports in the event of devaluations or a slowdown in the pace of privatization.

In light of these disagreements, the central Europeans increasingly voiced their disappointment with the attitude of the EC. In the spring of 1991 the stalemate led the eastern Europeans to walk away from the negotiations. Andrzej Olechowski, the head of the Polish delegation, stated publicly that if sensitive sectors were not included in the agreements, his country would reconsider its participation altogether. This moment constituted a test for the bargaining power of eastern governments. The stalemate, widely advertised by the western media, exposed publicly that, as a Czechoslovak trade official remarked, "in the field of trade, the proclaimed political will of the west has not been translated into practical deeds."[57] As a result of the crisis, the Commission obtained a new mandate from member states to negotiate the progressive opening of markets in sensitive sectors to an extent that, according to Polish negotiators, had been "out of the question" before. Negotiations in the summer did not, however, make much progress. Only with the failed coup attempt in Moscow in August 1991 and the disarray that ensued in the Soviet Union did political leaders in western Europe express a newfound political concern for eastern Europe to overcome protectionist lobbies.

Soon after the August coup, the Commission, strongly backed by the Dutch presidency of the Community, put before a meeting of foreign ministers a draft proposal for accelerating the rapprochement with eastern Europe. Above all, national governments were called on to make greater trade concessions to bring to a speedier close the three association negotiations. In addition, the Commission proposed extending similar associate status to Bulgaria and Romania as well as opening trade talks with Albania and the three Baltic states.

But the Commission's proposal drew sharp criticism from several member countries, with Portugal, Ireland, and Belgium hiding behind France's most vocal opposition to a modest 10 percent increase in one meat import quota. At that point the French government was facing strong protests from domestic meat producers, in part because of a cyclical pattern in the meat market and in part because of earlier increases in meat imports from the east as a result of the post-1989 concessions. To those who pointed out the discrepancy between the triviality of the problem and the broader stakes involved, French negotiators called attention to the disproportionate marginal effects of what appeared to be a small concession and to the irrationality of adding to existing Community surpluses and thereby sending the wrong signals to eastern European farmers. Again, eastern European negotiators voiced their dismay. As a trade official said at the time: "This is absurd. Through exports we can help ourselves. We believe in free trade, and that is why we have opened our markets. But here at home our own farmers, even foreign investors, are pushing in the direction of protectionism and import substitution. The EC is providing a terrible example and this is a time when we are urged to go in the direction of the market. We need the EC to lower barriers now, not in four or five years' time."[58] Finally, at the September 30 European Council meeting, as a result of strong pressure from France's main EC partners, a compromise was reached, including the linkage between association agreements and triangular trade in the area of food aid.[59] Up to the close of the negotiations on November 16, 1991, individual countries in the EC resisted certain sectoral liberalization measures. At the last moment Spain was persuaded to give its approval to the elimination of quantitative restrictions on steel imports on the condition of strengthening safeguard measures in the event of disruption.

The three final agreements were officially signed on December 16, 1991, following the Maastricht summit. Before the signing, the parties also agreed on the desirability of speeding up the implementation of the trade part of the association agreement. This was legally possible, since external trade was under sole Community competence. The rest of the agreement, which concerned mixed competences of member states and the Commission, would have to be ratified by the parliament of each country concerned. Under this scenario the "interim agreement," consisting of the trade portion of the agreement and the appendixes containing the agreed-upon schedules of concessions, was to come into force on March 1, 1992, only a month after agreement had been reached on the last technical details of the appendixes. The agreement also contained an evolution clause that would allow the parties to renegotiate some of the terms within three years.

The terms of the framework association agreements differed little among the three central European states. The specific schedules of concessions did, however, vary significantly in terms of product mix and pace of liberalization. In particular, Hungary, which up to then had been considered by far the most liberal of the three, adopted the most cautious approach to liberalization. The country's twenty years of experience with tariff reduction had allegedly led its decision makers to conclude the necessity of a "gradual" approach to opening domestic markets.[60]

Central European negotiators pointed out that the final results differed little from the Commission's initial mandate.[61] But the EC, and in particular the Commission, noted that the results represented major victories over sectoral interests.[62] The principle of asymmetry was reflected mainly in the lengthier liberalization period granted to the eastern side, but from the viewpoint of the east, according to a Hungarian spokesman, "there shouldn't be too much made of 'asymmetry'; in ten years' time, both sides will be on an equal footing."[63] The agreement represented an important commitment to liberalization for all parties in the area of industrial products. Approximately 55 percent of Poland's industrial exports to the EC and 50 percent of Czechoslovakia's were liberalized on March 1, 1992.[64] For most sensitive products, the Community committed to decreasing its tariffs by 15, 15, and 10 percent a year for Poland, Czechoslovakia, and Hungary, respectively (while increasing its quotas by 20, 20, and 15 percent a year), reaching complete liberalization within five years.[65] On their side, the three central European countries would open their borders completely within seven to ten years. The Community agreed to complete tariff liberalization on textiles, but only within six years, and to a gradual elimination of quantitative restrictions during a period equal to half the period to be decided in the Uruguay Round, but no shorter than five years, starting in January 1993. The central Europeans, for their part, were to liberalize textile imports within ten years. Overriding Spain's resistance, quantitative restrictions applied to steel exports were to be abolished on the entry into force of the agreement, but customs duties were to be eliminated only by January 1997.

The results obtained in agriculture, though still far from meeting the wishes of the three central European partners, were seen as major concessions on the part of the EC. For the majority of agricultural exports to the EC, tariffs would decrease by 20 percent on a three-year basis and quotas would increase by 10 percent on a five-year basis (for Czechoslovakia the average import duty as a result of the agreement was to decrease from 36 percent to 23 percent). Obviously, the final impact of these bargaining results depended on the initial level of protection in the EC, which was often very high. On the whole, east Europeans would be able to sell more fruit, vegetables, pork, or game to the EC, while mainstream items such as cereals, beef, lamb, or dairy products would continue to be protected by the EC's Common Agricultural Policy.

Free movement of goods constituted but one element of the negotiations, along with free movement of capital, people, services, and the related issue of freedom of establishment for foreign firms. In these areas the agreement only created the basis for later liberalization. To start with, these items were not included in the interim agreement and would therefore not come into force before at least 1993. Also, although the EC had dropped its call for a review halfway through the ten-year transition period for trade in goods, it refused to do so in these other areas. The modalities for gradual liberalization of the movement of capital were left for later discussions within the association council. As for the free movement of services and people, their implementation was largely left to future discussions.

Free movement of services constituted a largely uncharted terrain for central European countries, and the negotiations did not leave enough time to explore the issue in a systematic manner. In the communist tradition services were not seen as playing an important role in the economy. First, at an ideological level, the emphasis on heavy industry and the production of capital goods had carried over to favoring tangible production over intangible production. Because Marxist economics perpetuated the Smithian notion of services as unproductive activities, services were not even included in the calculation of gross domestic product (GDP).[66] Second, at a structural level the planning process had endogenized many of the traditionally market-based service functions in the west (accounting, financial, insurance, legal, marketing, advertising, consulting), implying that the economic and legal underpinnings of these activities needed to be reconstituted from scratch in the transitional phase to a market economy.

This overall neglect of the role of services initially carried over into the negotiations with the EC. Gradually, however, eastern European negotiators realized the importance of issues that were connected not with trade in tangible products but with the two related issues of movement of services and movement of people. In May 1991 Poland stressed that no agreement would be satisfactory if it did not include the free movement of temporary workers providing services. One million Polish expatriates, mostly illegal, in western Europe played a large role in this Polish stance, which would lead to the legalization of employment. Overall, the demands of the east on free trade in construction and transportation services, where they held a comparative advantage (transport represents two thirds of Czechoslovak services exports), were met by EC requirements that service providers meet EC standards in these sectors as a condition for market access. By refusing to engage in the mutual recognition of regulations in this field, the Community signaled its lack of willingness to extend its liberal stand on goods to more sensitive matters touching on issues of migration.[67] In this light, the Community also insisted that "key personnel" allowed to enter its territory on temporary contracts should not include all those with "specific knowledge of equipment" but should be defined on the basis of the narrower criterion of knowledge of "research equipment." On the issue of the free movement of professionals, the Community also refused to consider mutual recognition of diplomas and qualifications. To be sure, the EC in turn was eager to gain liberal rights of establishment for its financial services firms. But although eastern negotiators welcomed prospects of foreign investment in all sectors, they were somewhat hesitant to accept total loss of control over their financial systems. Ultimately, however, they yielded to EC demands, which led some observers to comment that in the area of services, asymmetry had been ensured in favor of the Community.[68]

Sustaining Eastern Trade: Slow Awakenings

The implementation of a free trade area between central Europe and the EC obviously helped enhance the prospects for redirection of trade toward the west. In the short term, however, the incapacity of many firms in central Europe to adapt rapidly to western consumer demand, combined with the sudden collapse of the Soviet market, created a crisis in the east that could not immediately be addressed by market access concessions by the west. What were western governments to do in the face of the situation?

Admittedly, western governments could first and foremost abstain from making matters worse. Yet, in the early phase of the transition period, EC policies actually worsened eastern Europe's prospects for trade with the Soviet Union. In the fall of 1990 subsidized exports from the EC to the Soviet Union had the immediate effect of displacing traditional food imports from eastern Europe.[69] This move, blatantly ignoring their needs, infuriated many trade officials in eastern capitals. While the Community later sought to amend itself, the event impressed in their minds the propensity of their mighty neighbor to deviate from free market solutions when the interests of its farmers were at stake.

Beyond abstaining from such blatantly counterproductive policies, western governments were called upon directly to help sustain intra-eastern trade. Providing credit for trade between eastern European countries and the Soviet Union could have simultaneously alleviated pressures for access to the west's own markets, helped cushion the transition for eastern economies, and addressed the urgent needs of the Soviet Union. Viewed in this light, the west's failure to act effectively constituted an instance of great institutional inertia.

Even though they had not foreseen its magnitude, eastern governments had sought early on to cushion the shock by appealing for support in the west. In the spring of 1990 Jiri Dienstbier, the foreign minister of Czechoslovakia, had already proposed that western countries aid the Soviet Union by providing credit for imports from eastern Europe, in line with the approach of the Marshall Plan, which in the postwar period had contributed so successfully to sustaining trade among western European countries. During the first half of 1991 the three governments of central Europe agreed to make this demand their foremost priority in dealing with the west. In July they conveyed a joint message to this effect at the London summit of the Group of Seven (Canada, France, Germany, Italy, Japan, the United Kingdom, and the United States), as well as in bilateral talks with the EC. The demand was reiterated after the August coup in Moscow.

In the first half of 1991 the European Council of Ministers was sharply divided on the issue of triangular trade. While the United Kingdom and Italy strongly favored the idea, France was at first vehemently opposed, presumably for fear of foreclosing an important outlet for its agricultural surpluses. The crisis brought about by their isolated stance against meat imports the fall of 1991, however, persuaded French officials that triangular trade might actually provide *un moindre mal,* a lesser evil. France therefore not only accepted the linkage between triangular trade and market access issues but used it for tactical purposes, as an argument for limiting market access: the Soviet Union, French negotiators argued, had up to then been the natural outlet for meat production from the east, and this should continue to be the case. In October 1991, after having discarded this option for months, Pierre Bérégovoy, the French finance minister, went on record arguing that the west should consider special payment mechanisms to revive trade among countries of the former Soviet bloc, a statement received favorably in central European capitals.

The triangular trade deal crafted by the EC in the fall of 1991 constituted notable progress but appeared to have limited implications. EC food credits to the Soviet Union, which had originally been tied to purchases in western Europe, were allowed to be used for imports of food from eastern Europe.[70] But because of the inherent limitations of the deal, these credits could at best constitute marginal stimuli for reinitiating trade between eastern Europe and the Soviet Union. First of all, credits applied only to food aid and pharmaceutical exports: they were far from serving as a new type of Marshall Plan favoring a broad spectrum of eastern European industries. Second, the compound costs of credit, transportation, and distribution diminished the appeal to eastern exporters. Third and most important, the 25 and 50 percent share allocated to the east in each of the two financial instruments respectively represented only ceilings, mere "marketing gimmicks" in the view of some critics. Any actual use of such credits depended entirely on the capacity of eastern producers to sign contracts with Soviet importers, who in most cases were more interested in food deliveries from the west, seen as more reliable and of higher quality. By early 1992 no credit at all had yet been disbursed by the EC in support of intra-eastern trade. Not surprisingly perhaps, trade relations had slowly been reinitiated between, in particular, Poland, Hungary, and the Soviet Union under the familiar solution of barter deals.

In the east and in the west, analysts disagreed as to whether the short-term benefits of sustaining intra-eastern trade would not in the mid- to long term stifle the necessary conversion of these economies. In general, the desirability of such a strategy varied according to economic sectors and their pace of conversion. Nevertheless, even as consensus was reached that some degree of support for agricultural trade was desirable, the institutional solutions reached were far from achieving even this reduced objective.

Learning from the West: The Association Agreement

The negotiation of association agreements between the EC and central European countries should not be analyzed merely in terms of their most immediate effect, the reciprocal granting of market access. These negotiations also constituted a more subtle means of integrating the newly democratic countries into the "western world" through the socialization of its elites.[71] The negotiations also helped clarify the conditions and prospects for long-term membership in the Community and provided an institutional anchor for what I have described as a strategy of anticipatory adaptation on the part of eastern governments. Learning did not occur only in one direction. In the wake of the 1989 revolutions, the Community also was faced with an unprecedented challenge, and the 1990–91 negotiations with its eastern neighbors constituted a test for its adaptive capacity as well as a test of the capacity of the Commission to claim authority over external trade matters.

Learning by Negotiating

Polish, Czechoslovak, and Hungarian officials, many of whom had had little experience dealing with the west, underwent an accelerated learning process during their year-and-a-half-long negotiations with the EC. At first they believed that the west Europeans did not fully grasp their new reality. Eastern negotiators commented: "We are still treated as a state trading partner and a nonmarket economy. Witness the EC's antidumping policy toward us"; or "The Community is unfair to us; we are much more liberal than they pretend." Often, they also perceived a lack of belief that their reforms would be successful, a "wait-and-see attitude" on the part of the European Community. Most important, eastern negotiators learned to deal with the discrepancy between political deeds and economic realities in western Europe: "We initially came into these negotiations thinking it would be like with the World Bank or the IMF: working together to solve a common problem. Instead, we quickly found out that we were talking from two opposite sides of the table and that we were engaged in tough political bargaining." More precisely, they learned about the power of sectoral interests in western democracies, and the fact that "in the Community, there is not enough political will to counterbalance political lobbies." An EC official concurred: "At first, they thought that the Community was deeply committed to the peaceful evolution of eastern Europe; now they have come to realize that its core motivation is to protect its special interests. As they see it, the fate of their fragile democracies hangs in the balance against the fate of Irish potato growers!"[72]

An obvious problem early on was the lack of experts on the EC within central European countries as well as the gap in expertise on specific substantive areas. As one government expert put it: "Fifteen people in Czechoslovakia know about the EC." Compounding these problems was the fact that government structures were in constant flux, with responsibility scattered among a plethora of ministries.[73] This structural situation made it difficult in turn to develop coherent national strategies toward the EC, which meant, for instance, that negotiations were always conducted on the basis of proposals drafted by the Community. As a Polish negotiator recalled: "At first, we did not recognize the importance of leading the process and simply agreed to negotiate on the basis of EC drafts."[74] As the negotiations unfolded, however, central Europeans learned to adopt the give-and-take strategies prevalent in such undertakings. By the middle of the negotiations they were "learning to mobilize support for [our] position on a country-by-country basis and concentrate on places of resistance." Moreover, they sought to make the stakes of the negotiations clearer through more systematic cost-benefit assessments of alternative agreements. Thus, for instance, in order to strengthen their case in the early summer of 1991, the Polish delegation came to the negotiating table with a macroeconomic model, developed by Polish economists, forecasting the relative gains from the EC-Polish free trade agreement.[75] Whatever the accuracy of the projected results, such an initiative on the part of Poland reflected a definite evolution in negotiation tactics.

Negotiators from Czechoslovakia, Hungary, and Poland also learned the value of cooperating among themselves. During their negotiations with the EC, they had been in constant contact, helped by the existence of strong cross-national ties among their leaders that predated the revolutions. Yet each country also had a sense of being a special case. Hungary most strongly believed that it deserved special treatment, since it had been the first among the Troïka to engage in economic reform and, after 1989, to engage in formal talks with the EC. Czechoslovakia saw its special relationship with Germany as an important asset, as did Poland with regard to France. More generally, the uphill battle throughout the 1980s for establishing bilateral relationships with the EC independently of the CMEA had left strong memories. "The irony," commented a Czechoslovak official, "is that we share the same destiny, but we don't want to admit that we are in it together."[76] But in the course of the negotiations, the central Europeans came to realize that none of them was going to get special treatment. A Polish official commented: "This is not a beauty contest; why does Hungary always want to be first?" In fact, EC negotiators who were cognizant of these competitive dynamics made sure that any concession granted to one country would be extended to the two others, except with regard to the specific schedules of trade concessions drawn on the basis of asymmetric reciprocity. Although such equitable treatment brought obvious advantages for the three negotiating partners, it could at times be disadvantageous when a concession by the Community was deemed impossible because of the threat constituted by one of them. For example, the Community might have allowed freer movement of people in the case of Poland's neighbors. Nevertheless, toward the end of the negotiations with the European Community, the need for regional cooperation became increasingly patent. The three countries realized that they could exchange valuable negotiating tips and that coordinating their position could strengthen their hand vis-à-vis the Community. They were careful nevertheless not to offend the EC: "We have consultation among ourselves but not coordination," said a Czechoslovak diplomat. At the end of the negotiations in November 1991 the three countries formally consolidated their position before going to Brussels, a move that would certainly have a bearing on future interactions with the EC.

Finally, the association agreement negotiations constituted a learning process not only in the east but also for western European negotiators, both from the EC Commission and from member states. The Common Commercial Policy had been a pillar of European integration since its inception in 1958, and numerous external trade deals had been negotiated since then. Moreover, the Community had worked through complex accession protocols for six new members between 1973 and 1985.[77] But, as member states and the Commission discussed a negotiating mandate for the latter in the year following the 1989 upheavals, there was clear awareness that Article 238 of the Treaty of Rome on the "association agreement" constituted a vague legal basis for the newly styled "Europe Agreement," and that mere reliance on precedents and the arsenal of available legal bases for external trade agreements would not suffice to address the new challenge from the east.[78]

The most politically contentious dimension of this learning process was that of the connection between "association" with and "membership" in the Community. EC member states were called on to define exactly what such "rights of association" or "rights of membership" should involve in the case of eastern Europe and the extent to which they were ready to transfer their bargaining authority to a supranational body, the Commission. Differences in the preferences of member states were significant both with regard to the connection between short-term association and foreseeable enlargement to the east, and with regard to the modalities of association with the Community. Indeed, after the events of 1989, it took EC member states an entire year to agree on a mandate for the negotiations to be conducted by the Commission with central European countries. Nonetheless, after this long preparatory phase the EC Council agreed to grant a relatively important margin of maneuver to the Commission, in contrast, for instance, with the traditionally strong oversight by Committee 113 during the GATT negotiations.[79] This left more room for Commission negotiators to innovate than in previous instances—within a tightly defined bargaining space, to be sure.

The Road to Membership: Unilateral Adaptation

While the Community recognized that the process of negotiating association agreements could lead to future accession, it was eager to stress throughout the negotiations that these agreements would be "of special value in themselves and should be distinguished from any commitment concerning the question of accession."[80] Nevertheless, "membership" became one of the most contentious issues during the negotiations: Would there be a reference to future membership in the agreement, and if so, would this amount to an implicit commitment? Central Europeans insisted that such a clause be included for "symbolic reasons." It was clear that ultimate accession would be determined by objective economic criteria rather than by such a commitment. But, as a Polish negotiator stated: "Our population is swimming in a storm; it needs one clear point on the horizon." And as another echoed: "To financial investors this would serve as a signal. As for the average citizen, he could start to imagine a mosaic of German supermarkets coming to his town!"

At first the Community simply refused to include any allusion to membership in the preambles to the agreements. Many in the EC simply doubted that even within a decade those countries would be in a position to meet the stringent requirements of the European Community. The Turkish precedent of embarrassing commitment to membership was also foremost in their mind. Therefore, although the ultimate desirability of membership was generally accepted, the Community resisted any hint in the agreement which could be construed as a "right" of accession. In the spring of 1991 the three preambles were finally amended to include formulas such as "recognizing the fact that the final objective of Poland is membership in the Community" and "having in mind that the final objective of Hungary is to become a member of the Community," which duly recorded the aspirations of these countries to join the EC, but did not convey the impression that the EC welcomed such aspirations. As the negotiations came to a close, and after the August coup, the Community finally accepted a suggestion by Poland to add to this wording "and that this association, *in the view of the parties,* will help to achieve this objective" (emphasis added). At the same time, Frans Andriessen, the EC commissioner for external relations, put forth the notion of "affiliate membership" for eastern European states, which would enable affiliate members, in the period prior to membership, to contribute fully to policy formulation in areas of common interest through enlarged sessions of the council of ministers and the European Parliament. In contrast with the EFTA countries, it was felt that in these countries political integration could be implemented faster than economic integration. This idea, however, was not acted on during the negotiations. By the end, the three central European countries had in any case come to realize the amount of internal adjustment that would be required for the implementation of the association agreements, and thus accepted, more or less enthusiastically, the rationale for the transitional phase provided for by those agreements. As underscored by Pablo Benavides, the EC's chief negotiator, at the close of the negotiations: "This is not an entrance ticket. It is a kind of trial run to see if they would like to become members later on."[81]

The discussions on the membership clause were not merely an abstract long-term debate but reflected a broader divergence of views about the role the Community should play in the east during the transitional phase. Whether or not future membership was an explicit goal included in the agreement, it was clear that central European countries would be actively working toward that goal. These countries did not question the fact that their membership in the Community could not be envisaged until their economic system was compatible with EC requirements. To what extent, however, was the Community responsible for helping them craft such "compatible" systems? In other words, was regulatory and legal change within eastern European countries seen as a *precondition* or an *effect* of closer ties with the Community?

As the negotiations with EFTA made clear, the Community expected candidates for membership to adapt simply by adopting Community laws and regulations, the *acquis communautaire,* into their domestic laws. But the EFTA countries had bitterly complained about the prospect of being left out of EC decision-making procedures while having to implement these decisions as associate members. In contrast, the central Europeans sought to adapt to EC norms and regulations *in anticipation* of membership negotiations, a strategy of anticipatory adaptation. In the course of 1990 each of these governments issued orders that no legislation should be passed without a check of its conformity with EC law. Hence, in the three countries all domestic laws and regulations were to be adjusted to fit Community requirements. Every ministry was to follow the procedure.[82] In Poland a special office in the Council of Ministers attached to the prime minister was charged with developing systematic ties with the Diet and ministries and with organizing an intergovernmental structure to coordinate the process of convergence with Community laws. A special legal counsel to the prime minister was asked to draft a white paper spelling out what adaptation to the *acquis communautaire* would be required. Yet, actually to ensure that domestic laws were compatible with EC laws was no small task. As a Polish official recounted: "When the Ministry of Patents and Standardization sends us a notification that 'all laws that come under our authority are "compatible" ' how do we know and how can we verify it?" He added: "We talked with the Swedes about their experience in integrating the *acquis communautaire* into their legal system. They told us that this required dozens of experts."[83]

The rationale underlying such a policy was clear: on the one hand, the central European countries found themselves in the unprecedented historical situation of having to create anew a legislative framework conducive to the workings of a market economy and to the new democratic and social goals set forth after the revolutions; on the other hand, they unequivocally sought eventual membership in the EC. The breadth of the *acquis communautaire* and the difficulty of translating it into national laws was made apparent in the concurrent EFTA negotiations. In this light the regulatory blank slate of the postcommunist regimes could be turned into an asset: why not harmonize with the Community *ex ante* instead of waiting for accession negotiations? Central Europeans were thus more ready to play a passive role than were the EFTA countries. "We want to adapt to the EC system in any case, so, why should we complain?" commented a Polish diplomat. To be sure, as another Polish negotiator stressed: "Some of our features are connected to the past, and we do want to preserve our national identity"; but these considerations did not carry much weight relative to the prospect of EC membership.

Not only was regulatory adaptation a unilateral initiative; it also became a commitment under the Europe agreements' section on "approximation of law."[84] Many of the areas listed in the agreement as necessitating "approximation" could be viewed as prerequisites for the building of a genuine free trade area, as had been shown by the history of internal EC integration itself.[85] Specific target areas included consumer protection and product liability laws, company law, banking law, rules of intellectual property, financial services, rules on competition, food legislation, indirect taxation, technical issues, and standards and transport.[86] While committing to such legal approximation dovetailed with their interest, central European negotiators were careful to circumscribe what it entailed.[87] What, then, was going to be the role of the European Community in supporting the regulatory adaptation process? In the agreement the Community committed to "provide these countries with technical assistance for the implementation of [the approximation] measures." But only as a result of insistence by Czechoslovak, Hungarian, and Polish negotiators were precise descriptions of assistance means also included in the agreement (exchange of experts, provision of information, organization of seminars, training activities, translation support).[88] EC bureaucrats were reluctant to interfere with their partners' domestic politics, fearing anti-European backlash down the road. More pragmatically, the Commission simply feared that it would not have enough resources to meet such a commitment.[89] In frustration, a Polish negotiator commented: "We understand that legal adaptation is our responsibility. Yet, it is in both of our interests, isn't it?"[90]

A second issue, though certainly a less apparent one, was bound to constitute a question in the future: What did it really mean to adapt to "EC legislation" when the European Community itself was made up of a complex mosaic of overlapping legislative jurisdictions? EC member countries had never succeeded in harmonizing the bulk of their laws and regulations, and under the 1986 Single European Act had acknowledged this fact by agreeing to a regime of mutual recognition, henceforth giving up the aim of harmonizing their legal systems. As a result, in many cases eastern Europeans were faced with twelve different legal systems with which to ensure future compatibility. To be sure, they could start by internalizing the "essential requirements" or "minimal standards" agreed to by EC states in the process of completing the European single market. But what else was expected from them was unclear.

While unilateral adaptation was expected from, and implemented by, eastern Europeans, the European Community did not act up to the end of 1991 to adapt its own institutional structure to the future requirements of a potential doubling of its membership. Indeed, during the 1989–1991 period, the EC's foremost priority had been to design ambitious new plans for monetary and political union. Nevertheless, there was broad agreement that the institutional structure of the EC was not adapted to the requirements of a future Community of twenty-four members or more. The new Treaty on Political Union, adopted at the Maastricht summit in December 1991, did not tackle the issue directly; but at the summit the heads of state asked the Commission to draft a proposal by mid-1992 examining the necessary institutional reforms in light of future enlargement. The accession of EFTA countries such as Austria and Sweden was clearly going to be first on the agenda, but accession by eastern European countries seemed likely to be considered before the year 2000.

Bargaining Outcomes and Institutional Functions

The relatively fast pace of institutionalization of external trade relations among eastern European countries from 1989 through 1991 testifies to the fact that the strategies of governments in response to the end of the Cold War were deeply conditioned by the existence of international institutions. From the viewpoint of both eastern and western governments, these institutions were the focal points of renewed relations. As Table 7.4 indicates, institutional membership served as an anchor for trade policy reform in the east, and trade institutions also served as bargaining forums for the granting of market access by the west. But western governments and institutions proved rather ineffective in addressing the short-term crisis brought about by the collapse of trade between eastern Europe and the Soviet Union. Beyond this overall assessment, one can attempt to draw some preliminary conclusions on the role of international institutions with regard to the three core questions posed in Chapter 6 of this volume: To what extent did international institutions constrain individual state strategies in both east and west? How did they affect the specific outcomes of the bargains struck between these states in 1989–1991, and how are they likely to affect such outcomes in the future? Are they likely to enhance the sustainability of post–Cold War arrangements?

State Strategies and International Institutions: The Institutional Nature of Unilateral Adaptation

The main premise of this volume is that one needs to take account of the degree of institutionalization of an issue area before one can understand state strategy with respect to the problem. Trade is certainly one of the most highly institutionalized areas in world affairs. Indeed, as eastern European and western states faced a choice between unilateral, bilateral, and multilateral approaches to their renewed trade relations, they were constrained by their membership in international institutions in several ways. First of all, the existence of GATT and the EC forecloses to a great extent bilateral options, making multilateral forums the only practical locus for bargaining over reciprocal trade concessions. EC member states in particular were bound by the mechanisms of their Common Commercial Policy.

Second, from a positive standpoint, all the major institutions concerned with trade are bound to a certain extent by the commitment contained in their charters to consider the requests of "worthy" candidates (this is in contrast with national constitutions, which obviously do not contain such an obligation). Therefore, not only did integration in these institutions quickly become a major objective for eastern European countries, but such an objective could not be disputed by western countries, in contrast, for instance, with membership in security organizations such as NATO.

Third, the existence of international institutions forces linkages among issues that might not otherwise have existed and influences states' priority ranking among external policy issues. To be sure, institutions may at times inhibit efforts at cooperation by forcing the attention of states toward alternative priorities. Thus, in the case at hand, eastern Europeans were certainly up against competing demands on the Community's policy agenda at a time when the Community was involved in both major internal (the single market and the monetary union) and external (the Uruguay Round) negotiations. These negotiations in turn affected Community producers' willingness to accept further market opening.

Arguably, the collapse of the CMEA, and the rapid decrease of trade among its former members which ensued, provides *a contrario* evidence for this aspect of the role of institutions. The highly negative symbolic connotation of the institution and its correlation with the Warsaw Pact led the new eastern European governments to preside hastily over its demise, while perhaps not assessing fully the adverse consequences of such a move, unmitigated by a functioning regional payment union. EC institutions may have contributed further to the dramatic decline of intra-eastern trade by displacing eastern exports with the Community's own subsidized exports. Moreover, the lack of preexisting institutionalized mechanisms for supporting intra-eastern European trade rendered such a strategy difficult, thereby speaking to the dominance of preexisting arrangements over the creation of new ones. In spite of inflated rhetoric, lessons from the success of the postwar Marshall Plan did not provide much guidance, at least during the period under consideration.

Last but not least, the norms embedded in multilateral institutions served as focal points for what I, and other authors in this volume, have described as eastern European strategies of anticipatory adaptation, guiding domestic adjustment efforts in advance of full participation in these institutions. We have seen that, in part to facilitate the bargains with international institutions, in part as a component of domestic structural reforms, the eastern European countries early on launched radical trade liberalization programs, mainly on a unilateral basis. The unilateral option was chosen for reasons of expediency, given the part played by trade policies in the overall liberalization objective. From the point of view of radical reformers, to have waited for reciprocal concessions from the west would have been inefficient. Internally, the legal norms embodied in international institutions served as a model for domestic reform in eastern Europe by providing a policy template for regulatory adaptation.

The impact of institutions through anticipatory adaptation is not limited to the behavior of state actors. Private actors operate on the basis of the signals issued by governments. It is obviously hard to assess the extent to which the dramatic shift of eastern European trade from east to west would have occurred irrespective of institutional arrangements. As we saw in the early part of this chapter, "closing the parenthesis" meant reverting to "natural" trade patterns focused on western Europe. But the prestige of the EC as well as expectations linked to intragovernmental negotiations over access contributed to making the EC market a magnet for eastern exporters. In turn, the redirection of their exports to the EC provided eastern governments with added incentives to adapt quickly to western European standards.

Therefore, unilateral liberalization of external trade norms and unilateral adoption of legal norms were the twin components of eastern strategies that, perhaps paradoxically, speak to the important role of international institutions. When defining international regimes as sets of norms and rules "around which expectations converge," analysts in international relations refer mainly to strategic behavior on the part of states.[91] In the case at hand, international institutions and regimes have shaped not only mutual expectations about external behavior but also domestic adaptation processes by signaling how individual countries can become "compatible" with their actual and potential trading partners. They serve as a means of creating and maintaining mutual understanding and mutual confidence between the two halves of Europe, and as a means of socializing new elites into international diplomatic networks. Finally, to the extent that national preferences are "learned" rather than given, especially in a context of complete policy reappraisal such as that characterizing eastern Europe after 1989, institutions may actually affect national preferences, the most far-reaching function identified in the conclusion to this volume. As Robert Keohane and Stanley Hoffmann state in that conclusion: "The Cold War collapsed not into a vacuum but into the new Europe." The desire to be part of this highly institutionalized new Europe was the main driving force behind eastern European state strategies after the Cold War.

Bargaining Outcomes: Do Institutions Mitigate Power Asymmetries?

The underlying power differential between east and west after 1989 was overwhelming. For each of the three central European countries, trade with the EC represented between 30 and 50 percent of its total trade, whereas each represented less than 1 percent of EC trade. In light of such asymmetrical interdependence, traditional "structural realist" explanations of bargaining outcomes based on relative power among actors would lead one to expect that the east would have to adjust to a much greater extent than the west. And indeed this is exactly what one could observe in 1989–1991. Eastern European countries underwent considerable adjustment to ensure the opening of their economies to the west, and were largely "regime takers." The process of unilateral adaptation which I have described contributed further to their relative weakness in that it involved making concessions prior to securing quid pro quos. Western countries, by contrast, only marginally adjusted their existing rules to adapt to the specific cases of these countries in transition, and generally catered to their own material interests in granting trade concessions to the east.

Yet, when the political and ideological changes that have occurred in the east are taken into account, asymmetric adjustment may just as well be attributed to existing domestic preferences as to power differentials: the east was willing to open its borders and adapt to western norms irrespective of the west's demands. If this is the case, the sustainability of current bargaining outcomes may be seen as rather unpredictable, as both eastern and western preferences may shift in the event of domestic resistance to change.

In this light, the fact that the rules embedded in western institutions have been adopted as the prevailing rules of the game does not necessarily imply that the costs of adjustment themselves will be borne asymmetrically. To be sure, irrespective of the international context, east Europeans have had to bear the inherent costs of adjusting to market economies. Moreover, while full parity of concessions in the context of the European agreements would hardly have been feasible, the central Europeans did not wish to sustain a pattern of dependency as initially projected by its their immediate inclusion by the EC as GSP beneficiaries in the aftermath of 1989. Yet, to the extent that western rules imply obligations to provide certain kinds of public goods to the east, and to the extent that prospects for instability in eastern Europe constitute a serious threat to western countries, the post–Cold War era may be characterized by "western hegemony" toward the east in analogy to American hegemony toward Europe in the postwar period. In this light the west as a whole, and western Europe in particular, would be partially responsible for providing welfare-increasing deals that involve short-term sacrifices and concessions for the sake of long-term gains. Therefore, given the institutional context in which the new relationship between eastern Europe and the west is embodied, asymmetries of power favoring the west are likely to coexist with asymmetry of contributions to the restructuring of the international trading system in favor of the east.

To what extent does the 1989–1991 period provide evidence for the emergence of such a pattern of "western hegemony"? Did the multilateral character of trade cooperation increase the pace and aggregate level of trade liberalization on the part of the west? To be sure, increased access to the west was not provided quickly enough to offset the shrinking of eastern markets. But, given the relatively depressed state of western economies at the time, a plausible argument can be made that western governments acting bilaterally may not have been able to justify concessions to their constituents short of the traditional use of multilateral obligations as scapegoats. The swift implementation of liberalization measures by the EC in the fall of 1989 also testifies to the impact of institutions in accelerating responses in time of crisis when standard operating procedures are available.

Negotiations over the terms of new membership in GATT—or, most important, renewed modalities of the terms of preexisting membership— were at times controversial, but on the whole, GATT contracting parties allowed eastern Europeans to depart from standard procedures in order to restructure their tariffs while at the same time benefiting from the standard MFN clause. Most important, these countries could most likely assume that they would be beneficiaries of the impending Uruguay Round agreements on an asymmetric basis.

What about the Association agreements with the European Community? In spite of the reluctance of some member states, the Commission was granted a sizable margin of maneuver by the member states for negotiating with central European countries. This move allowed the Commission to push toward bolder liberalization than if concessions had been left solely to individual member states. The multilateral character of the negotiations raised the incentives for cooperation, both by increasing the visibility of noncooperative behavior and by overriding resistance against liberalization from negatively affected national-level constituencies or isolated EC member states. Ultimately, Spain's resistance over steel, Portugal's over textiles, and France's over agriculture were partially mitigated by these institutional dynamics. The Commission played a crucial role in applying pressure against member states and reinitiating negotiations in times of stalemate. Such a role, however, should not be misconstrued as an unqualified factor for liberalization, given the ambivalent position of the EC Commission in such negotiations as both a mediator between the two sides and an agent of one. To some extent, EC institutions were more instrumental in smoothing out differences between member states than in raising their aggregate trade concessions. The outcomes of the trade agreements reflect in the first instance compromises reached within the EC.

Counterfactuals can at best serve only as stimulating thought experiments. Would Germany have been more liberal if it had been dealing with the central Europeans alone? Would France's partners have made more concessions over agriculture if they had not been forced to cater to its veto? Would continental Europe, absent U.K. resistance, have accepted greater freedom of movement for central European service providers? Would western countries have granted market access to the new eastern democracies more quickly had they not been bound by GATT's rules of procedures and the prohibition on discrimination between east Europeans and their Third World competitors? Even though one may find instances where such behavior may be plausible, at the aggregate level it would seem that the existence of multilateral trade institutions in the west contributed to greater overall liberalization than if eastern Europe had sought to reintegrate a world of pure anarchy and specific reciprocity.

Sustainability of the New Bargains

Finally, what can be said about the sustainability of the trade bargains that have been reached, or are in the process of being reached, by the eastern European governments?

As I have underscored, and as is well known from the study of trade politics, international cooperation, while enhancing aggregate welfare, also contributes to domestic adjustment problems. Although adjustment costs may fall on certain relatively high-wage sectors in western Europe, east Europeans may not, at least in the short run, benefit unequivocally from opening their relatively uncompetitive markets. Freeing trade may enhance efficiency and increase consumption, but it can also compound the costs of the broader adjustment difficulties faced by these countries.

On this count not all central European countries have made the same assessment. Whereas Poland consistently pursued a bold liberalization up to the fall of 1991, Hungarian policymakers were decidedly more cautious, allegedly because of the lessons drawn from a decade and a half of gradual liberalization. Will its relative caution make it easier for Hungary to absorb the shock of transition? Will the Polish strategy succeed by providing the "right" incentives to local producers? Whatever the inherent dynamics of each of these unprecedented domestic reforms, the existence of agreements with the west can help local governments forestall sectoral protests and sustain the gradual opening of their economies. Agreements with the west can also provide a predictable framework for adapting domestic trade policies to changing circumstances. In this vein, the association agreements with the EC provide flexible modalities for adapting trade concessions in view of domestic developments and for policymakers in charge of trade reform in the east to coordinate their action among themselves as well as with their western counterparts. Ultimately, however, the stability of the trade bargains between the western countries and eastern European countries will be a function of the stability of the social bargains struck to support them at the respective domestic levels.

Chapter 8

The Political Economy
of Financial Assistance to
Eastern Europe, 1989–1991

Stephan Haggard

Andrew Moravcsik

In the wake of the peaceful revolutions of 1989, western nations faced critical decisions regarding the extension of financial assistance to eastern Europe.[1] Humanitarian concern for the postrevolutionary regimes moved European publics, and market-oriented reform and democratization posed the prospect of profitable east-west commerce and an expansion of the liberal zone of peace across the entire European continent. But how much aid should be committed to support these objectives? Through what institutional channels, bilateral or multilateral, preexisting or newly created, should it flow? And what economic and political conditions, if any, should be attached? Between November 1989 and the end of 1991, the first two years of transition, these issues were addressed in almost continuous negotiations.

The outcome of these negotiations appears, at first glance, haphazard. Between $30 and $40 billion in aid were committed over two years, nearly equaling current western aid to the less developed countries (LDCs), yet this level was widely criticized as falling far short of the functional need, not to mention the standard set forty years previously by the Marshall Plan. The choice of institutional channels to distribute the aid appears perplexing. Relatively large bilateral aid commitments were made by some western governments, notably a newly reunited Germany, but not others. Some existing international financial institutions (IFIs), including the International

Monetary Fund (IMF) and the World Bank, played a decisive role, while others, such as the European Investment Bank (EIB), were nearly frozen out. Despite the presence of preexisting institutional alternatives, a wholly new organization was created, the European Bank for Reconstruction and Development (EBRD), while the Poland/Hungary Aid for Restructuring Economies (PHARE) program granted an unprecedented role in international aid coordination to the Commission of the European Communities—despite its near total lack of previous experience in the area. Finally, there was little disagreement over some major issues, such as the general desirability of swift flows of finance, the need to link aid explicitly to democratization, and the priority of the IMF in monitoring policy conditionality; yet more serious conflicts arose over other, often ostensibly less significant, issues, including the location and directorship of the EBRD, Soviet membership in international institutions, the proper proportion of aid to direct at the private sector, and levels of debt relief.

The lack of a readily apparent pattern to this complex set of outcomes poses a challenge to existing theories of international cooperation. The most widespread of these theories views cooperation as a public good. Institutionalist theory predicts that cooperation is likely to occur within existing international institutions, if such are available, since the high uncertainty and transaction costs of renegotiation mean that "regimes are easier to maintain than they are to create."[2] Hegemonic stability theory, a variant of realism, asserts that extensive cooperation requires the coordinating efforts of a single powerful state whose inducements and sanctions to other states prevent "free riding."[3] Yet our case study provides little evidence supporting either of these theories. New institutions and policies were launched, despite both the absence of a hegemon and the presence of preexisting organizations capable of performing the function.

Most realist writings focus on the priority of security concerns and the highly conflictual nature of interstate bargaining. These realists might predict that cooperation would be impossible in the absence of a common external threat; that western cooperation would be undermined by strategies aimed at achieving "relative gains"; and that the creation of a new European financial institution reflects a decisive shift in political power from Europe to the United States, resulting in a "desire to move beyond American hegemony altogether."[4] Yet the realist approach seems equally unsatisfactory: much western cooperation did take place and national security concerns appear to have played little role in western calculations.[5]

Our explanation for this complex set of substantive and institutional outcomes draws on two factors derived from liberal theories of international
relations: economic interdependence and domestic political pressure. It rests
on five arguments.

First, while western nations may have been concerned about the provision
of the "public goods" of peace and prosperity in eastern Europe, particularly
during the first year of the transition, their willingness to provide aid reflected
the extent and nature of "privatizable" national benefits, primarily commercial and financial though also political.

Second, given variations in national preferences, the institutional outcome
that best met the needs of governments was not the strong multilateral regime
called for by critics of western policy, but a more decentralized system in
which bilateral aid flows predominated, backed by ad hoc, often temporary
coordination.

Third, strong regimes were found only in areas where more than pure
coordination was required. The IMF provided technical expertise on macroeconomic policy and served as a unified "gatekeeper" for the west, while the
World Bank offered expertise in managing structural adjustment. Even these
organizations, however, were influential primarily because they provided
technical and monitoring functions for western governments. In other areas,
such as aid levels and debt relief, governments conducted negotiations in
relatively weak institutions such as the Paris Club and the Group of Twenty-
Four (G-24), both of which tacitly recognized the central role of unilateral
action.

Fourth, the transaction costs of institutional creation, understood as the
costs of negotiating and financing new institutions, were sufficiently low so
as to permit the creation of redundant institutions, such as the EBRD. The
creation of the EBRD was neither an effort by a unified Europe to free itself
from American hegemony, nor an attempt to fill a pressing functional need
that preexisting organizations could not fulfill. Rather it was a largely symbolic act by the government of François Mitterrand and other European states
to signal support for eastern Europe and perhaps garner some commercial
benefits while avoiding a financial commitment on the scale of that undertaken by Germany.

Fifth, the prospects for future compliance by east European governments
with western conditionality remain uncertain. A monopoly over financial
assistance gave western governments considerable leverage over east European economic policies, but the long-term stability of the "conditionality

bargains" between the western donors and their clients ultimately rests on real external economic constraints and domestic political support for liberalization. By the end of 1991 signs of a reaction against market-oriented reforms were visible in every east European country.

The evidence for and implications of these empirical arguments are examined in more detail throughout this chapter. The argument proceeds in four sections. The first section highlights the economic reasons why official aid to eastern Europe became necessary to avoid economic collapse. The second section analyzes variations in the willingness of western governments to provide aid and examines the choice between four alternative institutions through which the aid could be channeled: bilateral programs; ad hoc coordination through the G-7, G-10, G-24, the Paris Group, and the EC Commission; existing multilateral institutions such as the IMF and the World Bank; and the newly formed EBRD. The third section examines the domestic politics of compliance in the two most advanced east European countries: Poland and Hungary. The fourth and final section explores theoretical implications for international relations theory.

The findings of this study, and the outcome of the EBRD negotiations in particular, call into question a crucial assumption of contemporary institutionalist theory on which its predictions concerning the importance and persistence of multilateral international institutions are based: that the transaction costs of creating new institutions are high. Our study also makes us cautious about the empirical significance of public goods, which are often invoked to help explain international institutions. Future research should take the limits in the scope of institutionalist theory more seriously and examine with greater precision the underlying national preferences and social purposes that lead governments to cooperate.

Interdependence: The External Position of East Europe

During the first few months following the fall of the Berlin Wall, many believed that the transition to democracy and capitalism in eastern Europe would be swift. A corollary was widespread confidence that private sources could provide the bulk of the financing needed for the transition. By mid-1990 a reassessment was under way as it became clear that if the economic transition toward market economies was to take place without internal collapse or fundamental external disequilibrium, it would require far higher levels of public finance than expected.

The need for finance stemmed from three factors: the shortage of longer-term private investment, the debt burden left by past borrowing, and short-term balance of payments constraints. The east European countries had initially hoped to cover both short-term and long-term needs with high levels of direct foreign investment and commercial lending. But direct investment proved modest, while unresolved debt problems limited their access to international capital markets and external shocks buffeted their economies.

The debt positions of almost all the east European countries placed a burden on their economies, but the burden varied considerably across countries. Poland, Hungary, and Bulgaria had incurred substantial levels of debt. Poland, the largest debtor in absolute terms, had a history of debt problems dating to the early 1980s, culminating in a massive restructuring package covering over $8 billion on debt coming due between 1987 and 1993.[6] On a per capita basis, Hungary was even more heavily indebted in 1989 than Poland, but the country's debt profile was fundamentally different, since Hungary owed three quarters of its debt to the commercial banks, while over 60 percent of Poland's debt came from official sources, particularly bilateral aid programs. Bulgaria also owed the bulk of its debt to the banks, and although its gross debt appears smaller than that of Hungary, the rapid rise of debt in the second half of the 1980s and the country's weak export performance would culminate in debt servicing difficulties and the declaration of a moratorium in 1990.

Czechoslovakia and Romania faced significantly smaller debt burdens. Czechoslovakia was the most prudent of the five, borrowing modestly and not facing serious external difficulties. Romania represents the most bizarre case of "prudent" international debt management not only in eastern Europe but among all sovereign debtors. Like Poland, Romania signed rescheduling agreements throughout the 1980s. At horrible cost to the Romanian population, however, Nicolae Ceausescu decided in the late 1980s to repay all external obligations, including those to the international financial institutions. At the time of the Romanian revolution, the country enjoyed the dubious distinction of having liquidated its entire external debt.

The debt overhang partly offset western aid. Donors typically emphasize aid disbursements or commitments, but when reverse flows in the form of amortization and payment of interest to creditors are included, *net* financial flows to Poland, Hungary, and Czechoslovakia in 1990 actually turned *negative*. In mid-1990 it became clear that in order "to ensure the appropriate mix between adjustment and financing," the east European countries would require an estimated $4 billion more in aid than was available through existing multilateral and bilateral sources.[7]

These longer-term legacies of past borrowing were compounded by a series of profound shocks to the region that began to be felt as early as 1989, but became pronounced in 1990 and particularly 1991. The effects of expansionary macroeconomic policies, the virtual disappearance of trade with East Germany, increasing economic chaos in the Soviet Union, the January 1991 agreement to settle all trade among the Council for Mutual Economic Assistance (CMEA) countries (including imports of Soviet oil) in hard currency, and the rise in oil prices following the Iraqi invasion of Kuwait in late 1990 all contributed to deteriorating balance of payments positions.[8] Moreover, the institutional, policy, and legal changes required for the transition to a market economy—including privatization of state enterprises, the construction of fiscal and financial systems, current- and capital-account liberalization, currency convertibility, the abolition of monopolies, the deregulation of labor markets, and the creation of social safety nets—required a combination of expertise, administrative capability, and capital unavailable through the commercial credit markets.

The demands of economic reform, long-term debt, and short-term shocks created, according to estimates by the Group of Thirty (G-30), a total financing need for eastern Europe of between $237 and $252 billion for the period from 1991 through 1995. Of this approximately $160 billion was expected to come from private sources. Yet these figures vastly overestimate the potential contribution of the private sector, since the large private-sector figure includes short-term debt of less than one year in maturity; by G-30 estimates, 80 percent of total private financing during the period would take the form of short-term debt, mostly trade credits.

When short-term debt is removed, the picture changes dramatically. Private equity financing could be expected to cover only 12 percent of east Europe's *long-term* needs. Private long-term debt would account for another 25 percent—a figure that, given the attitude of commercial banks toward sovereign lending in the region, appeared overly optimistic.[9] Moreover, such figures underestimated the official role in the provision of finance in another way: much "private" lending has to be undertaken with some sort of official guarantee, in the form of either trade financing or private "co-financing" with official sources.

To summarize, the large debt overhang, severe balance of payments problems associated with external shocks, and the shortage of private longer-term finance needs catapulted public financing into a central role in meeting eastern Europe's needs in the 1989–1991 period.[10] In the medium run, official aid would have to cover more than half of east Europe's financial needs. Moreover, while aid to eastern Europe up to that point had almost exclusively taken the form of project lending, the external problems and the transition to capitalist economies required balance of payments support, funding to back the transition to convertible currencies, and loans to support policy reform and privatization. By 1990–91, ever-increasing amounts of "exceptional untied balance of payments assistance, complementary to support from the IMF," was needed to cover the "financing gap" in eastern Europe.[11] It is to the organization of this effort that we now turn.

National Preferences and Institutional Strategies

The potential for financial crisis and economic collapse in eastern Europe, along with political and economic interdependence between the two halves of Europe, raised the issue of official aid. But it determined neither the willingness of western governments to respond generously nor the proper institutional framework for administering the financial flows. In the discussion that follows, we begin with an analysis of bilateral aid. We then turn to the institutionalization of aid flows. Aid may be channeled through three types of institutions: bilateral or regional programs; existing multilateral organizations such as the IMF, EIB, World Bank, or International Finance Corporation (IFC); and multilateral organizations new to the issue area, such as the G-24, the European Community (EC) Commission, and the EBRD.[12]

Bilateral Aid and National Interests
Post–Cold War financial support for eastern Europe has been widely viewed as an act of enlightened statecraft, providing the public goods of peace and prosperity for all of Europe. One analyst writes: "Western democracies . . . wish to encourage change in Eastern Europe . . . because such change would improve the long-term security and stability of Europe as well as increasing the liberty of those in Eastern Europe."[13] This view, reiterated in speeches by western ministers and heads of government, suggests that a high level of western support for eastern Europe was self-evidently desirable. Western leaders hoped to ensure Soviet withdrawal from the region, prevent regional unrest, forestall westward migration, assist fellow Europeans, and establish a beneficial economic environment.

Whatever normative attraction these goals may have held for western states-men, however, the willingness of western governments to back rhetoric with action was in fact both strictly limited and highly variable. In general, enthusi-asm waned as it became clear that the estimated costs of transition increased and the danger of a Soviet resurgence receded. Many governments sought to minimize their commitment to the region, with several west European govern-ments going so far as to oppose explicit recognition, even in principle, of their eastern neighbors' right to apply eventually for EC membership.[14]

Large variations in the commitment of western governments help explain why approximately three quarters of western aid commitments, debt relief excluded, has come from bilateral or regional sources rather than multilateral organizations. Donor countries can benefit from bilateral or regional aid in two ways: through the general promotion of exports, investment, or other profitable economic links with the recipient country, and through direct procurement opportunities for domestic producers through "tied" credits and grants, which stipulate that the funds be spent in the donor country. Bilateral aid often limits consideration for service or goods contracts to domestic firms, while the EC limits such consideration to firms with their main establishment in the EC. The bulk of western project assistance committed to eastern Europe has been directed toward infrastructure development, including tele-communications and transport, areas in which there is substantial excess capacity in western Europe and in which the need for compatibility can bestow decisive "first mover" advantages. The EIB's focus on telecommuni-cations and transport contracts, as well as coal and steel exports, and the stiff competition among west European national champions, suggests that this concern is realistic.[15]

These specific "privatizable" benefits from economic relations with eastern Europe appear to explain much of the variance in aid levels. The distribution of aid commitments between the United States, Japan, and the EC countries (including EC institutions), which together account for about 90 percent of western aid, suggests diverging interests among them. Germany stands out as the largest single donor. In 1989 Germany acted "quickly and decisively," making unprecedentedly large pledges of aid to the Soviet Union and Poland.[16] During the next two years Germany provided nearly a third of total G-24 aid commitments (and two thirds of EC bilateral commitments), while financing a large portion of EC aid as well. Germany's contribution totaled over six times that of France, nearly twelve times that of Great Britain, and about twice as much as that of the United States and Japan combined.

Table 8.1. Assistance Committed to Eastern Europe, January 1990 through June 1991 (percent of total)[a]

Donor	Project Assistance	Macro Assistance	Export Credits	Private Investment Support	Total	% of All Grants
France	2.6	1.8	9.8	17.2	4.9	2.3
Germany	14.4	28.5	56.9	25.8	30.9	28.2
U.K.	0.7	8.6	4.5	—	2.6	0.6
EC Bilateral	24.2	40.2	81.4	57.8	46.6	21.6
EC/PHARE	21.1	28.7	1.0	2.9	14.1	22.4
EIB	10.7	0.0	—	—	11.7	—
National + EC	55.9	68.9	82.4	60.7	74.2	44.0
U.S.	20.1	2.5	3.8	19.0	7.7	16.6
Japan	9.8	15.2	6.4	—	8.6	8.1
Total	100.0	100.0	100.0	100.0	100.0	100.0

Source: Commission of the European Communities, "G-24 Assistance to Central and Eastern Europe: Summary Tables," document prepared for the G-24 Ministerial, November 11, 1991, Brussels.

a. Columns do not sum to 100 percent owing to excluded countries. Some categories of aid have also been excluded. Macro assistance refers to general balance of payments support, and funding for stabilization efforts. Dashes indicate negligible amounts.

Germany's leading role is readily explained by Germany's long experience and extensive commercial relations in the region. Moreover, the immediate geographic proximity of eastern Europe, and particularly the fear of migration, makes political stability in the region a higher priority for Germany than for some of its western partners. Finally, the acquiescence of the Soviet Union and others in German reunification was purchased in part through commitments of generous aid.

Realist arguments that link this dominance to Germany's relative economic and political power are unconvincing, since the German commitment far outstrips its relative economic capability. Instead, a more plausible view is that France and other western countries lacked an equal economic stake in extending more aid.[17] Nonetheless, given the sensitivities of other European countries, Germany maintained an extremely low profile during the negotiations—quietly but unenthusiastically supporting common initiatives—so as not to stir up overt opposition to its dominant commercial and financial position in eastern Europe. Only in late 1991, with a domestic fiscal crisis in the making, did Chancellor Helmut Kohl publicly criticize its partners for providing insufficient aid.

While much weaker than that of Germany, the general commitment of other west European governments to provide aid was nonetheless more substantial than that of the United States or Japan—reflecting the stronger economic, geographic and political relationship between the two parts of Europe (Tables 8.1, 8.2). Finance originating in EC countries accounted for almost three quarters of bilateral and regional assistance, of which 25 percent was channeled through EC institutions—either through the PHARE program, coordinated by the Commission, or through the semiautonomous European Investment Bank (EIB).[18]

From the beginning, EC aid was subject to political conditionality. In 1988 the EC had already moved to sign agreements with Hungary and Czechoslovakia, the former dealing with aid as well as trade. Despite a legal mandate, however, negotiations were not taken up with Romania and were suspended

Table 8.2. Assistance Committed to Eastern Europe, January 1990 through June 1991 (percent of total)[a]

Donor	Project Assistance	Macro Assistance	Of Which BOP	Export Credits	Private Investment Support	% of All Aid
France	10.8	10.2	—	66.1	10.1	100
Germany	9.5	26.0	—	60.0	2.8	100
U.K.	5.2	94.0	—	—	—	100
EC Bilateral	10.0	24.6	—	57.6	4.2	100
EC/PHARE	30.0	58.0	36.0	2.2	0.7	100
EC Total	15.8	26.9	7.0	37.1	2.8	100
U.S.	53.0	9.3	1.4	16.3	8.3	100
Japan	23.4	50.0	19.9	24.6	—	100

Source: Commission of the European Communities, "G-24 Assistance to Central and Eastern Europe: Summary Tables," document prepared for the G-24 Ministerial, November 11, 1991, Brussels.

a. Columns do not sum to 100 percent owing to excluded categories of assistance and double counting of balance of payments support. Dashes indicate negligible amounts.

with Bulgaria. No agreement was signed with East Germany. After the 1989 democratic transitions, aid was greatly increased (except to Romania), totaling from ECU 300 million in 1990 to ECU 785 million in 1991 and a projected ECU 1 billion in 1992.[19]

It would be misleading to think of EC aid as initiated and directed by the Commission. Some Commission initiatives, such as its proposal for food aid to Poland and Romania, its redirection of small amounts of EIB aid to Poland and Hungary, and improved access to EC markets for east European products, were accepted; others, such as Community-wide political and export risk insurance, a greatly expanded EIB role, and greater Commission initiative in selecting programs, have enjoyed no success to date, despite support from some business groups.[20] After committing between ECU 200 and 300 million to eastern Europe in 1989, the European Investment Bank made ECU 1 billion available for commitment in 1990–1992, plus an additional ECU 200 million for projects in coal and steel. Some joint EIB–World Bank projects have since been announced. Yet the basic priorities of these programs were set by the member governments.

In contrast to the EC countries, Japan and the United States each provided less than 10 percent of western aid, representing relatively low per capita figures. In neither country was there much business support for policies to exploit opportunities in eastern Europe. Despite strong advocacy at the highest levels of the Bush administration, U.S. programs to promote trade and investment in the region foundered on business apathy. Passage of the Support for East European Democracy (SEED) Act of 1989 signaled a certain willingness on the part of Congress, despite the skepticism of the president toward greater spending, to extend trade credits and investment guarantees to eastern Europe, but dollar totals remained modest. American interests in the region were initially defined almost entirely in military and political terms, while only the Polish ethnic minority in the United States constitutes a political force of any importance, which explains the emphasis on U.S. aid to that country.[21]

Despite Japanese Prime Minister Toshiki Kaifu's efforts to assume a high-profile role, for politically symbolic rather than economic reasons aid from Japan has remained modest, though it represents a per capita commitment larger than that of the United States. This is consistent with the public declaration of the Japanese government that "even in 10 years' time the government could not foresee Japanese trade with Eastern Europe rising above 1 percent of total trade."[22]

The importance of privatizable national interests, as opposed to public goods concerns, is further demonstrated by striking differences in the *form* of aid favored by different governments. Three categories account for over 80 percent of total aid by all countries: project lending (20 percent), balance of payments support (29 percent), and official export credits (33 percent). The distribution across these three categories varies considerably among countries. The EC and its members, eastern Europe's key trading partners, focus disproportionately on forms of aid that promote trade and investment, providing 80 percent of G-24 export financing and disproportionately low shares of balance of payments, project, and investment finance. Germany, the world's leading capital goods exporter, provides particularly generous trade credits, while general balance of payments support plays a significant but secondary role—a priority consistent with the dangerously high regional exposure of German banks. After trade credits, France tends toward project lending and investment guarantees. Britain, with a weak trading relationship with eastern Europe, provides very low overall levels of aid, offering no official export credits at all and concentrating 94 percent of its assistance on balance of payments funding.[23]

In contrast to the EC member states, the United States disburses over half its aid in the form of project lending, with official export credits playing a distinctly secondary role.[24] Moreover, U.S. aid, for reasons we have noted, is targeted heavily at Poland. U.S. investments in Hungary in 1992 appeared to be resulting in a shift of aid priorities toward that country.[25] For its part, Japan extends half of its aid in the form of balance of payments support, with secondary efforts equally divided between project lending and export credits. Japanese banks—like their German counterparts, but unlike those in the United States—are extended in eastern Europe.[26]

The result of these divergent interests has been that multilateral agencies acted more swiftly than many national governments in the initial period of the transition, but bilateral and EC aid flows have steadily been supplanting the role of multilateral donors since that time. A picture of the emerging balance between bilateral and multilateral sources of financing can be gained by examining estimates compiled by the IMF for 1991. One indicator of the shift from multilateral to bilateral aid is that during the period from January 1990 through June 1991, aid *disbursements* (debt relief excluded) were still dominated by the IFIs, but bilateral and regional aid *commitments* were dominated by bilateral and regional aid, totaling $32 billion (72 percent), while aid from international financial institutions totaled $12.9 billion (29 percent).[27]

Coordination: The G-7, G-24, Paris Club, and EC Commission

The G-7, G-24, and Paris Club were ad hoc organizations employed to "coordinate" western aid. The appropriate view of these organizations is that they served as negotiating forums for senior officials, ministers, or heads of state, who reached agreement without the assistance of strong norms or decision-making procedures. In late 1989, for example, a Polish stabilization fund, initially for one year, was announced by the G-24, although it consisted essentially of $1 billion in bilateral commitments, to be drawn as the need arose.[28]

It has been widely argued that these organizations served also to overcome a "coordination problem" in the provision of aid to eastern Europe. One analyst argues: "Six multilateral organizations . . . and the G-24 . . . are capable of more or less independent action . . . The scope for duplication, conflicting action and other forms of wasteful behavior is enormous. The risks involved in wasting the time of the relatively small number of people who can actually change anything in eastern Europe are high; there is the danger of bureaucratic fatigue in the recipient countries. The premium is therefore on coordination among the donors."[29] A corollary view is that the unprecedented and much publicized assignment of the coordination task to the Commission of the European Communities marked a significant power shift from the United States to the EC—a moment when the EC, led by the Commission, grasped world leadership.[30] Yet this view vastly exaggerates the political importance of the Commission's role—and that of the G-24 more generally. As we demonstrate later in this chapter, there is no evidence that coordination, in this sense, was a political problem requiring more than a designated negotiating forum and a bureaucratic agency at which to direct ex post reporting. Even the forum was eventually eliminated in favor of meetings between senior officials. Formal institutionalization had little independent impact on the level or substance of cooperation.

The G-7, G-24, and EC Commission   At the "Summit of the Arch" in Paris in July 1989, G-7 leaders agreed to "coordinate" bilateral aid to Poland and Hungary.[31] The primary purpose of coordination was to centralize the drafting of national programs for emergency food aid and technical assistance, and to report bilateral aid to a central site. An ad hoc group was created, the G-24, consisting initially of representatives from the Organization for Economic Cooperation and Development (OECD) countries, though the current membership numbers in the forties. At the inaugural meeting of the G-24 on August 1, 1989, the participants agreed to coordinate food aid for Poland, investment promotion (through joint ventures), improved access to western markets, cooperation in environmental protection, and vocational training.

From the beginning the coordination of G-24 support was seen as an administrative rather than political task. Germany, the logical choice as a coordinator, preferred to keep a low profile and declined the role, suggesting to the United States that the EC Commission assume the task instead, despite its lack of experience in such matters. Canada was dispatched to gain the support of the French government, which initially hesitated to approve additional powers for the Commission. Nonetheless, the Commission was named administrative coordinator, the official reason being its "greater familiarity" with the region and the greater resources being provided by the EC.[32]

The Commission responded to its new mandate with two "Action Plans"—both reflecting preexisting consensus in the G-7 and G-24 and drafted after consultations with the IMF and the World Bank. The first, transmitted in September 1989, restated the five priorities set forth by the G-24 for coordinated aid to Poland and Hungary in the form of the PHARE program. Under PHARE, which totaled just under $1 billion annually (as compared to approximately $10 billion in annual bilateral and regional aid, excluding debt relief), "coordination" meant in practice that intergovernmental working groups were created in various areas, such as vocational education, and Commission officials assisted recipient countries in drawing up national aid plans for submission. PHARE does not coordinate funding for stabilization efforts, export guarantees, or private investment guarantees, focusing instead on immediate needs, such as agricultural supplies and credits, environmental protection, and human resource development. In 1991–92 the program was expanded to include support for privatization, demonopolization, joint ventures, and small and medium-sized enterprises.[33]

Neither the G-24 nor the PHARE program actually pools common aid funds among donor countries.[34] In most areas recipient countries address requests to individual donor governments, and bilateral aid efforts are simply reported ex post facto to the Commission. PHARE proposals are drafted by officials in member states, with some assistance from the Commission, and then reviewed by an intergovernmental G-24 management committee.[35] Commission support for the G-24 takes the form of processing aid requests, compiling information, and drafting potential agreements. It lacks the independent power of proposal that makes it a powerful actor within the EC.

The Commission also lacks the administrative capacity to monitor aid closely, a task carried out by the IMF and World Bank, whose prior involvement and greater expertise in the area are generally recognized and, secondarily, by a "monitoring group of financial counselors or other representatives of the participating G-24 countries," who work closely with national authorities actually administering the programs. At the end of 1990 PHARE had a modest budget and only twenty-four staff members.[36] In an effort to strengthen its involvement, the Commission opened small offices in east European capitals (program management units or PMUs) to coordinate G-24 assistance, but G-24 members had already set up contacts in recipient countries, and thus "the PMUs . . . tend . . . to be by-passed."[37] Even within PHARE, economic conditionality is left to the discretion of national governments, subject only to IMF policy. "Where national interests diverge on how tough conditions should be," one commentator notes, "the G-24, as a very loose coordination mechanism, tolerates diversity . . . Each government remains free to subscribe or not to a given program."[38]

The most important task of the G-24 has been to set terms of political conditionality. The primary western concern was to ensure that only democratic regimes should receive aid.[39] The Commission's second Action Plan, transmitted May 2, 1990, addressed the extension of the program to other eastern European countries, an issue which had first been raised at the G-24 ministerial at Brussels on December 13, 1989, where the principle of extending aid to Bulgaria, Czechoslovakia, Yugoslavia, and the German Democratic Republic was accepted. On February 16, 1990, Romania was also taken under consideration but not approved. On May 22, 1990, the G-24 declared that aid and loans be made conditional on moves toward democratic rule and a competitive market economy. The granting of coordinated assistance was made subject to the five specific political or economic conditions: firm commitment to the rule of law, the respect for human rights, the introduction of multiparty systems, the holding of free and fair elections, and the development of market-oriented economies. In July 1990 the PHARE program was extended to Bulgaria, Czechoslovakia, Yugoslavia, and the GDR, but not Romania. U.S. Secretary of State James Baker hailed this as a victory for the U.S. policy of "democratic differentiation," whereby aid is conditioned on adherence to the rule of law, respect for human rights, a multiparty system, fair and free elections, and market economies. The Europeans did likewise.[40]

Yet the imposition of political conditionality granted no political discretion to the Commission, since there was already near-complete unanimity on standards among western governments meeting in the G-7 and G-24. EC practice before 1989, and the statements of George Bush, François Mitterrand, and other leaders tallied almost exactly. (The French position on the EBRD statutes on specific lending policies, discussed later in this chapter, constitutes the sole, partial exception.) Western governments had little difficulty imposing political conditions on Romania. Throughout, the Commission followed the dictates of ministerial and senior officials' meetings of the G-24. The Commission "prepares situation reports for the senior experts, but its major function is to act as a 'scorekeeper.'"[41]

However modest, the responsibilities of the G-24 and the Commission, with the exception of the latter's role as a central reporting site for bilateral aid, proved only temporary. In April 1991 finance ministers in the G-10 consultative group (consisting of the G-7, the Benelux nations, Sweden, and Switzerland), noting that "the G-24 has been created as a temporary mechanism designed chiefly to provide emergency support and to ensure that political considerations were taken into adequate account," determined that henceforth primary responsibility for overall strategy would go to G-10 finance ministers and central bank officials themselves, meeting as an ad hoc body, while macroeconomic policy would be managed by the IMF, structural adjustment by the World Bank, and industrial policy and privatization by the EBRD.[42] The reality of western decision making had never strayed far from this anyway, with the Commission and the G-24 shadowing G-7 decisions.

The Paris Club   The provision of official debt relief, coordinated by the Paris Club, where finance ministers and senior officials meet on an ad hoc basis, occasioned more significant disagreements among western countries. In January 1991 the finance ministers of the G-7 countries agreed to grant Poland substantial debt relief. The United States, whose strong domestic Polish lobby was calling for generous write-down, and France, where there was little official exposure, could not reach agreement with Germany and Japan, whose banks were more highly exposed and opposed more generous relief. Important U.S. congressmen tied the deal to American ratification of the establishment of the European Bank for Reconstruction and Development. The debate continued for nearly six months until May, when agreement to write off 30 percent of the Polish official debt was made more generous after Poland adopted its IMF program. It was also agreed to permit individual donor governments to make further voluntary reductions, essentially recognizing the fait accompli of unilateral French and American debt relief.[43]

The IMF and the World Bank: Gatekeeping and the Role of Expertise

Pure coordination, analyzed in the previous section, was not the most important function of international institutions in mobilizing the western aid effort to eastern Europe. The IMF and the World Bank played more essential roles, owing to their large pools of ready resources, expertise in policy-based lending, and unique position as "gatekeepers" imposing conditionality on developing and developed countries alike. The primacy of these institutions was unquestioned: "From the outset, the Community and the G-24 governments adopted the position that the multilateral financial institutions, and especially the IMF and the World Bank, should play the major role in providing financial assistance for the countries of Central and Eastern Europe in the context of comprehensive adjustment and reform programs."[44]

The IMF   The IMF's long-standing mandate is to assist in the management of external disequilibria, such as those that arose during the east European balance of payments crises of 1990–91. With its quota increase of SDR 45 billion, the IMF, unlike most national governments, was well positioned to respond to the crisis with swift financial aid. In 1990 IMF commitments to eastern Europe already totaled $923 million; in 1991 they skyrocketed to $8.6 billion. Even more important, IMF conditionality became the common standard of the G-24 countries: the prerequisite for PHARE assistance, bilateral aid, and the rescheduling of public debt at the Paris Club, as well as the renegotiation of private debt (in the so-called London Club). In addition, IMF and World Bank expertise was essential to nearly all the activities of the Commission and the EBRD.[45]

The general pattern of direct IMF involvement was similar in each country, following a three-step pattern, though the timing reflected local political and economic developments. The first step was typically a one-year standby to support financial stabilization. Poland and Hungary, both of which had been members of the IMF before the political transition, signed standby agreements in early 1990. In September of that year Bulgaria joined and Czechoslovakia rejoined the IMF; both quickly negotiated programs. Six months later Romania negotiated its first regular program since reactivating its membership. In Hungary and Poland standbys were followed by a second step: a three-year Extended Fund Facility (EFF) designed to sustain stabilization and structural adjustment. As the crisis deepened in 1991, the IMF took a third step, supplementing its traditional arrangements with additional resources from the Compensatory and Contingency Financing Facility (CCFF), designed to fund energy imports, which were directed toward all five countries of east Europe. Such improvisations suggest a measure of discretion in lending policy.

The full importance of the IMF is not, however, accurately captured by looking solely at the level and swiftness of its disbursements; even more crucial are the "gatekeeper" and "monitoring" functions that the IMF carried out in relation to G-24 assistance, bilateral aid, and negotiations over both public and commercial debt relief. The policy of following the IMF's lead in balance of payments matters was made official at the July 5, 1990, meeting of the G-24, where it was agreed that the IMF should be the first instance for all requests for financial support to overcome short-term external financial constraints, after which the G-24 could take up other issues. Approval by the IMF also serves as a decisive signal for private investors and lenders to enter the market.[46]

G-24 actions were explicitly required to be complementary with IMF efforts. All western governments officially endorsed "the leading role of the IMF and the consistency that has to be ensured between any conditionality attached to EC/G-24 assistance and the Fund agreement with these countries."[47] All G-24 evaluation and aid activities were to be carried out "in close collaboration with the IMF." The intergovernmental meetings of the "Brussels Network" and senior official groups included the IMF, as well as member government experts. In contrast, the Commission lacked the expertise to estimate aid requirements (such as the $4 billion for increased G-24 aid in 1991), and its recommendations to the G-24 relied on the expertise of the IMF and World Bank. The Commission's proposal for a "general facility" with ECU 10 billion in reserves to address balance of payments requirements and to build up reserves to facilitate currency convertibility was rejected by the G-24 in favor of a case-by-case approach, which maintained the privileged position of the IMF and intergovernmental forums.[48]

A striking example of the IMF's importance as a gatekeeper, even against the immediate political interests of powerful heads of government, occurred during the negotiations over the write-down of the Polish debt in early 1991—agreed to in the Paris Club and by the G-7 finance ministers but initially blocked by the lack of an IMF imprimatur.[49] Although EC leaders were, in Helmut Kohl's words, "under enormous pressure" to act on Poland

and Hungary, they refused to move on bilateral aid or to authorize the EIB and other EC aid until IMF certification had been given. EC Council aid decisions have also been held up for IMF approval.[50]

The World Bank   The World Bank was somewhat slower to respond to events in eastern Europe, in part owing to unique difficulties associated with project and structural adjustment lending in a postcommunist society, but reportedly also owing to the reticence of its leading shareholder, the United States. Nonetheless, it was the institution best positioned to provide an initial infusion of long-term project and program lending to the region. Moreover, as with the IMF, the World Bank faced no practical limit on available funds, since it had received a $75 billion general capital increase in 1988 and had since been unable to meet its targets for commitments and disbursements. During the 1989–1991 period, country coverage and total loan amounts by the World Bank increased rapidly.[51]

Most World Bank loans fell into one of three categories.[52] The first category consisted of structural adjustment loans (SALs), a form of balance of payments support aimed at achieving a particular reform objective such as privatization or financial sector development. The second category contained loans designed to restructure business in a particular sector by financing technical assistance and needed imports, usually of capital goods. These loans typically emphasize improving export performance and competitiveness. The final category included about 30 percent of World Bank commitments during the period, which were directed to the Bank's traditional "bread and butter" areas (basic transportation, energy, and telecommunications infrastructure), as well as support for environmental regulation and social welfare systems.

As with the IMF, an examination of direct funding activities, while significant on its own, underestimates the World Bank's importance. Behind the scenes, the Bank proved to be by far the most expert international organization in the provision of technical assistance and program evaluation. While the World Bank and the IMF have had to adjust their policy-oriented SAL and EFF loans in the face of the particular realities of the east European cases, the reforms being undertaken were broadly in line with those in which the two institutions have been engaged in developing countries for decades. Many G-24, EC, bilateral, and EBRD efforts depended on the World Bank to evaluate requirements in the area and to monitor the program.

The EBRD and the Problem of Institutional Redundancy

The European Bank for Reconstruction and Development, with its flamboyant director Jacques Attali, has captured the headlines. Despite the protestations of the bank's advocates, however, it is difficult to escape the conclusion that its creation was largely an act of symbolism and its contribution redundant.

Creating the EBRD   The genesis of the first official proposal for the EBRD can be attributed to Attali, then the close adviser to President Mitterrand, although the concept itself cannot. Similar proposals had already been publicized by Jacques Delors, Valéry Giscard d'Estaing, Adolf Herrhausen (former president of the Deutsche Bank), and various major European newspapers.[53] Mitterrand first floated the idea of a European bank in a speech before the European Parliament on October 25, 1989, and within weeks Attali had directed the French treasury to develop plans for such an organization. Informal discussions with EC partners were followed by a French proposal for the creation of a bank, modeled on the charters of the Asian Development Bank and the World Bank's private wing, the International Finance Corporation, at the Strasbourg meeting of the European Council December 8–9, 1989.[54]

The precise purposes of the French initiative remain unclear. One possibility could have been to gain an inside track on procurement contracts in eastern Europe. But unlike Japan and various small countries, France declined to support a proposal to limit procurement with EBRD funds to member governments, though such practices are the norm in multilateral development organizations. Still, participation may have been seen as a way to grant French firms a higher profile and facilitate their access to inside information.[55] A more plausible explanation is that the French government promoted the organization for reasons of political symbolism: as a visible counterbalance to Germany in eastern Europe, as a means of "tying" Germany into Europe, as a means of integrating the Soviet Union into multilateral organizations, as a way of expressing independence from the United States, or perhaps simply as a way to increase the personal stature of the French president after German reunification and the Soviet-German agreements, when French diplomacy appeared to be on the defensive.[56]

Mitterrand went public with the proposal before consulting his partners. The German government was "at most ambivalent" and joined the Netherlands, Italy, and Britain in expressing skepticism about the need for a new institution.[57] With eastern Europe looking for a sign of European good will, however, the EBRD became "a political appeal that no European Community government felt able to resist."[58] It appears likely that the German government, concerned not to appear to be exploiting its increased power post-reunification and having agreed to support Soviet requests for aid, was not in a position to oppose the proposal, which in some ways served its interests.

Although the proposal was swiftly accepted by European governments, certain important aspects had been altered.[59] The EC proposal made clear that rather than expanding the EC, as the Commission had urged, or creating an independent European organization, as the initial French proposal seemed to imply, the EBRD was reconceived as a global intergovernmental organization in which the EC countries, as well as their common institutions, held a bare majority stake of 51 to 55 percent. Moreover, its activities were clearly labeled as adjunct to, rather than as alternatives for, current activities of bilateral and multilateral donors.

Meetings of the G-24 to discuss the issue began with a conference of over thirty governments on January 15, 1990, in Paris under Attali's chairmanship. Agreement on the EBRD statutes was reached at a meeting of forty-two member countries on April 9, 1990, in Paris.[60] The United States, backed by the United Kingdom, was at first somewhat unsympathetic to the initiative and proposed a relatively low capitalization of $5 billion, while the French proposal called for $18 billion. Finding itself isolated and realizing that the Europeans would move ahead in any case, however, the United States soon moderated its objections. As Treasury Secretary Nicholas Brady put it: "Let's conjure up . . . the headlines . . . if we didn't join this. It's a kind of stark position to think us not as a member."[61]

From the beginning, the United States supported a majority stake for the EC in the bank. In the final agreement, the EC and its members held a 53.7 percent share of the capital of ECU 10 billion ($12 billion), a figure midway between the French and U.S.-U.K. proposals. During the final rounds of the negotiations, after having opposed higher funding, the United States also raised its contribution several times, at the expense of the USSR—suggesting that the United States wanted to retain bargaining power within the organization (Table 8.3).

The bargaining over Soviet membership took a similar course. The United States, backed by Japan, initially opposed Soviet membership, but this was an issue, like that of the size of the bank, over which the Europeans appeared

Table 8.3. Positions of Major Western States in the EBRD Negotiations

Issue	France	EC Majority	U.S.	Outcome
Soviet membership	Yes	Yes	No	Yes
Restricted lending to SU	No	Mixed	Yes	Yes
Capitalization	15 b	Mixed	5 b	10 b
Private lending	No rule	Mixed	Only	60%
Presidency	Attali	Mixed	Banker	Attali
Limitations on president[a]	No	Yes	Yes	Yes
Location of headquarters	No view	Mixed	Prague	London
Political conditionality	In principle	Mixed	Yes[b]	Yes
Economic conditionality	In principle	Yes	Yes	Yes
EC majority share	Yes	Yes	Yes	Yes
Use of ECU only	Yes	Mixed	No	No

Source: Paul A. Menkveld, *Origin and Role of the European Bank for Reconstruction and Development* (London: Graham and Trotman, 1991), p. 92.

a. We have added this category to Menkveld's.

b. The "yes" on U.S. support for political conditionality is a personal judgment. Menkveld codes the U.S. position as "mixed."

ready to move ahead on their own if agreement was not reached, and the United States relented.[62] Nonetheless, the United States, backed in this effort by the United Kingdom, Japan, and a number of smaller EC states, successfully opposed immediate lending to the USSR, suggesting that the reform process was not sufficiently advanced and that the USSR would crowd out other borrowers. Italy, France, and Germany supported immediate aid. In July 1990 the U.S. position, namely, that the USSR not be granted borrowing powers beyond its 6 percent share, was accepted for two and a half years, although the United States announced that it would not oppose individual efforts to extend assistance to the USSR. Since that time Attali has attempted without success to rescind these limits.[63]

The United States and Britain supported lending only to private-sector borrowers, while France opposed any minimum statutory quotas of lending directly to the private sector. The U.S. government itself came to view this proposal as unrealistic, and changes in Soviet law rendered much of the argument moot, while the remaining EC countries favored a primary but not exclusive emphasis on the private sector. Thus, the final compromise states that at least 60 percent of all loans must go to private-sector projects or sectors being privatized.[64]

Conflicts over the location of the bank and its first chairman were resolved in tandem at a May 1990 G-7 meeting. The bank was to be based in London, in exchange for the chairmanship going to Attali over the more qualified Dutchman H. Onno Ruding, a decision supported by the United Kingdom, some smaller EC countries, and some elements of the German government. (Germany declined to press its claims on behalf of Berlin.) As part of the deal, the French government renounced its claims on a position in the IMF hierarchy ahead of Britain—a long-standing dispute. Yet the United States and its allies limited Attali's power by successfully opposing his proposed by-laws, according to which there would be no second-in-command and the president would decide all major issues of policy, hiring, and firing. The United States insisted instead upon the designation of an American as second-in-command, a post given to Ronald J. Freeman of Salomon Brothers, and the formation of a twenty-three-member board of directors with the power of approval over projects. Subsequently these measures have proven effective at diluting Attali's influence over EBRD lending policies.[65]

The most skeptical countries, namely the United States, Japan, and the United Kingdom, were quite successful at limiting French demands.[66] On issues influencing the day-to-day operation of the bank, such as political and economic conditionality, the use of the European Currency Unit (ECU), and its internal structure, the United States imposed its views. Where U.S. pressure did not prevail, it often achieved its objectives in a more subtle, less symbolically significant way. It was not possible to deny Attali the presidency, for example, but his de facto power was vitiated. The United States found no support for Prague as a site for the bank, but London proved an acceptable substitute. The Soviet Union was permitted to join, but its lending rights remained narrow. Only on the capitalization of the bank and on the proposal for a purely private-sector bank was the United States forced to compromise; these were issues on which it had little choice.

The pattern of U.S. success in these negotiations can readily be explained by a simple bargaining model according to which noncoercive negotiations of this kind tend to reach equilibrium at the lowest common denominator, except where one or more parties can be credibly threatened with exclusion (or linkages are employed).[67] The United States, as the least forthcoming government, generally succeeded in limiting the organization to the lowest common denominator, except where the EC threatened to go ahead alone. On those issues (for example, membership for the USSR, the $12 billion capitalization, and the U.S. proposal for a purely private-sector bank) where the EC did take a strong position and was able tacitly to threaten the United States with exclusion from the organization, the EC position (though not, on capitalization and the private-sector bank, the position of France) prevailed. On most issues, however, the EC was either divided or opposed to the French position, and the United States prevailed. Moreover, the French appeared willing to compromise on numerous issues in order to gain the presidency. As one delegation leader from a small EC country remarked: "From the moment Attali was a candidate to the presidency, he did what had to be done to get the support of the US and Japan."[68]

Justifying the EBRD   The EBRD has suffered from a legitimacy crisis since its creation. Doubts about its apparent redundancy have been fueled by the far-reaching claims of its first president and primary advocate. Anglo-American and Japanese diplomats have quietly criticized the EBRD as redundant, while public attacks have been led by the *Economist,* which cited the celebrated observation: "If the EBRD did not exist, it would not need inventing."[69] The EBRD, it is charged, performs no functions that the World Bank, EIB, or G-24 cannot perform. Its capital base of $13 billion is relatively small by comparison with the EIB's subscribed capital (in 1991) of almost $70 billion and the World Bank, whose 1988 *increase* in capital base alone was even greater. The EBRD's capitalization permits it to lend no more than $2.5 billion a year, though $1.3 billion is a more realistic figure—a number far smaller than projected annual lending of the World Bank in eastern Europe.[70]

Since 1990 EBRD officials, led by Attali, have responded with a number of justifications for the new organization. None, however, withstands close scrutiny. The bank's modest lending, it is argued, will have a powerful "multiplier effect," since the EBRD intends to provide a small stake in many projects. Yet the multiplier effect in no way distinguishes the EBRD from other bilateral and multilateral programs involved in co-financing, domestic and international, private and public.[71] Indeed, the decision to take a small stake in many projects, justified by the multiplier-effect argument, is perhaps more properly seen as a means of compensating for the lack of internal EBRD expertise in project management.[72]

Attali also asserts that the EBRD is exploiting specialized niches not handled by other IFIs, such as training and technical assistance, aid to small and medium-sized enterprises, infrastructure building, and environmental protection. Yet nearly all of the EBRD priority areas are included in the mandate of programs by the World Bank, the European Community, and bilateral donors.[73] Nor is the EBRD unique, as Attali and others maintain, in lending to the private sector or taking equity shares—an ironic claim in light of the initial French suspicion of private-sector lending. The IFC has been expanding activities that began in Yugoslavia in 1968, Hungary in 1985, Poland in 1987, and Czechoslovakia in 1991.[74] The EIB, called "the European equivalent of the IFC," has also expanded its activities. In any case, private equity investments are projected to total no more than 10 percent of EBRD lending—a modest $140 million annually.[75] And as western interest in investment declined, the private-sector focus of the bank became as much a liability as an advantage, and efforts were made to focus on telecommunications, financial issues, and energy infrastructure, thereby creating even greater overlap with preexisting multilateral lenders.[76]

Attali frequently remarks that the EBRD is the only IFI able to impose political conditionality—another aspect of the organization that the French government initially opposed. This view, while strictly speaking true (since the charters of the World Bank and IMF prohibit explicit political conditionality), overlooks the de facto conditionality imposed by the west through the G-7, G-24, and even, in informal ways, the Bretton Woods organizations. Since the EBRD constitutes only a small percentage of the lending of these groups, its independent effect on political developments is in any case unlikely to be significant.[77]

Attali's most provocative and interesting justification for the bank is purely political. He argues that the EBRD is the only IFI to which all the east European countries (except Albania) belong. Universal European membership is important because "we needed to create an organization where all the nations of Europe could meet. Just as the European Coal and Steel Community (ECSC) in the 1950s served as the embryo for the Common Market, the European Bank signals a Continent-wide raising of consciousness to build a peaceful political future."[78]

This justification is intriguing but ultimately unconvincing. First and most obviously, an organization that includes the United States, Japan, and a host of NICs can hardly act as a catalyst for a European identity, as did the ECSC in its time. Second and more important, the primary European organization in which the east European countries are seeking, and will probably eventually gain, membership is surely the EC. Accession to the EC is the primary focus of all east European governments—a phenomenon termed "anticipatory adaptation" elsewhere in this volume. If support for pan-European institutionalization was a central goal of institutional design, therefore, the logical institutional choice would not have been a new organization open to the OECD, but the EC development bank, the EIB, with a capital base four times the size of that of the EBRD and lending activities under way in Poland, Hungary, and Yugoslavia. The EIB had assumed precisely this role with respect to Spain and Portugal before their accession, and some EC member governments supported a similar solution for eastern Europe.[79]

Yet the EBRD appears to have been deliberately designed to circumvent preexisting EC institutions. For a brief period between mid-1989 and mid-1990, the EIB seemed fated to become the leading European institution in the area, and associate status for eastern European countries would surely have been possible. Something similar was the aim of Delors's 1989 proposal, which would have dovetailed with subsequent Commission proposals, floated in 1991 by its vice president, Frans Andriessen, to permit partial participation of east European governments in the decision making of the council of ministers. But this possibility was soon preempted by French proposals for a bank independent of the EC; once these proposals were accepted, efforts to expand EIB lending in Czechoslovakia, Bulgaria, and Romania were easily blocked by France and Britain.[80]

This last point suggests an addendum to our interpretation of the European motivations for creating the EBRD. While the French preference for an independent "European" organization rather than one within the EC may be explicable through the traditional "Gaullist" views of the European future, it remains to be explained why *other* European governments, faced with the French proposal, did not turn to Delors's proposal for an expanded EC role.

The negotiating history suggests three possible explanations. The first is technical. The EIB mandate would have had to be altered, and "changing a well-established Community institution into something as of yet unknown was not very attractive."[81] The second explanation is that some countries may have preferred an organization that included all OECD countries. If this is true, however, it would have—as we have just seen—undermined Attali's primary justification for the organization, namely, that it provides the core for a new, uniquely European identity.

The third explanation focuses on the fact, explicitly recognized by Delors and Andriessen, that expanding EC activities would necessarily open the door to closer east European participation in EC decision making on foreign trade, financial, and aid policies.[82] Given the delicacy of the pan-European trade negotiations over agriculture, steel, and other sectors in which the EC already suffered from surplus capacity, east European participation in the council of ministers was surely to be avoided. The EBRD offered the symbolism of a united, largely European organization in which east European governments were members, without jeopardizing the essential intergovernmental organs of EC decision making. If this explanation is valid, then the advantage of the EBRD to EC members was not simply that it integrated the east Europeans into some European decision-making processes, but also that it excluded them from others.

Compliance: Domestic Politics and the Conditionality Bargain

The central theoretical and empirical problem in analyzing compliance with international agreements is to distinguish between underlying interests and strategic interaction, between consent and coercion. Governments may comply with conditions because they accept the underlying goals or because they are linked to external inducements or sanctions. In the case of compliance with economic conditionality, this problem is particularly sharply defined because reform measures impose domestic political costs. The pain of adjustment falls unevenly, and the (uncertain) winners do not necessarily constitute a political counterweight to the (often more certain) losers. Moreover, there is often a time inconsistency problem, in that reform may bring benefits over the longer run, but politicians frequently make calculations in response to short-term constraints.[83]

The international financial relations between the western donors and the east European countries during 1989–1991 involved just such a mixture of conflict and consensus, thus raising the central question of conditionality: To what extent did the terms under which aid was dispensed affect domestic political and economic policies in eastern Europe? There are two interpretations. On the one hand, liberalization may have resulted from—and will continue to result from—sharp asymmetries of power. East European governments were "regime-takers" because the western powers controlled desperately needed external resources. The dispensing of those resources hinged on judgments concerning the political worthiness of the recipient country and its willingness to undertake reform measures. Governments may also be constrained by severe external disequilibria, which leave no alternative to austerity, regardless of the political terms imposed on them.

On the other hand, compliance may not have been the result of the influence wielded by international financial institutions and the donor community more broadly. During this period the governments and societies of most east European countries were committed to economic reform and structural adjustment independent of any outside demands that were placed on them—a policy pattern of "anticipatory adaptation." Moreover, given the lack of understanding regarding the transition process, multilateral institutions exercised influence as much through persuasion and the transmission of policy expertise as through outright inducement or coercion.[84] If domestic factors are an important part of the explanation of compliance, as our case studies suggest, rising social resistance to stabilization and market-oriented policies may result in what Robert Putnam terms "involuntary defection."[85] Even though a government may negotiate in good faith, it can face substantial difficulties in ratifying and implementing the reform package at home.

The complexity of the conditionality bargain is illustrated by comparing the experiences of Poland and Hungary—the two most advanced east European economies, which together received approximately 50 percent of western aid in this period.[86] In many ways the two cases are similar. For both, internal and external economic equilibrium has been the fundamental political issue since before the transition to democracy. Unlike Czechoslovakia, Romania, and Bulgaria, they had a substantial legacy of economic reform efforts, often provoked by external disequilibrium, prior to the transition to democracy. Debates over economic management played a decisive role not only in the downfall of the communist regime but in subsequent changes of government. Governments moved a substantial distance toward austerity under the combined influence of external disequilibrium, pressure from western aid donors, and ideological commitment to rapid liberalization. In both cases it is difficult to disentangle the effect of these three factors, but it is plausible to argue that domestic opposition is increasingly calling the long-term sustainability of adjustment policies into question.

Yet Poland and Hungary also diverge in several key respects. The Polish case demonstrates the importance of anticipatory adaptation to western conditions. In 1989 Poland faced the most severe economic crisis in eastern Europe and the largest absolute debt burden of all five east European governments; but it was also the country in which western donors were most intimately engaged. On assuming power, the new Solidarity government initiated the most sweeping radical reform program in all of east Europe, winning substantial international support for doing so. Poland had the good fortune to owe most of its debt to official sources, who proved forgiving in the face of economic difficulties, thereby facilitating a quid pro quo with western donors.

Although Hungary began with higher per capita debt than Poland, its more competitive economy and highly developed structure meant that external disequilibria imposed a less binding policy constraint than in the Polish case. Moreover, the ideological impetus toward radical macroeconomic adjustment was less strong. Finally, although orthodox in its willingness to meet external commitments, Hungary found private banks less willing to write down debt in exchange for reform. The result of these factors was a much more gradual pace of economic reform.

Poland

Since the early 1980s the question of the relationship between economic reform and representation for the opposition has been the paramount question in Polish politics. Although Poland negotiated restructurings of its bank debt in 1983, 1984, and 1986, debt servicing costs remained high, exports were sluggish, and as a result the government remained vulnerable to balance of payments crises. After 1988 labor unrest in response to a rescheduling program, a mismanaged indexation scheme, the legalization of the black market for foreign exchange (which provided the opportunity to flee the currency), and the liberalization of food prices caused prices to explode into hyperinflation levels in the second half of 1989. In the June 1989 elections the Communist party attempted the gambit of maintaining political control while getting the Solidarity leadership to share some responsibility for the crisis and moderating the demands of its membership. This effort backfired completely as Solidarity won virtually all of the seats it was allowed.[87]

There were initially serious divisions within Solidarity about the wisdom of assuming responsibility for a deteriorating economy, but the overwhelming nature of Solidarity's victory made it difficult not to participate in government. Moreover, the deteriorating economic situation had catapulted radical reformers within Solidarity's ranks to the fore. In a speech to the Solidarity parliamentarians in the summer, Harvard professor Jeffrey Sachs convinced Solidarity leaders that they could gain politically through a radical "shock treatment" reform effort that would arrest the hyperinflationary spiral and initiate wide-ranging market-oriented reforms.

Thus Poland undertook its first posttransition adjustment program in advance of direct pressure from the IMF or the official donor community. Yet

Sachs and the Polish team had maintained that the program would require extensive external support, including debt relief. EC proposals concerning assistance to eastern Europe were already on the table, and a variety of diplomatic signals suggested that the new Solidarity government would enjoy substantial external support if it undertook strong adjustment efforts.[88] In short, inducements did exist.

This assessment proved correct. In comparison with the situation in other eastern European countries, the swiftness and comprehensiveness of the western response to Poland is striking.[89] By late October the EC emergency aid package of $669 million for Poland and Hungary had been set up, and this was soon expanded to include access to the European Investment Bank up to approximately $1 billion. In Tadeusz Mazowiecki's trips to western capitals in October and November he collected pledges of 4 billion francs ($640 million) over four years from the French, $400 million in export credits from Italy, and DM 3 billion in loans for specific projects, as well as a rescheduling of debts worth DM 2.5 billion from Germany.

Negotiations with the IMF for a standby proceeded relatively smoothly on the basis of the Sachs-Balcerowicz plan, and in late December Poland signed an IMF letter of intent. This immediately gave it access to a bridging loan of $215 from the Bank for International Settlements as well as access to the $1 billion stabilization facility provided to underwrite the move to convertibility. The final approval of the standby opened not only IMF coffers but World Bank lending as well. Moreover, predictions for the program in the short run were proven correct: the program stabilized the balance of payments while achieving convertibility, reduced inflation to single digits, and eliminated shortages. This success was achieved, however, through a sharp drop in output, a gradual but steady increase in unemployment, and growing dissatisfaction with the costs of adjustment.

The formation of Lech Walesa's first cabinet in the winter of 1990–91 further demonstrates the subtle but decisive influence that credibility with foreign creditors can play in domestic politics. When Mazowiecki could not be persuaded to stay on as prime minister, Walesa turned to a Solidarity lawyer, Jan Olszewski. A major issue in the formation of the cabinet, however, was whether Leszek Balcerowicz, clearly favored by the donor community, would stay. Balcerowicz threatened to resign if his plan were altered or his power diminished; and when Olszewski could not fully accommodate Balcerowicz's demands, it was Olszewski who was fired. Walesa turned instead to Krzysztof Bielecki, a leading figure in a small grouping known as the "Gdansk liberals," signaling to the creditor community that stabilization policy would not be sacrificed, despite Walesa's own election-year pledges. Through the spring of 1991 Walesa was careful to give the government free rein, even in the face of mounting protests from farmers and workers.

This strategy paid off handsomely. In a move that had potentially wide-ranging consequences for the management of other debtors, the United States succeeded in pushing the other Paris Club countries to erase half of Poland's $33 billion in public debt as a reward for the efforts undertaken up until that point. Less than a week later, Walesa came to Washington and received another $800 million in relief from President Bush, and in April the IMF agreed to an extended arrangement to run through 1993 totaling $1.665 billion, under which 25 percent of each disbursement would be set aside for debt reduction. The agreement eliminated one quarter of Poland's annual debt service, even though efforts to secure a similar agreement with the commercial banks proved much less successful, despite support from official creditors in the form of pressure on the banks to settle.[90]

Since the elections of October 1991, it has become increasingly unclear whether the equilibrium could be maintained as the effects of the structural measures such as privatization worked through the economic and political system. The transition has proved more socially and politically disruptive than expected. By late 1991 Poland had had five prime ministers in three years; Walesa had been forced to implement economic reform by decree; parties advocating continued reform had gained less than 20 percent in the most recent elections; inflation had reached 70 percent; the government budget was $1.7 billion in deficit; and EFF credits were being denied for failure to meet IMF conditionality.[91] These events suggest that the domestic capacity of Poland to comply with the conditionality bargain may be eroding.

Hungary

At the time of its political transition, Hungary had gone the farthest in undertaking reforms within the socialist framework, triggering an extensive literature about the limits and possibilities of "market socialism." Critics of gradualism pointed to the problems of the Hungarian economy during the 1980s, however, as evidence that such an approach was doomed to failure.[92] In addition to low growth and creeping inflation, the country experienced recurrent balance of payments and debt difficulties during the 1980s. By 1987 commercial lenders had become apprehensive; maturities shortened and terms hardened. The mounting economic crisis on both the domestic and external fronts triggered a wide-ranging internal debate on economic policy in the summer of 1987 and the development of a program that included not only stabilization but accelerated economic reform as well. While agreements were reached with international lenders, stabilization measures contributed to a further erosion of growth in the short run; GDP dropped in both 1988 and 1989.

By 1988 political debate in Hungary both inside and outside the party crystallized around the same question that had been posed by Poland's economic crisis: Could economic reform go further without political liberalization? As elsewhere in eastern Europe, pressures for more rapid change were reflected first in the ascent of reformist factions within the party, which eased János Kádár from power in May 1988. The reformist communist governments of 1988 and 1989 were divided on the pace and scope of reform. In May the IMF shocked the government by announcing that it was withholding the final tranche of the $350 million standby because Hungary had failed to meet a number of policy targets and risked a current account deficit twice that projected under the program. Although the government acted rapidly to guarantee that the budget deficit would not exceed targets, the incident, as well as the deterioration in the balance of payments, triggered a reformulation, sharpening, and deepening of previous reform efforts. This revised reform program was subsequently presented to the G-24 in the fall of 1989, prior to the completion of the political transition.

The interim government's reform program and the general enthusiasm of the European countries to assist the reform efforts of new democratic governments allowed the Hungarians to secure extensive financing during the transition process. By the end of the first quarter of 1990, pledges to Hungary through the G-24 already totaled over ECU 4.8 billion, and in March the IMF approved a standby for $200 million.[93] Yet the external support the country enjoyed rested on commitments made by the outgoing government. Given developments within the CMEA and with reference to oil pricing, the cushion of improvement in the current account and external debt picture could not be counted on indefinitely.

Political events contributed to policy drift. Not until May 24, 1990, did a coalition government, led by Josef Antall of the center-right Hungarian Democratic Forum, come to power. In an effort to stanch demand in the face of rising prices associated with the Iraqi invasion of Kuwait and the impending shift to convertible currency pricing of Soviet oil, the government was forced to impose a 66 percent increase in gas prices. Widespread protest ensued.[94]

One effect of the crisis was to accelerate a debate within the government about the pace of economic reform.[95] Although a "shock therapy" plan advanced by the state secretary for economic affairs on October 30 was rejected by the government, pressures from the IMF, particularly concerning fiscal policy, and declining trade prospects led the government toward a more rapid reform path. The new finance minister appointed in December 1990, Mihaly Kupa, was given relatively free rein in drafting a new four-year program that placed emphasis on speeding the pace of privatization, liberalizing prices, controlling inflation through tight monetary and fiscal policy, and moving toward convertibility. On the basis of the cabinet changes and preliminary drafts of the program, the IMF approved an extended three-year agreement that, together with contingency financing under the CCFF, would permit Hungary to draw over $2 billion.

Yet in the course of 1991 the government increasingly split over the pace of reform, particularly privatization and the management of the exchange rate. Even though the IMF continued to give the country its stamp of approval, Kupa threatened to resign in June over failure to implement the four-year program and concessions to the increasingly organized and mobilized unions.[96] Poland's ability to secure debt relief also triggered a debate about whether Hungary should continue to follow the orthodox approach of prompt repayment when declarations of moratorium seemed to be rewarded.

Hungary did not move in the radical reform direction of the Polish program. The opposition remained divided, and though the government's popularity fell over the course of 1991, Antall maintained and even increased his political hold over the government. But the main reason for the policy drift appears to have been economic: through the end of 1991 conditions were not as bad as had been feared and were certainly better than elsewhere in eastern Europe. The economy contracted in 1991, but only slightly, and inflation, which never approached the levels seen in Poland, Romania, or Bulgaria, appeared under control. The shock associated with the collapse of the CMEA affected Hungary less than other east European countries as a result of the rapid shift to western markets and the generosity of official donors.

Thus, despite an extremely heavy debt servicing burden, Hungary has not faced an inflation or balance of payments crisis of the magnitude of Poland's. These economic conditions allowed the country to pursue a more moderate adjustment strategy. While Hungary has met its debt payments and implemented significant microeconomic reform, it has stopped short of macro-economic shock treatment. Hungary's more gradual approach also reflected a different constellation of domestic political forces, but its reform program and debt repayment may similarly be threatened by the costs of future reform and Hungary's inability to gain concessions from private bankers at the London Club, who hold most of the country's debt.[97]

The Institutional Landscape

The findings of our examination of western official aid to eastern Europe between 1989 and 1991 can be summarized in the form of five empirical conclusions.

First, privatizable national benefits, rather than a common concern for the provision of international "public goods," appear to be the key determinants of the level and type (trade credits, debt relief, or project finance) of aid western governments extended to eastern Europe. To be sure, there was a minimum consensus on the desirability of ensuring regional peace and prosperity, given that private long-term finance was manifestly insufficient to prevent economic collapse. But the absence of an overwhelming threat and, except in Germany, a compelling economic interest—both decisive factors motivating Marshall Plan aid in the 1940s and 1950s—meant that assistance to eastern Europe on this basis remained relatively modest. In this negative sense, the pattern of national policies reflects realist calculations: the resulting contrast between today's programs and those of the Marshall Plan era are in part the consequences of the region's economic and strategic insignificance.) Yet an approach that stresses socioeconomic interdependence and domestic politics better predicts individual national policies. Variations in the willingness of western governments to commit resources to aid were closely correlated with concrete commercial, financial, and political interests. Despite legitimate humanitarian concerns, countries with few concrete interests contributed relatively little.

Second, these variations in the interests and commitments of western governments led them to reject multilateral solutions in favor of bilateral and regional aid, coordinated by single-purpose institutions that provided little more than a negotiating forum. Within the western consensus on the need to promote democratic legitimacy and financial orthodoxy, bilateralism provided room for governments with greater material interests in eastern Europe to pursue distinctive strategies. In the area of direct financial assistance, bilateral and regional commitments account for 75 percent of total funding. As for debt relief, ad hoc discussions over Poland at the Paris Club led to an outcome near the "lowest common denominator," with unilateral defection by those creditors with less exposure. In the first years of the transition the swift distribution of emergency aid was a top priority, and governments turned to multilateral organizations with ready finance at hand. But bilateral and regional sources, which are slower to come on line but which had always constituted the bulk of aid *commitments,* are now coming to dominate *disbursements* as well.

Third, the headlines grabbed by the formation of the EBRD and the unprecedented coordination activities of the EC Commission and the G-24 exaggerate their importance to the overall western aid effort. In particular, the widespread view, especially in Europe, that 1989 marked a watershed—a moment when the EC, led by the Commission, overcame its lack of power, cohesion, and expertise to assume decisive leadership in shaping postwar aid institutions— can be dismissed.[98] Both the EC PHARE program and the EBRD are, in fact, politically and financially secondary. The EBRD is modestly funded ($12 billion capitalization), compared to the World Bank, the EIB ($170 billion), and bilateral programs. Moreover, the United States and its allies, with support from EC moderates, were successful in blocking the more controversial French proposals to expand its discretion, although even the initial French proposal acknowledged its subordination to existing Bretton Woods organizations. With one exception—the need for Soviet membership—the EC was not cohesive, while Commission proposals were repeatedly brushed aside. The outcome of the negotiations can be predicted with a simple bargaining theory based on "lowest common denominator" outcomes (except where governments can credibly threaten to go it alone or exclude others). Finally, the lack of any coherent justification for the creation of the EBRD, given the manifest ability of the preexisting EIB and IFC to perform the same tasks, suggests that it was an act of political symbolism rather than functional necessity. The most striking evidence of the lack of functional justification is that many of those aspects of the EBRD that Attali now points to as virtues—its imposition of political conditionality, its private-sector focus, and its investment bank structure—are among the proposals he most vehemently opposed as a French official.

The coordination of emergency aid under the PHARE program has proven a narrow, transitional, and almost exclusively bureaucratic task occupying no more than a few dozen Commission officials, most without technical expertise in the area. The program was initiated by national governments, who first offered the task of coordination to the German government, which evidently saw little advantage in accepting it. In any case, cumbersome PHARE procedures were often circumvented by national officials. The lack of any essential need for an international organization is further demonstrated by the decision of G-10 finance ministers in April 1991 to transfer many Commission activities, along with some performed by the G-24, to other multilateral organizations and ad hoc senior officials' groups.

Fourth, the focus on new organizations diverts us from the real institutional continuities of the western response. In addition to the predominance of bilateral funding and ad hoc cooperation through the G-7 and the Paris Club, existing multilateral organizations — the IMF and the World Bank — made an essential contribution, as institutionalist theory would expect. Monitoring country risk, disbursing funds quickly, and providing a focal point for macroeconomic conditionality were tasks that these organizations could perform with unique competence and efficiency, and these were thus sources of real institutional discretion and persistence. Yet it is important not to exaggerate the independent importance of the IMF and World Bank in the overall direction of the aid program. The autonomy of the IMF and the World Bank was not truly put to the test because the western consensus on the need to impose conditionality, political and economic, was near total. No western government voiced dissatisfaction with IMF conditionality, World Bank structural adjustment programs, or the common political standards worked out in the G-7 and G-24. IMF approval was a necessary condition for granting official debt relief and rescheduling commercial debt, but these were still negotiated through the Paris and London clubs.

Fifth and finally, while conditionality clearly played a role in shaping the orthodox policies pursued by east European governments during this period, external economic constraints and domestic ideological commitments appear to have been even more decisive. Despite similar treatment by the IMF, for example, Poland and Hungary followed somewhat different paths of economic reform. Poland's orthodox program of "shock treatment" was in part a successful bid for debt relief. But macroeconomic constraints and liberal ideological currents in domestic politics also influenced reform policy. In both countries, as well as their east European neighbors, domestic factors are closely interwoven with international constraints. Rising political opposition to harsh austerity and adjustment policies may therefore undermine future efforts by east European governments to maintain their end of the "conditionality bargain."

Implications for Theories of International Cooperation

These findings make us cautious about public goods arguments for cooperation, and directly challenge the assumptions of institutionalist theory that the
transaction costs of international negotiation under anarchy are high. The
weakness of the public goods assumption has been discussed in the existing
literature on international cooperation; the weakness of the assumption about
high transaction costs has received less attention.

Institutionalist theory is quite clear that its arguments do not depend on the
assumption that international norms and rules necessarily constitute "public
goods." However, institutionalist theory does emphasize public goods as
helping to explain international institutions.[99] It is important, our findings
suggest, not to overemphasize this point.

In many aspects of aid policy toward eastern Europe we found the public
goods analogy unhelpful. Coordination by strong multilateral organizations
offered few advantages while having the added liability of limiting the
flexibility of governments to pursue specific "privatizable" interests. In such
circumstances all "pure coordination problems," bilateralism programs, or
minimal ad hoc multilateral institutions, which provide little more than a
forum, were preferred.[100] Even where some common gains may have been
possible, our findings suggest that the gains may well be outweighed by the
restrictions imposed by an international institution on bilateral diplomatic
flexibility.

Institutionalists may be tempted to interpret the weakness of multilateral
institutions in channeling western aid as a failure of collective action, in
particular as a failure to provide the public good of regional peace and
prosperity at an adequate level. Yet this argument would commit the fallacy
of imputing preferences to state leaders that they do not appear to have held.
Moreover, the failure of cooperation can hardly be attributed to the lack of
preexisting institutions; if anything, there have been *too many* potential
forums, coordinators, and initiators. Nor were leaders primarily concerned
about free riding or relative gains. Instead, most of them simply did not
believe that their country would gain from greater aid flows.

Two exceptions to the pattern of bilateralism and ad hoc cooperation were
the IMF and the World Bank, considered central to the western aid effort and
accorded more institutional discretion than the G-24, the Commission, or the
EBRD. Why did these multilateral organizations play an important autonomous role? One reason is that both the IMF and the World Bank could carry
out specific tasks that were difficult to replicate elsewhere: a large pool of

ready resources and long experience in extending official aid, for example, allowed them to disburse large sums more quickly than bilateral donors or new multilateral institutions. Their expertise in assessing country and project risk made the IMF and World Bank essential "gatekeepers" for aid.

A theoretically more interesting reason for the importance of the IMF is the advantage, when imposing macroeconomic conditionality, of employing a single global agent with expertise (in order to assess proper conditionality) and legitimacy (in bound negotiations in what may be a crisis situation) and, most important, autonomy (because it may be called upon at any time to impose conditionality on any country in the international system).[101] The last point is decisive. Were the purpose of the IMF simply to coordinate macroeconomic conditionality for eastern Europe alone, ad hoc coordination might have been adequate to the task. But the threat of external insolvency may face *any* government in the international system—a situation that can be thought of as an n-person Prisoner's Dilemma, in which any government might face an incentive to exempt itself. Hence the need for a relatively autonomous international actor to impose macroeconomic conditionality. In other words, because this task raised a collaboration problem rather than a coordination problem, the international institution that performed it was granted more autonomy.[102]

Yet the autonomy of the IMF should not be exaggerated. The case studies of Poland and Hungary demonstrate that while IMF approval was a precondition for aid, it was the intervention of individual governments, and particularly U.S. support for debt relief to Poland, that actually relieved the external constraints. The IMF and the World Bank, though necessarily autonomous, are nonetheless best understood as the extension of bilateral and ad hoc cooperation by major creditors.

These findings extend previous criticisms and extensions of institutionalism, which focused on the distinction between coordination and collaboration, to include the bilateral alternative.[103] Where interests diverge but do not conflict, bilateralism is an optimal institutional form; where pure coordination is sought, ad hoc cooperation is adequate to the task; and where a collaboration problem exists, owing to conflicts of interest and the resulting incentive to defect in certain circumstances, international institutions may be granted a measure of institutional autonomy.

A more fundamental challenge to institutionalist theory follows from our finding that western statesmen were willing to incur the transaction costs (in this case bargaining and overhead costs) of creating a functionally redundant organization, namely, the EBRD. This not only poses an empirical anomaly for institutionalism but calls into question the validity of one of its basic assumptions. The explicit recognition by most EC governments that modification of the EIB or IFC would have been *more* difficult administratively than creation of the EBRD undermines the foundational institutionalist assumption that the transaction costs of institutional creation are higher than those of institutional reform. Even more troubling, the amorphousness of justifications for the EBRD, the swiftness of its founding negotiations (despite their ad hoc forum), and even, in some cases, the ease with which expertise could be transmitted between institutions all suggest that the *absolute* costs of institutional creation are relatively low.

Recall that institutionalist theory advances two major predictions: first, levels of international cooperation are often suboptimal, owing to the lack of an appropriate international institution, and, second, cooperation is more likely to occur within preexisting international institutions because institutions are cheaper to maintain than to create. Both of these distinctive institutionalist predictions rely critically on the assumption of high transaction costs. Despite the vital importance of this assumption to current thinking on international institutions, it has not previously been subjected to empirical evaluation.[104] Our findings suggest that it may often be invalid.

To be sure, the persistence of two preexisting institutions, the IMF and the World Bank, is consistent with the predictions of institutionalist theory, but this does not constitute a strong confirmation of it, for there was no evidence of support among western leaders for serious alternatives. Only "inconvenient" commitments provide a properly controlled test of the strength of international commitments.[105] (Even adoption of the relatively isolated French proposal for larger funding for the EBRD, which might have undermined some World Bank activities, would not have reversed this conclusion.) Satisfaction with the results of its actions is a more straightforward reason for the persistent central role of the IMF and the World Bank, *despite* the fact that the transaction costs of creating a new organization had already been incurred.[106]

Implications for Empirical Research

Neither of these two objections to institutionalist assumptions seeks to deny that international institutions facilitate cooperation or, indeed, that under some circumstances they may be necessary conditions for cooperation to emerge. But these objections do challenge the notion that institutions can be thought of as *causes* of cooperation, either by *independently* increasing the probability of cooperation or by accounting for variance in cooperation across issues and countries.[107]

Our findings are more consistent with a pure liberal theory of cooperation, one which assumes that the demand for the functional benefits of cooperation tends to create its own supply. In this view, bargaining and other transaction costs are relatively low, and intergovernmental institutions persist above all because they satisfy the functional demands of participating governments more efficiently than the alternatives. This suggests that the causes of institutional stability may lie in the stability of underlying national interests or strategic problems more than in the institutional inertia that results from the high cost of renegotiation. In this view, international institutions are not *causes* of cooperation but mechanisms through which cooperation occurs.[108] If this alternative explanation is correct, then in order to generate reliable predictions, institutionalist theory must be embedded in a strong, detailed theory of national preference formation.

These findings point to the need for more narrowly bounded empirical applications of institutionalist theory, more precise theoretical specification of its predictions about institutional form, and, above all, closer attention to the social interests that underlie the preferences of governments for international cooperation. Just as an analysis of these social interests is the first step toward understanding the revolutions of 1989, it is also the starting point for an analysis of the international institutions that have followed in their wake.

Chapter 9

Foreign Direct Investment in Eastern Europe

Debora L. Spar

In the countries of central and eastern Europe[1] the question of foreign direct investment (FDI) has assumed a vivid importance. Prior to 1989 there was virtually no western investment in the region. With few exceptions, the communist governments of the Soviet bloc forbade the entry of western firms or western capital; the western governments likewise forbade the export of a wide variety of goods deemed to be of strategic value; and the potential investors themselves saw no reason to invest in an economy where all business was conducted under the auspices of the state, and where profit making was considered fundamentally illegal.

All of these conditions were changed, however, with the collapse of the Berlin Wall and the subsequent demise of the Soviet bloc and the Soviet-style communism that had prevailed within it. Almost immediately upon declaring their change in regimes, the new governments of eastern Europe pronounced themselves open to foreign investment. And almost immediately thereafter investors from the west rushed to declare their interest in the newly opened markets of the east.

Under these circumstances, FDI seems to offer a tremendous potential for cooperation and mutual gain. If it is carefully directed, private investment can bring the eastern European countries the capital, technology, and industrial infrastructure they need in order to modernize their economies and boost their

286

standard of living. Likewise, if they can enter the market successfully, eastern Europe offers western businesses substantial opportunities for wide-scale investment and long-term profits. The problem, however, is that the bargain also entails significant risks and uncertainties for both sides. For the eastern Europeans especially, the political risks would appear to be huge. They desperately need capital to resuscitate their economies, but they also need, after four decades of Soviet domination, to reassert control over their domestic social and political order. If foreign investment becomes too large, or too important to the economy, it may threaten the government's ability to implement the policies it desires. Moreover, because the political situation in eastern Europe is so fluid, even the *perception* of foreign dominance may be sufficient to push domestic opposition to an unsustainable level.[2] For the western investors, meanwhile, political unrest translates into great economic uncertainty.[3] They do not know when laws will change, how they will change, or even where on the political spectrum their host governments will eventually establish themselves. Tax laws, foreign exchange procedures, labor codes — things that investors usually take as given — are all in a state of flux and uncertainty. In order for investment to proceed, therefore, the governments of eastern Europe must find some way to codify their existing legal and economic structures and to guarantee the sanctity of western investment. Simultaneously, though, they need to ensure that the demands of western investors do not interfere with their own political and economic objectives.

In the area of foreign direct investment, therefore, the contours of the bargaining space are relatively clear. The west wants security, the east wants investment, and both demand clarity. On these grounds we should expect international institutions to play a large role: providing a forum for negotiation, signaling intentions, and codifying the evolving system of rules. What makes the position of international institutions somewhat awkward in this area, though, is that the most important players — the investors themselves — are private corporations, which have historically shied away from international attempts to regulate foreign direct investment.

And yet, despite this obvious constraint, the area of foreign direct investment is still littered with international institutions, and with international efforts to coordinate the evolution of investment practices in eastern Europe. The Organization for Economic Cooperation and Development (OECD), the European Bank for Reconstruction and Development (EBRD), and the World Bank's International Finance Corporation (IFC) are all active in the area, and promise to become even more so. The western European nations, meanwhile, have basically agreed to pool all of their investment assistance in the PHARE (Poland/Hungary Aid for Restructuring Economies) program, and the United States has demonstrated its commitment to joining the Europeans' efforts. Most tellingly of all, perhaps, the eastern Europeans themselves are rushing to embrace both the western institutions and the norms and rules they represent. Indeed, in a process the contributors of this volume term "anticipatory adaptation," the governments of the formerly socialist states are abiding by western laws and adopting western standards even before they are accepted into the organizations that formally embody these laws and standards. Some of this adaptation, of course, may be staged for the benefit of potential investors and some may be part of a broader phenomenon of eastern Europe's lust for nearly all western institutions. Nevertheless, it is still significant. Even when the leading players are not states, and even when there are significant opportunities for bilateral and unilateral arrangements, international institutions are proving to be a powerful force.

State Strategies: The Efforts of the East

If there is one thing that the governments of eastern Europe seem to have in common, it is a desire to attract foreign investment. They all want to regulate it, of course, and to set some guidelines for its role in their economies, but their first priority seems simply to attract wide-scale investment as quickly as possible.

The reasoning behind this desire is straightforward. After forty-five years of socialist control, the countries of eastern Europe are suddenly rushing to embrace capitalism. They are determined to establish private enterprise, open their borders to foreign goods, and rid themselves of the state-owned enterprises that have long dominated their economies. As these countries are quickly discovering, however, the transition from communism to capitalism is exceedingly difficult. To be successful, it demands a fundamental restructuring of the entire economic and social basis of the state. All at once, the countries of eastern Europe are struggling to create a financial infrastructure, realign their currencies, learn the basic rules of market competition, distribute the productive assets of the state, and privatize a vast industrial infrastructure. All of these tasks, of course, are extraordinarily complicated and intricately interlocked. They all require fundamental changes in the existing legal system and in the social structure that developed under communist control. If the changes do not occur in the proper sequence, or if they fail to produce the outcomes that the people of the region have come to expect, they risk pushing the already fragile political order of these states into chaos.

To make matters even worse, no one really knows the correct formula for enacting this transformation. Certainly the transition will require significant amounts of foreign aid, technical assistance, and debt relief. There seems to be a growing realization in the east that private investment—FDI—will play a crucial role in the transformation process. Aid donated by western governments—even massive amounts of aid—will not suffice, since the funds are only being channeled into economies that do not yet have the financial infrastructure to absorb them. Through the middle of 1992, for instance, nearly $175 million of World Bank funds were still sitting in the Central Bank of Poland, since the bank did not yet have a network to distribute the funds to small borrowers, or even the internal capacity to assess their creditworthiness. Similarly, most intragovernmental aid is likely to stay focused on the central government—precisely the opposite of what a move toward decentralization of the economy demands. In order for capitalism to take root, capitalists and capitalist enterprises must develop throughout the economy. And in order to develop, they need access to capital and the means to employ it.

This is where foreign direct investment comes in. The hope is that foreign firms will invest in the region, bringing with them the desperately needed capital and technology. They will buy the old industries from the state and revitalize them with capital infusion and western-style management. They will act as a spur to the development of local enterprise, both by providing an example and, more important, by providing start-up capital for the entire economy.

This last point is especially critical. In Poland, Czechoslovakia, and Hungary the governments have been engaged in dramatic programs of privatization designed to put all economic assets back into private hands. Although the specifics of each country's program differ widely, the basic idea is identical: to allow the citizens to buy the assets of the state. The problem, though, is that the citizens simply do not have sufficient capital to purchase these assets, much less to manage them profitably. There are ways to finesse this problem—by undervaluing assets, by selling them for vouchers, and so on—but none of these schemes can eliminate the basic need for capital. Someone simply has to put the money—real, hard, convertible currency—into these economies. And the best prospect for this role seems to be foreign investors. Thus, the governments of eastern Europe share a common strategy with regard to foreign direct investment: they want to attract it, and to keep it. The tactics they have employed in pursuit of this goal vary somewhat from country to country, but the basic thrust of their efforts is the same.

This chapter examines in some detail the policies that emerged between 1989 and 1991 in two of the region's most rapidly changing states: Poland and Czechoslovakia. Their stories, to be sure, are not entirely representative: Bulgaria and Romania still lag far behind them, and Hungary (which started with a considerably higher level of foreign investment) has been able to move more quickly and somewhat more smoothly. Nevertheless, the stories of Poland and Czechoslovakia provide a good illustration of the challenges that face eastern Europe in the area of foreign direct investment, and of the strategies they are formulating in response.

Poland

As of mid-1991, the Polish government was actively involved in creating the legal and financial structures that would be most conducive to the entry of foreign investors. Realizing that "the requirements of the great task of modernizing the Polish economy exceed the amount of domestic capital and technical capabilities,"[4] the Poles had embarked on a dramatic program of opening their country to foreign investment.

Officially, Poland had been open to foreign investment since 1976, when the Council of Ministers passed a regulation permitting the establishment of small-scale enterprises. Under these laws, however, the investors were significantly constrained both in the scale of their operations and in their potential profitability. They were not eligible, for instance, for credit at any Polish banks; they had to make an advance deposit of 30 percent of their project's cost to a Polish bank; and they were allowed to transfer only 50 percent of their export profits out of the country.[5] Under these conditions, it is hardly surprising that only nine minor firms chose to invest in Poland during the six years that these regulations were in place.[6]

In 1982 the Polish Sejm (parliament) moved to loosen the rules, and thus to attract greater investment in Poland. Under the terms of a then radical law,[7] the state recognized the legal basis of foreign investment and created a state guarantee for the invested capital.[8] Still, all investment under the law was limited to businesses with a maximum size of two hundred employees, and enterprises were prohibited from exporting anything but their own products or importing anything but their own needs. In 1986 another law extended the range of potential investment in Poland by permitting the creation of joint ventures with public-sector companies.[9] Under these more relaxed conditions, over fifty firms formed joint ventures in Poland; nevertheless, the terms of their involvement were still strictly constrained.

All of these conditions changed, however, along with the political changes that swept Poland in the late 1980s. By 1991, all investment in Poland was regulated by the 1988 Joint Venture Law[10] and an even more liberal foreign investment law was passed in June 1991. The brunt of these laws was to open the country to virtually any foreign investment. There was no minimum limit set on the amount of initial investment, and permits were required only for a handful of industries such as defense, air and sea ports, real estate, and wholesale trade in imported goods. Foreign companies were allowed to repatriate all of their capital, including capital gains, and to remit full profits and dividends. For companies with invested capital of more than ECU 2 million, or companies which exported more than 20 percent of their production, additional tax relief could also be obtained.

By any standard these laws created an extremely liberal climate for investment. Not only were foreigners given full national treatment, but they were also given investment guarantees, tax holidays, and capital export allowances which, arguably, were not available to the average Polish investor. Moreover, the laws virtually took foreign investment beyond the realm of government regulation. In effect, they announced that foreigners were free to engage in any business they desired, so long as they paid their taxes and brought hard currency with them. The result was a rapid increase in joint ventures between 1989 and 1991 (see Table 9.1), although most were small (see Table 9.2). German capital took the lead (see Table 9.3).

Thus, rather than regulate foreign investment, Poland chose to do all it could to attract it. In this context it is worthwhile to note the brief history of Poland's Foreign Investment Agency. Established under the 1988 Joint Ven-

Table 9.1. Joint Ventures, 1989–1991[a]

Year	Poland	Czechoslovakia	Romania	Hungary	Bulgaria
1989	867	22	5	180	30
1990	2799	1550	1502	4400	140
1991	4000	1318	2665	2420	366

Source: The Economist, September, 21, 1991.
a. First quarter of 1991 only.

Table 9.2. Joint Ventures in Poland by Value of Foreign Capital

Value of Foreign Capital ($ thousands)	Number of Companies
Over 3,000	10
1,000–3,000	12
500–1,000	17
200–500	54
100–200	136
60–100	217
50–60	287
50 or less	413

Source: Foreign Trade Research Center, Warsaw, 1990.

ture Law, the agency was responsible for all aspects of foreign investment. In practice, though, its main job was to review the extended applications that all potential investors were required under the law to submit. The agency approved virtually all of the applications it received; however, the length of the approval process was a source of tremendous frustration to both the investors and the agency's own officials. In 1991, at its own request, the agency was officially closed, the application process was eliminated, and a new foreign investment office charged solely with promotional duties was attached to the Ministry of Privatization.[11]

Part of Poland's enthusiasm for the free market approach has no doubt been driven by the overall imperatives of the Balcerowicz plan[12] and by its explicit intention to restructure the Polish economy as quickly as possible. With the launch of its "big bang" in January 1990, Poland lowered its trade barriers substantially, introduced currency convertibility, and eliminated virtually all domestic price controls. The next step, and perhaps the single most important one, was to redistribute state assets through a massive program of privatization. The details of this privatization program are extremely complex and go beyond the scope of this discussion. In general, though, the first "wave" of privatization was designed to include the sale of over four hundred enterprises which together constitute about 25 percent of Poland's industrial output.[13] If the process goes as planned,[14] it will entail distributing ownership of the state-owned companies among five to twenty newly created investment funds. All Polish citizens will then be given, free, equal shares in these funds. The hope is that the funds will act as both owners and managers of the firms under their control. By imposing western management skills and capitalist market discipline upon the firms, they will cut the wastage out of Poland's economy and make its firms competitive in the international economy. Simultaneously, the firms will also serve to bring capitalism to the Polish citizens without asking them to accept any real down-side risks.

Even under the most optimistic scenarios, however, the success of the Polish privatization scheme still rests largely with the western response to it. The funds themselves were slated to be run by western investment banks, which meant that Poland's Ministry of Privatization would have to attract these fund managers, find a suitable means of compensating them, and still ward off accusations that foreigners were running the country's economy.[15]

Table 9.3. National Distribution of Joint Ventures in Poland (by capital investment)

Country	Number of Firms	Value of Capital ($ millions)	Percent
Germany	404	42.6	29
Sweden	101	19.7	13
Norway	9	18.2	12
Netherlands	48	16.8	11
U.S.	73	10.6	7
Italy	47	10.5	7
Austria	74	8.9	6
Britain	49	5.7	4
Belgium	27	4.7	3
Switzerland	29	4.2	3
France	49	3.5	2
Canada	24	2.3	2

Source: Foreign Trade Research Institute, Warsaw, 1990.

At the same time, there was grudging agreement that foreigners would have to be involved as well at the level of the firm.[16] Firms that do not receive adequate capital and updated technology simply may not survive. And if enough of them die, they risk dragging the investment funds down with them as well.

Given these tremendous risks, it is not at all surprising that Poland has adopted such a liberal strategy with regard to foreign direct investment. What is especially noteworthy in the context of this project, however, is the extent to which Poland's evolving system appears to conform with prevailing international norms of foreign direct investment. Rather than merely removing its formal prohibitions against foreign investment, for example, the Polish government has been extremely careful to frame its new laws in the language of the west, and to adopt many of the same conventions. Most important, all of the recent regulation has attempted to increase the transparency and reduce the uncertainties of the business environment. Whenever possible the Poles have replaced a system of bureaucratic discretion with one of legal mandate. This trend is evident, for example, in the dissolution of the Foreign Investment Agency, in the elimination of most permits, and in the limiting of discretionary tax privileges.[17] In removing as many bureaucratic layers as possible, the Polish government has clearly recognized that its western investors prefer laws over discretion, and that these laws need to be as transparent and stable as possible. As one 1990 study urged: "The scale of inflow of foreign capital to Poland depends . . . not only on attractive legislation and investment opportunities but also on the legal infrastructure which is one of the factors determining the so-called investment climate."[18] Likewise, Poland has been quick to adopt the principle of national treatment, agreeing in virtually all cases with the western norm that "conditions of business activity created for investors of the other party cannot be less convenient than those created for home investors or investors from any other country."[19] The government has been quick to offer full guarantees that the investments of foreigners will be treated the same as those of Polish nationals, and that the government will offer full compensation in the case of nationalization or expropriation. Between 1988 and 1991 Poland signed nearly twenty bilateral agreements on investment.[20]

Internally, the Polish government is also attempting whenever possible to align its standards with those of the broader international community. Bank guarantees for joint ventures, for instance, are meant to conform to internationally recognized standards; new tax codes have been designed along the lines of those of the European Community; and the country's entire system of accounting is being redrafted to conform with that of the International Accounting Standards Committee as well as with principles in force in the European Community.

Poland thus seemed determined to adopt the legal norms of the west in order to meet "the requirements of the market economy and expectations of foreign investors."[21] Its strategy was to attract foreign investors by playing by the rules of their game. The overwhelming hope was that by adopting western norms, Poland could mitigate to some extent the chief barrier to foreign investment: uncertainty about the pace and direction of political change.[22]

To be sure, there was really no way that Poland could eliminate the uncertainty that investors—and the Poles themselves—faced. But in 1991, the Poles seemed determined to demonstrate their resolve by moving as quickly as they could, and by adopting whenever possible the norms, procedures, and legal standards of the west. "Why should we invent the wheel?" asked one government official. "We'll just take the rules that are available."[23] Even when the adoption of these standards threatened to compromise their existing social contract, they seemed determined to follow the western model. As a result, they were exceedingly open to any and all western institutions. Indeed, a common complaint voiced during the summer of 1991 was that the Poles had no time to work because they spent all day speaking with visitors from international agencies—from the World Bank, the International Monetary Fund, the European Community, the OECD, and many others. Even when guidance from these agencies was not forthcoming, Polish officials felt a need at least to entertain their western visitors—for fear of offending them, and in the hope of launching a longer-term relationship.[24] In addition, there was a general sense that membership in western institutions would make Poland look like a safer place to invest. "We need the Fund," said one former official, "to give them [foreign investors] security."[25]

By contrast, the Polish government showed no interest in cooperating on the subject of FDI with any of its former Soviet bloc allies. Surely there were significant gains for cooperation here; surely there were risks in competition, since Poland, Czechoslovakia, and Hungary were all attempting to attract a similar group of potential investors. Yet the countries were trying so hard to demonstrate their commitment to the west that they were loath to return to their eastern alliances, and to the practices symbolized by the Council for Mutual Economic Assistance (CMEA) and the Warsaw Pact.

Thus, without any desire to join in a common eastern strategy toward FDI, Poland chose the most aggressive course possible. It liberalized its entire economy, opened itself to the vagaries of the international marketplace, and removed virtually all barriers to investment. Moreover, it crafted a strategy that was explicitly tied to the rules of the game that prevailed in the west. It was a strategy grounded in the conviction that uncertainty was the single greatest barrier to foreign investment in Poland, and that the way to reduce uncertainty was through an increase in transparency, a renewed emphasis on rules rather than discretion, and a widespread adherence to western norms.

Accordingly, the Poles were very enthusiastic about joining western institutions and binding themselves to western rules. Where foreign investment was concerned, they made clear their intention to abide by all internationally recognized guidelines: the OECD codes, the Multilateral Investment Guaranty Agency (MIGA) codes, and the United Nations Center on Transnational Corporations (UNCTC) guidelines. The practical problem, however, was that the institutions themselves were not that powerful. The codes and guidelines, after all, had no binding force; and the institutions that supported them had no sanctions for noncompliance. The primary focus of these codes, moreover—the foreign investor—was not even a party to them.

Thus, in order to demonstrate even more strongly their commitment to an open investment climate, the Poles worked simultaneously on several fronts: with multilateral agencies, to be sure, but also with national governments and individual investors. Where the institutions were available, therefore, the Poles used them. But even where institutional capacity was limited, they sought to embed the international norms in other—bilateral or unilateral—arrangements.

Czechoslovakia

In many respects Czechoslovakia's strategy did not differ dramatically from Poland's. Like Poland, Czechoslovakia decided that it needed to pull foreign capital into the country, and that it had to liberalize and standardize its domestic laws in order to do so. Like Poland, it also recognized a basic need to play by western rules and conform to western standards. And, like Poland, it sought to demonstrate its commitment in a wide range of arrangements—in unilateral regulations and bilateral guarantees as well as in multilateral institutions. This discussion will therefore be relatively brief, and focus only on those areas where Czechoslovakia's policies have differed substantially from those of its Polish counterparts.

The most obvious difference concerns the pace of reform. Whereas Poland embraced the shock therapy of the Balcerowicz plan in January 1990, Czechoslovakia was much slower in opening up its economy to the full forces of capitalism. Indeed, even the most reform-minded Czech officials publicly voiced their determination not to liberalize the economy too quickly. After the Polish parliament passed its reform package, for instance, Czech Finance Minister Vaclav Klaus wrote: "We are afraid of the unrestrained reform romanticism of some of our colleagues. Reform is a very dangerous undertaking, and we do not want to put our fates again into the hands of irresponsible intellectuals."[26]

This same caution was evident in the area of foreign direct investment. The first Czech law that even permitted foreign investment was adopted in 1988.[27] Under the terms of this law, foreign investors were permitted to establish "foreign property participation enterprises," but they still needed to obtain the specific approval of either the Federal Ministry of Finance or the Czechoslovak State Bank, and their participation was still limited to 49 percent of any venture.[28] In 1991, however, a series of laws was adopted in order to liberalize the process of foreign investment and to encourage the entry of substantial foreign capital.[29] These laws proclaimed Czechoslovakia's intention to adhere to the principle of nondiscrimination, and thus to guarantee that foreign investors would be treated the same as nationals in the area of taxes, profits, and borrowings. In addition, the laws provided for a significant reduction in the regulatory role of government. In speeches and in private conversation, government officials stressed that the aim of the laws was to create an open, liberal, and transparent regime for foreign investment. Repeatedly they emphasized that the government's policy toward FDI would be based on the philosophy that what was not forbidden was allowed.

The precise terms of the law, however, were not quite as liberal as its proponents claimed. Although some investment could be undertaken without explicit approval of any government agency, a licensed approval was still required for all investment in the banking sector, for all projects established from state enterprises (that is, by way of privatization), or for any enterprise wishing to engage in foreign trade.[30] In addition to these specific constraints, moreover, there were many regulations which simply made the business environment less inviting. For instance, foreign companies were not legally permitted to purchase property in Czechoslovakia; Czech companies with 100 percent foreign participation[31] were able to purchase property, but they had to obtain permission from the Ministry of Privatization in order to do so. Similarly, even the reformed laws on convertibility and foreign exchange[32] still made it difficult for foreign investors to earn hard currency profits. All companies had to offer their foreign currency trade earnings to an authorized Czech bank in exchange for Czech korunas. Only those companies that could demonstrate a significant contribution to Czechoslovakia's foreign exchange balance were permitted to maintain a foreign exchange account. In order to pay debts incurred abroad, the company had to present evidence of the debts to a foreign exchange bank, which would then issue the foreign currency against the balance of the firm's local currency account. In order to repatriate its profits, the firm had to demonstrate to the state bank that the profit in question did indeed represent a return on investment.[33] Taken together, these regulations seem to suggest that Czech law in 1991 was not yet as open and transparent as the government—and potential investors—might have wished it to be. Although government officials were clearly aware of the need to "liberalize and demonopolize"[34] the Czech economy, the 1991 regulations still fell somewhat short of this goal.

Even more important, perhaps, Czechoslovakia moved more slowly than Poland in reducing the discretionary powers of the bureaucracy. For instance, in 1991 government agencies still had the power to determine the credibility of foreign exchange claims, to set the exchange rate on which these claims would be paid, to grant tax holidays and other preferential tax incentives, to regulate the issuance of debt instruments by private firms and set the rate of interest for this debt, and to give priority to foreign investment in certain sectors of the economy, including "public investment." This is not to say, of course, that the discretionary power still vested in the state was necessarily used *against* the interests of foreign investors. On the contrary, it appears that all elements of the bureaucracy were eager to draw foreign capital into the country. Nevertheless, just the existence of this discretionary authority raised the level of concern among foreign investors and left them somewhat more uncertain about the scope and direction of change in Czechoslovakia.[35]

In addition, the process of investment was further complicated by the sheer number of bureaucracies in Czechoslovakia, and by the often fuzzy division of responsibilities among them. Legally, Czechoslovakia was a federation composed of the Czech and Slovak republics, each of which maintained autonomy over its own internal affairs. As democratization progressed in the country, moreover, the republics—and especially the Slovak republic—called for a further devolution of power away from the central government. The result was that by 1991 many responsibilities in Czechoslovakia were split among three competing agencies—the Czech, the Slovak, and the federal. There were, for instance, three foreign investment agencies and three ministries of privatization. The result was a situation which continued to befuddle many potential investors even before agreement was reached in 1992 on the division of the country into sovereign Czech and Slovak rep.1blics.[36]

What was even more confusing to these investors, moreover, was the Czech program for privatization, and the role that foreign investors were expected to play in the process. Under legislation in force in 1991,[37] privatization was expected to occur in two stages. Small-scale privatization, which began early in 1991, involved the sale of one hundred thousand small and medium-sized businesses. These businesses were to be selected for sale by local officials, approved by the Ministry of Privatization, and offered to Czech citizens in two rounds of auctions. Foreigners were permitted to enter only the second round, and the final selling price in this round could not be less than 20 percent of the business's assessed value. Under the laws on larger-scale privatization, all large enterprises were to develop plans for their own privatization and submit them to the Ministry of Privatization. Where an enterprise was unable, or unwilling, to formulate a plan, it could be helped along by its founding ministry, which in most cases was the Ministry of Industry. All of the enterprises were to be legally transferred to state property funds organized on both the republic and federal levels. The property funds would then distribute the property, presumably by a combination of sales, agglomeration, and liquidation. Where they saw fit, the property funds were allowed to retain property for later sale or for future cash flow.[38]

The vast bulk of Czech enterprises, however, were expected to be privatized by the government's much-touted voucher scheme. The idea was to sell vouchers to the Czech citizens for a nominal fee, and then to allow them to use these vouchers to bid for shares in the privatized firms. As an alternative, Czechs could also use their vouchers to purchase shares of newly established investment funds, which would then invest their shares collectively.

In contrast to Poland's privatization program, the Czech plan did not depend explicitly on the involvement of foreigners. The presumption was that foreign investment would occur, but at the level of the firm rather than through the intervention of the state; that is, the government expected that Czech enterprises would negotiate their own arrangements with foreign investors as part of their individual privatization plans. And indeed this happened in a number of cases.[39] The other possibility, however, was that once the most profitable enterprises had been bought by foreigners, all other potential investors would postpone their decisions until after the effects of the privatization process were better known. If all of the foreign capital chose to wait, the Czechs would be hard-pressed to find the money and skills they needed to resuscitate all of the newly privatized industries.[40]

Perhaps as a way of alleviating this risk somewhat, the Czechs—like the Poles—repeatedly stressed their desire to play by western rules and adopt western norms of foreign investment. They applied for membership in the IMF and the World Bank, and made clear their intention to join the European Bank for Reconstruction and Development. They demonstrated a clear desire to cooperate with the European Community (EC) and the OECD, and applied for guest status in the Council of Europe.[41] They were creating a new system of taxation designed to be compatible with that of the EC. With specific regard to FDI, they voiced their commitment to the principles of nondiscrimination and most favored nation status.[42] Under the Act on Enterprises with Foreign Property Participation, and in accordance with a series of bilateral agreements, the Czech government promised to protect foreign investment against expropriation; if expropriation did occur, it could be done only in compliance with relevant laws, and with provision for just compensation in convertible currency.[43] Finally, the Czech government declared that any disputes between entrepreneurs were to be settled before the Economic Arbitration Court. If the court failed to resolve the dispute, the investor would be free to take his or her complaint either to a domestic court of arbitration, which would follow the arbitration rules of the United Nations Commission of International Law, or to the International Center for the Settlement of Investment Disputes in Washington, D.C.[44]

Thus, as was the case in Poland, the Czechs seemed determined to change their laws of foreign investment in accordance with international norms, and to participate in any international institution that dealt with investment issues. Like the Poles, they were clearly aware of the need to make their laws stable and transparent, and to reduce as much as possible the uncertainties that faced potential investors. By 1991, however, the Czechs appeared to have been slightly less successful in clarifying the procedures for foreign investment and in demonstrating their country's commitment to the full implementation of market reforms.

The Western Response

After decades of condemning the communist regimes in eastern Europe, the west became, after 1989, a boisterous supporter of the region's movement to capitalism and democracy. Western governments, institutions, and private citizens applauded the demise of Soviet-style communism, and flocked to eastern Europe to offer their suggestions, their assistance, and occasionally even their money.

At a certain level, then, the strategy of the west has been clear and unwavering: to support eastern Europe's transition to market capitalism and democracy. What was less clear in mid-1992, however, was precisely what the west would do to ease this transition, and how it would choose to channel and coordinate its efforts. With respect to foreign investment, the west appeared to have settled, on a three-pronged strategy. At the international level, western governments were pooling their efforts and expressing their desire that eastern Europe conform to international norms and join the relevant international institutions. Simultaneously, though, they were all working bilaterally, negotiating individually with the governments of eastern Europe, and signing separate investment treaties. And, finally, they were leaving the real task of investment to the private investors themselves.

The Role of International Institutions

In responding to eastern Europe's obvious demand for foreign investment, western governments were noticeably careful to coordinate their efforts whenever possible, and to bring eastern Europe into the existing network of multilateral economic institutions. Indeed, on virtually all fronts western governments declared their intention to work together in order to speed the pace of reform in eastern Europe. As one U.S. official explained his government's policy in 1991:

> Our answer has been to strengthen the entire web of East-West relationships. We have encouraged ties to the EC and EFTA, we have favored new institutional arrangements as part of the CSCE process, we have encouraged closer consultative ties with NATO through the liaison relationships the president proposed at the London NATO Summit last year. We have created a new status in the OECD for reforming Central and Eastern European countries to support economic reform and the transition to market economies; we hope this ultimately leads to OECD membership for countries that qualify. We have supported regional groups such as the Pentagonale and are using our own assistance programs as an incentive to greater regional cooperation by offering to finance cooperative efforts of two or more countries of the region to deal

with common environmental or energy projects. But more needs to be done in this area as well, and the reinforcement of this "web" is therefore a central U.S. priority for 1991 and 1992.[45]

Although perhaps somewhat optimistic in its portrayal, this speech does capture what seemed to be the intention of most western governments: to cooperate in the extension of investment assistance to eastern Europe. They all agreed to participate in the EBRD, to coordinate their economic assistance through the Group of Twenty-Four (G-24), and to let the European Commission play a lead role in this organization. With specific regard to foreign direct investment, intergovernmental cooperation was evident in the export credits provided by the World Bank, the European Investment Bank, and the EBRD; by the establishment of an EC reinsurance pool;[46] and by the establishment of the PHARE program to coordinate, among other things, efforts to improve the investment climate in eastern Europe.[47]

On their part, the international organizations themselves appeared extremely eager to play an active role in the area of foreign direct investment. Indeed, virtually all of the international economic organizations, and many of the purely political ones, created a division or declared an intention to study the promotion of foreign direct investment in eastern Europe. The EBRD, for example, made clear its intention to concentrate on promoting and investing in eastern Europe's private sector.[48] Likewise, the United Nations Industrial Development Organization (UNIDO) undertook to complete industrial feasibility studies in Poland and Hungary, and the World Bank's International Finance Commission provided extensive assistance in the area of privatization.[49] Another World Bank affiliate, the Multilateral Investment Guaranty Agency, also turned its attention to eastern Europe,[50] while the World Bank itself, along with the International Monetary Fund (IMF), was the principal source of long-term credit and credit guarantees. Other international organizations which sought to play an advisory role of some sort include the European Investment Bank, the United Nations Economic Commission for Europe, and the OECD.

Finally, the Conference on Security and Cooperation in Europe (CSCE) seemed in 1990–91 to be emerging as a key institutional player. In March and April 1990 the CSCE's members met in Bonn and produced a fairly remarkable document concerning the prospects for economic cooperation in Europe. Although not legally binding, the Bonn treaty prescribed that each of its signatories would facilitate commercial ventures on a nondiscriminatory basis, produce regular trade statistics that conformed to international standards, and protect industrial, commercial, and intellectual property rights. The signatories also agreed to cooperate through the EBRD and other multilateral institutions and to continue to channel their cooperative efforts through these multilateral agencies. While the treaty acknowledges that the prospects for cooperation ultimately rest with governments and with the "initiative of the enterprises directly concerned," it is nevertheless a powerful statement on the role of international cooperation in the field of foreign direct investment.[51]

Overall, however, the role of international institutions in the area of FDI remained somewhat ambiguous. While there was clearly a tremendous surge of institutional activity in this area, it was not apparent by mid-1992 where all of this activity would lead. There was a general consensus among western governments to coordinate their activities with regard to foreign direct investment, and a number of international organizations were vying to play a role in the coordination process, but there was little involvement in the actual process of foreign direct investment. In the terminology of this volume, by the end of 1991 there was neither a selection of forum nor any delineation of institutional authority. Instead, there was an emerging system of rules and norms, and a general determination to cooperate.

Alternative Strategies
Meanwhile, the western governments were also pursuing bilateral options. In particular, they signed bilateral treaties guaranteeing the protection of foreign investment and avoiding the double taxation of this investment. In addition, many western governments also took steps to ensure more directly the sanctity of their citizens' investments in eastern Europe. In 1989, for instance, the United States established a $100 million growth fund for eastern Europe under the auspices of OPIC (Overseas Private Investment Corporation). In keeping with OPIC's mandate, the bulk of the money was designed as investment insurance—that is, to cover U.S. investors in eastern Europe against the risk of currency inconvertibility, expropriation, and political violence. In addition, OPIC also provided for extensive loans to U.S. firms investing in eastern Europe.

Another way in which western governments addressed the problems of investment in eastern Europe was through the provision of technical advisers. The United Kingdom, for example, created a Know-How Fund, which paid for British accountants and investment bankers to advise eastern European governments on privatization and other related matters. Italy created an organization to assist small enterprises in creating joint ventures, and Belgium and Canada advised Poland on the development of its banking system. French experts assisted the development of the Polish stock market; and the U.S. Agency for International Development (AID) launched a wide-ranging program which would fund U.S. teams to participate in privatization programs throughout eastern Europe.[52] In addition to the AID and OPIC programs, the United States extended Export-Import Bank eligibility to include eastern Europe, and established the Polish-American and Hungarian-American Enterprise Funds, as well as more general private enterprise programs with an emphasis on technical training and the creation of private business organizations. All of this was in addition to more traditional forms of foreign assistance, including debt relief.[53]

The Role of Investors

Before turning to the broader implications of national and institutional strategies toward foreign direct investment, let us take a brief look at the strategies of one other key set of actors—the investors themselves.

Arguably, the investors are the single most important set of actors in the area of foreign direct investment. The eastern European countries can adopt strategies to attract investment; the western countries can support and encourage investment initiatives; but ultimately it is up to the investors—private firms and citizens—actually to make the investment. Thus we need to understand their motives, their strategies, and their response thus far to the opportunities in eastern Europe.

When the countries of eastern Europe first declared themselves open to investment, the western business community responded with great enthusiasm. Western businessmen flocked to Warsaw, Prague, and Budapest, over-running scarce tourist facilities and overwhelming local bureaucrats.[54] In 1988 there were 165 joint ventures registered in eastern Europe. By June 1989 the figure had risen to 1,375, and by December it had reached 3,300.[55] By the end of 1990, 9,700 joint ventures had been registered in Poland, Czechoslovakia, and Hungary alone.[56] By March 1990 American and western European companies had pledged nearly $500 million in regional investments.[57] Major deals were announced in rapid succession: Fiat's launching a joint venture to make cars in the Soviet Union; General Electric's purchase of 50 percent of Hungary's Tungsram; Schwinn Bicycle Company's agreement to manufacture bicycles for export from Budapest. In the wake of the largest multinationals came a horde of medium-sized and small firms, all determined to examine for themselves the business potential of eastern Europe. As one executive described it: "Exploring opportunities in eastern Europe has simply become a must."[58]

Very quickly, however, the initial enthusiasm subsided, and was replaced by a set of more realistic concerns about the prospects of doing business in the east. Potential investors realized that there was no commercial infrastructure in the region—no office space, no computer facilities, virtually no telephones. There was, moreover, no financial infrastructure—no capital funds, no foreign exchange facilities, no banks. And most critically, there was no legal infrastructure.[59] The newly elected governments were proclaiming their commitment to reform, but these reforms had yet to be embedded in a comprehensible legal framework. For many investors, these legal uncertainties made investment in the region—already a risky proposition—too risky to handle.[60]

Throughout 1990 and 1991 western investment in eastern Europe continued at a pace that many described as a "steady trickle." The westerners were still coming, but their total investment was far less than the east European governments had expected. Moreover, the investment appeared to be primarily of two sorts. There was some very large investment being made by western firms such as Volkswagen, Procter and Gamble, and Coca-Cola, but even here a lot of the investment was in sales outlets or small factories rather than in major industrial operations.[61] The bulk of the investment, meanwhile, was being made in small businesses such as casinos, import-export, and consulting. There was not much investment at all in medium-sized, high-value-added industry—precisely the kind of investment that the eastern European countries needed in order to jump-start their economies. The firms that could make these investments, for the most part, decided to wait for the political situation to stabilize, for legal reforms to be implemented and codified, and for the economic parameters of investment to become considerably less murky.[62] In particular, many investors expressed their intention to wait until Poland, Czechoslovakia, and Hungary had completed their privatization programs. The problem, of course, was that the fate of privatization rested, to a certain degree at least, on the involvement of western capital. Moreover, if privatization failed to meet the expectations of the east European people, or if its economic costs became too burdensome, then the political situation was likely to deteriorate, in turn making foreign investment an even riskier proposition.[63] The eastern European governments were painfully aware of this cycle, as were the international agencies concerned with economic reform in the region. The governments could create new laws as fast as their political systems would allow,[64] and the international agencies could help them write these laws so as to conform as closely as possible with prevailing western norms. Ultimately, though, this still might not prove sufficient to erase the uncertainties that the investors perceived. And as long as they remained uncertain, many of them would continue to wait.

To a large extent the entire issue of foreign direct investment in eastern Europe was marked by a remarkable congruence of interests. The governments, both east and west, the international secretariats, and the investors all wanted to see economic liberalization in eastern Europe, and all of them concurred that, in order to succeed, the liberalization process had to be fueled by an infusion of foreign capital. All of the players understood, moreover, that this investment would come only once it was made secure, and once certain levels of transparency and legality were established.

The bargaining space in this area thus included considerable room for cooperation. Given that interests were so similar, and the potential gains so large, we could have expected to find the players coordinating their efforts in the regulation of foreign direct investment. And indeed the evidence suggests that they did. Rather than trying to use foreign investment as a lever of any sort, and rather than insisting on the relative gains it offered, states and investors alike seemed committed to the development of an equitable, consistent, mutually beneficial set of rules. They agreed to abide by all of the existing codes and guidelines, and to formulate their investment policies on a cooperative rather than a competitive basis. In both eastern Europe and the west, national governments repeatedly voiced their support for the work of the OECD, the EBRD, the IFC, and the MIGA. Likewise, they repeatedly stressed their intention to coordinate their efforts in the area of foreign direct investment and to play by the established rules of the game. In particular, the countries of the European Community worked closely in presenting a common policy front to the east.

By the same token, however, although institutions were involved in the policy-making process, they were not integral to it. They had no formal powers or authority, and key questions about forum selection and institutional scope had not even been addressed, much less resolved. As of the end of 1991, it appeared that the primary function of international institutions was to serve as a source of information for new entrants into the game. For instance, the OECD has suggested that it prepare a list of legislative arrangements in the eastern European countries.[65] Likewise, the G-24 created a survey of the international investment climate and a "scoreboard" listing the specific actions governments have taken in support of privatization and investment guarantees.[66] Certainly this information function was an important one, not to be overlooked. Still, it seemed a much smaller role than that which was being assumed by international institutions in other areas, and smaller, too, than the demand for coordination in the area of foreign direct investment suggested.

How, then, are we to understand the relatively limited reach of international institutions in this area? There was an explicit demand for international institutions, and an ample supply of international organizations willing to meet this demand. Why did a broader transfer of functions not occur?

The answer to this puzzle lies in the nature and capacities of the institutions themselves. In contrast to other issue areas covered in this volume, foreign direct investment has long been notable for its distinct *lack* of institutions.[67] There is no GATT (General Agreement on Tariffs and Trade) for investment, no organization with the stature of the IMF or the World Bank or NATO. There are only guidelines, stuck onto a handful of institutions whose primary function lies elsewhere. When the issue of foreign direct investment arose so suddenly in the eastern European context, there was no obvious focus, and no obvious forum to which the would-be participants could turn.[68] Thus, in an environment that was not richly endowed with international institutions, it was not surprising that countries should define their strategies primarily in terms of noninstitutional options.

Of course, it would have been conceivable to create a new and more powerful institution to deal with the issue of foreign direct investment. Indeed, this may yet happen, as it already has in the areas of public assistance and environmental protection. What seems to militate against this possibility, however, is the fact that there are no obvious "regime-makers." The actors with the greatest interest in doing so—the eastern European governments—do not yet have sufficient power. For the foreseeable future they will be only "regime-takers." By the same token, there is no obvious group among the western countries that is likely to take the initiative. The only group that is really concerned about foreign investment is the business community. And traditionally businesses, even multinational businesses, have looked to their own governments to secure protection for their investments. Moreover, decades of controversy about the politics of foreign investment have made many western corporations extremely reluctant to politicize—or even publicize—

their overseas activities. Thus, while most western investors are likely to favor international regulation of foreign direct investment because of the greater certainty it would provide them, few are likely to initiate it.

Given this dearth of institutional options, states responded as one might expect: by concentrating on unilateral and bilateral options. We find, therefore, a host of bilateral investment treaties, a score of bilateral assistance arrangements, and even significant competition among western advisers to gain the attention of eastern European officials.[69] On the eastern side, we find a pattern of unilateral regulation and an emerging system of national laws.

What is most significant in the context of this project, however, is that all of these unilateral and bilateral strategies still conform to the rules that have been established at the international level. That is, rather than using national policies to avoid international norms or to achieve competitive advantages, states used their policies to support the international rules of the game. As in other issue areas covered in this volume, one sees in foreign direct investment a process of anticipatory adaptation, even when states were adapting to rules that had not yet been codified in a formal institutional structure.

Thus, the evidence presented here suggests that even if international institutions cannot play a direct role in shaping firm or state strategies, the rules and norms embedded in these institutions most certainly can. We have seen, for example, how quickly the governments of Poland and Czechoslovakia adopted the international norms of nondiscrimination, most favored nation status, and no expropriation without just compensation. Likewise, we have seen their willingness to accept a broad range of western standards—in accounting, statistics, asset valuation, tax treatment, and environmental protection. And most important, perhaps, we have seen their willingness to embed these norms in their own legal systems as well as in bilateral agreements.

As of the end of 1991, formal compliance with these norms existed only in these domestic statutes and bilateral treaties; there were no significant mechanisms established at the international level. Still, the extent of compliance with recognized international standards suggests that foreign direct investment in eastern Europe was already being governed by an informal regime. Because the area is marked by such grave uncertainties, all of the actors—the host states, the home states, and the corporations—were eager to find some means to structure change in a predictable way, and to make all of the evolving laws of investment in eastern Europe as transparent as possible. Regimes mattered in this case by offering a convenient shortcut to transparency, and thus by lowering the risks and uncertainties involved.[70]

By mid-1992 it was still too early to tell whether any legal or informal guarantees would be sufficient to reduce the uncertainties of eastern Europe to a more comfortable level. Even where legislation was in place, potential investors still had reason to suspect that it would not be implemented as planned, or that it would be overwhelmed by political events and unstable economic conditions. Even if an effective institutional forum were to emerge, therefore, it still would not, by itself, magically draw investors to eastern Europe. Unlike other issue areas reviewed in this volume, foreign direct investment occurs largely beyond the realm of government intervention. Governments can regulate and legislate and cooperate, but they still cannot force investors to invest.

Nevertheless, the recent history of foreign direct investment in eastern Europe reflects the power of international institutions, even when these institutions are weak, and even when compliance with them is informal. Through a process of anticipatory adaptation, the governments of Poland and Czechoslovakia aligned themselves with western norms and produced an investment climate that reduced, as much as possible, the political and economic uncertainties. In this process of adaptation they may well have strengthened the institutions themselves.

Chapter 10

East-West Environmental Politics after 1989: The Case of Air Pollution

Marc A. Levy

Environmental protection was an immediate priority of each post-1989 government in central and eastern Europe, owing to the horrible damage wrought by the communist regimes and widespread public support for cleanup; in some cases environmentalism had played a significant role in the political opposition. But not only had the communist regimes despoiled their own environments; they had inflicted such damage for years on their neighbors in the west as well. In fact, pressure from the west for eastern environmental cleanup predates the end of the Cold War by several years. Post-1989 environmental protection in the east became an international issue very quickly, therefore, as western governments saw an opportunity to manage existing patterns of interdependence (which they had attempted to do before 1989 unsuccessfully) in new and, they hoped, more effective ways. International institutions figured prominently in the environmental strategies of both east and west. This chapter examines the status through August 1991 of east-west institutional politics concerning transborder air pollution. In the first section I portray the nature of the status quo ante and show how the events of 1989 changed the issue. The second section then describes strategies adopted toward three institutional questions: international legal instruments, monitoring and joint scientific research, and financial and technical assistance. In the third section I indicate how these international institutional politics are affecting the domestic politics of Poland and Czechoslovakia, the largest polluters in eastern Europe.

I find institutions playing central roles in three basic processes: anticipatory adaptation, cooptation, and socialization. Regarding international and domestic legal norms, eastern governments have adopted western standards because they anticipate that regulatory harmonization is necessary for their goal of eventual membership in the European Community (EC). In this process of anticipatory adaptation the east Europeans are making all the significant adjustments. In the realm of pollution monitoring and collective scientific research, there is a process of cooptation going on. Both western and eastern governments share an interest in more fully integrating the east into institutions, and secretariats of international institutions favor such a policy as well. There have been disagreements concerning how far such integration should proceed and how much control the west should cede to the east, and so far western governments have not had trouble in setting their own limits. The most extensive integration of monitoring and research is being planned by the European Community's new European Environment Agency, open to eastern membership. Finally, the most penetrating interactions are taking place at the level of financial and technical assistance. In what can be called a process of socialization,[1] western donors are working themselves deep into the structure of east European states and using the leverage their funds provide to help thoroughly revamp the processes and institutions involved in shaping environmental policy in these states. This is not an imperialistic process—many eastern government officials share the same goals as the donors—but it is highly interventionist.

The Politics of East-West Environmental Relations before 1989

In Europe, air pollution generates patterns of interdependence by crossing borders and causing damage. About half the European countries get more of their air pollution from foreign than from domestic sources. Because of meteorological and ecological conditions, the pattern of interdependence is such that the countries of Scandinavia and central Europe are especially vulnerable, and those of northwest and southern Europe less vulnerable. The international political response has taken its most concrete form in the Convention on Long-Range Transboundary Air Pollution (LRTAP), signed in Geneva in 1979. The convention commits signatories to the principle of reducing transborder air pollution as much as is economically feasible, and to cooperate in monitoring and studying such pollution. Separate protocols have been signed under the Convention which commit states to specific reduction targets for sulfur dioxide (1985), nitrogen oxides (1988), and volatile organic compounds (1991).

LRTAP was the outgrowth of negotiations under the auspices of the Conference on Security and Cooperation in Europe (CSCE), and was the result of a convergence of interests on the part of the USSR, which wanted to engage the west in cooperation on non–human rights issues, and Scandinavia, which wanted reductions in acid rain. Secretariat functions are handled by the United Nations Economic Commission for Europe (ECE), which has virtually the same membership as the CSCE.[2]

Because of its origins in the politics of détente, all the east European states except Romania and Albania have been members of LRTAP from the beginning. Bulgaria, Czechoslovakia, Hungary, and the Soviet Union signed the sulfur protocol; and these four plus Poland signed the nitrogen protocol (see Table 10.1). All of these countries face domestic environmental catastrophes brought about by the cruel combination of Stalinist industrial and environmental policies. For forty years the world's dirtiest industries operated under the most lax environmental controls. Many of the most devastating effects were of a local nature, however; in terms of transboundary air pollution, by far the bulk of the problem was centered in East Germany, Poland, and

Table 10.1. East European Participation in LRTAP

Country	Signatory to		
	LRTAP	SO_2 Protocol	NO_x Protocol
Albania			
Bulgaria	x	x	x
Czechoslovakia	x	x	x
Hungary	x	x	x
Poland	x		x
Romania	x		
USSR	x	x	x
Yugoslavia	x		

Czechoslovakia, which accounted for 74 percent of eastern Europe's sulfur emissions in 1988.[3] These countries burn massive quantities of low-quality coal in factories and electricity-generating power plants. A variety of technologies exist to remove sulfur either before or during combustion, but with very few exceptions the only good applications of such technology are all in the west.[4] The Geneva Convention failed to improve this situation. East European compliance with the convention and protocols is considered poor.[5] Of the east European signatories to the 1985 sulfur protocol, only Hungary has a chance at meeting the 1993 deadline for achieving 30 percent reductions. The weak east European performance through 1989 came on the heels of some very serious air pollution reduction activities in the west. Since 1980 six countries had reduced their sulfur dioxide emissions by half or more, and five had reduced by 40 to 50 percent. Eastern Europe accounted for approximately 64 percent of Europe's sulfur emissions in 1988, as compared to 56 percent in 1980.[6] Some west European countries had therefore grown increasingly vulnerable to eastern emissions, relative to their own or to other western sources.

This was especially the case for the Nordic countries. As Table 10.2 shows, by 1988 the five Nordic Council members (Denmark, Finland, Iceland, Norway, and Sweden) received from 15 percent to 47 percent of their sulfur dioxide (SO_2) pollution from east bloc states. A single power plant in East Germany emitted more sulfur than all sources in Sweden.[7] Because these countries have some of the most sensitive ecosystems in Europe, reducing these remaining sources has been considered an important political objective. These countries all have among the most stringent domestic air pollution standards in Europe and have been very active in promoting acceptance of similar standards on the part of other countries, especially within the framework of the Geneva Convention. The Scandinavians are all members of the Nordic Council, which seeks to harmonize policies and adopt common action programs.

The countries of the European Community (EC), by contrast, receive much less eastern air pollution. With the understandable exception of Greece, all receive less than 15 percent of their pollution from the east. The EC plays a more active role than the Nordic Council in both environmental policy and foreign assistance. The organization harmonizes domestic environmental regulations to avoid trade distortions and, increasingly since the passage of the Single European Act in 1987, adopts common environmental policies even if the trade implications are less obvious. The EC has an extensive

Table 10.2. West European Countries and Their Regional Economic Institutions, by Percentage of Sulfur Pollution from Eastern Europe (1988 data)

Country	Percent of SO$_2$ from Eastern Europe	European Community	EFTA	Nordic Council
Greece	47	x		
Finland	47		x	x
Austria	34		x	
Sweden	32		x	x
Norway	24		x	x
Iceland	18		x	x
Denmark	15	x		x
Italy	14	x		
Germany	12	x		
Switzerland	8		x	
Netherlands	4	x		
France	4	x		
Luxembourg	3	x		
Belgium	3	x		
U.K.	1	x		
Spain	0	x		
Ireland	0	x		
Portugal	0	x		

Source: EMEP/MSC-W Report 2/90 (August 1990).

environmental directorate, as well as considerable foreign assistance expertise. It operates the European Investment Bank (EIB) to provide concessionary financing for economic development in Europe, as well as humanitarian foreign assistance programs in developing countries.

One way of characterizing the situation as of 1989 is that a number of states had entered into an agreement characterized by diffuse reciprocity and unlinked bargaining.[8] That is, they had exchanged pledges to reduce air pollution emissions but were not able to target such reductions at fellow reducers, and were unable or unwilling to connect cuts to specific actions in other spheres such as foreign assistance.[9] Among west Europeans, this form of bargaining had worked fairly well. There were some problems with Mediterranean countries and Britain, but these exceptions had reached a satisfactory political solution by 1989, and by and large countries that reduced their air pollution exports were reciprocated with reductions in imports from western countries.

Even before the dramatic changes of 1989, the limits of diffuse, unlinked bargaining had been realized. As Table 10.3 shows, a clear pattern of relative winners and losers had emerged. The relative contribution of transborder air pollution from eastern Europe was increasing, threatening some western countries with serious ecological harm despite the expensive corrective measures they had taken. A UN Development Program–ECE joint program was begun in 1988 aimed at promoting the transfer of clean power production technology to eastern Europe and other low-income European countries. A LRTAP Task Force on Exchange of Technology was created in November 1988, headed by Finland. An explicit aim of both efforts was to promote compliance of these countries with their LRTAP commitments, or to permit additional states to make such commitments.[10]

In addition to these multilateral developments, bilateral environmental agreements between east and west European governments were started, many of which concerned transborder air pollution. Most of these bilateral programs offered concessionary financial assistance from the west for air pollution reduction measures in the east. There was only very limited success with such ventures, however. Serious pollution reduction often required large transfers of western technology. One study estimated that eastern power plants (not including those in the USSR) would require $40 billion in investment.[11] This estimate may be too low; Germany is spending an estimated DM 30 billion just to bring the former East German electricity generation industry

Table 10-3. Changes in Sulfur Emission and Deposition, 1980–1987 (percent)

Country	Emission	Deposition	Emission minus Deposition
Sweden	-50	- 8	-42
Austria	-58	-27	-31
Norway	-29	- 3	-26
Netherlands	-42	-21	-21
Finland	-44	-23	-21
Ireland	-24	- 3	-21
Luxembourg	-45	-30	-15
Belgium	-39	-25	-14
France	-48	-34	-14
Iceland	0	14	-14
Portugal	-13	0	-13
West Germany	-36	-24	-12
Switzerland	-51	-42	- 9
U.K.	-21	-13	- 8
Denmark	-29	-25	- 4
Spain	- 3	0	- 3
East Germany	0	2	- 2
Czechoslovakia	- 6	- 6	0
Italy	-34	-39	5
Hungary	-13	-19	6
Poland	10	3	7
USSR	-20	-30	10
Greece	-10	-21	11
Romania	0	-19	19
Turkey	22	0	22
Albania	0	-23	23
Yugoslavia	0	-25	25
Bulgaria	9	-20	29

Source: Emission and deposition figures from *Acid Magazine* 8 (September 1989), 5.

Note: Countries at the top of the list reduced their own emission a great deal but witnessed only small reductions in deposition on their territory, owing to emissions from foreign countries. Those at the bottom saw their deposition levels drop even though they made little effort to reduce emissions. Those in the middle saw their efforts reciprocated by upwind neighbors.

in line with western standards.[12] Western governments were unwilling to transfer such amounts without considerable guarantees for its efficacious use (under communist governments such guarantees were hard to obtain). By the time of the changes of 1989, the only such east-west environmental agreements of even modest success were by and large confined to the special relationship of East and West Germany.[13]

One final feature of the pre-1989 situation deserves mention. In the first ten years after LRTAP was signed in 1979, enormous advances were made in both the quality of scientific knowledge and the degree of consensus around it concerning the transport mechanisms and effects of long-range air pollution. There was a widespread desire to utilize this new state of understanding to move beyond the rather arbitrary form of protocols (30 percent reductions in the case of the 1985 sulfur protocol, freeze in the case of the 1988 NO_x protocol) by developing more sophisticated regulations that would connect varying national emission reduction targets with desired levels of improvement in ecological conditions. National officials and experts, in working groups organized by LRTAP, have prepared maps showing the sensitivity of ecosystem regions to acidic deposition. Sensitivity is measured in terms of "critical loads," which is the amount of deposition believed to be sustainable without ecological damage. Critical loads vary a great deal across Europe, depending on geological and biological conditions. These maps can easily be compared with actual deposition maps and transfer matrixes to obtain an indication of how various reduction strategies compare with respect to environmental improvement. Negotiators are attempting to base the new sulfur protocol on critical loads, and this will almost assuredly mean that countries will be asked to take on varying emission targets. These targets will be based in part, LRTAP negotiators hope, on computer modeling indicating where emission reduction achieves the best mixture of abatement costs and environmental benefits, across Europe as a whole.[14]

Such an approach tends to place the greatest emission reduction responsibility on those countries that have low marginal abatement costs and are upwind from sensitive ecosystems. In practical terms this means Poland and Czechoslovakia will be expected to make among the largest percentage reductions. They face marginal pollution reduction costs of about one tenth of those of some west European countries, and are directly upwind from the most sensitive ecosystems in Europe. One 1991 model estimated that Poland and Czechoslovakia would have to take reductions 69 percent and 73 percent greater, respectively, than their present policies called for. Germany would have to reduce by only 23 percent more, and the Scandinavian countries would even be permitted increases.[15] Because eastern Europe has little ability to pay for such reductions, however, negotiators began thinking more directly about financial and technological transfers, or burden sharing, as a potentially integral component of future LRTAP protocols. This change in thinking predates the end of the Cold War by several years.

Strategies Adopted after 1989

After the dramatic changes of 1989, the nature of east-west environmental relations changed fundamentally. Whereas before the largest polluters in eastern Europe had been either unwilling to take on air pollution reduction commitments (as in Poland) or willing to sign but unwilling to comply (as in Czechoslovakia), the new governments indicated a consistent willingness both to sign and to make the serious adjustments required for compliance. And the governments in the west were now more interested in providing technical and financial assistance, both because they saw a greater chance that such aid would be put to good use, and because environmental assistance was considered an appropriate humanitarian response. The effect that 1989 had on east-west environmental relations, therefore, was to open up new possibilities for managing extant patterns of interdependence.

But such new possibilities required many difficult problems to be solved. An institutional home (or homes) had to be selected for east-west agreements on air pollution. The nature of the rules or institutional authority had to be agreed on. And the precise terms of the quid pro quo had to be settled. The remainder of this section will review the evolution of thinking about these questions on the part of national and international actors. Some of these questions are still in flux. I review the state of play concerning international legal instruments, monitoring and scientific research, and environmental financial and technical assistance.

International Legal Instruments
The question of where to locate international legal instruments governing transboundary flows exhibited the least deviation from the status quo. There was no expressed desire in the west to shift such activity away from the ECE, where multilateral east-west air pollution treaties had resided since 1979. Although the Council of Europe had expressed some desire to get involved in east-west environmental treaties, most governments and international

institutions were content to leave the negotiation of protocols and treaties to the ECE for the time being. The ECE had considerable experience fulfilling this function, and, alone among European organizations, possessed virtually the same membership as the CSCE. A number of bilateral environmental treaties had been signed between east and west since 1989, but none of these contained regulatory rules; they were more akin to "friendship" treaties.

The governments of eastern Europe also were committed to working within the ECE framework to negotiate international commitments. They additionally sought regional agreements among themselves. Through 1991, however, none of the attempts at regional treaties resulted in binding air pollution reduction commitments. Czechoslovakia and Poland both import about twice as much sulfur dioxide from western Europe as they do from fellow east Europeans. Their long-term commitment is to pan-European instruments. The impetus to attempt regional agreements in the short term is attributable to the fact that pollution from fellow east Europeans, though of lesser magnitude than western pollution, is often highly concentrated along border regions. The "black triangle" in the region bordered by the former East Germany, Poland, and Czechoslovakia has been said to suffer the worst air pollution in the world.

Eastern Europe's relations with the EC may affect the region's approach to international commitments as well. Although the European Community's environmental directives apply only to EC members, EC environmental law is having strong influence beyond the twelve. The governments of eastern Europe want, in general, to play as active a role as they can with the European Community. At the highest level, the east Europeans all hoped to obtain associate status by 1992, toward the goal of full membership within a decade or so. This goal, whatever one thinks of how realistic it is, exercised a powerful force on these countries' processes of environmental reform. All began seeking to harmonize their environmental legislation with EC legislation, and made this a high priority in the legislative process.

Although this process of harmonization will have a strong impact on the air pollution reduction policies of eastern Europe, the EC is not likely to be the forum for new international legal instruments involving eastern Europe. The association agreements negotiated in 1991 and signed in 1992 required no immediate harmonization, though they specified that further integration would require that legislation "be compatible with Community legislation at the time when [the country] becomes a member of the Community."[16] Any step beyond associate membership will occur much too late for it to have any immediate effect on transborder pollution commitments.

All governments, then, looked to the ECE to house European transboundary air pollution treaties and protocols for the near term. Officials of the Organization for Economic Cooperation and Development (OECD) had no interest in taking on the task, and the Council of Europe, which did want to make more of a mark in the environmental field, did not get involved in transborder pollution.[17]

One can imagine, however, scenarios in the medium to long term in which the ECE's importance diminishes. If the CSCE acquires an operational capability (which some have argued it should), then it may reverse its historic pattern of deferring to the ECE on such matters and may seek to control environmental negotiations itself. The air pollution secretariat at the ECE is quite small (five professional positions), and could easily be supplanted by an ambitious and competent CSCE. Another plausible longer-term scenario would entail heightened regional cooperation on transborder air pollution within eastern Europe analogous to what takes place within the European Community and the Nordic Council. In such an event there would be little left to negotiate in a pan-European context, though governments may continue to codify their regional agreements within LRTAP protocols.[18] Finally, if the governments of eastern Europe continue to take the goal of EC harmonization seriously, then as the EC takes a more direct role in setting transborder pollution standards, these will be transmitted, with some changes, to the east. All of these scenarios are plausible only in the longer term, and for no government (east or west) did they represent an alternative to the strategy of working within the ECE in the immediate aftermath of 1989.

Monitoring and Scientific Research

If the location of legal instruments was straightforward during 1989–1991, the story was rather different when it came to monitoring environmental quality and disseminating scientific information and technology. This role had been played largely by UN agencies, with some bilateral activity as well. The executive body of LRTAP, operating within the framework of the Senior Advisers on Environmental Matters to the ECE, operates several working groups, task forces, and cooperative research programs pertaining to various aspects of air pollution monitoring, effects, and control. These working groups have coordinated scientific research on environmental effects, economic studies on cost-effective pollution abatement, and pan-European monitoring of pollution flows and acidification. In addition, there have been task forces and programs charged with promoting the exchange of pollution-control technology.

By virtue of its wide membership, the ECE was unique in being able to serve as a pan-European home to this kind of activity before 1989. Once the political differences separating east and west had dramatically shrunk, however, the ECE lost much of its comparative advantage. In fact, some of the former advantages were seen as weaknesses. For example, participants often complained about the strict adherence to UN rules of procedure in most international meetings. Especially for fulfilling informational functions involving scientists (more at home in technical, informal settings than the politically sensitive formalities associated with the UN), the benefits of conducting such work within the ECE came under question. The chief alternatives to the ECE which emerged include the OECD, a new EC-operated European Environment Agency, a Regional Environmental Center in Budapest, and an abortive proposal promoted by officials in Czechoslovakia.

The OECD actively considered ways to involve the east Europeans more directly in its activities. In March 1990 it created a Center for Cooperation with European Economies in Transition, and in June started a Partners in Transition program with a more operational emphasis aimed at countries desiring OECD membership.[19] These decisions were made at high levels for reasons having little to do with the environment. Once they were made, however, environmental areas were found to be good candidates for eastern participation in the OECD. A meeting of OECD environment ministers in January 1991 strongly recommended increasing OECD participation in east European environmental reform. The OECD's primary emphasis in dealing with the east has been on disseminating information relevant to policy design, which it considers to be its organizational comparative advantage. The environment directorate created a new position for east European issues, and developed a program organized around analyzing environment-economy linkages, transferring OECD member states' experience to eastern Europe, and assessing environmental conditions and policy performance. It considered extending its newly begun practice of conducting environmental policy reviews of OECD countries, analogous to its ongoing economic policy reviews, to eastern European countries in the future.[20] In 1991 reviews were undertaken of the Polish, Czechoslovak, and Hungarian environmental information systems.[21]

The EC opened its environmental information and monitoring activities to the east as well. Following a June 1989 proposal by the European Commission, the EC decided in March 1990 to create a European Environment Agency, to serve primarily information gathering and dissemination functions. While this decision was grounded fundamentally on an assessment by the Commission of the needs of the member states, the community decided to permit nonmember states to participate in the agency, on terms to be negotiated between prospective participants and the Community. This provision was aimed at EFTA (European Free Trade Area) members as well as the new regimes in eastern Europe.[22]

All the east European governments saw their participation in the agency as a high priority. The prime benefits they sought were access to western expertise and participation in Europe-wide monitoring programs. While they welcomed the chance to participate in an environmental institution less bureaucratically cumbersome than the ECE, many east European officials regretted that this particular setting did not include the United States. They consider the United States to be at the forefront of many environmental science and regulatory developments.

Although the accident of the timing of the agency's creation benefited eastern Europe by putting its concerns on the agency's agenda, another accident of timing worked to its detriment. A dispute among EC member states over the site of the European Parliament spilled over into a deadlock over where to locate the new Environment Agency. The agency could not begin operations until its location was settled. In effect, the new agency was held hostage by France, which wanted Parliament to remain in Strasbourg, and as a result the opening of the agency was delayed indefinitely.[23]

Although the new agency was not explicitly an enforcement agency (Commission President Jacques Delors claimed that the Community was not "sufficiently mature" for such an institution),[24] some member states hoped that it would nonetheless help put pressure on EC members to comply with environmental directives and regulations. The agency could operate within its "information only" domain and still play a role in compliance questions. It could examine national legislation and implementation measures required by EC law, and it could collect and disseminate environmental quality data relevant to such directives. If there were widespread east European participation in the agency, then it could play a similar role with respect to east European countries and their international environmental commitments. As of mid-1992 the only comparable practice was occurring within the context of the LRTAP process, in which national air pollution reduction policies and strategies were reviewed annually, with major reviews every four years.[25] These reviews were probably of limited utility in encouraging compliance, however. The reviews reported only information supplied by national governments, and no independent judgment was made as to who was actually in compliance and who was not. With the important exception of actual emissions data, which most observers considered to be fairly reliable, these policy reviews amounted to a forum in which governments were invited to report (and exaggerate) their successes without fear of cross-examination. Many western governments, especially in Scandinavia, would have welcomed new mechanisms to highlight patterns of compliance with LRTAP protocols.[26]

Another institution devoted to primarily informational functions was the Regional Environment Center in Budapest, founded in September 1990. The Regional Center was incorporated as a nongovernmental organization (NGO). It began with U.S. financing, though it later received funding from many sources, including the European Community. The center's initial months' activity bore the marks of an ad hoc response (foreign donors had apparently decided to create the organization before deciding exactly what they wanted it to do). By mid-1991 the Regional Center had begun to focus its efforts on "the development of civic society in the environmental field," which in practical terms meant providing financial support for east European environmental NGOs.[27] It provided somewhat less than $2 million per year in grants.

Monitoring and information dissemination functions in post–Cold War Europe were to be fulfilled, then, by many different institutions, some new and some old. They represented a wide range of evolutionary patterns, including the continuation of previous activity (ECE), the extension of ongoing activity from one geographical region to another (OECD), creation of a new institution with an eastern element added (European Environment Agency), and creation of a new, eastern-specific agency (Regional Center). This presented a need to coordinate the actions of these various institutions. The preexisting institutions—the OECD, ECE, and EC—already had a long history of coordination, and easily arranged joint participation in a review of the "State of the European Environment" planned for 1992. Cooperation between the EC and the Regional Center occurred on specific events,[28] and the European Bank for Reconstruction and Development (EBRD) began discussions with the center as well.

All these responses probably constitute what Ernst Haas calls "adaptation." New activities were added incrementally, without any examination of the broader purposes on which the incrementalism was grounded.[29] The lack of depth in this process is what leads me to characterize it as cooptation: international institutions were used to facilitate coordination of activities in which conflicts of interest were practically absent. No government was opposed to coordinating scientific research and environmental monitoring, and the west succeeded, unsurprisingly, in framing the terms according to which the coordination took place.

The Czechoslovak government, especially its environment minister Josef Vavrousek, promoted a more radical institutional response without much success. Vavrousek recommended that the two ad hoc conferences of European environment ministers (in Dublin in 1990 and Dobris in 1991) be institutionalized into an annual event. This permanent conference might also take on a more operational identity as a Council of European Environment Ministers with a small staff, analogous to the EC's Council of Environment Ministers. Vavrousek proposed that such a council run the EC's Environment Agency, and offered to seat the agency in Prague. Such a council would also "oversee the evaluation of the environmental situation of our continent, set priorities for action and targets for achieving them, coordinate the processes of building up a European environment monitoring and information system, strengthen and unify European environmental legislation, and develop a pan-European strategy for environmental revival, which must include concrete programmes and projects together with sufficient financial support and a system of environmental education."[30]

If Vavrousek's recommendations regarding the EC's Environment Agency were to be adopted, they would transform the agency from an EC institution into a thoroughly pan-European agency. Neither of Vavrousek's proposals received much governmental support outside Czechoslovakia. The most vigorous objections came from western governments wary of creating new institutions, especially one in which western governments would have less control.[31] What is less understandable is the lukewarm response Vavrousek's proposal generated in other east European capitals.[32] As Vavrousek points out, the collapse of the Council of Mutual Economic Assistance (CMEA) left eastern Europe the only European region lacking an institution to promote regional integration. He intended his proposals to fill this void in the environmental area. While there were clearly alternative means to achieve this end, it is somewhat striking that the question received so little attention outside of Czechoslovakia. Some officials pointed to the Regional Center in Budapest as fulfilling some of the needs highlighted by Vavrousek, but the direction in which the Regional Center was heading, as part of its effort to define a focused niche, was away from intergovernmental collaboration and toward NGO-based transnational cooperation.

Although Vavrousek's proposal was greeted with hostility by western governments, it had elements in common with the European Commission's vision for the agency. The Commission's initial proposals called for the agency to play a bigger role in developing policy proposals, but member states insisted on a narrower mandate, limited to information gathering and monitoring. And the Commission wanted the agency to be run by a management board operating by simple majority vote; member states changed this to a two-thirds majority, partly to prevent being outvoted by non-EC members.[33] Vavrousek's specific proposal to institutionalize the annual meetings of environment ministers was not warmly received by the Commission, however. Such a development would have threatened the Commission's growing competence in environmental matters; the Commission preferred to build pan-European environmental agendas through the European Environmental Agency and existing institutions.[34]

Financial and Technical Assistance

The provision of financial assistance for the amelioration of environmental conditions in eastern Europe was negotiated and managed in a variety of institutional forums, with no clear, dominant pattern established by the end of 1991.[35]

Several countries launched bilateral assistance programs with eastern Europe. Many of these, especially in the beginning, took the form of specific, linked reciprocity. That is, they provided western money and technology in exchange for measures which promised direct emissions reductions. None of these programs, however, entailed explicit commitments to reduce emissions on the part of the countries of eastern Europe. Rather, the western donors provided funds for measures which, it was hoped, would ipso facto reduce transborder pollution flows.

In July 1989 the western Group of Twenty-Four (G-24) countries agreed to coordinate their bilateral assistance programs, and assigned coordinating function to the European Commission. The Commission hosted a series of meetings with representatives of national governments and multilateral institutions, including meetings specifically devoted to environmental assistance.[36] However, the degree of coordination of bilateral environmental programs was considered "relatively ineffective."[37] Commission officials reported low interest among donor countries for coordination of bilateral environmental programs.

The poor record of coordination is part of the reason why there is little reliable data on bilateral environmental assistance programs: governments provided only limited data to the Commission. Many of these programs entailed significant participation of donor-country firms, and some observers in the Commission and eastern governments speculated that governments were unwilling to share information concerning activities in which they were seeking benefits for domestic firms.[38] A 1991 report from PHARE (Poland/Hungary Aid for Restructuring Economies) concerning bilateral environmental assistance was clearly missing information from key countries.[39] It lists only three Swedish aid projects, without funding levels, and only a single German project, but identifies twenty-six Dutch projects, including precise budget figures. Since Sweden and Germany have among the most active bilateral environmental aid programs for eastern Europe, the Commission's data were obviously incomplete. A 1990 report from the Polish government, for example, indicated that Sweden was the single largest donor in environmental aid projects, at a level of $46.6 million over three years.[40] The World Wildlife Foundation went to great lengths to attempt to secure comparable data on bilateral environmental aid, with poor results owing to the unwillingness of governments to supply information.[41]

While failing in its attempt to serve a coordinating role, the Commission fared better in operating its own assistance program directly to eastern Europe, which had a significant environmental component. The PHARE program began in 1990 with a budget of ECU 500 million, and was set to continue at least through 1992, for which ECU 1 billion had been authorized.[42] There was no fixed percentage allocated to environmental projects. Priorities were determined in consultation with each country; Czechoslovakia specifically requested a large environmental component of its PHARE aid while others requested less. In 1990 about 20 percent of the total PHARE budget went for environmental projects.

These bilateral programs and the PHARE program both went through a similar evolution over 1990–91. They shared a heavy emphasis at the beginning on discrete, high-visibility projects, many promising significant transborder consequences, and then moved toward an approach promising more diffuse benefits through increasing the capacity of environmental regulatory institutions in east European governments. In the terms used by the PHARE coordinators, the change was from a "shopping list" to a "more integrated programme concept" of environmental assistance.[43] In essence, the initial response can be characterized as an increase in the intensity of prior attempts at east-west environmental cooperation (direct linkage) without a change in strategy. After a year of disappointing results, the strategy changed as well.

The early results were considered disappointing because the promises of early, dramatic reductions in pollution never materialized. The governments of eastern Europe proved unable to implement the recommendations of western advisers because they lacked the institutional capacity. They were unable to weigh alternatives, set priorities, develop implementation plans, and carry out large-scale projects.

The initial aid efforts, tied to specific pollution reduction projects, quickly ran into bargaining and implementation problems. The key issue was the inability of the eastern recipients credibly to assure western aid providers that they had the capacity to manage these projects effectively so that pollution levels would stay low. Negotiations on a project to reduce emissions from nickel smelting on the Kola Peninsula in the Soviet Union, for example, dragged on inconclusively for three years.[44]

The new "programmatic approach" was designed to redress these weaknesses. Programmatic environmental assistance emphasizes monitoring, training, and institutional reform. It begins to put in place the national political and administrative capacity in the east which facilitates bargaining with the west and increases reassurance that pollution control projects have the backing of the government as part of a comprehensive environmental and industrial policy.

The multilateral development banks emphasized a more programmatic approach from the beginning, and many observers credit their influence with promoting the abandonment of the shopping list approach both within eastern European governments and among western donors. A World Bank mission to Poland resulted in an $18 million loan to improve the management of environmental policy in the country. It included funds for monitoring equipment, staff training, and preparation of policy plans. The report accompany ing the loan specified in detail the rationale behind the institution-building approach, and was apparently instrumental in securing consensus within the Polish government behind this approach, and in turn in convincing other foreign donors to shift their assistance toward this form.[45] The World Bank planned to complete similar studies for all countries in eastern Europe by mid-1992, many in conjunction with the EC, the U.S. Environmental Protection Agency, and other international agencies. A joint study of environmental problems in Czechoslovakia was completed in late 1991. By that time the Bank had not set specific targets for environmental loans.

The brand-new EBRD was the other development bank operating in the region, and it did so with a decidedly green bent. Quickly after western governments agreed to create it in 1990, a concerted campaign on the part of western and eastern environmental NGOs was launched to promote an environmental dimension to the Bank's activity. The World Wide Fund for Nature (WWFN) spearheaded the effort, producing a carefully designed set of recommendations for the Bank in time for a key meeting.[46] Virtually all of WWFN's recommendations were adopted, and the EBRD declared itself to be the only development bank with an explicit environmental mandate. In practice, this mandate meant both that the environmental impact of all loans would be reviewed, and that projects promising environmental improvement were being actively sought.[47] The Bank announced no specific targets for environmental loans by the end of 1991. It began operations in April 1991 with a capitalization of $10 billion.

The EBRD shared the World Bank's philosophy of building institutional capacity. In addition to its project and merchant financing operations, it planned a series of workshops and seminars to alleviate what it saw as some of the key knowledge and skill gaps in eastern Europe. Some of these were to be organized in coordination with the Regional Center in Budapest.

The Nordic countries provided financing through two multilateral venues.[48] The Nordic Investment Bank allocated about 15 percent of its lending volume (or about $150 million) for projects outside the Nordic region. It intended to use part of these funds for environmental projects in eastern Europe; these were still in the planning stages in 1991. In October 1990 the Nordic countries created the Nordic Environment Finance Corporation to promote joint ventures between Nordic and east European firms with positive environmental impacts. The corporation approved loans for three joint ventures through 1991, with more under consideration. Its original capital was $56 million.

The European Investment Bank, an arm of the EC, was primarily devoted to financing infrastructure projects within EC member states. Over 1985–1989 these investments included ECU 1.7 billion for environmental projects, primarily water and air pollution reduction.[49] The EIB was also a vehicle for EC foreign aid programs, including the Lome Convention and a Mediterranean cleanup program. In November 1989 the EIB was authorized by the EC to provide ECU 1 billion in infrastructure loans to Poland and Hungary, and in 1991 was authorized to provide an additional ECU 700 million in loans to Czechoslovakia, Romania, and Bulgaria. The EIB claimed that the environment was to be a high priority in its east European lending. A likely focus was the energy sector, where the Bank already has experience within the member states. Poland and Hungary had already received ECU 65 million in energy sector loans by mid-1991.[50]

As opposed to the bilateral aid programs, in which coordination was all but absent, the multilateral financial institutions were more accustomed to coordinating as a matter of course. It is standard operating procedure for a development bank to serve as lead institution for a particular project and then solicit co-financing from other institutions. Bilateral programs, by contrast, commonly entail smaller-scale projects and tie their aid to expenditures in the donor country.

The pattern described so far of international financial assistance, then, was one in which there were few explicit links to transborder pollution reductions from the east, although many of the planned projects will reduce transborder emissions. There were alternatives in which the linkage would have been more explicit.

One explicit form of linkage, pursued actively by the Polish government, would tie pollution reduction to debt reductions. In this case the connections would be less automatic than in the bilateral shopping lists, but also less diffuse than with the multilateral banks. In other words, there would be explicit linkage between debt relief on the one hand and transborder pollution reduction on the other, but the reductions were to be achieved by Polish initiatives utilizing resources freed up by debt reduction. The Polish proposal was still under negotiation with western lenders at the end of 1991. Norway and the United States, among others, were especially supportive. The plan, developed in collaboration with Norwegian officials, called for approximately $200 million per year, diverted from debt servicing, to be spent on "problems of international importance." These problems included transboundary air pollution, pollution of the Baltic Sea, greenhouse gas emissions, and loss of biological diversity. Funds for alleviating these problems would come from an agreed-upon percentage of retired external debt, which would be placed in a trust fund supervised by an international board of directors.[51] Operation of the trust fund would be in coordination with the World Bank and EBRD, which would co-finance many of the investments.

The transborder aspects of the debt-for-environment proposal were made explicit by both sides. Norwegian officials highlighted the consequences for Norway's environment. Prime Minister Gro Brundtland, in announcing support for the initiative, referred to the "increasing acid rain originating from SO_2 emissions on Poland," and said that "a debt-for-environment swap may help creditor countries improve their own environment by means of projects in Poland . . . We must give priority to those efforts which give the greatest effect at the lowest cost."[52] Polish officials focused on the trust fund's international control, permitting "geographic preferences" to be taken into account, and included only high-salience global and transborder measures in the list of fund priorities. They stressed the fund's role in enabling Poland to meet its international environmental obligations, such as the LRTAP Convention.

Debt-for-environment was a potentially viable option for Poland (depending on the west's response) because of the massive size of its external debt. Even setting aside a small percentage of the face value of its debt could generate sizable resources for pollution abatement. On April 21, 1991, a Paris Club agreement reduced Polish official debt by half, and included provisions for an additional 10 percent reduction through voluntary swaps. This 10 percent, which would have represented $3.1 billion, was the focus of the Polish debt-for-environment proposal.[53] Other eastern European countries had considerably less external debt, however, and debt-for-environment was a less plausible option for them.

Another alternative to the diffuse approach inherent in the multilateral development banks would have been a European Environmental Fund. Such a fund had been proposed by Sweden in the context of LRTAP, beginning in 1989, and negotiators considered the idea in talks concerning revisions of the sulfur dioxide protocol set to expire in 1993.[54] The rationale for a European Environment Fund, in the context of a revised SO_2 protocol, was that European states could contribute to a fund based on some combination of ability to pay and degree of benefits achieved by reductions in deposition, while the disbursement of such funds could be directed to those locations where ability to pay is low but emission reduction benefits are high. In essence, it would institutionalize a bargain between wealthy vulnerable states and poor polluting states, especially northern and central Europe, respectively. If such a fund were established in conjunction with LRTAP, the linkage between aid transfers and emission reductions would be much more specific.

However, LRTAP negotiators were largely unenthusiastic about such a fund; they recognized that financial transfers are required to secure meaningful participation of the new regimes of eastern Europe, but some felt that a reliance on the EBRD and World Bank would be preferable to the establishment of a new fund. One possibility, considered by some EBRD officials but not on government negotiators' agendas during 1989–1991, would be for governments to contribute separately to a facility within the EBRD for transborder pollution projects. Such a facility could be modeled after the Global Environment Facility within the World Bank.[55] The virtue of such a facility is that it would reduce the need for additional institutional infrastructure, since EBRD staff could manage it, and it would simplify coordination with ongoing multilateral projects affecting transborder pollution.

Another possibility would be to organize a task force similar to one currently operating for the Baltic Sea. The Baltic Task Force attempts to coordinate the provision of financial assistance from multilateral sources toward the goal of ensuring east European compliance with the 1974 Helsinki Convention for the Protection of the Baltic Sea. Sweden, which originally raised the issue of a European Environment Fund, by mid-1991 had come to prefer an arrangement similar to the Baltic Task Force model. Among the reasons Swedish officials cited were the desire to reduce institutional proliferation and the increased financial flows already under way among the initiatives described earlier.[56] The Baltic Task Force attempts to identify priority projects and promote their financing. The World Bank, EBRD, Nordic Investment Bank, European Investment Bank, and Commission of the European Community (as operators of PHARE) are members.

The issue of whether to link new SO_2 reduction commitments explicitly to financial assistance could not be resolved until the protocol negotiations neared completion, slated for 1992–93. The protocol signed in November 1991 to control volatile organic compounds generated no discussion of such assistance. This protocol was not based on the critical loads concept, which lends itself more readily to financial linkages, though even with flat rate reductions the east Europeans faced the same problems of having less money to finance pollution control. Rather than linking reductions in the east to financial transfers, however, the volatile organic compounds protocol attempted to accommodate eastern concerns by permitting a two-track approach, with some countries (principally in the east) permitted a freeze of emissions while the rest (principally in the west) adopted a 30 percent reduction.[57] Eastern government negotiators did not raise the aid question during negotiations; they preferred to do as much as they could without explicit aid so long as the two tracks permitted them to participate in the protocol. The west shared the east's interest in being included in the protocol, and was willing to tolerate smaller eastern reductions in order to achieve it.[58]

Assessment of Institutional Strategies

Between 1989 and 1991 national governments and international institutions responded to the pattern of interdependence created by transborder air pollution flows with a variety of strategies. Across the board, virtually all international institutions having something to do with either east Europe or the environment made adjustments to incorporate east European environmental issues into their area of work. International legal instruments remained the home of the ECE, the institution making the least adjustment owing to its historical origins. Policy-level information was staked out by the OECD as its niche, while more technical information was to be collected and disseminated by the ECE and the EC's new Environmental Agency. The Regional Center in Budapest, with a much smaller budget and poorer access to governments, appeared to be taking a relative back seat. Financial transfers were handled by the extant multilateral banks and the new European Bank, as well as in a plethora of bilateral initiatives.

The resulting pattern is not exactly perplexing, but there are some puzzles. It is not obvious, for example, why new institutions should have figured so prominently. There were extant alternatives to the EBRD and the European Environmental Agency (the World Bank on the one hand and the OECD and ECE on the other). Why weren't these used to a greater extent? The consequences of opting for new institutions appear potentially significant. Both the EBRD and the European Environment Agency (once it gets off the ground) represent more radical responses to east European environmental concerns than the agencies whose role they are in part supplanting. This appears to be due to the greater openness to outside influence of these agencies during the period of their creation. Compare the rapid greening of the EBRD in response to NGO pressure to the much slower response of the World Bank.

I accept the argument made by Stephan Haggard and Andrew Moravcsik that the EBRD is a largely redundant exercise in political symbolism,[59] and suspect that the decision to extend participation in the European Environmental Agency to eastern governments was motivated in large part by a perceived opportunity to garner similar symbolic laurels. Such an interpretation is consistent with the EBRD's apparent desire to appease environmental pressure groups; such a strategy promises greater symbolic benefits, which a functionally redundant institution needs more than one such as the World Bank. However, such an interpretation is not inconsistent with the possibility that, in the 1990s, the EBRD will make a significant difference in eastern environmental adjustments. While the EBRD is not *necessary* for the west to assist the east in serious environmental adjustment, it is also true that such adjustment is fairly low on the west's list of priorities. Therefore, creating an institution which is vulnerable to charges of redundancy, and which therefore cultivates constituencies such as environmentalists, may have the effect of boosting the long-term position of environmental protection on the multilateral assistance agenda. The EBRD may result in the west's funding projects it would not otherwise have funded, even though, if it had wanted to fund them, it would not have needed the EBRD to do so.

The possibility of the EBRD's serving to maintain long-term commitment in the west to eastern environmental protection is potentially important because there are no clearly compelling reasons why environmental concerns have occupied such a prominent role in the west's response to the east. It does not appear to be explainable in instrumental terms. The Scandinavian countries have obtained direct domestic benefits for some of their expenditures, but the EC countries and the United States were spending no less, proportionately, yet they suffer very little direct harm from east European air pollution (as indicated in Table 10.3). This suggests, perhaps, the power of dominant ideas. Environmentalism was a highly salient issue, and international institutions wanted to be seen to be on the right side of it.

An unsurprising outcome is the low degree of coordination among institutions and governments (the exception of a rather precise division of labor between the OECD and ECE predates the end of the Cold War). In the absence of extensive interinstitutional coordination, one could have expected that the pattern in place in 1991 would have been subject to change as a result of competitive pressures. The most vulnerable institution was probably the ECE, where its principal source of comparative advantage (pan-European membership) was losing relative value. If the EC's Environment Agency became operational and successfully incorporated east European, Nordic Council, and EFTA participation, for example, then government interest in current ECE informational activities might greatly diminish. As of 1991 there was no agreed-upon division of labor between the new agency and the ECE comparable to that between the OECD and the ECE.

The Consequences of International Institutions on State Strategies

In this section I look at east-west environmental relations the other way around, focusing on the effect that international institutions have had on European state strategies. There was little effect on state strategies in the west, where governments continued prior policies, with the exception of providing additional financial assistance to the east. In the east, by contrast, changes at the level of international institutions were closely connected to serious changes at the domestic level. The process was a dynamic and ongoing one, making it hard both to discern cause and effect and to judge outcomes. Nevertheless, by the end of 1991 some interesting patterns had emerged. In brief, what one sees is that, for Poland and Czechoslovakia at least, strategies regarding foreign environmental policy objectives were driven by an overwhelming desire to gain credibility in international institutions. When it came to taking concrete steps to achieve these objectives, however, serious differences emerged.

The similarly ambitious foreign environmental policy objectives across eastern Europe reveal the powerful impact of international institutions on domestic politics. With little difference across countries, eastern governments paid serious attention to compliance with existing agreements and strove quite hard to take on rigorous new commitments. This was consistent with the broader foreign policy of these countries with respect to international institutions, in which they attempted to sever all ties with the Soviet-dominated institutions of the past and gain membership in as many western institutions as they could. At the level of stated objectives, the foreign environmental goals had widespread support in these countries. Polish and Czechoslovak industrialists did not oppose them; parliaments passed quite stringent legislation; and industry ministries offered a degree of support that would be enviable among environment ministries in the west.[60]

Poland and Czechoslovakia both placed their LRTAP commitments high among their environmental priorities. Poland announced plans to achieve a freeze in sulfur emissions at 1980 levels by 1993, and to achieve 30 percent reductions by 2000.[61] The Czech Republic (which accounts for most of Czechoslovakia's air pollution) did not provide a target date, but said that "an important task will be the fulfillment of Czechoslovak international obligations issuing from the agreement on long-distance atmospheric pollution, particularly the protocol requiring a 30 percent reduction of SO_2 emission by 1993."[62]

Part of this uniformity of ambition was due simply to similarly abhorrent environmental conditions. There was domestic political pressure to correct the abuses of communism, and the new elite that had taken over the environment ministries had been planning such corrections for decades. The breadth of support in other segments of these societies, however, probably had more to do with the hopes for international economic integration. Industrialists and economic policymakers pinned their hopes on rapid, high levels of economic integration with the west, which means at a minimum membership in the IMF, negotiation of lower tariffs with the west, and inflow of foreign investment capital. Even the maximalist goal had widespread support, and this meant entry into the European Community by the end of the 1990s. Industrialists presumed that these goals, especially the maximalist goal, required deep environmental reforms. The negotiation of association agreements with the EC, seen in eastern Europe as an interim step toward inevitable full membership, undoubtedly helped to speed up the desire to achieve harmonization with EC standards. The process of environmental policy reform in the east is therefore a clear instance of the general pattern of anticipatory adaptation, a topic discussed in greater detail in Chapter 6 in this volume. This adaptation is evocative of Ernst Haas's description of "the expansive logic of sector integration," but with a twist. For Haas, European integration began with a desire for gains from trade (and broader political goals), and expanded as each stage of integration bred additional benefits from continued integration; integration spilled over from one sector to another.[63] This process accurately captures how harmonization of environmental policies entered the EC process.[64] The east Europeans were acting as if spillover pressures had already emerged, and were adjusting their environmental policies (and a host of other policies) to meet what they perceived to be the requirements for a level of integration which, under the most optimistic scenario, was a decade away.

The effect of east European countries' broader international institutional goals on their environmental policies indicates the enormous significance that sequencing (or more simply history) can make. In the late 1980s environmental objectives were much less prominent in the international institutions deemed most important by eastern governments. Before the 1987 Single European Act environmental policy was a much lower priority in the EC. Spain and Portugal were able to join the Community in 1986 despite serious differences in environmental policies that persisted into the 1990s. It was only since 1988 that environmental issues routinely found their way into Group of Seven (G-7) economic summit communiqués, corporate policy objectives, and political party platforms across the spectrum. If the changes in eastern Europe had occurred five years earlier, it is doubtful that these governments would have been united behind such ambitious environmental objectives. Industrial interests would almost certainly have been pitted against environmentalist and electoral interests much more sharply than they are today.

But goals are one thing, performance another. On this question it is of course too early to pass judgment, yet initial differences in strategy emerged between Poland and Czechoslovakia that are worth pointing out. The reason for these differences appears to be connected in part with differences in how domestic and international institutions have interacted in a process I refer to as socialization. In the case of Poland, the influence of international institutions reached much deeper than in Czechoslovakia, exerting a profound effect on emerging structures to deal with transborder air pollution. In Czechoslovakia international institutions had a less profound impact.

The interaction between the Polish environmental reform process and international institutions centered on the World Bank. As we have seen, a mission in late 1989 was followed by negotiations in early 1990, culminating in an $18 million loan for environmental management. World Bank officials believed that because of the enormous disparity between environmental needs and available resources, the first priority had to be to put in place the institutional capacity to evaluate and implement difficult trade-offs. This required high-quality information about Poland's environmental situation, and the skills to conduct and evaluate cost-benefit and feasibility studies. All of this was lacking except at a rudimentary level. The World Bank loan attempted to rectify this situation by providing funds for technical advice to environment ministry officials on management and legislative techniques, for improved monitoring systems, and for conducting policy designs in a limited number of key priority areas.[65]

The World Bank loan required that the ministry establish a Project Implementation Unit as an office within the environment ministry to oversee not only the World Bank project but all other multilateral and bilateral assistance programs as well, in order to ensure that such programs contribute to consistent environmental and investment policy. The unit would in essence serve as a gatekeeper between the ministry and foreign donors, to provide the coordination that many of the donors were failing to engage in themselves, and to ensure that foreign assistance is used in priority areas.

Following the World Bank loan in April 1990, Polish environmental policy showed a very serious commitment to engage in the kind of prioritizing and institution building recommended by the Bank. Such measures had been supported by some officials before the World Bank program but had been resisted by many others. Officials concluded that the World Bank report, and its $18 million soft loan, helped those who favored such a process of rationalization and prioritization to convince their colleagues in internal debates.[66] The government released its National Environmental Policy in November 1990, which made explicit attempts to delineate short, medium-, and long-term priorities. It identified further institutional capacity building as one of three priorities for future foreign assistance.[67] Other institutional changes enacted in Poland over 1989–1991 included an environmental impact assessment requirement for new investments, and an environmental fund to collect pollution fines and disburse grants for cleanup projects. The fund also became the principal shareholder in a new Environmental Protection Bank, which made subsidized loans for priority environmental investments. Polish officials report that the World Bank program, subsequent to consolidating Polish government support behind the goal of institution building, was also instrumental in reorienting bilateral and PHARE assistance toward similar objectives, away from the initial emphasis on high-visibility discrete investments.

Czechoslovakia, by contrast, made much less progress in reforming its environmental institutions in the initial aftermath of 1989. There was little attempt to prioritize environmental problems; there was no requirement for environmental impact assessments; and there was no environmental fund to assist compliance with new norms. Part of the difference can be attributed to the fact that Czechoslovakia's reform process began later than Poland's. In addition to the obvious factor of simply providing a later starting point, the difference in timing meant that Czechoslovakia's domestic reform process occurred in a different multilateral environment. As one of the earliest to change, Poland was able to have a World Bank environment mission when Czechoslovakia was still run by the Communist party. By the time of Czechoslovakia's change, which occurred more suddenly as well as later, the EC's PHARE program exerted more of an initial influence, and PHARE officials had a much less programmatic emphasis than the World Bank, especially during 1990. As I have shown, the early PHARE emphasis was on quick, discrete projects. The PHARE program did ask Czechoslovakia to establish a Project Implementation Unit analogous to Poland's, but the unit engaged in far less actual coordination than Poland's and was organized entirely differently. World Bank and EBRD officials, upon beginning talks with Czechoslovakia, recommended major reforms in the coordination process, but these recommendations were resisted.[68]

In addition to the accident of timing, Czechoslovakia's federal structure was undoubtedly an independent factor accounting for the relative slowness of reforms. Power was divided among a Czech Ministry for the Environment, a Slovak Environmental Commission, and a Federal Committee for the Environment. The bulk of the technical expertise resided in the republic governments, yet responsibility for national planning, external relations, and priority setting rested with the federal committee. Although there was a formal understanding regarding the division of rights and responsibilities, every major environmental initiative at the federal level was challenged by the Slovak government. The government sought the right to establish its own air pollution emission standards and to engage in direct talks with foreign donors, as well as provoking many other challenges to federal authority. On many of these issues the government eventually conceded, but the added layer of political bargaining greatly delayed the change process.[69]

Another possible factor accounting for the swifter progress in Poland's domestic reforms has to do with the greater openness of Polish society prior to the events of 1989. In 1989 there was a critical mass of Polish economists and lawyers familiar with cutting-edge environmental economics and law. Economists were able to study principles of environmental economics based on neoclassical microeconomics at the University of Warsaw, and to travel abroad for more in-depth exposure. Environmental economists quickly began playing a major role in the Polish environmental ministry, and sought to apply western principles virtually identical to those espoused by the World Bank and the EBRD (the Poles are much more ambitious than any western government in seeking to use economic instruments to design and implement environmental policy).[70]

In Czechoslovakia, by contrast, there was a much smaller number of lawyers and economists familiar with western principles. It was not possible to study such material openly in the country, and it was more difficult to leave for such study elsewhere. World Bank and EBRD officials report much greater difficulty discussing basic concepts such as cost-benefit analysis with Czech officials than with Polish officials.

In summary, in the Polish case international and domestic environmental institutions appear to have interacted in a synergistic fashion, with initial tendencies at the international level reinforcing a latent tendency at the domestic level. This in turn seems to have influenced other international actors, and one should expect an additional consolidation on the part of domestic institutional reformers. Through 1991 the international and domestic tendencies appeared compatible and stable. In Czechoslovakia, however, the interaction was less synergistic. World Bank and EBRD exhortations to build institutional capacity and develop prioritized programs found a less hospitable home.

It would be wrong to exaggerate the differences between Czechoslovakia and Poland. As I have emphasized, both governments were firmly committed to environmental reforms along western lines and took their cues from the most progressive regulatory models in the west. At the end of 1991 it seemed possible that the institutionalization gap would be resolved in the near term, heading off the possibility of a later implementation gap. It was also possible for either country to experience serious backsliding. In both countries environmental politics are highly sensitive to broader concerns, including the still uncertain state of constitutional conflicts and relations with foreign investors. As the decision in 1992 to divide Czechoslovakia showed, the patterns of 1989–1991 could easily be altered dramatically.

The response to the perceived need to integrate the new regimes of eastern Europe more fully into existing norms, rules, and institutions concerning transborder air pollution varied greatly across management functions. The smallest degree of institutional change occurred in the area of formal commitments, where the status quo was largely retained intact. This small institutional change nonetheless was matched by a dramatic change in the behavior of eastern governments, which adopted highly ambitious policies to honor their commitments. They did so, I argue, in anticipation of later benefits from greater economic integration with the west. Somewhat more institutional change can be detected in the area of monitoring and information exchange. Here two new institutions were created, although one appears to have been originally planned as a western agency and subsequently modified to allow eastern participation (the European Environment Agency), and the second has a very low budget and fairly low profile as well (the Regional Environment Center). Adjustments in this functional area were not enormously costly, and disagreements centered on control questions. Not surprisingly, western governments retained the bulk of the control in the face of challenges from the European Commission and from eastern governments. In the case of financial transfers there was also significant institutional change. The PHARE program represented a new effort on the part of the G-24 countries, though its coordinating function was considered a failure. The EBRD was a new creation, and with $10 billion of initial capitalization and a major environmental commitment it could be a major factor in the future; through 1991, however, it remained redundant with the World Bank and EIB activities. All other multilateral lending agencies active in Europe seriously addressed environmental concerns in eastern Europe as well. These new aid programs meshed with domestic reform processes, with greater success, so far, in Poland than in Czechoslovakia.

The major institutional lacuna in 1992 remained regional environmental cooperation. There was very little information sharing within eastern Europe, and even less political cooperation. It was not clear at that point whether the relative lack of attention to regional cooperation within eastern Europe was a mistake. Through 1991 all eyes seemed to be on Brussels, whether that meant participating in the European Environment Agency or harmonizing environmental standards with the hope of eventual EC membership. The argument that the Brussels-based approach was best did not necessarily rest on one's assessment of the likelihood of east European membership in the EC. Many east European officials pointed to the considerable time savings involved in using the EC as a focal point, as opposed to developing standards from scratch, either in a purely domestic context or, even more difficult, in a regional one. Time was vital in the legislative processes of 1990–91; these governments were trying to make up for some forty-five years of lost time as quickly as they could. Adopting EC and EC member states' laws as frameworks helped them move faster. And if each country adopted environmental reforms in harmony with EC standards, then the de facto result would be considerable regional harmonization.

Analytically, international institutions played their most profound role in orienting domestic change in the east. They were not used to set new multilateral standards governing transboundary pollution, nor to establish cost-sharing mechanisms for pollution abatement. In fact, the politics of negotiating pan-European emission standards *after* 1989 looked surprisingly like they did *before* 1989. What was radically different after 1989 was the rapidity and seriousness of the domestic policy changes undertaken in the east. In this regard institutions played two roles, one passive and one active. The passive role was probably the more important: the institutions of the west, especially the European Community, exerted a magnetic pull on the east that was so strong that it kept alive a domestic consensus in the east for rapidly harmonizing pollution standards with those of the west. The active role was critical as well: the World Bank and other aid organizations combined financial and technical assistance in a way that transferred the skills and expertise necessary for harmonization to succeed. Especially in Poland, this process appeared to help consolidate significant reorientation in government practices. Together the magnetic pull and the transfer of expertise generated a profound degree of socialization of eastern governments in accord with western norms and practices.

Chapter 11

Pursuing Military Security
in Eastern Europe

Richard Weitz

Recent developments in Europe allow for a rewarding inquiry into how governments employ international institutions to promote their military security.[1] From a theoretical perspective, most students of multilateral institutions have focused on their role in areas of "low politics"—commerce, the environment, international law, and so on—and not on the "high politics" of military security. From a practical point of view, understanding how governments use international institutions to further their security could shed light on an important tool of statecraft.[2] This essay seeks to explore these questions: What military security policies did east European governments employ during the immediate post–Cold War period?[3] How did multilateral security institutions affect their strategies (that is, the tactics they employed to attain their goals)? What factors in turn most influenced shifts in the nature and resources of these institutions?[4]

This chapter first reviews how the great powers and the east European states interacted to produce changes in the two dominant international institutions affecting the European security environment. It then outlines the strategies east European governments employed to promote their military security after the Cold War. The conclusion explores the reasons for variations in national behavior, the surprisingly numerous tasks institutions performed in the military security area, and the superiority of approaches to international relations that stress the importance of relative power in accounting for institutional outcomes. Although international institutions performed a variety of roles beneficial to the east European governments in the military security area, the great powers largely determined the authority and resources allocated to these structures.

International Institutions

The various country studies in the first part of this volume explore how the great powers sought to promote their security interests in Europe. To avoid needless repetition, I concentrate here on how Europe's two dominant multilateral security institutions changed their structure and policies as a result of these great power interactions. These institutions arose in a Europe divided into two rival blocs. The collapse of the Soviet empire and the reunification of Germany rendered many of their traditional purposes obsolete. Yet these same developments meant they could now assume new functions that would define their role in European international politics for years to come. In line with their often conflicting national interests, the member governments had to redetermine these institutions' precise functional mandates, authority, resources, and rules and decision-making procedures. The national representatives also had to determine the new boundaries between their often overlapping functions.[5]

The North Atlantic Treaty Organization (NATO)
Since the country studies in this volume have already discussed great power disputes over NATO's future, this section focuses on the alliance's response to east European pleas that it assume a larger security role in their region. Although sympathetic to their concerns, NATO officials took steps to limit their involvement in eastern Europe while still maintaining the organization as Europe's preeminent military security structure.[6]

NATO first responded to post-1989 developments by increasing diplomatic exchanges with east European officials. Delegations from WTO (Warsaw Treaty Organization) states met senior NATO personnel in Brussels, and NATO Secretary-General Manfred Woerner and representatives from a variety of NATO committees visited several east European capitals. These exchanges involved not only specialists in military matters but also economic, ecological, and scientific experts.[7] During these consultations NATO officials made clear that continued improvements in bilateral relations depended on the east European governments' sustaining their domestic reform programs. For example, Woerner told Romanian Foreign Minister Adrian Nastase in February 1991 that, in return for improved ties with NATO, Romania must continue to democratize.[8] At their July 1990 summit in London, the NATO governments stated that they accepted the WTO governments as partners in security and invited the WTO members to establish "regular diplomatic liaison" with the NATO secretariat.[9] In subsequent months the governments of Bulgaria, Czechoslovakia, Hungary, Poland, and the USSR accredited their ambassadors to Belgium to NATO as well.[10] Although pleased by their enhanced links with the alliance, several east European governments desired much stronger ties, including, if not formal membership, at least some form of security guarantee.

NATO officials dismissed suggestions that the east European countries could soon join the alliance. They expressed concern about their nationality problems and warned that membership could unduly alarm Soviet conservatives. Belgian Foreign Minister Mark Eyskens told journalists: "We are not closing the door, but we say that their security has to be put in the context of a formula . . . which should not lead to unnecessary provocation or misunderstanding with the Soviet Union."[11] The same concerns also made NATO governments reluctant to consider extending the east European countries a limited security guarantee or agree in advance to undertake peacekeeping functions in the region. "If there's a problem with the Turkish population in Bulgaria, or trouble between the Czechs and the Slovaks, you think NATO is going to send in the troops to keep the peace?" pondered a NATO diplomat. "Forget it."[12]

NATO officials tried to reassure east European officials by pointing out that NATO's mere existence deterred Soviet aggression against them. Woerner told reporters: "The presence of our alliance contributes to the security of the whole of Europe . . . [and] to deter any idea that the use of force . . . might produce good results."[13]

Although they displayed a strong reluctance to accept a prominent role in eastern Europe, NATO officials fought hard to preserve their alliance's pre-eminent position among European security institutions in the face of the collapse of the Soviet threat, German reunification, and other major changes on the European scene. In particular, they questioned the ability of other institutions to assume a larger role in the defense field. In mid-October 1990 Woerner said: "The European Community cannot replace NATO. It will take a long time before it can really establish a defense structure. And even then, are you sure that the Europeans could, with their forces alone, balance Soviet power?"[14] Many NATO officials preferred that continental governments seek to create a strong European pillar within the alliance and that NATO and the European Community (EC) develop "creative parallelism," which presumably meant that, while the two organizations would coordinate their policies more, the EC would concentrate on European economic affairs while the Atlantic Alliance would focus on military issues.[15]

Although NATO officials accepted that the CSCE (Conference on Security and Cooperation in Europe) could help promote European security and the political and economic liberalization of the east European countries, they stressed that the organization could not fulfill this task alone. Woerner warned the Poles in mid-September 1990: "I know that there are many in the newly democratizing nations of central and Eastern Europe, as in our alliance nations, who see it [CSCE] as a replacement for the existing security organizations . . . [But] the interests of each of its members, their social structures and value systems, at least for the foreseeable future, are too diverse to enable them to act collectively to preserve security in the event of crisis."[16] The following month Woerner also cautioned that the CSCE lacked the means to enforce its decisions: "With 34 very different countries, each with a right to veto, what can we do if a real conflict breaks out?"[17] NATO leaders maintained that the CSCE could realize its full potential only in conjunction with the EC and the Atlantic Alliance.[18]

NATO officials acknowledged the need to establish a new European security system, but they insisted that such a structure should be "a supplement and not a replacement for our alliance."[19] They claimed that NATO was adapting well to the changes in Europe and that it had an important role to play in maintaining peace and stability on a still unsettled continent. After recounting at a gathering of the North Atlantic Assembly the numerous problems plaguing eastern Europe and the USSR, Woerner observed in late November 1990 that NATO was "the only collective security and defense structure that can secure stability and protect the member states from [these] threats and risks to their security and their territory."[20]

The Conference on Security and Cooperation in Europe (CSCE)

NATO was not the only institution that, having attained most of its original objectives, now had to adapt to a new international environment. The CSCE,[21] established in the mid-1970s to make the bipolar Cold War order more stable and bearable, also confronted a more complicated but perhaps more tractable environment. Rather than codify balance-of-power arrangements among competing great powers, the CSCE now had to guide international change, including the disintegration of authoritarian empires, and oversee disputes among antagonistic nationalities. Although the new situation strengthened the CSCE as an institution, some of the great powers, particularly the United States, succeeded in combating east European proposals to fortify it greatly.

The east European governments favored an expansion of the CSCE's authority and resources for several reasons. First, the institution offered them the same rights and privileges as western countries, and guaranteed that they had some influence on international developments. During the Yugoslav crisis, the east European governments had the greatest effect on the international response when the world community dealt with the conflict mainly through the CSCE. Once the EC and the United Nations became more involved, their relative influence declined precipitously. Second, participation in the CSCE clearly identified countries as members of the European commonwealth. Although acknowledging the CSCE's continued weaknesses, a British diplomat justified the effort at the Paris summit to restructure the institution by observing that "at least it gives the East Europeans a feeling of belonging to the European club."[22] Third, the CSCE remained the only security institution, besides the even more tenuous links provided by the United Nations, connecting the east European governments with the United States. As many east European officials explained to me in private interviews, these countries wanted Washington to play a prominent role in pan-European security issues because they believed an American withdrawal could destabilize the continent.[23] Fourth, the numerous meetings held under the institution's auspices granted east European officials an extensive dialogue with western representatives and with one another. These meetings provided the CSCE members with broad knowledge about other countries' practices in areas such as human rights, economic management, and military security. Given their lack of information during their years under communism, the new political elites presumably highly valued the knowledge transmitted through the various CSCE forums. Fifth, the east European governments could more easily request the CSCE to carry out a fact-finding mission or implement other tasks than press NATO to pursue similar measures. At this time NATO intervention in eastern Europe would have encountered strong French resistance and might have alarmed Soviet officials. Sixth, the CSCE's existence facilitated the east Europeans' campaign to weaken the WTO. Not only could they proceed against the pact knowing that they would retain membership in an alternate security organization, but also the Soviet Union's membership in the CSCE made it easier for Moscow to relinquish the WTO. Seventh, once the WTO dissolved, the CSCE remained the only security institution whose membership included the USSR. The CSCE's continued existence thereby helped the east European governments attain their goal of preventing the USSR's isolation. Finally, many east European officials had been active dissidents before 1989. They drew inspiration from the Helsinki process during their struggle for human rights. Having benefited so much from the CSCE before their revolutions, they expected the institution to provide additional advantages following the disappearance of the communist governments that had thwarted the attainment of CSCE norms.[24]

Until recently the CSCE was more a process, an itinerant forum of discussion and negotiation for its member governments, than an organization with defined structures. It lacked a permanent headquarters, and its three major review sessions on compliance with the Helsinki Final Act, as well as the more numerous but still intermittent expert meetings it sponsored, occurred in various locales. Yet the increase, starting in the mid-1980s, in the frequency and length of CSCE review sessions, regularly attended by the same group of national officials, allowed the CSCE to develop an institutional identity.[25] A group of CSCE specialists developed within each member country's foreign policy bureaucracy and the deadlines produced by CSCE meetings became routinized in national planning processes.

In addition to blessing German reunification in two paragraphs of its final document which were written largely by German officials,[26] the November 1990 CSCE summit in Paris decided to endow the institution with several permanent organs whose precise functions will take years to delineate. These included a Council of Ministers, consisting of the foreign ministers of the member governments, and a subordinate Committee of Senior Officials. The two bodies' functions were to determine CSCE policies and to prepare for the biannual summits of the CSCE heads of state. The Vienna-based Center for the Prevention of Conflict furnished governments with a forum to consult on what participants considered "unusual military activities" in other member countries (such as unscheduled exercises or other actions that may foreshadow a surprise attack). Calling a meeting did not require a consensus, but any government (including the country where the activities occur) could veto proposed measures. The Office of Free Elections in Warsaw not only helped supervise ballots, but also provided governments, legislatures, and private organizations with information about elections and democratic principles. The Paris summit participants also agreed to endow the CSCE with a parliamentary body consisting of representatives from all the national legislatures. At a two-day meeting held in Madrid at the beginning of April 1991, representatives from thirty-four countries decided to establish a 245-seat assembly that would meet every July in a different city. Although its precise functions remain undetermined, the parliament clearly lacks enforcement powers over national legislatures. Finally, the member governments decided to provide the CSCE with a permanent secretariat based in Prague. Despite its many tasks, the frugal-minded Paris summit participants refused to endow the secretariat, or any of the other permanent organs, with large staffs, spacious headquarters, or extensive budgets.

The "Charter of Paris for a New Europe" provides a comprehensive listing of the norms associated with the CSCE.[27] Among other things, the charter commits all CSCE participants to promote the free market, respect the rule of law, uphold the rights of national minorities, treat "human rights and fundamental freedoms" as "the birthright of all human beings," and hold free and fair elections. An unusual feature of these norms is the extent to which they attempt to affect the member governments' domestic policies. Not only do the CSCE accords proscribe numerous abhorrent internal practices, but the periodic review sessions and expert meetings permit members to evaluate the implementation of the rules. The linkage is deliberate. The CSCE posits a close connection between how well a government respects human and civil rights at home and its proclivity toward conflict abroad.

In the area of military security, the CSCE's major norms have been the peaceful settlement of disputes, the prevention of surprise attacks, and the inviolability of existing national frontiers.[28] The rules drafted by the member governments within the CSCE framework to attain these military security objectives consist of two basic types. The first kind, known as confidence- and security-building measures (CSBMs), seek to improve openness and predictability ("transparency and confidence" in the words of the Paris Charter) in the security area, and thus reassure governments of one another's peaceful intentions. They restrict how member governments can use their armed forces in Europe. For example, certain provisions of the 1986 Stockholm accords and the 1989 Vienna Document require signatories to notify neighboring states of planned maneuvers involving more than a fixed number of troops, to exchange information on military strength, and to invite observers and permit short-term ("challenge") inspections to enforce compliance. Other important CSBMs include the promotion of military-to-military contacts such as multinational seminars on military doctrine, emergency meetings when one member government perceives "unusual military activities" in another, and a communication hot line linking CSCE governments. The other type of CSCE rule concerning military security limits the size of the member governments' conventional military establishments in Europe. The 1990 Treaty on Conventional Armed Forces in Europe (CFE), which the participants negotiated autonomously but under the CSCE framework, constitutes the most extensive agreement in this area. Both types of rules promote the creation of stable expectations among the member states and dampen the injurious effects of worst-case military planning.

The CSCE member governments decided their rules by consensus. During the period under study this unanimity requirement engendered increasing criticism when, to the professed despair of many governments, the USSR singlehandedly blocked the efforts of various Soviet republics—including Armenia, Ukraine, and the Baltics—to participate officially at CSCE meetings. Although they adopted a mechanism (described later in this chapter) to convoke emergency meetings of the Committee of Senior Officials, the CSCE members dismissed proposals to alter other decision-making procedures or concentrate authority among certain countries. Allowing some governments more votes than others or establishing an executive committee of states with special powers would have alienated the weak countries that most benefited from existing procedures.

Although the CSCE has been highly active in combating latent conflicts, until recently it lacked experience stopping active military disputes. Before the 1986–1989 Vienna Review Conference, the institution concentrated on conflict prevention, not conflict resolution. The CSCE expert meetings on dispute settlement that met in 1978 and 1984 made little progress. Only during the Vienna conference did the members resolve to seek "a generally accepted method for the peaceful settlement of disputes" that would entail "the mandatory involvement of a third party when a dispute cannot be settled by other peaceful means."[29] The participants at the Paris summit reiterated their support for compulsory third-party involvement, and a subsequent meeting of legal experts in Valetta, Malta, refined the procedures by which member states selected third-party mediators. Yet they continued to agree that the arbitration should not be legally binding on the parties in dispute. The mediators could propose solutions but not enforce them.

The member states took their most important step to forestall imminent interstate conflict when they established a procedure to convene emergency meetings of the Committee of Senior Officials. After diluting more ambitious proposals to meet Soviet and Turkish objections about noninterference in their internal affairs, the first CSCE Council of Ministers session agreed in Berlin on a mechanism for consultation in emergency situations. In a significant departure from CSCE norms, the participants decided that no government (not even the country under discussion) could veto the request of another member state for clarification of what it perceived as "a serious emergency situation which may arise from a violation of one of the Principles of the [Helsinki] Final Act or as the result of major disruptions endangering peace, security or stability." In an unprecedented break with CSCE tradition, the ministers agreed that if the complaining government remained dissatisfied, it could call an emergency meeting of the Committee of Senior Officials in Prague, provided at least twelve other countries supported the request. The government complained against could not veto such a meeting, but any member, though unable to prevent the discussion of an issue, could still impede the committee from adopting resolutions or taking concrete actions.

This ability of the USSR or other governments to block measures to overcome emergencies left east European officials dissatisfied. One diplomat complained: "What could the new system do if hardliners get into power in the Soviet Union and threaten military action against Poland, or Czechoslovakia or Romania? The new agreement means the Helsinki process is better equipped to deal with dangerous disputes and that is a good thing. But it does not give us the collective security arrangements which we need. We do not feel we can turn to the Helsinki process to answer a threat to our borders or to our internal security."[30]

The CSCE's weak response to the Yugoslav crisis strengthened the pessimism. Largely because of Soviet objections that the CSCE should prevent only conflicts *between* countries and not interfere in disputes *within* states, the CSCE as an institution did little to halt the escalating civil war beyond adopting ineffectual resolutions. For example, at the urging of Yugoslav Foreign Minister Budimir Loncar, the Berlin session of the Council of Ministers in June 1991 expressed "friendly concern and support for [the] democratic development, unity and territorial integrity of Yugoslavia." The statement also declared the member governments' support for continued dialogue among all the parties in conflict and their desire that "the existing constitutional disputes should be remedied and a way out of the present difficult impasse should be found without recourse to the use of force and in conformity with legal and constitutional procedures."[31]

Seeking endorsement of its own peace initiatives, the European Community, operating through the government of Luxembourg, in early July successfully invoked the CSCE's two-week-old emergency consultation and cooperation mechanism. The crisis session provided another opportunity for Loncar to attempt to employ the institution to deter further challenges to his central government's authority from either the federal army, which seemed increasingly independent of civilian control, or the separatist governments of Slovenia and Croatia. The Committee of Senior Officials adopted a resolution whose provisions matched those then advocated by the EC and the Yugoslav federal government. The text backed the concurrent EC mediation efforts, asked all military forces to subordinate themselves to political authority, and urged Slovenia and Croatia to suspend their declarations of independence for three months. The resolution also called on the federal army and Slovene defense forces to end their hostilities immediately, release all prisoners of war, and return to their barracks. In the face of Soviet and Yugoslav objections to stronger measures, such as the dispatching of a mission to help the various parties resolve their differences over Yugoslavia's constitutional structure, the delegates could do little but issue declarations, dispatch a fact-finding mission to monitor the EC-sponsored cease-fire, and offer Yugoslavia a CSCE "good offices mission" that would "be at the disposal of the Yugoslav authorities as long as they deem it necessary."[32]

In late June, Austria, alarmed by developments in its southern neighbor, first implemented the related CSBM procedure that allowed the member governments to request information on "unusual military activities" in other states. Although this procedure had been designed to uncover covert operations that might augur a military assault, the Austrians, with the approval of other governments, employed the mechanism to express dissatisfaction with ongoing (but open) military developments in Yugoslavia.[33] The resulting emergency meeting of the Conflict Prevention Center could only agree to call on the parties to halt their conflict.[34] CSCE members did not even attempt to activate the CSCE Procedure for the Peaceful Settlement of Disputes because the register of mediators had not yet been established, and because, as British Foreign Secretary Douglas Hurd bemoaned, "you can only mediate between people who are willing to accept mediation, and we are not in that position now."[35]

Another emergency meeting of the Committee of Senior Officials met in early August under the shadow of a failed EC peace mission. Now that fighting between Serbia and Croatia had commenced in earnest, the Serbian-dominated federal government sought to employ the CSCE to prevent unwanted EC interference. The Yugoslav representative blocked efforts to secure CSCE endorsement of a proposed EC-sponsored peace conference and compelled the adoption of yet another favorable resolution. The declaration backed the federal government's vow to begin peace talks immediately and called on all parties to respect its cease-fire order. The resolution, as well as the concurrent CSCE decision to supplement the EC cease-fire monitors then in Yugoslavia with five hundred additional observers from non-EC states, could not prevent the conflict's escalation.[36] CSCE members turned increasingly to other institutions such as the EC and, somewhat later, the UN.

The CSCE's failure to halt the Yugoslav crisis demonstrated its weaknesses. When faced with a threatening situation, either within one country or among several, CSCE members could do little but convene emergency meetings. The requirement that all measures except discussion obtain a consensus allowed any dissatisfied party to veto proposed actions. In contrast, only the five permanent members of the Security Council enjoyed this privilege in the UN. The unanimity principle resulted in actions reflecting the lowest common denominator. The member governments' desire to avoid international criticism and remain members of good standing in the European club represented the only decisive factor militating against efforts to block CSCE decisions. Although acknowledging that the CSCE "cannot force a member to do anything if they [sic] are not willing to cooperate," one delegate to the CSCE emergency meeting on Yugoslavia in early July 1991 claimed that "the fact that the CSCE contains all European states and the United States and Canada does carry a lot of political weight in itself."[37] But unlike NATO, the CSCE could not offer countries a military guarantee and lacked military forces (or even a multinational planning staff) to enforce its decisions. Unlike the UN Security Council, the institution did not yet enjoy a procedure to deploy peacekeeping troops in areas of conflict. It was not even clear how the CSCE could expel governments that violated its norms.

Western governments, particularly the United States, successfully circumscribed the CSCE's military role and retained NATO as Europe's primary security institution.[38] Although it provided the east Europeans with a mechanism for expressing their defense concerns, the new CSCE bore little resemblance to the powerful institution proposed by Czechoslovakia in 1990 and favored by other east European officials. A collective security system requiring all its members to combat any state that behaves aggressively would at a minimum have disrupted relations among NATO members accustomed to working as a team. Countries strongly committed to the alliance's long-term survival succeeded in focusing CSCE efforts on confidence building and crisis management rather than on collective security or defense. Soviet objections then largely prevented the CSCE from developing procedures to take actions (as opposed to merely debating problems) without a consensus. Although other governments shared Soviet concerns about intervening in a dispute within a member country, before the failed coup attempt Soviet officials took the lead in restraining CSCE actions during the Yugoslav civil war for fear of creating precedents others might employ against Moscow's efforts to hold the USSR together.[39]

State Strategies

Let us turn to a review of how east European countries promoted their military security after the Cold War. Three issues preoccupied their governments between 1989 and August 1991: German reunification, unpredictable Soviet policies, and the civil war in Yugoslavia. The next section highlights the strategies that several east European governments employed to meet these perceived threats. For reasons of space, the analysis restricts its review to Poland, Czechoslovakia, Romania, and Albania. (I hope to explore the policies of Bulgaria, Hungary, and other east European countries in a subsequent study.) These focused reviews of the military security policies of a few states toward a common threat provides theoretically enlightening comparisons.[40]

Dealing with German Reunification
Poland: Bilateral and Limited Multilateral Balancing Polish authorities perceived a serious threat in Germany's reunification. Although acknowledging the Germans' right to reunify, the Polish government insisted that Bonn officially accept without reservation the existing border between Poland and the German Democratic Republic. The Poles presumably recognized that their leverage over Germany on this issue would decline after reunification.

Although Foreign Minister Krzysztof Skubiszewski stressed that the newly unified German state "must be fully integrated into what is now called the new architecture of Europe, whatever that term specifically means," [41] Polish officials employed primarily bilateral and limited, noninstitutionalized multilateral means to meet the perceived German threat. They held numerous direct discussions with their German counterparts. They also attempted to exploit their ties with the USSR to control Germany's external behavior. For example, after Prime Minister Tadeusz Mazowiecki met with President Mikhail Gorbachev and other senior Soviet officials in November 1989, Polish government spokesperson Malgorzata Niezabitowska described the USSR as a "guarantor" of Poland's security.[42] As I will show, Polish officials did not push for the removal of Soviet troops stationed in Germany until after Bonn had confirmed the existing frontiers. In addition, they implied that, out of fear of a united Germany, Poland would remain close to the USSR even if the WTO dissolved.

The Polish government's multilateral measures centered mainly on participation in the noninstitutionalized "two-plus-four" talks.[43] Established in February 1990 to resolve the external questions pertaining to Germany's reunification, this group originally consisted exclusively of the foreign ministers of France, Britain, the USSR, the United States, and the two German states. It was not designed as a permanent institution. Citing the need to avoid a second Yalta conference (where Poles believe the great powers had decided Poland's fate without their consent), Polish officials successfully demanded the right to participate in the two-plus-four discussions concerning the Polish-German border. Polish policies contributed to the German government's decision in mid-November 1990 to sign a formal treaty affirming the Oder-Neisse line as its eastern border. The June 1991 Polish-German treaty of cooperation and neighborly relations, which included a clause renouncing the use of force or threats against one another, further reduced Polish perceptions of a German threat.[44]

Czechoslovakia: Unilateral Restraint   President Vaclav Havel and Foreign Minister Jiri Dienstbier expressed complete backing for Germany's reunification provided the new German state remained democratic and emerged within the context of a new Europe-wide security system.[45] During his sojourn in Washington in February 1990, Havel evinced a very liberal faith in the benign external behavior of republican governments: "I wouldn't be afraid of a democratic country if it had 100 million people, but I would be afraid of a totalitarian country with a million people."[46] Shortly thereafter in Moscow, Dienstbier and Soviet Foreign Minister Eduard Shevardnadze issued a joint communiqué that stated: "The unification of Germany must take place in harmony with the all-European process, and with the formation of a principally new multilateral European security structure which will replace the blocs and reliably ensure equality and stability on the Continent."[47] Czechoslovak officials repeatedly stressed their desire to avoid recriminations over past wrongs, and Havel even suggested that his countrymen had to confront the morality of their forceful expulsion of approximately 2 to 3 million Sudeten Germans after World War II.[48] In addition to issuing their favorable unilateral statements, Czechoslovak officials held frequent bilateral discussions with their German counterparts to discuss the reunification process and other issues of joint concern.

Starting in August 1991 a new source of tension arose between Germany and Czechoslovakia when they made slow progress negotiating a successor to their 1973 bilateral treaty. Czechoslovak officials blamed Bonn for failing to demonstrate "political courage" and resist demands for extensive compensation and the right of resettlement for those Germans expelled from Czechoslovakia after World War II. They also advanced their own claims for compensation for damages during the Nazi occupation. The Czechoslovak ambassador to Germany, Jiri Grusa, impoliticly referred to "a certain conference in Munich" in arguing against the German claims. Although his public remarks drew a sharp rebuke from German Chancellor Helmut Kohl, Czechoslovak officials refrained from multilateralizing their dispute.[49]

Confronting an Unstable Soviet Union
Poland: Diverse Unilateral and Bilateral Measures The newly installed noncommunist government's initial preoccupation was to secure Moscow's toleration of its continued existence. Mazowiecki himself indicated to the Soviet government news agency, TASS, his concern about "the doubts which I think exist in certain Soviet circles about the stability of the situation in Poland and about whether it creates a threat to the situation in Europe and to our neighbors. We would like such doubts to be dispelled precisely because we are committed to cooperation with the Soviet Union."[50] In the past Moscow had relied on the east European communist parties to keep these countries loyal, and the new Polish government now sought to prove that it (and by extension noncommunists in other east European countries) could pursue policies benign to Soviet interests.

Polish authorities relied mostly on unilateral and bilateral means to counter the perceived threat of Soviet intervention in Poland's domestic affairs. First, they unilaterally sought to assuage Moscow's concerns by appointing pro-

Soviet communists to leading positions in the defense and internal security ministries.[51] (The previous July enough Solidarity representatives in the Polish legislature had voted for General Wojciech Jaruzelski to elect him president. His presence in 1989 and 1990 provided yet another guarantee to Moscow of Poland's fidelity.) Polish authorities also took care to downplay and combat anti-Soviet sentiment among the Polish population, particularly after Soviet commentators criticized such manifestations.[52] Finally, during their first few months in power, Polish officials repeatedly stated that they did not intend to withdraw from the WTO or the Council for Mutual Economic Assistance (CMEA). As Mazowiecki explained in an interview with the Soviet government newspaper *Izvestiya* shortly after assuming office: "We are aware of the geopolitical situation in which Poland finds itself. We will remain true to alliance commitments which follow from our membership in the Warsaw Pact."[53] Polish officials drew a distinction between spheres of influence, which they rejected, and spheres of security, which they accepted for the time being. The former grants a government influence over another state's internal policies; the latter influence over only its foreign policies. As the government newspaper expressed it: "Respecting the right of our eastern neighbor to a security cordon and regarding it as the principal guarantee of our own security, we desire to arrange our own affairs in a sovereign manner."[54] As part of this effort to reassure the other WTO leaders about its external behavior, the Polish government adopted toward them a "policy of nonantagonism" and refrained during the summer and fall of 1989 from assisting the popular movements seeking to overthrow them.[55] Polish officials also held numerous high-level bilateral talks with their Soviet counterparts, including Gorbachev and Shevardnadze.

Although accepting Moscow's right to influence Poland's foreign policy, Polish officials took steps to increase their maneuvering room. As early as the fall of 1989, Niezabitowska said: "Our goal is the liquidation of spheres of influence in Europe. We want a Europe of states that are sovereign in international politics and independent in internal policy."[56] The Polish government pursued three specific objectives toward this end. First, Polish officials attempted to remove the approximately fifty thousand Soviet troops then based in Poland. Second, they endeavored to reform the WTO so that it was no longer controlled by the Kremlin nor concerned with ideological questions or its members' domestic policies. Third, they sought to avoid signing another bilateral treaty with the USSR like the 1965 accord which had granted Moscow extensive influence over Poland's foreign policy.

Monthly bilateral talks between Polish and Soviet representatives to discuss the withdrawal of the USSR's military contingent from Poland began only in November 1990. Before this period, the government held that the troops should remain until "military blocs were no longer necessary."[57] Although their desire not to provoke Moscow influenced their policies, Polish authorities also apparently wanted the troops to moderate Germany's stance on the frontier question.[58]

At first, Polish officials considered allowing Soviet troops to remain for perhaps four years, providing they left after Soviet forces had completed their evacuation of eastern Germany.[59] But by early 1991 they had become increasingly insistent that all Soviet troops withdraw before the end of that year. Soviet representatives complained about the difficulties associated with such a swift pullout and stressed the need to maintain troops in Poland while Soviet forces departed Germany through Polish territory. They proposed 1994 as the date for the withdrawal of the last Soviet unit.[60] Complaining that Poland should not receive a "worse deal" than Czechoslovakia and Hungary,[61] Polish authorities started in January 1991 to prevent convoys carrying Soviet soldiers and military equipment from entering Poland.[62] Emboldened by the conservative reaction then apparent in Moscow, the senior Soviet commander in Poland, General Viktor Dubynin, menacingly remarked that "if the Polish side does not agree with the Soviet protocol settling legal, property and financial issues and does not show good will, the Soviet army will nevertheless enter the territory of the superpower, the Soviet Union, following our plans and routes we have planned. In this case, we will be responsible only for the lives and health of Soviet citizens. We will shake off responsibility for the Polish side."[63] Two days later the Soviet military intervened in Lithuania. In response to Moscow's continued intransigence, the Polish government, which had not been consulted in advance by Soviet and German representatives about their bilateral departure agreement, threatened to withdraw permission for Soviet units to remain on its territory and to deny the approximately 380,000 Soviet troops based in eastern Germany the right to transit Poland.[64] Skubiszewski blamed the Soviet military's "general dissatisfaction" for the USSR's hardline position. He told journalists: "They are having to leave all these countries so they are saying, 'Let's hang on in the last one.'"[65] The despondent but ever circumspect Lech Walesa said his government recognized that "this is a nuclear power, and no forces are capable of threatening, pushing it away or chasing it away."[66] As the talks progressed, the financial costs of dismantling Soviet facilities in Poland and transferring Soviet military units over vulnerable Polish bridges and roads also became increasingly a point of contention. The prolonged stalemate embittered Soviet-Polish relations.

Polish officials used the WTO both to balance Germany and to appease Moscow. They initially expressed support for the continued existence of a reformed WTO. Although he called in September 1990 for the dissolution of the pact's military organ and a diminution of its political functions, Skubiszewski said that Europe's heightened instability argued against the alliance's complete dismantling.[67] The Polish government's reluctance to break decisively with the WTO resulted from concerns about Germany and from the presence of large numbers of Soviet troops on Polish territory.

Polish authorities also tried to do what they could to prevent either civil war in the USSR or the reversal of Gorbachev's reform program. To counter these perceived threats, Polish officials repeatedly declared their backing for Gorbachev's reform program. Skubiszewski declared that the success of his government depended on "the maintenance of Mikhail Gorbachev's internal and foreign policies."[68] They also stressed in public that any new European security structure must take legitimate Soviet interests into account.[69] Finally, although in theory they advocated the Soviet republics' right to national self-determination, in practice they declined to recognize the independence claims of some of their governments or otherwise support them in disputes with Moscow.[70] Such a policy was particularly difficult for Poland to carry out toward Lithuania, whose claims for self-determination enjoyed widespread support in Poland.[71] At the time of the Soviet military crackdown there, the realist Walesa contended: "It's not a good time to anger the bear."[72]

In May 1991 the Soviet and Polish governments initiated negotiations to draft a comprehensive bilateral treaty to define their new relationship. Polish authorities had made clear that they would not negotiate further bilateral military treaties with the USSR,[73] so the formal talks focused on other areas. Soviet efforts to incorporate clauses denying Poland the right to "enter into alliances and to cooperate with other countries" or to "facilitat[e] foreign activities that might be hostile to the Soviet Union," as well as a proposed provision permitting the USSR "to transit through Polish territory," produced a deadlock.[74] Polish officials declined to follow the example of the Romanian government, which had assented to similar wording in its bilateral treaty with Moscow.

Polish authorities soon came to realize NATO's existential value in meeting the Soviet threat. Although they recognized that they could not soon become NATO members because, as Skubiszewski put it, the alliance had to take "Soviet sensibility" into account, they expressed interest in obtaining some kind of "associate status" and in receiving the alliance's help with their security problems.[75] Walesa said that the alliance "is very needed" given that the Soviet bloc's collapse had left the east European countries security "orphans."[76] Jerzy Makarczyk, secretary of state at the Foreign Ministry, told visiting U.S. Vice President Dan Quayle in late April 1991 that "Poland viewed NATO, and in particular, American participation in NATO, as one of the principal elements in the present system of European security."[77] Skubiszewski openly welcomed the communiqué of the June 1991 NATO ministerial session in Copenhagen, which stated that the allies' security was inseparable from the safety and freedom of the other European states.[78]

Czechoslovakia: Multilateral Balancing Czechoslovakia's security interests with regard to the USSR were complex. On the one hand, Czechoslovak officials wanted to lessen Moscow's influence over their country's security policies and remove its military forces from their territory. On the other hand, they did not want to embitter their relations with their powerful eastern neighbor whose military strength might counter a German threat.

The new Czechoslovakian ambassador to Moscow, Rudolf Slansky, aptly explained the essence of his government's aims toward the USSR: "The great issue is to finish changing our relationship from unequal to equal."[79] Czechoslovak officials thought they had attained this goal in principle at the end of February 1990 when, following bilateral talks, Havel and Gorbachev signed a joint declaration that stated their relations would develop "on the basis of equality and complete mutual respect for state sovereignty."[80] In the minds of Czechoslovak officials, the declaration replaced de facto the 1970 bilateral treaty of friendship between the two governments.[81] Yet, in the negotiations for a new, nonideological friendship treaty, Czechoslovak diplomats confronted Soviet efforts to place a clause in the document prohibiting either side from joining an alliance directed against the other. Given their country's higher probability of entering NATO or the EC, Czechoslovak officials believed that the proposal burdened them more. Havel complained at a press briefing that "such a clause would limit our sovereignty as well as that of our freedom of decision." Although denying that a quest for NATO membership motivated his opposition, he did express concern that, with the EC considering a stronger security dimension, the Soviet proposal could prevent Czechoslovakia's membership in the Community.[82]

Among the various specific security issues affecting their relationship, the Czechoslovak officials' top priority was to secure the removal of the Central Group of Soviet forces from their territory. Soviet authorities had based these approximately seventy-five thousand troops in Czechoslovakia since August 1968, when the USSR and other Warsaw Pact countries had invaded the country to depose the "Prague Spring" reform movement. Czechoslovak officials resolved this issue through bilateral negotiations with their Soviet counterparts, despite the parallel efforts of the Hungarian (and, much later, Polish) governments to obtain the withdrawal of Soviet military forces from their territory. The negotiations began in January 1990, with Czechoslovak officials urging that all Soviet troops leave by the end of the year. They ended the following month with a bilateral agreement providing for a phased withdrawal of Soviet forces, with the last soldiers and their families leaving by July 1, 1991. During the negotiations Czechoslovak officials encouraged popular demonstrations against the Soviet presence, despite negative commentary by TASS. The last Soviet forces departed on June 26, a few days ahead of schedule.[83]

Like their Polish counterparts, Czechoslovak officials wanted the USSR's new policies to continue. They feared that a reversal of Gorbachev's reform program could end Moscow's uncharacteristically moderate European policies. One Czechoslovak parliamentary representative warned that "if conservative forces in the Soviet Union take over power, the term of the withdrawal of Soviet troops could be considerably prolonged, e.g., under the pretext of a united Germany."[84]

To prevent the emergence of a "Versailles complex" among Soviet leaders, which could have led to a future backlash, Czechoslovak authorities strenuously sought to keep the USSR involved in European affairs and expressed their support for Gorbachev's concept of a Europe without blocs. They insisted that the Soviet Union participate in any new European security system and the institutions associated with it. When he visited NATO headquarters in March 1991, Havel warned that any effort to exclude the USSR from Europe would only aid Soviet conservatives. First Deputy Chief of the General Staff Lieutenant General J. Vincenc rejected proposals by Henry Kissinger and others that Austria, Czechoslovakia, Hungary, and Poland formalize their unsought status as a "neutral belt" on the grounds that Moscow would interpret such a step as aiming at its isolation.[85]

Although Havel attempted to reassure Moscow by agreeing before forming his government that he would not change Czechoslovakia's relations with the WTO,[86] during the spring and summer of 1989 Czechoslovak officials wavered over whether to retain the organization as a political organ. Havel's February 1990 statement obfuscated the issue sufficiently to keep all options open: "I think the aim of our activities should be a gradual abolition of the Warsaw Pact. We would not help this process very much if we unilaterally left it. I think if it is going to be transformed into something else, it must be done as a unifying step. It can't be changed by just some of its members. But we think there is a good chance all of its members would like to change it. So why should we do it in a controversial way when we can do it in peaceful negotiations?"[87] In June 1990 Dienstbier stressed that, because the WTO kept the USSR involved in Europe, "for the first time, the Warsaw Pact is useful to us."[88] By late 1990, however, Czechoslovak officials had called for the institution's disbanding in the near future.[89] A few days after the Soviet military crackdown in Lithuania, a large majority of the Czechoslovak parliamentarians called for the WTO's dissolution.[90] On February 4, 1991, Havel said that Czechoslovakia probably would withdraw from the pact by the end of the month unless the member states abolished its military structures.[91] When the WTO governments agreed to the proposal at the end of the month, Dienstbier called it "a great day for Czechoslovakia."[92]

Besides their dependence on declining Soviet oil deliveries, which Czechoslovak officials acknowledged constrained their foreign policy,[93] the most significant remaining point of contention between Czechoslovakia and the USSR concerned Moscow's policies in the Baltic region. Havel and other Czechoslovak officials, though failing until August 1991 to extend official recognition to the self-proclaimed independent state of Lithuania, expressed full support for the Baltic republics' quest for independence, established direct diplomatic ties with Lithuania, and condemned the January 1991 Soviet military action in the republic as a "gross violation" of international standards of behavior that "undermined confidence in the democratic changes taking place in the Soviet Union." Although Soviet authorities resented this stand, neither government allowed their differences on this matter to spill over into other areas.[94]

Shevardnadze's decision to resign as foreign minister, which he announced December 20, 1990, and the apparent end of the Soviet reform program in the winter of 1990–91, evoked trepidation in Prague. Apprehensive Czechoslovak officials stepped up their efforts to attain a security guarantee from the west once it appeared that reactionary forces were regaining influence in the

Kremlin. The realities of confronting Soviet power caused Czechoslovakia's new leaders to reassess the relative utility of the CSCE and NATO.

Leading Czechoslovak decision makers, particularly Dienstbier and other Foreign Ministry personnel, initially urged the establishment of a new all-encompassing European security structure based on the CSCE process. In early April 1990 Dienstbier addressed a memorandum to all thirty-five governments involved in the CSCE process. It called for the creation of a Europe-wide security system centered in the first instance on a new Commission on Security in Europe, whose membership would have consisted of all CSCE participants. The European Security Commission would have gradually assumed the functions of the existing alliances. At some unspecified future date the European states would have formed a confederation that would have behaved as a single foreign policy actor.[95] In an address to the Parliamentary Assembly of the Council of Europe on May 10, Havel outlined further how his government hoped to strengthen the CSCE. Of particular interest was Havel's proposal that the participants in an enhanced CSCE bind themselves "to provide mutual assistance in the case of an attack from the outside and [accept] the duty to submit to arbitration in the case of local conflicts."[96] Although the Paris summit participants agreed to carry out elements of Dienstbier's proposal, by this time Czechoslovak officials had already scaled back their grandiose plans for the organization. In justifying his newfound appreciation of NATO, Havel wistfully observed: "We are not giving up the idea [of a European security structure centered on a powerful CSCE], but it appears we cannot dream of the future only."[97]

After assuming office, Havel and Dienstbier at first called for the rapid disbanding of both NATO and the WTO. Sacha Vondra, Havel's diplomatic adviser, explained in March 1990: "All our acts aim at the creation of a Europe which is no longer divided into two contrary blocs, but is united under a new system of security."[98] Rather than rely on the extension of the western bloc into eastern Europe, most Czechoslovak officials initially believed that all-European structures not tarnished by exclusive past association with the west or the east would best serve their country's (and Europe's) security. Czechoslovak policymakers urged the departure of all foreign (including American) military forces based in Europe. In an interview with the Cable News Network, Havel stated: "I think American troops can leave Europe and they are not necessary there anymore."[99]

After meeting with President George Bush and other senior U.S. policymakers during their visit to Washington in February 1990, Czechoslovak officials began to indicate that American troops should remain in Europe for the time being because they played a stabilizing role.[100] They also began to display a greater appreciation for NATO. During a visit to London in April, Dienstbier remarked: "There's nothing wrong with NATO except that we don't belong to it."[101] At the Paris CSCE summit in November, Havel went out of his way to praise the western alliance and proposed that NATO consider offering east European countries "association agreements."[102] In early February 1991 Havel, alluding to the "very dramatic changes" taking place in Soviet politics, stated that he favored closer ties between Czechoslovakia and the alliance because it represented Europe's "only functioning, democratic security structure." He suggested that NATO could constitute the nucleus of a new all-European security system.[103] In mid-March 1991 Havel acknowledged that, even without membership, closer contacts with NATO provided "a sort of guarantee" to Czechoslovakia. Yet, during his address at NATO headquarters, he lamented that "we realize . . . our country cannot become a regular member of NATO for the time being. At the same time, we believe . . . an alliance of countries united by the ideals of freedom and democracy should not be forever closed to neighboring countries that are pursuing the same goals."[104]

By mid-1991 Czechoslovak officials appeared to have accepted the argument of some NATO officials that the alliance's mere existence, even without formal east European participation, exerted a kind of "existential deterrence" on great power aggression in Europe. In a domestic radio address following his talks in Brussels, Havel argued that the growing contacts with NATO would help ensure Czechoslovakia's security.[105] During a visit to Washington in June 1991, Czechoslovak Defense Minister Lubos Dobrovsky denied that his country wished to join NATO, but added that his government appreciated the alliance's contribution to European security.[106] A Czechoslovak official involved with NATO affairs explained to me in August 1991 that although Czechoslovakia could not soon become a member, his government would remain satisfied provided NATO continued to consider the interests of the central European countries when formulating its policies, as it did in its London and Copenhagen communiqués.

Romania: Bilateral Bandwagoning and Emphatic Support for CSCE Norms
The signing of its controversial bilateral treaty with Moscow, combined with its initial strong support for the WTO and its efforts to resist popular pressures to confront Moscow over Moldavia, suggests that during the appar-

ent reactionary recrudescence in the USSR before August 1991, the Romanian government saw a need for close security ties with the still communist-dominated Soviet Union.

Romanian authorities initially renounced any intention of seeking the return of Soviet Moldavia (with its approximately 3 million ethnic Romanians) or other areas seized by the USSR in 1940. On January 25, 1990, for instance, the newly appointed Romanian ambassador to the USSR told Moscow television that his country, in accordance with CSCE norms, was "fully committed" to Europe's existing frontiers.[107]

Although this stance avoided giving Hungary justification to demand the return of Transylvania, where approximately 2 million ethnic Hungarians resided, and which Romania had acquired in the mid-1940s, it proved difficult to sustain at home after the Soviet government took action against nationalist movements in Moldavia and elsewhere during the winter of 1990–91. As Romanian public opinion became increasingly vocal in its opposition to Moscow's policies,[108] government officials felt compelled to condemn anti-Romanian agitation in Moldavia. They also stated in public that Moldavia consisted of former Romanian territory and that history would eventually restore the region to its rightful owner.[109] In March 1991 Ion Iliescu openly supported the Moldavian republic's decision to boycott the all-union referendum on the future of the Soviet federation. The president declared that Moscow's endeavors to compel the republic's inhabitants to participate had "nothing to do with democracy."[110] Anti-Russian demonstrations in Romania provoked by the referendum, during which some protesters had shouted slogans against Iliescu, may have prompted the president's announcement.[111] In June the Romanian parliament, despite the executive branch's evident concerns over Moscow's reaction, unanimously passed a declaration condemning and declaring invalid the USSR's incorporation of the former Romanian territories of Bessarabia and northern Bukovina and called for measures to eliminate the "consequences" of the Hitler-Stalin pact that had made the Soviet annexation possible.[112]

Despite their domestic problems, the Romanian authorities stressed their continued adherence to the CSCE norms concerning the inviolability of Europe's existing frontiers and the nonuse of force. A spokesperson for the Romanian Ministry of Foreign Affairs declared in late 1990 that "in its relations with all European states, therefore with the Soviet Union included, *our government firmly observes the principles of the CSCE final act in Helsinki* reasserted in the Paris charter for a new Europe. Within these limits we follow with special attention but also with worry the events in and connected with the Moldavian SSR." He added: "In approaching those issues, the Romanian government starts from its consistent stand to observe the principles of frontiers [*sic*] inviolability and territorial integrity of all European states as well as the other principles in the Helsinki Final Act."[113] In a speech to the parliamentary session that enacted the declaration described earlier, Nastase said that Romania could not make "territorial demands" of the USSR because of certain "unfortunate realities." Not only had Moscow altered the region's ethnic composition by encouraging Russian immigration, but because Romania had adhered to the CSCE accords confirming the present borders, other member countries would not support Romanian irredentism.[114]

The signing by Iliescu and Gorbachev of a fifteen-year "Treaty of Cooperation, Good Neighborliness, and Friendship" in early April 1991 constituted an important element of Romania's security policy. The new accord replaced the 1970 treaty of alliance that had included ideological clauses. According to the new document's provisions, the two governments accepted their borders' inviolability and pledged not to employ aggression or force in their relations or to interfere in each other's domestic affairs. They also agreed to consult in situations that threatened international peace or their security interests. The commitment both sides made in the fourth paragraph not to join or aid any alliance directed against the other constituted the most controversial feature of the accord.[115] Not only did Romanian opposition figures criticize it,[116] but other east European governments vociferously refused to accept such a provision in their planned bilateral treaties with Moscow. In justifying his acceptance of the terms, Nastase subsequently claimed that the WTO's disbanding "generated the need for the protection of [the] national security interests of the East-European countries in new terms, complying with the CSCE documents and the charter of Paris." The foreign minister added that, "under the Paris Charter on Co-operation and Security in Europe, all the countries of Europe are now supposed to be friends."[117]

Support for the WTO represented another element of the government's strategy to remain close to Moscow. Reversing Nicolae Ceausescu's policies and disregarding the preferences of the other east European governments, Romanian officials did not initially seek to loosen their ties with the Warsaw Pact, one of the few European security institutions that accepted them as full members. Instead, they backed Soviet efforts to convert the alliance into a predominantly political organ. In late February Foreign Minister Sergiu Celac told foreign journalists: "I see no reason to suggest major policy changes in my government's position toward the Warsaw Treaty."[118] But Romanian officials soon lost faith in the WTO's utility as an institution. In early May, Romanian Prime Minister Petre Roman told the Yugoslav state news agency: "It is my opinion that we must all strive for greater bloc disengagement, which implies also a transformation of the existing military structures in Europe. The process must move in the direction of stronger cooperation and even of the creation of alliances, but on a political and economic basis and not a military one."[119] In October 1990 Roman seemed skeptical that the pact could play even a political role in the future: "We now ask the question if the political component is useful and . . . whether it can contribute to stability in Europe . . . We have to ask questions on this and find answers—if they exist."[120] When the signatories disbanded the WTO's military structure in March 1991, Iliescu said that the development had resulted from "an objective process reflecting reality."[121]

Given the WTO's demise and NATO's patent lack of interest in playing a key role in the Balkans, Romanian officials soon concluded that, from their perspective, the evolving CSCE structure represented the most useful security institution for the foreseeable future.[122] They argued that the CSCE process, an institution in which they enjoyed full membership and whose norms sanctified Europe's existing frontiers (and hence Romania's retention of Transylvania), should play a "very important" role in preserving European security and dealing with the problem of ethnic minorities.[123] When some CSCE participants proposed proceeding beyond the existing structure and creating a new European security system, Romanian officials became concerned that other states would attempt to exclude them. Employing rather immoderate language, Nastase warned in an interview with the Reuters news agency on July 6, 1990:

I have heard some ideas that perhaps we should develop a Europe, not up to the borders of the Soviet Union or even to the Urals, but create a Europe which finishes at the western border of Romania . . .

Any trend which does not take into account all the countries in Europe in the CSCE will not be credible and successful. I think it would be ridiculous to keep Romania outside this process. If Romania is kept outside, in order to survive it will have to connect itself with other places and areas, and I do not think this would be good for economic ties or political stability.

In an arduous effort to overcome western concerns about their commitment to civil rights and liberal democracy, Romanian officials unilaterally introduced a series of reform measures. As the newly appointed foreign minister Nastase explained: "If we succeed to do good things in terms of domestic policy, then we can change our foreign image."[124] The government made it easier for Romanians to travel abroad. It invited observers from the United Nations, the Council of Europe, and other CSCE members to help supervise the May 1990 national elections (which, despite some irregularities, most observers deemed free and fair).[125] Romanian officials also made a vigorous effort to persuade various international institutions of their commitment to democracy, capitalism, and human rights. For example, at a CSCE-sponsored conference on human rights in Copenhagen in June 1990, Celac told the assembled delegates that the Romanian revolution had "put an end for good to a totalitarian dictatorship and inaugurated an irreversible process leading to the establishment of a pluralistic society based on the rule of law, a market-oriented economy and on freedom, democracy and human rights."[126] Over time such measures succeeded in improving the government's image in the west and ensured Romania's continued involvement in the CSCE process.

In another effort to avoid becoming too dependent on Moscow, Romanian officials sought to strengthen ties with the United States. On January 7, 1990, for instance, Celac indicated he desired increased American involvement in the region to "counterbalance" the growing role of the USSR in Romania.[127] Yet the Bush administration's repeated denunciations of the Romanian government's human rights abuses, culminating in the decision to have the U.S. ambassador boycott President Iliescu's inauguration, and its refusal to renew most favored nation trade status led Iliescu to complain that the U.S. government was "waging an economic war [against Romania] that is impossible to understand."[128] To improve relations, Romanian authorities offered to provide U.S. forces during the Persian Gulf War with mineral water and access to Romania's unused oil refining capacity (for jet fuel) and luxury resorts.[129] Such gestures, combined with the government's increasing commitment to human rights and the free market, succeeded by mid-1991 in bettering ties with Washington. But Romania, like the other east European countries, found the United States unwilling to assume a high-profile security role in eastern Europe.

Containing the Yugoslav Civil War

Romania: Unilateral Measures Romanian officials became increasingly concerned about the ongoing collapse of Yugoslavia. Liviu Muresan, deputy chairman of the ruling National Salvation Front, lamented: "We are caught in a vise, situated as we are between two countries—the Soviet Union and Yugoslavia—that are on the brink of civil war."[130] Romanian officials especially worried that Yugoslavia's breakup could inspire Transylvanian secessionists. On July 1, 1991, Iliescu said that the chaos in Romania's Balkan neighbor could have unpleasant repercussions "not only for Yugoslavia but also for the stability of the whole area."[131] A spokesperson for the Hungarian Democratic Union in Romania (HDUR) acknowledged that "there are many Hungarian extremists . . . who might seek to use the Slovenian and Croatian precedent to press their claims for a redrawing of borders."[132]

To contain the conflict, Romanian authorities relied primarily on unilateral declarations. They repeatedly endorsed the preservation of Yugoslavia's existing federal structure and denied any intention to intervene in the dispute. They resolutely dismissed allegations that they planned to annex parts of Yugoslavia if the federation disintegrated and that Romanians, perhaps acting independently of their government, were aiding Serbian or Croatian forces. The Foreign Ministry observed that "such claims [of Romanian participation in the fighting] cannot be true because it would be contrary to the policy of good neighbourly relations which Romania implements consistently."[133] In addition, Romanian officials also urged Yugoslavia's other Balkan neighbors "to refrain from acts that might increase tension in the area or endanger [that country's] unity and territorial integrity."[134] Though opposing the intervention of Albania, Bulgaria, and especially Hungary in the civil war, Romanian officials did support other countries' efforts to defuse the conflict.[135]

In addition to their unilateral statements, Romanian officials resorted to limited unilateral actions and bilateral measures to support Yugoslavia's integrity and Romania's defense. Sometime in the spring the Romanian military assumed a higher alert status. Defense Minister Nicolae Constantin declared on May 10: "There is instability in Yugoslavia. It is natural that the military should be in a certain state of alert. The state of alert should be strengthened, and steps have already been taken to this effect."[136] In an effort to enhance the Yugoslav government's legitimacy through bilateral measures, Romanian authorities continued to cooperate with federal officials in such forums as the Romanian-Yugoslav Commission for Economic Collaboration.[137]

Albania: Bilateral Balancing and Multilateral Bandwagoning Albanian officials evinced increasing alarm at the chaos in neighboring Yugoslavia. The
dominant Serbian republic was pursuing ever harsher measures against the
approximately 2 million–strong Albanian majority in neighboring Kosovo,
a region many of the 3 million Albanians living in Albania proper consider
part of their nation. "The disintegration of Yugoslavia could bring about a
dangerous situation for the Balkans and all Europe," President Ramiz Alia
warned. "It presents a great danger for Albania."[138] Like the Czechoslovak
leadership, the Albanian authorities eagerly employed international institutions to help them counter perceived threats.

Despite the holding of the first meeting in over forty years between an
Albanian president and a Yugoslav minister, and the Albanian government's
continued refusal to call for Kosovo's incorporation into Albania, relations
between Albania and Yugoslavia deteriorated in 1990.[139] The expanding
sway of democratic politics in Albania, which increased the importance of
popular support as a source of political power, encouraged politicians to issue
ever harsher denunciations of Serbian repression. After Albanian opposition
leaders complained about the government's failure to act more forcefully on
behalf of the Albanians in Kosovo, the authorities felt compelled to take a
stronger stand.[140] In September 1990 Alia told the United Nations that,
although his government wished to improve relations with Yugoslavia, it had
to consider that in Kosovo "crimes are being committed that would have been
considered monstrous even in the dark Middle Ages."[141]

In early June 1991 Albanian Foreign Minister Mehmet Kapllani made an
unprecedented journey to Croatia, Serbia's major opponent in the Yugoslav
civil war. During his stay Kapllani met with the republic's premier and
foreign minister. At the same time Alia began to confer with ethnic Albanian
leaders from Kosovo.[142] A month later relations between Serbia and Albania
plummeted. Yugoslav and Albanian border guards exchanged fire, and Serbian authorities accused Albanians of overturning frontier markers and insti-
gating unrest in Kosovo. In a statement the Serbian government accused
Albania of interfering in Yugoslavia's internal affairs and warned that it
would respond "decisively with all available means" to any challenges to
its sovereignty. The head of the Albanian army announced that Albania's
military had assumed a higher alert status because of Yugoslavia's escalating
civil war.[143]

Reversing their previous policies, the Albanian authorities also pursued
improved bilateral ties with the superpowers to dissuade them from exploit-

ing domestic unrest in Albania and to deter Serbia from aggressive actions. On July 30, 1990, Albanian and Soviet officials signed a protocol normalizing relations. Albania's efforts to restore relations with the United States made much slower progress. Although Albanian officials expressed appreciation for the U.S. government's protests against Serbia's repressive actions in Kosovo,[144] American officials repeatedly complained during bilateral meetings about their slow pace of domestic reform.[145] U.S. representatives also reportedly obstructed Albania's initial efforts to join the CSCE because of its poor human rights record.[146] But in March 1991 U.S. officials restored diplomatic relations and agreed to reopen the American embassy.

Besides responding to their heightened sense of threat through unilateral and bilateral balancing, Albanian authorities displayed an unprecedented interest in deepening their involvement with international institutions. In addition to the expected security benefits, they believed that participation would enhance their domestic legitimacy. As one British correspondent observed in October 1990 regarding Albania's campaign to enter the CSCE: "The CSCE decision is crucial, for if membership is not forthcoming it could spark off another wave of unrest as young people protest at their leaders' failure to integrate the country in a process which places great emphasis on European values and human rights."[147]

In explaining his government's reversal on the CSCE, which Albania, unlike every other European country, had refused to join in 1973 when the rules granted automatic membership, Alia said participation in the process "responds to the times and to Albania's interests."[148] In June, Albanian representatives attended a CSCE meeting in Copenhagen as observers. At the talks an Albanian official formally announced that his country wished to become a full member and would "adopt all the rules of the conference and take care to accept what has been accepted by other participant countries."[149]

Although Albanian representatives attended the November CSCE summit in Paris as observers, the other delegations refused to accept them as full members until Albania had introduced further domestic reforms. Western representatives seemed particularly disturbed by the brutal means Albanian officials had employed during the July 1990 refugee crisis.[150] A western diplomat commented: "Albania's problem is that the threshold has been raised. What was acceptable in the middle of the Cold War is not acceptable any longer."[151]

The Albanian government expressed "surprise and incomprehension" after learning of the summit's decision. It issued a statement declaring that the refusal to grant Albania full membership failed to respect the "spirit and the letter of the CSCE."[152] During the preparatory meetings Albanian officials had pleaded that "you cannot expect things to change overnight," and complained: "No country can set an absolute standard of behavior, not the U.S., not Britain. What we are trying to do is commit ourselves to an international standard."[153]

To gain admission to the CSCE, Albanian authorities made a sustained effort to overcome other governments' concerns about their domestic policies. In a process of anticipatory adaptation to the norms associated with CSCE membership, Albanian officials implemented unilateral reform measures to strengthen their candidacy and enhance their popular support. Throughout 1990 hesitant and divided Albanian leaders introduced major policy changes, including reducing reliance on the death penalty, permitting greater religious freedom, and allowing Albanians to travel abroad. In September 1990 the Albanian Council of Ministers, in presenting their demand for CSCE membership, avowed that "the changes made and that are actually being made to the Albanian legislation allow the application of the principles of the Helsinki charter and of the decisions of the CSCE."[154] In his UN address Alia, after stressing his government's intention to participate in the CSCE, proclaimed that "any decision or suggestion contributing to the defense of human rights and national and democratic freedoms will have Albania's full support."[155] Opposition leaders' demands that the government adhere to the Helsinki process and publish translated versions of CSCE documents also prompted the government's new approach.[156] In June 1991, after Albanian communists had accepted a multiparty government, the CSCE granted Albania full membership.

Issues, Institutions, and Outcomes

The themes of this chapter, as related to the volume as a whole, can be summarized by examining national security behavior, institutional activities, and outcomes.

Variations in National Security Behavior

The international system constrains state behavior but still allows some room to maneuver. All four of the governments studied perceived security threats, whether from German reunification, the chaos in the USSR, or the collapse of Yugoslavia. Despite confronting similar types of problems, these governments pursued divergent security strategies. Czechoslovakia and Albania placed great faith in international institutions, while Poland and Romania relied primarily on other means to enhance their security. It is possible to speculate on the reasons for this divergence.[157]

Situated between Germany and the USSR, Poland possessed an unenviable geopolitical position. Because its powerful neighbors enjoyed a vast superiority in military resources, unilateral resistance could not have sustained it in a major conflict with either country. Although Polish officials sought strong allies in western Europe, these states were too distant and not sufficiently powerful compared with Germany or the USSR to provide effective deterrence or timely assistance. The American government did not show an interest in guaranteeing Poland's security. Although they could have relied on institutional balancing, Polish officials consistently displayed little interest in such a strategy. Unlike in Czechoslovakia, the dominant shapers of Polish security policy, particularly the foreign minister, were not dissidents who had developed a great appreciation for the efficacy of international security institutions in their years out of power; rather they were largely the type of professional international affairs experts (academics and diplomats) who previously had determined Poland's security policies.[158] Given the perceived ineffectiveness of other strategies, Polish officials logically concluded that their optimal policy was to seek to balance Bonn and Moscow against each other.

In terms of the composition of its national security elite, Czechoslovakia's political revolution produced a sharper break with the past than in the other three countries. During their dissident years Havel, Dienstbier, and other future Czechoslovak officials developed an ideal (and idealized) vision of a future European security system without military blocs or bilateral alliances. In their first year in power they sought to realize their vision, but they overestimated the great powers' willingness to establish a new pan-European security structure centered on the CSCE. As the threat of a reversal in Soviet policy increased, Havel in particular altered course and, against the advice of senior Foreign Ministry officials,[159] sought membership in NATO, then the only viable European security institution. Although the west European governments rebuffed these efforts, Czechoslovak leaders soon contented themselves with the belief that NATO's mere existence helped deter Soviet aggression in eastern Europe.

Domestic factors played a larger role in shaping Romanian and Albanian policies. Seeing themselves as fellow reforming communists, Romanian authorities concentrated on establishing good bilateral ties with the USSR in order to gain a great power patron whose leader shared many of their values and whose country's resources might help improve Romania's economy. Although Albanian officials feared that remaining the only government outside the CSCE and other European institutions would leave them isolated during a period of heightened conflict in the Balkans, they also believed they needed CSCE membership to enhance their domestic political legitimacy.

The governments under evaluation did not rely heavily on self-help policies or regional diplomacy. In response to the exigent need to restructure their economies, they all reduced their armed forces and their defense spending. They also displayed more interest in strengthening ties with west European security institutions than in improving cooperation among themselves. When the Soviet military crackdown in Lithuania induced Havel to seek to contact Walesa, his aides realized they did not even have his phone number![160]

A common factor explains the relative lack of interest in both strategies. Even collectively, the east European governments were weak. They did not possess the resources to establish a credible defense against states such as Germany and the USSR. As Polish Solidarity leader Bronislaw Geremek said when discussing east European foreign economic policies: "People aren't interested in alliances with poor neighbors. They want to be with the rich countries."[161]

Robert Rothstein cogently concluded from his analysis of the weaker European countries' behavior before World War II that "one factor which has obviously remained constant for Small Powers is that the solution to any 'security-dilemma' must come from an outside source . . . When Small Powers are threatened by Great Powers, they must turn to other Great Powers for support."[162] Yet, although east European governments such as Poland and Romania relied heavily on bilateral balancing and bandwagoning, their ability to employ this option with outside great powers was constrained. Not only did their relative military weakness mean they could offer little to potential allies, but their history of mutual strife and their numerous latent conflicts exacerbated other governments' fear of entrapment. The country studies in the first part of this volume also show that western powers saw little reason to seek bilateral alliances with the east European countries: the USSR was dying, and Germany remained subdued.

The Role of Institutions

At first glance it would appear that institutions had little independent effect on east European governments' defense strategies. Despite their equally good ties with international security institutions, Poland and Czechoslovakia pursued radically different policies toward similar security problems. (The response of Romania and Albania demonstrated more similarity: both pursued great power patrons and sought close ties with European security institutions.) The lack of common behavior indicates that other factors— such as their domestic coalitions, the legacy of history, and the personalities within the national security elite—besides multilateral institutions shaped these states' response to external military threats.

Yet the relative abundance of international institutions in post–Cold War Europe did affect the east European security environment. As one might expect, governments attempted to employ multilateral institutions as instruments to attain specific goals. But their effect on state behavior went beyond serving as tools of statecraft. Despite common assumptions that governments either exploit or ignore institutions when it comes to the high politics of military security, during the period from 1989 to August 1991 multilateral security institutions also exerted an independent impact on state behavior. Although the most powerful governments decided what role institutions could play in European security affairs, once established, they acted as intermediate variables in affecting governments' policies. Institutions exerted a feedback effect on their founders and shaped the policy choices of governments aspiring to membership. They did not determine states' ultimate goal of survival, but their presence confronted governments with both opportunities and constraints that influenced their security strategies.[163]

Governments employed multilateral institutions as tools to strengthen their military security in several ways. First, they used them to signal their future intentions. For example, the initially fearful Poles tried to reassure Moscow of their foreign policy fidelity by continuing to participate actively in the WTO. Only after Germany's benign intent and the Soviet government's willingness to permit widespread security changes in eastern Europe became clear did the Polish government push for the pact's dissolution.

Second, governments used institutions to legitimize their behavior. German officials inserted paragraphs in the Paris charter blessing German reunification, and thereby secured the endorsement of all European countries except Albania. Both the Soviet and the Yugoslav central governments attempted to employ the CSCE to strengthen their position vis-à-vis their subordinate republics. The Soviet government vigorously fought to keep its various constituent republics out of the CSCE process to prevent them from strengthening their claims to independent statehood. Loncar took pains to attain CSCE resolutions that implied international support for his central government's efforts to hold Yugoslavia together. For the east European regimes, membership in institutions with western members symbolized their "return to Europe." The Albanian government sought to enter the CSCE partly to demonstrate to other countries and its own anxious citizens that it too belonged to the European club. Fear of losing such status partly explains Romanian officials' patent concern to remain active in the CSCE.

Third, institutions can provide governments with information about other states' behavior and practices. Czechoslovak officials stressed that they would feel secure only if German reunification took place simultaneously with a strengthening of Europe's institutional structures because such a development would enhance the accuracy of their expectations about Germany's future security policies. Lacking archives, researchers, and other data resources, east European legislators treasured the information they obtained from the North Atlantic Assembly and the Institute for Security Studies of the West European Union.[164] All European governments appreciated the enhanced intelligence they derived from the CFE agreement and related CSCE confidence-building measures.

Fourth, governments can employ one institution to affect another. Seeking to reinforce its own mediation efforts in the Yugoslav civil war, the EC successfully obtained the CSCE's endorsement of its peace proposals at the July 1991 emergency meeting of the Committee of Senior Officials. More frequent examples exist of governments' using institutions to combat other institutions. The prospects of a strengthened CSCE facilitated east European endeavors to secure Moscow's approval of the WTO's dissolution. Yet the east European states normally lacked the power to execute this strategy successfully. Czechoslovak officials failed in their initial effort to render NATO superfluous by fortifying the CSCE. The more powerful states played this game better. After initial skepticism toward the institution, U.S. officials in 1990 offered the prospect of a somewhat stronger CSCE as a mechanism to quiet east European appeals for much closer ties with NATO.[165]

Fifth, institutions can provide states with "disinterested intervention." Parties in dispute more readily accept third-party arbitration from international institutions than from other governments. These structures appear more concerned with solving the dispute and less preoccupied with advancing their particular interests. The value of their intervention is of course lessened when institutions appear to be instruments of less disinterested blocs, which is why conflicting parties should more readily accept mediation from the CSCE than from NATO or the EC. When the July 1991 emergency meeting of the Committee of Senior Officials decided to offer a "good will" mission to Yugoslavia, it made sure that no members came from neighboring countries.[166]

Finally, governments employed international security institutions as forums to strike favorable bargains and gain the attention of policymakers in other countries. Polish insistence on participating in any two-plus-four talks about Poland's frontier with Germany proved a rewarding strategy because the institution strengthened its hand against Germany. Rather than confronting Bonn in direct bilateral negotiations on this issue, a forum that would have exacerbated Poland's relative weakness, the government institutionalized French, British, Soviet, and American involvement in the dispute. Because these states favored the Polish position, their presence diluted Germany's relative strength vis-à-vis Poland. Similarly, WTO meetings provided east European countries with forums for presenting common demands to Soviet officials, first to reform the institution and later to destroy it. Both CSCE meetings and the biannual sessions of the North Atlantic Assembly provided east European officials and legislators with access to their counterparts in other governments. Given the difficulty and travel costs involved in gaining the attention of U.S. officials in particular, these institutions played a helpful role in reducing the east Europeans' transaction costs.

In addition to serving as tools of statecraft, international institutions also exerted an independent impact on state behavior. First, the institutions had an existential effect: their mere existence affected the strategies of states that were not even members. Even if they could not join NATO, the east European governments favored the alliance's persistence because they believed its presence acted to control Germany and deter the USSR. NATO's presence made them feel more secure and thus reduced their incentives to bandwagon with Germany or balance against the USSR. In this example NATO is not serving as a tool of statecraft because the east European governments neither were alliance members nor had an appreciable effect on the institution's policies. International institutions are like any other background factor (the distribution of power, the nature of weaponry, and so on) that governments must consider when determining their strategies. Of course, the east Europeans had little influence on NATO decisions, but neither can governments easily control other background variables affecting their security. The invention of new weapons can render existing ordnance obsolete; allied governments can alter their policies or lose power; and shifting popular sentiment at home can disrupt defense programs. Institutions provide as reliable a guarantee of security as other changeable background variables and deserve as much research as the other factors receive.

The east European governments' support for NATO's persistence despite their exclusion from the institution presents a puzzle for international relations theory. Notwithstanding the argument of scholars such as Joseph Grieco who stress that relative gains matter more to statesmen than absolute gains, and despite the finding by Celeste Wallander and Jane Prokop in Chapter 2 that Soviet leaders feared security institutions they could not join, the east European governments came to back an institution that worsened their position relative to the member governments. This example demonstrates the complexities of applying the relative versus absolute gains debate to a concrete problem involving many states. Although the east European countries benefited absolutely from NATO's presence, and perhaps relatively vis-à-vis the institution's target, the USSR, their position with respect to the west European countries weakened. In situations concerning more than one dyad, testing the hypothesis that relative gains matter more to statesmen than absolute gains (or vice versa) becomes difficult.[167]

A second way in which international institutions affect state behavior is through "anticipatory adaptation," defined in this volume as the unilateral adoption of a set of norms associated with a multilateral institution by a government before it has acquired full membership in that institution or even received guarantees of entry. As in the other issue areas, security institutions have occasionally brought about this process. The perceived need to enter the CSCE, combined with the collapse of the other communist regimes in eastern Europe, prompted the Albanian government to reform its political system in conformity with CSCE norms. Similarly, Romanian officials' concern about possible exclusion from the CSCE or any successor security institution encouraged them to raise their domestic human rights policies to west European standards. If the CSCE had not existed, both governments would have felt less external pressure to reform.

The process of anticipatory adaptation does not only affect governments. Various domestic groups can perceive the norms associated with international institutions as focal points to govern their preferences. For over a dozen years the Helsinki process motivated a variety of east European reformers to challenge their governments' policies. During the 1989–1991 period, Albanian opposition leaders successfully pressured the government to join the CSCE and respect its norms concerning human rights and political democracy.

A final though less important manner in which international institutions affect state behavior is that they can influence when governments make policy decisions. For example, NATO summits served as temporal mechanisms to force the member governments to decide how to adapt the institution to accommodate developments in the east. Institutional sessions involving senior officials produce deadlines that force decisions.

Variation in Institutional Outcome

Approaches to international politics that highlight the importance of relative power in explaining outcomes also best explain the results of recent bargaining in the issue area of European military security. Weaker countries traditionally favor international institutions. In theory they can reduce the effect of disparities in military power among states by placing restraints on the great powers and by resolving disputes through voting (sometimes even among electoral equals) rather than through engagements among military unequals. They also can enhance the attention weaker states receive from great powers.[168] Yet, just as weaker countries have historically favored an increased role for multilateral institutions, the great powers regularly have shaped the resources and impact of these structures so that they promote great power interests. The result, as Thucydides observed long ago, is that the strong do what they can and the weak accept what they must.

The same pattern occurred during the period from 1989 to August 1991. Despite the strenuous efforts of small countries such as Czechoslovakia to join NATO or construct a new, more equitable European security environment centered on a more powerful CSCE, those states with the most capabilities again determined forum selection and institutional authority and rules. In the issue area of military security, the great powers were the regime-makers and the east European countries the regime-takers. Western governments made a few changes in Europe's institutional structure to accommodate the east's defense interests, but they carefully avoided sacrificing resources to uphold the east Europeans' security. The United States, Britain, and other NATO members overrode the preferences of the USSR and some east European countries for a new security structure that would have replaced NATO as the strongest European security institution. American and other western officials also successfully fought to keep the CSCE's military functions and resources limited while retaining NATO as a collective self-defense organization for the North Atlantic area alone. Having largely renounced the option of remaining allied with Moscow, and being too weak to fight alone against Germany or the USSR, the east European countries lacked any real leverage over the west. Their weakness, their lack of potential allies, and their belief that they could satisfy western demands made their decision to bandwagon with the west overdetermined.[169]

Despite its effectiveness in highlighting the diverse roles institutions can perform even in the high politics of military security, a functional approach to international institutions is less helpful in explaining outcomes in this issue area.[170] The changing patterns of security interdependence in eastern Europe did engender stronger demands among regional governments for a new international regime. East European officials recognized that, without the USSR to act as their military guardian, their responsibility for their countries' defense had increased. They also realized that their ability to integrate with western Europe depended not only on developments within their particular country but also on trends within the larger region. The approach also correctly predicted that countries favored providing existing European security institutions with additional functions rather than creating new structures. Preexisting institutions were privileged as channels of negotiation and as forums for the institutionalization of new east-west bargains. In addition, the functional approach helps explain why east European officials, concerned to establish their government's international reputation, so often stressed their commitment to CSCE norms. These represented the most widely accepted guidelines for interstate security behavior in the new Europe. Yet the institution that assumed the most prominent role between 1989 and August 1991 in guaranteeing east European governments' security, the CSCE, was patently less efficient than NATO. The latter institution was better institutionalized and better endowed with resources, and focused predominantly on security issues. The CSCE, despite its new centers and staff, was still rickety. It also served a variety of functions in nonsecurity areas.[171]

The east European countries today are theoretically very vulnerable to military assault. Their national defenses are weak. Potential great power allies keep their distance. They cannot rely on any institution to come to their defense automatically. NATO has refused to commit itself; any member can block CSCE decisions; and the five permanent members of the Security Council can veto collective defense actions by the UN. As a result, east

European officials have to rely on a weak CSCE, the existential deterrent value of NATO, and their diplomatic skills to ward off external dangers.

Fortunately, it is hard to perceive who would threaten the military security of the east European countries. Despite an increase in its diplomatic activity, Germany has shown no interest in threatening military action against its neighbors. The USSR has disintegrated into smaller states whose main security preoccupation seems directed toward one another. But developments during the past few years have made clear how hard it is to predict Europe's future. The east European governments must proceed knowing that should a challenge to their military security arise, their fate could lie in the hands of other governments, many of whom might perceive little need to defend them. Whereas during the Cold War the superpowers felt less militarily secure than their European allies, now once again Europe's smaller countries appear more vulnerable to international trends beyond their control.[172]

Conclusion: Structure, Strategy, and Institutional Roles

Robert O. Keohane
Stanley Hoffmann

The end of the Cold War, marked by the withdrawal of the Soviet military from central Europe and the reunification of Germany, forced major European powers to adapt their strategies quickly to new realities. For the west, these policy changes took place not in a fragmented international system of mutually suspicious and rival states, but in one that had become highly institutionalized. The policies of the United States and its west European allies revolved around sets of rules and organizations, ranging from NATO to the European Community to global international organizations such as the International Monetary Fund (IMF). In the east, by contrast, those international institutions that had existed within the Soviet bloc were soon dissolved. This volume has explored the effects of these historically conditioned patterns of institutionalization on strategies of both states and international organizations between the fall of 1989 and the fall of 1991.

The principal theme of this concluding chapter is that how governments reacted to the end of the Cold War was profoundly conditioned by the existence of international institutions. Europe was an institutionally dense environment in which the expectations of states' leaders were shaped by the rules and practices of institutions, and in which they routinely responded to initiatives from international organizations, as well as using those organizations for their own purposes. Particularly important were the European Community (EC), which had pooled members' sovereignty on major economic issues through the Single European Act of 1985, and the North Atlantic Treaty Organization (NATO), which displayed remarkable resilience throughout the period studied in this volume. European governments and the United States had many institutional levers in their hands, and used them with considerable skill throughout these two uncertain years.

The principal focus of attention was Germany and the significance of its unification for the new European order. In Germany itself, as Jeffrey Anderson and John B. Goodman show in Chapter 1, membership in international institutions such as NATO and the EC acquired intrinsic or "reflexive" significance: these institutions were "embedded in the very definition of state interests and strategies." Other western powers, on the whole, viewed international institutions more instrumentally, but the strategies of the United States, Britain, and France were nevertheless profoundly affected by the nature of existing institutions. It is hardly surprising that in a period of rapid and unanticipated change governments were more likely to attempt to use what was available than to try to redesign international institutions to meet their own standards of perfection. Institutions that continue to serve state purposes tend to persist, as the authors of Chapter 6 indicate, so long as they perform specific functions that are useful to their powerful members, and especially where preexisting arrangements and linkages among issues raise the costs associated with bilateral strategies or new multilateral institutional configurations. Creating new multilateral institutions is usually a costly strategy of last resort.

While major west European powers, and the two superpowers of the Cold War, focused on the significance of Germany's unification for the new European order, the east European states emphasized measures they could take—unilaterally, bilaterally, or through international institutions—to obtain help from and hasten their integration into the west. Thus, priorities were not the same across the former Iron Curtain. Since institutionalization was so weak in the east, it is not surprising that in their search for support and integration, east European governments vacillated between unilateral and bilateral approaches on the one hand and multilateral ones on the other. Poland followed unilateral and bilateral security strategies, while from the outset Czechoslovakia emphasized multilateral institutions; but on environmental issues Poland's policies were more multilateral than those of the Czechs. Since the IMF and World Bank served as "gatekeepers" for loans and debt relief for eastern Europe, east European states had to orient their policies toward these multilateral institutions. However, on issues of direct foreign investment, unilateral and bilateral policies prevailed, reflecting the lack of international institutions in this issue area—largely because multinational enterprises and home country governments had for decades opposed the creation of institutions that would effectively regulate such investment. Soviet policies lacked coherence, being apparently based unrealistically on the assumption that the Soviet Union could reshape security arrangements and join western economic institutions.

The findings of this volume support the institutionalist argument that international institutions—both organizations and regimes—are significant not because they exercise control over states (with few exceptions they do not) but because they are useful to states. They do not substitute for common or complementary interests: they depend on such interests, but they may also amplify them. International institutions in Europe remained significant insofar as their functions could be altered to fit new circumstances: the activities of NATO, the EC, and the IMF could be adapted in many ways to serve state purposes, whether these involved dealing with a unified Germany, signaling peaceful intentions to the Soviet Union, encouraging democratization, or devising fiscal and monetary policies to encourage privatization and capitalist development in eastern Europe. As Part II of this volume shows, in a number of issue areas, including public financial assistance and trade, bilateral ties were also important, and in the former area a new organization, the European Bank for Reconstruction and Development, was created. Nevertheless, preexisting institutions had the advantage not only of organizational inertia but also of fitting well into the complex matrix of relationships and agreements in each issue area.

In this concluding chapter we seek first to account for the broad patterns of state strategies described in the foregoing chapters. This interpretation seeks to be sensitive to the effects of both state power and the activities of international institutions. The latter part of the chapter is more descriptive and more detailed; it seeks to identify what international organizations and regimes did during the two years after August 1989, and how states sought to use the forums, rules, and organizations provided by international institutions to achieve their purposes during this transition.

Structure and Strategy

In 1776 Adam Smith declared that "defence is more important than opulence," and as long as an active military threat existed, whether that of France in the eighteenth century or the Soviet Union in the twentieth, this dictum applied. NATO, the central institution linking the United States with the defense of Europe, was after 1949 the central security institution for most west European governments, a precondition for their confident economic reconstruction and growth. As the chapters on British, German, and American policy indicate, during the 1989–1991 period its members clung to it for protection against the vaguer but pervasive uncertainty that the fall of the Berlin Wall brought. NATO displayed both remarkable persistence and adaptability. Toward the end of 1991, the collapse of the Soviet Union into a collection of sovereign republics, several equipped with nuclear weapons, further increased both uncertainty and fear of chaos, making NATO seem even more essential as an insurance policy against disaster.

Yet the structure of the situation that NATO faced had fundamentally changed. Since NATO was no longer essential to protect its European members from the Soviet Union, the American security guarantee against the Soviets, which had always been at the root of the NATO bargain, had been devalued, from protection against a credible threat to insurance against uncertainty.[1] It was clear to governments and NATO officials alike that the alliance would have to change its central mission. Just as west European governments could begin to question NATO's role, or even its permanence, the states of eastern Europe developed a growing interest in association with or even membership in NATO because of their anxiety about the turbulence and uncertainties in the convulsed Soviet Union. Ironically, the former objects of NATO's military plans became its most enthusiastic champions. NATO's members were—with the usual French "difference"—eager to provide some reassurance, but not to extend the alliance's formal guarantees beyond Germany.

While the nature and immediacy of security threats to western Europe shifted abruptly, the structure of world politics was changing in two ways. With the collapse of the Soviet superpower, bipolarity under any meaningful definition had collapsed as well. The United States was militarily preeminent. However, in the world political economy both Europe and Japan had become more important. The structure of the European political economy was being irrevocably shaped by the European Community, not by NATO, bilateral relations with the United States, or ancillary organizations such as the General Agreement on Tariffs and Trade (GATT) or the Organization for Economic Cooperation and Development (OECD). The collapse of the Community would mean economic and political crisis for its members.

Considerable upheaval, and perhaps political and economic conflict, could ensue were GATT, the OECD, or even NATO to vanish; but their disappearance would be less momentous for their members than the collapse of the EC. None of these organizations was so closely linked to the domestic political and economic structures of their members as were the institutions of the Community. Hence, any analysis of the implications of the end of the Cold War for international politics and institutions in Europe must pay special attention to the European Community.

The European Community in 1989 contained twelve members with a population of 340 million people and a gross economic product of over $5 trillion. As an economy it was equivalent in size to that of the United States. Its scope of authority and decision-making procedures were unprecedented in the history of modern international society: it could not be readily compared with other international organizations, all of which looked puny by comparison. The Community makes decisions principally through inter-governmental action, although its supranational executive, the Commission, plays a significant initiating and negotiating role. Yet this is intergovernmentalism with a difference, characterized by qualified majority voting on major issues concerning the internal market, an extensive set of committees linking national bureaucrats to the Community structure, and a European Court of Justice that has successfully institutionalized the superiority of Community over national law.[2] The end of the Cold War thus did not take place in a fragmented, balance-of-power Europe, but in a political space increasingly dominated by a single organization, so that even rivalry and competition among the members are shaped by and channeled through the common rules and institutions. Three factors seem particularly important in analyzing the interplay between structural change in political-military relations and the institutions of the New Europe: the vulnerability of Europe to extra-European events; asymmetries of power between the Community and its neighbors; and shared expectations for the future. The first of these factors conditions and qualifies the intra-European dominance that the second and third confer on the Community.

Threats to European security were not eliminated by the collapse of the Soviet Union, but they were transformed by this epochal event. New or continuing dangers included possible fragmentation of control over Soviet nuclear weapons, the outbreak of ethnic violence and national strife in eastern Europe and the former USSR, mass migrations of peoples in the wake of such violence and strife, or military action outside Europe, as in the Middle East.

Facing the extra-European threats, whether of nuclear forces in the former Soviet Union or of expansionist states in the Middle East, would for the foreseeable future require American assistance. Thus, even apart from NATO's staying power as an institution, the security interests linking Europeans to the United States could be expected to maintain the support of most Europeans (although not the French) for a NATO that had been reformed so that it could deal more effectively with relatively small conflicts in a wider geographic area. But the French, with increasing German support, have been eager to develop a capability for coping with such conflicts by the Community itself, through the long-dormant West European Union.

Indeed, within Europe the Community—built on the assumption of a divided Europe—became vastly *more* significant and powerful as a result of the Soviet collapse. The chapters in this volume that concentrate on eastern Europe particularly reflect this power shift, which was most pronounced in trade (see Chapter 7) and least pronounced in financial assistance (see Chapter 8). The economies of all fourteen nonmembers in Europe, to the west of the Soviet Union, were inconsequential compared to that of the Community. Thus the EC's partners were all vulnerable to its actions but incapable of any effective response. Since vulnerability was so asymmetrical, the power discrepancies were also extreme.[3] The bargaining, if one can call it that, over a "European Economic Space" between 1989 and 1991, between the Community and former EFTA (European Free Trade Area) members, provides a case in point. Essentially, the Community laid down conditions that its would-be partners had to accept. It did not change its rules or reform its institutions to hasten the integration of east European states. Recognizing this reality, most of them rapidly made plans to adapt their laws, as in the areas of direct foreign investment (see Chapter 9) and environmental protection (see Chapter 10), to Community law. They also sought where possible to join the Community. Subject to its rules in any event, they preferred to have some representation in their formation.

The third element of this situation is perhaps even more important, albeit more elusive. Although European elites differed with respect to the desired pace of change and the institutional strength of the newly reconstituted Community, in the end they shared the assumptions that the Community would become institutionally more authoritative and broader in functional scope in the future (although not necessarily through a smooth process), and that Europe would gradually expand—if not "from the Atlantic to the Urals," at least to a Europe of eighteen to twenty states, and eventually, if political developments in eastern Europe were favorable, to twenty-five states or so.

The implications of these assumptions were clear to both members and nonmembers. First, members must seek to shape the rules to accord with their preferences. The intense conflict over rule making that characterized 1991, in preparation for the two intergovernmental conferences in December, reflected not a collapse of integrative momentum but the opposite: precisely because the rules mattered, struggle was intense and bargaining tough. Second, in the view of European leaders (although perhaps not of the voters, as the Danish referendum of June 1992 indicated), exclusion from Europe would be disastrous for any state. Fear of exclusion was the key to British concessions in the 1980s, and would be similarly critical to other concessions, by isolated members and by nonmembers, in the 1990s.[4] Thus, in December 1991 at Maastricht this fear led the British finally to accept (albeit with a possibility of exit) a Monetary Union with a Central Bank and single currency, and a considerable expansion of the functional scope of the EC, except in one area: social policy, where the British Conservative government thought that the exclusion was in Britain's interest.

In view of these structural and institutional features of the European environment and these expectations, what strategies made sense for the major players? Can we infer strategy from structure and institutions? In thinking about how this could be done, it may be useful to draw an analogy with the distinction drawn by some writers on alliances between "balancing" and "bandwagoning." States balance when they join either the weaker or the less threatening side, depending on whether they focus on capability or threat; states bandwagon when they join the stronger party.[5] This distinction has been used chiefly in the context of adversarial political-military relations; in such situations bandwagoning is harmful to the interests of weak or threatened states and may (depending on the intentions and success of the most powerful or threatening state) be self-defeating as well. Often, states bandwagon because they calculate that they have no better alternative, especially when the major powers have failed to balance effectively against the threatening state, as in Europe between 1933 and 1939.

In analyzing the policies of European states between 1989 and 1991, we are concerned with less precarious situations, where no immediate military threat exists. But balancing strategies could still be followed and, according to many realists, are likely to be pursued. Such strategies focus on the maintenance of political influence through autonomy as states seek to limit the power of others in order to preserve their own independence or freedom of action. The contrast that we draw with balancing is not bandwagoning in the usual sense, that is, joining the more powerful or threatening state out of fear. Rather, it is the pursuit either of multilateral strategies or coordinated and noncompetitive bilateral and unilateral strategies, which sacrifice some degree of autonomy and independently exercised influence in order to enable rich and strong states to act more effectively on a collective basis, and to permit poor and weak countries to gain acceptance into a club of prosperous states, governed by rules that apply to all members. Such strategies can be called regime-oriented, in that they imply subscribing to a set of rules whose acceptance is required for inclusion within an international regime, and that define procedures for joint decision and action. Regime-oriented states give up the chance to demand specific reciprocity for their concessions in exchange for benefiting from the diffuse reciprocity applied to all members of a coalition, which may (like the European Community) be highly institutionalized, with organizations and rules of its own.[6] Strong members of such a coalition may be able to exercise substantial influence within it, on the basis of patterns of asymmetrical interdependence, but they must do so within the constraints imposed by institutional rules. Weaker members may be forced to defer to their partners' preferences in return for material benefits.

Throughout the Cold War, Soviet policy balanced against western Europe and the United States (just as NATO balanced against the USSR). Mikhail Gorbachev essentially abandoned this balancing strategy for a regime-oriented one—most notably in his July 1990 agreement on German re-unification in return for large financial payments and vague acceptance into the circle of European states. The Soviet Union sought to become a member of western international economic institutions; but in security affairs it sought to redefine those institutions. However, this strategy was rendered inoperative by the reality of Soviet weakness: as Celeste Wallander and Jane Prokop explain in Chapter 2, in Soviet–east European military affairs there simply was no bargaining space. Hence, Gorbachev's rapid retreat was only partially covered by his ambiguous and often confused institutionalist rhetoric. The Soviet Union in 1989–1991 was a former superpower without a coherent political strategy. By the end of 1991 its principal successor, Russia, had inherited the Soviet Union's dilemmas, with some additional potential difficulties. It ran the risk of being doubly separated from western Europe: geographically by Belarus, Ukraine, and Poland; culturally by centuries of isolation and distrust. Although Boris Yeltsin seemed keen on pursuing Gorbachev's attempt at reintegration into the "civilized world community," domestic turmoil and potential conflict with its partners in the new Commonwealth of Independent States rendered the success of such efforts problematical. Russia's strategic policy—apart from the failing effort to keep the former Soviet Union's armed forces under a single command—was focused on the nuclear issue, and therefore on bilateral negotiations with the United States. Its appeals to western countries in general centered on its desperate need for food and other forms of aid. On the western side, the U.S. response was tepid, and the vast German effort at promoting a peaceful transition in the former eastern superpower through subsidies and credits was at odds with the far more costly integration of the former German Democratic Republic into the new Germany.

The collapse of Soviet power meant that Germany no longer had to balance against the Soviet Union. It could turn to a traditional sphere-of-influence strategy in eastern Europe, although such a strategy would almost certainly bring forth a balancing coalition to limit its power. Or it could (and did) choose a regime-oriented strategy, with itself as the leading state, and the arena of action Europe as a whole. Such a strategy implies, as Jeffrey Anderson and John Goodman argue in Chapter 1, seeking to create a strengthened European Community in its own image. This regime-oriented strategy had another, distinctive aspect, since Germany is the only country in modern history whose leaders seem more afraid of their own people than of their neighbors: the German Ulysses seeks to tie himself to the European mast.

As a result, German foreign policy has been marked by a highly distinctive feature. Ever since Konrad Adenauer (whose disciple Helmut Kohl has proven to be), Bonn has seen in the west European communities not merely (like its partners) an instrument for regaining status and for economic influence but a good in itself, the very framework of its policy. Unlike France and Britain, which still insist on national autonomy (however circumscribed by the Community), German officials and scholars like to describe their country as a "postnational" state. Such a conception can be viewed, outside Germany, as a clever ploy: after all, especially since unification, German power has the capacity to shape the framework and to mold the Community's policies. And outsiders do not fail to note that Germany thus has two roads to influence: the public road, through the Community, and a private one, through the activities of German industrialists and investors in eastern Europe and the former Soviet Union. But the other side of the coin is equally significant: fears expressed outside Germany in 1989 that the new Germany would be tempted to escape from the confines and constraints of the EC have so far remained unrealized. By the end of 1991 the identification of Germany with the Community was a source of relief for Germany's weaker partners, although Germany's great influence in the Community was also a source of concern.

If Germany found it worthwhile to follow a regime-oriented strategy, so did the nonmembers of the European Community to the north and east. The collapse of British balancing against Europe around 1970 spelled the doom of an effective European Free Trade Area, even though some of the latter's members were slow to recognize this fact. Only the strategy of joining the European Community was viable, given the weakness of the remaining EFTA members.[7] Likewise, the collapse of Soviet power means that balancing against the Community is impossible in the east. During 1990 all post-communist governments in eastern Europe sought to acquire membership in the Community (see Chapter 7 by Kalypso Nicolaïdis). In the security realm, Poland used unilateral and bilateral means to ensure recognition, in 1990, of its border with Germany, which allowed the Poles to abandon the hints of a balancing strategy that they had earlier displayed, and instead to insist on rapid withdrawal of Soviet troops from Polish territory and the dismantling of the Warsaw Treaty Organization. Czechoslovakia, by contrast, had welcomed German reunification from the start, seeking through a regime-oriented strategy, rather than through balancing, to ensure its security.

In economic and environmental issue areas, as the chapters in Part II of this volume show, regime-oriented strategies in the east took the form of "anticipatory adaptation," by which the newly democratic governments sought to align their policies, practices, and laws with those of the European Community. The weakness of east European states seeking economic development under democratic rule means that, once their security vis-à-vis Germany has been assured and insofar as they remain internally coherent, they have very strong incentives to follow regime-oriented strategies.[8] Thus the functional studies in this volume show variations on a theme, which is evident in all five issue areas surveyed: in trade, as discussed by Kalypso Nicolaïdis; financial assistance, analyzed by Stephan Haggard and Andrew Moravcsik; private investment, described by Debora Spar; control of emissions causing acid rain, on which Marc Levy's chapter focuses; and provision of security, discussed by Richard Weitz. However, variations among issue areas also existed. For example, global rather than European international organizations (the World Bank and the IMF but not the EBRD) played the most important roles in financial assistance; the United States was a member of the key security organizations (NATO and the CSCE) but not of the central organization in the European trade area (the European Community); international organizations competed in environmental regulation but were lacking in the issue area of direct foreign investment.

Powerful states have more opportunities to shape the nature of the institutions to which they belong. France and Britain, although linked irrevocably to the European Community, can pursue strategies of "institutional balancing"—using institutions in which they have influence to limit the power of states they deem threatening or too powerful, and to affect the terms of bargains on economic or security issues. Their options were not identical. Britain, as Louise Richardson indicates, clung to NATO as a means of avoiding being swallowed up by the continental powers. "Institutions," she writes in Chapter 5, "can be used against other institutions and against other states, both inside and outside the institution." France continued to distrust NATO because of American dominance and therefore sought to use the European Community to balance growing German power, although as Stanley Hoffmann shows in Chapter 4, this strategy was weakened by France's contradictory desires both to exploit the EC economically—which required German support—and to retain a "margin of independence" for itself. Yet as the vicissitudes of both the British and French strategies suggest, policies of institutional balancing are problematical when one's own economy is so tied to the dominant institution that one could not afford to disentangle from it, and when "je refuse" therefore sounds more like a cri de coeur than a negotiating position. Interestingly, Germany (its earliest champion), Britain, and France all found the Conference on Security and Cooperation in Europe (CSCE) too weak an institution to play a major role in their strategies. So did the Soviet Union, which had hoped to use it as the "royal way" to its return to the west. For the Soviet Union, the gradual shrinking of options resulted from Gorbachev's increasing unwillingness to pursue the kind of superpower (or imperialistic) policy that the USSR had played in Europe and in the world since 1945. Soviet diffidence and acceptance of radical change in political control in eastern Europe then contributed to the collapse of superpower status which its domestic economic weakness had initiated. Those who, like Henry Kissinger, feared that the Soviet Union might play its "German card" by offering German unity in exchange for German neutrality realized belatedly that the Soviets had no cards left to play, except perhaps the threat of their own collapse, which turned out not to be worth much.

As for the one remaining superpower, the United States, it has an economy of roughly equal size to that of Europe. It could follow a mercantilist balancing strategy, an option that is preserved by its efforts to create a North American Free Trade Area (NAFTA). In security terms, the United States needs Europe much less than before the Soviet collapse. Europe also needs the United States somewhat less, with the threat of conventional invasion eliminated; but the war in the Persian Gulf should remind those on the Old Continent that Europe is not an island, sufficient to itself. Indeed, the capacity of the United States to act militarily, in a way that the EC can only aspire to in a hypothetical distant future, remains its major source of political leverage over European politics. The United States also has considerable "soft power," as Joseph Nye has explained, including proficiency in English as a world language and centrality to NATO and other Atlantic institutions.[9] One could also include the fact that it is a single country, not a confederation, and the unparalleled and perhaps excessive self-confidence of its leadership class. Yet, although Washington's need for European bases for security is now diminished, its dependence on European (as well as Japanese) support in order to sustain its claim to "single superpower" status remains high.

In an anarchic world of sovereign states, absent international institutions, the United States would presumably balance against Europe in the world political economy, as Europe would balance against the United States in the security realm.[10] But international institutions change realities and expectations. Indeed, they have helped to prevent such options from being put seriously on the political agenda. Hence, so far at least, the United States has pursued a strategy of institutional cooperation toward Europe. American policy has supported European unification and has sought to use its influence in NATO to magnify its impact on European developments in general. The United States, more than any other state, has managed to keep its options open: influence on and within Europe if possible, balancing against it if necessary.

Strategy follows from the interplay of structure and international institutions, at the international level, with national preferences and domestic constraints. At the international level, it is not just state power that matters but the other kind of structure provided by international institutions. Europe is an area of dense institutions, at the center of which is the European Community: the Cold War collapsed not into a vacuum but into the New Europe. This New Europe has strong institutional ties with the United States, and more distant economic and political links to eastern Europe, broken for half a century. Since history matters, both links remain important. Indeed, in eastern Europe, feelings and policies rejected the immediate past. They aimed at erasing from people's minds the forty-five years of communism or of Soviet control, and at returning to the pre-1945 past—for better (as in the case of trade patterns flowing from east to west, as is shown in Chapter 7 by Kalypso Nicolaïdis) or for worse (as in the case of Serbs and Croats bloodily settling the accounts of the Second World War as if Tito had never ruled). But strategy is essentially forward-looking: beginning where history has left them, actors seek to take advantage of future trends. Their expectations shape their policies as much as does their actual situation. States seek to achieve future gains and to avoid future losses. State strategies and institutional evolution after the end of the Cold War can be understood only if one is well aware of the growing strength of the European Community and its increasing significance for the political economies and domestic political systems of its members, as well as recognizing the continuing significance of strong global or Atlantic organizations such as the World Bank, the IMF, or NATO.

Roles Played by International Institutions

The interplay between state strategy and international institutions can be viewed from another perspective: that of the institutions themselves and the roles they play. The chapters in Part II adopt one such vantage point, asking about evolving rules and practices within the somewhat distinct areas of trade, environmental protection, and public or private investment. The authors point out that in those areas one finds many instances both of conflict and of cooperation. Concerning the latter, the negotiation of trade agreements by the EC and by western countries with Poland, Czechoslovakia, and Hungary and the convergence of policies between west and east on the environment (with, as Marc Levy puts it in Chapter 10, the western "victims" paying, and the eastern polluters accepting western norms enthusiastically) are perhaps the best examples. Most of the chapters point out that among the countries of eastern Europe, by contrast, the amount of cooperation has been limited, partly for historical reasons, partly because of the fear that successful and institutionalized cooperation among them might provide the west Europeans with an excuse for keeping the newly liberated states out, partly because in areas such as financial assistance and foreign direct investment these states were in competition with one another (in the realm of security they could only have pooled their weaknesses).

As for outright conflict, there has, in eastern Europe, been continuing tension between Romania and Hungary about the treatment of the Hungarian minority in Romania (an issue that even communist regimes had not been able to sweep under the rug), and of course the most tragic case has been the civil war in Yugoslavia. In the realm of trade, as Chapter 7 shows, there are major conflicts of interest which the cooperative arrangements mentioned earlier have not eliminated. Between western and eastern Europe these conflicts focused on the effects of opening markets, a policy that could contribute to the wiping out of previously protected industries in the east, and to the difficulties of "sensitive" sectors such as steel, textiles, and agriculture in the west; within western Europe such an opening of markets would disproportionately help German exporters but hurt French or Spanish producers threatened by cheap eastern imports. The introductory chapter to Part II also points out areas of potential conflict: between western trade concessions to eastern Europe and the pressure for trade concessions to EFTA countries or to the United States in GATT; between western governments providing financial assistance to eastern European countries and recipients incapable of meeting the conditions they had promised in exchange for receiving such aid; between private western investors swamping certain sectors of the east European economies and the ability of these nations' governments to carry out their public policies. One could add to the list a potential conflict between western aid to eastern Europe and western aid to the states of the new post-Soviet Commonwealth (or to the poor countries of North Africa, Africa, and the Middle East, other possible providers of masses of unwelcome immigrants and refugees).

The authors of the issue-area studies also discuss the relative importance of unilateral, bilateral, and multilateral options open to and used by the west and the east Europeans. On the whole, the governments of the west European nations have often preferred bilateral policies so as to reach particular objectives, for instance in order to shape public aid programs, as Chapter 8 by Stephan Haggard and Andrew Moravcsik points out; foreign investment codes have sometimes been the objects of bilateral deals. The east Europeans themselves, as stated in Chapter 6, have often grown impatient with the intricacies of multilateral bargaining, and the common front of western governments and western pressure groups with which they had to contend in such bargaining. In the case of foreign direct investment, where there are very few international norms and agencies, unilateral measures by donors and by recipients have prevailed, with Germany (as Debora Spar shows in Chapter 9) playing a leading role among the donors. The remarkable phenomenon of unilateral adaptation, in the east, will be discussed later in this concluding chapter. Nevertheless, the authors of this volume show how broad the range of multilateral cooperation has been. Such cooperation partly reflects what Chapter 6 calls the east European strategy of "joining every western institution, leaving every eastern one." But it is the result also of western policies, including the jurisdiction of the EC over foreign trade, western public donors' interest in coordinating aid and debt relief, the role of regional and international banks in shaping environmental policies in the east, and attempts both by the CSCE in its November 1990 meeting in Paris and by NATO in 1991 to address the security fears and needs expressed by the east Europeans. Indeed, as Chapter 6 suggests, the existing international institutions and norms "imply obligations on the part of the west to provide certain public goods to the east, regardless of the short-term costs."

This brings us to the main point of this section: analyzing six major roles played by international institutions, viewed as complexes of rules and organizations. Since international rules are largely set by governments, and international organizations rarely act on their own, we focus on the nexus linking states and institutions. That is, we ask, across countries and issue areas, how states are making use of these institutions for their own purposes. We chiefly use the language of *roles,* although it would be legitimate also to speak of *functions.* We do not wish to imply a deterministic functional explanation for the patterns that we identify.

Most of the roles played by international institutions are instrumentalist, either fully or in large part: that is, they reflect the calculating use of institutions by governments to achieve their own purposes. These roles can be aligned roughly along a continuum, from those conventionally recognized by realist writers through those emphasized more recently by institutionalist analysts. Yet the sixth role that we discuss, whereby international institutions help to shape the preferences, or even the identities, of states, goes beyond instrumentalism.[11]

Six Roles of International Institutions

Realist thinkers emphasize that states seek to attain their purposes through the exercise of power. International organizations and regimes are potential sources of leverage for ambitious governments; thus we should expect, in a period of rapid change, to see them used as arenas for the *exercise of influence.* Germany is not only the most economically and financially powerful member of the European Community; it also (unlike Britain or even

France) has a set of preferences about policy that provides it with many natural allies within the Community. Moreover, it now can sometimes get what it wants from its partners by threatening or suggesting unilateral action (as France used to do in the Gaullist days). Thus Jeffrey Anderson and John Goodman predict in Chapter 1 that it is likely to reshape the institution in its own image with the participation and consent of its partners. In the imbroglio over Yugoslavia, Germany used the threat of unilateral action (that is, the recognition of Slovenia and Croatia) as a way of forcing reluctant states such as Britain and France to agree on a common policy that was the policy Bonn wanted; they did so in order to prevent German unilateralism and to erase the bad impression created by the Community's split during the Gulf War. Having obtained a consensus, Germany nevertheless moved ahead of its partners anyway. At Maastricht the agreement on Economic and Monetary Union (EMU) entailed German acceptance of a "Europeanization" of the Bundesbank; in exchange, however, Germany's partners had to endorse the idea of a totally independent central bank and of a convergence of economic and monetary policies around those preferred by the Bundesbank. If they had balked, they would have perpetuated a status quo that was far more advantageous to Germany than to them.

Comparably, Britain and the United States emphasized the role of NATO, in large part because its membership and policy orientation were likely to give them more influence than alternative security arrangements centered on the European Community, linked to a revived Western European Union. Gorbachev's Soviet Union vainly tried to reinforce the role of the CSCE, of which it was a member, since it was excluded from both the EC and NATO: "The real value of the CSCE for the Soviets," write Celeste Wallander and Jane Prokop in Chapter 2, "was that it was the only major existing European institution (other than the twenty-two-nation CFE talks) in which it was a member."

The western powers have used financial, trade, and environmental institutions to influence jointly the politics of east European countries. These countries were typically eager to meet western terms, thus giving western states the upper hand in bargaining. However, international institutions created some opportunities for effective maneuver by eastern countries. With respect to public financial aid, as Stephan Haggard and Andrew Moravcsik indicate in Chapter 8, Poland has been skillful at extracting substantial concessions from the donors. And as Kalypso Nicolaïdis remarks in Chapter 7, in bargaining with the eastern countries, the western ones had to respect their own rules implying obligations to provide certain kinds of resources to the east. Hence, asymmetries of power are to some extent offset by the general principles and norms institutionalized in international regimes governing trade or financial assistance.

When states pursue influence within international institutions, the rules of the institutions affect outcomes. Hence a second role of international institutions is to *constrain bargaining strategies.* They may thereby facilitate agreement, and they typically provide advantages for some states, disadvantages for others. This role of international institutions depends on *conflicts* of interest, not harmony: state interests must diverge sufficiently so that constraints on bargaining strategies facilitate agreement. Yet there must also be complementary interests: collective action must hold out the prospect of producing joint benefits, and neither party to the conflict must be able to impose a solution on its own. Among the issues surveyed in this volume, these conditions were met most closely by the "two-plus-four" negotiations over German reunification. Wallander and Prokop show that the so-called two-plus-four negotiating framework institutionalized Soviet arguments that German unification must take into account the rights of the four victorious World War II allies. Likewise, as Richard Weitz indicates in Chapter 11, when Poland demanded that it participate in discussions concerning its border with Germany, these talks also provided a forum for the formal resolution of that issue. Anderson and Goodman comment that "'two-plus-four' proved to be a flexible vehicle for resolving the difficult questions relating to the sovereignty, alliance status, and territorial borders of a uniting Germany." On economic and environmental issues, by contrast, the western powers held all the high cards; hence, institutional rules constrained the east European countries (which had to adapt to them) rather than their western partners. The contrast with U.S.-European negotiations in GATT was striking: GATT rules were significant in affecting the outcomes of U.S.-European trade disputes precisely because of the pressure which either side could bring to bear on the other through the operation of reciprocity.

Bargaining in international institutions reflects states' efforts to exert influence but is also affected by institutional constraints: thus it has a realist aspect insofar as it promotes the interests of states, and an institutionalist aspect insofar as it provides a cooperative solution that is not merely a compromise reflecting power differentials or the bargaining advantages of certain states but also an increase in the authority of an international institution. The association agreements negotiated by the EC with EFTA and with

Poland, Czechoslovakia, and Hungary have reduced conflict within the EC and reinforced it as an institution while also reducing conflict with its negotiating partners. As Weitz indicates, the CSCE has been able to establish a center for the prevention of (interstate) conflicts, an office to monitor free elections, and a permanent secretariat, although it remains unclear how effective such organizational innovations will be.

So far international agencies have been notably unsuccessful in preventing civil strife, and the record of ameliorating civil conflict once it has broken out remains ambiguous. Both the CSCE and the EC failed in their attempts— brief in the first case, protracted in the second—to deal with the Yugoslav civil war. The CSCE was handicapped by the principle of unanimity, and therefore the veto exercised by Yugoslavia (that is, by Serbia); the EC was plagued not only by its members' divisions but also by the fact that during the period when it tried to tame the tigers of civil war, neither a victorious Serbia nor a Croatia eager to reverse the trend was willing to accept a cease-fire unconditionally. By the middle of 1992 the United Nations Security Council had not been notably more successful.

A third role of institutions is, like the first two, consistent with aspects of both institutionalist and realist thinking. International institutions can serve as instruments to *balance against* or *replace* other institutions. France has sought to foster a greater security presence within the European Community to limit the importance of NATO, while the United States has attempted to bolster NATO's role, and Britain has used the Western European Union to limit the role played in military affairs by the EC. Such patterns of competition among institutions—or between states using institutions for their own purposes—appear even more clearly when analysis is undertaken by issue area.

Some central European officials expressed the futile desire to use the United States as an ally to balance overwhelming dependence on the EC on trade issues, which would necessarily have involved GATT. However, as Nicolaïdis argues, neither the necessary degree of U.S. interest or of institutional involvement existed to make this hope realistic. Indeed, the EC is overshadowing the GATT in "closing the parenthesis": increasing the EC's share to roughly 50 percent of the total trade of Czechoslovakia, Hungary, and Poland, as in the years before the Great Depression. In Chapter 8 Haggard and Moravcsik describe the competition between the nascent (and in their view redundant) European Bank for Reconstruction and Development (EBRD), on the one hand, and the World Bank and the European Investment

Bank (EIB) on the other. Interorganizational competition may also occur with respect to environmental monitoring and scientific research, which had been coordinated largely by UN agencies such as the Economic Commission for Europe (ECE). The end of the Cold War means, as Marc Levy explains in Chapter 10, that the ECE has lost its comparative advantage—its ability to bridge the east-west gap—and has enhanced the salience of frustrations over UN procedures and bureaucracy. The OECD has started to involve itself in this set of activities, but as usual the EC is the major player. In March 1990 it decided to establish a European Environment Agency, which may well overshadow the ECE's activities in the future.

A fourth role played by international institutions is to enable policies toward institutions to *signal governments' intentions,* providing others with information and making policies more predictable. Soviet observers believed that the deepening of integration in the EC would clarify the role of a united Germany in Europe, and therefore make the Soviet foreign policy environment more predictable. Germany used its support for NATO and the EC to allay the doubts of its western allies as well as those of its eastern neighbors. Franco-German statements, in April 1990 and in December 1991, about the reform of EC institutions and the expansion of the Community's functions were aimed at showing that the two countries wanted to remain the motor or axis of progress in the EC and at signaling their continued commitment to it despite the changes in the structure of power. The United States' opposition to incorporating eastern Europe into NATO, and its willingness to devise a new NATO strategy at the July 1990 NATO meeting in London, helped to reassure the Soviet Union about its intentions, just as the reform of the NATO forces' structure and the organization's statement of concern about threats to eastern Europe in June 1991 were aimed at reassuring Poland, Czechoslovakia, and Hungary, which had become anxious about developments in the Soviet Union and about the effects of a possible reduction of the American military presence in Europe. Czechoslovakia used its support for the CSCE process as a way of accommodating Soviet concerns about its demands for dismantling the Warsaw Treaty Organization and the withdrawal of Soviet troops from its territory.

Using institutions as signals is consistent with realism as well as with institutionalist analysis. Also consistent with realism's cynicism about state policy is the fact that signals transmitted through institutions are not necessarily more accurate than those conveyed in other ways. According to Richard Weitz in Chapter 11, in 1989 Poland's prime minister declared in an interview in *Izvestiya* that Poland "will remain true to alliance commitments which follow from our membership in the Warsaw Pact." One can interpret these remarks either as balancing against Germany, pending final confirmation of Germany's eastern borders, or as misleading signals intended to calm Soviet fears. Institutions also helped forge connections between east and west during the 1989–1991 period. One way to view this process is as one of cooptation, as Marc Levy indicates in his chapter on environmental issues. Cooptation does not require cognitive or organizational change within a country. As Levy has expressed it: "A state is coopted when it is given an opportunity to do something it already wants to do, but under terms and conditions set by the state doing the coopting."[12]

Cooptation is reflected in a fifth role of international institutions: to *specify obligations* that guide state action, thereby serving as "templates" for policy choice (see Chapter 6). The result in eastern Europe was a pattern of *anticipatory adaptation,* by which states use institutional norms to guide changes in domestic law and policy. In Poland and Czechoslovakia, as Levy argues, "strategies regarding foreign environmental policy objectives were driven by an overwhelming desire to gain credibility in international institutions." As a result, even in the absence of changes in formal commitments, east European governments have changed their policies in an effort to comply with *anticipated* commitments, to achieve benefits from increased economic integration with the European Community, and to weaken resistance to faster integration. As Kalypso Nicolaïdis shows in Chapter 7, Czechoslovakia, Hungary, and Poland all "issued orders that no legislation should be passed without a check of its conformity with EC law. Hence, in the three countries all domestic laws and regulations were to be adjusted to fit Community requirements." Foreign direct investment in eastern Europe, according to Debora Spar, is "already being governed by an informal regime" whose rules reflect international codes such as the OECD guidelines.

This pattern of anticipatory adaptation can be explained as a consequence of both east European bargaining weakness and the absence of established internal law suited to the political economies of pluralistic democracies. Weakness means that nothing is to be gained by holding back one's concessions as "bargaining chips" with the Community, which is unwilling to enter into give-and-take negotiations. The absence of established internal law means that these countries need coherent sets of rules quickly: those that have been agreed to by the west, in the context of their international institutions, constitute convenient "focal points" for policy coordination.[13] Under these conditions, international institutions not only provide a salient solution to problems of coordination but also exert a substantial effect on domestic politics and law.

The implications of cooptation are not limited to weak states: the coopters themselves may take advantage of the process to send signals as well as to exercise influence. In the negotiations on monetary and political union, Germany has sought to ensure the irrevocability of its own commitment to the European Community, as well as that of others. On security affairs, the government officials sought to create European institutions that would "restore consensus in German foreign policy" on their terms, according to Jeffrey Anderson and John Goodman in Chapter 1. More broadly, Germany's political elite has pursued the objective not of maximum autonomy and national influence but of becoming "a consequential but *semi-sovereign* member of a supranational authority," as Anderson and Goodman put it. It seeks not self-help but a combination of influence and constraint.

Our sixth and final role of international institutions goes beyond instrumentalism. Under certain conditions—so far the exception rather than the rule—international institutions can affect not merely the *interests* of states, by affecting constraints and opportunities (thus incentives), but also their more fundamental *preferences*. Such effects on preferences are most evident with respect to states that lack a successful continuous history of independent action. The new democracies of eastern Europe underwent after 1989 a rapid process that John Ikenberry and Charles Kupchan refer to as socialization, "a process of learning in which norms and ideals are transmitted from one party to another" and accompanied by material inducements.[14] The new east European democracies adapted to western laws and norms not only because they had to, but also because they admired western institutions and sought to imitate them, to become western-style democracies. In his chapter on environmental policy, Marc Levy shows how Poland's policies have been sharpened and its environmental institutions reformed under the influence primarily of the World Bank. The existence of international security organizations, particularly NATO, affected the east European governments' political-military strategies, as Richard Weitz demonstrates. Czechoslovakia, for instance, shifted from hostility to military alliances to an interest in joining NATO.

With respect to powerful states, this volume suggests three examples of how international institutions may affect states' preferences, and therefore play roles that go beyond instrumentalism. Joseph S. Nye and Robert O.

Keohane note that after 1989 the United States did not undertake an "agonizing reappraisal" of the institutional strategies it had followed for forty years, but rather reinforced those strategies and adapted them to the new conditions of the international system. The institutional orientation of America's policy toward Europe had, it seems, acquired a "taken for granted" quality over four decades. In France, after a few weeks of wavering, the president acted in the same way with respect to the Community. He ignored suggestions from neo-Gaullists and from nationalists within his own Socialist party, who argued (remarkably like Mrs. Thatcher) that the new Germany might dominate the EC and that a much looser "Europe of states" enlarged to the east would be more in France's interest. Much more strikingly, as Jeffrey Anderson and John Goodman argue in Chapter 1, in the Federal Republic of Germany international institutions deeply affected the terms of domestic political discourse and the identity of the country itself. Not only did German leaders seek to use institutions to reassure others (an instrumental function), but they also viewed the Federal Republic as having an identity distinct from its predecessors as a result of its institutionalist, nonnationalistic orientation. Only in Germany did state policy rest, to a significant degree, on a belief in the *intrinsic* value of international institutions.

Even before the events of 1989, western Europe had become densely institutionalized. Between 1989 and 1991 this pattern of institutionalization began to be extended to eastern Europe, through the European Community and other international institutions, including NATO, the IMF and World Bank, and the CSCE. The Community has been an especially strong magnet. Its own members found that the high costs of isolation create incentives to compromise, even when the consequence is stronger institutions than they would prefer. Weak nonmembers have had to adjust to the rules and practices of the Community to obtain benefits that are crucial to their economic development, and that often seemed essential to the growth of pluralistic democratic institutions. The United States has sought to use the Community as one of the pillars of its leadership but, lacking membership in it, remains somewhat ambivalent about it and seeks to maintain the strength of other institutions, such as NATO, in which it plays a leading role.

Although the European Community is the central institution in the new post–Cold War Europe, it is by no means alone. During the transition phase between 1989 and 1991, it often took a back seat to NATO, or even to less highly institutionalized arrangements such as the CSCE or the two-plus-four talks. The diplomacy of the two transition years used a variety of international institutions in traditional ways: for instance, as arenas for the exercise of influence and ways to reduce the impact of institutions less favorable to their own objectives. But institutions have themselves constrained state strategies and therefore affected outcomes, and they have been used to signal intentions (accurately or not). Furthermore, they have fostered cooptation, facilitating anticipatory adaptation by nonmembers, by which policies of democratic capitalism become "locked in" to the domestic politics of east European countries. Finally, for the Federal Republic international institutions have become intrinsically valuable; and they have been part of a process of socialization for the east. Institutions have been flexible instruments of state policy, constraints on policy, and even, for some countries, sources of intrinsic value.

Recent events have underlined the difficulties, even the folly, of forecasting in international relations. Nevertheless, by mid-1992 it seemed to observers within Europe and across the Atlantic that while western Europe was likely to continue to be an area of peace and extensive cooperation (if not of harmony), and would probably become more united, the former Soviet Union and the Balkans would remain more fragmented for the indefinite future than during the Cold War. The collapse of the Soviet Union at the end of 1991 gave pause to those who had thought that Europe could readily jettison American political and military support; although the long-term future of NATO was in doubt, in the short run there was little question of Europeans' attachment to it. Since international institutions, like other institutions, have a remarkable tendency to persist, even when some of their functions change, NATO should not be counted out.

In the current Europe threats of attack on countries of the EC from the east are unlikely to be taken seriously, but threats of instability and the concomitant distress—including both mass immigration and the military and ecological side effects of civil war or civil collapse—would be more dangerous. The ever-widening wars in the former Yugoslavia could conceivably draw in one or more neighboring countries. The prospects of another Chernobyl disaster in one of the republics, of the acquisition of formerly Soviet nuclear weapons by terrorists, or of warfare within Russia or between Russia and Ukraine are frightening, even if still relatively remote. Western Europe will need new, unconventional security strategies to deal with these problems. In coping with these threats, economic means of statecraft seem likely to become increasingly influential: the European Community and the United States will seek to provide economic resources to prevent chaos in the east and economic incentives to promote democracy, or at least moderation, there. As the United Nations actions of May 1992 against Serbia and Montenegro indicated, economic sanctions are likely to be the preferred policy instrument, in Europe as well as elsewhere, of concerned governments seeking to end regional warfare.

Despite the ineffectiveness of the European Community in coping with the Yugoslav disaster, and ambiguities associated with ratification of the Maastricht Treaty, the EC remains the major long-term force to reckon with for east European countries. States to the east and north of the EC will have to pursue policies that are oriented toward the Community in order to be treated as fully European and to obtain the intangible respect and material benefits they seek. In the short run, of course, EFTA states such as Austria and Sweden will find it easier to become members of the EC than any of the states of formerly communist eastern Europe. The EC remains in control of entry, and the failure of its members at Maastricht to revamp its institutions seriously may provide those (like France) who want to slow down the process of enlargement with an additional argument; for the current institutional system would be severely strained by a Europe of even fifteen or sixteen states, and the necessary institutional reforms might run into formidable domestic obstacles in France and in England.

Partly because the EC, for all its might, has only limited institutional coherence and commands only partial loyalty from individuals within its boundaries, and partly because it lacks military force, Europe is not yet a world power. Indeed, it discovered during 1991–92 that it was incapable of carrying out an effective policy even in Yugoslavia, and at Maastricht in December 1991 it proved unable to transcend the principle of unanimity in areas as crucial for its future as diplomacy, defense, social security, and immigration. Yet the shadow that its future casts loomed even larger than its current bulk. To leaders in both eastern and western Europe in 1991, when our interviews were conducted and analysis undertaken, the institutional and political evolution of the Community seemed likely to shape increasingly the international politics of the continent.

Notes
Contributors
Index

Notes

Introduction

Particular thanks are due to Stephan Haggard and Stanley Hoffmann for valuable critical readings of earlier drafts of this chapter.

1. A crude indicator is provided by data compiled by Michael Wallace and J. David Singer in 1970. European memberships in intergovernmental organizations doubled from 865 to 1,608 between 1920 and 1960; virtually all of that increase occurred after 1945. See Wallace and Singer, "Intergovernmental Organization in the Global System, 1815–1965: A Quantitative Description," *International Organization,* 24 (Spring 1970), 272.

2. On democracy and war, see Michael Doyle, "Kant, Liberal Legacies, and Foreign Affairs, Part I," *Philosophy and Public Affairs,* 12, 3 (Summer 1983), 205–235; Zeev Maoz and Nasrin Abdolali, "Regime Types and International Conflict, 1816–1976," *Journal of Conflict Resolution,* 33 (March 1989). On complex interdependence among pluralist democracies, see Robert O. Keohane and Joseph S. Nye, Jr., *Power and Interdependence: World Politics in Transition* (Boston: Little, Brown, 1977).

3. See Peter J. Katzenstein, ed., *Between Power and Plenty: Foreign Economic Policies of Advanced Industrial States* (Madison: University of Wisconsin Press, 1978), Peter J. Katzenstein, *Small States in World Markets: Industrial Policy in Europe* (Ithaca: Cornell University Press, 1985).

4. Robert O. Keohane and Joseph S. Nye, Jr., "Power and Interdependence Revisited," *International Organization,* 41, 4 (Autumn 1987), 725–753.

5. See Kenneth N. Oye, ed., *Cooperation under Anarchy* (Princeton: Princeton University Press, 1986).

6. For an excellent critique of the concept of anarchy, see Helen V. Milner, "The Assumption of Anarchy in International Relations Theory: A Critique," *Review of International Studies,* 17, 1 (January 1991), 67–85.

7. For a similar argument, see James M. Goldgeier and Michael McFaul, "Core and Periphery in the Post–Cold War Era," *International Organization,* 46, 2 (Spring 1992), 467–492.

8. John J. Mearsheimer, "Back to the Future: Instability in Europe after the Cold War," *International Security,* 15, 1 (Summer 1990), 47.

9. Stanley Hoffmann, *Contemporary Theory in International Relations* (Englewood Cliffs, N.J.: Prentice-Hall, 1960), pp. 40–53.

10. With respect to the former Soviet Union, the *Financial Times* reported that "the way in which the Bretton Woods institutions and the newly created European Bank for Reconstruction and Development (EBRD) have assumed the main burden of both technical and financial assistance has reduced a potential conflict between the European Community and the US over who should provide 'leadership' during the traumatic period of transition." *Financial Times,* May 26, 1992, p. 2.

11. See Robert Jervis, "Security Regimes," in *International Regimes,* ed. Stephen Krasner (Ithaca: Cornell University Press), pp. 173–194, esp. pp. 178–184.

12. See Charles Kindleberger, *The World in Depression, 1929–1939,* 2nd ed. (Berkeley: University of California Press, 1986), and Barry Eichengreen, *Golden Fetters: The Gold Standard and the Great Depression, 1919–1939* (New York: Oxford University Press, 1992). On the gold policies of the Bank of France, see Kindleberger, pp. 49–53, and Eichengreen, pp. 210–212. Kindleberger stresses French animosity toward Britain, Eichengreen statutory constraints on the Bank of France.

1. Mars or Minerva?

The authors are grateful to Peter Katzenstein, Glenn Snyder, and Celeste Wallander, as well as the members of the project on the post–Cold War settlement in Europe, for their comments on an earlier draft of this paper. In addition, John Goodman would like to acknowledge the financial support of the Harvard Business School Division of Research.

1. The term "semi-sovereign" is Peter Katzenstein's; see his *Policy and Politics in West Germany: The Growth of a Semi-Sovereign State* (Philadelphia: Temple University Press, 1987).

2. Carl Lankowski, "Modell Deutschland and the International Regionalization of the West German State in the 1970s," in *The Political Economy of West Germany: Modell Deutschland,* ed. Andrei Markovits (New York: Praeger, 1982), pp. 90–115.

3. The EC also provided an anchor for democratization in the early years of the republic. German elites and masses found themselves embedded in a thoroughly western, liberal "community of values" *(Wertegemeinschaft).* See Rudolf Hrbek and Wolfgang Wessels, eds., *EG-Mitgliedschaft: Ein vitales Interesse der Bundesrepublik Deutschland?* (Bonn: Europa Union Verlag, 1984), and Bernhard May, *Kosten und Nutzen der deutschen EG-Mitgliedschaft* (Bonn: Europa Union Verlag, 1982).

4. Arnulf Baring, *Machtwechsel: Die Ära Brandt-Scheel* (Stuttgart: Deutsche Verlag, 1982), and Clay Clemens, *Reluctant Realists: The CDU/CSU and West German Ostpolitik* (Durham: Duke University Press, 1989).

5. See Simon Bulmer and William Paterson, *The Federal Republic of Germany and the European Community* (London: Allen and Unwin, 1987), pp. 67–68. Regarding détente, tensions came to the surface over issues such as the Soviet gas pipeline, the neutron bomb, and the question of intermediate nuclear forces. See also Angela Stent, *From Embargo to*

Ostpolitik (Cambridge: Cambridge University Press, 1981); Sherri Wasserman, *The Neutron Bomb Controversy: A Study in Alliance Politics* (New York: Praeger, 1983); and Thomas Risse-Kappen, *The Zero Option: INF, West Germany, and Arms Control* (Boulder, Colo.: Westview Press, 1988).

6. Historical analyses of German belligerence between 1871 and 1945 have relied heavily on international structure as an explanatory factor. The destabilizing aspects of German foreign policy, including its seesaw policy between east and west and the militarization of society, are seen as direct consequences of its geostrategic position as "das Land der Mitte." This view has competed with domestic explanations of German foreign policy. These include explanations based on culture—Germans are by nature aggressive and authoritarian—and on the efforts of German elites to cement domestic unity with the pursuit of aggressive external policies. This chapter focuses primarily on the structural arguments. For a summary discussion of the German *Sonderweg* prior to defeat and division, see Charles Maier, *The Unmasterable Past* (Cambridge, Mass.: Harvard University Press, 1988), pp. 100–120.

7. Joanne Gowa, in a piece written before the dramatic events of 1989, outlines the negative consequences of a breakdown of bipolarity for economic cooperation in western Europe. See "Bipolarity and the Postwar International Economic Order," in *Industry and Politics in West Germany: Toward the Third Republic,* ed. Peter J. Katzenstein (Ithaca: Cornell University Press, 1989), pp. 33–50.

8. Anneliese Herrmmann, Wolfgang Ochel, and Manfred Wegner, *Bundesrepublik und Binnenmarkt '92: Perspektiven für Wirtschaft und Wirtschaftspolitik* (Berlin: Duncker and Humbolt, 1990).

9. For assessments of the Single European Act, see Wayne Sandholtz and John Zysman, "1992: Recasting the European Bargain," *World Politics* 42 (October 1989): 95–128; Andrew Moravcsik, "Negotiating the Single European Act: National Interest and Conventional Statecraft in the European Community," *International Organization* 45 (January 1991): 19–56; and David Cameron, "The 1991 Initiative: Causes and Consequences," in *Euro-Politics,* ed. Alberta Sbragia (Washington, D.C.: Brookings Institution, 1992), pp. 23–74. On EMU, German monetary policy, and the process of monetary integration, see John B. Goodman, *Monetary Sovereignty: The Politics of Central Banking in Western Europe* (Ithaca: Cornell University Press, 1992), and John Woolley, "1992, Capital, and the EMS," in Sbragia, *Euro-Politics,* pp. 157–190. On Europe's foreign and defense policy, see Reinhardt Rummel and Peter Schmidt, "The Changing Security Framework," in *The Dynamics of European Integration,* ed. William Wallace (New York: Pinter Publishers, 1990), pp. 261–275.

10. See Karl Kaiser, "Germany's Unification," *Foreign Affairs* 70 (Winter 1991): 179–205, and Elizabeth Pond, "A Wall Destroyed: The Dynamics of German Unification in the GDR," *International Security* 15 (Fall 1990): 35–66.

11. See Horst Teltschik, *329 Tage* (Berlin: Siedler Verlag, 1991).

12. Leslie Lipschitz, "Introduction and Overview," in *German Unification: Economic Issues,* ed. Leslie Lipschitz and Donogh McDonald (Washington, D.C.: International Monetary Fund, 1990), p. 5.

13. Wages, salaries, and rents were converted into deutsche marks at a rate of M 1 = DM 1 instead of at the Bundesbank's proposed conversion rate of M 2 = DM 1. The final form of German economic and monetary union also provided for a graduated conversion scale for individual savings accounts and the conversion of all other domestic financial liabilities and assets at a rate of M 2 = DM 1.

14. The rapid introduction of a single currency eliminated the exchange rate as an adjustment mechanism for the East German economy, which only intensified the collapse as the region sank in a flood of more attractive western products. The subsequent decline in production, with attendant bankruptcies and layoffs, added to the fiscal burdens of the federal government. In 1991 the government spent approximately $83 billion in the East, 60 percent of which went toward consumption (for example, unemployment benefits and subsidies). A Bundesbank estimate projected that the budget deficit of German public authorities, measured as a percentage of GNP, would increase from a little under 0.5 percent in 1989 to just over 5 percent in 1991—a tenfold increase in two years. If one takes into account the borrowing of state and local authorities, the figure approaches 8 percent. See "Din of Renewal in East Berlin," *New York Times,* July 5, 1991, p. D4; "Bruttolöhne im Osten durchschnittlich 1357 DM," *Frankfurter Allgemeine Zeitung,* April 24, 1991, p. 15; "Germany: Darkness and Light," *Economist,* July 6, 1991, pp. 50–51; "Eastern German Jobless Level Is Over a Million," *New York Times,* August 7, 1991, p. D3; Deutsche Bundesbank, *Annual Report for the Year 1990,* p. 31; "Germany: Rudderless," *Economist,* July 20, 1991, pp. 49–50.

15. Deutsche Bundesbank, *Annual Report for the Year 1990,* pp. 1, 49.

16. Kaiser, "Germany's Unification," pp. 189–190.

17. Kaiser refers to the widespread consensus on this point (ibid., p. 195), and Elizabeth Pond mentions the "abortive debate" in early February 1990 on NATO membership for a united Germany, led principally by SPD figures such as Oskar Lafontaine and Egon Bahr ("A Wall Destroyed," p. 64). What if the Soviets had said no to Germany in NATO? Those of our respondents who addressed this question maintained that the price would have been two Germanys—that is, confederation instead of unification. Pond argues that domestic public opinion would have forced German politicians to purchase unity at the price of NATO membership. That this did not even make it onto the national agenda is testimony to the convergence of diplomatic opinion from Vancouver to Vladivostok that continued German membership in NATO enhanced regional stability.

18. See Chapter 2, "Soviet Security Strategies toward Europe," by Celeste Wallander and Jane Prokop, in this volume, and Hannes Adomeit, "Gorbachev and German Unification: Revision of Thinking, Realignment of Power," *Problems of Communism* 39 (July–August 1990): 1–23.

19. This proposal stipulated that until the completion of the Soviet troop pullout from eastern Germany in 1994, no NATO command troops, German or otherwise, could be stationed in the region (Berlin excepted). Only German territorial defense units were allowed in the area. After the Soviet pullout, the special status would continue insofar as Germany pledged not to station foreign forces, nuclear weapons, or nuclear carriers there. See Kaiser, "Germany's Unification," pp. 196–198.

20. For a detailed discussion of the legal reasoning behind this controversial position, see Clemens, *Reluctant Realists*.

21. Pond, "A Wall Destroyed," p. 64n.

22. Kaiser, "Germany's Unification," p. 200.

23. A civil servant in the Ministry of Economics stated ruefully that this is no longer an active concern among Germany's EC partners, in view of the collapse of East German industry and the general unattractiveness of consumer products produced for export.

24. Jeffrey Anderson, "Skeptical Reflections on a Europe of Regions: Britain, Germany, and the European Regional Development Fund," *Journal of Public Policy* 10 (October–December 1990): 417–447, and Gary Marks, "Structural Policy and 1992," in Sbragia, *Euro-Politics,* pp. 191–224.

25. Final Commission approval of the assistance package was made contingent on Bonn's ability to push through a reduction in the assisted-area coverage of its domestic regional program, which occurred in January 1991. In this manner EC assistance gave the Commission leverage over the German government.

26. Kaiser, "Germany's Unification," p. 198.

27. See Chapters 7 and 10 in this volume.

28. This was a particularly sensitive issue within the CSU and the right wing of the CDU, where refugee and expellee groups wield considerable organizational (if not numerical) power. In May 1991 the government's pledge to ratify the German-Polish treaty by June 17 was jeopardized temporarily by CSU objections that the treaty did not go far enough in protecting German minorities in Poland. In the context of German-Czech negotiations Theo Waigel, the chairperson of the CSU and federal finance minister, demanded a seat at the table for the Sudeten Germans and the CSU itself. The official Bonn position was to secure the viability of German ethnic enclaves within these various eastern European countries while rejecting demands for territorial claims or for measures that would call into question the citizenship of these individuals.

29. There were tangible differences of ministerial opinion within Bonn on this point; the Chancellory and the Foreign Ministry were much more inclined to reach into the German till to address what they saw as mounting crises in the East.

30. In May 1991 the minister of economics announced that the government was in the midst of preparing a memorandum that would establish principles for future German economic aid to the Soviet Union. Specifically, assistance would be governed by three guidelines: first, aid would be part of a total package that would take into account not only Soviet requests for financial transfers but also the requirements of German unification; second, untied aid to the USSR would henceforth be granted as part of joint packages arranged by the western allies, and not on the basis of bilateral relations in which the German government provided the sole guarantee; and third, German financial assistance would be linked to specific investment projects in the USSR or to concrete import contracts involving eastern German firms.

31. "Wie den Ländern Osteuropas helfen?" *Frankfurter Allgemeine Zeitung,* June 24, 1991, p. 5.

32. Kohl was quoted in an interview with the *London Daily Mail* as stating: "I do not order around the Bundesbank . . . But I was not in agreement with the bank's decision and did not want it." However, he went on to defend the basic principle of an independent central bank, and recommended it without reservation for Europe. "Kohl tadelt Bundesbank-Beschluss," *Frankfurter Allgemeine Zeitung,* February 15, 1991, p. 15.

33. Thus, NATO continued to perform, albeit much more implicitly, the function of "double containment." See Wolfram Hanrieder, *Germany, America, Europe: Forty Years of German Foreign Policy* (New Haven: Yale University Press, 1989), pp. 6–11.

34. See Chapter 11 by Richard Weitz, "Pursuing Military Security in Eastern Europe," in this volume.

35. Where this threshold of acceptability lay was unclear: witness Soviet objections to the August 1991 French proposal to send in WEU forces to maintain a cease-fire in Croatia. Soviet officials also expressed skepticism about the desirability of an out-of-area capability for the WEU; see Chapter 2 in this volume.

36. Officially, American policymakers objected to a strengthened WEU on two counts: first, as the WEU took on new functions and capabilities, it would weaken NATO's foundation; and second, the imperfectly overlapping memberships of the two organizations create undesirable and even dangerous inefficiencies in the NATO decision-making process. On U.S., British, and French views on European security, see, respectively, Chapters 3, 5, and 4 in this volume. Unofficially, Washington feared a loss of influence if it were forced to deal with a unified bloc of European alliance partners. The Germans, who assumed the chair of the WEU on July 1, 1991, convinced the Bush administration that they would not allow the WEU to undermine NATO's vital functions; American rhetoric on the WEU softened noticeably in mid-June.

37. Quoted in Karl Lamers, "Selbstverständnis und Aufgaben des vereinten Deutschland in der Aussenpolitik," unpublished essay, April 1991, p. 21.

38. "Golfkrieg hat eine Katharsis im Denken bewirkt," *Frankfurter Allgemeine Zeitung,* May 2, 1991, p. 2.

39. In the aftermath of the crisis, Chancellor Kohl called on NATO to clarify the application of Article 5 of the NATO treaty, which regulates the alliance obligations of members.

40. These demonstrations received a great deal of attention in the domestic and international press. Nevertheless, opinion polls taken during the same period showed that three quarters of the German public were in favor of the war against Iraq. As to whether Germany should come to the aid of Turkey in the event of an Iraqi attack, the results were much more ambiguous: 48 percent said yes, whereas 47 percent said no. "Drei Viertel der Westdeutschen für den Krieg gegen den Irak," *Frankfurter Allgemeine Zeitung,* January 29, 1991, p. 1.

41. Politicians pointed to the hefty financial contribution made by Germany to the war effort, which came to approximately $11 billion, as well as the massive logistical support required to transport American forces from Germany to Saudi Arabia. One CDU member of the Bundestag confessed that he was taken aback by the speed with which world opinion about unification had shifted from fears of "Germany the imperialist" to complaints about "Germany the pacifist."

42. "Kohl: Es darf keine Flucht aus der Verantwortung geben," *Frankfurter Allgemeine Zeitung*, January 31, 1991, p. 1.

43. The SPD position, the subject of considerable internal strife between the left-wing factions of the party and the more centrist leadership, was cobbled together at the Bremen party conference held in late May 1991.

44. The minesweeper decision occurred before the formal declaration of a cease-fire and yet drew no objection from the SPD.

45. Lamers, "Selbstverständnis und Aufgaben des vereinten Deutschland in der Aussenpolitik," p. 2.

46. SPD opposition to the macroeconomic policies of the Christian-Liberal coalition government, as well as to German rearmament and European integration, drove the party into an electoral ghetto. Escape came with the Bad Godesberg program of 1959, in which the party rejected much of its socialist heritage and jumped confidently into the left channel of the political mainstream.

47. The Bonn government had come under considerable pressure from the CDU/CSU parliamentary caucus, as well as public opinion, both of which evinced much sympathy for the underdog republics. Government officials were quick to stress that acceptance did not entail full diplomatic recognition of independence.

48. Indeed, one might argue that the German government placed itself in a potentially awkward, even explosive, position with respect to the German ethnic minorities in Poland, Czechoslovakia, and other eastern European countries. The position also drew the critical attention of Soviet President Gorbachev and one of his deputy foreign ministers. "Yugoslavs Reach Slovenian Accord on Border Posts," *New York Times*, July 8, 1991, p. 5. In any event, Germany's challenge to the EC's stance was consistent with the general emphasis on "Europeanization" in current German thinking, which brings with it a concomitant deemphasis on the importance of national borders.

49. The Soviets warned that any foreign intervention in Yugoslavia could lead to full-scale European conflict. "Fragile Truce in Yugoslavia," *New York Times*, August 8, 1991, p. A8.

50. Germany's leverage is considerable here; 20 percent of Yugoslavian trade is with the Federal Republic, and Yugoslavia's current account balance is heavily dependent on the foreign remittances of the over 600,000 Yugoslavian guest workers employed in Germany. "Kohl Threatens Serbia over Cease Fire Violations," *New York Times*, August 8, 1991, p. A8.

51. One emerging issue of contention between Russia and Germany is the status of the 2.5 million Volga Germans. When Boris Yeltsin appeared to retract his promise of an independent republic for the Volga Germans in January 1992, Bonn was quick to register a strong complaint. The German government had welcomed the Russian president's earlier pledge and had set aside $130 million in foreign aid for 1991 and 1992, with promises of more to follow. German concerns centered on the fear of an influx of refugees in the event that the Volga Germans' demands for autonomy should go unmet; each of these Russian citizens is entitled to German citizenship under the terms of the Basic Law. There are clear fault lines on this issue within the German government; the Interior

Ministry, which is responsible for refugee policy, has taken a hard line, while the Foreign Ministry has cautioned against allowing this matter to poison relations between the two countries.

52. The rationale, according to Foreign Ministry officials, is both economic and political. Not only will EC members save money in erecting the necessary diplomatic infrastructure, but they will contribute to the goals of a common foreign policy set out at Maastricht.

53. Government officials argued that the understanding between Europe and Japan over Japanese automobiles presented a special case. The seven-year period of voluntary restrictions on imports and transplants, they noted, was by definition transitional in nature: "Full liberalization lies at the end of the road." On the 1992 program as it affects automobiles, see Alasdair Smith and Anthony J. Venables, "Automobiles," in *Europe 1992: An American Perspective*, ed. Gary Clyde Hufbauer (Washington, D.C.: The Brookings Institution, 1990), pp. 119–158.

54. According to this official, neither the agricultural ministry nor the French government was consulted in this revision of the Bonn position, which was announced in February 1991. The turnaround in German policy reflected the fear of U.S. retaliation: "If the GATT round failed, it would accelerate protectionist trends in the U.S., which would have a negative impact on the multilateral trading system. Given our export dependence, this would constitute a huge setback."

55. See Stanley Fischer, "International Macroeconomic Policy Coordination," NBER Working Paper no. 2344, May 1987, p. 41.

56. As it turned out, the amendments to the Treaty of Rome on Economic and Monetary Union follow the main outlines of the 1989 Delors committee report. During stage one, members agree on the basic principles of economic and monetary union and on the outlines of the three-stage plan. All members would join the exchange rate mechanism and remove restrictions on capital mobility. Stage two, which would take effect on January 1, 1994, required the creation of a European Monetary Institute—an embryonic central bank—which would have no decision-making power but would be responsible for policy coordination. For stage three to take effect, member states had to meet four performance conditions: convergence of inflation rates to within 1.5 percent of the three best-performing member states; convergence of long-term interest rates to within 2 percent of the three best-performing member states; budget deficit not in excess of 3 percent of GDP; and no devaluations within at least two years. If a majority of member states meet these criteria by the end of 1996, then EMU can proceed. If by the end of 1996 no date has been set, then in mid-1998 EC leaders will decide who has met the criteria, and a minority can go ahead with EMU in 1999.

57. This demand was characterized in the press and within political circles as a concession to the Länder, whose support will be necessary for ratification of the inter-governmental conferences' decisions.

58. Some officials saw the "threat of widening" as a lever to use against intransigent Community members in the bargaining rounds leading up to the Maastricht summit in December 1991. The need to bring democratic eastern bloc countries in from the cold rapidly, both to forestall a spillover of immigrants and conflicts into western Europe and

to promote the economic utility of these countries to EC members, would require getting one's own house in order quickly.

59. Officials in the Ministry of Economics expected that the larger farms in eastern Germany, once rationalized and modernized, would place substantial pressure on the smaller, less efficient Bavarian farming sector. Properly encouraged by CAP reforms, this could lead to a major upheaval in the political landscape in Germany, since Bavarian farmers constitute one of the principal power bases of the CSU.

60. The goal of establishing trade relations with the eastern bloc countries arose in part out of a domestic economic concern to restore production and employment levels in the five new Länder. According to officials, this goal complemented the far more important objective of securing stability to Germany's east.

61. Ronald Asmus, "Fragen unter Freunden," *Die Zeit,* February 22, 1991, p. 4.

62. Wolfram Hanrieder, *The Stable Crisis: Two Decades of German Foreign Policy* (New York: Harper and Row, 1970), p. 193.

63. Peter Gourevitch, "The Second Image Reversed," *International Organization* 32 (Autumn 1978): 881–912, and Robert Putnam, "Diplomacy and Domestic Politics: The Logic of the Two-Level Games," *International Organization* 42 (1988): 427–460.

64. On the subject of "exiting" and "buying" regimes, see Keohane, *International Institutions and State Power* (Boulder, Colo.: Westview Press, 1989), p. 106. As institutionalist approaches predict, German foreign policymakers were aware of the tradeoffs between self-aggrandizement and self-preservation, and sought to manage these tradeoffs, made all the more salient by the changed distribution of capabilities on the continent by way of institutions (ibid. p. 47).

65. Rudolf Hrbek and Wolfgang Wessels, "Das EG-System als Problemlösungsebene und Handlungsrahmen," in Hrbek and Wessels, *EG-Mitgliedschaft,* p. 521.

66. Institutions embody valued patterns of behavior that may originally have been grounded in instrumental rationality, but which at some point take on value in and of themselves. In short, the support of participants transcends rational cost-benefit analysis. James G. March and Johan P. Olsen, *Rediscovering Institutions* (New York: Free Press, 1989). In the case of Germany, this process may have been facilitated by the emergence of networks of officials whose responsibilities and ultimately careers have become intertwined with multilateral decision-making forums and foreign negotiating counterparts.

67. Keohane, *International Institutions,* p. 167.

68. Andrei Markovits and Simon Reich adopt a Gramscian theoretical framework that highlights the role of ideas, as opposed to structural resources, in the consolidation of Germany's hegemonic position. They correctly point out that Germany's ability to export valued goods extends beyond BMWs and machine tools to include ideas and institutional arrangements. This confers an immense amount of influence on Germany. Influence, however, remains conceptually distinguishable from hegemony. Their case for a Gramscian hegemony needs to address a number of issues, including the implications of sovereignty giveaways to the EC. See Andrei Markovits and Simon Reich, "The New Face of Germany: Gramsci, Neorealism, and Hegemony," Center for European Studies Working Paper Series no. 28, Harvard University, 1991.

69. In 1991 Germany's budget deficit exceeded the performance criterion agreed to at Maastricht.

2. Soviet Security Strategies toward Europe

We would like to thank Ulrich Brandenburg, Bruce Porter, Thomas Risse-Kappen, Stephen Rosen, and Glenn Snyder for their comments on an earlier version of this paper. Any errors remain our responsibility.

1. This chapter is based in part on Louise Richardson and Celeste A. Wallander, "A Comparison of British and Soviet Adjustments to Structural Change in Europe," paper prepared for the meeting of the International Studies Association, Vancouver, British Columbia, March 19–23, 1991.

2. John J. Mearsheimer, "Back to the Future: Instability in Europe after the Cold War," *International Security* 15, 1 (1990), 5–56; Jack Snyder, "Averting Anarchy in the New Europe," *International Security* 14, 4 (1990), 5–41; Stephen Van Evera, "Primed for Peace: Europe after the Cold War," *International Security* 15, 3 (1990–91).

3. Robert O. Keohane, *After Hegemony: Cooperation and Discord in the World Political Economy* (Princeton: Princeton University Press, 1984); Robert O. Keohane and Joseph S. Nye, *Power and Interdependence: World Politics in Transition,* 2nd ed. (Boston: Little, Brown, 1989); "Back to the Future, Part II: International Relations Theory and Post–Cold War Europe," correspondence by Stanley Hoffmann, Robert O. Keohane, and John Mearsheimer, *International Security* 15, 2 (1990), 191–199. Institutions are persistent and connected sets of rules, formal and informal, that prescribe behavioral roles, constrain activity, and shape expectations (Keohane [1989], chap. 1). Although this chapter tends to focus on international organizations (the most formalized type of institution), regularized patterns and state contacts such as U.S.-Soviet arms control talks are clearly institutions as well.

4. Neorealists also focus on the intersection of individual state choices but argue that national leaders base their choices on zero-sum calculations. This distinction is the source of the "relative gains" versus "absolute gains" debate. See Joseph Grieco, "Anarchy and the Limits of Cooperation: A Realist Critique of the Newest Liberal Institutionalism," *International Organization* 42, 3 (1988), 485–508; Robert O. Keohane, *International Institutions and State Power* (Boulder, Colo.: Westview Press, 1989), chap. 1, pp. 10–11; Robert Powell, "The Problem of Absolute and Relative Gains in International Relations Theory," *American Political Science Review* 85, 4 (December 1991), 1303–20; Duncan Snidal, "International Cooperation among Relative Gains Maximizers," *International Studies Quarterly* 35, 4 (1991), 387–402.

5. Celeste A. Wallander "Third-World Conflict in Soviet Military Thought: Does the 'New Thinking' Grow Prematurely Grey?" *World Politics* 42 (October 1989); Celeste A. Wallander, "Soviet Policy toward the Third World in the 1990s," in *Third World Security in the Post–Cold War Era,* ed. Thomas G. Weiss and Meryl A. Kessler (Boulder, Colo.: Lynne Rienner, 1991).

6. USSR Foreign Ministry, "Glava I: Natsionalnaya bezopasnost i natsionalnye interesy SSSR na sovremennom etape" (Chap. 1: National security and national interests of the USSR in the present period), in "Vneshnepoliticheskaya i diplomaticheskaya deyatelnost SSSR—Obzor MID, noyabr 1989 g.–dekabr 1990 g" (Foreign policy and diplomatic work of the USSR—foreign ministry overview 1989–90), published by *Mezhdunarodnaya Zhizn* (March 1991), 12–14.

7. On Gorbachev's "turn to the right," see Bruce D. Porter, "The Coming Resurgence of Russia," *The National Interest* 23, 1 (1991), 14–23.

8. "Nobelevskaya lektsiya M. S. Gorbacheva" (M. S. Gorbachev's Nobel prize lecture), *Pravda,* June 6, 1991, p. 4.

9. Defense Minister Marshal Dmitriy Yazov, "Vysokiy rubezh istorii" (The high frontier of history), *Krasnaya Zvezda,* November 29, 1990, pp. 1–2.

10. FBIS-SOV-91–122 (June 25, 1991), from *Frankfurt/Main Frankfurter Allgemeine,* June 7, 1991, p. 2.

11. On the basic distinctions and their role in new thinking, see Vadim Udalov, "Balance of Power and Balance of Interests," *International Affairs* 6 (1990), 14–22. (Udalov was first secretary of the Scientific Coordination Center of the Ministry of Foreign Affairs.)

12. For a full discussion of the concept of "anticipatory adaptation," see Chapter 10, "East-West Environmental Politics after 1989," by Marc Levy in this volume.

13. USSR Foreign Ministry, "Glava III, Izmeneniya v Yevrope i novyye podkhody k obespecheniyu bezopasnosti. Stroitelstvo 'obscheyevropeyskogo doma" (Changes in Europe and new approaches to safeguarding security. Development of a common European home), pp. 41–42.

14. See Vlad Sobell, *The CMEA in Crisis* (New York: Praeger, 1990), p. 78.

15. "ES soglasno, no . . . s usloviyami" (The EC agrees . . . but with conditions), *Pravda,* August 6, 1990; *Bulletin of the European Communities,* no. 12 (1990), 112; *Bulletin of the European Communities,* no. 4 (1991), 44.

16. See "'Troika' v tsentre Yevropy" ("Troika" in the center of Europe), *Pravda,* January 25, 1991, p. 4. The Soviet Union was itself a participant in one subregional grouping formed to promote economic cooperation between states in the Black Sea region; FBIS-EEU-91–123, June 26, 1991, p. 10; FBIS-EEU-91–125, p. 13; and Douglas Clarke, "Central Europe: Military Cooperation in the Triangle," *RFE/RL Research Report* (January 10, 1992), 42–45. The Czech-Hungarian bilateral treaty was concluded January 21, the Czech-Polish treaty February 27, and the Hungarian-Polish treaty March 20, 1991; "Bez Uchastiya SSSR" (Without the participation of the USSR), *Izvestiya,* September 21, 1990, p. 3.

17. "Otvety M. S. Gorbacheva i Dzh. Busha na voprosy zhurnalistov" (Answers of M. S. Gorbachev and George Bush to questions of journalists), *Pravda,* December 5, 1989, pp. 1–2.

18. "Otvetstvennost' pered budushchim" (Responsibility facing the future), *Izvestiya,* January 31, 1990, p. 1; FBIS-SOV-90–024, February 5, 1990, pp. 33–35, from interview with Soviet Foreign Minister Eduard Shevardnadze, reported in TASS international

service, February 2, 1990; "Otvety M. S. Gorbacheva na voprosy" (Answers of M. S. Gorbachev to questions), *Pravda,* February 21, 1990, p. 1.

19. "A pravda takova" (But the fact is . . .), interview with A. P. Bondarenko of the Soviet Foreign Ministry, *Trud,* February 18, 1990, p. 3.

20. FBIS-SOV-90–037, February 23, 1990, p. 5, from Shevardnadze interview in TASS International Service, February 22, 1990; "Otvety M. S. Gorbacheva na voprosy korrespondenta Pravdy" (Answers of M. S. Gorbachev to questions of a *Pravda* correspondent), *Pravda,* March 6, 1990, pp. 1, 5.

21. FBIS-SOV-90–072, April 13, 1990, p. 22, from Shevardnadze-Baker meeting, reported in TASS International Service, April 12, 1990; FBIS-SOV-90–083, pp. 38–39, from Shevardnadze statement on Germany in TASS, April 27, 1990.

22. "Ubezhdat' pravdoy" (To convince with the truth) *Ogonyok,* no. 11 (March 1990), 2–6.

23. "Preserving the Momentum," *Vestnik* (July 1990), 27–29, quote at p. 29.

24. "Declaration of the Warsaw Treaty Member States," *Vestnik* (July 1990), 44; "What Are the Options?" *Vestnik* (July 1990), 36–38, quote at p. 38.

25. Eduard Shevardnadze, "O vneshney politike" (On foreign policy), *Pravda,* June 26, 1990, p. 3.

26. FBIS-SOV-90–138, July 18, 1990, p. 3, from TASS, July 17, 1990; "Politics Is the Art of the Possible," *Vestnik* (August 1990), 29–35, quote at p. 31.

27. FBIS-SOV-90–216, November 7, 1990, pp. 16–19, from Vadim Zagladin, "The Soviet View of German Reunification," Moscow IAN press release (in English).

28. USSR Foreign Ministry, p. 54, emphasis added; FBIS-SOV-90–196, October 10, 1990, pp. 38–41, from *Der Standard,* October 6, 1990; "Interv'yu zamestitelya ministra inostrannykh del SSSR Yu. Kvitsinskogo diplomaticheskomu korrespondentu TASS" (Interview of Deputy Foreign Minister of the USSR Yu. Kvitsinskiy by the TASS diplomatic correspondent), *Vestnik MID,* no. 5 (March 15, 1991), 20–23.

29. FBIS-SOV-90–184, September 21, 1991, pp. 20–23, from TASS, September 20, 1990 (in English).

30. FBIS-SOV-91–078, April 23, 1991, pp. 15–18, from interview with Yuliy Kvitsinskiy, deputy foreign minister, "The Treaty Means More Than Money," *Novoye Vremya,* no. 12 (March 1991), 18–20.

31. The priority and attention given to these negotiations in the USSR Foreign Ministry document is solid evidence of this. See especially Glava III and Glava XII, "Dvukhstoronniye otnosheniya SSSR s zarubezhnymi stranami" (Bilateral relations of the Soviet Union with foreign countries).

32. For example, see Gorbachev's interview from *Der Spiegel,* "Intervyu M. S. Gorbacheva zhurnalu 'Shpigel,'" *Izvestiya,* March 25, 1991, p. 4.

33. FBIS-SOV-91–102, May 28, 1991, p. 23, from Hamburg DPA (in German), May 27, 1991. (The Soviet reportage of Möllemann's visit [pp. 22–23 of this issue of FBIS]) stressed Germany's willingness to "render further assistance to transformations in the Soviet Union," while Hamburg DPA made no mention of German commitments beyond the immediate agreement reached. *New York Times,* July 28, 1991, p. E5.

34. "Nemtsy i my" (We and the Germans), *Pravda,* November 14, 1990, pp. 1, 5.

35. USSR Foreign Ministry, p. 43.

36. FBIS-SOV-91–115, June 14, 1991, pp. 2–6, Obminskiy interview from Moscow All-Union Radio, June 13, 1991.

37. "Vystupleniye A. A. Bessmertnykh na zasedanii komiteta ministrov soveta Evropy v Madride, 21 fevralya" (A. A. Bessmertnykh's speech at the February 21 session of the Committee of Ministers of the Council of Europe, Madrid), *Vestnik MID,* no. 5 (March 15, 1991), 19–20.

38. "'7 + 1': my vybrali pravilnyy put. Nas podderzhivayut" (7 + 1: we chose the correct path. They support us), *Izvestiya,* July 19, 1991, pp. 1, 5. This is an interview with Deputy Prime Minister Vladimir Scherbakov.

39. FBIS-SOV-91–115, Obminskiy interview; FBIS-SOV-91–139, July 19, 1991, pp. 14–17, from Moscow Central Television, First Program, July 17, 1991.

40. In his November 1990 television interview Gorbachev described how the Soviet Union's new course in foreign policy had emerged from domestic imperatives. See "Intervyu M. S. Gorbacheva dlya sovetskogo i frantsuzskogo televideniya."

41. Interviews given by Deputy Prime Minister Scherbakov were most often the medium chosen to deliver the more specific messages regarding convertibility. See "'7 + 1': my vybrali pravilnyy put. Nas podderzhivayut."

42. FBIS-SOV-90–171, September 4, 1990, p. 1, interview with Deputy Foreign Minister Viktor Karpov from Warsaw PAP, August 31, 1990 (in English); "Ekonomicheskiye i iuridicheskiye aspekty stroitelstva obshcheyevropeyskogo doma" (Economic and legal aspects of the building of a common European home), in *Mirovaya Ekonomika i Mezhdunarodniye Otnosheniya,* no. 11 (1990), 138–142; Shevardnadze's interview in *New Times,* no. 26 (June 26–July 2, 1990), 5–8; FBIS-SOV-91–128, July 3, 1991, pp. 1–3, from TASS International Service, July 1, 1991 (in Russian); FBIS-SOV-91–139, July 19, 1991, pp. 5–6, from TASS International Service, July 18, 1991 (in Russian).

43. For a succinct overview, see Leonard Geron, *Soviet Foreign Economic Policy Under Perestroika* (London: Royal Institute of International Affairs, 1990).

44. USSR Foreign Ministry, pp. 44–47.

45. Ibid., pp. 98–99.

46. Ibid., pp. 46, 97. To date, however, the EBRD has proven to be of less help than expected. The maximum loan allowed the USSR for 1992–1994 was determined by its contributions to that bank, and amounted to no more than $220 million. See FBIS-SOV-91–143, July 25, 1991, p. 5, from *Izvestiya,* July 23, 1991, p. 1; "Intervyu M. S. Gorbacheva dlya sovetskogo i frantsuzskogo televidenia."

47. Colonel V. Markushin, "Germaniya. Yevropa. Bezopasnost" (Germany. Europe. Security), *Krasnaya Zvezda,* September 28, 1990, p. 3; "Parizh: i nadezhdy, i opaseniya" (Paris: hopes, and fears), *Izvestiya,* November 20, 1990, p. 1.

48. FBIS-SOV-91–116, June 17, 1991, pp. 5–6, from TASS International Service, June 14, 1991 (in Russian).

49. FBIS-SOV-91–140, July 22, 1991, pp. 6–10, from Moscow Central Television Vostok Program and Orbita Networks, July 19, 1991 (in Russian).

50. A state's membership in a given international organization (IO) could serve either to reduce or to enhance its vulnerability vis-à-vis other states, depending on the IO's structure and rules. For example, an IO might reduce vulnerability by acting as a neutral middleman for the distribution of goods such as information; or by forcing states to provide equal access to one another (for instance, GATT and most favored nation status), thus widening the range of choices facing any given states. Or an IO could "institutionalize" asymmetrical vulnerability through its rules, procedures, and functions (for instance, the pegging of the international monetary system to the dollar under Bretton Woods).

51. *Pravitel'stvennyy vestnik,* no. 3 (January 1991), 10 (see also USSR Foreign Ministry, p. 102); "'Tayfun' peremen" ("Typhoon" of changes), *Pravda,* 13 (March 1991), 5; Budapest Domestic Service, May 16, 1991, translated in FBIS-EEU-91–097, May 20, 1991, pp. 20–21; Nikolay Shishlin, "Vtoroye dykhaniye pridet" (A second wind will come), *Pravda,* July 8, 1991, p. 7.

52. See Valerie Bunce, "The Empire Strikes Back: The Evolution of the Eastern Bloc from a Soviet Asset to a Soviet Liability," *International Organization* 39, 1 (1985), 1–46.

53. The first agreement of this sort, dealing with economic relations and scientific-technical cooperation, was concluded between Czechoslovakia and the Russian Federation. See FBIS-EEU-91–058, March 26, 1991, pp. 20–21, from Prague CTK, March 25, 1991 (in English). In December 1990 Hungarian enterprises were already anticipating trade at the republic and even regional level. See "'Ikarus' Moskvu ne minuyet" ("Icarus" doesn't escape Moscow), *Izvestiya,* December 1, 1990, p. 5.

54. The stubborn stance taken by the USSR probably reflects the asymmetrical dependence between the countries. Soviet oil is critical to the economies of nearly all the east European countries. In the 1970s Hungary, Czechoslovakia, the GDR, and Bulgaria depended on the USSR for approximately 90 percent of their oil. Robert Hutchings, *Soviet–East European Relations: Consolidation and Con*flict, 1968–1980 (Madison: University of Wisconsin Press, 1983), p. 193. The degree of dependence may have been in part a function of the abnormally low price of Soviet oil for eastern Europe. Price increases were introduced first in 1975, and of course the most dramatic jump in price occurred in January 1991. In the first half of 1991 Hungary purchased slightly over 50 percent of its oil from the USSR (1.4 million out of 2.6 million tons). See FBIS-EEU-91–140, July 22, 1991, p. 19, from Budapest MTI, July 19, 1991 (in English). The CPSU Central Committee memorandum (cited earlier) states that the "question of energy exports to eastern Europe must be regarded as a very important instrument in our overall strategy in this region." Furthermore, some degree of specialization was achieved within the CMEA, which meant that the east European countries had a significant amount of industrial capacity which was oriented solely on the Soviet market.

55. USSR Foreign Ministry, p. 50.

56. FBIS-EEU-91–033, February 19, 1991, p. 32, from *Warsaw Rzeczpospolita,* February 13, 1991, pp. 1, 9.

57. FBIS-SOV-91–128, July 3, 1991, pp. 1–3, from TASS international service, July 1, 1991 (in Russian).

58. FBIS-SOV-91–139, July 19, 1991, pp. 33–35, from *Novoye Vremya,* no. 26 (June 1991), 14–16.

59. Lieutenant Colonel P. Vladimirov, "Kogda raspadayutsya bloki" (When blocs fall apart), *Pravitelstvennyy Vestnik,* no. 11 (March 1991), 11; FBIS-SOV-91–088, May 7, 1991, pp. 12–13, from interview with Deputy Foreign Minister Yuli Kvitsinskiy, in *Nepszabadsag* (Budapest), April 29, 1991, pp. 1, 6. A few days after the military structure of the WTO ceased to exist, General Mikhail Moiseyev pointed out this asymmetry in institutions. The preservation of NATO's military structure meant that "equal security will not be obtained" and NATO might seek to use its position of strength. This situation would require the Soviet Union to weigh its security interests anew and "rely not on illusory nonbloc security but on the organization of the country's defense independently, within national borders." M. Moiseyev, "Problemy bezopasnosti: neobkhodim vzveshennyy podkhod" (Security problems: a balanced approach is needed), *Izvestiya,* April 5, 1991, p. 6. Surprisingly, he admitted that the chief reason why the Soviet Union agreed to the CFE agreement "was for lightening our own military burden, helping the country to extricate itself from the economic crisis, and raising Soviet people's living and everyday conditions."

60. The Soviets sought to reinterpret CFE limits on their coastal defense and transferred a number of tanks east beyond the Urals so that they would not be included in reductions.

61. Yazov, "Vysokii rubezh istorii."

62. FBIS-SOV-91–140, July 22, 1991, pp. 1–3, from TASS international service, July 19, 1991.

63. On the early period of this process, see Stephen M. Meyer, "The Sources and Prospects of Gorbachev's New Political Thinking on Security," *International Security* 13, 2 (1988), 124–163.

64. For a concise overview of the CSCE's structure and history, see Chapter 11, "Pursuing Military Security in Eastern Europe," by Richard Weitz in this volume.

65. Yazov, "Vysokiy rubezh istorii"; FBIS-SOV-90–216 (Zagladin article).

66. USSR Foreign Ministry, p. 43.

67. E. A. Shevardnadze, "O vneshney politike" (On foreign policy), *Pravda,* June 26, 1990, p. 3; FBIS-SOV-90–224, November 20, 1990, pp. 1–3, from Moscow Radio, November 19, 1990.

68. For example, on his way to the Berlin CSCE meeting in June 1991 Yuriy Deryabin (head of the Foreign Ministry CSCE Administration) quoted Foreign Minister Bessmert-nykh's position: " [Our approach] is that the CSCE process should be a priority from the viewpoint of creating future security and cooperation structures in Europe. We admit that in the current transitional period there are structures that have proven their worth and that they should be used. But it would be wrong to try to perpetuate them. European security and stability presuppose the need for a deep transformation of all structures and their unification so that new structures would cover the entire continent." FBIS-SOV-91–122, June 25, 1991, pp. 1–2, from TASS, June 24, 1991 (in English).

69. USSR Foreign Ministry, p. 49.

70. FBIS-EEU-91–140, July 22, 1991, pp. 22–23, from *Warsaw Zycie Warszawy,* July

17, 1991, pp. 1, 3; FBIS-EEU-91–039, February 27, 1991, p. 9, from Budapest domestic service, February 25, 1991.

71. Vladimirov, "Kogda raspadayutsya bloki."

72. Moiseyev, "Problemy bezopasnosti."

73. Vice President Gennadiy Yanayev described the new agreements as "a new treaty base for mutual relations that is capable of creating a stable international and legal foundation for progressive development and cooperation in all fields . . . At the same time questions concerning the mutual provision of security must occupy an important place, we are convinced, in the treaties that are being concluded." See FBIS-SOV-91–128, July 3, 1991, pp. 1–3, from TASS International Service, July 1, 1991 (in Russian). USSR Foreign Ministry, p. 50; FBIS-SOV-91–088, May 7, 1991, pp. 12–13, from Nepszabadsag (Budapest), April 29, 1991.

74. FBIS-SOV-91–112, June 11, 1991, p. 31, from Izvestiya, June 5, 1991. Also FBIS-EEU-91–124, June 27, 1991, p. 12, from Prague CTK, June 26, 1991 (in English). According to the Bulletin of the Atlantic Council of the US 2, no. 7, the Soviets insist that a treaty without the security clauses would be rejected by the Supreme Soviet.

75. FBIS-SOV-91–122, June 25, 1991, pp. 19–20.

76. Moiseyev, "Problemy bezopasnosti"; "Shto gryadet za peremenami" (What is coming after the changes), Pravda, March 18, 1991, p. 7.

77. As the Foreign Ministry reported: "Efforts to restrain by force the objective historical process not only would have violated the principles of civilized society but would have been inconsistent with the plan for securing Soviet national interests. These interests may be threatened not by the process of democracy as such but by social, political, or ethnic conflicts." USSR Foreign Ministry, pp. 40–41.

78. A notable exception is Poland, which fears the German specter perhaps more than any other state. A Polish vice minister of defense stated in an interview that Poland very much wishes to continue its military cooperation with the USSR. See FBIS-EEU-91–123, June 26, 1991, pp. 25–27, from Warsaw Rzeczpospolita, June 19, 1991, p. 6.

79. E. Fadeyev, "Yugoslaviya: vse spokoyno?" (Yugoslavia: is all calm?), Pravda, July 6, 1991, pp. 1, 6; "Vashington: prizyv k prekrashcheniyu ognya v yugoslavii" (Washington: call for a cease-fire in Yugoslavia), Izvestiya, July 4, 1991, p. 1; "Yugoslavia: storony prokhodyat k kompromissu" (Yugoslavia: the sides approach compromise), Izvestiya, July 8, 1991, p. 1; FBIS-SOV-91–128, July 3, 1991, p. 25, from Pravda, July 1, 1991; New York Times, August 8, 1991, pp. A1, A8.

80. "Vstrechi na nemetskoy zemle" (Meetings on German soil), Pravda, November 12, 1990, p. 4.

81. Coit D. Blacker, "The Collapse of Soviet Power in Europe," Foreign Affairs, America, and the World 70, 1 (1991), 88–102.

3. The United States and International Institutions in Europe after the Cold War

1. John Gerard Ruggie, "Multilateralism: The Anatomy of an Institution," *International Organization* 46, 3 (Summer 1992), 571.

2. Glenn H. Snyder, "The Security Dilemma in Alliance Politics," *World Politics,* 36, 4 (July 1984), 461–495.

3. *IMF: Direction of Trade Statistics Yearbook,* 1984, p. 385.

4. See Robert O. Keohane, *After Hegemony: Cooperation and Discord in the World Political Economy* (Princeton: Princeton University Press, 1984).

5. For such an argument, see Keohane, *After Hegemony,* pp. 258–259, and Joseph S. Nye, Jr., *The Making of America's Soviet Policy* (New Haven: Yale University Press, 1984), chap. 13.

6. Snyder, "Security Dilemma," p. 495.

7. Lawrence Eagleburger, testimony before the Subcommittee on European Affairs of the Senate Foreign Relations Committee, June 22, 1989, in *Department of State Bulletin,* 89, 2142 (October 1989), 38–39.

8. See Judith Goldstein, "Ideas, Institutions, and American Trade Policy," *International Organization,* 42, 1 (Winter 1988), 179–217.

9. Richard N. Gardner, *Sterling-Dollar Diplomacy in Current Perspective,* rev. ed. (New York: Columbia University Press, 1980), p. 373.

10. See Alan S. Milward, *The Reconstruction of Western Europe, 1945–51* (Berkeley: University of California Press, 1984). Milward makes stronger claims for European influence but in our judgment understates the cumulative impact of U.S. initiatives.

11. John F. Kennedy, quoted in Stephen Woolcock, "US Views on 1992," *National Institute Economic Review* (November 1990), 86–92, quote on p. 86.

12. Dean Rusk, "Trade and the Atlantic Partnership," *Department of State Bulletin,* 51, 1327 (November 30, 1964), 767.

13. Henry Kissinger, quoted in Helmut Sonnenfeldt, "The European Pillar: The American View," *Adelphi Paper 235,* "The Changing Strategic Landscape," pt. 1 (Spring 1989), 91–105, quote on p. 93.

14. William Wallace, "European Defence Co-operation: The Reopening Debate," *Survival,* 26, 4 (November/December 1984), 254.

15. See Robert O. Keohane and Stanley Hoffmann, eds., *The New European Community: Decisionmaking and Institutional Change* (Boulder, Colo.: Westview Press, 1991).

16. *IMF Survey,* November 29, 1982, p. 369.

17. M. Peter McPherson, deputy treasury secretary, *New York Times,* August 5, 1988, p. D-1; Alfred Kingdon, retiring U.S. ambassador to the EC, *Financial Times,* May 6, 1989, p. 3.

18. *Financial Times,* May 2, 1989, p. 4; *Financial Times,* May 27, 1989, p. 3.

19. Eagleburger testimony, p. 37.

20. George Bush, remarks to residents of Leiden, the Netherlands, July 17, 1989, in

Public Papers of the Presidents, George Bush (Washington, D.C.: Government Printing Office, 1989), 2: 978.

21. *Economist,* March 5, 1988, p. 54.

22. "American Public Opinion about Western Europe," a 1990 Gallup survey sponsored by the European Community's Press and Public Affairs Office in Washington, D.C., pp. 4–5.

23. "The New Europe: The Reshaping of Global Business: An American Perspective," a survey prepared by KPMG Peat Marwick, September 1990, pp. 3–4, 6.

24. Chicago Council on Foreign Relations poll, quoted in John E. Reilly, "Public Opinion: The Pulse of the '90s," *Foreign Policy,* no. 82 (Spring 1991), 79–86, quote on p. 91.

25. "American Public Opinion," pp. 17–19.

26. *Economist,* June 10, 1989, p. 47.

27. George Bush, news conference in Helena, Montana, September 18, 1989, in *Public Papers of the Presidents, George Bush, 1989,* 2: 1221.

28. *Wall Street Journal,* February 17, 1989, p. A10.

29. Stephen Ledogar, "European Defense Cooperation outside the NATO Context: A U.S. View" (unpublished, 1986), quoted in James B. Steinberg, "Rethinking the Debate on Burdensharing," *Survival,* 29, 1 (January/February 1987), 56–78, quote on p. 75.

30. *Economist,* July 22, 1989, p. 22.

31. *Financial Times,* October 15, 1991, p. 1.

32. James Baker, address before the National Committee on American Foreign Policy, "The Common European Interest: America and the New Politics among Nations," printed in *U.S. Department of State Dispatch,* September 3, 1990, p. 37.

33. James Baker, Council of Ministers' Meeting of the CSCE, Berlin, June 19, 1991, "Economic Transition in Central and Eastern Europe," printed in *U.S. Department of State Dispatch,* July 1, 1991, p. 465.

34. On the U.S. advisory committee process, see Sylvia Ostry, *Governments and Corporations in a Shrinking World* (New York: Council on Foreign Relations, 1990), pp. 18–25.

35. Richard Cooper, "Trade Policy Is Foreign Policy," *Foreign Policy,* no. 9 (Winter 1972–73), 18–36.

36. On imperial overstretch, see Paul Kennedy, *Rise and Fall of the Great Powers* (London: Unwin and Hyman, 1988).

4. French Dilemmas and Strategies in the New Europe

1. See my contribution "Balance, Concert, Anarchy, or None of the Above," in Gregory Treverton, ed., *The Shape of the New Europe* (New York: Council on Foreign Relations, 1992), pp. 194–220.

2. See Frédéric Bozo, *La France et l'OTAN* (Paris: Masson, 1991), pp. 191ff. Chapter 11 gives the best account and analysis of the Franco-American contest over NATO in 1991.

3. See Anne-Marie Le Gloannec, "Le sens de la puissance allemande", in *L'ordre*

mondial relâché, ed. Zaki Laïdi (Paris: Presses de la Fondation Nationale des Sciences Politiques, 1991).

4. I happened to be the *rapporteur* of this committee, which attracted a large number of political personalities and representatives of European and international institutions. In his final speech the French president, who had only then been informed of his plan's fate, beat an elegant retreat.

5. Ratification of the Maastricht treaties might prove more difficult than that of the Schengen accords. The French constitution states that treaties that contradict it cannot be ratified until it has been revised. The provisions on European citizenship require such a revision, and the neo-Gaullists have warned that they object to allowing non-French citizens to run for office. If parliament does not provide the government with the required qualified majority, the constitutional reform may have to be done through referendum. Elements of the opposition also assert that the treaty on EMU, by transferring monetary power to a European central bank, clashes with the constitution.

6. On the subjects discussed in this essay, see also Steven Philip Kramer, "The French Question", *Washington Quarterly* (Autumn 1991), 83–96; Philippe Moreau Defarges, 'L'Allemagne et l'avenir de l'unification européenne," *Politique etrangère* (April 1991), pp. 849–858; Anne-Marie Le Gloannec, "Mitterrand et l'Allemagne," *French Politics and Society* (Summer-Fall 1991), 121–129.

5. British State Strategies after the Cold War

1. This chapter is in part adapted from Louise Richardson and Celeste A. Wallander, "A Comparison of British and Soviet Adjustments to Structural Change in Europe," paper presented at the meeting of the International Studies Association, Vancouver, British Columbia, March 20–23, 1991.

2. Here I am using Robert Keohane's definition of institutions as persistent and connected sets of rules, formal and informal, that prescribe behavioral roles, constrain activity, and shape expectations. See Robert O. Keohane, *International Institutions and State Power* (Boulder, Colo.: Westview Press, 1989), chap. 1.

3. For an elaboration of the neorealist position, see, for example, Kenneth Waltz, *Theory of International Politics* (Reading, Mass.: Addison-Wesley, 1979), and John Mearsheimer, "Back to the Future: Instability in Europe after the Cold War," *International Security,* 15, 1 (1990), 5–56. For the institutionalist position, see, for example, Robert O. Keohane, *After Hegemony: Cooperation and Discord in the World Political Economy* (Princeton: Princeton University Press, 1984), and "Back to the Future, Part II: International Relations Theory and Post–Cold War Europe," correspondence by Stanley Hoffmann, Robert O. Keohane, and John Mearsheimer, *International Security,* 15, 2 (1990), 191–199.

4. See Chapter 4, "French Dilemmas and Strategies in the New Europe," by Stanley Hoffmann in this volume.

5. See Karl Kaiser, "Germany's Unification," *Foreign Affairs, America, and the World,* 70, 1 (1990/91), 179–205.

6. Ibid.

7. See *Independent,* July 6 and 7, 1990.

8. For a more measured presentation of Ridley's views, see Nicholas Ridley, *My Style of Government* (London: Hutchinson, 1991).

9. For the text of the interview, see *Spectator,* July 14, 1990 pp. 8–10.

10. MAI UK Market Research. See *Independent on Sunday,* July 15, 1990, pp. 1–3.

11. The leaked minutes of the meeting are reprinted in full in *Independent on Sunday,* July 15, 1990, p. 19.

12. Ibid.

13. For an eloquent expression of this position, see Timothy Garton Ash, "Germany Unbound," *New York Review of Books,* November 22, 1990.

14. These commitments are defined in *Statement on the Defense Estimates,* vol. 1 (April 1990), HMSO, p. 19.

15. For details of the proposals, see Hansard, House of Commons Debates, July 25, 1990, HMSO, and *Independent,* July 26, 1990.

16. For details, see Defence White Paper, July 1991, HMSO; Hansard, House of Commons Debates, July 9, 1991; *Independent,* July 10, 1991; *Guardian,* July 10, 1991; *Economist,* July 6, July 13, 1991.

17. Boxes containing 800,000 signatures demanding a reversal of the cutbacks in Scotland alone were handed in to the House of Commons. See defense debates in Hansard, October 14, 15, 1991, and June 18, 19, 1990.

18. On the question of foreign direct investment in eastern Europe, see Chapter 9, "Foreign Direct Investment in Eastern Europe," by Debora Spar in this volume.

19. House of Commons, Treasury and Civil Service Committee, Seventh Report, "International Monetary Arrangements: Eastern Europe," session 1989–90, HMSO; hereafter cited as HC 431.

20. Cited by treasury official in evidence before the Treasury and Civil Service Committee, May 26, 1990, HC 431.

21. On the role of the EBRD, see Chapter 8, "The Political Economy of Financial Assistance to Eastern Europe," by Stephan Haggard and Andrew Moravcsik in this volume.

22. *Economist,* September 21, 1991, survey, p. 25.

23. *Economist,* April 7, 1990.

24. "International Monetary Arrangements with Regard to Eastern Europe," memorandum submitted by the Bank of England to the Treasury and Civil Service Committee, May 13, 1990, HC 431.

25. *Financial Times,* November 6, 1990.

26. Overseas Trade Statistics, CSO, reprinted in HC 431.

27. HC 431, p. xvii.

28. EC 114, "The Community's Relations with Eastern Europe: A Framework."

29. Ibid.; also *Financial Times,* January 9, 1990.

30. House of Commons, session 1989–90, Defence Committee, Tenth Report, "Defence Implications of Recent Events," July 11, 1990, HMSO, p. 36.

31. Ibid., pp. 1–18.

32. Ibid., p. xxxiii.

33. *Guardian*, July 10, 1991.

34. Ibid., July 14, 1991.

35. Douglas Hurd, press conference, Berlin, December 10, 1990.

36. House of Commons, session 1989–90, Defence Committee, Tenth Report, "Defence Implications of Recent Events," July 11, 1990, HMSO, p. 63.

37. *New York Times*, November 8 and 9, 1991.

38. The WEU grew out of the Brussels Treaty, a mutual defense pact signed in 1948 by Britain, France, the Netherlands, Belgium, and Luxembourg. After the failure of the EDC in 1954, it was decided, largely on the initiative of Anthony Eden, to rearm Germany within the framework of this security organization. Germany and Italy were invited to join. A deal was made whereby Germany would accept restrictions on its forces and prohibitions on the manufacture of certain types of weapons in return for membership in NATO. To assuage fears of German rearmament, Britain made an unprecedented pledge not to reduce its forces on the continent without the consent of the WEU. Over the years the WEU has served as a consultative body bereft of power. It has a council, consisting of foreign ministers or ambassadors for coordination of defense policy, an agency for the control of armaments, and a standing armaments committee for coordination of military procurement. The WEU assembly, composed of the representatives sent by the member states to the Consultative Assembly of the Council of Europe, actively debate defense policy, but its recommendations have rarely been accepted by national governments.

39. Excerpts from the white paper are published in *Guardian*, July 10, 1991.

40. See Douglas Hurd, interview with ITN, February 4, 1991, and press conference, Brussels, February 4, 1991.

41. John Major, press conference, Maastricht, December 11, 1991.

42. Harold Macmillan, *Britain the Commonwealth and Europe* (London: Conservative Political Centre, 1962), p. 2, cited in Geoffrey Howe, "Sovereignty and Interdependence: Britain's Place in the World," *International Affairs*, 66, 4 (1990), 687–688.

43. He made the same point repeatedly thereafter. See, for example, *Financial Times*, November 13, 1991.

44. "The Fates lead on those who are willing; those who are unwilling, the Fates drag along anyway." Cited in Howe, "Sovereignty and Interdependence," p. 689.

6. Integrating the Two Halves of Europe

For comments on earlier drafts, we are indebted to Robert O. Keohane, Joseph S. Nye, Debora L. Spar, Stanley Hoffmann, and Richard Weitz.

1. Chapter 11, Richard Weitz's case study of national security policies in eastern Europe, was prepared independently of the other four chapters in this section, and it does not review the domestic policy problems of implementation and compliance.

2. The separation of the liberal tradition from the variant of regime theory variously

termed neoliberal institutionalism or modified structural realism can be found in Robert O. Keohane, "Neoliberal Institutionalism: A Perspective on World Politics," in Robert O. Keohane, *International Institutions and State Power: Essays in International Relations Theory* (Boulder, Colo.: Westview Press, 1989), pp. 1–20.

3. Regime theorists maintain that regimes are *intervening* variables: they mediate between power and preferences on the one hand and outcomes on the other. Nonetheless, the essential empirical question remains: What portion of observed variance in interstate cooperation and conflict is explained by the background patterns of power and preferences and what portion by intermediating institutions? See Stephen Krasner, "Structural Causes and Regime Consequences: Regimes as Intervening Variables," in *International Regimes,* ed. Stephen D. Krasner (Ithaca, N.Y.: Cornell University Press, 1983); Andrew Moravcsik, "Liberalism and International Relations Theory," paper presented at the Program on International Politics, Economics, and Security, University of Chicago, January 9, 1992.

4. Alexander George and Timothy McKeown, "Case Studies and Theories of Organizational Decisionmaking," in *Advances in Information Processing in Organizations,* ed. Robert Coulam and Richard Smith (Greenwich, Conn.: JAI Press, 1985).

5. Robert O. Keohane, *After Hegemony: Cooperation and Discord in the World Political Economy* (Princeton: Princeton University Press, 1984); Krasner, "Structural Causes."

6. Moravcsik, "Liberalism."

7. John J. Mearsheimer, "Back to the Future: Instability in Europe after the Cold War," *International Security* 15 (Summer 1990), 5–56. Cf. Moravcsik, "Liberalism."

8. We elaborate the definition of Ernst Haas by defining issue areas as substantively connected sets of relations in which the terms of interdependence are—or, we would add, could be—politically managed. Ernst B. Haas, "Why Collaborate? Issue-Linkage and International Regimes," *World Politics* 32, no. 3 (April 1980), 362.

9. For an argument that there are "liberal" and "realist" variants of institutionalism, with most current theories falling into the latter category, see Moravcsik, "Liberalism." On the lack of empirical confirmation, see Robert O. Keohane, "Multilateralism: An Agenda for Research," *International Journal* 45 (Fall 1990), 731–764.

10. Robert O. Keohane, "The Demand for International Regimes," in Krasner, *International Regimes,* pp. 141–171.

11. Keohane, "Demand for International Regimes," pp. 155–156.

12. Keohane, "Demand for International Regimes." This hypothesis is closely connected with the so-called modified structural realist position.

13. For this argument from an institutionalist perspective, see Hildegard Bedarff, *Die Osteuropapolitik der Europäischen Gemeinschaft: Zur Institutionalisierung der Ost-West Beziehungen* (Muenster: LIT Verlag, 1992), pp. 56–59.

14. The precise extent to which this promoted integration where it would not have been possible before remains unclear.

15. Bedarff, *Osteuropapolitik,* pp. 73–75.

16. Kalypso Nicolaïdis, in Chapter 7 in this volume, is quite critical of the EC for failing to promote cooperation among eastern countries, which, at least in the short run, would

have helped ease the pains of adjustment while at the same time alleviating pressure for access to its own markets. See also Bedarff, *Osteuropapolitik,* pp. 79-87. See also Richard Portes, "The European Community's Response to Eastern Europe," in *The Economic Consequences of the East* (London: CEPR, 1992), pp. 8-11.

17. This was also the primary effect of the initial negotiation of the common external tariff of the European Economic Community in the 1960s. See Andrew Moravcsik, "National Preference Formation and Interstate Bargaining in the European Community, 1955-1986" (Ph.D. diss., Harvard University, 1992), pp. 254-255.

18. The landmark decision of the European Court on this point is *Commission v. Council* 22/70 (March 31, 1971), ECR 263, commonly referred to as ERTA. The court's reasoning is precisely that uncoordinated external policies would threaten the integrity of the internal market.

19. Keohane, "Demand for International Regimes." This sort of linkage is to be sharply distinguished from tactical or institutionally induced issue linkages. For an argument that such linkages are important in the EC, see Lisa L. Martin, "Institutions and Cooperation: Sanctions during the Falkland Islands Conflict," *International Security* 16 (Spring 1992), 143-178. The case studies report no evidence of tactical issue linkage; the linkages are inherent in the substantive issue area and previous patterns of institutionalization.

20. For a critique of western policy, see Portes, "European Community," pp. 10-20.

21. Moravcsik, "Liberalism."

22. Alan S. Milward, *The Reconstruction of Western Europe, 1945-1951* (Berkeley: University of California Press, 1984).

23. See John Gerard Ruggie, "International Regimes, Transactions, and Change: Embedded Liberalism in the Postwar Economic Order," in Krasner, *International Regimes.*

24. Joanne Gowa, "Bipolarity and the Postwar International Economic Order," in *Industry and Politics in West Germany: Toward the Third Republic,* ed. Peter Katzenstein (Ithaca, N.Y.: Cornell University Press, 1989), pp. 33-50.

25. Robert D. Putnam, "Diplomacy and Domestic Politics: The Logic of Two-Level Games," *International Organization* 42 (Summer 1988), 427-460.

26. Ruggie, "International Regimes, Transactions, and Change."

7. East European Trade in the Aftermath of 1989

This chapter is based on research and interviews conducted in Warsaw, Prague, Brussels, and Paris during 1991-92, supported by a grant from the post-Cold War settlement project of the Center for International Affairs, Harvard University. In addition to the numerous individuals interviewed during this period, the author thanks in particular Stephan Haggard and Lisa Martin for their comments on an earlier version of this chapter, Anna Jancewicz for her invaluable support in Warsaw, as well as the other participants in the project for their stimulating intellectual companionship.

1. This chapter uses *eastern Europe* as a shorthand term to refer to the eight central and eastern European countries (Albania, Bulgaria, Czechoslovakia, Hungary, Poland, Roma-

nia, and Yugoslavia) and *central Europe* to refer exclusively to Czechoslovakia, Hungary, and Poland. Although Czechoslovakia became the Czech and Slovak Federal Republic during the period under consideration, the older name is used here for the sake of consistency. When not otherwise indicated, trade figures cited in this chapter are drawn from *The Direction of Trade Statistics* (IMF), and *Eurostat Statistics* (Office of Publication of the EC).

2. As laid out in the introductory chapter to this volume, our purpose is to put forth an institutionalist account of post–Cold War cooperation, not so much in contrast but as a crucial supplement to dominant theories of international relations, for example, liberal theories of international institutions according to which patterns of cooperation mostly reflect underlying convergence or divergence of policy preferences among the countries involved, and realist theories for which such patterns mostly reflect the distribution of power between states and their respective bargaining leverage. For a more detailed account of institutionalist, realist, and liberal theories of international relations, see the introductory and concluding chapters in this volume, as well as Chapter 6. See also Kenneth Waltz, *Theories of International Politics* (Reading, Mass: Addison-Wesley, 1979), and Robert Keohane, *After Hegemony: Cooperation and Discord in the World Political Economy* (Princeton: Princeton University Press, 1984).

3. EFTA—created in 1961 as an alternative free trade area to the EC—included Austria, Iceland, Liechtenstein, Norway, Sweden, and Switzerland.

4. Czechoslovakia, for example, produced domestically 65 percent of all categories of industrial goods of the Standard International Trade Classification (SITC), a larger proportion than Japan, whose GNP was twenty times higher. See John Williamson, *The Economic Opening of Eastern Europe* (Washington, D.C.: Institute for International Economics, 1991).

5. For a discussion of earlier negotiations, see Leah Haus, "The East European Countries and GATT: The Role of Realism, Mercantilism, and Regime Theory in Explaining East-West Trade Negotiations," *International Organization*, 45, 2 (Spring 1991), 163–182.

6. See Susan M. Collins and Dani Rodrik, *Eastern Europe and the Soviet Union in the World Economy* (Washington, D.C.: Institute for International Economics, 1991).

7. To be sure, attempts at reforming the CMEA had actually started in the mid-1960s and had systematically failed. The very logic of the planning system and the refusal to introduce any degree of liberalization left virtually no room for reform. In the wake of perestroika planners loosened their control over foreign trade, but trade flows were left under administrative controls. The structural problem remained the same: no country had an interest in sustaining a surplus, so trade was limited to the potential of the weakest trading partner. Constraints on liberalization were enormous, from the most mundane, such as naming products, to the most structural, such as the fact that the USSR was channeling all negotiations with the outside world.

8. This led to the paradoxical situation that while Poland bore a trade surplus with the Soviet Union of $500 million in nonconvertible currency, it had a deficit in hard currency of $470 million by the end of the first half of 1991.

9. Polish officials estimated that between one half and two thirds of the decline in gross national production in 1991 was due to the free fall of exports to the USSR (from 23 to 5 percent of Polish production between 1990 and 1991, according to the Foreign Trade Research Institute in Warsaw). In the first couple of months of 1991, thirty Polish companies went bankrupt for lack of orders from the Soviet Union.

10. Other informal regional cooperation groupings include the twin conferences of the Baltic states and the Baltic cities held in September 1990 and 1991 and the Pentagonale initiative.

11. The fact that a similar model had been envisaged in the mid-1980s within the institutional context of the CMEA was a serious drawback. Advocates needed to argue forcefully that this did not amount to a survival of the CMEA but was a means of managing the transitional period. An alternative that was considered but not adopted was to settle for an arrangement reminiscent of the CMEA days in the form of barter or clearing arrangements settled every quarter through convertible currency.

12. The major asset supporting such cooperation was political and economic similarity among the central European countries. Yet such similarity also implied that these countries represented less trade potential for one another compared to the huge Soviet market or more complementary markets such as Bulgaria.

13. Martin Palous, deputy minister, Federal Ministry of Foreign Affairs, Prague, July 1991.

14. Interview with Maciej Perczynski, director, Polish Institute for International Affairs, Warsaw, June 1991.

15. The Pentagonale was officially created on August 1, 1990, and initially included Czechoslovakia, Hungary, Yugoslavia, and Austria, along with Italy, its only EC member. Poland at the time was busy with the German question and became a full member of what then became the Hexagonale in July 1991. Bulgaria and Romania expressed their interest in joining but were met with refusal. Pentagonale members created working groups on transport, environment, culture, technology, and energy but purposely excluded any trade agreement from their cooperation, staying careful not to take any steps which might be interpreted as the creation of a trade bloc. On the contrary, in the view of the non-EC members a central purpose of the initiative was to accelerate member countries' readiness for membership in the EC. Yet the Pentagonale did promote trade by focusing on developing regional infrastructures. Interview with Josef Wiejacz, Ambassador Plenipotentiary for Baltic Cooperation, Pentagonale, and Human Environment, Warsaw, June 1991.

16. Interview with Jerzy Wieczorek, adviser to the minister, Ministry of Foreign Affairs, Warsaw, June 1991.

17. Interview with Jaroslaw Mulewicz, director, Department of International Economic Relations, Ministry of Foreign Affairs, Warsaw, June 1991. In the case of Poland, the 1 million Polish Americans obviously contributed greatly to this sense of closeness.

18. Interview with Zdenko Pirek, deputy foreign minister, Prague, July 1992. In this vein the French project for a European Confederation including the Soviet Union but excluding the United States was ill received by the eastern Europeans, who ultimately opposed such exclusion.

19. In GATT, for instance, "we will just be forced to be closer to the European line of thinking than to the American line of thinking." Interview with Miloslav Had, head of Analysis and Policy Planning, Federal Ministry of Foreign Affairs, Prague, July 1991.

20. EFTA as a whole absorbed 8.7 percent of Czechoslovakia's exports in 1991, with Austria alone absorbing 5.8 percent.

21. Interview with Miloslav Had. In the course of 1991 all eastern European countries nevertheless initiated negotations of free trade agreements with EFTA.

22. One analyst in Poland expressed a somewhat different opinion: "We are worried that Europe would become German, when what we want to see is Germany become European. An enlarging that could hamper so-called deepening and therefore the stronger anchoring of Germany in the Community would not be in Poland's interest. It seems better to wait and deal with a strong EC partner, firmly containing Germany, than to precipitate enlargement and weaken the Community. It would not be realistic to expect further deepening for a while once eastern Europeans had become members." Interview with Maciej Perczinski.

23. Interview with Maciej Perczinski.

24. Interview with Miloslav Had.

25. Interview with Marek Kulczycki, director, Department of Foreign Economic Relations, Ministry of Foreign Economic Relations, Warsaw, June 1991.

26. Interview with Antoni Kaminski, director, European Affairs, Ministry of Foreign Affairs, Warsaw, June 1991.

27. See Chapter 8 by Stephan Haggard and Andrew Moravcsik in this volume.

28. According to the dominant viewpoint in the east, foreign trade could play a much greater role than direct assistance, and that technical assistance could be of more use than financial assistance. In short, according to one official in Poland, "there is no lack of capital [in our countries]; millions of dollars are sitting in our banks unallocated. What we need is management skills, investment projects, a risk-taking spirit, and market opportunities abroad to back it up."

29. See Chapter 9 by Debora Spar in this volume.

30. Interview with Zdenko Pirek.

31. Interview with Peter Palecka, director general, Multilateral Trade Policy Department, Federal Ministry of Foreign Trade, Prague, July 1991. In addition, Czechoslovakia never used antidumping complaints under the subsidies code, or the government procurement code.

32. Only a few peak tariffs, however, exceeded 20 percent. In Hungary 90 percent of imports were freed, and in Czechoslovakia only oil, gas, arms, and drugs were exempted from liberalization.

33. In 1990 and 1991 Czechoslovakia went through seven waves of gradual liberalization. Starting in May 1990 foreign trade organizations, each of which under the CMEA held a trade monopoly according to commodity specification schemes, were detached from the supervision of the Ministry of Foreign Trade and transformed into joint stock companies. These companies were allowed to start competing with one another and to find partners. Private persons acquired the same rights to trade as legal entities. Require-

ments for import permits were gradually eliminated (limited export licensing was kept in place in particular to avoid speculation through exportation of goods that would need to be reimported at higher prices). The right to export armaments was extended to every individual firm, a development dear to Slovakia. Simplified registration procedures were put in place, and finally a new trade bill was introduced in parliament. By the end of 1990, 3,500 companies were engaged in foreign trade. In the fall of 1991 the GATT secretariat produced its first review of an eastern European country's trade policy on Hungary. While it generally praised the changes which had occurred in the two previous years and called for the west to open its markets further, the review also stressed that much still needed to be achieved before Hungary could claim to be in full conformity with GATT. In particular, the report stressed the discretionary character of administrative decisions regarding trade policies. See *Country Trade Policy Report—Hungary* (Geneva: GATT, 1991).

34. Bulgaria liberalized most imports in 1991 while introducing tariffs. Albania, which had until then followed a policy of self-sufficiency, abolished foreign trade organizations in August 1990 and introduced trade licensing in December 1991. Import liberalization was introduced in August 1991, followed by a ban on food exports.

35. In 1990 the GNP fell by 10 to 25 percent—depending on methods of estimation— in all eastern European countries and contracted further by a regional average of 12 percent in the first quarter of 1991. The various estimates differed on the scope of GNP decrease, but as a Polish analyst stated: "Whether the decline is 16 or 30 percent, it is still enormous!" Indeed, such levels of economic recession had not been seen since the Great Depression of the 1930s.

36. Interview with Deputy Komarec, chairman of the Foreign Policy Committee, Federal Parliament, Prague, July 1991.

37. Interview with Dariusz Rosati, director, Foreign Trade Research Institute, Warsaw, June 1991.

38. The internal controversy around arms export was particularly telling. By unofficial estimates Slovak arms production for export employed 80,000 persons directly and 200,000, including suppliers, indirectly; and one third of Slovakian firms had a connection with arms production. President Vaclav Havel's morally driven decision to ban arms sales, in particular tank sales in the Middle East, not surprisingly met with strong protests in Slovakia and was quietly abandoned in order not to strain further the relationship between independence-prone Slovakia and the federal government.

39. Czechoslovakia was a founding member of the multilateral trade organization, but, as we have seen, its participation therein had been largely symbolic. In the 1960s, de-Stalinization and the willingness of the west to encourage diversity in the east had opened the path for Poland, Romania, and Hungary to develop ties with GATT, in which they became observers in 1957, 1957, and 1966, respectively. The three countries joined the organization in 1967, 1971, and 1973 respectively. (Bulgaria had become an observer in GATT in 1967, but, given its close association with the Soviet Union, its bid for membership was systematically rebuffed until 1990.) The terms of participation embodied in their protocol of accession duly accounted for the fact that reciprocal access could not be expected on the part of nonmarket economies. The EC, in particular, had insisted on

terms of agreement that permitted members to apply bilateral and discriminatory quantitative restrictions, as well as discriminatory safeguards, against the east European members of GATT. For its part, the United States had unilaterally extended most favored nation treatment to Poland in 1962, but not to other eastern members, in accordance with its 1962 Trade Expansion Act, which prevented granting MFN status to products "of any country or areas dominated or controlled by Communism" (section 231). In sum, membership in GATT had been dictated by political objectives, and, as most observers agree, had had little impact on the trade patterns of nonmarket economies. For a detailed historical overview, see Leah A. Haus, *Globalising the GATT: The Soviet Union's Successor States, Eastern Europe, and the International Trading System* (Washington, D.C.: The Brookings Institution, 1992).

40. See Chapter 3 by Joseph Nye and Robert Keohane in this volume.

41. In an interview in the spring of 1991 that was perceived as a major setback by eastern Europeans, President François Mitterrand spoke of possible membership "in several decades." See Chapter 4 by Stanley Hoffmann in this volume.

42. See note 12. The idea of the Pentagonale had emerged in Rome prior to the 1989 revolutions. Italy's intention at the time was to play a special role as a bridge builder between east and west, while at the same time catering to the independent ambition of its regions, especially Venice, which had been organizing a conference of European regions since 1982.

43. In 1991 Germany represented more than half of Czechoslovakia's imports from the EC. For a discussion of Germany's ambivalent attitude toward the east, see Chapter 1 by Jeffrey Anderson and John Goodman in this volume.

44. The joint declaration signed in Luxembourg on June 25, 1988, was a simple agreement establishing official relations between the two parties, leaving the negotiations over trade concessions to the bilateral level. See Bull. EC 6–1988, point 1.5.1. et seq.; O.J. 1988, L 157/35.

45. The signing of the agreement with Romania was delayed until October 1990 as a result of the disruption of relations following the violent events in Bucharest in June 1990. By the summer of 1991, Albania was the only eastern European country that had not yet signed such an agreement.

46. The EC Generalized System of Preference was extended to Poland and Hungary in December 1989 and to Bulgaria, Czechoslovakia, and Romania on October 18, 1990. The GSP for 1991 covered ECU 28 billion in exports from developing countries and saved them approximately ECU 13 billion in terms of waived EEC import duties. The quantity of goods covered was 13 percent more than in 1990 and applied to all manufactured goods not covered by special sectoral arrangements. "Brussels to Widen Trade Favours in East Europe," *Financial Times*, October 18, 1990.

47. In 1988 two thirds of GDR foreign trade was with CMEA partners.

48. In addition to multilateral EC commitments, the Federal Republic of Germany also pledged to honor the former East Germany's trade contracts with Comecon countries, with a total cost estimated at DM 6 billion. "German Concern over Bottom Line of Redrawn Borders," *Financial Times*, September 28, 1990.

49. The EC established its first mission in Warsaw at the beginning of 1990 but still did not have an official mission in Prague by the summer of 1991.

50. According to Community law, the EC can conclude trade agreements with nonmember countries either on the basis of Article 113—as for the GATT Rounds—or on the basis of Article 238, whereby "the Community may conclude with a third state, a union of states or an international organization agreements establishing an association involving reciprocal rights and obligations, common action and special procedures." In addition, when treaty instruments are insufficient and the scope of provisions required exceeds that of the Common Commercial Policy (CCP), the Community has come to rely on Article 235, which provides for the expansion of Community competence. For a discussion, see Dan Horovitz, "EC–Central/East European Relations: New Principles for a New Era," *Common Market Law Review,* 27 (1990): 259–284.

51. In addition, an association committee would meet at a senior level and deal with technical issues, and a parliamentary association committee would provide a forum for discussion between members of parliament from the associated countries and members of the European Parliament. This committee would make recommendations to the association council.

52. Special links with Yugoslavia were also to be upgraded, and the situation in Romania, Bulgaria, and Albania—lagging somewhat behind their northern counterparts—was to be monitored with a view to extending exploratory talks to those countries. With regard to economic cooperation with the Soviet Union, see Chapter 2 in this volume by Celeste Wallander and Jane Prokop.

53. Interview with Peter Palecka.

54. According to a Polish official, half of all Polish exports to the EC came under some kind of import restriction.

55. Agriculture constituted 25 percent of Polish exports.

56. It is estimated that 800,000 people are employed by the textile industry in Poland. Textile exports represent 15 percent of Polish exports. In Czechoslovakia the director of a shirt factory from Moravia went on national television to denounce the EC quotas.

57. The EC at the time was criticized by a number of EC analysts. See, for instance, *The Community and the Emerging European Democracies: A Joint Policy Report* (June 1991), published jointly by six prominent international affairs institutes throughout Europe. In its final recommendations on trade the report advocated "a rapid granting of market access" in sensitive sectors, warning that "if trade liberalization is not achieved quickly now, it will prove more difficult in the future" (p. 82).

58. Quoted in "Don't Give Up Now," *The Economist,* September 21, 1991.

59. France had to yield to the priority given to imports, but EC member countries were allowed to deduct from their agreed-upon import quotas the amount of EC-financed exports from eastern Europe to the Community.

60. Interview with Péter Gottfried, general secretary of the Hungarian mission in Brussels, January 1992.

61. Interview with Jan Truszczynski, Polish mission in Brussels, January 1992. At the close of the negotiations, Andrzej Olechowski, Poland's chief negotiator, while welcom-

ing the agreement, underscored its "shortcomings and the lack of cohesion" between its approach to industrial and agricultural goods. According to one Hungarian government estimate, export growth as a result of the agreement could be as low as $100–200 million per year.

62. Interview with Willy Vanderberghe, Directorate General, Commission of the European Community, Brussels, January 1992.

63. Interview with Péter Gottfried.

64. Interview with Jan Truszczynski.

65. Sensitive products such as footwear, chemicals, and cars represent 23 percent of Polish exports.

66. As a corollary, the study of services was not academically rewarding, which explains why the few economists who studied these issues in the east were mostly women. For further discussion of services issues in eastern Europe, see *Services in Central and Eastern European Countries* (Paris: OECD Publication Service, 1991).

67. The Commission had hoped to persuade member states to open up their labor market more, in particular by "communitarizing" immigration quotas granted by individual EC states, but this was opposed by the United Kingdom.

68. Of the three countries, Hungary was ultimately the most reluctant to grant the right of free establishment for foreign banks and insisted on keeping in place its current system of rather liberal licensing. In part, Hungary's argument was that, in conformity with the new EC single market, its own banks should be granted the right to operate on the basis of home country control within the EC. Interview with Péter Gottfried.

69. In the fall of 1990 the Community extended an ECU 500 million loan in food credits to the USSR, tied to imports from the EC.

70. The Community adopted two financial instruments of ECU 500 million and ECU 1.25 billion, respectively, in the food aid package to the Soviet Union in which triangular trade figured prominently: up to 25 percent of the first and up to 50 percent of the second instrument could be devoted to the financing of eastern European imports.

71. For a discussion of socialization in the field of environment, see Chapter 10 by Marc Levy in this volume.

72. Interview with Alan Mayhew, Directorate General, Commission of the European Community, Brussels.

73. In Poland, for instance, at least five ministerial departments were directly connected with the negotiations. In Czechoslvakia the Foreign Ministry headed and coordinated the delegation, but ministries involved included the Ministry of Finance, the Ministry of Strategic Planning, the Ministry of the Economy, the Ministry of Foreign Trade, formerly in charge of the CMEA, and the corresponding republican ministries.

74. Interview with Renata Stawarska, Council of Ministers, European Integration Office, Warsaw, June 1991.

75. The study contrasted two basic scenarios, one based on the EC proposal and the other on the Polish proposal, and made two main points: first, that under any scenario benefits for the Community would be higher than for Poland; and second, that under the EC proposal the net growth benefits would be 2.5 times higher for the EC than for Poland.

See "The Analysis of the Macroeconomic Effects of Alternative Reg. of the Agreement on the Association between Poland and the EC," Office of the Undersecretary of State for European Integration and Financial Assistance, Council of Ministers, Poland.

76. Interview with Martin Palous.

77. Pablo Benavides, the head of the Commission negotiating team, had himself been Spain's head negotiator in the early 1980s at the time of his country's accession negotiations.

78. Interview with Willy Vanderberghe.

79. Interview with Jacques Teyssier d'Orfeuil, Direction des Relations Economiques Extérieures, Paris, January 1992.

80. See "Communication from the Commission to the Council and Parliament: The Development of the Community's Relations with the Countries of Central and Eastern Europe," SEC (90) 196 final, February 1990.

81. *Financial Times*, November 23, 1991.

82. Upon receiving such an order, the Polish agriculture ministry allegedly faxed the Polish representative in Brussels asking him to fax back the EC agricultural law. The reply came in the form of a question: "Minister, would you settle for a shipment by truck or by train?"

83. Interview with Piotr Daranowski, European Integration Office, Council of Ministers, Warsaw, June 1991.

84. Under this title, Article 68 reads: "The Contracting Parties recognize that the major precondition for [the country]'s economic integration into the Community is the approximation of that country's existing and future legislation to that of the Community. [Country] shall act to ensure that future legislation will be compatible with Community legislation at the time when it becomes a member of the Community."

85. See Kalypso Nicolaïdis, "Mutual Recognition among Nations: Europe 1992, the Uruguay Round, and Trade in Services" (Ph.D. diss., Harvard University).

86. Article 69. In addition, two other areas would require major efforts to achieve compatibility: social regulations, particularly in the workplace, and environmental regulations.

87. For instance, the Poles insisted on changing the Community's original wording calling for their legislation "to comply" with that of the EC to the notion that legislation should "be compatible." Interview with Pavel Telichka, second secretary of the Czech and Slovak Federal Republic, Brussels, January 1992.

88. Article 70.

89. To help in this process, the PHARE program started to create a data bank on EC laws.

90. Interview with Piotr Daranowski.

91. See Stephen Krasner, ed, *International Regimes* (Ithaca, N.Y.: Cornell University Press, 1983).

8. The Political Economy of Financial Assistance to Eastern Europe, 1989–1991

1. We are grateful to Shannon Pierce for research assistance and to Karen Geiffert, Robert Keohane, Thomas Risse-Kappen, Steve Weber, and members of the project on the post–Cold War settlement in Europe for their comments.

2. Robert O. Keohane, *After Hegemony: Cooperation and Discord in the World Political Economy* (Princeton: Princeton University Press, 1984), p. 100.

3. Robert Gilpin, *U.S. Power and the Multinational Corporation: The Political Economy of Direct Foreign Investment* (New York: Basic Books, 1975). For a critique of hegemonic stability theory, see Keohane, *After Hegemony,* chap. 3.

4. On the realist prediction of western conflict, see John J. Mearsheimer, "Back to the Future: Instability in Europe after the Cold War," *International Security* 15 (Summer 1990), 5–56. On the putative transatlantic shift in power, see Jeanne Kirk Laux, "Beyond Bretton Woods: Reintegrating East Central Europe," paper presented at the International Conference of Europeanists, Chicago, March 26–29, 1992, pp. 2, 34, from which source the final quotation is taken. On realism and relative gains-seeking, see Joseph M. Grieco, "Anarchy and the Limits of Cooperation: A Realist Critique of the Newest Liberal Institutionalism," *International Organization* 42 (Summer 1988), 485–508.

5. Jack Snyder, "Averting Anarchy in the New Europe," *International Security* 14 (Spring 1990), 5–41.

6. International Monetary Fund, *International Capital Markets: Developments and Prospects* (Washington, D.C.: IMF, 1990), p. 96.

7. Richard Feinberg, "Paltry Aid to Eastern Europe," *Challenge,* 39 (January-February 1992), 36–43; Commission of the European Communities, "Framework for Community/G-24 Medium Term Balance of Payments Assistance to Central and Eastern European Countries," Brussels, Document SEC (91) 1090 final, June 6, 1991, p. 9.

8. John M. Kramer, "Eastern Europe and the 'Energy Shock' of 1990–91," *Problems of Communism* (May-June 1991).

9. The eastern European countries were reluctant to extend blanket guarantees to the commercial banks as they had in the past. Nor does the bond market present a viable option. By 1990 Hungary had completed bond issues of $4.7 billion, the Czech and Slovak Federal Republic (CSFR) had raised $500 million, and Bulgaria $200 million. These amounts are not insignificant, but it is unlikely that Poland, Romania, and Bulgaria will have the same success in tapping the bond market as Hungary and Czechoslovakia, and Hungary's debt position is likely to limit its future access as well. Julie Sychrava, "Curtain Up, Project Financiers," *Euromoney* (April 1990), 55–64; see also Chapter 9 by Debora Spar in this volume.

10. Laux, "Beyond Bretton Woods," pp. 3–4, cites European Commission and United Nations reports; J. M. C. Rollo, *The New Eastern Europe: Western Responses* (New York: Council on Foreign Relations, 1990), pp. 63–99; Chapter 9 in this volume.

11. Commission of the European Communities, "Framework," p. 3; "Declaration of Ministers of the Group of 24 Countries on Coordinated Economic Assistance to the

Countries of Central and Eastern Europe (the CEEC)," Brussels, mimeographed, November 11, 1991, p. 2; Commission of the European Communities, "External Financing Requirements of the Countries of Central and Eastern Europe and the Potential Need for Complementary Financial Support," Brussels, mimeographed, October 15, 1990.

12. See the introduction to this volume. See also Steve Weber, "Origins of the European Bank for Reconstruction and Development," Center for European Studies Working Paper no. 40, Cambridge, Mass., 1992.

13. Rollo, *New Eastern Europe,* p. 100.

14. See Chapter 7 by Kalypso Nicolaïdis in this volume.

15. Commission of the European Communities, "Relations with Central and Eastern European Countries: New Initiatives of the European Commission in the Field of Export Credits and Investments," Brussels, mimeographed, November 7, 1990; Commission of the European Communities, "PHARE: Assistance for Economic Restructuring in the Countries of Central and Eastern Europe: An Operational Guide," draft, July 19, 1991, p. 4; interview with EC official, Brussels, June 1992.

16. Weber, "European Bank," pp. 10–11.

17. This motivation is suggested by Weber, who argues, incorrectly in our view, that France lacked the "power resources" to play a major role in eastern Europe. See Weber, "European Bank," pp. 11–13. For a provocative yet unconvincing attempt to account for acquiescence by Germany's allies through a sort of "false consciousness," see Andrei S. Markovits and Simon Reich, "The New Face of Germany: Gramsci, Hegemony, and Europe," Center for European Studies Working Paper, Harvard University, 1992.

18. We treat EC flows as a subset of bilateral flows, extended on similar terms; PHARE aid *is,* for the most part, national aid. Commission of the European Communities, "PHARE," p. 4.

19. For historical overviews, see *The European Community and Its Eastern Neighbors,* European Documentation (Luxembourg: European Communities, 1990); Valérie Assetto, *The Soviet Bloc in the IMF and the IBRD* (Boulder, Colo.: Westview Press, 1988); Rollo, *New Eastern Europe,* chaps. 1–3.

20. Robert Scallon, "Political Risk Insurance Could Be EC Stimulus to Invest in Soviet Union," *Financial Times,* July 30, 1991, p. 15; Commission of the European Communities, "EC Assistance to Central and Eastern Europe: Progress Report, July 1991," Brussels, DG X Background Brief, July 9, 1991, p. 2; interview with EC Commission official, November 1992.

21. Nonetheless, Poland, termed a "big winner," gained no more than $225 in assistance. Weber, "European Bank," pp. 17–20.

22. Ibid., p. 16.

23. Although EC institutions, with a heavy emphasis on macroeconomic financing (particularly balance of payments support) and project lending, somewhat counterbalance the bilateral emphasis of France, Germany, and other member states on trade credits, the net effect is nonetheless as described. Commision of the European Communities, "EC Assistance."

24. Governments differ in the percentage of aid they disburse in the form of grants.

Among the major European Community countries, Germany disburses a relatively high percentage of aid—nearly 23 percent—in the form of grants, twice as large a percentage as that of France and four times that of Britain. But the German grant levels are no higher, in percentage terms, than those of Japan. Perhaps reflecting its focus on project finance, it is the United States that is the most generous in this regard, extending almost 55 percent of its aid in the form of grants.

25. This point is based on research by Karen Geiffert.

26. Weber, "European Bank," pp. 14–15, 17–18, 22. Weber suggests that the Japanese focus primarily on tied-aid export credits, but aggregate statistics do not support this.

27. Between them the World Bank and the IMF were supplying between 15 and 40 percent of total funding needs, with bilateral and regional aid channeled through the G-24 process (described in more detail later in this chapter) supplying the rest. These figures may exaggerate the role of the G-24 relative to the Bank, since some share of G-24 lending is co-financing for projects on which the World Bank has taken the lead. Commission of the European Communities, "G-24 Assistance to Central and Eastern Europe: Summary Tables," document prepared for the G-24 Ministerial, November 11, 1991, Brussels, mimeographed, November 6, 1991.

28. Commission of the European Communities, "Framework," pp. 3–4.

29. Rollo, *New Eastern Europe,* p. 101.

30. Jacques Pelkmans and Anna Murphy, "Catapulted into Leadership: The Community Trade and Aid Policies vis-à-vis Eastern Europe," Brussels, Center for European Policy Studies Working Documents no. 56 Economic, August 1991. Karen Geiffert advances the same argument in a more nuanced form in "Is the European Bank for Reconstruction and Development Just Another Multilateral Development Bank?" (M.A. thesis, University of Chicago, 1992).

31. Jacques Delors's May 1989 intiative for EC and G-7 action on Polish debt was greeted coolly by Britain, France, and the Netherlands, but the strength of reformist pressures in the summer of 1989 appears to have changed the minds of European leaders. David Buchan, "EC Cool on Loans for Poland to Encourage Reform," *Financial Times,* May 23, 1989, p. 2. Delors had not publicly proposed that the Commission adopt this role. See Pelkmans and Murphy, "Catapulted into Leadership," pp. 11–12.

32. Weber, "European Bank," p. 21; Laux, "Beyond Bretton Woods," p. 9; interview with former U.S. National Security Council official, November 1992.

33. Commission of the European Communities, "PHARE," pp. 5–12.

34. The funds contributed by the EC itself constitute an exception.

35. Commission of the European Communities, "First Annual Report from the Commission to the Council and the European Parliament on the Implementation of Economic Aid to the Countries of East and Central Europe as of 31 December 1990," Brussels, Document SEC (91) 1354, July 24, 1991, p. 8.

36. Commission of the European Communities, "Framework," p. 8. Monitoring includes enforcement of common rules for contributors, overseeing the disbursement of funds, exchanges of information on economic reform programs, and assessment of the impact of support. Commission of the European Communities, "First Annual Report,"

pp. 4, 17; "Declaration of Ministers of the Group of 24 Countries" p. 2; Commission of the European Communities, "External Financing Requirements of the Countries of Central and Eastern Europe and the Potential Need for Complementary Financial Support," Brussels, mimeographed, October 15, 1990.

37. World Wildlife Fund, "Who Knows Where the Money Goes? A Survey of Investments in Central and Eastern Europe," London, mimeographed, March 1991, p. 3.

38. Laux, "Beyond Bretton Woods," p. 24. Existing international organizations held observer status at all G-24 meetings (ibid., p. 10). See also Commission, "PHARE," pp. 5–12.

39. This was not true of all aid to the Soviet Union, where the special bargain between Germany and the Soviets regarding withdrawal from East Germany precluded the imposition of such a restriction.

40. Although technically the standards applied only to PHARE programs, they were applied to national programs as well.

41. Laux, "Beyond Bretton Woods," p. 11, also p. 18.

42. "Communiqué of the Ministers and Governors of the Group of Ten," Washington, D.C., April 29, 1992, cited in Laux, "Bretton Woods," p. 52. Technical assistance was to be handled by the OECD.

43. Peter Riddell, "Row in G-7 over Polish Debt Write-Off," *Financial Times,* February 4, 1991, p. 20; Stephen Fidler, "US Pushes for Write-Off Deal on Polish Debt," *Financial Times,* March 1, 1991, p. 6.

44. Commission of the European Communities, "Framework," p. 5.

45. John M. Starrels, *Assisting Reform in Eastern Europe* (Washington, D.C.: International Monetary Fund, 1991), pp. 10–11, and Feinberg, "Paltry Aid," pp. 39–40, 43.

46. Karl-Heinz Klaine and Ernst Thien, "The Role of the IMF and the World Bank in the Former Eastern Bloc Countries," *Intereconomics* (January-February 1992), 21.

47. Commission of the European Communities, "Framework," p. 9; also "First Annual Report," p. 14. By 1990 the IMF and the World Bank had already worked out macroeconomic adjustment policies for Poland and Hungary, which provided a "basic framework" within which EC and PHARE aid was developed.

48. Other Commission initiatives to coordinate aid have been limited to relatively specific projects, generally environmental or educational, and generally managed in coordination with other donors. Coordinated G-24 appraisal and co-financing have been slow to develop. Commission of the European Communities, "First Annual Report," pp. 15–16; Pelkmans and Murphy, "Catapulted into Leadership," p. 20. On the proposal for a general facility, see also "A Financial Safety Net for Central and Eastern Europe," speech by Frans Andriessen, Euromoney Conference, Berlin, June 11, 1990, pp. 9–11.

49. Stephen Fidler, "Eastern Europe in Transition," *Financial Times,* February 4, 1991, Survey, p. 12.

50. Ian Davidson, Robert Mauthner, and David Buchan, "EC Heads Pledge Economic Help for Eastern Europe," *Financial Times,* November 20, 1989, p. 1; David Buchan, "More Aid to Poland Endorsed," *Financial Times,* October 4, 1989, p. 2. On the leading role of the IMF in the EC, see Pelkmans and Murphy, "Catapulted into Leadership,"

pp. 22–23. One cannot exclude the possibility that member governments, faced with public and diplomatic pressure to provide aid, were all too pleased to permit the IMF to tie their hands.

51. The discussion in this section follows Feinberg, "Paltry Aid," pp. 39–40. Part of the ambiguity of the World Bank's position concerned the proper sequencing of reform efforts—a point contested among expert and academic observers.

52. The activities of the International Finance Corporation (IFC), the World Bank's private arm, are treated later in this chapter.

53. Paul A. Menkveld, *Origin and Role of the European Bank for Reconstruction and Development* (London: Graham and Trotman, 1991), pp. 25–26; Commission of the European Communities, "The European Bank for Reconstruction and Development," Brussels, Background Brief, December 11, 1990, p. 1. Attali himself called it "an obvious idea."

54. The first decision on the EBRD appears to have been taken at a "working dinner" of the EC heads of government called by Mitterrand in the wake of events in Berlin and held in Paris on November 18, 1989. This "impromptu summit" detailed Felipe González, Charles Haughey, and Mitterrand to examine the possibilities of setting up a European development bank. An implicit link to democracy was already forged. In Mitterrand's words: "We are ready to cooperate by all available means toward the creation of healthier economies, in exchange for . . . a verified return to democracy, respect for human rights, and the calling everywhere of free and secret elections." Geiffert, "European Bank," p. 24.

55. This discussion follows Menkveld, *Origin and Role*, pp. 32–44, 50–51. It is unclear how significant the decision not to restrict contracts is, given that nearly every OECD government and a substantial number of newly industrializing countries were already involved. Menkveld maintains that the latter probably did join in order to gain contracts.

56. This closely resembles Mitterrand's tactic in 1983–84 concerning the relaunching of Europe. See Andrew Moravcsik, "National Preference Formation and Interstate Bargaining in the European Community, 1955–1986" (Ph.D. diss., Harvard University, 1992), pp. 572–574.

57. "Friends in High Places," *Euromoney* (June 1990), 28; Menkveld, *Origins and Role*, pp. 24–26, 32–37. A German Ministry of Finance official states that the Germans did not play an active role because "the proposals correspond to our conception of the project."

58. British Overseas Development Institute, "The European Bank for Reconstruction and Development," September 1990.

59. Anthony J. Blinken, "Jacques of All Trades," *New York Times Magazine,* October 13, 1991, pp. 46–48.

60. The members included the G-24, the seven east European countries, Yugoslavia, Cyprus, Malta, Liechtenstein, Israel, Egypt, Morocco, South Korea, Mexico, and the European Community/European Investment Bank.

61. Menkveld, *Origin and Role,* p. 174n.

62. Ibid., p. 56. According to some public justifications by American officials, the United States backed down for this reason.

63. The "soft" German position may have resulted from the Soviet-German bargain, which committed Germany to support aid to the USSR, at least symbolically, despite doubts about the appropriateness of such aid. Leyla Boulton, "Attali Calls for Easing of EBRD Restrictions on Soviet Union," *Financial Times,* June 17, 1991, p. 1; Menkveld, *Origins and Role,* pp. 51–55; Pelkmans and Murphy, "Catapulted into Leadership," pp. 48–51.

64. Weber, "European Bank," p. 44; Menkveld, *Origin and Role,* pp. 61–63. The EBRD was also authorized to take equity positions and underwrite security offerings. Weber points out that the initial French position was not, strictly speaking, inconsistent with support for private lending.

65. Blinken, "Jacques," p. 48. See also Weber, "European Bank," p. 50; "Friends in High Places," p. 26; interview with EBRD official, March 4, 1992.

66. Geiffert, "European Bank," pp. 7–9, 31–34.

67. For an application of this bargaining model, which relies on the "opportunity costs of nonagreement and exclusion," known among negotiating theorists as bargaining on the basis of the "best alternative to negotiated agreement," see Moravcsik, "National Preference Formation."

68. Menkveld, *Origin and Role,* p. 57.

69. Blinken, "Jacques," p. 37.

70. *EIB Information* 65 (July 1990), 1; Feinberg, "Paltry Aid," p. 41; cf. Weber, "European Bank," p. 5.

71. For a sophisticated defense of the EBRD's uniqueness, see Weber, "European Bank," passim. Michel Camdessus points out that the IMF assumes a multiplier of 5. See Lionel Barber, "Camdessus Wins Second Term in Top IMF Post," *Financial Times,* October 1, 1991, p. 5.

72. "Particularly at the outset, the EBRD will cooperate with bilateral donors and existing multilateral development institutions, cofinancing projects already on-line through the World Bank and IFC. Key to the Bank's eventual identity, however, will be its ability to define specific niches among the already existing panoply of international lenders." Feinberg, "Paltry Aid," p. 41.

73. Blinken, "Jacques," p. 48; Feinberg, "Paltry Aid," p. 41; Weber, "European Bank," pp. 52–54.

74. It is therefore hard to know what Attali means when he argues that the "investment bank" structure of the EBRD allows for unique flexibility. See Attali, "The Bank of Europe's Post–Cold War Program," *Harvard International Review* (Fall 1990), 8–11. Menkveld (*Origin and Role,* p. 37), who participated in the negotiations, reports: "Both the IFC and the EIB were starting their own operations in Central and Eastern Europe and were well capable of extending their respective roles in this region." Weber considers the IFC "the major potential competitor to the BERD" ("European Bank," pp. 26–31). On IFC activities, see World Bank Memorandum, "The World Bank Group's Support for Economic Transformation in Central and Eastern Europe," Washington, D.C., June 5, 1991; World Wildlife Fund, "Who Knows," p. 29 and annex 3; IFC, *1991 Annual Report* (Washington, D.C.: IFC, 1991), pp. 44–50; Menkveld, *Origin and Role,* pp. 23, 33–36, 48.

75. On the EIB, see Geiffert, "European Bank," p. 26; Blinken, "Jacques," p. 48; Attali, "Bank of Europe's Post–Cold War Program," pp. 8–11; Menkveld, *Origin and Role,* pp. 23, 29–32, 36–37.

76. Interview with former NSC official, November 1991. See also the testimony of David Mulford, U.S. Department of the Treasury, on European Bank for Reconstruction and Development, Senate hearings before the Subcommittee on International Economic Policy, Trade, Oceans, and Environment, Committee on Foreign Relations, 101/2, March 22, 1990, pp. 13, 57–62.

77. Blinken, "Jacques," p. 48; Weber, "European Bank," p. 5.

78. Blinken, "Jacques," p. 48.

79. Menkveld, *Origin and Role,* p. 37.

80. David Gardner, "Brussels Seeks Closer Links with EC's Eastern Neighbours," *Financial Times,* August 22, 1991, p. 4; Lucy Kellaway, "Conservatism Characterizes Bank's Record—The EIB," *Financial Times,* November 16, 1990, Survey, p. v; Stephen Fidler, "East European Finance," *Financial Times,* November 30, 1990, p. 2.

81. Menkveld, *Origin and Role,* p. 46; see also pp. 30–32.

82. Interview with EC Commission official, November 1991.

83. Stephan Haggard and Robert Kaufman, "Introduction," in *The Politics of Adjustment: International Constraints, Distributive Politics, and the State,* ed. Stephan Haggard and Robert Kaufman (Princeton: Princeton University Press, 1992).

84. For a discussion of these two models of influence, see Miles Kahler, "External Influence, Conditionality, and the Politics of Adjustment," in Haggard and Kaufman, *Politics of Adjustment.*

85. Putnam, "Diplomacy and Domestic Politics."

86. Laux, "Beyond Bretton Woods," p. 15.

87. See Bartlomiej Kaminski, "Systemic Underpinnings of the Transition in Poland: The Shadow of the Round-Table Agreement," *Studies in Comparative Communism* 24, no. 2 (June 1991), 173–190, for an overview of the round-table talks. Also David Lipton and Jeffrey Sachs, "Creating a Market Economy in Eastern Europe: The Case of Poland," *Brookings Papers on Economic Activity,* no. 1 (1990), 109ff.

88. Barbara Bailey, "The IMF in Eastern Europe: The Role of Financial Assistance and Access to Financing" (M.A. thesis, University of Chicago, 1992), p. 31.

89. Economist Intelligence Unit, *Country Report: Poland 1989,* no. 4, pp. 16–17.

90. Prior to the February Paris Club meeting, at least one meeting had taken place between public and private creditors to arrive at a common position, but the banks were unwilling to provide a "breathing space" in interest payments. Economist Intelligence Unit, *Country Report: Poland 1990,* no. 2, p. 16. Also *Washington Post,* March 21, 1991, p. A32; *New York Times,* March 16, 1991, p. A1.

91. Bailey, "IMF in Eastern Europe," p. 33.

92. For a review of these debates, see Janos Kornai, *The Road to a Free Economy: Shifting from a Socialist System: The Example of Hungary* (New York: Norton, 1990).

93. Economist Intelligence Unit, *Country Report: Hungary 1990,* no. 1, p. 23.

94. Alfred Reisch, "Prime Minister Replaces Key Ministers," *Report on Eastern Europe,* February 8, 1991, pp. 11–14.

95. Karoly Okolicsanyi, "The Debate over Economic 'Shock Therapy,'" *Report on East Europe,* January 11, 1991, pp. 11–13.

96. In December the IMF agreed to continue the extended arrangement through 1993, contingent on approval by the parliament of the government's proposed budget deficit. See *Eastern Europe Reporter,* December 9, 1991, p. 154.

97. Bailey, "IMF in Eastern Europe," p. 28.

98. For the argument about the EC's coming of age, see Pelkmans and Murphy, "Catapulted into Leadership."

99. For critiques of generalized acceptance of the public goods assumption, see Keohane, *After Hegemony,* p. 38 and chap. 5, esp. n. 5, p. 83; Joanne Gowa, "Rational Hegemons, Excludable Goods, and Small Groups: An Epitaph for Hegemonic Stability?" *World Politics* 41 (1989), 307–324; Duncan Snidal, "The Limits of Hegemonic Stability Theory," *International Organization* 39 (Autumn 1985), 207–232.

100. For an analogous argument regarding informal agreements, see Charles Lipson, "Why Are Some International Agreements Informal?" *International Organization* 45 (Autumn 1991), 495–538.

101. Feinberg, "Paltry Aid," p. 43.

102. Arthur A. Stein, "Coordination and Collaboration: Regimes in an Anarchic World," *International Organization* 36 (Spring 1982), 299–324.

103. Stein, "Coordination and Collaboration"; Duncan Snidal, "Coordination versus Prisoner's Dilemma: Implications for International Cooperation and Regimes," *American Political Science Review* 79 (December 1985), 923–942.

104. In a sense, these criticisms result from taking the assumptions of the model seriously. For clear statements of these assumptions, see Robert O. Keohane, "The Demand for International Regimes," in *International Regimes,* ed. Stephen Krasner (Ithaca, N.Y.: Cornell University Press, 1983), pp. 141–171, and *After Hegemony,* chaps. 5 and 6.

105. Robert Keohane, "U.S. Compliance with Commitments: Reciprocity and Institutional Enmeshment," seminar paper presented at Program on International Politics, Economics, and Security, University of Chicago, October 24, 1991.

106. Only cooperation in the face of "inconvenient" commitments would constitute strong confirmation of institutionalist prediction. See ibid.

107. This argument follows Moravcsik, "Liberalism and International Relations Theory," which also suggests some broader implications of a pure liberal theory of international institutions.

108. See ibid. In other words, they intervene between the independent causes, found in liberal or realist theory, and state behavior. In direct contradiction to existing regime theory, our findings suggest that as intervening variables they add little to the explanation.

9. Foreign Direct Investment in Eastern Europe

1. For the sake of simplicity, I refer to the formerly communist countries of central and eastern Europe as "eastern Europe."

2. See Steven Greenhouse, "East Europe's Sale of the Century," *New York Times,* May 22, 1990, p. D1.

3. See *The Economist,* "Don't Rush In," June 16, 1990, pp. 14–15.

4. Mikokaj Breitkopf, "Foreign Direct Investment in Poland," Working Paper no. 13, Institute of Finance, Warsaw, 1990.

5. See Breitkopf, "Foreign Direct Investment," p. 24, for full reference.

6. Ewa Sadowska-Cieslak, Roland Pac, and Wojciech Kozyra, "The Goals of Direct Investments and Analysis of Relevant Legislation," in *Foreign Investments in Poland: Regulations, Experience, and Prospects* (Warsaw: Foreign Trade Research Institute, 1990), p. 14.

7. Law on the Principles of Running Small-Scale Industry Businesses by Foreign Persons, *Bulletin of Legislation,* Dz. U. Nr. 19/82 poz. 146.

8. Sadowska-Cieslak, Pac, and Kozyra, "Goals of Direct Investments," p. 14.

9. Law on Companies with Foreign Capital Participation, *Bulletin of Legislation,* Dz. U. Nr. 17/86 poz. 88.

10. Act of Parliament on Economic Activity with the Participation of Foreign Parties, *Bulletin of Legislation,* Dz. U. 41/88.

11. Jerzy Maslankiewicz, "Foreign Investment in Poland," mimeographed, Foreign Investment Agency, Warsaw, June 15, 1991.

12. The Balcerowicz plan (also known as the Sachs plan, after its U.S. adviser, Jeffrey Sachs) is a fairly radical package of macroeconomic stabilization measures intended to push Poland as quickly as possible toward a free market system while simultaneously guarding against inflation. As implemented, the plan entailed the rapid elimination of virtually all price controls; the devaluation and convertibility of the zloty; a severe reduction in government spending on subsidies, the military, and internal security; and the rapid privatization of all state-owned assets. For some of the aftereffects of the plan, see Natalia Wolniansky and Leon P. Garry, "Poland Races toward a Free Market Economy," *Management Review* (April 1991), 37–40; and Stephen Engelberg, "Strikes and Lack of Investors Threaten Polish Austerity Plan," *New York Times,* April 25, 1990, p. A10.

13. "Voucher Power," *The Economist,* Survey: Business in Eastern Europe, September 21, 1991, pp. 18–19.

14. At the time of this writing the exact course of the program was in considerable doubt. The Polish government was already lagging behind the deadlines it set for itself, and growing political opposition (as manifest in the elections of late October 1991) seemed certain to slow the privatization process even further.

15. For an excellent discussion of these risks, see Charles Jonscher, "The Role of Foreign Investment in Poland's Privatisation Programme," in *The Social and Political Consequences of Privatization,* ed. Robert Beschel and Shirley Williams (Cambridge, Mass.: Project Liberty, Harvard University, 1991).

16. See Committee on International Investment and Multinational Enterprises, "Foreign Direct Investment in Central and Eastern Europe," OECD, 1990, p. 8.

17. It is interesting to note in this context that the largest western investors, the ones that Poland most wants to attract, were never really tempted by the tax holidays initially offered. On the contrary, they feared that the holidays were evidence of too much administrative meddling, and preferred a system of more straightforward laws. This point was stressed to me repeatedly in interviews.

18. Sadowska-Cieslak, Pak, and Kozyra, "Goals of Direct Investments," pp. 32–33.

19. Ibid., p. 33.

20. The countries included Great Britain, France, China, North Korea, Austria, Belgium, Italy, and Sweden. Not all of these have yet come into force. For an example, see the Treaty between the Republic of Poland and the United States of America Concerning Business and Economic Relations. For a discussion of the need to guarantee protection of investment, see "New Proposals for Polish Legislation for Foreign Investors," Foreign Investment Agency, Warsaw, June 1991.

21. Ewa Sadowska-Cieslak, "Proposals for Changes of Principles of Functioning Companies with Foreign Capital Participation," Foreign Trade Research Institute, Warsaw, 1990, p. 97.

22. Recognition of the costs of uncertainty is prevalent in all writings on the current changes in Poland. See, for instance, Mikokaj Breitkopf, "Foreign Direct Investment in Poland," Working Paper no. 33, Institute of Finance, Warsaw, 1990, p. 18; Jonscher, "The Role of Foreign Investment in Poland's Privatisation Programme"; and Jerzy Maslankiewicz, "Foreign Investment in Poland," Foreign Investment Agency, mimeographed, June 15, 1991. This point was also confirmed to me in numerous interviews.

23. Interview, Warsaw, June 25, 1991.

24. This point was borne out repeatedly in interviews.

25. Interview, Warsaw, June 24, 1991.

26. Quoted in Suzanne Leoffelhoz, "The Paradox," *Financial World,* March 6, 1990, p. 33. See also Vicky Pryce and David Brown, "Economic Fundamentals in a State of Flux," *Accountancy* (August 1990), 75.

27. Act 173/1988 Coll.

28. "Investment Guide to Czechoslovakia," Federal Agency for Foreign Investment, Prague, 1991; and Ivan Zelenka, "Czechoslovakia: The Curtain Rises on Joint Ventures," *Accountancy* (August 1990), 76–78.

29. Two of the most important laws were the Large-Scale Privatization Act (Act 92/1991 Coll.) and the Decree of the Government of the Czech and Sloval Federal Republic 132/1991 Coll. In addition, the Joint Ventures Act was formally amended.

30. "Investment Guide," pp. 5–6.

31. This is the standard way of avoiding laws which restrict the activities of foreign companies. Basically it just entails the formation of an enterprise under Czech law.

32. The two most relevant laws are the Foreign Exchange Act of November 28, 1990 (instituted on January 1, 1991), and the State Bank of Czechoslovakia Announcement 15 (issued February 22, 1991).

33. Andy Sack, "Direct Foreign Investment in Czechoslovakia," Agency for Foreign Investment, Ministry for Economic Policy and Development, June 25, 1991. See also Charles Leadbeater, "Czechoslovakia to Ease Curbs on Joint Ventures," *Financial Times,* January 12, 1990, p. 5A.

34. For example, see statements in "Memorandum of the Government of the Czechoslovak Socialist Republic to the Commission of the European Communities as the Co-ordinator of the Group of 24," February 1990, mimeographed.

35. A similar though more gentle conclusion appears in Financial Services Volunteer Corps, "Mission to the Czech and Slovak Federal Republic: Observations, Findings, and Recommendations," April 10, 1991. See also "Less Talk, More Action Please," *The Economist,* February 16, 1991, p. 54.

36. See, for instance, Natalia Wolniansky and Leon P. Garry, "Go East, Young Capitalist: Czechoslovakia," *Management Review* (January 1991), 40.

37. Small-Scale Privatization Act 427/1990 Coll., and Large-Scale Privatization Act 29/1991 Coll.

38. Sack, "Direct Foreign Investment in Czechoslovakia," pp. 17–18.

39. The best-known example is Volkswagen's purchase of 50 percent of Skoda, the Czech auto maker.

40. See "Voucher Power," Survey: Business in Eastern Europe, *The Economist,* September 21, 1991, p. 19.

41. Memorandum of the Government of the Czechoslovak Socialist Republic, February 1990, p. 2.

42. Ibid., p. 8.

43. The bilateral treaty between Czechoslovakia and Great Britain, for example, establishes that "investments of investors of either Contracting Party shall not be nationalised, expropriated or subjected to measures having effect equivalent to nationalisation or expropriation . . . in the territory of the other Contracting Party except for a public purpose related to the internal needs of that Party on a non-discriminatory basis and against prompt, adequate and effective compensation."

44. "Investment Guide to Czechoslovakia," pp. 12–13.

45. Testimony of Ambassador Robert L. Barry before the Senate Committee on Appropriations, Subcommittee on Foreign Operations, April 16, 1991, pp. 6–7.

46. Commission of the European Communities, "Relations with Central and East European Countries," Spokesman's Service, November 7, 1990.

47. See World Wildlife Fund, "Who Knows Where the Money Goes: A Survey of Investments in Central and Eastern Europe," March 1991, pp. 2–6.

48. This concentration does not preclude the possibility of public-sector loans as well. See "All Europe's a Stage," *The Economist,* March 16, 1991, p. 489; and Steven Greenhouse, "Talks on Bank to Aid the East Bloc End in Dispute," *New York Times,* January 17, 1990, p. A10.

49. "Foreign Direct Investment in Central and Eastern Europe," seminar held June 21–22, 1990, Centre for Cooperation with the European Economies in Transition, OECD, Paris, 1990, p. 10.

50. Alver Carlson, "Political Upheavals Giving World Bank Unit Bigger Role," *Boston Globe,* September 10, 1990, p. 21.

51. *Document of the Bonn Conference on Economic Cooperation in Europe of the Conference on Security and Cooperation in Europe* (Washington, D.C.: U.S. Government Printing Office, 1990), pp. 6, 7, 9, 15, 11.

52. See OECD, "Foreign Direct Investment." For a country-by-country summary of projects, see World Wildlife Foundation, "Who Knows Where the Money Goes," pp. 15–24.

53. For specific provisions, see the Support for East European Democracy Act of 1989; and the Foreign Operations, Export Financing, and Related Programs Appropriation Act, Public Law 101-53, 101st Congress, November 5, 1990.

54. Media reports from early 1990 are filled with stories about the adventures of western businessmen turning to the east. See, for instance, Patrice Duggan, "These Countries Are Up for Sale," *Forbes,* December 25, 1989, p. 130; and Barry Newman, "Gold Rush," *Wall Street Journal,* April 11, 1990, p. 1.

55. According to the United Nations Economic Commission for Europe, cited in *International Management* (April 1990), 24.

56. "Eastward Ho! The Pioneers Plunge In," *Business Week,* April 15, 1991, p. 51.

57. *Financial World,* March 6, 1990, p. 26.

58. Quoted in *International Management* (April 1990), 24. More cynically, perhaps, a Pole remarked: "It's the fashion. Everyone wants to come to Eastern Europe." Newman, "Gold Rush," p. 1.

59. In one survey executives ranked "political uncertainty" as the primary obstacle to investment, followed by "uncertainty about economic policies," "ability to expatriate earnings and/or capital gains," and "lack of legal protection for private property" (all ranked equally). See Susan M. Collins and Dani Rodrik, *Eastern Europe and the Soviet Union in the World Economy* (Washington, D.C.: Institute for International Economics, 1991), pp. 141ff.

60. After a six-day tour of Hungary, for instance, one U.S. executive concluded that "there are no rules." Added his colleague: "An investment here will be a leap of faith." Quoted in Steve Weiner, "On the Road to Eastern Europe," *Forbes,* December 10, 1990, p. 220. See also Alan Murray, "Poland's Hope for Strong U.S. Investment May Be Misplaced, at Least in the Short Run," *Wall Street Journal,* December 7, 1989, p. A11.

61. See "Less Talk, More Action Please," p. 54.

62. See, for instance, Julie Sychrava, "Curtains Up, Project Financiers," *Euromoney* (April 1990), 55–58.

63. Already the privatization program in Poland appears to be falling prey to political opposition arising from the economic toll that liberalization is imposing. See Stephen Engelberg, "In Polish Vote, a Clear Slap at Reform," *New York Times,* October 29, 1991, p. 3.

64. As of June 1991, the Polish parliament had adopted one hundred new economic laws and was working on drafts of one hundred more. Jerzy Maslankiewicz, "Foreign Investment in Poland," Foreign Investment Agency, mimeographed, June 15, 1991.

65. OECD, "Foreign Direct Investment," p. 21.

66. Commission of the European Communities, "PHARE: Coordinated Support for the Restructuring of the Economies of Certain Central and Eastern European Countries," Meeting of the Group of 24 at Senior Official Level, mimeographed, January 30, 1991, p. 8.

67. On this point, see DeAnne Julius, "Foreign Direct Investment: The Neglected Twin of Trade," Occasional Papers no. 33 Group of Thirty, Washington, D.C., 1991.

68. On the relationship between institutional richness and international cooperation, see the "Introduction" to this volume, by Joseph S. Nye, Jr., and Robert O. Keohane.

69. In some cases the sheer number of advisers seems to be a source of irritation to the east Europeans. Many of them are grumbling that the advisers do not stay long enough, or know enough about the specific problems of the region. In addition, there is considerable resentment that western governments are using eastern money to pay their own consultants, rather than injecting it more directly into the economies of eastern Europe. One highly placed official in Poland, in fact, pleaded with me to "tell them [the western governments] not to send any more management consultants!"

70. In addition, acceptance of international codes such as the OECD guidelines can minimize the risk that the eastern European countries will compete among themselves to attract scarce western investment. This point is stressed in Blanka Kalinova, "The Macro-Economic and Micro-Economic Environment for FDI," IEWSS Conference, Stirin, Czechoslovakia, July 3–7, 1991. See also OECD, "Foreign Direct Investment." On the role of institutions in reducing risk and increasing predictability, see the "Introduction" to this volume.

10. East-West Environmental Politics after 1989

This chapter is based on research conducted in Prague, Warsaw, Geneva, Brussels, and London during the summer of 1991. I am indebted to the many officials who granted me interviews and access to documention. For financial support, I am grateful to the Center for International Affairs and Center for European Studies at Harvard University. I thank Hildegard Bedarff, Abram Chayes, Margaret Karns, Robert Keohane, Michael Schecter, participants in the November 16, 1991, post–Cold War settlement workshop at Harvard, and members of the MIT Study Group on East European Environmental Policy for helpful comments on earlier drafts. I owe much to Anna Jancewicz and Romney Resney for valuable research assistance.

1. The distinction between cooptation and socialization is in part a matter of degree. Cooptation does not require internal change at either the cognitive or the organizational level. A state is coopted when it is given an opportunity to do something it already wants to do and can do, but under terms and conditions set by the state doing the coopting; giving Ukraine a seat at the UN is cooptation. Socialization implies either resistance or lack of capacity overcome by deliberate strategies of the socializer. Training the Ukraine government in principles of civilian military control is socialization. John Ikenberry and Charles

Kupchan define socialization as "a process of learning in which norms and ideals are transmitted from one party to another," often accompanied by material inducements. John G. Ikenberry and Charles A. Kupchan, "Socialization and Hegemonic Power," *International Organization* 44, 3 (Summer 1990), 289. I consider transfer of skills to be an important component of socialization as well.

2. The origins of LRTAP are described in Evgeny M. Chossudovsky, *East-West Diplomacy for Environment in the United Nations* (New York: UNITAR, n.d.). I discuss the workings of LRTAP in "European Acid Rain: The Power of Tote-Board Diplomacy," in *Institutions for the Earth: Sources of Effective International Environmental Protection,* ed. Peter M. Haas, Robert O. Keohane, and Marc A. Levy (Cambridge, Mass.: Harvard University Press, 1993).

3. Data from European Monitoring and Evaluation Program (EMEP), EMEP/MSC-W Report 2/90, August 1990, p. 8.

4. UN Economic Commission for Europe, *Energy Reforms in Central and Eastern Europe—The First Year* (New York: United Nations, 1991), pp. 24–26.

5. The Soviet Union represents a special case. The Soviet government insisted on a clause in the 1985 sulfur dioxide protocol permitting a signatory to reduce either its total emissions or its transboundary flows by 30 percent. Because the prevailing winds blow from west to east, and the USSR has such a large land mass, this clause permits it to comply without much costly adjustment simply by shifting dirty power production eastward. Nuclear power was concentrated in the west in part for this reason. This chapter does not deal with Soviet relations with the west on environmental matters.

6. Data from EMEP Report 2/90, p. 8. Percentages include Soviet emissions.

7. Bo Thunberg, "East Germany's Modernest Lignite-Fired Power Station: Emissions as High as All of Sweden's," *Acid Magazine* 8 (September 1989), 15–18.

8. Diffuse and specific reciprocity are discussed in Robert O. Keohane, "Reciprocity in International Relations," *International Organization* 40, 1 (Winter 1986), 1–27. On linked versus unlinked bargaining, see James K. Sebenius, *Negotiating the Law of the Sea* (Cambridge, Mass.: Harvard University Press, 1984), 182–207.

9. The 1988 NO_x protocol did contain articles mandating that states facilitate exchange of technology. However, these articles are much less precise than the emissions control articles, and it is difficult to imagine how a state could fail to comply with them.

10. "Means and Measures, Including Financial Mechanisms, to Promote the International Exchange of Technology for Abatement of Air Pollution from Stationary Sources," ECE/UNDP/AP/15/R.10, September 14, 1990.

11. Economic Commission for Europe, *Energy Reforms in Central and Eastern Europe,* p. 26.

12. *Acid News,* no. 3 (October 1991), 12.

13. A survey of bilateral east-west environmental agreements conducted in late 1989 reveals that seven of the thirteen agreements were between East and West Germany. Helmut Schreiber, "East-West Cooperation in the Environment in Europe: Problems, Strategies, Perspectives," study for the National Energy Administration of Sweden, January 1990. Inter-German environmental cooperation is reviewed in Helmut Schreiber,

"Inter-German Issues of Environmental Policy," in *To Breathe Free: Eastern Europe's Environmental Crisis,* ed. Joan DeBardebelen (Baltimore: Johns Hopkins University Press, 1991).

14. K. R. Bull, "The Critical Loads/Levels Approach to Gaseous Pollutant Emission Control," *Environmental Pollution* 69 (1991), 105–123. The most comprehensive maps to date have been published in Jean-Paul Hetteling, Robert J. Downing, and Peter A. M. de Smet, eds., "Mapping Critical Loads for Europe: CCE Technical Report No. 1," LRTAP Coordinating Center for Effects, Netherlands National Institute of Public Health and Environmental Protection, Bilthoven, RIVM Report no. 259101001, July 1991.

15. "Economic Principles for Allocating the Costs of Reducing Sulphur Emissions in Europe," *Air Pollution Studies,* no. 7 (1991), UN ECE/EB.AIR/26, pp. 63–80.

16. See Chapter 7 by Kalypso Nicolaïdis in this volume.

17. Interview with OECD officials, Paris, January 22, 1991. On the Council of Europe, see the council's presentation to the Environment for Europe Conference, Dobris, Czechoslovakia, June 21–23, 1991.

18. Much the way North America and Scandinavia do at present.

19. As of June 23, 1991, Poland, Hungary, and Czechoslovakia had signed memoranda of participation in the Partners program. These countries and Bulgaria, Romania, and the Soviet Union participate in the center.

20. Interview with OECD officials, January 22, 1991. See also the statement of the OECD to the Environment for Europe Conference, Dobris, Czechoslovakia, June 21–23, 1991: "The OECD considers that the role it is best equipped to play in supporting an environmental strategy for Europe is to continue to serve as an international forum for policy analysis and policy dialogue, focusing especially on the relationships between economic growth and environmental management objectives" (p. 4).

21. OECD Statement to Environment for Europe Conference, pp. 13–16.

22. European Communities, "The European Environment Agency," Information Sheet 1, May 1, 1990; and "The European Environment Agency and Third Countries," Information Sheet 2, May 21, 1990.

23. *Presse Environnement* (Paris), June 6, 1991, p. 1; see also *Financial Times,* April 28, 1991, p. 4.

24. *Presse Environnement* (Paris), June 30, 1989, p. 2.

25. UN Economic Commission for Europe, "Strategies and Policies for Air Pollution Abatement: 1990 Review," ECE/EB.AIR/27, 1991. The 1986 review can be found in ECE/EB.AIR/14.

26. Compliance questions are receiving much closer scrutiny in current protocol negotiations in LRTAP.

27. Regional Environmental Center, statement to Environment for Europe Conference, Dobris, Czechoslovakia, June 21–23, 1991. See also the Center's *Information Bulletin* 1, 2 (March 1991), and *International Environment Reporter,* February 27, 1991, pp. 110–111.

28. The Commission held a seminar at the center, for example, for east European government and private-sector representatives on EC environmental law.

29. Ernst B. Haas, *When Knowledge Is Power: Three Models of Change in International Organizations* (Berkeley: University of California Press, 1990), p. 3.

30. "The Environmental Dimension of European Integration," Statement of Josef Vavrousek to Environment for Europe Conference, Dobris, Czechoslovakia, June 21–23, 1991, p. 2.

31. There are reports that western officials attended the second European Environment Ministers conference in Dobris, Czechoslovakia, under duress (because of the political need to support Vaclav Havel) and complained about its being a waste of time.

32. Interview with officials in Poland, European Commission, Economic Commission for Europe.

33. U.K. House of Commons Environment Committee, "The Proposed European Environment Agency," Session 1988–89, Seventh Report with Minutes of Evidence, London, HMSO, November 13, 1989.

34. Interviews with Commission officials, Brussels, July 11–12, 1991.

35. For a thoroughly researched review of the state of such assistance as of early 1991, see World Wildlife Fund, "Who Knows Where the Money Goes," March 1991.

36. G-24 coordination consists formally of an annual ministerial meeting to review developments, quarterly meetings of senior officials to prepare common strategies, more regular meetings of a "Brussels Network" of Brussels-based G-24 officials to monitor coordination, and regular meetings of sectoral working groups (including an environment working group) and task-specific ad hoc groups. "G-24 Progress Report: Strengthening the Coordination," paper presented at meeting of the Group of 24 at Senior Officials Level, Brussels, June 13, 1991.

37. European Commission, "Environment Sector Strategy for Central and Eastern Europe," June 15, 1991, p. 3.

38. The dominance of particularistic over common goals applies to the G-24 assistance overall. See Chapter 8 by Stephan Haggard and Andrew Moravcsik in this volume.

39. European Commission, PHARE, G-24 Coordination Unit, untitled document, April 29, 1991.

40. "Information about Initiatives and Existing Projects in the Field of Bilateral and Multilateral Financial Cooperation of Poland and Countries of ECE Region of Relevance to Environmental Protection," Institute of Environmental Protection, Warsaw, August 5, 1990.

41. World Wildlife Fund, "Who Knows Where the Money Goes," pp. 15–23.

42. PHARE originally stood for Pologne Hongrie—Aide à la Reforme Economique. The name has stuck even though assistance is now also provided to Czechoslovakia and Romania. The term is sometimes used to refer to coordinated G-24 assistance as a whole.

43. European Commission, "Environment Sector Strategy for Central and Eastern Europe," p. 6.

44. The initial aid efforts were consistent with the Coase theorem; their rejection in favor of more diffuse programmatic aid represents the realization that the conditions required by the Coase theorem were not present in eastern Europe. According to the Coase theorem, externality problems (such as pollution crossing a border) can be solved,

regardless of how property rights are distributed, by making side payments; a victimized state can reach a favorable outcome by paying the polluting state to reduce. See Ronald Coase, "The Problem of Social Cost," *Journal of Law and Economics* 3 (1960), 1–44. For a discussion concerning environmental politics, see Ralph C. d'Arge and Allen V. Kneese, "State Liability for International Environmental Degradation: An Economic Perspective," *Natural Resources Journal* 20 (July 1980), 427–450. The preconditions which did not obtain in eastern Europe were the absence of transaction costs and the presence of perfect information.

45. Consultation of confidential World Bank reports, interviews with World Bank, Polish Government, and PHARE officials, June–July 1991.

46. World Wide Fund for Nature, "The European Bank for Reconstruction and Development: An Environmental Opportunity," October 1990. The Center for International Environmental Law also played an instrumental role in pressuring member states to include environmental safeguards in the EBRD's charter.

47. Interview with EBRD officials, July 31, 1991. Some environmentalists consider the EBRD's environment measures to fall seriously short, particularly their provisions for public participation and access to information. See Center for International Environmental Law—U.S., "Promoting Sustainable Development and Democracy in Central and Eastern Europe: The Role of the European Bank for Reconstruction and Development," Washington, D.C., July 1991.

48. This information comes from "Statement from the Nordic Investment Bank," Environment for Europe Conference, Dobris, Czechoslovakia, June 21–23, 1991; and World Wildlife Fund, "Who Knows Where the Money Goes," p. 25.

49. European Investment Bank, "Environmental Protection," 1990.

50. European Investment Bank, statement to Environment for Europe Conference, Dobris, Czechoslovakia, June 21–23, 1991.

51. "Redirecting Debt Service for Environmental Recovery Purposes," memorandum of Poland's Ministry of Environment, March 5, 1991; and Republic of Poland, "Government Initiative on Environmental Fund," June 11, 1991.

52. "Norway Assists Poland in Linking Debt to Environment," Norwegian government press release, June 11, 1991.

53. Republic of Poland, "Government Initiative on Environmental Fund." This document outlines the technical terms of the proposal as follows: Poland would be permitted to reduce its payments to the Bank for International Settlements by an amount equal to qualifying Trust Fund expenditures, up to a maximum of 20 percent of the debt stream following the Paris Club agreement (or 10 percent prior to the agreement). The annual rate of available expenditure would begin at approximately $120 million and increase over time along with the Paris Club debt service profile.

54. See UN Economic Commission for Europe, "Economic Principles for Allocating the Costs of Reducing Sulphur Emissions in Europe," pp. 61–78, in *Air Pollution Studies 7: Assessment of Long-Range Transboundary Air Pollution*, ECE/EB.AIR/26 (New York: United Nations, 1991). The idea is also discussed in Schreiber, "East-West Cooperation in the Environment," pp. 38–40.

55. The Global Environment Facility accepts voluntary contributions from developed countries, which it uses to finance environmental projects in developing countries. It was established in November 1990 with initial commitments of about $1.5 billion. See "The Global Environment Facility," *Finance and Development* 28, 1 (March 1991), 24.

56. Interview with Swedish environment official, February 1, 1991. A Swedish Environmental Protection Agency review found 180 international environmental bodies requiring active participation.

57. A third track is intended to permit countries with large land masses or very low transborder pollution flows (such as Russia) to restrict emissions only in certain parts of the country. The protocol is intended as an admittedly arbitrary first step, to be followed by more precisely framed regulations based on critical loads. See *ENDS Report,* no. 193 (February 1991), 39.

58. Interview with protocol negotiators, January–February 1991, Geneva. See Levy, "European Acid Rain," for more details.

59. See Chapter 8 in this volume.

60. Interviews with Polish and Czechoslovak government officials and parliamentarians. The Czech industry ministry endorsed new air pollution legislation which was modeled on one of the strictest air pollution laws in Europe—Germany's—and which adopted tougher standards in some cases than many western countries have (Czech interviews). A Polish industrialist announced approvingly in October 1990 that the government would adopt EC environmental standards within ten years. *International Environment Reporter,* October 24, 1990, p. 435.

61. Government of Poland, Ministry of Environmental Protection, Natural Resources, and Forestry, "National Environmental Policy," Warsaw, 1990. LRTAP's sulfur protocol requires 30 percent reductions by 1993, which Poland has concluded it cannot meet.

62. Bedrich Moldan et al., *Environmental Recovery Program for the Czech Republic* (Prague: Academia, 1991), p. 38.

63. Ernst B. Haas, *The Uniting of Europe: Political, Social, and Economic Forces, 1950–1957* (Stanford. Stanford University Press, 1958), pp. 283–317. For a critical discussion of the spillover concept, see Robert O. Keohane and Stanley Hoffmann, "Institutional Change in Europe in the 1980s," in *The New European Community,* ed. Robert Keohane and Stanley Hoffmann (Boulder, Colo.: Westview Press, 1991), pp. 18–22.

64. The Treaty of Rome made no provisions for environmental policy, yet the EC grew increasingly active in the field, largely to manage the potential trade distortions of unharmonized policy. The Single European Act of 1987 provided a legal basis for environmental policy per se. See Stanley Johnson and Guy Corcelle, *The Environmental Policy of the European Communities* (London: Graham and Trotman, 1989).

65. Unpublished World Bank documents and interviews with Bank and Polish officials, June–July 1991.

66. Interview with Polish government officials, June–July 1991.

67. Government of Poland, "National Environmental Policy."

68. Interviews with Federal Committee for the Environment, World Bank, and EBRD officials, July 1991.

69. In the summer of 1992 it appeared that the Czech and Slovak Federal Republic (Czechoslovakia) was destined for dissolution. Environmental officials in the Czech Republic indicated, in conversations in June 1992, that dissolution, regardless of its overall results, was expected to streamline environmental policy-making.

70. See Tomasz Zylicz, "National Environmental Policy: Outline of Economic Instruments," Ministry of Environmental Protection, Warsaw, September 1990; Tomasz Zylicz, "Socio-Economic Environmental Research in Poland: Background, Priorities, Cooperation," photocopy, Warsaw, November 1990. Zylicz is economics director of the Polish Ministry of Environmental Protection.

11. Pursuing Military Security in Eastern Europe

I would like to express my appreciation to the other members of the post–Cold War settlement group as well as Robert Art, Michael Desch, Grzegorz Ekiert, Samuel Huntington, Kenneth Oye, several European officials and academics, and members of the Radio Free Europe/Radio Liberty (RFE/RL) Research Institute and the Center for Foreign Policy Development at Brown University for commenting on earlier drafts of this manuscript. I would also like to thank the NATO research fellowship program and the institutions and Academy Scholars programs at the Center for International Affairs for financial assistance. None of these individuals or organizations bear any responsiblity for my conclusions.

1. Each analyst tends to employ the term *national security* to encompass a different range of issues. This chapter, while recognizing the importance for a nation's survival of factors such as economic development and social stability, nevertheless focuses on military threats perceived from other states. Concentrating on defense against armed aggression allows for analytic clarity and a manageable scope. In addition to the other chapters in this volume, for perspectives on Europe's broader security problems, see Jacques Delors, "European Integration and Security," *Survival,* 33, no. 2 (March/April 1991), 99–109; Jenonne Walker, "Keeping America in Europe," *Foreign Policy,* no. 83 (Summer 1991), 128–142; and Robert E. Hunter, "The Future of European Security," *Washington Quarterly,* 13, no. 4 (Autumn 1991), 55–68. For a defense of the traditional approach to European security, see Richard H. Ullman, *Securing Europe* (Princeton: Princeton University Press, 1991), p. xii.

2. Although this chapter focuses on how states relate to international institutions, it recognizes both that governments employ a variety of means to pursue their objectives and that institutions may not always represent the most effective instruments for ensuring military security.

3. Because the two independent variables that most affected the east European countries' security policies—the collapse of Soviet power and the reunification of Germany—occurred in 1989 and 1990, this chapter focuses on the period from 1989 to the aborted Soviet coup of August 1991. The subsequent disintegration of the USSR so changed the

European security environment that an analysis of the east European governments' defense policies after August 1991 must await a later study.

4. Unlike the other issue area studies, this chapter does not speculate about the domestic sustainability of the new east-west bargains. I believe that developments outside the region, particularly the policies of the great powers, will most affect the compliance of the east European countries with the post–Cold War security settlement.

5. For a useful typology of the decisions architects of institutions must consider, see Ernest B. Haas, *When Knowledge Is Power: Three Models of Change in International Organizations* (Berkeley: University of California Press, 1990), pp. 59–61.

6. For more detail than can be presented here, see Richard Weitz, "NATO and the New Eastern Europe," *Report on Eastern Europe,* May 24, 1991, pp. 30–35; and Richard Weitz, "Explaining NATO's Persistence: State Behavior and Institutional Survival in a Changing World Order" (Ph.D. diss., Harvard University, forthcoming).

7. Erich Hauser, *Frankfurter Rundschau,* March 22, 1991.

8. RFE/RL correspondent (Michael Bartholomew), February 14, 1991.

9. For an analysis of the London declaration, see Herbert Kremp, *Die Welt,* July 12, 1990.

10. Reuters, *Sueddeutsche Zeitung,* August 11, 1990; "Regulaere Beziehungen zwischen Polen under der NATO," *Neue Zuercher Zeitung,* August 11, 1990; and Radio Sofia, August 30, 1990.

11. Cited in Reuters, March 21, 1991.

12. Cited in Reuters, November 20, 1990.

13. Cited in Reuters, March 21, 1991.

14. *Liberation,* cited in AP, October 17, 1990.

15. RFE/RL correspondent (Michael Bartholomew), December 14, 1990.

16. Cited in AP, September 13, 1990.

17. *Liberation,* cited in AP, October 17, 1990.

18. RFE/RL correspondent (Michael Bartholomew), September 6, 1990; and "Zeiten der Konfrontation vorbei," *Frankfurter Allgemeine Zeitung,* September 7, 1990.

19. Cited in "Gorbatschow nimmt Einladung Woerners zu NATO-Besuch an," *Die Welt,* July 16, 1990.

20. Cited in DPA, November 29, 1990. See also Woerner's remarks cited in "Zeiten der Konfrontation vorbei," *Frankfurter Allgemeine Zeitung,* September 7, 1990; and "Osten sieht NATO als stabilisierend an," *Sueddeutsche Zeitung,* December 1, 1990.

21. For more detail on the CSCE's new structures and procedures than space here allows, see Richard Weitz, "The CSCE's New Look," *RFE/RL Research Report,* February 7, 1992, pp. 27–31.

22. Cited in R. C. Longworth, *Chicago Tribune,* November 18, 1990.

23. The North Atlantic Assembly also provided several east European legislators with an opportunity twice a year to discuss security issues with their American counterparts. Given their lack of funds, the expense involved in traveling to the United States, and the difficulty of attempting to secure meetings with U.S. congressmen, the east Europeans

highly valued the assembly and the CSCE because these institutions significantly reduced the transaction costs associated with meeting U.S. policymakers (interview with an official of the North Atlantic Assembly).

24. Interviews with east European officials and security experts.

25. Stefan Lehne, "Vom Prozess zur Institution: Zur aktuellen Debatte ueber die Weiterentwicklung des KSZE-Prozesses," *Europa-Archiv,* no. 16 (1990), 500.

26. RFE/RL correspondent (Roland Eggleston), November 21, 1990.

27. The preamble to the 1990 CFE (Conventional Forces in Europe) Treaty, the 1990 Bonn declaration on economic principles, the 1989 Copenhagen declaration on human rights, the 1989 Vienna Concluding Document, and the 1975 Helsinki Final Act provide other comprehensive statements of principles.

28. Borders can be changed by peaceful means only when all concerned parties agree to such alterations and the revisions take place in accordance with international law.

29. Cited in James E. Goodby, "A New European Concert: Settling Disputes in the CSCE," *Arms Control Today,* 21, no. 1 (January/February 1991), 5.

30. Cited in RFE/RL correspondent (Roland Eggleston), June 24, 1991.

31. Cited in Michael Binyon, *The Times* (London), June 20, 1991.

32. Cited in Hansjakob Stehle, *Die Zeit,* July 12, 1991; and Reuters, July 5, 1991. See also Martin Winter, *Frankfurter Rundschau,* June 29, 1991.

33. For information on the original intent of the Conflict Prevention Center's emergency procedure, see "Die KSZE-Mechanismen im Fall Jugoslawien," *Neue Zuercher Zeitung,* July 3, 1991.

34. "Erste Erprobung der KSZE-Krisenmechanismen," *Neue Zuercher Zeitung,* July 7, 1991.

35. Cited in Reuters, June 28, 1991.

36. For a review of this meeting, see Tim Judah and Gerard Davies, *The Times* (London), August 9, 1991; *New York Times,* August 10, 1991; and "KSZE entsendet weitere Beobachter nach Jugoslawien," *Sueddeutsche Zeitung,* August 10, 1991.

37. Cited in Reuters, July 5, 1991.

38. For a discussion of the United States' role in keeping the CSCE weak, see Barry James, *International Herald Tribune,* November 16, 1990; Edward Mortimer, *Financial Times,* November 16, 1990; Robert C. Toth and Norman Kempster, *Los Angeles Times,* November 18, 1990; Peter Pringle, *The Independent,* November 19, 1990; Daniel N. Nelson, "Europe's Unstable East," *Foreign Policy,* no. 82 (Spring 1991), 155–156; Walker, "Keeping America in Europe," pp. 137–138; James Goodby, "Commonwealth and Concert: Organizing Principles of Post-Containment Order in Europe," *Washington Quarterly,* 14, no. 3 (Summer 1991), 83–84; and Weitz, "Explaining NATO's Persistence."

39. Sarah Helm, *The Independent,* June 20, 1991; Alan Philips, *Daily Telegraph,* June 20, 1991; Gerard Davies, *The Times* (London), July 5, 1991; Robert Mauthner and Arlane Genillard, *Financial Times,* July 5, 1991; Karl-Peter Schwarz, *Die Presse,* July 5, 1991; Robert Mauthner, *Financial Times,* July 6, 1991; "Erste Erprobung der KSZE-Krisenmechanismen," *Neue Zuercher Zeitung,* July 7, 1991; and "KSZE befuerwortet zwei Missionen," *Sueddeutsche Zeitung,* July 8, 1991. As Celeste Wallander and Jane

Prokop demonstrate in Chapter 2, Soviet officials had originally been among the leading proponents of strengthening the CSCE.

40. For a discussion of the analytical value of such focused pairing, see Peter Gourevitch, *Politics in Hard Times: Comparative Responses to International Economic Crises* (Ithaca, N.Y.: Cornell University Press, 1986), pp. 66, 68.

41. Krzysztof Skubiszewski, "Change versus Stability in Europe: A Polish View," *World Today,* 46, nos. 8–9 (August/September 1990), 149.

42. Thomas Urban, *Sueddeutsche Zeitung,* January 25, 1990.

43. Polish leaders also urged the USSR to agree to Germany's remaining in NATO. They expected membership to moderate Germany's external behavior (interview with Czechoslovak official).

44. Public opinion polls illustrated the changed perception. Jan B. de Weydenthal, "The Polish-German Reconciliation," *Report on Eastern Europe,* July 5, 1991, p. 21.

45. In private Dienstbier stressed to western officials the need to prevent the Germans from developing another "Versailles complex" of alienation from the new European order (interview with a Czechoslovak official).

46. Cited in AP, February 20, 1990.

47. "Sovetsko-chekhoslovatskie peregovory," *Pravda,* February 28, 1990.

48. Jonathan C. Randal, *Washington Post,* February 8, 1990; CTK, April 14, 1991, and April 21, 1991.

49. For a review of the issue, see "Prague Promised New Pact by Kohl," *The Times* (London), May 10, 1991; "Sudeten Issue Mars New Treaty," *The Independent,* August 7, 1991; and Reuters, August 7, 1991. The first quote is from *The Independent,* the second from Reuters, August 7, 1991.

50. TASS, November 22, 1989.

51. The Soviet authorities had made known in advance their desire that Polish communists retain the senior positions in the defense and interior ministries "and perhaps the Foreign Ministry." L. Toporkov, "Pol'sha: nazhachen Prem'er-Ministr," *Izvestiya,* August 20, 1989. The announcement of the appointment of two communists occurred only after a senior Solidarity official had returned from talks with Soviet policymakers in Moscow. John Gray, *Toronto Globe and Mail,* August 29, 1989.

52. For examples of Polish efforts to downplay the level of anti-Soviet sentiment in Poland, see Mazowiecki's remarks in his interview with TASS, November 22, 1989. During his visit to Moscow later that month, Mazowiecki apologized for the incidents of vandalism against Soviet graves and memorials in Poland. Francis X. Clines, *New York Times,* November 25, 1989; and Stefan Dietrich, *Frankfurter Allgemeine Zeitung,* November 27, 1989. For Soviet expressions of concern about the Polish government's failure to combat the rise of anti-Sovietism in Poland, see "Neponyatnoe molchanie," *Trud,* September 29, 1989; and Thomas Urban, *Sueddeutsche Zeitung,* December 11, 1989.

53. "Novoe pravitel'stvo—novaya filosofiya," *Izvestiya,* August 24, 1989. Shortly thereafter Soviet Foreign Ministry spokesperson Yuri Gremitskikh said that his government was "happy to hear" of Mazowiecki's pledge (cited in AP, August 25, 1989). For additional examples of such statements, see Bill Keller, *New York Times,* August 21, 1989;

Pravda, August 25, 1989; John Gray, *Toronto Globe and Mail,* August 29, 1989; PAP, September 21, 1989; Reuters, October 18, 1989; Anna Swidlicka, "Polish Government Spokesman Presents Foreign Policy Aims," *Radio Free Europe Research,* October 19, 1989, pp. 1–2; Mazowiecki's interview with TASS, November 22, 1989; Michael Parks, *Los Angeles Times,* November 25, 1989; "Mazowiecki findet bei Gorbatschow Verstaendnis fuer seine Politik," *Frankfurter Allgemeine Zeitung,* November 27, 1989; and Thomas Urban, *Sueddeutsche Zeitung,* January 25, 1990.

54. *Rzeczpospolita,* cited in John Tagliabue, *New York Times,* October 24, 1989. See also Swidlicka, "Polish Government Spokesman Presents Aims," p. 3; "Vor einer Bestandsaufnahme der polnisch-sowjetischen Beziehungen," *Frankfurter Allgemeine Zeitung,* October 25, 1989; Skubiszewski, "Change versus Stability in Europe," p. 150; and Adam Ulam, *Expansion and Coexistence: Soviet Foreign Policy, 1917–73,* 2nd ed. (New York: Holt, Rinehart and Winston, 1974), pp. 360, 399–400.

55. Swidlicka, "Polish Government Spokesman Presents Aims," p. 2. See also Michael Dobbs, *Washington Post,* November 26, 1989.

56. Cited in Mary Battiata, *Washington Post,* October 25, 1989.

57. Cited in Thomas Urban, *Sueddeutsche Zeitung,* October 24, 1989. See also Bill Keller, *New York Times,* November 26, 1989; and Anna Sabbat-Swidlicka, "Polish Senate Contemplates Policy on Eastern Neighbors," *Radio Free Europe Research,* September 7, 1990, pp. 2–3.

58. See, for example, the remarks of President Jaruzelski cited in "Polen verlangt Beobachter-Status bei der Sechser-Konferenz ueber Deutschland," *Frankfurter Allgemeine Zeitung,* February 15, 1990. See also Josef Riedmiller, *Sueddeutsche Zeitung,* February 23, 1990.

59. See, for example, the remarks of Polish Deputy Defense Minister Janusz Onyszkiewicz, cited in RFE/RL correspondent (Stuart Parrott), September 6, 1990.

60. "Die Positionen Warschaus und Moskaus weit auseinander," *Frankfurter Allgemeine Zeitung,* February 14, 1991; and Stephen Engelberg, *New York Times,* April 10, 1991.

61. Cited in AP, January 10, 1991.

62. Ibid.

63. Cited in Stephen Engelberg, *New York Times,* January 17, 1991.

64. BBC World Service, February 14, 1991.

65. Cited in Reuters, March 11, 1991.

66. Cited in Stephen Engelberg, *New York Times,* March 18, 1991.

67. "Woerner: Wir respektieren jede Entscheidung," *Frankfurter Allgemeine Zeitung,* September 14, 1990. See also Skubiszewski's statement in April 1990, cited in Tanjug, April 18, 1990.

68. Cited in Jan B. de Weydenthal, "Polish Foreign Policy," *Radio Free Europe Research,* April 27, 1990, p. 3.

69. See, for example, Walesa's remarks, cited in AFP, April 3, 1991.

70. However, Skubiszewski did support the Baltic states' efforts to attain observer status at the CSCE (Reuters, October 2, 1990).

71. Klaus Bachmann, *Die Presse*, March 27, 1990; and Ulrich Schmidla, *Die Welt*, February 4, 1991. Approximately 300,000 residents of Polish extraction live in Lithuania.

72. Cited in Roger Boyes, *The Times* (London), February 19, 1991. He remarked to foreign journalists that the developments in Lithuania foreshadowed an attempt by the Soviet empire to recoup its losses of the previous two years and placed Poland in "mortal danger." Cited in "Neue sicherheitspolitische Ueberlegungen in Polen," *Neue Zuercher Zeitung,* January 23, 1991.

73. See, for example, Deputy Defense Minister Janusz Onyszkiewicz's statement, cited in PAP, November 15, 1990.

74. Cited in Jan B. De Weydenthal, "Prospects for Polish-Soviet Relations," *Report on Eastern Europe,* September 20, 1991, p. 13. See also Jan B. De Weydenthal, "Building a National Security System," *Report on Eastern Europe,* June 14, 1991, p. 15; and Rowland Evans and Robert Novak, *Washington Post,* June 21, 1991.

75. "Warschau sucht Annaeherung an die NATO," *Sueddeutsche Zeitung,* February 28, 1991; "The Limbo People," *The Economist,* November 17, 1990, p. 60; PAP, January 10, 1991; and interview with a Polish official (citation in PAP, January 10, 1991).

76. Cited in AP and AFP, April 3, 1991.

77. Cited in PAP, April 26, 1991.

78. Statement before the Sejm, June 27, 1991; English text provided by the Polish embassy in Brussels.

79. Cited in Henry Kamm, *International Herald Tribune,* February 14, 1990.

80. The declaration is reprinted in "Rabochiy vizit," *Pravda,* February 27, 1990.

81. Interview with Czechoslovak official.

82. Cited in Reuters, April 29, 1991, and CTK, April 29, 1991.

83. For a review of the negotiations, see Jonathan C. Randal, *Washington Post,* February 8, 1990; Reuters, February 25, 1990; Francis X. Clines, *New York Times,* February 27, 1990; "Gorbatschow und Havel besiegeln Truppenabzug," *Frankfurter Allgemeine Zeitung,* February 27, 1990; Bernhard Kueppers, *Sueddeutsche Zeitung,* February 28, 1990; and Jan Obrman, "Withdrawal of Soviet Troops Completed," *Report on Eastern Europe,* July 26, 1991, pp. 14–20.

84. Cited in CTK, February 26, 1990.

85. Jan Obrman, "Interview with First Deputy Chief of the General Staff," *Report on Eastern Europe,* July 20, 1990, p. 15; see also the subsequent joint declaration of the Czechoslovak and German foreign ministers (cited in ADN, April 11, 1991).

86. John Tagliabue, *New York Times,* December 16, 1989.

87. Cited in Lally Weymouth, *Washington Post,* February 18, 1990.

88. Henry Kamm, *New York Times,* June 13, 1990, cited in Jan B. de Weydenthal, "Changing Views on Security in Eastern Europe," *Report on Eastern Europe,* July 20, 1990, p. 47.

89. See, for example, the citations in Jan Obrman, "Putting the Country Back on the Map," *Report on Eastern Europe,* December 28, 1990, pp. 11–12; and Daniel N. Nelson, "Europe's Unstable East," *Foreign Policy,* no. 82 (Spring 1991), 149.

90. *Neue Zuercher Zeitung,* January 17, 1991, cited in Curt Gasteyger, "The Remaking of Eastern Europe's Security," *Survival,* 33, no. 2 (March/April 1991), 118.

91. CTK, February 5, 1991.

92. Cited in AP, February 27, 1991.

93. Czechoslovakia's ambassador to the United States, Rita Klimova, stated that "we have to ask ourselves how dependent are we . . . and to what extent do we have to adapt our foreign policy to this factor." Cited in RFE/RL correspondent (Robert Lyle), March 1, 1991. In an interview with Radio Free Europe, Czechoslovak Prime Minister Marina Calfa said that the country's dependence on Soviet oil had constrained the government's support for the Baltic governments: "Whether one likes it or not . . . [Czechoslovakia] has got to protect its own economic interest. You have to balance these things — economic interest and the desire for independence in foreign policy." RFE/RL correspondent (George Stein), April 16, 1991.

94. For information on this issue, see Edward Lucas, *The Independent,* June 1, 1990; AFP, November 19, 1990; Obrman, "Putting the Country Back," p. 13; CTK, February 13, 1991; and Carol J. Williams, *Los Angeles Times,* February 16, 1991. The text of the condemnation is cited in Mary Hockaday, *The Independent,* January 14, 1991.

95. RFE/RL corrrespondent (Stuart Parrott), April 3, 1990; Reuters, April 6, 1990; de Weydenthal, "Changing Views on Security," p. 46; and Obrman, "Putting the Country Back," p. 12. Czechoslovak officials never precisely defined or even thought out their proposal for a confederation (interview with Czechoslovak official).

96. Cited in Peter Corterier, "Transforming the Atlantic Alliance," *Washington Quarterly,* 14, no. 1 (Winter 1991), 36.

97. Cited in AP, February 11, 1991.

98. Cited in Pierre Haski, *Liberation,* March 19, 1990.

99. Cited in Reuters, February 20, 1990.

100. Obrman, "Putting the Country Back," p. 11; and interview with Czechoslovak official. During their consultations Bush stressed that NATO and the United States would continue to play a security role in Europe (AP, February 20, 1990).

101. Edward Mortimer, *Financial Times,* April 17, 1990, cited in Ullman, *Securing Europe,* p. 74.

102. Reuters, November 27, 1990.

103. Cited in AP, February 11, 1991. According to the source, Havel added: "Changes in the Soviet Union are of great concern to us . . . instabiility in one part of the world exudes instability elsewhere . . . We are in [the] direct neighborhood of this colossus, undergoing very dramatic changes." Czechoslovak officials also claimed that their newfound desire to enter NATO resulted from the unexpectedly rapid demise of the WTO and the resulting security vacuum in eastern Europe (interview with Czechoslovak official).

104. Cited in Reuters, March 21, 1991. See also Joel Havemann, *Los Angeles Times,* March 22, 1991.

105. CTK, March 24, 1991.

106. RFE/RL correspondent (Foley), June 14, 1991.

107. See also TASS, January 4, 1990; and Viktor Meier, *Frankfurter Allgemeine Zeitung*, March 8, 1990.

108. In early November demonstrators in Bucharest, accusing Ion Iliescu of having made a secret deal with Gorbachev not to demand Moldavia's return, shouted in the streets: "Down with the Molotov-Gorbachev-Iliescu pact!" and "Bessarabia is part of Romania. The Moldavians are our blood brothers. We'll never leave them alone!" Cited in Mary Dejevsky et al., *The Times* (London), November 5, 1990.

109. See, for example, Rompres, November 8, 1990; Jean-Jacques Mevel, *Le Figaro*, November 23, 1990; and Boris Kalnoky, *Die Welt*, December 5, 1990.

110. Cited in Rompres, March 16, 1991.

111. Reuters, March 17, 1991; and Rompres, March 23, 1991.

112. Vladimir Socor, "Annexation of Bessarabia and Northern Bukovina Condemned by Romania," *Report on the USSR*, July 19, 1991, pp. 23–27. For background information on the Bessarabia issue, see F. Stephen Larrabee, "Long Memories and Short Fuses: Change and Instability in the Balkans," *International Security*, 15, no. 3 (Winter 1990/91), 85.

113. Cited in Rompres, December 27, 1990; emphasis added.

114. Cited in Socor, "Annexation of Bessarabia," p. 25.

115. According to Radio Bucharest: "Starting from the principle of nonaggression stipulated by the UN Charter and in the definition of aggression adopted by the United Nations in 1974, the treaty emphasizes that Romania and the Soviet Union will not participate in any alliance directed against each other. The two countries pledge not to tolerate the use of their territories by a third state to commit an act of aggression against the other side and not to support such a state" (March 23, 1991). The treaty also dealt with matters relating to economics, tourism, the environment, and other bilateral issues. Vladimir Socor, "The Romanian-Soviet Friendship Treaty and Its Regional Implications," *Report on Eastern Europe*, May 3, 1991, pp. 25–33.

116. For a review of their critique, see "Rumaeniens Beziehungen zur UdSSR—umstrittener bilateraler freundschaftsvertrag," *Neue Zuercher Zeitung*, May 25, 1991.

117. Citations in Rompres, March 28, 1991; and Hella Pick, *The Guardian*, May 11, 1991. Romanian officials subsequently claimed that the treaty would not prevent Romania's entry into NATO or the EC because, among other reasons, these organizations no longer had hostile designs on the USSR (interviews with a Romanian official and an official at the Institute for Security Studies of the West European Union).

118. Cited in AP, February 24, 1990.

119. Cited in Tanjug, May 8, 1990.

120. Cited in AP, October 23, 1990. See also AFP, October 23, 1990.

121. Cited in Reuters, April 5, 1991.

122. Interview with a Romanian official.

123. Adrian Nastase, cited in Steven Greenhouse, *New York Times*, July 16, 1990. See also Rompres, October 3, 1990. Iliescu even requested at the Paris CSCE summit that the CSCE countries establish a European center for the peaceful resolution of disputes in Romania (Reuters, November 20, 1990).

124. Cited in Steven Greenhouse, *New York Times,* July 16, 1990.

125. AP, February 24, 1990; and RFE/RL correspondent (Eggleston), June 6, 1990.

126. Cited in RFE/RL correspondent (Eggleston), June 6, 1990.

127. AP, January 7, 1990. See also Celac's remarks in Glenn Frankel, *Washington Post,* January 27, 1990; Deputy Foreign Minister Romulus Neagu's statements in Reuters, February 8, 1990; and Deputy Foreign Trade Minister Ion Aurel's comments in Reuters, February 22, 1990.

128. Cited in AP, September 26, 1990. Iliescu later denied ever making such remarks. Dan Ionescu, "Transylvania and Romanian-Polish Relations," *Report on Eastern Europe,* October 11, 1991, p. 24. But a Romanian official complained to me at the time that his government could not understand the American position because Romania could serve as an important economic market for U.S. merchants, was certainly as deserving of most favored nation status as China or the USSR, and would make more progress toward democracy if it were not isolated.

129. Stuart Auerbach, *Washington Post,* September 5, 1990; Reuters, September 25, 1990; and Rompres, September 26, 1990. For a general review of Romania's policies during the Gulf conflict and its effects on Romania, see Anneli Ute Gabanyi, "Rumaenien in der Golfkrise: Akute Schwierigkeiten, chronische Probleme," *Suedosteuropa,* 40, no. 1 (1991), 21–39.

130. Reuters, August 21, 1991, cited in Ionescu, "Transylvania and Romanian-Polish Relations," p. 24.

131. Rompres, July 1, 1991, cited in Dan Ionescu, "Concern over the Yugoslav Crisis," *Report on Eastern Europe,* July 19, 1991, p. 25. See also the allegations of some Romanian newspapers, cited ibid., pp. 26–27.

132. Reuters, July 4, 1991, cited in Ionescu, "Concern over the Yugoslav Crisis," p. 26.

133. Reuters, May 7, 1991. See also the statements cited in Ionescu, "Concern over the Yugoslav Crisis," pp. 25–26; and Tanjug, February 14, 1990.

134. Romanian Foreign Ministry statement, cited in Ionescu, "Concern over the Yugoslav Crisis," p. 25.

135. Ionescu, "Concern over the Yugoslav Crisis," p. 25.

136. Cited in Reuters, May 10, 1991.

137. Ionescu, "Concern over the Yugoslav Crisis," p. 26.

138. Cited in C. L. Sulzberger, *International Herald Tribune,* June 29, 1990.

139. Yugoslavians termed the two officials' discussion "long, frank, polemical, and very correct." Cited in Louis Zanga, "Approaching the European Mainstream," *Report on Eastern Europe,* December 28, 1990, p. 3.

140. For examples of opposition statements, see AP, January 26, 1991.

141. Cited in Louis Zanga, "Ramiz Alia Renews Albania's International Contacts," *Report on Eastern Europe,* October 26, 1990, p. 2. Alia's parents came from Kososvo. "Tyrant of Tirana," *The Times* (London), January 11, 1990.

142. AP, June 2, 1991.

143. AP, July 10, 1991; and Tanjug, July 25, 1991. Citation in AP.

144. Louis Zanga, "Albania Makes Overture to Superpowers," *Report on Eastern Europe,* May 11, 1990, p. 1.

145. Norman Kempster, *Los Angeles Times,* March 13, 1991.

146. UPI, June 27, 1990.

147. Richard Bassett, *The Times* (London), October 29, 1990.

148. Cited in Zanga, "Albania Makes Overture," p. 1; see also Alain Jacob, *Le Monde,* May 10, 1990.

149. Cited in "Albania Seeks to End Isolation," *The Independent,* June 7, 1990.

150. Louis Zanga, "Approaching the European Mainstream," *Report on Eastern Europe,* December 28, 1990, p. 3. In response to the flight of thousands of refugees into western embassies, the government attempted to seal off the capital's diplomatic quarter. An American diplomat complained that "in the rest of Europe walls are coming down, and in Albania the walls are still going up" (cited in Reuters, October 17, 1990).

151. Cited in Reuters, October 17, 1990. When the CSCE was established in 1973, any European government, as well as those of Canada and the United States, could participate as full members or observers. Afterward, states could join only with the unanimous consent of existing members.

152. Citations in Reuters, November 20, 1990.

153. Cited in Reuters, October 17, 1990.

154. Cited in ATA, September 15, 1990.

155. Cited in Zanga, "Ramiz Alia Renews Contacts," p. 1.

156. "Albanien auf dem Weg zum Mehrparteiensystem," *Neue Zuercher Zeitung,* December 14, 1990. Opposition figures also urged the CSCE to admit Albania to strengthen the hand of the country's democratic forces. See, for example, the remarks of exiled writer Ismail Kadare in "M. Ramiz Alia annonce le developpement d'un 'Etat de droit,'" *Le Monde,* November 16, 1990; see also "Vorsichtiger Reformkurs in Albanien," *Neue Zuercher Zeitung,* November 3, 1990.

157. I am grateful to Samuel Huntington and especially Robert Art for encouraging me to address this puzzle. I hope to offer a more thorough explanation in a subsequent study as to why governments adopt divergent responses to common security issues. Extensive exploration of this question has already occurred in the international political economy scholarship; see, for example, Peter A. Gourevitch, *Politics in Hard Times* (Ithaca, N.Y.: Cornell University Press, 1985); Peter J. Katzenstein, ed., *Between Power and Plenty: Foreign Economic Policies of Advanced Industrial States* (Madison: University of Wisconsin Press, 1978); and David A. Lake, *Power, Protection, and Free Trade: International Sources of U.S. Commercial Strategy, 1887–1939* (Ithaca, N.Y.: Cornell University Press, 1988). For a discussion of the theoretical complexity of this issue, see Kenneth N. Waltz, *Theory of International Politics* (Reading, Mass.: Addison-Wesley, 1979), pp. 71–72, 122–123.

158. My assessment of the foreign minister's skepticism about the efficacy of international security institutions is based on an interview with a Polish academic.

159. Interview with a Czechoslovak official.

160. Roger Boyes, *The Times* (London), February 19, 1991. Personal relations between the two presidents were notoriously poor.

161. Cited in Flora Lewis, "Bringing in the East," *Foreign Affairs,* 69, no. 4 (Fall 1990), 16. For the east European governments, the two strategies were also probably contradictory. Any effort to develop a significant military force would likely alarm neighbors and could produce a regional arms race. For a description of how this process could work, see Robert Jervis, *Perception and Misperception in International Politics* (Princeton: Princeton University Press, 1976), pp. 62–67.

162. Robert L. Rothstein, *Alliances and Small Powers* (New York: Columbia University Press, 1968), pp. 24, 169.

163. This finding is of course tempered by the fact that the states concerned were weak, but the other chapters in this volume indicate that international institutions affected the behavior of more powerful governments as well.

164. Interviews with officials at these organizations.

165. Interview with an official at the Institute for Security Studies of the Western European Union.

166. "KSZE befuerwortet zwei Missionen," *Sueddeutsche Zeitung,* July 8, 1991.

167. For more on this debate, see Joseph M. Grieco, *Cooperation among Nations: Europe, America, and Non-Tariff Barriers to Trade* (Ithaca, N.Y.: Cornell University Press, 1990); Robert Powell, "Absolute and Relative Gains in International Relations Theory," *American Political Science Review,* 85, no. 4 (December 1991), 1303–20; and Duncan Snidal, "International Cooperation among Relative Gains Maximizers," *International Studies Quarterly,* 35, no. 4 (December 1991), 387–402.

168. Rothstein provides additional reasons why weak countries favor an increased role for international institutions (*Alliances and Small Powers,* pp. 39–40).

169. According to Stephen M. Walt, these are the three conditions that most favor bandwagoning; see *The Origins of Alliances* (Ithaca, N.Y.: Cornell University Press, 1987), pp. 173–178. From the perspective of the Romanian and Albanian governments, who were not preoccupied with German intentions, adhering to western democratic norms constituted bandwagoning.

170. For an example of such an approach applied to international economic institutions, see Robert O. Keohane, *After Hegemony: Cooperation and Discord in the World Political Economy* (Princeton: Princeton University Press, 1984).

171. Since 1989, however, security has become the CSCE's chief function, while the Council of Europe has assumed the dominant role in the area of human rights, and a variety of other institutions have a greater effect on pan-European economic issues (interview with Peter Ludlow, director, Centre for European Policy Studies).

172. Rothstein similarly concludes that during the interwar period "the ultimate fate of central and southeastern Europe was determined by the Great Powers, not by the Small Powers who inhabited the region" (*Alliances and Small Powers,* p. 168).

Conclusion

We gratefully acknowledge the comments and criticisms of our collaborators, especially Stephan Haggard and Andrew Moravcsik, on earlier drafts of this chapter.

1. Glenn Snyder, "The Security Dilemma in Alliance Politics," *World Politics*, 36, no. 4 (July 1984), 461–495.

2. See Robert O. Keohane and Stanley Hoffmann, eds., *The New European Community: Decisionmaking and Institutional Change* (Boulder, Colo.: Westview Press, 1991).

3. On asymmetrical vulnerability and power, see Robert O. Keohane and Joseph S. Nye, Jr., *Power and Interdependence: World Politics in Transition,* 2nd ed. (Boston: Little, Brown, 1989).

4. See Chapter 5 by Louise Richardson; Andrew Moravcsik, "Negotiating the Single European Act," in Keohane and Hoffmann, *The New European Community,* esp. p. 56.

5. Kenneth N. Waltz, *Theory of International Politics* (Reading, Mass: Addison-Wesley, 1979), p. 126; Stephen M. Walt, *The Origins of Alliances* (Ithaca, N.Y.: Cornell University Press, 1987).

6. For a similar discussion of bandwagoning, see James M. Goldgeier and Michael McFaul, "Core and Periphery in the Post–Cold War Era," *International Organization,* 46, no. 1 (Spring 1992), 480–481. On specific and diffuse reciprocity, see Robert O. Keohane, "Reciprocity in International Relations," *International Organization,* 40, no. 1 (Winter 1976), 1–27.

7. Walt argues that "the weaker a state, the more likely it is to bandwagon rather than to balance" (*Origins of Alliances,* p. 29).

8. Yugoslavia followed tragically different policies, not as a result of concerns about its external security but owing to internal collapse.

9. Joseph S. Nye, *Bound to Lead: The Changing Nature of American Power* (New York: Basic Books, 1990), p. 111.

10. Kenneth N. Waltz made the latter prediction in a conference on the end of the Cold War at Cornell University, October 19, 1991.

11. See Robert O. Keohane, *After Hegemony* (Princeton: Princeton University Press, 1984), esp. chap. 7; and Keohane, "International Institutions: Two Approaches," *International Studies Quarterly,* 32, no. 4 (December 1988), 379–396.

12. Levy used this phrase in an earlier draft of Chapter 10.

13. Geoffrey Garrett and Barry Weingast make this point nicely in "Ideas, Interests, and Institutions: Constructing the EC's Internal Market," paper prepared for a project on ideas and foreign policy organized by Judith Goldstein and Robert O. Keohane, November 1991. A revised version will appear in Goldstein and Keohane, *Ideas and Foreign Policy* (Ithaca, N.Y.: Cornell University Press, forthcoming).

14. John G. Ikenberry and Charles A. Kupchan, "Socialization and Hegemonic Power," *International Organization,* 44, no. 3 (Summer 1990), 283–316.

Contributors

JEFFREY J. ANDERSON, Assistant Professor of Political Science, Brown University, is author of *The Territorial Imperative: Pluralism, Corporatism, and Economic Crisis* (1992) and "Skeptical Reflections on a Europe of Regions," *Journal of Public Policy* (1990).

JOHN B. GOODMAN, Associate Professor of Business Administration, Harvard Business School, is author of *Monetary Sovereignty: The Politics of Central Banking in Western Europe* (1992) and "The Politics of Central Bank Independence," *Comparative Politics* (1991).

STEPHAN HAGGARD, Professor, Graduate School of International Relations and Pacific Studies, University of California, San Diego, is author of *"Pathways from the Periphery": The Politics of Growth in the Newly Industrializing Countries* (1990) and coeditor of *The Politics of Adjustment* (1992).

STANLEY HOFFMANN, Douglas Dillon Professor of the Civilization of France and Chairman of the Center for European Studies at Harvard University, is author of *Dead Ends* (1983) and *Janus and Minerva* (1986) and coauthor of *The Mitterrand Experiment* (1987).

ROBERT O. KEOHANE, Stanfield Professor of International Peace, Harvard University, is author of *After Hegemony: Cooperation and Discord in the World Political Economy* (1984); and coeditor, with Peter M. Haas and Marc A. Levy, of *Institutions for the Earth: Sources of Effective International Environmental Protection* (1993).

MARC A. LEVY, Assistant Professor of Politics and International Affairs, Princeton University, is coeditor, with Peter M. Haas and Robert O. Keohane, of *Institutions for the Earth: Sources of Effective International Environmental Protection* (1993).

ANDREW MORAVCSIK, Assistant Professor of Government, Harvard University, and Research Associate, Program in International Politics, Economics and Security, University of Chicago, is author of articles in *Daedalus, Survival, International Organization*, and elsewhere on the foreign economic and technology policies of advanced industrial democracies.

KALYPSO NICOLAÏDIS is a doctoral candidate in political economy in the Department of Government and the Department of Economics at Harvard University. She is coeditor of *Strategic Trends in Services* (1989) and author of articles on European integration and international political economy which have appeared in *International Organization* and in edited volumes.

JOSEPH S. NYE, JR., Clarence Dillon Professor of International Affairs and Director of the Center for International Affairs at Harvard University, is author of *Bound to Lead: The Changing Nature of American Power* (1990) and *Nuclear Ethics* (1986).

JANE E. PROKOP is a doctoral candidate in the Department of Government, Harvard University, working on a dissertation on politics in the former Soviet Union.

LOUISE RICHARDSON, Assistant Professor of Government; Associate, Center for European Studies; Head Tutor, Department of Government, Harvard University, is author of "Avoiding and Incurring Losses: Decision Making in the Suez Crisis," *International Journal* (1992).

DEBORA L. SPAR is Assistant Professor at Harvard Business School. She is coauthor with Raymond Vernon of *Beyond Globalism: Remaking American Foreign Economic Policy* and *Iron Triangles and Revolving Doors: Cases in U.S. Foreign Economic Policymaking*.

CELESTE A. WALLANDER, Assistant Professor of Government, Harvard University, is author of "International Institutions and Modern Security Strategies," *Problems of Communism* (1992), and "Third-World Conflict in Soviet Military Thought: Does the New Thinking Grow Prematurely Grey?" *World Politics* (1989).

RICHARD WEITZ, Academy Scholar and a doctoral candidate at the Center for International Affairs, Harvard University, is author of "The Soviet Retreat from Third World Conflicts: The Importance of Systemic Factors," *Security Studies* (1992), and "Insurgency and Counter-Insurgency in Latin America, 1960–80," *Political Science Quarterly* (1986).

Index